D1543236

*Eddie Cantor*

# Eddie Cantor
## A Life in Show Business

*by Gregory Koseluk*

McFarland & Company, Inc., Publishers
*Jefferson, North Carolina, and London*

*Frontispiece:* Cantor in the early thirties during his tenure as radio's number one star and host of *The Chase and Sanborn Hour* (collection of Brian Gari)

British Library Cataloguing-in-Publication data are available

Library of Congress Cataloguing-in-Publication Data

Koseluk, Gregory, 1958–
    Eddie Cantor : a life in show business / by Gregory Koseluk.
      p.   cm.
    Includes bibliographical references and index.
    ISBN 0-7864-0096-X (lib. bdg. : 50# alk. paper) ∞
    1. Cantor, Eddie, 1892–1964.  2. Entertainers—United States—
Biography.  I. Title.
PN2287.C26K67   1995
791′.092—dc20
  [B]                                  94-48782
                                           CIP

Manufactured in the United States of America

*McFarland & Company, Inc., Publishers*
  *Box 611, Jefferson, North Carolina 28640*

To my wife, Cyndi,
with all my love

# *Acknowledgments*

I would like to thank many individuals, without whose assistance this effort would have been more difficult. Shawn Levy, Louis Chunovic, and Dr. Charles Stansfield gave valuable advice to a first-time author. Joe Swaney of Turner Broadcasting and my brother Chris Koseluk offered invaluable aid in helping track down some of the harder to find Cantor films. Chris also provided advice and encouragement. Maureen Sullivan offered encouragement, support, and taxi service. David Hicks provided friendship and insight.

I would also like to express my appreciation to Brian Gari, Cantor's grandson, for his efforts on my behalf, and special thanks go to Joe Franklin for hours of interviews and enthusiastic support. In my studies and travels, Franklin was the only person I encountered that was a bigger Eddie Cantor fanatic than myself.

I would also like to thank the staffs of the various libraries and institutions where I conducted the bulk of my research: Princeton University Library, the Annenberg Communications Library of the University of Pennsylvania, the Special Collections Library of UCLA, the University of Delaware, and the Motion Picture and Recorded Sound Divisions of the Library of Congress.

My deepest gratitude also goes to those friends and family members who took the time to read the roughest drafts of this book, especially my father, Ronald Koseluk, and my mother-in-law, Diane Peterson. An extra special roll of those banjo eyes goes to my wife, Cyndi, who not only painstakingly proofread my manuscript, but also offered unfailing support and encouragement over the last four years, spent her vacations in libraries, watched endless Eddie Cantor films, and happily allowed me to warble Cantor songs to her at our wedding.

Thank you all.

# Table of Contents

# Introduction

Eddie Cantor. Now there's an unlikely subject for a book. Not because he wasn't a major star. On the contrary, as the following pages will document, Eddie Cantor was easily a superstar in an era when that title had not yet been worn out by chronic overuse. Cantor was at various times throughout his career at the zenith of vaudeville, the Broadway stage, films, radio, and television. Yet today, in the last years of the twentieth century, decades after his death, the man who as much as any of his contemporaries was for several decades a ubiquitous show business force is all but forgotten.

For more than twenty-five years after his death in 1964, no books were written about Eddie Cantor. Unlike his contemporaries W. C. Fields and the Marx Brothers, no cult has sprung up devoted to the kinetic little fellow with the bulging banjo eyes.* Today he is recalled to life primarily by a few old-timers, most of whom did not experience Cantor in his prime. Although wildly pro–Eddie, I am not among those dwindling fans who heard or watched Cantor when he was still alive.

I first encountered Eddie Cantor approximately ten years after his death via a Sunday afternoon telecast of his 1933 film *Roman Scandals*. I was a teenager and an avid devourer of vintage films, especially comedies. While I laughed more at the antics of Laurel and Hardy and the Marx Brothers, there was something unmistakably appealing and vital about this fellow who sang, cavorted, and wisecracked across the screen. I was enchanted by our initial contact and was hungry for more.

Unfortunately, because of the restrictions of the pre–VCR era, my first taste of Cantor was tantalizingly brief. It would be another decade before technology allowed me to investigate Eddie further. Even then, only a handful of his films were available on tape, but by that time I had been bitten by the Cantor bug. In an odyssey which could be titled "Desperately Seeking

---

*I am delighted to report, however, that an appreciation society devoted to Mr. Cantor's life and career has been formed. Those interested may write to The Eddie Cantor Appreciation Society, P.O. Box 312, Mount Gay, WV 25637.

Eddie," I began to search for every available scrap of Cantor performances. The films, television shows, and radio programs could be found, but when I looked for books to tell the story behind those wonderful movies and shows, and the man who made them, I came up empty-handed. I was shocked. Except for Eddie Cantor's own autobiographies, there have been no volumes on the man. This book, then, seeks to remedy that situation, and I hope that it will satisfy some of the curiosity of students and devotees of show business and Eddie Cantor.

While looking back at Cantor's fabulous career, one thinks of many questions. What happened to Eddie Cantor? Why isn't he as popular as so many of his contemporaries whom he once outshone? Why is he forgotten by subsequent generations? Initially, one might ascribe his fadeaway to the infrequent showing of his films — a condition I once ascribed to his regular use of blackface. This is too easy an answer, however. In actuality, the difficulty is not in the answer, but rather the question. The problem needs to be turned around. Instead of asking why Eddie Cantor hasn't retained his popularity, we need to inquire why Cantor was popular at all. That question might seem heretical coming from a Cantor-booster, but nonetheless, it is valid.

George Burns has stated that Cantor's appeal was due to his high energy performances. "Maybe Eddie didn't sing so well," Burn wrote in *All My Best Friends*, "and he wasn't a great dancer, and most of his jokes really weren't that funny, but he did so much so fast that the audience didn't have time to notice. Slow-motion replay could have killed Cantor's career."

Burns is right. If you dissect the components which make up Eddie Cantor the entertainer, you will find that anything he did, someone else did better. There were better singers. Funnier comedians. Much better dancers. Yet intact, running at top speed, no one was as popular for so long as Eddie Cantor. Many point out that Cantor was a distant second to the great Jolson. At times, yes. But unlike Jolson, who fell from popularity in the 1930s only to experience a huge comeback in the 1940s, Cantor never needed a comeback. Eddie Cantor was never a has-been; he was popular throughout his long career.

Cantor's zestfully infectious performing style was an essential ingredient of his appeal. His energy alone, however, could not have sustained a career that lasted more than half a century. More than anything else, Eddie Cantor built his career on hard work coupled with a secret ingredient: an amazing sense of what would work in show business. While others around him were better comics, singers, and dancers, Eddie Cantor was unsurpassed as a businessman in the field of entertainment — a show businessman.

Performers who are remembered beyond their own lifetimes are generally thought of as artists. As much as it might be denied by those men themselves, we speak, for various reasons, of the art of Laurel and Hardy, the art of Buster Keaton, or the art of W. C. Fields. Their insight and craft lives on to speak to future generations because it remains relevant (and funny in the case of comedians). Artists, usually subconsciously, work for posterity. In this sense, Eddie Cantor was not an artist. True, like those others mentioned above, Cantor had the same goal—to elicit laughs from an audience—but I believe that Fields or Keaton strove first to do what they thought was funny, rather than seek out the audiences' tastes. They pleased themselves first. Cantor, as a show businessman, sought to provide his audiences with what they wanted. To Cantor, it was a business arrangement.

Show businessmen like Cantor and Harold Lloyd worked extremely hard to please their audiences, and while they succeeded wildly, one is left with the impression that they did not have to be entertainers. Their business sense would have made them as successful in other fields of endeavor. Cantor, an orphan, first chose show business for the feeling of acceptance it provided. Perhaps if his parents had not died in his youth, he would have gone on to be a highly successful manufacturer.

All this is not to say that Cantor's character was cold and calculating. On the contrary, Eddie was an extremely engaging, warm, and funny performer. But he belongs, for the most part, to another era—his own era. He tailored his career for popularity among the audiences of his own time, and from them he reaped the rewards of his work with very little left for future generations. Who can fault this approach? It was the smart business decision.

This book is a labor of love, an attempt by a devoted fan of Eddie Cantor to record the details of a fabulous career. The chapters, for the most part, are arranged according to career vehicles. Because this is the first book on Eddie Cantor, aside from the autobiographies, I wanted to write a volume which would put down the facts about his public life, facts culled for the most part from the newspapers, magazines, and personal accounts of the era.

Those looking for juicy details or gossip will be disappointed by this work. This is not to say that Eddie Cantor was a saint. He was not. He was a human being with his share of faults, including a hot temper, a large ego, and at times a devastatingly harsh, facetious manner. Nor was his fabled home life all that audiences were led to believe it was.

My purpose, however, is not to titillate the casual reader looking for Hollywood gossip. I mention the above behavior only to show that while I am not hiding these details of Mr. Cantor's personal life, neither do I choose to spotlight them. My purpose in writing this book is to explore the career of one of the twentieth century's top stars and show business pioneers.

# CHAPTER 1

# *East Side Orphan*

"Tell me about yourself. What were your parents' names?"
"Papa and Mama."
"Oh, I mean where do you come from? What's your pedigree?"
". . . All my people came from the hospital. My father died two
years before I was born. My grandfather passed away when he was
still a baby, and my mother was so sick she was never allowed to
marry. When I was three years old I had the measles, and you know
what happened? It was fatal!"

—*Palmy Days*

Perhaps Eddie Cantor's "pedigree" was not quite as grim as the one he described in his 1931 film, *Palmy Days*, but it was as bleak a beginning as one could imagine. Cantor's father, Michael Iskowitz, was twenty years old when he and his wife, Maite, immigrated to the United States from Russia in the early 1890s. Michael had no real trade, but had a definite talent for daydreaming and playing the violin. The young couple's passage was paid by Maite's mother, who hoped Michael would be able to make a living in America, the fabled land of opportunity.

Michael wasn't looking for streets paved with gold; in fact, he wasn't even looking for a job but rather was content to dream and fiddle away his days. Cantor later summed up his father by saying that he was "evidently a lovable ne'er-do-well who played the violin," and he reasoned that Michael, "thinking people should throw money through the windows, wouldn't even have gotten up to open the door!"

The young couple's situation changed when Maite, already a frail woman, became ill while pregnant with their first child. Michael, unprepared to shoulder the responsibilities of a family, sent for his mother-in-law. Maite's mother, Esther Kantrowitz, was a strong woman used to struggle and hard work. Widowed at the age of thirty, Esther raised three sons and one daughter by hand-rolling cigars. Known in her home province near Minsk as "Esther the cigarmaker," she rolled enough to send her entire family, including the aforementioned Iskowitz branch, to America. She accomplished all this in spite of the fact that she had no license to ply her trade and consequently was arrested several times for illegal rolling.

Upon receiving Michael's urgent plea for help, Esther sold her unsanctioned shop and left for New York with her life savings, a small bag of silver rubles. When she arrived in late 1891, Esther found Michael and Maite half-starved living over a Russian tearoom on Eldridge Street in lower Manhattan. Immediately, Esther took charge of the situation: cooking, cleaning, and caring for her pregnant daughter. She also would slip Michael a few dollars on the side each week so that he could pretend to Maite that he was working for their livelihood.

Eddie Cantor would later say that his birth on January 31, 1892, occurred "at about the time the regular overtures began on Broadway." In his often sentimental 1928 autobiography (written with David Freedman), Cantor paints the night of his birth as a festive, celebratory occasion. The Iskowitzes' tiny flat was crowded with relatives and well-wishers, who made themselves sick drinking slivovitz to the new arrival's health while Michael played the violin in accompaniment to the balalaikas in the tearoom below. In the next room, a midwife tended to Maite while Esther served double duty, comforting her daughter primarily, but finding time to pass out cakes and fill glasses between labor pains. The baby, a boy, was named Isidore.

As with all the other unmet challenges in his life, Michael Iskowitz failed to provide for his growing family. Try as he might, he could never hold a steady job. Soon Maite wearied of encouraging him to do so and resigned herself to their plight. Cantor later wondered why his father never thought of joining a musicians' union, where he could at least pick up some money with his fiddling. That, however, would make music into work, and in his son's words, "he loved life too well to make a business of it." Instead, Michael went on dreaming bigger dreams while Grandma Esther, her savings depleted, supported the family by peddling candles, matches, and pins from tenement to tenement.

If nothing else, Michael Iskowitz proved himself successful as a progenitor, and within the year Maite was expecting their second child. The young father's world, built as it was on a fragile foundation of dreams, collapsed around him when his wife died during childbirth. Unable to accept Maite's death, Michael took to wandering the streets. Supposedly, Michael Iskowitz died a year later of pneumonia, though no death certificate has ever been found.

At the age of sixty-two, Grandma Esther found herself starting all over again in a new world with a two-year-old grandson to raise. First the pair moved in with one of Esther's daughters-in-law and her three children. The arrangement worked out well enough until little Isidore developed a talent for dropping the family silverware and china down the stairwell from the family's fifth floor apartment. From there Esther and her "little Itchik," as she called Isidore, moved into a two-room basement flat on Henry Street.

Their new home was not lonely by any stretch of the imagination. In an attempt to boost their income, Grandma Esther had quit peddling and opened an employment agency. She supplied girl domestics, mostly Polish immigrants, at a dollar a head to families in the area. The girls, not knowing anyone else in New York, slept on the basement floor until Esther could place them. Cantor remembered as many as eight or nine girls at a time living in their tiny flat. He recalled women stopping by looking for a girl to clean, cook, and care for the children. They gave Grandma Esther their specifications and paid their dollar. After the customer departed, Esther would pick out a suitable employee, hoist the girl's trunk on to her own back, and deliver them both to the client's home. Often, if her Itchik was home, she would perform a perfect imitation of the lady who had just left for his amusement. "She was a great mimic," Cantor, himself an impressionist early in his career, noted, "in fact, that's where I got the idea."

With most of Grandma Esther's time taken up with her employment agency, she spent precious little time with her grandson. On any given day, Isidore would awake to find his grandmother already out on business. Before going out for the day, she would be careful to provide for her Itchik's meals.

"She was so busy eking out an existence that there were few hot meals," Cantor would recall. "She would leave me a nickel on the kitchen sink each morning. That would buy me four cents' worth of salami and a penny's worth of bread. By the time I was thirteen, I'd consumed more delicatessen than most people eat in a lifetime."

To balance out his diet, Cantor became quite adept at swiping fruit off the neighborhood pushcarts. He later boasted of elevating pilfering to an art. "I used to pack a peach into my mouth with one snap of the jaws and look deeply offended when the peddler turned suspiciously upon me. With steady practice I got so that I could gulp a banana at one swallow and appear absolutely famished with a plum in each cheek!"

When he wasn't devouring forbidden fruit, Isidore was running with the local gangs, even though most of the other kids were twice his age. According to Cantor, the gang's main activity was staying out late singing the popular songs of the day. Occasionally, in spite of their musical inclinations, there would be battles between rival gangs. During one of these fights, Isidore was hit in the forehead by a jagged brick that knocked him unconscious. The wound ran deep, and Grandma Esther took Itchik to the local druggist to sew it up. Unfortunately, the cut was not properly cleaned out and within two days the young warrior's forehead swelled up with an infection. Panic-stricken, Grandma Esther carried her grandson to the nearest dispensary, where the wound was properly treated. The incident left Cantor with a scar across his forehead, which he later covered up by combing his hair over it in a distinctive bang, a practice which he continued into his professional career.

Some semblance of discipline entered young Isidore's life when his grandmother enrolled him in school. Probably the biggest change came not in his mind, but in his name. While she was registering her grandson, the registrar of Public School 136 asked Esther the boy's name. Thinking she was being asked her own name, Grandma Esther started to reply "Kantrowitz," but stopped halfway through because she was confused. The registrar wrote down "Kanter" and so it remained until Isidore left P.S. 136 for P.S. 2 and changed the spelling to "Cantor."

Isidore Kanter's talent for schoolwork fell far below the levels of achievement he had attained in the fields of salami eating and banana swallowing. Since he had absolutely no head for figures or dates, Isidore would dodge the teacher's questions by talking his way out of them. He became such an accomplished speaker that his teachers would loan him out to other classes for recitations. Around the school he became a rhetorical sensation for such pieces as "Benedict Arnold — The Traitor's Deathbed" and "The Soul of the Violin." By Cantor's own account, he passed through seven terms on the strength of his oratory.

Isidore would have graduated except for the intervention of his last teacher. This last instructor was, by Cantor's own recollection, "a narrow-minded schoolmaster of the old birch-rod type who insisted on treating me like one of the class and refused to promote me for a little thing like failing in all my subjects." Isidore's final achievement in the halls of organized learning was hitting this unbending educator on the jaw with a blackboard eraser. After his parting shot, young Cantor left school for good.

It is said that most clowns and comedians establish their lighthearted exteriors out of an underlying insecurity or unhappiness. In the case of Eddie Cantor, it can be argued that he learned dramatics as a substitute for studying. He learned to sing to be part of the gang, but he took up clowning to escape the tenements of the city.

When he was ten years old, Isidore took his first comedy act on the road, not to vaudeville, but to summer camp. The Surprise Lake Camp, in Cold Springs, New York, was run by the Educational Alliance, a lower East Side welfare organization. For $1.50, the price of the transportation to the camp, a boy from the tenements of New York City could spend two weeks in the country. For a kid who spent his entire life in the congestion of lower Manhattan, the camp was indeed a surprise. "Cold Springs was a strange place," Cantor wrote twenty-five years later, "It was not a network of brick walls covered with patches of sky like metal ceiling. It had no walls of any kind and it was all sky. And green stretches of grass rolled like plush carpets over wide, endless playgrounds."

Aside from an environment 180 degrees removed from the city's slums, Isidore found other differences at camp. For a boy raised on delicatessen fare, the three balanced meals a day made quite an impression. The people who ran the camp were different too. Unlike the city with its hostile shop-keepers and policemen, at Surprise Lake the counselors treated him with kindness, even when he stole an extra blanket for his cot or broke a window.

The two weeks were a revelation to Cantor, who immediately tried to figure out a way to prolong his stay in paradise indefinitely. Every Saturday night the entire camp would gather around a roaring campfire to roast marshmallows, sing songs, and tell stories. Cantor reasoned that if he could make a hit reciting his specialties at the weekly campfire perhaps they would hold him over for an extended stay. It was worth a try; after all, the scheme had been a proven success in more than half a dozen school terms.

That Saturday night, determined to reduce his fellow campers to uncontrollable tears, Isidore pulled out all the stops with his renditions of "The Traitor's Deathbed" and "The Soul of the Violin." Unfortunately, the young would-be Barrymore pulled out too many stops. In his attempt to portray the height of drama, Cantor exaggerated his soul-wrenching grimaces to such a degree that he crossed the line between tragedy and comedy. Instead of tears, his efforts were greeted with gales of laughter. Cantor became the hit of the evening and was asked to stay on for an additional two weeks at the camp. His fellow campers nicknamed Cantor "Happy" for his impersonations of popular comic strip character Happy Hooligan. The widespread approval and acceptance Isidore received encouraged him to clown even more, and he soon became the unofficial camp comedian. One summer his efforts produced a seven-week stay.

Despite the wholesome environment of Surprise Lake, Cantor's real world for most of the year lay in the slums of Manhattan. At age thirteen, Cantor was hired by Pock-faced Sam, one of the local thugs, to join his gang of strikebreakers and strong-arms. Although he was the smallest of the group, Cantor used his acting abilities to present a sufficiently tough exterior to satisfy his boss. In street fights, however, Cantor later confessed that he stood mainly on the sidelines, making scary facial contortions to frighten the opposition. As the smallest member, Cantor was able to make another, more tangible, contribution to the gang. He was the gang's number one choice when it came to climbing through the transoms of stores targeted for burglary. Their favorite mark was a neighborhood bicycle shop; the gang would rob it by night and then sell back the stolen stock the next day to the intimidated shopkeeper.

Still, Cantor longed for the ego stroking only an audience could provide. The hurly-burly arena of city politics gave Isidore an ideal platform — the soapbox. Just barely a teenager, and a rather scrawny one at that, Cantor took to delivering emotional campaign speeches for the local politicians, regardless of party affiliation or platform. Not being of voting age or a member of any party, Isidore delivered his orations for the sheer pleasure of being before an audience. While he personally made no money for his efforts, the local pickpockets profited by working the crowd while Cantor held everyone's attention.

One night Cantor delivered a stinging attack on a Democratic candidate after praising the same man the night before. Some angry party members knocked Isidore off his platform and beat him up. Then and there the young free-lance speaker decided that if he was to survive in politics, he had better become a loyal Democrat. Cantor remained a Democrat the rest of his life, becoming an ardent campaigner and friend to Al Smith, Franklin D. Roosevelt, and Harry Truman, among others.

Political stumping may have given Cantor satisfaction, but its lack of monetary compensation worried Grandma Esther. At the time, Cantor recalled, he felt there was only one type of work for him—play. "I was still one of those simple children of art who thought that to get paid for work was a sin." Still, Esther, perhaps with the memory of Michael Iskowitz's similar philosophy fresh in her mind, urged her grandson to find a line of employment that would yield a tangible paycheck.

Cantor found himself a job down on William Street in the financial district with an insurance company. He worked in the mail room, where he was in charge of the stamps. After two weeks, company officials noticed a marked increase in the amount of correspondence that the firm was producing. Their findings were based on the number of stamps being used. Strangely enough, a decrease in stamp consumption corresponded to Cantor's dismissal from the company.

After being fired from the insurance company, Cantor consoled himself by taking up a new hobby, which consisted of standing on the street corner making funny faces at the passers-by. Roughly around the same time, Isidore had his first love affair. Her name was Fanya, and she was a sixteen-year-old Russian girl who had found work through Grandma Esther's employment agency. One day Esther walked in on the pair while they were kissing. Furious, she ordered Fanya to "put the child back in his cradle" and leave. "If she goes, I go with her!" Cantor announced in a fit of chivalry. Grandma Esther agreed. So, at the age of fourteen, Esther's little Ishtick moved in with an older woman in order to prove he was a man.

Cantor quickly tired of his new domestic arrangement and longed to be free of his Russian sweetheart and back with his grandmother's meatballs. Ditching Fanya was not so easy, however, and Cantor couldn't muster up the nerve to make a quick, clean break. The situation was complicated by the fact that Fanya was supporting Isidore under the ruse of him being her sickly little brother. Fortunately though, it was summer, and Cantor was still living the life of an unemployed gentleman of leisure. This meant spending his days at the summer recreation grounds of P.S. 1 and P.S. 177. Although he could beat most of the boys at the playground games, there was one person there, a girl, whom Cantor could not top. Her name was Ida Tobias.

By Cantor's own account, Ida Tobias was the belle of Henry Street. "Despite her athletic prowess," Cantor recalled, "she possessed a soft, girlish grace; a frank, bright countenance mellowed by two caressing eyes." Isidore was smitten, but a romantic conquest of Ida was definitely an uphill struggle. Ida's mother had long warned her daughter against all the "potential good-for-nothings" in the neighborhood "who could make wonderful love but a very poor living." Cantor was firmly ensconced in this category, especially since his local reputation was founded on his ability to hang out on the street corner all day making funny faces.

In lovemaking, as with school and camp, Cantor quickly realized that any edge he might possess lay in his ability to amuse others. To this end, Cantor convinced the recreation director to let him sing with the small brass band that gave playground concerts. With a robust performance of "My Mariuch She Took-a de Steamboat" (a big hit that summer), Cantor won the applause and admiration of the fair Miss Tobias. After a follow-up song the next night, Ida let Isidore walk her home, and a romance began.

Eddie Cantor's lack of a visible means of support put a decided crimp in their courtship. Whereas Ida's other suitors could afford to take her skating or to Coney Island, with Isidore Cantor she had to settle for nights and Sundays of sitting on the steps outside the school. Cantor's main competition came from a pair of twins, Louis and Leo Rosner, who often dated Ida and her sister Minnie. Ida's mother approved of the duo because they wore starched collars and brought boxes of candy when they came courting. In addition, the brothers had good, solid, steady jobs working in the post office. Given Cantor's track record with postage stamps, it was unlikely he could hope to build a similar career. Ida would see Louis on Saturdays, but would reserve all day Sunday for sitting in the schoolyard with Isidore Cantor. The only worldly pleasure they shared, aside from each other's company, was the box of candy Louis Rosner had given Ida the night before.

Ida provided Isidore with more than Louis Rosner's candy; she also gave him a new name. One of Ida's friends had a brother named Eddie. Ida thought the name cute and decided it fit her new beau better than "Isidore." It did. And so Isidore Iskowitz, then Kanter, then Cantor, finally became Eddie Cantor.

Falling in love brought about other changes in Eddie. He began to consider his future and his reputation. After all, Mr. and Mrs. Tobias were not likely to give their daughter's hand to a fellow who pretended to hang himself from street lamps for a living. In addition, there was still the ongoing affair with Fanya that continued to provide grist for the neighborhood rumor mills. His burgeoning love for Ida gave Eddie the extra courage he needed to finally break free from his Russian paramour.

One night Fanya came home with the news that she had just been given a raise at work. To celebrate she gave Eddie $4 to buy two of the best seats available for *The Talk of New York*, starring Victor Moore. Cantor bought the tickets for the next day's performance as instructed, but then turned around and asked Ida to the show. He explained his windfall to Ida by telling her, "I'm coming up in the world." That night when he got home he told Fanya he had lost the money.

The following day Eddie cleaned up his best suit, such as it was, and called for Ida at her parent's home, an honor usually reserved for more prestigious suitors. Now Eddie Cantor surpassed even the candy-toting Louis Rosner—he was a theater goer. The day was perfect. Perfect that is until the couple reached the theater, where Fanya was waiting to chase her unfaithful love up and down Eighth Avenue with her rapier-like hat pin.

With not enough money for a hotel room and too much pride to go back to Grandma Esther, Eddie spent the next few nights sleeping on park benches and tenement rooftops. One night a particularly heavy cloudburst washed the last vestige of independence from him, and Eddie retreated to the friendlier climate of Grandma Esther's basement flat. Esther welcomed her Itchik back with loving, open arms and one firm stipulation: he must go to work.

The following Monday, Eddie landed a job as a clerk in a broker's office for the salary of $5 a week. The second day on the job he wrote Ida a letter, on the company's letterhead, apologizing for his hasty retreat from the theater. Eddie went on to explain that he had been working with the broker all along; in fact, he would probably be made a member of the firm soon. When he received no reply, Eddie blamed it on a plot by postal employee Louis Rosner to subvert mail from rival suitors. It was evident to Cantor that he would have to become a business success to get back in good with Ida. To that end, Eddie resolved to buckle down and make good at his new job.

Unfortunately, it didn't take very long for Eddie the entertainer to overcome the efforts of young Mr. Cantor, the industrious office boy. At the end of his first week on the job, Eddie became so elated at the prospect of receiving his pay that he jumped on a desk and began to dance a jig for his fellow employees. Regrettably, the company's president walked in on the performance (which incidentally was being executed on the firm's weekly market letter) and fired Eddie.

Undaunted, Eddie quickly found a job as a stock clerk with the National Cloak and Suit Company for an even higher salary — $7 a week. Here his job history improved dramatically; this time it took three weeks for Eddie to get fired. Again he was dismissed for clowning for his co-workers. His new act consisted of mincing around the model's platform while wearing a ladies fur coat. One day a group of company officials caught his act and released him back into the job market. The only other critique of his performance came from his fellow employees, who urged their bosses to fire Cantor since his antics, funny though they were, proved too distracting from their vital work of hanging up coats.

Finding himself in the now familiar position of being out of work, Eddie Cantor was at a crossroads. He couldn't resort to his usual life of bumming on the streets if he hoped to win back Ida's love. On the other hand, his attempts at breaking into the business sector met with less than ringing results. For someone with Eddie's penchant for performing, where the laughter of the crowd meant more than the money in the pay envelope, there was only one route left open — show business.

# CHAPTER 2

# *Professional Dreams and Amateur Nights*

Eddie Cantor's show business career—not counting his schoolhouse oratory or summer camp clowning—began as half of a team along with his best friend Daniel Lipsky. Oddly enough, Dan, who had a sober reputation and eventually wound up being a prominent banker, was assigned the role of the comedian, while Eddie, one of the neighborhood's more colorful characters, was given the more dramatic pieces of business. However, just as water must seek its own level, a true comedian cannot play it straight for too long, and eventually the pair switched roles. The team worked at local weddings, bar mitzvahs, parties, and any venue that provided them with an audience. Their act borrowed liberally from vaudeville acts of the day. Their act usually opened with Cantor, decked out in a long crepe beard, using a line from comedian Joe Welsh: "If I had my life to live over again I wouldn't be born." Other times, they would parody such popular material as Little Lord Fauntleroy (with Eddie in blonde wig and blacked out teeth), and Snow White—where they both appeared as dwarves. No mention is made of who played Snow White or the other five dwarves.

One day, while performing their dwarf act, the pair was offered a dollar to go to a nearby club to do one of their routines. They jumped at the opportunity and went immediately to the club. They went over so well that the manager of the Clinton Street Music Hall, who happened to be at the club, offered them $2 to repeat the act on his stage.

Excited at the prospect of appearing on a professional stage, Eddie and Dan put their all into their performance at the Music Hall. Despite their best efforts, however, every one of their jokes was met with silence from the audience, or as Cantor recalled: "Every gag we tried fell flat like eggs on a cake of rice." Mystified, the duo retreated in defeat to the wings. It was there, while watching the other acts, that they discovered the reason for their failure—all the other performers were speaking another language. In their haste to make good, they hadn't realized they were playing a Yiddish theater.

The next night, after translating their jokes, Eddie and Dan convinced the manager to let them go on again for free. Now speaking a tongue their audience understood, the boys were received with laughter and applause. The experience taught Cantor that the audience was never wrong, and as he later wrote: "If a performance failed to go across it was either the fault of the material or the manner of presentation. By carefully correcting the one or the other or both with an eye to the peculiarities of the audience I could never fail a second time."

Despite their success in Yiddish, however, the team soon fell apart due to lack of work. Dan Lipsky's sober side convinced him to take a position in an engineer's office, leaving Cantor without a partner and no job prospects. Again, Eddie took to the streets, having too much pride and too little work to return home to face Grandma Esther. He survived by sleeping on rooftops and bumming change from his friends, but as weeks passed, even this became increasingly difficult as his already slim credit line dried up.

Eddie's friends, tired of giving out their hard-earned money, challenged him to appear on the bill of the amateur night program at Miner's Bowery Theatre. Even if he got the hook, they reasoned, Eddie would be paid a dollar, a dollar that they wouldn't have to loan him later. After some cajoling, Eddie, weakened because he had not eaten for the past two days, agreed to try out his act on the burlesque house's stage. The gang adjourned to the theater, but only after one member swapped Eddie's torn pants for his own. For the trouser rental, Eddie would pay him fifty cents out of his dollar, well worth it to preserve at least some of his dignity in front of the tough amateur night audience.

Standing in the wings waiting to go on, Eddie was gripped by fear as he witnessed act after act being booed, jeered, and hooked off stage. At first, he considered prefacing his act with a hard luck story about being a starving orphan. Maybe then, he reasoned, they would feel sorry for him, or perhaps put padding on the hook. After what seemed like enough acts to put on two editions of the *Follies*, it was finally Eddie's turn.

In his two autobiographies, Cantor gives conflicting accounts of what happened next. In his 1957 book, *Take My Life*, Cantor recalls being pushed out onto the stage only to receive a barrage of rotten fruit and Bronx cheers. After ducking the produce for a moment or two, Eddie stamped his foot, held up his hand, and whined, "Oh, dat makes me so mad!" which, at the time, was a famous catch phrase of burlesque comic Sam Sidman. The audience roared its approval, let Eddie go on with his act, and the rest was history.

His earlier book, *My Life Is in Your Hands*, gives a somewhat different account. First, according to Cantor, Edward was considered something of a sissy name in 1908, so when the M.C. announced "Mr. Edward Cantor, Impersonator," the tough crowd responded with a hail of derisive hoots and laughs. Next the M.C., a large man named Isham, raised his hands to silence the audience, then told them, "He's a new one, boys. Give him a chance."

With the audience stilled, Eddie went into his repertoire, starting with an imitation of Cliff Gordon, a local congressman with a thick German accent. "Nowadays effery von goes out on shtrike!" Eddie began in his best Deutsch dialect. "Soon vile de vifes vill go out on shtrike, too. But can you himachin de scabs coming in to take deir blazes?" He had the audience's attention; some even laughed at his jokes—ones they had doubtlessly heard before in other burlesque houses. One man called out from the balcony, "Stick to it, kid, you're lousy!"

Cantor next launched into his version of comic Harry Thompson, who was known as the "Mayor of the Bowery," presiding at court. He played judge, lawyer, and various defendants, while going through a pastiche of worn but accepted courtroom gags. For example, a pickpocket appears before the judge and is fined $10 but only has $3 on him. "Send him loose in the crowd, till he gets the other seven." Or a woman is brought on charges of not making the payments on her sewing machine. Her defense? "The salesman told me the machine would pay for itself in time!"

Eddie's finale consisted of an imitation of popular comedian Junie McCree. McCree would usually play a dope fiend, delivering his jokes in slow moving, languid drawl. Being one of the most distinctive acts of the day made him the favorite subject of amateur mimics, but not their audiences, who groaned in anticipation of yet another interpretation of McCree. Unperturbed, Eddie continued with gags like this one: "I'm so broke, that if they were selling steamboats for a nickel, I couldn't buy an echo of a whistle." Or, "My son came home the other day, took a jab of the needle, and bought St. Louis. 'Take another jab,' I told him, 'and pay the rent.'"

By the time Cantor finished, not only had he avoided the dreaded hook, he found himself picking up coins the audience had showered on him, along with their laughter and applause. After the final amateur had gone on and the entire bill gathered on stage for the judgment of the crowd, Eddie was awarded the $5 grand prize. His closest competition came from a pair of artistic dancers.

Cantor's friends greeted him with warm congratulations; he was no longer just a street corner clown, he was a prize-winning, wage-earning comedian. To celebrate his triumph, Eddie took the gang to Chinatown, where they quickly devoured his prize money in the form of a chop suey dinner. Later that night, while bedding down on a rooftop, Eddie became suddenly and violently ill. In his revelry, he had made the mistake of throwing three bowls of Chinese noodles and fried onions on top of a stomach that had just gone through a two-day fast. He sat up alone shivering and crying through the night. Despite the sudden attack, Cantor later recalled: "Even this sad anti-climax did not wholly obliterate the new vistas opened to me. I felt certain of one thing now: I would be an actor."

Eddie wasted no time in starting his new career, making the rounds of New York's amateur contests. One burlesque house, the London, offered Eddie a regular position with them, but he turned it down because he lacked self-confidence. Instead, he continued as a professional amateur, picking up prizes and new material as he went along. The new material was picked up from headlining comics such as Harry Thompson and Walter Kelly. Eddie would then change the material just enough to make it seem new and at the same time fit his own developing style. He called this "Burbanking" after Luther Burbank, the famous botanist who developed new hybrids from existing plants.

Just what Eddie Cantor's style was at this point is difficult to ascertain. From his own recollections, his act seems to have consisted of imitations, jokes, and an occasional song or nonsense poem. Even without the poems, the act seemed steeped in a healthy dose of nonsense. Often Cantor would close his performance by coming back on stage while the audience was still applauding; he would lift his arms to quiet the crowd and then proclaim dramatically, "I too am a mother!" Although he claimed it always got a laugh, even Cantor could never understand why.

Finally, after building up his act and his confidence through countless burlesque amateur nights, Eddie Cantor went professional. His opportunity came from a traveling burlesque review run by Frank Carr entitled *Indian Maidens*. Eddie's salary came to $15 a week, out of which he had to pay for four different costumes for his four separate roles: a tramp, a Hebrew comedian, a waiter, and a bootblack. The troupe left New York in late November to play small towns, many of which were one-night stands. As the tour progressed, business got progressively worse. Finally, the show came to an end on Christmas Eve in Shenandoah, Pennsylvania, where the company walked out on stage to be greeted by an empty theater. To make matters worse, even the company's manager had beat it back to New York.

Alone and stranded on the holiday, Eddie's initial flush of euphoria at being a professional actor vanished in the snow of Shenandoah. He wired Grandma Esther, who sent her little Itchik the fare to come back home. Back in New York, Eddie used the occasion of his return as an excuse to call on Ida Tobias. After all, months had passed since his infamous retreat from the theater at the point of Fanya's stickpin; besides Eddie was no longer just a neighborhood character—he was now a professional.

By the time Eddie returned, however, Ida and her sister Minnie had taken up again with the Rosner brothers. To make matters worse for Eddie, Ida's sister Jennie was getting married, and the announcement of Minnie's and Ida's betrothals was likely to come at their sister's wedding. Eddie met Ida one more time at the schoolyard to tell her of his undying love, but his pleas fell on deaf ears. Ida was convinced that her father was right: Eddie Cantor would not amount to anything, least of all a good husband. At best, Ida reasoned, he would become an itinerant actor, making petty wages and wiring home for return train fare.

In the first part of the century, East Side weddings were often huge affairs which were open to the public as long as they paid their way in. Eddie was an accomplished wedding crasher, becoming so adept at his craft that he was often called upon to read telegrams, offer toasts, and occasionally sing. He was, however, definitely barred from Jennie Tobias' wedding. As the festive wedding party, including Ida and Louis Rosner, left for the hall, Eddie watched from a distance, then went home to cry himself to sleep. At the wedding, however, only Minnie's betrothal was announced, with the understanding that Ida and Louis were next after that. Eddie greeted the news as a reprieve and determined not only that he would be invited to the next Tobias wedding, but that he would make it a showcase for his success. Full of resolve, all he needed now was the success.

The next day he set out for Coney Island, where he landed a job singing at Carey Walsh's saloon for $3 a night. "Carey Walsh's saloon aspired to the dignity of a cabaret," Cantor said, recalling the atmosphere and adding: "While bottles were thrown occasionally, the guests aimed only at one another, never at the entertainers." Singing almost one hundred times on a busy night afforded Eddie the dual opportunity to expand his musical repertoire and polish his delivery, all while building up a bankroll to impress the Tobiases.

While he was singing, Eddie noticed that the waiters were making considerably more than him, for not only did they receive tips, but out of every $5 in drinks they sold, they got to keep fifty cents. With such a potential windfall staring him in the face, Eddie became a waiter — a singing waiter. It was while he was working at Carey Walsh's that Eddie met a young piano player, who coincidentally lived just around the block from Eddie. His name was Jimmy Durante. The two became fast friends, riding the elevated train to work and back together, wandering around Coney Island before Walsh's opened, and occasionally shilling for the skill games on the boardwalk.

Eddie, Jimmy, and the other three singing waiters at the saloon decided to pool their tips to reduce any unfair competition that might spring up between them. They decided to keep all the tip money in a cigar box on top of Jimmy's piano, with the booty to be divided at the end of each work week. By the end of the first week of this arrangement, roughly $125 had been deposited in their cheroot vault, meaning a windfall of $25 for each of them. Unfortunately, that Monday, the day that they were to have split the tips up, Durante approached the others with tears streaming down his face.

"How could they do this," Jimmy cried, "somebody stole it! Somebody stole the money! A hundred and twenty-five bucks out of the cigar box!"

The four waiters did all they could to console their partner, assuring him that they would make up the loss somehow. They never discovered the culprit, not until years later, that is.

One day while he was sitting in the Hunting Room of the Astor Hotel in New York, Eddie Cantor felt a slap on his back. He turned to see his old friend, Jimmy Durante; both of them were now big stars.

"I'm lookin' all over for you," Jimmy growled in his distinctive gravelly voice. "Here," Durante said, handing Cantor $25. It seems that Durante had taken the money and given it all to his father, who used the pinched funds to bring Jimmy's brother over from Italy.

Jimmy explained that he was looking for the other waiters in order to repay them their long pilfered tips. "Two of the guys croaked," Durante said sadly, but not too contritely, adding: "What a break! What a break!"

Together Eddie and Jimmy made extra tips by filling special musical requests from the customers. Durante recalled, to Gene Fowler in his book *Schnozzola*, that there wasn't a song they couldn't deliver, especially since, rather than lose a tip, they made up any number they didn't know:

> If a guy wanted "The Hills of Kentucky" which I didn't know or ever heard of, I'd fake a melody and Eddie could sing, "The Hills of Kentucky are far, far away, and when you're from them hills, you're away from them hills, yes, away from them hills of Kentucky." So the guy who asked for the song and slipped us a couple of bucks for it, would object, "What the hell did you sing to me?" Then Eddie would say, "Why, 'The Hills of Kentucky.'" Then the guy would say "What? That ain't the words." And Eddie would say, innocent like, "Are there two of them? Well, gee, I'll ask the piano player does he know the other one." And then we'd go on from there, and we'd make a regular routine out of it, and Eddie would say to the man, "Oh," he'd say, "you must mean this one." And he'd sing the title right in guy's kisser and turn to make double talk like he's singin' some lyrics, and I'd follow him on the piano: "Old Kentucky in the hills, which we love so dear . . ." And the guy would yell his brains out, "Stop it! That's not it either." He'd say "What are you guys? Wise guys?" Eddie with his big brown eyes, would shed real tears and sob. "No," he'd cry, "and if you want the money back, we'll give you the money back!" But as he says this he's walkin' away from the guy. The money is in his shoe already, and the guy wants his money back; but Eddie walks away too fast. What a guy, that Eddie! He's tops!

Eddie thought Jimmy was terrific too, so much so that he often tried to persuade Durante to quit Carey Walsh's and join him in a vaudeville act. As hard as Cantor tried, however, Durante refused to leave his piano playing. Eddie urged him to look to his future.

"I know you want to be a piano player, but piano playing is going to get you nothing," Cantor reasoned. "You'll be a piano player till you're a hundred years old. You gotta look further than that. People like you a whole lot. So why don't you get up on the floor and say something to the people? Make remarks while you're playing the piano?"

"Gee, Eddie, I wouldn't do that," Durante responded. "I'd be afraid people would laugh at me."

In the end Durante remained playing piano at Coney Island for three more years before eventually teaming with Eddie Jackson and Lou Clayton for their legendary act. One can only speculate on the kind of an act or career which would have resulted from the teaming of Eddie Cantor and Jimmy Durante. At least, their saloon partnership enabled Cantor to build up a healthy bankroll (by 1909 standards) of $400, enough to make an impression at Minnie's wedding. All he needed now was an invitation.

Fortunately, Ida had still kept in touch with Eddie, hoping against hope that he would prove himself successful enough for her parents to allow their courtship to resume. Eddie told Ida of his job; the actor in him embellished the position, however. Instead of a waiter, he told Ida he was the manager.

His lie was safe, Eddie reasoned to himself, since Coney Island was too far away for a casual visit and, in addition, he never specifically mentioned which "restaurant" he was managing.

Naturally, Ida quickly found out where Eddie was working and along with her sister Jennie and her husband dropped into Carey Walsh's saloon to surprise Eddie. Fortunately, Eddie spotted the Henry Street expedition before they sighted him waiting tables. Quickly, the make-believe manager threw off his apron and started barking orders at his fellow waiters, who merely stood there agape at Eddie. After making a sufficient display of his managerial talent, Eddie ushered the trio out, explaining it was his night off and he would join them outside. He then went back to the kitchen, changed his coat, snuck out the back door, and proceeded to spend the rest of the evening escorting Ida around Coney Island.

The next day he had to do a lot of explaining in order to keep his job, but it was all worth it. His ruse had worked, and he was invited to Minnie's wedding.

With his $400 backing him up, Eddie pulled out all the stops for Minnie's wedding. With the first $100, he rented the swankiest tuxedo he could find, hired a car, and bought an impressive wedding present. The remaining $300 went just as quickly at the wedding for tips and countless rounds of champagne for the guests. By the time the last of his fortune had been drained, along with the last drops of champagne, Eddie was something of a Henry Street hero. Impressed by "Eddie Cantor—the businessman," David Tobias all but agreed to the wedding of Eddie and Ida. Now that Eddie had proven himself, Mr. Tobias had the perfect business for him—a haberdashery store.

Any thaw in David Tobias' opinion of Eddie quickly refroze when Eddie pushed aside his future father-in-law's suggestion and proclaimed that he still intended to be an actor. "Young man," Tobias warned, "if you don't forget acting, you'll have to forget Ida." When Eddie protested, Mr. Tobias informed him that when he had saved up $2,500 (the amount needed to start the men's store), then he could come back to ask for Ida's hand in marriage. Eddie looked to Ida for support in the argument, but her silence made it clear that she agreed with her father. The choices were clear, either sell men's furnishings and marry Ida or become an actor and lose her. Eddie Cantor did the only thing he could, given the alternatives. He would follow a career in show business—in secret.

# CHAPTER 3

# *Bedini and Arthur*

At first, keeping his clandestine career in show business a secret was not at all difficult for Eddie Cantor. He decided to start big and in New York that meant Broadway, only it was extremely hard to get work on Broadway without an agent. Even with an agent it was hard. For Eddie it was extremely hard to even find an agent.

With the last of the cash from his saloon singing, Eddie bought his first tailor-made suit, a gray pinstripe model that cost him $25. He had enough left over to have cards printed that read: "Eddie Cantor, Dialectician." With his cards in hand and his suit on his back, Eddie went to the office of an agent by the name of Joe Wood. Wood listened to Cantor's skimpy professional résumé and shook his head. "This is a business for professionals," the agent explained.

Eddie reminded Wood that all professionals started out as amateurs, but Wood would not take him on as a client. Determined to bring Wood around to his line of reasoning, Eddie Cantor became a professional nuisance, hanging around Wood's outer office all day, everyday. Finally, Joe Wood asked Eddie to show him his act. Eddie started performing the routines that had made him the hit of amateur nights all over New York. Halfway through, Wood shook his head, but handed Eddie his card and told him to report to Gaine's Manhattan Theatre on 34th Street and Sixth Avenue.

When he arrived at the theater, Eddie discovered that he was only one of twenty acts. The usual number needed to fill a bill was seven. In the days before actors' unions, such overbooking was standard operating procedure. Several agents would send down a handful of acts; all would go on for the matinee, then the theater manager would pick seven and send the others home.

Eddie went on and performed his usual act, but instead of laughter the matinee audience greeted him with silence. Despite the inauspicious tryout, the manager called Joe Wood and told him he was keeping Cantor, reasoning that although he hadn't gone over, he was "different" and bore watching. That night when Eddie went on for the seven o'clock show, he was a hit with exactly the same material. "It was the same every day," Cantor later wrote.

"I flopped every afternoon and was a hit at night." No explanation was ever given, but at least his part-time success before an audience impressed Joe Wood enough that he agreed to represent Eddie.

After Eddie's stint at Gaine's Theatre, Wood booked him throughout the Northeast for about $20 a week, out of which Wood received 10 percent. After paying his own way to his bookings, Eddie would shell out another $2 a day for room and board at the local boarding house. With careful budgeting, he could wind up with a dollar at the end of the week.

Once, after performing his routine at a Harlem theater, Eddie was approached by a man who introduced himself as Joseph M. Schenck. Schenck was president of the People's Vaudeville Company, which he owned along with his brother Nicholas, Adolph Zukor, and Marcus Lowe. Joe Schenck explained that he and his partners owned a small chain of four vaudeville houses in New York and New Jersey. He offered Cantor a week at the Lyric in Hoboken, followed by another at the New Lyceum in Elizabeth at the same salary he was now receiving. Eddie jumped at the chance.[1]

Eddie did so well on his opening night in Hoboken that Joe Schenck offered him a full run of their tiny circuit (the aforementioned New Jersey houses along with the Royal and Lyric, both in Brooklyn): four weeks at $20 per week. In addition, Schenck offered Eddie further runs, but only if he could come up with new material. Again, Eddie readily agreed.

At the end of the initial four weeks, however, Cantor was faced with a problem. The surefire act he was currently using was built up over many months and was mostly lifted and adapted from big-time acts. Any hastily thrown together new material would clearly be second rate. After racking his brains, Eddie came up with an idea. Maybe he wouldn't have to change his material. Perhaps all he needed was a change in his outward appearance.

In the following months, Eddie Cantor played the four theaters of the People's Vaudeville Company, a total of sixteen weeks with essentially the same act, only different makeups and dialects. The exact order is uncertain (accounts differ even in Cantor's own autobiographies), but Eddie went on as a Dutch comic, a Hebrew Comic, and a blackface comic. Although Cantor thought the audiences must have learned his patter by heart, surprisingly enough, Joe Schenck never caught on. In fact, by the time Eddie was completing his fourth circuit with the same lines, Schenck complimented him, telling him: "You know, Eddie, I like this last act of yours better than the other three."

Although his experience with the People's Vaudeville Company would seem to be of little consequence at the outset, it did have two long-term effects on Eddie Cantor's career. First, it introduced blackface into his act. He stumbled across the use of blackface almost by accident. In his attempt to change his makeup, Cantor was experimenting with some burnt cork, trying to sketch age lines into his youthful face. Eddie's awkward makeup attempts left his face too streaky. While trying to tidy up the lines, he wound up smearing the cork all over his face.

Gazing in the mirror, Eddie quickly realized a new character was staring him in the face. He defined the character even further by adding a pair of white spectacles, which he first used so he wouldn't have to put as much makeup around his eyes, thereby reducing the risk of getting cork dust in them. Besides, the glasses added a look of intelligence, a novel departure from the standard blackface portrayal of the time.

The second result of his success in small-time vaudeville was that Eddie became something of a local hero back on Henry Street. He was no longer the street fool, hanging from a lamp post, or even just a kid with dreams of becoming an actor. No, after working sixteen steady weeks on the stage, Eddie Cantor was now a professional.

Eddie would often spend his days off hanging around Henry Street, performing his act upon request. One Sunday a crowd from nearby Jefferson Street was parading their favorite son, vaudevillian Roy Arthur, up and down Henry Street to show him off. Arthur was one half of Bedini and Arthur, a big-time vaudeville team whose act consisted of juggling and travesty.

Not to be out done by Jefferson Street, the Henry Street crowd called for their favorite vaudevillian, Eddie Cantor, to do his stuff. Eddie pulled out all the stops performing for the appreciative neighborhood throng, but his act was aimed at only one man. "I went through my whole repertoire as if it were a tryout, keeping my eye on Arthur." Cantor later wrote, "The crowd applauded, but that didn't matter; what mattered was this man from another world, the world of top-line theaters."

Despite Eddie's best efforts, Roy Arthur's reaction seemed only one of indifference. Before he left, however, Arthur told Eddie to stop by and see him the next week at Hammerstein's theater. To the anxious small-time vaudevillian, "next week" meant Monday afternoon during intermission. Roy Arthur introduced Eddie to Jean Bedini, the head of the act, whose first words to Cantor were, "How would you like to join our act?" Cantor accepted at once at the hefty salary of $30 a week.[2]

Although Eddie immediately left the employ of the People's Vaudeville Company, his dealings with its partners were not finished. He would work with each of them again, directly or indirectly, in motion pictures. He played in two silents in the late 1920s at Paramount Pictures, whose president was Adolph Zukor. During the early thirties when Joseph Schenck was chairman of United Artists, the company distributed Cantor's films made for Sam Goldwyn. Then in 1937 Eddie made *Ali Baba Goes to Town* at 20th Century–Fox, where Joseph Schenck was chairman and co-founder. Nicholas Schenck was president of Lowe's Incorporated, MGM's parent company, which produced Eddie's film *Forty Little Mothers* in 1940. Although Marcus Lowe died in 1927, Eddie did work for the company Lowe founded for the aforementioned film.

Not wanting to burst the bubble of success that had so swiftly lighted on him, Cantor didn't ask Jean Bedini what he was to do or even when he would start. He just stayed with the pair throughout the rest of the day's performances, waiting for Bedini to tell him he was on next. He never did go on stage that day, or the next, or any day that week. Instead, Eddie Cantor ran errands, packed and unpacked the trunks, and looked after the makeup and costumes—all while waiting for Bedini's signal to get into costume. Another one of Eddie's duties would be to buy crockery from the five-and-dime, take it back to the theater, and crack it just enough so that it would smash well when dropped "accidentally on purpose" during the show.

At the end of the week, Eddie was paid his $30, dispelling the thought in his mind that it was all a joke. Although he longed to become more than a backstage valet, Eddie suffered in silence, while at the same time soaking up the rich surroundings of the big time, and studying the business of show business. "I watched my 'acting partners' keenly," Cantor later told David Freedman, "listened to their careful discussion of every piece of stage business, and while they performed, I peeked through the wings and wandered into other dressing rooms. I was getting paid to inhale atmosphere. Stage life seeped in through every pore."

Finally one day in the dressing room, with a cast of vaudeville all-stars present, Jean Bedini let Cantor do his act for the cast. "I want you to hear this boy and tell me what you think of him," Bedini said. Eddie went through his entire routine of impersonations that had served him so well in the past, only now he wasn't on before a small-time house, his audience were big names in the big time.

Cantor recalled their response was less than enthusiastic. "When I finished it was very quiet and even chilly in the room. All those who watched me knew the originals intimately and turned up their noses at my imitations." Eddie continued as Bedini and Arthur's silent and unseen partner.

After weeks of waiting, Eddie Cantor's opportunity finally came when Bedini informed him that he would be used in the next day's performance. Cantor thought he would be doing one of his impersonations, but Bedini wanted Eddie to try a different skill. "You'll just stand in the wings," the juggler explained, "and at a certain signal you'll bring on a plate, give it to me, and go off. That's all."

Disappointed, but still determined, Eddie spent hours readying his costume and makeup; he, like Roy Arthur, appeared in blackface to offset and draw attention to Jean Bedini, who performed in whiteface. In addition, Eddie carefully considered exactly how he would hand his boss the plate. If he couldn't be on stage for a lengthy period of time, Eddie reasoned, at least he would get a laugh in the brief moment he was on stage.

The next day when Eddie received his cue, he strolled leisurely out on stage, paused, languidly eyed Bedini and Arthur, and then haughtily looked out over the audience. Bedini and Arthur just stared at each other at the cheeky, unexpected display their new assistant was putting on. The audience roared. Having gotten his laugh, Cantor handed over the plate, turned, and exited to a nice round of applause.

Upstaging your employers was a risky thing to do, but in Cantor's case it paid off. Jean Bedini began to realize that Eddie had talent beyond small-time imitations. He could originate his own bits of business. Starting the next week, Cantor's role expanded when Bedini started to teach him how to juggle. Eddie's first assignment was to practice rolling a hat down his arm and catching it. With this minor feat mastered, Eddie graduated to performing the same trick, but with a plate.

Once he had the plate roll down pat, the bit was incorporated into Eddie's walk-on. Now Eddie would come on, hand the plate to Bedini, who would proceed to roll it down his arm and catch it at the last moment. Arthur would then try to duplicate the trick, only to have the plate crash on the floor. Eddie would then take another plate, slide it down, catch it, and snap his fingers disdainfully at Arthur. Roy Arthur would then chase Eddie around stage, swinging wildly at him with a hammer, while Eddie intoned in Oxford English, "He means to do me bodily harm!"

The audience roared even louder than before, partly because they had never heard a character in blackface speak in such a refined manner. From then on his character, a high-toned, effeminate black man, complete with round white spectacles, was a mainstay of the act, especially when he was paired against Roy Arthur in the role of the loutish bully.

As time went by, the act became filled with more nonsense comedy — initiated by Eddie — and less juggling. Jean Bedini eventually told Eddie that he could come out on stage to interrupt the act anytime he had something to add, provided it was funny. At first, Cantor was careful not to abuse the privilege, but as his ad-libbing skills sharpened and his timing got better, Eddie was interrupting the duo constantly. By now Eddie was enough of the act to get billing. The act was now "Bedini and Arthur, Assisted by Eddie Cantor."

Ironically, once Eddie had developed his own individual style, Bedini and Arthur started using him in their parodies of other acts on the bill with them. To add insult to injury, the spoofs would often include the other performer's own scenery "borrowed" for the occasion. They used Molasso's own sets to do their outrageous comic version of the violent Apache dance that the Frenchman had just introduced to America — directly after he had performed it straight.

Probably their best-known and most successful parody was a takeoff on the popular drama *Madame X*. Their version of that play's courtroom scene, which they entitled *Madame 10*, was the hit of Hammerstein's Victoria in Manhattan and was held over for ten weeks.

Often they would mimic famous women performers with Eddie, still blacked up, in drag. Once, while Eddie was playing Salome, dancing to Mendelssohn's "Spring Song," he lost his dress by accident. It stopped the show as the audience howled. Of course, it became a regular routine for the act, used every time Cantor appeared in drag. Especially when they needed a solid laugh, Bedini would signal, "Drop the dress!" And off it would fall.

The training Cantor received under Bedini and Arthur was to prove invaluable to him. The more adept he became at it, the more he realized comedy was a serious business. "Here I learned one of the basic lessons in the delivery of comedy," Cantor later revealed, "never to consciously point one's fun, but to do one's comedy very seriously, almost grimly, and let the audience pick the laugh itself."

One of Eddie's stock routines—usually coming right after the dress had been dropped—illustrates perfectly his use of nonsense delivered seriously. Just before his exit, Eddie would step up to the footlights, pause for a moment's reflection, then wistfully recite:

> Twinkle, twinkle, little star.
> How I wonder what you are!
> Up above the world so high—
> Oh, what care I?
> Oh, what care I?

Not terribly funny in itself, but coupled with Eddie's delivery it never failed to get a big laugh, after which Eddie would exit, skipping off stage. As Eddie received more of the lion's share of the laughs, he longed for more.

Bedini and Arthur were what was known as a "full stage act"—that is, they used the entire stage. Given the roughhouse style of their act, the stage-hands often needed five to ten minutes to clear the stage of the broken plates and mass destruction the team left in its wake. Initially, Bedini and Arthur would fill the time before the next act by performing before the curtain, but even this would cut it close with the clean-up crew. Eddie suggested to Jean Bedini that he could give them extra time by doing a song or two in front of the curtain. "By all means, Eddie," Bedini told him half-seriously, "learn a song and each time we open in a new place rehearse it just in case."

Months later when an extra number was needed to pad out the program, Eddie got his chance to go on.[3] He walked out in front of the curtain carrying a normal-sized violin case, from which he pulled a tiny toy violin. He plucked a few sour notes and announced, "You wouldn't believe this, but two weeks ago I couldn't play this thing at all!" From there he launched into a rousing rendition of "Ragtime Violin," one of the first hits from an up-and-coming songwriter by the name of Irving Berlin. The number was a smash, and Eddie had to do half a dozen encores. Singing, as he was, from an advanced copy, Eddie Cantor made "Ragtime Violin" the first in a long series of songs that he either introduced or was instrumental in popularizing.

This first singing appearance also helped to form another trademark of Cantor's style—his frantic, energy-filled delivery. Although he had been waiting weeks to try out his voice on stage, when the opportunity finally presented itself, Cantor was extremely nervous. Aside from Carey Walsh's saloon, he had never sung professionally, and, as he later put it, this was "on stage and before sober people!" His nerves, coupled with the peppy tempo of the song, caused Cantor to pace the stage, bob up and down, and clap his hands in time to the music. The effect on the audience was electrifying.

Never before had a singer performed with such energy—nervous or otherwise.

Cantor's song was such a hit that later in the dressing room he shared with Roy Arthur, Eddie overheard the theater manager arguing with Jean Bedini to give "that skinny little guy in blackface" more time. For Eddie opportunity was not only knocking, but yelling through the walls. Quickly, he took off his makeup and rushed next door to ask for a raise. Before Bedini could object, Eddie reminded him that he was "that skinny little guy" the manager had just been praising. Bedini gave in and raised Eddie $5 a week (not a bad deal for Bedini since the act was receiving an additional $75 with Cantor on the bill). In addition to the raise, Eddie's number before the curtain was kept in the act and expanded to ten minutes, including a monologue.

Eddie traveled the big vaudeville circuits with Bedini and Arthur for two years, starting as a gofer and becoming a polished vaudevillian who could get a laugh, put over a song, or assist in catching turnips. This later feat occurred in Kansas City in 1911 as a publicity stunt. The team was performing at the Orpheum Theater when Jean Bedini bet the *Kansas City Post* $250 that he could catch a turnip dropped from the fourteenth floor of the Waldheim building on a fork held in his teeth. According to newspaper accounts, the stunt attracted in excess of ten thousand spectators.

After a test turnip was dropped to demonstrate its impact, the local fire chief dropped a second turnip over two hundred feet towards a special platform built for the occasion. Bedini caught the vegetable on his fork. The turnip then split in two as Bedini tumbled back off the platform and was caught by his two assistants. A front-page photograph shows Bedini just before the trick giving last minute instructions to the fire chief. Next to him, wearing a pith helmet (perhaps as protection against other falling produce), is Eddie holding two turnips.

As Eddie's share of the act became larger, it was only a matter of time before he moved on to bigger things. The two years with his senior partners had transformed him into a professional, but after all, the act was still "Bedini and Arthur." The seeds for Eddie's next move were planted towards the end of the 1912 season when the act was playing Atlantic City. Also on the bill was Gus Edwards and one of his "kid" acts. Edwards was famous, not only for discovering many future stars as children, but in his own right as a performer and writer of hundreds of songs, including the standards "School Days" and "By the Light of the Silvery Moon."

Edwards was also known for bringing his acts along after the show to perform at benefits and private functions. One night Edwards and the boys in his act were appearing at a stag party at the Chelsea Yacht Club. Gus invited Eddie to tag along, and he did.

By the time the performers had arrived, the party was in full swing with most of the revelers having more than a few drinks under their belts. Half-tight, the all-male audience was in no mood for the sentimental songs Gus

Edwards was singing, and they started to get rowdy. Cantor jumped up on stage and began telling the audience two or three risqué stories, which he followed up with a slightly dirtied-up imitation of the vaudeville team Smith and Dale that he had thrown together on the way over with young Georgie Jessel, a member of Edwards' troupe. Cantor had saved the performance.

On the way back to the hotel, Edwards gushed with praise for Eddie. "My boy," he said, "you made the hit of the evening, and if you're ever out of a job, come to me!" Not wanting to be accused of stealing talent from another act, Edwards added, "You understand Bedini is a very dear friend of mine, and I couldn't just take you from him. It wouldn't be right. But if you ever should quarrel with him—it's liable to happen, you know—always remember, you can count on me."

Like a persistent fly, Edwards' offer buzzed inside of Eddie's head. In a Gus Edwards act, Eddie would be the featured player, perhaps even have an act built around him. It was the opportunity to be a star, not just an "assisted by." The only way he could accept Edwards' offer in good conscience, however, was to get Jean Bedini to fire him. That was not going to be easy. After all, any boss who gives you the license to interrupt and upstage him at will is not easily offended.

Suddenly, Eddie became argumentative and temperamental over everything in the act. At first the tolerant and easy-going Jean Bedini let Eddie's behavior slide, but over the span of several months even Bedini's patience was near an end. While they were planning their new act for the upcoming season, "Dandy Girls," Eddie complained his part was too small—this after he had managed to squeeze himself in every scene of the show. Finally, Bedini lost his temper. "If you don't like it, quit!" Bedini shouted.[4]

Feigning deep hurt, Cantor cried, "I quit!" He then rushed out to the nearest pay phone to call Gus Edwards, who was playing at a nearby theater. When Edwards got on the line, Eddie told him, "I quarreled!"

"Meet me at my office in New York the first thing tomorrow morning," Edwards replied. Eddie Cantor's apprenticeship was over.

## REVIEW

(The following press clipping is taken from one of Eddie Cantor's personal scrapbooks. Unfortunately, no notation is made of the date or place.)

> One of the clever entertainers at the Orpheum this week was not on the program as it was his first appearance and the advance printing did not include his name. He is Eddie Cantour [*sic*], the third man in the juggling act billed as Bedini and Arthur. Bedini says: "He is a clever boy. I discovered him about a year ago in his home, New York, where he was playing small houses and clubs. I have kept him with me, expecting at some time to work him into the act. Last Sunday the chance came. He has made good and will be a big card at some future day." Those who have seen him heartily indorse [*sic*] Mr. Bedini's opinion.

## *Notes*

1. Although he landed the People's Vaudeville booking by himself, Eddie continued to pay a commission to Joe Wood. After joining Bedini and Arthur, however, he decided he was his own best agent and for the next few years represented himself. Ironically, years later, his first agent after signing on with the William Morris Agency was Georgie Wood, Joe Wood's son.

2. Accounts as to how and when Cantor started to work with Bedini and Arthur vary, even by Eddie Cantor's own recollection. The account given is based on the more detailed version presented in his 1928 autobiography. According to his 1957 autobiography, he was not hired on the spot by Jean Bedini. Rather he hung around the theater doing odd-jobs for the pair while Roy Arthur tried to convince his partner that they could use Cantor in the act. When Bedini finally gave in, Cantor was hired at $35 a week.

3. Depending on conflicting accounts, Cantor's first singing performance in vaudeville either occurred at the Keith Theatre in Louisville or at Shea's Theatre in Buffalo.

4. According to Cantor's second autobiography, he didn't quit but was fired when Bedini told him, "One more word out of you and I'll fire you!" To which Cantor replied, "You wouldn't dare!"

# CHAPTER 4

# *Gus Edwards' Kid Kabaret*

Not having an agent, Eddie Cantor had to negotiate his own contract with Gus Edwards. The night before his meeting with Edwards, he consulted his childhood friend, Dan Lipsky, on the finer points of salary negotiation.

"I've been getting thirty-five a week from Bedini," Cantor explained, "but I think Edwards should do better than that." Dan told Eddie he thought a $5 a week raise should be fair, but in order to get that Eddie would have to ask for $50 a week.

The next day when Cantor met with Edwards he tried to present his demands forcefully, but he didn't quite have the nerve to ask for the salary he had rehearsed the previous night. Before Eddie could deliver his "exorbitant" demands, Edwards told Cantor that he wouldn't think of starting him at any less than $75 a week. Eddie quickly tabled his own demands and signed on.

The vehicle Gus Edwards had in mind for his newest performer was called *Kid Kabaret*. The idea behind the act was charmingly simple. A wealthy couple go out for a night at the theater and later a cabaret, leaving their young son home alone with the butler. In his parents' absence, the boy invites all his playmates over to stage their own cabaret. The framework provided a natural way for the young actors in the troupe to display their songs and impersonations. The rich boy (Carlton Terrace, Jr.) was played by Eddie Buzzell, who, after a stage career, would go on to become a director at MGM. The butler was played by Cantor, performing in blackface.

Cantor's part provided him with the lion's share of the laughs and allowed him to do imitations of Eddie Leonard and Al Jolson. According to Eddie, the audience was always on the side of someone in a servile position, and they loved it when he would talk back to his rich little master. The size of his part, coupled with the fact that he was the only adult in the cast, gave Eddie featured billing status. It was quite a promotion for Eddie to have the act listed as "Gus Edwards' *Kid Kabaret*, featuring Eddie Cantor."

Another member of the troupe was fourteen-year-old Georgie Jessel, whom Cantor had worked so well with back in Atlantic City. After Cantor,

Jessel was the principal comedian of the act, playing the role of "Muttky," a character the program described as "a little bit of Yiddish." Jessel was getting so many laughs of his own that Cantor soon asked Gus Edwards to change the billing to give Georgie featured status also. Edwards agreed.

This move made Eddie Buzzell so jealous that he began intentionally blowing his lines and throwing off Cantor's and Jessel's cue lines in an attempt to make them look bad. That night after the performance Cantor went to Buzzell's room and in his words, "gave him a good talking to, with both fists." Buzzell saw the logic behind Eddie's argument and apologized to Cantor and Jessel. Afterwards, the three became close friends.

Although Jessel's mother also traveled with the troupe, as wardrobe mistress, Jessel roomed with Cantor. Like Eddie, Georgie also had no father, brothers, or sisters. The two developed a close, lifelong friendship, often calling each other "brother." Like the closest of brothers, however, the pair often clashed. Eddie, being six years Jessel's senior, was the more cautious and frugal of the duo, while Georgie was a fast and loose free spirit.

Barely into puberty, Jessel had a voracious appetite for the opposite sex, one that would last throughout his life — to which his many marriages, often to girls much younger than he, would attest. (Cantor later remarked that Jessel was "a boy destined to make a career of alimony.") The girls also found Georgie, with his head of dark, curly hair, attractive.

Cantor immediately took Jessel under his wing, instructing him in the mysteries of regular bathing (with soap), proper diet ("so he never ate a thing he liked," cracked Cantor), and saving money. It was this last point that encountered the greatest resistance. The frugal Cantor tried to get the spendthrift Jessel to put away some of his earnings for the future. Saving wasn't so hard for Eddie, he had a goal. In addition to sending money to Grandma Esther, Eddie sent most of his salary home to Ida in order to build up the bankroll required to win her father's consent. At one point, Jessel suggested they open a joint bank account for emergencies. Cantor, thinking all his economics lectures had finally gotten through to Jessel, readily agreed. The financial partnership ended, however, when Eddie realized that he was doing all the saving, and Georgie was having all the emergencies.

Finally, Jessel started his own bank account of sorts in the form of a diamond stickpin. Whenever a financial emergency arose, Georgie would hock the pin, which was usually good for a quick $5 at the local pawn shop. Given Jessel's economic health, Eddie would often see his pal without the pin. When Eddie would ask where it was, Georgie would reply, "Oh, it's back in the hotel room on the dresser." When Eddie would press him to go back and retrieve it, Jessel would smile sheepishly, shrug his shoulders, and pull the pawn ticket out of his pocket.

Years later, long after Cantor had left the *Kid Kabaret* and was a featured performer in the *Ziegfeld Follies*, Eddie was still trying to get Georgie to economize. The Christmas issue of *Variety* traditionally carried ads from actors wishing their friends and co-workers seasons greetings and a happy

New Year. In the 1919 edition, Eddie took out a full-page ad which read: "Eddie Cantor pays $77.50 for this 'ad' so that he can advise his friend George Jessel to save his money!"

In all fairness to Jessel, Cantor could be too frugal at times. After Cantor had become a movie star, he moved into a home in Beverly Hills which didn't have a swimming pool. When a friend suggested he put a pool in, Eddie said he didn't need one. "Besides," he reasoned, "they're too expensive." When the friend cited the old adage "you can't take it with you," Jessel quickly noted, "If Cantor can't take it with him, he'll send it on ahead."

On the road the two friends were always trying to economize, Cantor to save money and Jessel because he never had any. Once in San Francisco, Jessel met a girl whose father owned a restaurant. Georgie assured Eddie that his charms would keep them eating on the cuff for their entire stay in the city. True to Jessel's promise they ate free for two weeks. "But you know," Cantor recalled years later, "you can get awfully tired of chow mein."

As Jessel's "older brother," Cantor would also try to steer Georgie away from what Eddie considered trouble. Once, while the act was in New Orleans, Cantor kept his friend from going into a brothel, claiming Jessel was too young to be frequenting such places. Jessel begged Cantor, reasoning that in each city they stopped in Eddie had taken him to see the famous sites of the town. If they visited the White House in Washington, D.C., according to Georgie's logic, then he should be allowed to visit a whorehouse in New Orleans. Finally Georgie broke into tears, and Eddie agreed, "Okay, okay, Friday!"

Jessel's youthful maturity came back to haunt Cantor in other ways. As the oldest actor in the company and an experienced vaudevillian, Eddie was put in charge of the troupe's train tickets. In order to get half-price fares, Cantor had the girls dress in short skirts and the boys in knickers, even though some of the "kids" were as old as sixteen. Once a conductor pulled Cantor aside and asked him to identify the members of the company riding at half-fare. Eddie led the conductor through the cars, pointing out his young colleagues. Not one of the discount fares was disputed until they reached the club car. There they found Jessel in his short pants, to be sure, but also wearing a derby, smoking a big black cigar, and regaling the traveling salesmen in the car with a succession of dirty jokes. "That's a kid?" the conductor growled. "Oh, well," Eddie said, shrugging his shoulders, "boys will be boys."

In the two years he spent touring with the *Kid Kabaret*, Eddie Cantor met two men who would have a great influence on his career, Al Jolson and Will Rogers. Jolson had come up through vaudeville in Docksteader's Minstrels, then in a solo act, and finally in his own starring vehicles at Broadway's Winter Garden Theatre. Cantor first saw Jolie perform at Hammerstein's vaudeville back while Eddie was still a gofer for Bedini and Arthur. Jolson was just starting out as a solo performer, but he made an immediate impression on Eddie. "From the first time I heard him at Hammerstein's, he was

**Apparently a teenaged Georgie Jessel doesn't share Eddie's enthusiasm for the moon in this photo taken during the pair's *Kid Kabaret* days (c. 1912) (collection of Brian Gari).**

my idol," Cantor recalled. "There was something electric about him that sent a thrill up your spine."

Years later, when the *Kid Kabaret* played Oakland, Eddie found out that Jolson was in the city visiting his wife. Cantor and Jessel immediately set out to find Jolson. They found out all of Jolie's haunts and starting haunting them themselves in an effort to meet their idol. After a week of hanging around Oakland, they had still not found Jolson. Then one day, after their matinee performance, the stage doorman came back and told Eddie and Georgie that Al Jolson was waiting to see them. They both laughed, each thinking the other had sent the stage doorman back as a joke.

"Let him wait," Jessel laughed. "Sure, let him wait," Cantor agreed. They then leisurely took off their costumes and makeup and changed into their street clothes. Only after they walked out of the theater and saw Al Jolson waiting for them did they realize that the message had been on the level.

Jolson, in spite of cooling his heels waiting for the pair, told them he had enjoyed the act and thought they were a couple of talented kids. He then treated the stunned duo to dinner at a nearby kosher restaurant. The meal was entirely Jolson, as the star-struck Cantor and Jessel were too in awe of Jolie to speak. At the end of the meal, Jolson excused himself and visited the men's room. As soon as he left the table, Eddie and Georgie flipped a coin to see who would follow the great Jolson into the bathroom. Cantor won, and a few minutes later he rushed out to proclaim, "Georgie, that Jolson! He does it like anybody!"

Eddie Cantor first met Will Rogers when they played together on the same program at the Orpheum Theatre in Winnipeg in 1912. *Kid Kabaret* was heading the bill (going on last), while Rogers, with his cowboy roping act, was fourth from closing. According to Cantor, Will Rogers did the most amazing roping tricks, but had not yet spoken on stage. By Jessel's account, Rogers was already famous as a monologist. Actually, as reviews bear out, he was only just starting to use talking in his act when Cantor and Jessel met him.

Rogers took an immediate liking to Eddie and the rest of the kids. Eddie idolized Will, calling their time on the bill together "the happiest engagement I ever played." For ten weeks they were on the same circuit; during this time, Will organized and outfitted a baseball team made up of himself and the members of the *Kid Kabaret*. On their last night together, Cantor and Jessel went on stage during Rogers' act to present him with a silver cup for his efforts as their manager. The emotional Rogers cried and kissed them both before hurrying back to Oklahoma, where his wife had just given birth to their first daughter.

Years later, after they had been reunited in the *Ziegfeld Follies*, Will would remind Eddie of when they had first met on the Orpheum circuit. Whenever Eddie scored a hit with the critics, with whatever show he happened to be in at the time, Will Rogers would send him a wire reading, "These critics are a little late, I knew this back in Winnipeg."

When they weren't playing baseball with Will Rogers or scouring Oak-land for Al Jolson, Cantor and Jessel would fill their leisure time by amusing themselves on stage. Unfortunately for the victim, this happened during someone else's act. Once the duo broke in on the climax of what Cantor called, "a perfectly boring mystery thriller." As the actor on stage cried out in a fit of histrionics, "Where is my daughter?" Eddie and Georgie, in black-face, walked across the back of the stage with brooms slung over their shoulders like rifles. The audience broke up, as did any hopes for completing the performance.

Another time, they sabotaged the solos of Betty Washington, a violinist who was in the *Kid Kabaret*, their own act. Washington, Cantor noticed, had been getting more applause "than was healthy for her." The next night as she took her bow, she was stunned to find Cantor and Jessel on either side of her, violins in hand, sharing her curtain call. Obviously, for whatever reason, this girl was a favorite victim of the pair. A few nights later, just as she had finished her playing but before the applause could begin, Cantor suddenly appeared in one of the theater's boxes, making a loud campaign speech. The audience forgot about Washington and lavished their laughter and applause on Cantor. Eddie later admitted the tricks weren't very ethical, but were an old established tradition of the theater.

Eddie Cantor was part of Gus Edwards' *Kid Kabaret* for two seasons on the Orpheum circuit. The number one booking available in vaudeville and the jewel in the Orpheum crown, was the famous Palace Theatre in Manhat-tan, which the *Kid Kabaret* played in 1913. The circuit took the company throughout the United States and Canada. Edwards and his wife ran the troupe like a family, and they usually celebrated birthdays and holidays to-gether.

One charming newspaper clipping out of Eddie Cantor's scrapbook tells of the Christmas of 1913 in Lake Charles, Louisiana. After the audience had gone home, the local theater manager, a Mr. Little, and his wife threw a holiday party for the "Kids." After a sumptuous meal, the cast spent the rest of the evening entertaining the Littles and themselves with impromptu specialties. "Eddie Cantor," the article recounts, "'Cantored' about the stage, doing nothing but make noise, but keeping everyone in laughter. Eddie it seems, took three foolish powders before he started, and was primed for the work."

Although he enjoyed the camaraderie of the stage, Eddie would still rather have been spending his holidays back in New York with Ida. For two years Ida had been saving every penny that Eddie had sent her. By the spring of 1914, the couple had amassed $2,500. In addition, Eddie had saved enough to buy Ida a dazzling diamond ring. Since he was on the road, how-ever, he would have to wait until he got back to New York to present it to her. For safekeeping, Eddie wore it himself, even on stage, cutting a hole in one of the fingers of his glove in order to get it on over the diamond.

With $2,500 in the bank and a woman's engagement ring on his finger,

**Cantor (right) mugs while Jessel (center) ignores him (collection of Brian Gari).**

Eddie Cantor left the *Kid Kabaret* at the end of the second season. Eddie had saved the amount Ida's father had required of any serious suitor for his daughter's hand. Contrary to David Tobias' plans, however, Eddie had no intention of opening a haberdashery with the money. All actors, in Mr. Tobias' opinion, were bums, and no bum would marry his daughter. True, he had given Eddie permission to stay in show business while courting Ida, but only until Eddie had saved enough to go into a respectable profession.

"If you don't open a gents' furnishings store," Tobias cautioned Eddie, "you'll be sorry for the rest of your life. And remember David Tobias warned you!" He added, "After all, how long do you think people will go on paying good money for such foolishness like dancing and singing. Some day they'll get wise to themselves, and then where will you be?"

Cantor evidently believed that people would need entertainment long after neckties had gone out of fashion. Instead of a frontal argument, however, he appealed to his future father-in-law's sense of pride. "A man as big as David Tobias should have a son-in-law with only one store?" Eddie reasoned. "It should be three minimum. One in the Bronx, one in Manhattan, and one in Brooklyn!" To realize his vision of a haberdashery empire, Eddie argued, he would have to stay in show business longer to raise enough capital.

Although Mr. Tobias finally consented to the wedding of Eddie and Ida, he was never completely convinced that Eddie wouldn't have been better off owning a nice men's furnishings store. Cantor liked to tell the story of the time in 1933 when he was in New York for some personal appearances. His father-in-law came down to the theater to see him. Cantor took Mr. Tobias outside to the front of the theater and pointed to the marquee, which proclaimed in huge letters "Eddie Cantor in Person." Eddie then drew his attention across the street, where a movie theater advertised "Eddie Cantor in Roman Scandals." From there he took him around the corner to another movie house, which was showing a reissue of *Whoopee!* Throughout the tour Tobias never said a word. Finally, David Tobias pointed to a sign over a storefront which read "Nat Lewis's haberdashery" and broke his silence, saying, "*That* sign will always be there!"

## REVIEWS

Most of the following reviews come from Eddie Cantor's personal scrapbook. Unfortunately the names of the newspapers were not included with the clippings. It was also the practice of most newspapers not to give bylines to their vaudeville critics.

> Gus Edwards appears to have lost his "cunning" in the presentment of "kid" acts. His latest can scarcely be designated a hit for the reason that he hasn't a single performer in the cast who may be signally mentioned for the individual honors, unless it be Eddie Cantor as a blackface butler. — *Variety*, September 6, 1912

> "A Kid Kabaret in Kidland," one of the latest offerings of Gus Edwards, is the headliner at the Orpheum this week. Twenty "kids" take part in it and the company has for its principals Eddie Cantor and Georgie Jessel, who are wonderful fun makers. During the Kabaret several clever songs are sung by the youngsters, who show much dramatic as well as musical ability. — Omaha, Nebraska, October 31, 1913

Gus Edwards' Kids "kome back" this week at the Orpheum. To do it they stage a "Kid Kabaret" and before it winds up in A No. 1 cabaret fashion, there's enough music, tomfoolery and fun to make up a musical comedy. The audience joins in the frolic along towards the end and when favors are dispensed the offering takes on cafe caliber.

Like Gus Edwards' "Song Review" the act goes rapidly. Eddie Cantor as the butler-in-chief and announcer keeps things hustling to a whirlwind finale, all the while scattering comedy right and left. — Portland, Oregon, July 14, 1913

Gus Edwards' Kid Kabaret tops the bill. It is further an elaborate act with about twenty youthful fun makers in the cast. Eddie Cantor, as the negro butler, put over a good line of comedy and keeps the audience laughing constantly.

Eddie Cantor as the butler rises far over the rest in ability; they are "just cute kids"; yet he is the comedian that seems to lend the whole performance its dash and zest — he "kiddifies" the kids. — Salt Lake City, Utah, September 26, 1913

Eddie Cantor in the blackface is an able juvenile comedian, and Bettie [sic] Washington, child violinist, is some musician. The act drags occasionally, an expected difficulty where juveniles are concerned. — Spokane, Washington, June 19, 1913

# CHAPTER 5

# *Cantor and Lee —*
# *Master and Man*

If David Tobias was leery about his daughter marrying Eddie Cantor, Eddie's Grandma Esther was delighted. Esther had approved of Ida from the first time they met back when Eddie was courting her in the schoolyard. She smiled approvingly at Ida, then turned to Eddie and said, "Goot, mein kinde." As the years moved on, Grandma Esther prayed for Eddie and Ida's marriage, knowing Ida would care for her little Itchik after she had passed on.

After much cajoling, David Tobias consented to Eddie and Ida's wedding. Unlike his other daughters, however, Ida would not have an elaborate wedding in a rented hall. Instead, due to Tobias' lack of faith in his prospective son-in-law's future, the couple was married in the family's apartment on June 9, 1914. Only a handful of close relatives were invited. "When they started to give the presents," Cantor later quipped, "I realized how close they were!"

Immediately after the ceremony, the couple, armed with $700 in savings, departed on the *Aquitania* for a working honeymoon in Europe. Eddie, along with a straightman, Sammy Kessler, was booked for a week at the Oxford Theatre in London. Cantor had been teamed with Kessler by theatrical agent Max Hart, who had begun to represent Eddie after he had left Gus Edwards' employ.

After a week on the high seas, second class, in order to save money, Eddie and Ida arrived in London in time for his booking. Cantor recalled the week at the Oxford as one of the most notable flops of his career. The trouble, as the old stage joke goes, wasn't with the material, but with the audience. Eddie, along with Kessler, delivered a pastiche of his best material, but since most of that consisted of imitations of American stars, the audience sat in baffled silence. After all, it's very difficult to judge whether or not you're seeing a good impression of Eddie Leonard or Al Jolson if you've never seen Eddie Leonard or Al Jolson.

After an increasingly successful career on American stages, the week-long debacle at the Oxford, coupled with the added responsibilities of supporting a new wife, left Eddie frightened. Fortunately, Ida still believed in Eddie and implemented a strict regime of economy till the crisis was past. The couple started budgeting carefully for every meal and took to doing their own laundry in the hotel washbasin. Once when they went out for tea, the waitress brought by a tray loaded with pastries. Eddie asked how much they cost. The waitress told him the price, roughly twelve cents in American money. Thinking they had bought the entire tray, Eddie and Ida forced themselves to eat every pastry in front of them. It was only after they had stuffed themselves that they found out that the price was twelve cents each.

Luckily, Eddie didn't have to wait long for another booking. He wired Max Hart for advice, and Hart told him to go see Andre Charlot. Charlot, famous in England for producing high-class reviews, had seen Eddie at the Oxford Theatre and hired him, without Kessler, to appear in his latest show, *Not Likely*. Realizing the failure at the Oxford wasn't Eddie's fault, Charlot encouraged Eddie to drop the imitations and be himself. In *Not Likely*, Eddie came out in blackface and did ten minutes of jokes, mostly about the other acts in the show. He closed his act with a song called "I Love the Ladies." The number went over so well that Eddie was called on nightly to sing encores. *Not Likely* had so much repeat business that before long the audience started accompanying Cantor.

Eddie played in *Not Likely* for a month, with Ida watching each performance, either from the last row of the balcony or from the orchestra pit. The Cantors' honeymoon was cut short by the storm clouds of World War I, which were quickly gathering over Europe. Eddie and Ida returned to New York July 29, 1914, on the last ship to arrive before the war broke out. The ship, the *St. Paul*, creaked and strained the entire crossing and according to Cantor sank soon after the last passenger had disembarked.

That same day they got back to New York, Eddie was in Max Hart's office showing him the clippings from his London success, trying to get work as a solo act. To a seasoned agent like Hart, however, the reviews were not strong enough to book Eddie as a single. Instead, Hart offered to team him yet again, this time with Al Lee, considered one of the top straightmen in vaudeville. Immediately, the team of Cantor and Lee was formed.

Eddie, who again appeared in blackface, wrote their act, which he called *Master and Man*. The routine was, in Cantor's words, "strictly a nut act," filled with nonsense jokes and silly asides. *Master and Man* opened with Lee, in whiteface, and Cantor doing four minutes of patter. With the war raging in Europe, Eddie told Al he would soon be off to battle.

"You'll have to let me go," Eddie exclaimed.

"Why?"

"To fight in the war, for my mother country Russia!"

"Russia?"

"Darkest Russia," the blacked-up Eddie replied.

"I didn't know you were Russian," Lee would say incredulously.

"Oh yes," Eddie assured him, "my relatives are all in the war. My father's General Petrovich, my uncle's General Ivanovitch. General Itzowitch, and Eczema. . . ."

"Eczema?" Al interrupted.

"Yeah," Eddie said, "that's another itch!"

Aside from the war, the jokes ranged across a gamut of topics from love to family matters.

"I passed your house last night," Lee would start. "Next time you make love to your wife, pull down the shade!"

"The joke's on you," Cantor would laugh. "Last night I was in Philadelphia!"

"My father's an engineer," Lee would brag. "He makes engines."

"That's nothing," Cantor would counter. "My father's a commuter . . . he makes two trains a day!"

After their jokes, Al Lee would sing a ballad, or rather would attempt to sing a ballad, for Eddie would interrupt Al between every line of the song. Usually the song would be a tearjerker, like "The Curse of an Aching Heart."

"You made me what I am today," Lee would sing.

"If there were chickens in a lunatic asylum," Eddie would interrupt, "would they lay cracked eggs?"

"I hope you're satisfied," Lee would continue.

"I know where you got that collar," Eddie would proclaim.

"Where?" Al answered.

"Around your neck!"

"You dragged and dragged me down until the soul within me died," Lee went on, trying to ignore his partner.

"Speaking of necks," Cantor would say, "your neck reminds me of a typewriter — Underwood!"

After destroying Al Lee's solo attempts, Eddie would close the act with three or four songs of his own. One of them, "Down in Bom-Bom-Bay," an early jazz number, became a hit.

Cantor and Lee made their debut at the Star Theatre in upper Manhattan in August 1914. Eddie Cantor's own recollection of their first appearance is somewhat in question. In his first autobiography, he proclaims the act a hit from its first performance. In his 1957 book, he recounts that Max Hart told them to get some better material, leaving the team to scour the pages of humor magazines in an attempt to punch up the act. Either way, Max Hart managed to keep the act working steadily.

Steady work was just what Eddie needed. He and Ida were subletting a room in the apartment of Ida's sister in the Bronx. They dreamed of one day owning a home of their own and set aside $50 a week towards their goal. (Cantor was making $115 a week with Lee, not including commissions or expenses.) Although Eddie spent most of his time touring the act with Al Lee, the need for living space became even more acute on March 31, 1915, when

**Eddie Cantor in a solo portrait from his days with straightman Al Lee (1915) (collection of Brian Gari).**

Ida gave birth to their first child. "We called her Marjorie," Cantor later noted, "because it was a girl."

Cantor and Lee did fairly well on the vaudeville circuit, playing throughout the country. For the first time in his stage career, Eddie Cantor was working on developing his own professional identity, rather than relying on imitations of established stars. The process of Eddie finding his own style and hitting his stride was accomplished in fits and starts, with many difficulties on the way. When the act played the Majestic Theatre in Milwaukee, however, Eddie experienced what was probably his worst week in show business. Usually vaudeville bills would open with a visual act, an acrobat, or animal act, one that didn't require much talk, so the act wouldn't be disturbed by late arrivals finding their seats. From there the bill would build until by the fourth act the audience could expect a big number, one that would fill the stage.

In Milwaukee that particular week, the show opened with a banjo player performing before the curtain (or "in one"), followed by a pianist, then Will Rogers, also in one. Cantor and Lee were slated to go on in the fourth position. By the time they appeared, however, the audience expected the curtain to open for a full stage act. Instead, it opened to Eddie and Al standing alone before a backdrop doing jokes. "The audience wondered what the hell was going on," Cantor recalled. In protest, they sat in silence, refusing to laugh or applaud.

To add insult to injury, Cantor and Lee were demoted to the opening spot for the next performance. With half the audience still getting settled in their seats, the act continued to founder. Now, instead of being snubbed by the audience, Eddie and Al were just plain ignored by a large majority of them. After a few performances, Eddie was ready to quit, but Al talked him into seeing the week out.

At the end of the week, the theater manager, a man named Higler, took Eddie aside and gave him some friendly advice. Higler encouraged Eddie to get out of show business. "In this business," he told Eddie, "there are people who have it and people who haven't. You just haven't got it!" Citing Eddie's responsibilities as a family man, the manager advised him to quit as quickly as possible.

It was one thing to hear that lecture from David Tobias, but from a theater insider it was especially devastating. In tears Eddie walked out of the theater and prayed for a beer truck to hit him (he was in Milwaukee, after all). In the weeks to come, whenever the act went over poorly, Eddie thought of Higler, and wondered if perhaps he hadn't been right.

Cantor and Lee's tour eventually brought them back to New York for an engagement at the Palace. Although they were doing fairly well, they found that they weren't being paid on an equal scale to similar acts on the bill. It was then that they found out that Max Hart had been throwing them in at a bargain rate to theaters that booked his headline acts. Again Cantor had to chalk it up as another lesson in the school of show business and go on.

It was during his time with Al Lee that Cantor also dropped his "anything for a laugh" approach to comedy. The team often played club dates for lodges and smokers after their regular vaudeville turn. At one such performance before a group of visiting firemen in Rochester, Eddie pulled out all the stops, giving the stag audience the dirtiest routines they'd ever heard. The audience howled with laughter, and Cantor felt sure that he'd been a hit. Later back at the hotel and out of his blackface makeup, Eddie ran into some of the firemen. They were talking about Cantor and Lee. Since they didn't recognize Eddie without his makeup, he was able to eavesdrop on their conversation.

"Pretty funny, wasn't it," one of the firemen said.

"He seemed to be such a young fellow, though," another commented, adding, "How could such a fellow that young have such a filthy mind?"

Crestfallen, Cantor went back to his room and took an oath to himself that he would never again use obscene material. "Telling a dirty story is like seeing a couple of hundred pigeons flying and firing into the flock," Cantor noted years later. "It's too easy, there's no sport to it. And it isn't necessary."

For the most part, Eddie Cantor kept his word. Although his act would, in the future, contain what at the time may have been considered risqué material, he was sensitive to criticism. He often—though not always—removed questionable jokes or lyrics if they were found to be offensive. Once, while on tour with *Make It Snappy*, the drama critic for the *Detroit Times* expressed surprise that a comedian of Cantor's standing would resort to performing the song "Steady, Eddy," which he considered vulgar. Cantor permanently dropped the song from the show and apologized in writing to the *Detroit Times* and Detroit.

## REVIEW

Act opens with talk on war, pertinent and to the point. Carries a good quota of laughs.

Cantor in blackface and Lee playing straight. After war talk, Lee sings "Carolina," and Cantor comes on for "Victrola" and "Snyder's Grocery Store."

Cantor does some travesties on pictures that are laughable. Cantor also pulls a lot of "sissy stuff," unusual in blackface. Act ends with brisk duet.

Went so well at the Palace [Chicago] Cantor had to make a speech. Good comedy act out of the beaten rut.—*Variety*, November 20, 1914

# CHAPTER 6

# *Canary Cottage*

Cantor and Lee played the Orpheum circuit for a year and a half steady with only one break (actually it was Al Lee who got the break to go back to New York to see a sick relative). Eddie continued the act with straightman Fred Warren of Warren and Conley, who played with Cantor in addition to his own partner until Lee returned. Late in February 1916, Cantor and Lee were playing an extended engagement at the Orpheum Theatre in Los Angeles. Nightly they played to celebrities and bigwigs from the growing motion picture industry. With all those influential people in the audience, it was a good place to be "discovered." After all, Mack Sennett had plucked Charlie Chaplin from vaudeville just a few years back, and Charlie was now earning $670,000 a year in the movies.

Eddie Cantor was also plucked from vaudeville while playing the Orpheum in Los Angeles, but ironically it was not for the movies, but for the legitimate theater. One night Earl Carroll, a young songwriter fresh off his first hit, *So Long, Letty* with Charlotte Greenwood, spotted Eddie in his act with Al Lee. Carroll was impressed by Cantor's strong delivery and his unbounded energy on the stage. He thought Eddie would be perfect for a supporting role in his latest show, *Canary Cottage*, which would star Trixie Friganza, a popular comedienne. After the show he came backstage and told Cantor that his producer, Oliver Morosco, wanted to see him the next afternoon. The next day Carroll told Morosco: "This fellow Cantor ought to be good for our show. He sings songs like nobody's business and covers the stage like liquid fire!"

The following afternoon Eddie met with Oliver Morosco and was offered the part of a black chauffeur to Trixie Friganza's character. Morosco explained the show would open in Los Angeles, then work its way east, and eventually play Broadway. There was one catch, however; Morosco only wanted Cantor, he had no need of Al Lee. Valiantly, Eddie turned down the part, explaining that he didn't work without his partner.

Feeling noble for his decision, Eddie went back to that afternoon's matinee at the theater and told Al what he had done. Lee told Eddie he was crazy. "If you want the job then take it! Besides," Lee explained, "I wouldn't

44

be tied up in a town like this at any price, I'm Broadway." Eddie rushed back to Morosco's office and took the part. Rehearsals were scheduled to begin in a month.[1]

Aside from Trixie Friganza, the cast of *Canary Cottage* included Charlie Ruggles, Louise Orth, and Walter Johnson. Cantor, a newcomer to the legitimate stage, was listed fifth. Eddie's part was rather small, but he did have two songs to perform, "It Ruined Marc Anthony" and "I'll Marry No Explorer." Still, after paying his dues for so many years in vaudeville, Eddie was determined to make his first appearance in musical comedy memorable.

Throughout rehearsals Eddie would ad-lib jokes and bits of business in an effort to juice up his role. Each time he inserted something new, Earl Carroll, Oliver Morosco, and Elmer Harris, author of the book, would laugh at Eddie's efforts. The next day, however, whenever Eddie would start to repeat the previous day's ad-lib, he would be told that his new line had been dropped. Instead of increasing his part, Eddie found that bit by bit his role was dwindling to a few meager lines of little consequence.

Eddie was tipped off to what was happening by a frequent visitor to the rehearsals, Raymond Griffith. Griffith himself had been a successful actor, but he had injured his vocal chords and his voice was now a mere hoarse whisper. Although this ended his stage career, later, in 1922, Griffith turned to silent comedy and became a popular movie star in a series of feature films at Paramount. Cantor and Griffith had met when Eddie was playing the Orpheum with Al Lee. The two hit it off immediately and soon became friends.

When Griffith saw what was happening to Eddie, he took him aside and told him that Trixie Friganza was responsible for his troubles. Whenever Eddie inserted a line that got a laugh, Friganza, jealous for her own position as star of the show, would complain to Morosco. Since she was a proven star and Eddie only a supporting player, Eddie's suggestions were invariably thrown out.

"Don't let Friganza worry you," Griffith advised. "Write down whatever you think is funny, but don't do it at rehearsals." Griffith told Eddie to bide his time, wait for opening night, then use all the material he had saved up. Eddie heeded his friend's advice and kept his mouth shut, speaking only the few lines he had left. After five weeks of rehearsals, *Canary Cottage* moved down to San Diego for a three-day tryout before the Los Angeles opening. Still Eddie kept quiet, saving his punches for the important L.A. critics.

On opening night in Los Angeles, Cantor let loose. Whereas in rehearsal and in San Diego he had performed his tiny part with hardly a whimper, in L.A. he roared. Fortunately for Eddie, so did the audience. Cantor had fifteen entrances and exits; drawing on all his previous show business experience, Eddie managed to work some laughs into each one. "When I came on to dust the furniture I also dusted the fruit bowl and the fruit, and, taking up three oranges, I did my juggling act from the Bedini and Arthur days," Cantor recounted. "On another exit I worked in my ventriloquist bit that I had developed while with Gus Edwards. A third time, as Trixie Friganza, who was all dressed in white and weighed about two hundred and forty pounds, left the stage, I exclaimed, looking after her: 'My God! A milk wagon!'"

While the audience ate up Eddie's performance, his flagrant upstaging ate up the insides of the show's star, Trixie Friganza. After the show, producer Oliver Morosco came backstage to visit each dressing room with words of congratulations. He didn't stop to say a word to Cantor. Dejected, Eddie went to see his adviser, Raymond Griffith, for some consolation. Griffith was ready with a bottle of champagne. He told Eddie they had reason to celebrate. "So maybe you'll be fired," Raymond told him. "Tomorrow there'll be a hundred jobs waiting for you!"

The next day when Eddie arrived at the theater for the matinee performance, the stage doorman informed him that Mr. Morosco wanted to see him before he went to his dressing room. As Eddie took the walk to Morosco's downtown office, he felt certain that he had played his last performance of *Canary Cottage*. When Eddie reached the producer's office, he found Morosco sitting behind his desk with a stern look on his face.

"Eddie Cantor," he began, "what you did last night is the most unforgivable thing that can happen in the theater." Cantor braced himself for the boom to be lowered, but instead Morosco smiled and continued, "Now you go right back to the matinee and do everything you did last night, exactly the same way!" Morosco went on to predict stardom for Eddie and christened him "the apostle of pep" for his frenetic stage presence. Eddie's gamble had worked; not only had he scored a hit with the audience, but with his producer and the Los Angeles critics as well.

Predictably, Cantor's enlarged role did not go over well with Trixie Friganza, who waited until the next afternoon's rehearsal to voice her complaints. There, before Morosco, Carroll, Harris, and the entire cast, the show's star delivered her ultimatum. "Either this amateur goes or I leave, Mr. Morosco," Friganza threatened. Calmly, Oliver Morosco informed his star that he intended to keep Cantor for the run of the play. Friganza settled down and withdrew her demands. In time she even warmed up to Cantor, hiring him to write material for her club dates. She paid him $200—all of it in $20 gold pieces.

The extra money Eddie Cantor earned writing material for Trixie Friganza came in handy, especially since he now had another mouth to feed. On April 27, 1916, while Eddie was still in rehearsals for *Canary Cottage*, Ida gave birth to a daughter, their second. They named the baby Natalie.

With *Canary Cottage* enjoying a successful Los Angeles run and Cantor having a run-of-the-play contract, it was impossible for him to get back to New York to see his newest daughter. By the time September rolled around, between his vaudeville act and his current play, Cantor had been away from home for more than nine months and was getting homesick. Eddie wrote frequently to Ida complaining of his West Coast exile, which, though it had been good for his career, was keeping him away from his family. He also wrote to Max Hart, asking his agent if perhaps there wasn't work for him back in New York.

Finally, desperate to get back east, Eddie had his brother-in-law send him a telegram telling him to rush home because Ida was ill. (In another version of this same story, Cantor says that Ida, her sister, and Max Hart conspired to send the wire.) Upon receipt of the bogus message, Eddie ran to Oliver Morosco. Shedding crocodile tears, Eddie begged Morosco to release him. Sympathetically, Morosco agreed to put on Eddie's understudy, Lew Cooper, leaving Cantor free to return to New York.

Eddie was packing for his homecoming when another telegram, this time a real one, came from Max Hart. Hart wired Eddie that he had just booked him for twenty weeks on the New Amsterdam Roof in Florenz Ziegfeld's *Midnight Frolics*. It seems that Ziegfeld, along with his actress wife, Billie Burke, had caught Cantor in *Canary Cottage* during a recent trip to Los Angeles. Ziegfeld was impressed by Eddie's lively performance and thought he might be equally successful in the *Frolics*. Unbeknownst to Eddie, however, was the fact that Ziegfeld had only authorized a one-night tryout on the New Amsterdam Roof. Max Hart had told him he had a full-season contract in order to keep Eddie from getting overly nervous and ruining his audition.[2]

Although the details surrounding Eddie Cantor's departure from *Canary Cottage* are obscure in spots, the fact remains that he was heading home. And not only was Eddie returning to his family, but he would be working—for one night, at least—for Broadway's top producer.

## REVIEW

"Canary Cottage," opening at the Morosco Sunday, is the best comedy with music Oliver Morosco has produced, and it is a hit, pronounced here a better show than "So Long Letty."

Morosco and Elmer Harris wrote the book, which is rather Parisian. Earl Carroll supplied the score and lyrics. These far surpass anything Carroll has previously done. His "Canary Cottage," "I Never Knew," and "California Orange" songs leave an impression. There are other musical hits also.

Eddie Cantor is the bright spot, though held down. Trixie Friganza hasn't enough to do and the same may be said for Herbert Corthell. — *Variety*, May 26, 1916

## *Notes*

1. Oddly enough, Eddie Cantor in two separate autobiographies gives two different accounts of exactly how he landed his role in *Canary Cottage*. The first account, in his 1928 book, *My Life Is in Your Hands*, places him and Lee back east when Earl Carroll caught the act. In addition, Cantor has Morosco wanting both of them, with Al Lee refusing to go to California. Cantor's later book, *Take My Life*, tells the story as it is presented

here. Vaudeville booking schedules from *Variety* in 1916 place Cantor and Lee in Los Angeles at the time *Canary Cottage* was being cast, verifying the later account.

2. According to Charles Higham's book on Ziegfeld, Cantor was informed of his try-out backstage in Los Angeles by Ziegfeld himself, after which Eddie bragged to other cast members that he had a five-year guarantee with the producer. By all of Cantor's own accounts, he did not personally meet Ziegfeld until he arrived in New York and only found out that his opening at the *Frolics* was an audition the day after his debut.

# CHAPTER 7

# *Midnight Frolics*

Whether Eddie Cantor knew that his first night in Ziegfeld's *Midnight Frolics* could very well have been his last night is pure conjecture. Either way, Eddie arrived back in New York in October 1916, and after a quick family reunion (including an introduction to daughter number two, Natalie), he rushed down to the roof of the New Amsterdam Theatre. The New Amsterdam Roof was, in Cantor's words, "a unique pleasure center, neither theater nor cabaret, but a blend of both. It was a supper club where it cost a person five dollars to sit down and a good deal more to get up." Actually, front row seats went for $3, which Ziegfeld raised to a $4 top during Cantor's first run on the Roof. Nevertheless, late night supper entertainment at those prices in 1916 attracted only the cream of New York: the Vanderbilts, the Astors, and Diamond Jim Brady to name but a few. It was as if the great Ziegfeld was adorning his rooftop playhouse the way he adorned his *Follies* girls, with only the most opulent, richest, and glittering baubles he could find. This was Eddie's first peek at the polish that was Ziegfeld. Other Broadway producers were just show business; Ziegfeld's class put him in a league by himself.

Florenz Ziegfeld, Jr., was born in Chicago in 1867. His father, a German immigrant, was head of Chicago's Musical College. After graduating from high school, Flo Jr. became treasurer of the Musical College. Unfortunately, young Flo's extravagant fiscal style made it a short-lived appointment. Having been greatly influenced as a boy by Buffalo Bill's Wild West Show, Flo decided to try his hand at theatrical promoting. Among his first acts were "The Dancing Ducks of Denmark" (in reality they were from a local farm and danced when their metal stage was heated from below) and "The Invisible Brazilian Fish" (an elegantly lit empty bowl). Neither act made the young producer much money.

When Ziegfeld Sr. was appointed musical director of the 1893 Chicago Colombian Exposition, he dispatched his son to Europe to sign up the finest musical performers the Continent had to offer. Instead, Flo brought back a raft of various musical hall performers, including trapeze artists, jugglers, and acrobats. His budget exhausted, the elder Ziegfeld was forced to open his hall, the Trocadero, with such acts as were on hand. Business was disappointing.

In an attempt to increase attendance, Flo Jr. went to New York in search of one big name draw to put the Trocadero over the top. He returned with the Great Sandow, a German strong man. The younger Ziegfeld surrounded Sandow with a brilliant promotional campaign that made the behemoth the sensation of the fair and netted Ziegfeld $30,000.

After spending the next few years touring the country with the Great Sandow, Ziegfeld began to branch out into producing plays. It was in France, while looking for a girl for one of his shows, that he discovered Anna Held, a young Polish-French singer with a provocative figure and even more provocative manner. As he had done with Sandow, Ziegfeld used clever publicity to turn Anna Held into a show business sensation. Aside from making Anna into the sex symbol of the first decade of the twentieth century, Ziegfeld also made her his first wife. In return, Anna Held helped make her husband several fortunes.

Unfortunately, Flo Ziegfeld had a habit for spending all the money he made just as quickly as he earned it. What he didn't spend on more and more elaborate stage productions, he lavished on adorning himself and his women with the most expensive clothes and accessories money could buy. Every time Ziegfeld found himself broke, however, he also found himself an idea to make money. It was in 1907, after going through approximately his third fortune, that he produced the *Ziegfeld Follies of 1907*. (The actual credit for the *Follies* goes to Ziegfeld, Anna Held, or Abe Erlanger, depending on which version suits you.)

Initially presented on the rooftop of the New York Theatre, which Ziegfeld redid to look like a Parisian cafe, the *Follies* was a rapid succession of variety acts, songs, comics, and most of all, beautiful girls in the most sumptuous costumes ever seen on a stage. It was a sensation which grew more elaborate and expensive every year. The *Follies* was also a springboard to stardom for many of its featured performers. Among Ziegfeld's *Follies* "discoveries" were Fanny Brice, Will Rogers, W. C. Fields, Bert Williams, Marilyn Miller, Ruth Etting, Marion Davies, Ed Wynn, and of course, Eddie Cantor.

In 1913, after the *Follies* had moved to the New Amsterdam Theatre, Ziegfeld decided to use the rooftop for a new production, the *Midnight Frolics* (also referred to as the *Ziegfeld Frolics*, or just the *Frolics*). The original concept was to have eight or ten beautiful girls, along with a comic, perform for a late supper crowd. The *Frolics* also developed into a valuable proving ground for talent in which Ziegfeld was interested. If an act, heretofore unseen on Broadway, did well before the sophisticated roof audience, then it was probably safe to promote them downstairs in the *Follies*. It was imperative then to Eddie Cantor's career that he went over well on the Roof.

Eddie reported for rehearsals on the New Amsterdam Roof and introduced himself to Ziegfeld. When the producer took little notice, he tried again. "I'm Eddie Cantor," he started, then by way of a reminder added, "Max Hart is my agent. Max Hart?"

"Oh yes, Max Hart," Ziegfeld replied. "And what do you do?"

"Oh, I'm marvelous!" Eddie assured him.

"How do you know?" Ziegfeld asked.

"Why, Mr. Ziegfeld," Eddie grinned, "I wouldn't lie to you!"

Ziegfeld asked for a sample of his act. Eddie handed the piano player his music and started in on a spirited rendition of "Oh, How She Could Yacki Hicki Wicki Wacki Woo," a popular Hawaiian-style song of the day. As he sang, he plucked at a broken ukulele.

"You wouldn't believe it, last week I couldn't play this thing at all!" Eddie quipped.

Throughout the performance Ziegfeld sat grim-faced, a habit he acquired at the gambling tables he was fond of frequenting. When Eddie finished, the chorus girls and the band applauded.

"Mr. Kiraly'll tell you what time you go on tonight," Ziegfeld intoned. "He'll assign you a dressing room."

Eddie was as excited as Ziegfeld was calm. He rushed home, threw together his costume and makeup, and flew back to the theater, just in time to wait for hours before the midnight show began. Finally, at a quarter to one in the morning, in blackface and wearing his white horn-rimmed glasses, Eddie bounded on stage.

"I'm not a regular actor," Cantor told the high society crowd. "I work for a plumber in Hastings and yesterday something went wrong with the plumbing at Mr. Ziegfeld's house. He heard me singing in his bathroom and thought this would be a good gag. So, it doesn't matter if you applaud me . . . tomorrow I'm going back to plumbing!"

After his opening remarks, Cantor produced a deck of playing cards. The society audience, not familiar with Eddie from his vaudeville bookings, were led to believe he was a magician of sorts. For the same reason Eddie was not familiar with the influential members of the audience. Playing it straight, Cantor asked for volunteers to assist him with his act. Without knowing just whom he was picking, Eddie chose William Randolph Hearst (because, Cantor later recalled, "he was tall"), "Diamond Jim" Brady, and Broadway producer, Charles Dillingham. After telling them to stand up, Eddie gave each man a few cards and instructed them to hold them high above their heads so the audience could see them. With his society stooges set, Eddie launched into his nonsense song:

> She had a Hula, Hula, Hicki, Boola, Boola in her walk,
> She had a Ukulele Wicki Wicki Waili in her talk,
> And by the big Hawaiian moon,
> Beneath a banyan tree we'd spoon
> I've been trying to learn "Hawaiian,"
> Since that night in June . . .

At first the audience sat in puzzled silence waiting for the trick to become apparent. Cantor continued to sing, completely oblivious to the card-holding pillars of society he had set up. Slowly the audience began to realize the ridiculous picture that Cantor had painted for them, and they began to giggle. By the time he went through several choruses Cantor had brought down the house. Eddie collected the cards to generous applause. His future with Ziegfeld seemed set. He thanked his unsuspecting fall guys, then expressed his appreciation to the audience.

"I may not go back to plumbing after all," he began. "Still it might be good to have two jobs. Mother needs me now that Dad's gone," he continued, casting his eyes downward. "With good behavior he may be out in ten years. You know how it is, when you work in a bank you just can't take home samples!"

The next morning Cantor received the first in a series of hundreds of telegrams that Ziegfeld, a chronic Western Union user, would send him over the next fifteen years. The first said: "Enjoyed your act, you'll be here a long time." At first "a long time," meant a contract to do twenty weeks on the New Amsterdam Roof at $200 per week. Twenty weeks in the *Midnight Frolics* was an unusual booking; due to the review's repeat clientele, most acts exhausted themselves in less than a month. Any act that could prove itself with an extended roof run clearly was headed into the *Follies*.

After a few nights doing the same material, Eddie discovered he wasn't getting as many laughs as he had on opening night because he was playing to the same people. Also in the *Frolics*, appearing as the star comic, was Will Rogers, Eddie's rope twirling friend from vaudeville. Rogers had now begun to talk in his act, and his comments on events of the day were the hit of the Ziegfeld shows. Eddie noticed that each morning as they were leaving the theater, Rogers would buy up all the morning papers in order to glean material for that night's performance. Taking his cue from Rogers, Eddie started revamping his material on a daily basis.

With a twenty-week contract in his pocket for a booking on Broadway he could commute to, Eddie Cantor seemed set. Trouble arose late in November, however, when he decided to pick up some extra bookings in vaudeville. Since the *Frolics* didn't start until midnight, Eddie could easily appear on an evening bill and still be at the New Amsterdam Roof in plenty of time for his show there. With this in mind, he found work at the Colonial Theatre through the United Booking Offices.

When Ziegfeld heard of this booking, he forced Eddie to withdraw after the initial performance. Ziegfeld reasoned that if any of his entertainers appeared outside of a Ziegfeld production it would cheapen the value of both the performer and the Ziegfeld show. The incident had all the earmarks of developing into a feud between Ziegfeld and the UBO, with the booking agency threatening to prohibit their big-name vaudeville acts from picking up time in legitimate shows. Fortunately, both sides soon cooled down, and Cantor restricted his public appearances to the *Frolics*.

In January 1917, with Cantor's short-term contract quickly running out, Ziegfeld decided it was time to nail down the apostle of pep. Technically, despite his success in the *Frolics*, Eddie was scheduled to join the cast of *Canary Cottage* when it arrived in the spring for its New York run. Deciding it was infinitely preferable to be featured in a Ziegfeld show over any other, Eddie signed an exclusive two-year contract with Ziegfeld for $400 a week, twice what he had been making on the New Amsterdam Roof.

Any celebration was tempered, however, by the death of Grandma Esther, on January 31, Eddie's 25th birthday. She was eighty-four. Despite Eddie's success, she had refused to take advantage of it. Her only concession to her grandson's hard-won affluence was moving from the basement apartment on Henry Street to one on the ground floor. After the funeral, Eddie and Ida returned to her flat to collect her belongings. There they found $400 and a note which simply read, "For my funeral, please."

## REVIEW

Ziegfeld's "Midnight Frolic," fourth edition, on the Amsterdam Roof is a larger show than its predecessors, in point of numbers, acts and people. Gene Buck and Dave Stamper have again written the words and music, with Joseph Urban attending to the scenic display. There are eight acts and nine song numbers (ensembles). Plenty of pretty girls for a roof show provide the necessary drawing attraction for the addition of the Ziegfeld name. "The Midnight Frolic" is now charging $3 per for the front table seats, with $2 in the rear. That tells the strength of the attraction better than anything else could. The show runs in two parts and until 1:45, about 20 minutes longer than it did, still starting at the same hour, midnight.

A stranger to the roof is Eddie Cantor, called on the program "A New Nut." Mr. Cantor, once of an Edwards school act, sang a couple of Hula songs in blackface, tried to mildly kid with "impromptu stuff" and left the impression of a hybrid Al Jolson–Will Rogers. He did fairly well for a spot so far down, and might have gone better in the position given to Milo in the first part. Milo, with his dirty tramp make up and imitations, would not be suspected of making any decided sort of a success on a restaurant floor, but he did well enough, and as well as Cantor. — *Variety*, October 20, 1916

# CHAPTER 8

# Ziegfeld Follies of 1917

After a solid twenty-seven weeks in the *Midnight Frolics*, it was a foregone conclusion that Eddie Cantor would be promoted downstairs into the *Ziegfeld Follies*. Still, when Eddie and his agent, Max Hart, sat in Ziegfeld's office working out the details of his upcoming appearance in the *Follies*, Eddie was more than a little nervous. Ziegfeld explained that Cantor would appear in a sketch penned by the review's regular writers. In addition, Eddie would be called upon to do a "specialty," which he would have to write himself. When the producer asked Eddie if he was up to the challenge, Eddie stammered, "Mr. Ziegfeld, you'll never regret this. I'll never let you regret it. It's frightening, but, but, I'll do my darnedest!"

Rehearsals on the eleventh edition of the *Ziegfeld Follies* were called for early May, with a cast list so studded with stars that *Variety* announced the show would have no one star, rather all the performers would be "featured" players. The cast included Fanny Brice, Will Rogers, W. C. Fields, Bert Williams, all *Follies* veterans, with Walter Catlett and Cantor new to the show.

Aside from his solo, done in front of the curtain to allow for scene changes, Eddie appeared in a comedy sketch with Bert Williams, a veteran black comedian/singer who had been with the *Follies* since 1910. Although he was black, Williams appeared in blackface makeup because he felt it was a matter of showmanship, not race. Born in either 1874 or 1875, Williams worked his way up through music halls in a comedy act with his partner, George Walker. When Walker died in 1908, Williams continued with ever increasing success as a solo act in such shows as *Banana Land* and *Mr. Load of Koal*. In 1910 he signed a long-term contract with Flo Ziegfeld, who had been an acquaintance and admirer of Williams for many years.

Cantor was also an admirer of Bert Williams (years later he confessed that in his teens he was "the hottest fan Bert Williams ever had"), but he was apprehensive about being teamed with the veteran comic. Eddie felt that Williams might be resentful about performing with another blackface comedian, especially a white one. All his fears were quickly dispelled at the first rehearsal, when Williams offered Cantor his hand, smiled, and said in his rich, low voice, "Young man, you and I are going to be good friends."

54

Williams and Cantor's *Follies* sketch was perfectly suited for their characters. Bert played a Grand Central Station porter who had collected enough tips to send his son, played by Eddie, to an Ivy League university. Before Cantor's entrance, Williams bragged to his colleagues about his big, strong son, the college football hero. When he got off the train, Junior turned out to be a skinny, effeminate little wisp with white horn-rimmed glasses.

"Daddy!" Eddie cried out in girlish voice.

"Uh-uh!" Bert moaned, "So you been to college!"

Ignoring his father's disdain, Eddie chirped, "Look, Daddy, I carry matches!" The other porters roared as Williams slowly burned. In frustration, Bert slowly clenched his fist as if to hit Eddie.

"Remember, Daddy," the diminutive Eddie cautioned, "I have a temper!"

"I'll show you where you got it from," Bert snarled back.

After ten minutes of similar nonsense, the sketch ended with the university-educated son firmly following in his father's footsteps. Bert took off his porter's cap, slapped it on Eddie's head, and announced his retirement.

"Pick up them bags," Williams ordered. "This is my graduation and your commencement!"

The sketch was one of the biggest hits of the *Follies*.

They not only worked well onstage, they also built a warm "sonny and papsy" relationship offstage, according to Cantor. Eddie found Bert Williams to be not only a good friend and father figure, but an excellent teacher. A master of pantomime and timing, Williams would instruct Eddie on how to make the most of a comic situation. Once when Eddie bounded all over the stage in their sketch, Bert softly told him: "Look, son, don't push too hard. You can afford to underplay this character because the situation almost carries the scene." Cantor took the advice and as a result won even bigger laughs.

Cantor later recalled that it wasn't only Williams' advice that was good, but the way he offered it, never criticizing in public but only in the privacy of the dressing rooms. He fondly recalled Williams' disarming way of "discussing" a fellow performer's most obvious gaff by starting his critique with, "I see what you're trying to do, and that's good, but I think you'll find it might work a little better if you try it this way."

Bert Williams' kindness towards others arose from a firsthand knowledge of what it was like to feel hurt. In the highly segregated theater of the early 1900s, Williams was one of the first great black stars to appear in otherwise all-white shows. When he first signed with Ziegfeld, many in the cast and crew threatened to strike in protest. To the producer's credit, he called their bluff and said he would fire anyone who did not fall in line behind Williams. Still, Williams was often the target of prejudice. Once in St. Louis, Williams ordered a drink in bar. The bartender hesitated, then informed his black customer that drinks were $50 a glass. Williams calmly took out his wallet, laid $500 on the bar, and ordered ten of them.

As a concession to Williams' stardom, otherwise segregated hotels allowed him to stay with the rest of the *Follies* cast when they were on the road. In turn, Williams would use the service elevator, so he would not embarrass the management of the hotel. Only once did Cantor hear his friend complain about the arrangement, when he added, "It wouldn't be so bad, Eddie, if I didn't still hear the applause ringing in my ears."

Once when W. C. Fields and Will Rogers sought to play a practical joke on Eddie, it was Bert Williams who took the edge off of it. One night after a performance in Buffalo, Fields, Rogers, Williams, and Cantor were invited to a late dinner at the home of former boxing champ Jack Sullivan. By the time they arrived, Eddie was ravenous with hunger, only to find that the main course was pork chops. Starving, but eating only kosher, Eddie politely refused them. His host noticed and offered to bring Eddie some eggs. When they arrived, the eggs were covered with bacon. As Eddie stared incredulously at the plate, Sullivan started to giggle as Fields and Rogers exchanged knowing glances. It soon became painfully apparent to Eddie that he was the butt of a cruel joke.

Just as Eddie was beginning to wonder if there was anything but pork in the house, Bert Williams leaned over and whispered, "There's a package in my coat for you, son." They went out in the hall, where Williams pulled out a brown paper wrapper with a sirloin steak in it. Bert had caught wind of the others' plan back at the theater and brought the steak to make sure Eddie would have something to eat. Williams then proceeded to the kitchen, where he cooked the steak for his young partner.

Eddie's specialty in the *Ziegfeld Follies of 1917* was an even bigger hit than his sketch with Bert Williams. In between jokes, Eddie sang "The Maiden's Prayer" and introduced the lively "That's the Kind of a Baby for Me," performed in his trademark animated delivery, complete with legs hopping, hands clapping, and eyes rolling. Rarely had a Broadway audience witnessed such a raw burst of energy. "The audience seemed to lay bets on what chorus I'd drop in and have to be carried out," Cantor later quipped.

On opening night, "That's the Kind of a Baby for Me" went over so well Eddie had to do eleven or twelve encores, effectively stopping the show. The applause did not abate until well into the next act. A few minutes later, Will Rogers stopped by Eddie's dressing room to congratulate him. He found Eddie sitting with his head buried in his hands, quietly sobbing.

"What are you crying about?" Rogers asked. "They're still clapping downstairs. This should be the happiest night of your life!"

"It would be," Eddie explained, "if only my grandmother had been here to see it."

Rogers put his arm around Eddie's shoulder and reassured him. "Eddie, I have a feeling she did see it, and from a very good seat."

The next day when the reviews came out, Cantor found himself swamped with praise for his performance. That week Ziegfeld took out a half-page ad in *Variety* congratulating his new star, "the unqualified hit" of the *Follies*, Eddie Cantor. His solo had been so well received that two days after the opening Eddie recorded "That's the Kind of a Baby for Me" for the Victor recording company.

Although Ziegfeld prohibited his performers from appearing in other shows, he did allow them to play at private functions. With his newfound fame, Eddie was in great demand almost nightly at lodge meetings, banquets, and private parties thrown by the elite of New York society. Eddie's relatively light schedule in the *Follies* gave him plenty of opportunities to add considerably to his $400 a week salary.

Their newfound prosperity allowed the Cantors to move out of the apartment they shared with Ida's sister and into a flat of their own. Being in their own home for the first time meant Ida would now have to prepare the family's meals. After her first dinner, which Cantor later described as "horse's hip on toast," a cook was hired. Eddie also bought a car and hired a chauffeur to motor him to his various performances in the style befitting a Ziegfeld star.

The cook and chauffeur weren't the only employees on the Cantor payroll. As his success became known all over New York, Eddie was besieged by a steady stream of friends from the old neighborhood, along with several down-and-out actors who had known Eddie "when." Despite his increased income, Eddie's increased out-go was beginning to catch up. Cantor soon joked that he was taking home less money than his driver.

In September 1917, after doing record business on Broadway, the *Follies* left New York on its annual road tour. Transporting the *Follies of 1912*, with a cast of over 140 (including the entire original cast, except Walter Catlett), it was a logistic feat never before attempted in the theater. The effort was definitely worth it, however, because the latest edition of the *Follies* eclipsed all previous box office records in Boston, Philadelphia, Baltimore, Pittsburgh, Washington, and Detroit. The *Follies* knocked all competing shows, as *Variety* described it, "into a cocked hat." The only deterrent to the show's gross was America's entry into World War I. Not only did inflated food prices and war bond drives on the home front cut into the public's entertainment budget, but the government also instituted a "war tax" on all theater tickets sold. In addition, theaters were closed each week for a "showless Tuesday" in an effort to conserve heating oil and electricity.

Eddie Cantor's life on the road with the *Follies* was quite different from the touring he had known in vaudeville. The biggest adjustment was his roommate, W. C. Fields. Fields, after an impoverished youth, was convinced the only way to experience life was first class. This meant the finest food and the best liquor. Fields also detested train travel; he insisted that the most healthful way to get from one point to another was in his Cadillac convertible with the top down. This was fine in summer, but most of the *Follies'* tour was during the winter. Eddie, who accompanied Fields on most of these cross-country jaunts, would quickly turn blue from the experience of traveling seventy miles an hour with the top down in the middle of January. Fields was not totally unfeeling, however; when Cantor's knees would start knocking, Fields would insulate them with newspapers held on by rubber bands.

Sometimes, if the weather was nice, Fields would stop for a picnic. Other times they would eat at the best local restaurants they could find. If Fanny Brice was along for the ride, as she often was, she would cook dinner for Fields and Cantor up in her room. In her luggage, Fanny would carry the contents of a small kitchen, including hot plates, utensils, and condiments. One night after arriving in Cincinnati, Fanny prepared one of her specialties, spaghetti. Fields and Cantor sat hungrily as Fanny's cooking filled the room with tantalizing aromas. When dinner was finally ready and they dug in, first Fields started foaming at the mouth, then Cantor, and finally Brice. In her field kitchen, Fanny had mistakenly put soap power in the Parmesan cheese jar.

The *Follies* closed out the year, as they always did, with ten weeks in Chicago. The show again did record business and was turning away customers through the last week of the run. With business so good, Ziegfeld gave Eddie a raise, signing him to another two-year contract.

While the Windy City was good to the *Follies*, it was less kind to Cantor. Eddie came down with pleurisy and was forced to leave the show. His income suddenly cut off, albeit briefly, Eddie had time to ponder his sorry financial condition. Just as Eddie was considering wearing disguises to dodge his payday friends, he received a call from his childhood friend and first partner, Dan Lipsky. Since getting out of show business on the ground floor, Lipsky had learned stenography and entered the banking field, eventually becoming the private secretary to the president of the Manufacturers Trust Company. He had also married Eddie's cousin Anne.

After seeing the shambles of Eddie's financial situation, Dan offered to become his business manager. For a salary of $10 a week, Lipsky quickly put the Cantors on a budget, fired the chauffeur, and arranged for Eddie to be paid in a weekly check to head off any more stage door "loans." In addition, Lipsky instituted a strict savings plan whose goal was the building of a house for Eddie and Ida. Within a year under Dan's supervision, Eddie had saved $10,000.

## REVIEW

The new annual Ziegfeld "Follies" (11th edition) is a blaze of wealth, in looks and cost. That alone will carry the show to a bigger success than it has ever had, if that is possible, and it appears to be absolutely necessary to secure Flo Ziegfeld in his investment. If Ziegfeld has a bank account left after putting on that show, he must be standing in with a mint.

After the wealth comes the people, a large number programmed, with three distinct hits among the principals Fannie Brice, Eddie Cantor and Walter Catlett. The strictly specialty acts, like Will Rogers, Bert Williams, Fred Heider, W. C. Fields and Policeman Vokes and "Don" all heavily scored. Mr. Fields did a lawn tennis bit of ball juggling in a tennis set, amidst plenty of fun, furnished by himself though well assisted by Walter Catlett. Rogers, with his speaking voice and lariat, came on in the next to closing spot of a show that ended Tuesday night at 11:40, but no one walked out when they saw the only gum-chewing Williams [Rogers] appear.

Eddie Cantor, in blackface, who also was liked in a scene he had with Mr. Williams, sang "The Maiden's Prayer," written by McDonald & Hanley, as his first number, it proving a strong applause maker for him, he returning with a strictly "stage song," "The Kind of a Baby for Me" (by Eagan), for a riotous finish to his act that also contained a semi-monolog.

The new "Follies" will likely undergo expected changes, excepting with the production. There's so much to see in the show without watching the performance that maybe the Ziegfeld scheme is to draw 'em twice, once to watch the scenery and clothes, and the next time the performance. "The Follies" this season is certainly worth double price. It's a "sight show" of a kind never before shown.—Sime, *Variety*, June 15, 1917

# CHAPTER 9

# *Ziegfeld Follies of 1918*

During his recuperation from pleurisy, Eddie Cantor busied himself with writing, not only for his own act in the upcoming edition of the *Follies*, but for his old friends from the *Kid Kabaret*. Both Eddie Buzzell and Georgie Jessel were still in vaudeville: Jessel as a solo, Buzzell in a double with Peggy Parker. To help out his old comrades, Cantor supplied them with solid vaudeville acts, which, by the terms of his Ziegfeld contract, he couldn't perform himself. The acts did well enough that Eddie took out an ad in *Variety* announcing:

Eddie Cantor (author)
Will write material for a limited number of acts
Line forms at 1102 Palace Building
offices of Rose & Curtis who represent the author

Eddie Cantor (actor)
"Ziegfeld Follies" — New Amsterdam Theatre
under management of Max Hart

Eddie didn't have to wait for the 1918 *Follies* to get back on stage. As soon as the road company returned to New York, Ziegfeld put Cantor, along with other *Follies* principals, Will Rogers and Lillian Lorraine, into the ongoing *Midnight Frolics* on the New Amsterdam Roof. A return to the Roof was not a demotion, but a chance to try out new material in a relaxed atmosphere, in addition to picking up a little extra cash. Eddie would take similar advantage of his appearances in the *Frolics* throughout his career with Ziegfeld.

Eddie's latest appearance in the *Frolics* was not completely new material. In his specialty, he performed two songs; the first, "Cleopatra," was fresh. His second song, however, was his hit from the previous season, "That's the Kind of a Baby for Me," leaving *Variety* to note that Cantor was really "making the song stand up." It didn't seem to matter to the audience, who voted Eddie the hit of the review via their applause.

Aside from his solo, Cantor appeared with Will Rogers in a sketch featuring a series of impersonations. They started off with Eddie doing his version of Flo Ziegfeld while Will played Gene Buck, the *Follies'* writer. Rogers as Buck explained the show didn't need a script, all Ziegfeld had to do was "just bring on the dames!" Next, they demonstrated the contrasting walks of Ziegfeld and rival producer Charles Dillingham. Finally, they gave their impressions of each other, with Rogers jumping around the stage clapping his hands and Cantor chewing gum and twirling rope. Any plans to move the act downstairs to the *Follies* were probably forgotten after critics called the bit too long and opined that the two comics had hurt their reputations performing it.

While a Will Rogers–Eddie Cantor stage partnership was evidently ill-conceived, offstage their friendship, which had begun during their vaudeville days, strengthened in their *Follies* days. Ziegfeld, who usually gave little notice to his comics, had warm feelings for both Cantor and Rogers, and along with W. C. Fields, called them "my three musketeers."

Part Cherokee Indian, Will Rogers began his adult life as a cowboy in his home state of Oklahoma. His skill as a horseman served Will well when he decided to join a traveling Wild West show. Rogers thrilled audiences with his roping tricks, and after the show played New York he went solo, albeit with his horse, into vaudeville. On stage, Rogers was silent. When he occasionally spoke to explain an upcoming trick, his Western twang was invariably met with laughter.

This embarrassed Will so much that he resolved never to speak onstage. His fellow performers, who knew Will's easy, natural offstage wit, tried to explain that they weren't laughing at Will but at what he said. Gradually, Rogers spoke more and more until he became America's greatest monologist. By the time Rogers joined the *Follies* in 1915 his act consisted of standing before the curtain, twirling a rope, and giving his homespun, yet insightful, commentary on current events.

Eddie Cantor, though a great admirer of Rogers wit, was more impressed by Will Rogers the man. If Bert Williams had given Eddie invaluable advice on how to behave onstage, Will Rogers showed him, by example, how to act in real life. By the end of his career, Cantor would be famous for raising large amounts of money for all types of religious and charitable organizations. It was Will Rogers who first invited Eddie along to benefits and taught him, again by example, the human value of doing charity performances.

In return, Eddie taught Will the benefits of kosher cooking. When the *Follies* was on the road, Will would often ask Eddie to join him for dinner. Eddie, having been raised to observe strict dietary laws, would beg off with the excuse that he had friends in town. Eddie would then go off alone and find a kosher restaurant. It didn't take Rogers long to figure out that no one could have so many friends in so many different cities.

The next time Eddie refused Will's invitation, Will asked him if he'd been "kosherin' up some place." When Eddie confessed, Will asked why he'd never invited him along. Within the hour, the skinny Jewish kid from the East Side and the cowboy from Oklahoma were sharing a table at the nearest kosher restaurant. Will especially took to the chopped chicken livers, downing plate after plate while muttering, "I guess it's too late." When Eddie asked what it was too late for, Will responded, "It's too late for me to turn Jewish!"

In return for introducing him to the wonders to kosher food, Rogers would drag Eddie along on his constant quest for the world's finest chili. The search often led the wealthy stars to the seediest, toughest-looking joints in town. The surroundings never bothered Will, all that mattered was the chili. Cantor on the other hand, despite his gutter childhood, was often afraid of the places his pal dragged him. It was okay with Eddie, however, because as he put it, "Will Rogers was crazy about chili, and I was crazy about Will Rogers."

As close as the relationship between Will Rogers and Eddie Cantor was, it was not free from practical jokes, usually instigated by the other "musketeer," W. C. Fields. On many occasions, Rogers had told stories to Fields and Cantor about his closest boyhood friend, a fellow Oklahoman named "Clay McGonigle." Whatever the tale, Will always ended it slightly misty-eyed over his old pal whom he would give the world to see again. After hearing more than their fill of McGonigle stories (W. C. Fields liked the sound of the name so much that he would adopt it for his character in the 1934 film *The Old Fashioned Way*), Fields and Cantor decided it was time for Rogers to hear from Clay again. With the help of Rogers' valet, who supplied the conspirators with the secret nickname that Clay had dubbed Will, Fields and Cantor sent the following note:

> Dear Chickenchief [Cantor's cleaned-up version of McGonigle's nickname for Rogers],
> Will be out front tonight watching your show. Will see you for the last time. Tomorrow I'm on my way to France.
> Your old pal,
> Clay McGonigle

When Rogers received the letter, he hurried to show it to Fields and Cantor, who both expressed straight-faced astonishment that Clay McGonigle had turned up after all these years. That night, in honor of his pal who was going off to the war, Rogers devoted his entire monologue to reminiscences about the good old days. The audience sat in puzzled silence as Rogers began each sentence with either, "Clay, remember when we did this" or "Clay, how about the time . . . ." Backstage Fields and Cantor were doubled over with laughter as their fellow musketeer played his entire act to a man who wasn't even there.

After the show, Rogers rushed out front to catch Clay as he left the theater, but of course there was no Clay. Reasoning that McGonigle would go back to his dressing room, Rogers hurried backstage, again to find no Clay. After searching all the local hotels and nightclubs to no avail, Rogers sadly concluded that he must have said something from the stage to offend his old pal. Guilt-stricken at a joke turned sour, Fields and Cantor kept silent. It was only years later, when Cantor's first autobiography was published, that Rogers found out the truth about the mysterious disappearance of Clay McGonigle. In typical Will Rogers style, he held no grudge.

The *Ziegfeld Follies of 1918* went into rehearsals in the first week of May, with an Atlantic City tryout scheduled one month later. The announced cast included Will Rogers, W. C. Fields, Eddie Cantor, Bert Williams, Van and Schenck, Lillian Lorraine, Ann Pennington, Frank Carter, and singer Marilyn Miller, whom Ziegfeld had just stolen from the Shubert brothers. The show, again written by Gene Buck, with music by Dave Stamper and Louis Hirsch, was designed as a patriotic spectacular, reflecting the mood of World War I America. The *Follies* also included a song by Irving Berlin, who had promised Ziegfeld an exclusive number if Ziegfeld would send the New Amsterdam Roof chorus girls out to Camp Upton to entertain the troops.

The 1918 edition of the *Follies* went through many changes in material and personnel before it opened in Atlantic City. The first change was in the number of acts. Ziegfeld had assembled such a huge raft of talent and venues in which to display them that the cost of the latest *Follies* shot up to $140,000, an increase of over 25 percent from the 1917 show. The final dress rehearsal ran over seven hours. Cantor had to edit down his material to conserve time. This, coupled with his new contract, gave him even higher pay for less stage work. Bert Williams, a *Follies* mainstay since 1910, left the show altogether because he couldn't find the right material. After a few months off, Williams resumed his Ziegfeld career on the New Amsterdam Roof in the *Frolics*.

Eddie Cantor, though he had less time to perform, made the most of it with a comedy sketch in which he played an aspiring aviator taking his pilot's test. The routine was an excuse for cast member Frank Carter to give Eddie a violent physical examination as a prelude to his flying test. *Variety* felt it contained the strongest comedy in the entire show, and audiences loved watching Carter toss the diminutive Eddie around the stage like a rag doll. The bit would be repeated in one form or another in every Cantor show for years to come.

As much as audiences and critics liked to see Cantor getting bounced around the stage in the aviator sketch, they did not feel the same about his specialty number. The problem was not a lack of effort but of material; he needed a strong hit song like the 1917 "That's the Kind of a Baby for Me" or "Oh, Gee! Oh, Gosh! Oh, Golly! I'm in Love." Instead, Cantor performed a medley of popular songs with the words changed to satirize Ziegfeld and himself. Apparently the number was too much of an in-joke to appeal to a wide segment of the audience. Later in the *Follies*' run, Cantor inserted Irving Berlin's latest hit, "Oh, How I Hate to Get Up in the Morning," into his specialty to give his solo a boost.

The *Follies of 1918* marked a turning point for Cantor; it was the first time he appeared whiteface since back in his early days with the People's Vaudeville Company. He had first adopted blackface in an attempt to get an extra week's work; now ten years later the burnt cork was starting to restrict his career. Max Hart, Eddie's agent, had gotten Ziegfeld's tentative approval to let Eddie perform the aviator sketch without blacking up. Opening night in Atlantic City, however, Ziegfeld pulled the number, fearing audiences might not accept Cantor white. Feeling his future was at stake, Cantor demanded that the aviator's sketch be in the show, or he would be out of it altogether. The next night, without the aid of burnt cork, Cantor did the routine and was as popular as ever.

Another reason that Ziegfeld may have been opposed to the aviator sketch had nothing to do with Cantor's blackface, but rather the producer's own jealousy. For sometime Ziegfeld had been pursuing his newest star, Marilyn Miller. His rival for Marilyn's affection was one of his featured singers and Cantor's sketch partner, Frank Carter. Although Ziegfeld lavished expensive gifts and *Follies* stardom on Miller, she still preferred the much younger and more handsome Carter.

While Flo Ziegfeld was making romance as difficult as possible for the couple, Eddie Cantor was smoothing out true love's path. Eddie and Frank were good friends and occasionally roomed together on the road. When Eddie saw the difficulty Frank was having wooing Marilyn, he started arranging secret rendezvous for the couple away from the disapproving gaze of the Great Ziegfeld. When the producer found out, he was furious, not only with Miller, who he felt had used him, but also with Carter and Cantor. When Frank and Eddie first came to Ziegfeld with the idea for the aviator sketch, they were turned down flat. Only Gene Buck, the *Follies* writer, could finally convince his boss the bit was good. Even then, as previously stated, Ziegfeld almost killed it at the last minute. As for the offstage drama, in the end young love triumphed and Miller and Carter were married in May 1919, following the road run of the *Follies of 1918*.

The 1918 edition of the *Follies* opened on Broadway June 17. Although the show ran to near capacity throughout its summer run in New York, only after the company went on the road did the production start running in the black. Between the all-star cast, seventy-four chorus girls, and the most expensive production values on Broadway, Ziegfeld was lucky to meet his expenses. After the initial fourteen weeks at the New Amsterdam, however, the show was usually near the break-even point and poised to make its profits. The 1917 *Follies* had made over $200,000, most of that coming on tour.

Soon after they arrived in Boston on September 16 for the start of their annual tour, the city, and eventually most of the nation, was hit by the Spanish flu epidemic. All Massachusetts theaters were closed for ten days, then reopened, then closed again as the disease spread. Even after the theaters were allowed to reopen, all shows, even the mighty *Follies*, played to half-empty houses. With people dying at the rate of over one hundred per week from the flu, the public had much more on their minds than pretty show girls and comics. Ziegfeld lost over $3,000 from the Boston cancellations alone, a tidy sum for 1918.

Eddie Cantor, along with others in the *Follies'* cast, packed up and went home to New York to wait out the epidemic. Back in New York, Eddie went back into the *Frolics* while waiting for the *Follies* to open again somewhere. In an attempt to recoup some of his losses, Ziegfeld reopened the *Follies* in mid–October at New York's Globe Theatre (the New Amsterdam was housing another show at the time). The flu had reached New York, however, and the box office at the Globe was pitifully low.

Over 90 percent of all theaters in the United States were closed in October, with only New York and San Francisco houses still in operation, though just barely. Ticket prices were cut in half, to little effect, with many Broadway theaters closing in an attempt to cut their losses.

Aside from closed theaters and unemployed actors, the epidemic started taking a more serious toll on show business. At the height of the tragedy, *Variety* became filled with death notices and memorial ads, prompting the editors to comment, "Nothing in the annals of American theatricals has so disastrously affected the entire amusements field nor forced such a complete shut down of theaters in so wide a territory as the epidemic of Spanish influenza." Several memorials were taken out by Cantor, to pay tribute to ex-vaudeville friends and music pluggers who had succumbed to the flu.

If the events of September and October almost ruined the American theater, November saw it roar back to life. The lifting of the epidemic, coupled with the end of World War I, brought audiences out in droves. The *Follies* left the Globe and moved down to Philadelphia, where it did standing-room-only business. Records also fell as the show moved on to Washington, D.C.—where Will Rogers was invited to the White House and kept President Wilson up all night with his common sense humor—then Pittsburgh, Baltimore, Cleveland, and Detroit. Ziegfeld quickly forgot Boston, as the *Follies* raked in an average weekly profit of $10,000. Chicago topped them all. In a ten-week holiday run, the *Follies of 1918* broke all Chicago box office records, playing to standing-room-only crowds and averaging well over $30,000 a week.

One night in Chicago, Gus Van of the singing team of Van and Schenck approached Eddie for advice. Van had invested $2,500 in some bad stock and had to recoup his losses quickly before his wife found out about them. Eddie had a solution. During his specialty, Eddie had been making nightly casual references to a product called Green River Lime Juice Drink, for which the drink's advertising agency paid him $100 a week. Eddie would work it into his jokes wherever he could. (One night he even had a fake telegram delivered to him during his number. "It's from Ziegfeld," Eddie would inform the audience, "He's heard that I'm advertising Green River Lime Juice Drink, and he warns me not to use the name Green River Lime Juice Drink in my act. So, why antagonize him? Tonight I won't even mention Green River Lime Juice Drink!")

The next day Cantor, Van, and Schenck visited the Green River's advertising agency with a proposition. The three of them had written a song extolling the virtues of this marvelous lime juice. With the backing of not one, but two, *Follies* acts it was sure to become a nationwide hit. The agency head sat back as the trio belted out the worst impromptu jingle probably ever heard:

> For a drink that's fine with a kick,
> Try Green River,
> It's the only soft drink you should pick,
> Try Green River!

The earnestness of the performance did the trick, and the agency offered them $5,000. They balked, however, when Cantor demanded $10,000, and Gus Van nearly fainted. The next day a counteroffer came in for $7,500 to be split three ways. Van, Schenck, and Cantor quickly accepted. Van was out of his financial jam, Cantor and Schenck made a quick $2,500 each, and Green River Lime Juice Drink had a jingle which no doubt contributed to its eventual disappearance from the market place.

Soon after they had put one over on Green River, Van and Schenck conspired to put one over on Eddie Cantor. One night in St. Louis, Van and Schenck went out with Cantor for a late night supper after the show. While Cantor got them a table, Gus Van pulled the restaurant manager and the waitress aside to warn them about Eddie. "That fellow," Van started, pointing to Cantor, "has just been released from a sanitarium, but he's still slightly deranged." The problem, Van explained, was a rare mental malady caused by the consumption of too much milk. He went on to warn them that Cantor was to be served no milk, no matter how strongly he demanded it, lest he turn violent. Of course Cantor was on a diet at the time, the mainstay of which was milk.

When the waitress took their order, Eddie finished by asking for a glass of milk. Nervously, the waitress suggested he substitute cocoa or tea. Cantor was firm, however, and demanded milk. Finally the waitress told him they were all out of milk. Looking around at the other tables, Cantor noticed plenty of milk drinkers. "They've all got milk," Eddie noted. "Where did they get it?"

"They, they, brought it in with them," the waitress stammered.

Finally, Eddie demanded to see the manager. Cantor's appeal for a glass of milk was so rational the manager almost gave in, and probably would have acceded if it were not for Gus Van whispering: "No milk! He'll calm down! No milk or he'll get violent!" After several more minutes, Eddie resigned himself to a cup of cocoa (made at that time from hot water, cocoa powder and sugar).

## REVIEW

The newest "Ziegfeld Follies" is a big spectacular production. It's so big and holds so much that the eye wants to see, it is certain to draw, more so probably than "The Follies" always does.

But with a great deal it still misses much, and nearly all of the much is comedy. It's the sight end of the performance that's going to attract. There were several comedy scenes without much comedy, but those that held Eddie Cantor were funny because of Mr. Cantor's personality. He makes his comedy material laughable, and did so especially in the aviator's test scene. This particular bit is, by the way, the only legitimate comedy scene of the performance.

But Mr. Cantor could not make his material either funny or good in his single specialty. His first song was a parodied medley on popular numbers about Mr. Ziegfeld and himself, then some stories and a fast song to close, but there was nothing in the turn Cantor did that was really there or worthwhile. Otherwise, however, as far a comedians go, he is the backbone and hit of the show. — Sime, *Variety*, June 19, 1918

# CHAPTER 10

# *Ziegfeld Follies of 1919*

Of all the shows in which Eddie Cantor ever performed, the *Ziegfeld Follies of 1919* was his favorite. "The 1919 show," Eddie later wrote, "was one of those ideal organizations of entertainment that bespoke the last word in stage generalship and the most perfect harmony of actors and material. Each specialty, no matter what its character, was performed by the acknowledged master of that field."

It's only natural that Cantor would recall the *1919 Follies* so fondly. With two *Follies* under his belt, Eddie was a proven Broadway success and could afford to enjoy himself more. The show's cast, after two years together, were like old friends, some even like family. Will Rogers, W. C. Fields, Bert Williams (back after a season on the New Amsterdam Roof), Fanny Brice, Van and Schneck, Marilyn Miller, Ann Pennington, and others in the show were all seasoned veterans. For production values, Ziegfeld once again topped himself, spending so much that ticket prices had to be raised, making the *Follies* the most expensive show on Broadway.

Musically, the *Follies of 1919* boasted more hits than any of its previous editions. Gene Buck and Dave Stamper, the show's regular song writing team, came up with "Tulip Time." Harry Tierney and Joseph McCarthy, who would go on to write the songs for Cantor's later hit *Kid Boots*, scored with a number entitled "My Baby's Arms." Probably the biggest hits in the production came from Irving Berlin, who contributed the future standards, "Mandy" and "A Pretty Girl Is Like a Melody." The latter summed up Ziegfeld's "glorifying the American girl" philosophy so well that it became the unofficial anthem of the *Follies*.

Irving Berlin also supplied Eddie Cantor with a song for his specialty number. "You'd Be Surprised," with its humorous lyrics and bouncy melody, was tailor-made for Cantor.

> "She's not much good in a crowd,
> But when you get her alone,
> You'd be surprised!"

Irving Berlin was so sure he had a hit on his hands, he asked Eddie not to give it his usual frenetic delivery. "Eddie," the song writer advised, "for this one you don't have to move. You don't have to get the song over, it'll get you over." Berlin was right, and the song became one of Cantor's biggest hits. Not long after he introduced it in the *Follies*, Eddie make a recording of "You'd Be Surprised." It sold over a million copies.

Eddie repaid Irving by ruining the songwriter's reputation in Atlantic City. Berlin came down to the resort for the out-of-town opening of the *Follies*. While there, he shared a suite with Cantor at one of the resort's finest hotels. Berlin was unexpectedly summoned back to New York in the middle of the week, and he told his music secretary, future songwriter Harry Akst, to pack his bags. Eddie volunteered to help and proceeded to cram Irving's luggage with every picture hanging on the hotel room walls. Back in New York the bags were unpacked by Berlin's valet, so Irving never knew he had unwittingly taken the pictures. A few weeks later Berlin received a letter from the hotel manager. The manager expressed surprise that a gentleman like Irving Berlin would stoop so low. He ended his letter by asking Irving why he hadn't taken the walls while he was at it.

Cantor became so strongly identified with "You'd Be Surprised" that the song once kept him out of trouble with the law. About nine years after he had introduced the song in the *Follies*, a motorcycle cop stopped Eddie for speeding. The officer scrutinized his driver's license. "Are you Eddie Cantor?" the cop asked. Eddie assured him that he was, but a two-day growth of beard made the officer suspicious. "Got any other identification?" Eddie showed him an engraved watch Ziegfeld had given him. Now the cop was even more wary, thinking that instead of a speeder he had stopped a tramp who had stolen Eddie Cantor's watch and car. Finally the policeman tried one more test before hauling the apparent robber in. "If you're Eddie Cantor," he challenged, "then sing a song called 'You'd Be Surprised.'" It took several choruses before the cop showed his satisfaction with the vocal evidence and let Cantor off with a warning.

Apart from his specialty, in which he also introduced the postwar hit "How Ya Gonna Keep 'Em Down on the Farm? (After They've Seen Paree)," Eddie appeared in a comedy sketch which would become, in various incarnations, a mainstay of his act. The osteopath sketch was actually a takeoff from the previous *Follies'* aviator sketch, which was little more than a excuse for straight man Frank Carter to rough up Cantor while supposedly giving him a physical exam. In the 1919 version of the bit, Eddie played a patient, with George LeMaire playing the osteopath. LeMaire was one of the top straight men of the day. "If you couldn't be funny with him," Cantor later recalled, "you'd better quit."

LeMaire twisted Cantor around on the therapy table like a pretzel as Eddie alternated cries for help with snappy one-liners. The audience loved it, so much so that the routine was repeated, with minor alterations, in the *Broadway Brevities*, *The Midnight Rounders*, *Make It Snappy*, *Kid Boots*, and the films *Palmy Days* and *Thank Your Lucky Stars*.

Before opening on Broadway, the *Ziegfeld Follies*, like most shows, opened out of town in order to work the bugs out of the performance. The *Follies* usually spent the week before its New York premiere in Atlantic City, which also afforded the cast a working vacation at the popular seaside resort. Unfortunately, Atlantic City's proximity to New York made it possible for Broadway critics to sneak down and catch the show while it was still under revision.

Eddie Cantor, for one, did not want the important New York critics seeing his act before he had a chance to try it out and tighten it up. In an attempt to circumvent the critics, Eddie instituted a tryout for the tryout. Under an assumed name, he would get bookings at small, out-of-the-way uptown Manhattan vaudeville theaters to test his material and prune away any deadwood. When he and George LeMaire wanted to preview the osteopath sketch for the 1919 *Follies*, they took the act out under the name of "Kathryn Perry and Company," Kathryn Perry being the actress who had a bit as a nurse in the scene. Ziegfeld, who had previously barred Cantor from any vaudeville appearances, thought the idea was great. Cantor later employed the system when polishing material for other shows such as *The Midnight Rounders.*

The *Ziegfeld Follies of 1919* opened on Broadway on June 16 to strong notices for the show in general and Eddie Cantor in particular. The show was just as big a hit with audiences, who packed the New Amsterdam to capacity nightly. Business was so good Ziegfeld was able to raise ticket prices again without a murmur of protest from the public. Although another show, *Hitchy Koo*, was scheduled to move into the New Amsterdam Theatre in September when the *Follies* departed for its annual tour, Ziegfeld was having second thoughts. *Variety* speculated that the *Follies* showed no sign of slowing down and could have an indefinite Broadway run. As it turned out, the decision on how long the 1919 *Follies* should run was not in the hands of Flo Ziegfeld.

On August 7, 1919, the Actors' Equity Association, then a fledgling actors' union, called the first-ever strike against the Producing Managers' Association. The AEA was striking primarily over working conditions. Unlike Flo Ziegfeld, most producers did not pay their casts for the time when a show was in rehearsal. Actors and actresses could spend weeks, sometimes months, working without pay, only to have the show close on opening night. In addition, casts rarely received extra pay for special holiday performances, which were usually called at the discretion of the theater manager or producer.

Eddie Cantor's position during the strike seemed to be in a constant state of flux. As a member of the Equity Association council, he fully supported the walkout. The problem, however, lay with Flo Ziegfeld's position in the producers' association, which was vague at best. When the first strike call went out, Eddie, hearing that Ziegfeld had sided with his fellow producers, went out with it. Already in the theater district, Eddie went on a busman's holiday and took in a performance of George White's *Scandals*, which was exempted from the union action. When Ziegfeld found out, he tracked Cantor down and assured him that he was not a member of the producers' group and indeed the *Follies* was also an exempt show. Convinced, Cantor came back in time to perform his routines.

For a number of days, while the majority of Broadway theaters had closed their doors, the *Follies* played on. Both the producers and Equity claimed that Ziegfeld was on their side. Ziegfeld himself kept a low profile and was unavailable for comment. On August 11, however, Ziegfeld came out of hiding, firmly on the side of the Producing Managers' Association and with a restraining order against the AEA. The court order, claiming that $175,000 would be lost if the *Follies* closed, was handed out to each cast member that night as they arrived at the theater. Cantor, as an Equity board member, was specifically cited in the suit.

Two days later, in spite of the court order, Eddie Cantor, along with fellow cast members Van and Schenck, Johnny and Ray Dooley, Eddie Dowling, and John Steele, left the *Follies*, forcing its closure. Before he walked out, Eddie stopped at the box office and drew the half-week's salary due him, which he then donated to the AEA strike fund. In response, Ziegfeld announced he would reopen the *Follies* the following week without his striking principals, adding "their absence will not be material." To add injury to insult, the producer filed a $250,000 damage suit against Cantor, Van and Schenck, and the Dooleys.

In reply, Cantor told *Variety*, "I am with the Equity Association and will go back to the cloak and suit trade if they lose in their fight against the manager." Rather than go into haberdashery, as his father-in-law had always advised, Eddie went back on the stage, but for the union, not Ziegfeld. The AEA started to run strike benefits at the Lexington Opera House that featured the biggest stars on Broadway. The cast including Eddie Foy, Marie Dressler, Ethel and Lionel Barrymore, Ed Wynn, Cantor, and W. C. Fields, to name just a few. Fields had also been in the *Midnight Frolics*, which was not affected by the strike since it was considered part of vaudeville, but he walked out in sympathy to the Equity Association.

Eddie's turn on the bill consisted of his usual repertoire of songs, along with jokes about the strike. At one point, after one of his more energetic numbers, Cantor stopped and said, "I'm surprised I've got so much pep without being paid for it!" Then after thinking for a moment he added: "It's all right. I'm getting as much as Ethel Barrymore anyhow!" Not long after he started appearing in the AEA benefits, Cantor was served another injunction from Ziegfeld. In this one the producer stated that since Eddie still had forty-five weeks remaining on his contract, he could not appear in any production other than the *Follies*.

The benefit show, which ran daily, did well at the box office, especially since it was one of the few shows left on Broadway. Those shows that were exempt from the strike or were using scab casts were soon shut down when stagehands started walking out in sympathy with the actors. Any shows that still managed to remain open could count on disruptions from members of Equity. Cantor and W. C. Fields, along with others, had a favorite ploy to lure patrons away from non–Equity shows. They would park in front of the offending theaters and pretend to have car trouble. While trying to fix the car, they would start clowning around, thereby drawing prospective theater patrons away from the box office. The show on the sidewalk was so much more entertaining than the scab performance inside that the trick turned many customers away.

Aside from demolishing automobiles on the sidewalks of New York, Eddie Cantor and W. C. Fields had developed a very close friendship. Despite their closeness, an odder mismatch could not be found. Their beginnings were similar, however; Fields started life on the streets of Philadelphia and Cantor grew up on New York's Lower East Side. Fields, who began his professional career as a juggler, left home at the age of eleven to take a job as an actor in a nearby town for $5 a week, $3.50 after subtracting the agent's commission. From there he moved on to Atlantic City, where he would work in beer gardens at night and as a professional drowner by day (faking drownings in order to draw crowds for his boss). Fields soon went into burlesque, then vaudeville, and in time became the greatest comic juggler in the world.

Fields rarely spoke on stage, depending instead on his juggling and pantomime prowess to make audiences laugh. His silence allowed him to play not only English-speaking countries, but also the Continent, where he performed before numerous crown heads. He expanded his act to include his famous pool, tennis, and golf routines. It was in these classic bits which he used in the *Follies* that he first began to mutter comic gems in that now famous nasal voice.

The first night he roomed with Fields in Boston in 1917, Eddie returned to their suite after the show to find three large bottles of champagne in the living room. Bill (as Fields' friends called him) entered with two glasses and suggested they celebrate the successful opening. "Let's drink to your health, son," Fields drawled. They kept downing the bubbly till 3:00 A.M., by which time Cantor was sick as a dog. "We kept drinking to my health," Cantor recalled, "till we damn near ruined it!" Bill Fields, as always, showed no effect whatsoever to the alcohol. After that, Bill never encouraged Eddie to drink. Whenever they entered a night club, Fields would instruct the waiter: "Bring the boy with the big eyes a little milk, he's got a weak constitution."

Fields' reputation for consumption of strong drink was well founded. Once Fields returned to their suite and announced to Cantor he had just come from donating blood to the Red Cross. When Eddie expressed his surprise, Fields added, "Yes, the doctors were very pleased with my blood. They told me there was so much alcohol in it they'd use it to sterilize their instruments!"

W. C. Fields, as did Bert Williams and Will Rogers, took Eddie under his wing, seeing to it that Cantor received a liberal education. Fields, like

Cantor, had little formal schooling. In the early days of his career, in an attempt to correct this deficiency, Fields embarked on his own educational program. One day, just prior to a tour of Australia, Fields lugged a huge steamer trunk into a San Francisco book store. "Fill 'er up," the comedian told the clerk. When the puzzled clerk asked with what, Fields replied: "Books! Fill the trunk with books! I want books by the finest authors in English literature!" Fields then spent his entire South Seas tour reading Shakespeare, Dickens, Chaucer, Milton, and other classic authors.

By the time Eddie Cantor started rooming with him, Fields had worked up to three large trunks full of literature. When Bill discovered Eddie had been a P.S. 2 dropout, he fished a copy of *Oliver Twist* out of one trunk and gave it to Eddie. When Cantor finished that, Fields started him on *Les Misérables*. Not only would Eddie read the books, but each night after the show he would discuss the previous day's reading with his tutor. Each morning Bill would walk Eddie through the newspaper, reading and analyzing each story.

Fields also helped educate Cantor on the business world. "When we get to the end of the season," Fields advised, "Ziegfeld will start sending you critical telegrams. He'll criticize you so that you'll be glad to work next year for the same money you got this year. Don't be fooled like I was. You're making $400 a week this year, next year hold out for $600."

Although Ziegfeld called them his three musketeers, Fields once suggested that Will Rogers, Cantor, and himself form a type of covenant that traced its origins back to Omar Khayyam. Khayyam had once made an agreement with two competing tent makers that stated if any misfortune ever fell upon any one of them, they could always come to one of the others for food and a place to rest. Although none of the comedians ever had to take advantage of the agreement, the three remained friends for the rest of their lives.

The musketeers' offstage alliance did not translate well to the stage. Ziegfeld once suggested they all appear in a sketch together. The producer thought it would be the comic highlight of all the *Follies*. Fields would play a clerk at the patent office, while Rogers and Cantor would be inventors. Each night Will and Eddie would dig up some new gadget or whatnot and then explain what it was they had invented. The bit was, in Cantor's own estimation, "one of the worst in *Follies*' history." A week after it premiered, it was dropped from the show.

Fields, in spite of his affection for Eddie, loved playing practical jokes on his young friend. When Eddie was performing in the porter sketch from the *Follies of 1917*, he made his entrance skipping on stage, carrying two suitcases. One night Fields filled the valises with bricks and telephone books. Eddie remembers nearly breaking his neck trying to pick them up and hop out on stage at the same time. When Cantor found out who had perpetrated the practical joke, he invited Fields out for a game of golf that weekend. Eddie had led Bill Fields, himself a very serious golfer, to believe that he was in for a grueling match. On the first tee, Fields found Cantor waiting for him in his pajamas and slippers. Although he first had to laugh, Fields soon became embarrassed as Cantor followed him around the course ready for bed.

By the end of the third week, *Variety* reported that the strike had cost both sides over $1,500,000. After thirty days, a compromise agreement was hammered out that gave Actors' Equity most of their demands. In the future, actors would not work for more than four weeks in rehearsal without pay. In addition, there would be extra compensation for holiday performances, and producers with a bad business record would be required to post a bond to insure that their casts would receive their salary.

As great a victory as the AEA had won, it was bittersweet for Eddie Cantor. Although he was elated for the acting profession, Cantor's relationship with Flo Ziegfeld had been strained by the strike. Before the strike, Ziegfeld had agreed to make Eddie a star in a new production, not just a featured player in the next *Follies*. Once the strike was settled and the cast of the *Follies* reconvened, Ziegfeld wouldn't even talk to Eddie, let alone talk about putting him in his own vehicle, even though they had a written agreement for the project. Most likely the show Ziegfeld had in mind turned out to be *Sally*, with Marilyn Miller. Next season *Sally* would be the hit of Broadway, while Eddie Cantor would spend that entire time on the road in the *Midnight Rounders*.

To celebrate the end of the actor's strike and at the same time try to recoup some of the losses from it, Ziegfeld not only reopened the *Follies*, but moved his all-star cast upstairs for a special edition of the *Frolics*. In the rooftop review, Eddie assisted Fanny Brice in a slapstick parody of the risqué Apache dance. *Variety* reported that the team was "excruciatingly funny in [a] burlesque way. Miss Brice sacrifices all sense of dignity, permitting Cantor to administer kicks upon her posterior." This special edition would be the *Frolics* last hurrah. Within another year, the rooftop cabaret would close when prohibition began. (To reflect America's nonalcoholic outlook, Eddie introduced a song into his *Follies* specialty entitled: "It's the Smart Little Feller Who Stocked Up His Celler That's Getting the Beautiful Girls." It did not become a hit.)

The *Follies*, which resumed business September 10, played to standing-room-only crowds for weeks after the strike was settled. Business was so good that the show, which usually left town by the start of autumn, stayed till the second week of December, making it the longest Broadway run of the *Ziegfeld Follies* up to that time. Because of the extended New York run, the *Follies of 1919* skipped many of its regular road stops such as Boston and Philadelphia and moved on to Detroit for two weeks. As usual the show celebrated the holidays in Chicago, remaining until spring and breaking all records in that city for a Ziegfeld show.

After the road tour, Eddie returned to his apartment in the Bronx to find it empty and up for rent. He called his friend and business manager, Dan Lipsky, to find out what was going on. "Don't worry," Dan assured him,

"Ida needed a little rest and took the kids up to Mount Vernon." While Dan was driving him up to Mount Vernon, Eddie thought to himself that Ida was pregnant again (daughter number three, Edna, had been born the previous spring while the *Follies* were in their Atlantic City tryout). They soon stopped in front of a beautiful country home. When Eddie asked at whose house Ida was staying, Dan informed him, "It's your house, you've earned it." Ida had decided to surprise Eddie and had picked out the house herself. Lipsky's savings plan had taken just two years; the Cantors were now homeowners.

## REVIEWS

Eddie Cantor figured conspicuously in several contrasting features of the production, and usually elicited loud laughter and applause, but much of his material was more vulgar then even sophisticated New York may stand for. It seemed to be the consensus of the New York crowd that in its present form there is too much Cantor and not enough of the Dooleys, who, however, are on and off recurrently and always to howls coming and going. — *Variety*, June 13, 1919, Atlantic City opening

The one outstanding [comedy] bit was "At the Osteopath's" with George LeMaire and Eddie Cantor doing rough low comedy. No straight faces. If Cantor can survive the knocks and hot weather while he is being pounded about, [this] will prove the hit of every performance.

Mr. Cantor was a riot as usual with his specialty songs and mannerisms. — Sime, *Variety*, June 20, 1919, Broadway opening

# CHAPTER 11

# *Transition: 1920*

As soon as the road company of the *Ziegfeld Follies of 1919* arrived back in New York, rehearsals began for the *Follies of 1920*. Preparations for the new show began without Eddie Cantor. Eddie was still waiting for Ziegfeld to announce the particulars of the starring vehicle he had promised him. By the terms of their agreement, the producer was to provide Cantor with an author for the show by March 1. March 1 came and went with no author and no word from Ziegfeld.

Although their relationship was definitely strained by the recent Actors' Equity strike, Ziegfeld's foot-dragging was not totally uncharacteristic. One *Follies* principal told *Variety* that Ziegfeld had often promised them that they would have their own starring vehicle "next season." But next season by Ziegfeld's calendar, as many performers unhappily found out, was always one season away. Whether or not a starring show materialized, Eddie was definite on one point, he was not going back into the *Follies*.

At one point, Eddie decided that if Ziegfeld couldn't come up with a stage property for him, he would do it himself. Cantor, along with Georgie Jessel, announced they would present a show entitled *Troubles of 1920*. A review, *Troubles* was to be written by Cantor and Jessel, with music and additional material by Bert Kalmar and Harry Ruby. According to *Variety* the show would be mainly comedy scenes based on current events such as the Versailles peace conference, prohibition, and "the shimmy craze." Eddie Cantor wasn't the first Ziegfeld regular to attempt his own version of the *Follies*. George White, another graduate of the review, had done it with his long running *George White's Scandals*. *Troubles of 1920* evidently had more than its share of its own troubles, however, and the production never came off.

In the meantime, the *Follies of 1920* had premiered in Atlantic City. The review, without Cantor, Bert Williams (whose contract had run out), and Will Rogers (who had gone to Hollywood to make movies for Sam Goldwyn), was decidedly short on comedy. A small army of writers moved in to try to juice up the *Follies*. Additions and cuts were made at a frenzied pace, with over $60,000 worth of production material being removed. With his services obviously in need, Cantor still insisted he would not appear in the current *Follies*. Eddie offered to bet any takers $10,000 that when the *Follies* opened on Broadway it would do so without him.

The *Follies* premiered June 22, 1920, at the New Amsterdam Theatre. Listed as a surprise starter was Eddie Cantor. Ziegfeld had made a last minute appeal to Eddie to fill a much needed comedy spot in the second act. Cantor agreed, and his act nearly stopped the show. Being the hit of yet another *Follies* was not the same to Eddie Cantor as starring in his own show, however. Impatient for Ziegfeld to act, Cantor left the *Follies* before it had even completed its New York run. Instead, Eddie went back into vaudeville, headlining at the Palace for $2,000 a week. According to his agreement with Ziegfeld, Eddie's show was to open by the third week in September. Ultimately, when no show materialized, Cantor left Ziegfeld to look for his own show.

## REVIEW

Cantor, projected into the performance to fill a bad wait near the finale of the second act, dragged Ziegfeld on the stage with him, but the manager slipped away from the singing comedian, who immediately afterward sang two new songs to a walloping hit. Cantor would have stopped the show if it could have been stopped, for the applause was deafening while Granville, Donahue and Randall were singing the opening of the finale. It only stopped when the action went into full stage. Cantor's numbers were lively. Of his few stories, the best was that of the Hotel Claridge, when he said, "Over there you can get a room, bath and house detective for $5." — Sime, *Variety*, June 25, 1920

# CHAPTER 12

# *Broadway Brevities*

Immediately after he parted ways with Flo Ziegfeld, Eddie Cantor was swamped with offers, none of them quite what he was looking for. *Variety* speculated that Cantor would take *What's in a Name*, an established Broadway production, out on tour. In addition, the B. F. Keith Circuit, the biggest in vaudeville, offered Cantor several weeks as a headliner. At the same time, Eddie had a standing engagement to perform at the Winter Garden Theatre's Sunday night concert at $1,000 per appearance. To accept the Keith offer would tie him up Sundays, however, so Eddie declined. The Lowe's vaudeville theaters also offered Cantor engagements, with the added stipulation that he would have Sundays off to perform at the Winter Garden. Eddie turned them down also, not so much over money, as over medium. Although he had fought Ziegfeld in the past for the right to play vaudeville dates, Cantor felt a full-time return to vaudeville, even as a headliner, would represent a step backwards for his career. In the future he would make many appearances in vaudeville shows, but always as a stage, film, or radio star appearing as a nostalgic visitor, not a vaudeville fixture.

His three-plus years with Ziegfeld had made Eddie a name performer. He left Ziegfeld when he was on the threshold of having his own starring vehicle; for his next show, nothing less than that would do.

The Shubert brothers, Lee and J. J., approached Cantor with an offer for him to provide the comedy for one of their musical reviews. Two of the biggest producers in show business, the brothers had begun as ushers in Syracuse and they eventually controlled a vast theatrical empire which they ran with clockwork efficiency. Lee took charge of their real estate and business holdings, and J. J. produced as many as ten to fifteen shows a year. It was under the Shuberts' aegis that Al Jolson had become the biggest star on Broadway.

Cantor signed a two-year contract with the Shuberts for a weekly salary of $1,450, plus extra money whenever he appeared in their Sunday night shows at the Winter Garden. Ironically, the contract stipulated that the brothers would have Cantor in a starring vehicle by January 1, 1921, the exact date to which Ziegfeld had tried to postpone his promised Cantor-led production. To assure Cantor that they would have a show ready by the new year, the Shuberts posted a $20,000 bond which would be forfeited to the comedian if their promised vehicle did not materialize.

Immediately after Eddie signed with the Shuberts, they loaned him out to another review, *Broadway Brevities*, which was currently on tryout in Philadelphia. *Broadway Brevities* was the first attempt at producing by George LeMaire, the former straight man in the *Ziegfeld Follies*. (He had worked with Eddie the year before in the osteopath scene.) The show also boasted Bert Williams, who had recently left Ziegfeld when his five-year contract with the producer had expired. Williams reportedly put up half of the $80,000 in production costs for *Broadway Brevities*, with LeMaire providing the other half.

Aside from Cantor, who joined the company in mid–September at Philadelphia's Lyric Theatre, the *Brevities* was constantly changing personnel in advance of its Broadway premiere. At first, the featured performers were LeMaire, Williams, and Dorothy Jardon, a former vaudeville singer who eventually would wind up singing with the Chicago Opera Company. Soon after Cantor was added, Jardon withdrew from the show and was replaced by Edith Hallor. Also inserted into the cast were dancers Ula Sharon, Alexis Kosloff, and William Sully and singers Eddie Buzzell (Cantor's friend from back in the *Kid Kabaret*), Peggy Parker, Genevieve Houghton, and Maxwell Francis.

Like its cast, the show's musical numbers were in a constant state of flux. Songs and dance numbers were inserted and deleted from one performance to the next. The evolving score was composed by a young George Gershwin, working with a trio of lyricists. Gershwin had recently had his first big hit song in "Swanee." Unfortunately, no such standards were forthcoming for the score of *Broadway Brevities*. Additional numbers for the show were provided by the songwriting team of Bert Kalmar and Harry Ruby.

*Broadway Brevities* opened September 29, 1920, at Broadway's Winter Garden Theatre to mixed reviews. The consensus opinion was that LeMaire had bitten off more than he could chew in his first crack at producing. Although critics felt the show was not in the same league as the Ziegfeld or Shubert reviews, it was thought that *Broadway Brevities* would probably do strong business on its road tour. Since Eddie Cantor was on loan and was only scheduled to stay with the show through its New York run, *Variety* expressed doubts whether George LeMaire's name had sufficient drawing power on the road.

It should come as no surprise, with its three stars being recent veterans of the *Follies*, that *Broadway Brevities* would be a musical review featuring all the elements, in one form or another, of the Ziegfeld extravaganzas. *Brevities* had a similar program of songs, skits, production numbers, and specialties featuring its two main stars, Bert Williams and Eddie Cantor. Eddie's main bits included a comedy turn with George LeMaire in which they attempted to pick up girls and date them on a meager budget of only $11. *Variety* reports that laughs in that skit were "scattered at best."

Cantor's specialty, which went on just before the show's finale, started well but faltered when a trick fell flat. After his first song, Eddie, in blackface, ran backstage only to seemingly appear a moment later performing a violin solo. After the instrumental number, Eddie exited and then came back pretending to be blind; this supposedly made his violin virtuosity all the more remarkable and "amusing." Unfortunately, the violinist who doubled for Cantor had none of his characteristic stage energy, and this caused the audience to murmur throughout the routine over the identity of the ersatz Eddie. A subsequent monologue and song did little to recover the audience's attention after this confusing episode.

In his monologue, Eddie included a bit about his recent front porch campaign to educate the newly suffraged women voters. "Last night," he began, "I had a private session in the attic. I taught a Republican girl how to be Democratic." Reviewers also complained that Cantor's material was a shade too "blue" (risqué), even for Cantor.

Eddie Cantor's biggest number in *Broadway Brevities* was a reprise of the osteopath routine which he performed in the previous season's *Follies*. LeMaire repeated his role as Eddie's torturer/straightman. In an attempt to make the piece seem more original to the *Brevities*, the scene started out in a dentist's office, but it quickly reverted to the osteopath theme.

Eddie played a patient visiting dentist LeMaire. In an attempt to find out what was wrong with Eddie's teeth, LeMaire employed a variety of slapstick devices, before finally ending up in the chair straddling his hapless patient. As if this type of patient abuse humor wasn't enough like the osteopath bit, the scene lapsed into the very routine it was obviously based upon. While probing deep inside Eddie's mouth, LeMaire discovered that the problem wasn't in his teeth, but his spine. LeMaire then jumped off Eddie, pulled back a screen to reveal a therapy table and launched into a carbon copy of the osteopath sketch. The only change from then on was the ending, in which a pretty girl enters and sits in the dentist chair only to have Cantor jump on her as the scene blacks out.

While the reviewers and the audience didn't seem to mind seeing the osteopath routine in its latest incarnation, Flo Ziegfeld did. Within days of the opening of *Broadway Brevities*, Ziegfeld threatened to sue LeMaire and Cantor for lifting the material from his *Follies of 1919*. As the *Follies* producer, Ziegfeld reasoned he was the owner of any scenes that had appeared in his show. LeMaire, on the other hand, contended that the routine was his since he had created it, besides which the scenes were dissimilar in dialogue and presentation. *Variety* reported that the bit as it appeared in the *Brevities* had been "somewhat changed from the original." Cantor's run with the show ended before an injunction could bring a legal stop to the routine.[1]

Despite unenthusiastic reviews, *Broadway Brevities* did strong business at the box office, averaging over $30,000 a week for its first month and topping all other musicals then on Broadway, mostly on the strength of former Ziegfeld regulars, Cantor and Williams. After Cantor left the show, however, the receipts dropped swiftly, and "doctors" were brought in to fix the show. Their efforts resulted in five new numbers but failed to boost the sale of tickets. *Broadway Brevities* ended its New York run in early December but went on to a long and profitable road tour, fulfilling opening night predictions to that effect. Eddie Cantor, after a brief interim engagement at upper Manhattan's Fox Audubon, also went on the road for the better part of the next year as the star of his own show.

## REVIEW

To sum up the assets of the performance [of *Broadway Brevities*] in order of precedence as of the Blue Book of Broadway, it developed thus:

**Eddie Cantor** — good in a dentist scene and, of course, great in the osteopath scene, the same as in last year's "Follies"; as good as could be asked in a tedious dining and flirting scene with LeMaire, lines terrible; when he got into blackface for his next-to-closing specialty he did only three numbers, all very blue but typically Cantor. Although Cantor got a great reception the Winter Garden was still not "home" to him, and his specialty, further gummed up by a strange trick in which a "double" ragged on a violin, did not go as Cantor's specialty always has and always should. — *Variety*, October 8, 1920

## *Note*

1. LeMaire was also accused by another producer of stealing a production number which that producer had recently purchased from a London review.

# CHAPTER 13

# Midnight Rounders

If there were any doubts about the star of the Shuberts' new review, they were quickly dispelled by a full-page advertisement in *Variety* which proclaimed:

EDDIE CANTOR
in
The Century Promenade Review
"MIDNIGHT ROUNDERS"
Shubert Theatre, Philadelphia

The show, which was often referred to simply as *The Eddie Cantor Show*, was a departure from the usual way a show was presented. Most frequently a show would open for a few weeks out of town, usually within a few hundred miles of New York. Then, after the bugs were worked out, the production would move on to Broadway. Following a run of a few months (depending on its success), the show would tour the road (Boston, Chicago, Detroit, etc.) for anywhere from three to six months.

The *Midnight Rounders* on the other hand, was a combination of two reviews that had played on the roof of the Shuberts' Century Theatre, in a setting not unlike Ziegfeld's *Midnight Frolics*. Usually these midnight musical reviews would not have gone out on the road except that the Shuberts were stuck with a pair of problems. First, the Century Roof was due to close for an extensive remodeling, leaving the two shows playing there without a theater. Second, under the terms of their contract with Cantor, the Shuberts had to provide him with a starring vehicle before the first of the new year. Killing two birds with one stone, they decided to combine the two reviews into one show, ship it out of New York for an extended road run, and put Cantor at the head of it all, to supply the needed comedy and drawing power.

Since all the supporting numbers in the show had already been seen in New York, the *Midnight Rounders* entire year-long run took place on the road, leaving Eddie Cantor to wait over a year to become the star of his own show on Broadway. Perhaps as a concession to his disappointment, the Shuberts agreed to give Eddie 10 percent of the gross instead of the $1,450 per week agreed to in his two-year contract.

After a month of rehearsals, the *Midnight Rounders* moved down to Philadelphia in December 1920. In his 1928 autobiography, Cantor vividly recalls arriving at the Shubert Theatre and seeing his name for the first time in the starring position above the show's title. "Instead of thrilling me," he wrote, "the sight of this display made me weak and a sinking fear tugged at my heart." For the first time, Eddie Cantor *was* the show, quite a departure from his days with Ziegfeld. "If I got sick in the *Follies*," Cantor said, "I might be missed, but the show could still go on. Now the burden of the whole revue was pivoted on me and if I failed to appear, the doors of the theater would be locked."

Backstage, Eddie asked J. J. Shubert if they might be jumping the gun by featuring his name so prominently. Maybe they should wait and see if he could carry the show. "Don't be foolish, Eddie," Shubert replied, "You'll be a knockout!" And he was, but not before going through one of the most frantic opening nights of his career.

The *Midnight Rounders* was made up of twenty-nine scenes unrelated to one another. In fact, they were also unrelated to the title of the show, which had nothing to do with dissolute persons and was not performed at midnight, as it had been in New York. Throughout the premier performance, J. J. Shubert, as often was his habit, would run backstage and order last minute changes in the show—substituting songs, reversing the order of numbers, and cutting some scenes altogether. To complicate matters further, J. J. called for Cantor before his cue, telling him to go out and stall for time. Despite the fact that Eddie was only half made-up for his next number and still in his bathrobe, Shubert told him to go out on stage and "Do anything. Only keep 'em laughing!"

Having nothing prepared for just such an emergency, Eddie went out and told the truth. "Jake Shubert sent me out to stall while they change the show around," Eddie explained to the audience. "It may take weeks!" Eddie continued his half-dressed monologue until they signaled that the next number was ready, and he went back to his dressing room. A few minutes later J. J. called Cantor back, telling him to go stall some more. This time Eddie had finished making up, but went out on stage in his undershirt. After a few minutes, the show went on, and Cantor went back to try and finish dressing. No sooner had he made it back to his dressing room than the call boy burst in to tell him that Mr. Shubert wanted him immediately. This time Eddie was fully dressed except for his pants.

"Go out and stall," Shubert commanded.

"What! Without my pants!" Eddie cried. "At least give me a hat!" Eddie quickly put on a derby to complete his ridiculous outfit and went out for one final turn. His stalling monologues went over so smoothly the audience thought they were a prearranged part of the show. They were so successful, in fact, that they were kept in for the full run of *Midnight Rounders*.

Afterwards, J. J. Shubert assembled the cast backstage, put his arm around Eddie and proclaimed, "Ladies and gentlemen of the cast. I want to introduce you to Broadway's newest star—Eddie Cantor." High praise, except that Eddie would not really play Broadway in a starring show until *Make It Snappy* almost seventeen months later.

After the show, to celebrate, Eddie took out twenty of his friends who came from New York for the opening. He reserved tables at the nearest Childs, an inexpensive restaurant chain, and arranged for a budget menu of baked apples and cream. When members of the formally attired party protested, Cantor quieted them. "Which would my friends rather have," Eddie reasoned. "A big hit or a big banquet?" When they replied a big hit, Eddie nodded, said, "That's what I thought" and sat down to eat his apple.

The *Midnight Rounders* did smash business in every city it visited, usually out-grossing every other show it ran against. Even though the show was not on Broadway, J. J. Shubert was right about one thing—Eddie Cantor was a bona fide box office draw. In addition to making him a star, the *Midnight Rounders* was quickly making Cantor a rich man, thanks to his percentage agreement with the Shuberts. In the show's opening engagement in Philadelphia alone, Cantor's cut amounted to over $2,500. Quite an improvement over the $800 a week he had received from Flo Ziegfeld the previous year.

Although he had his own show and was earning considerably more money, Eddie missed working for the Great Ziegfeld. Years later Cantor recalled the difference between working for the Shuberts and Ziegfeld. "I was on percentage [with the Shuberts] that ran my salary to two and three, four times what I'd made with Ziegfeld. But I'd have gone back gladly, Mr. Ziegfeld was class. The Shuberts were just show business."

The *Midnight Rounders* consisted of five comedy sketches, seven production numbers, six dance numbers, and specialties. Cantor appeared in three of the comic bits, along with his specialty, and the aforementioned stalling turns between the other acts. Altogether, Eddie was on stage over an hour, or more than a third of the total running time.

Cantor's first and longest skit took place in a cabaret setting, with Eddie as a waiter, Joe Opp as the manager, and Lew Hearn, Harry Kelly, and several beautiful girls as patrons. Although details of this number are few, from the casting, the running time (twenty-five minutes), and the various musical bits interspersed throughout, it would seem that its inspiration, in part at least, came from Cantor's vaudeville experiences with Gus Edward's *Kid Kabaret*. In fact the entire *Midnight Rounders*, according to *Variety*, had the look of "Advanced Vaudeville" because most of the cast were alumni of the circuits.

A second comedy bit, entitled "Insurance," was yet another rehashing of the osteopath scene, with new jokes added to freshen up the physical comedy. In the skit, Eddie played a patient being examined for his life insurance with the Disreputable Insurance Company. "Do you drink anything?" the doctor asked. "Anything," Eddie replied. Despite the recycling of old material, the skit went over well with audiences and critics alike. Much of "Insurance," minus the roughhousing, can be seen virtually intact in the early talkie short of the same name which Cantor filmed in 1929.

The biggest comedy hit of the show came from a brand new number, "Joe's Blue Front." In "Blue Front," Cantor played a tailor's assistant in Joe Opp's clothing shop, with Lew Hearn playing the much abused customer who comes in looking for a suit. In the bit, Cantor and Opp are so determined to make a sale that they resolve not to let Hearn leave without first enriching the cash register.

All the customer wants is something with a belt in the back, exactly what they don't have in stock. In the course of the skit, Eddie tries selling Hearn a striped suit (with the stripes made of freshly applied tailor's chalk), a Prince Albert coat, and even a little boy's sailor suit. Each time, however, the customer protests that all he wants is a "belt in the back," and in response, Eddie raises his hand to strike Hearn before being stopped by Opp.

At one point, Eddie puts one coat on Hearn and remarks that the garment will make him look like a new man. "Go out in the light and see for yourself," Cantor tells him. When Hearn comes back in, Eddie strides up and asks how he can help. "It's me!" Hearn cries, "Me! The fellow who was just in here to try on a suit!" "You?" Eddie replies in amazement. "See? Even I didn't recognize you!" The skit ends with the totally confused Hearn running out of the store in his long underwear, leaving even his own suit behind.

After its Philly run, the *Midnight Rounders* continued on the road, playing in Atlantic City, Boston (where Cantor was a big draw, especially with the students from nearby Harvard University), Detroit, and Baltimore among other cities. In Chicago, the *Midnight Rounders* played for over three months despite the fact that the Shuberts forced the show into a smaller theater halfway through the run to make room for the new vaudeville circuit the brothers were attempting to launch. Even after moving from the Apollo to the tinier Great Northern, Cantor's name continued to pack in the crowds, setting records for both theaters and closing the Chicago run with bigger business than the show opened with.

Further proof of Cantor's star status — and especially sweet evidence to Eddie personally — arrived when the *Midnight Rounders* hit Milwaukee for Christmas week. On opening night, a large basket of flowers was delivered over the footlights to Eddie. Eddie was mystified until he examined the card, which read, "A lot of success and best wishes from the manager who made you open the show at the Majestic." The bouquet was from Higler, the manager who had urged Eddie to quit show business a scant six years earlier.

The *Midnight Rounders* finally rounded its last bend in early 1922 after more than a year touring the road. Except for missing a few performances in Cincinnati because the show's scenery was lost, the *Midnight Rounders* had played continuously since the fall of 1920. In addition to their regular slate of performances, the cast members would often spend their free afternoons putting on charity shows for local hospitals.

Eddie was on the road for so long that he again missed the birth of one of his daughters. On September 16, 1921, while the show was in Chicago, Eddie received word that Ida had delivered a fourth daughter, Marilyn. It was soon after Marilyn's birth that Eddie fully realized just how much he had been away from home. While playing a nearby city, Eddie decided to make a quick trip back to New York to see the new baby. When he rang the doorbell, six-year-old Marjorie opened the door, gave Eddie a strange look, then ran up the hall calling, "Mama! That man is here again!" Needless to say, Cantor fitted the kiddie quip into his nightly monologue.

Another incident that found its way into Cantor's specialty occurred just after the show had left Pittsburgh en route to its next engagement. Seated in front of Eddie on the train were two men whose conversation he couldn't help but overhear, especially because they were talking about him.

"I saw Eddie Cantor in the *Midnight Rounders*," one of them began. "Do you think he's such a nice fellow off the stage?"

"Nice fellow?" the other replied, "Why he's a relative of mine!"

Startled, Eddie leaned forward to get a better look at his mystery cousin. After he had settled in his own mind that he'd never seen the man before, Eddie sat back to listen further to the yarn the pretender was spinning.

Eddie's "relative" related apocryphal stories of his close friendship with the star—how Eddie visited them often in Pittsburgh, his favorite foods, and other personal and totally fictitious information. Finally, the tall tales got to Cantor, and he interrupted.

"You know Eddie Cantor?" he asked, careful not to give his identity away.

"Sure I do," the impostor bragged.

"And he visits you at your home?" Eddie probed.

"He was over only last night."

Not being able to stand the man's boasting anymore, Eddie admitted to knowing Eddie Cantor pretty well himself. "I'll bet you, you wouldn't know Eddie Cantor if you saw him."

"Okay," the man agreed, "I'll bet you ten dollars."

"And you'd know him if you saw him?" Eddie said, relishing the thought of exposing the braggart.

"Sure, he even told me he's leaving for New York tonight, and if he's on this train, he'd look me up."

"Well," Cantor challenged, "if he's on this train, who is he?"

"You are," the man laughed.

The two men had seen Eddie get on the train and had put on the entire conversation just to get his attention. Cantor paid the $10, not an unreasonable amount to pay for a story which immediately went into his act.

## REVIEW

Cantor's two best bits, aside from his own specialty, are the comedy scene, called "Insurance," resembling in some respects the "doctor's office" bits used by him before, and a new idea for a screaming comedy interlude called "Joe's Blue Front," a 20-minute farce, with Cantor playing a capital character bit as proprietor of a "pull-'em-in" clothing store, who forces misfit raiment upon his customers. — Rush, *Variety*, February 11, 1921

# CHAPTER 14

# *Make It Snappy*

No sooner had the exhausting run of the *Midnight Rounders* come to an end than the Shuberts went into production on their next vehicle for Eddie Cantor. Lee and J. J. Shubert no doubt rushed into Cantor's next review because not only did they need a show for the summer run at the Winter Garden Theatre, but Eddie's two-year deal was also almost half over.

That Cantor was not satisfied under the Shubert's aegis was evident from various items which appeared in *Variety* throughout 1922. In one article, Cantor was sending out a call for suitable scripts for future starring shows. The scripts would have to be farces or comedies because he did not want to be featured in any more musical reviews. The piece went on to say that "Regardless of what management he may be under in the future, Mr. Cantor says, he will insist the script selected by him shall be produced." In addition, Eddie also hinted that he might be in the market for a good film scenario for himself, playing either in white or blackface, since it would only be a matter of time until he appeared in "comedy pictures."

As the months remaining on Cantor's contract dwindled down, further reports circulated that several producers were competing for his future services. One of the offers reportedly came from Flo Ziegfeld's backer A. L. Erlanger, but the Great Ziegfeld himself apparently was not interested in his former star. Occasionally, while he was working for the Shuberts, Eddie would hint to his agent, Max Hart, that he was interested in working for Ziegfeld again. "Don't be silly," Hart would reply. "Ziegfeld won't have you."

A cattle call for forty chorus girls went out in late January for the new Cantor show; two thousand girls showed up, swamping the tryout held at the Century Theatre. The new show, which like *Midnight Rounders* was to be another plotless review, was initially titled *Kiss Me*, although the producers admitted that a title of *Laughs and Ladies* was just as likely. As in the case of the previous production, the title really didn't matter since it would probably have nothing to do with the show's content. Rehearsals were well under way when J. J. Shubert overheard a pushy elevator boy corralling passengers into his car by telling them to "Make it snappy!" Shubert immediately rushed to the office and announced, "I have the title for our next Cantor show! We'll call it *Make It Snappy*." And they did.

After five weeks of rehearsals, *Make It Snappy* opened at Philadelphia's Shubert Theatre in late February for a four-week run. Originally the show was scheduled to go directly to Broadway in the middle of March for an initial opening at either the 44th Street or Astor theaters. The Shuberts, probably on the strength of the Philly box office, decided to save *Make It Snappy* for the larger Winter Garden Theatre, which would be available April 24. The date was changed several times while the review went on an extended pre–Broadway tour that included runs in Buffalo, Cleveland, and Pittsburgh.

After seven weeks on the road, during which time numerous changes were made to the cast, *Make It Snappy* finally had its Broadway debut on April 13, 1922. The cast contained many carryovers from *Midnight Rounders*, including featured artist Nan Halpern and Eddie's comic foils Joe Opp and Lew Hearn. The inclusion of Opp and Hearn was important since they were featured prominently in *Make It Snappy*'s biggest comedy scene—"Joe's Blue Front," which was transplanted verbatim from *Rounders*, as the program explained, "by request."

The show was liberally laced with comedy, with Cantor playing a sheik, a police recruit, and a taxi driver, in addition to the tailor in the "Blue Front" sketch. All these characters were done in whiteface. The only time Eddie blacked up was for his musical specialty at the finale.

The absence of Eddie's blackface character in the comedy sketches reflected the full-fledged Broadway star status he achieved with *Make It Snappy*. As his career progressed from burlesque to vaudeville to featured Broadway player to Broadway star, his use of blackface tapered off, and it would continue to do so. In its place, Cantor developed the little fellow who was usually naive, but at the same time quick with a wisecrack. The character reflected the childhood Cantor spent on the streets of New York, where his small size made quick wits a necessity. Also, Cantor's stage character was definitely Jewish and often used Yiddish and Hebrew throwaway lines delivered with a Hebrew inflection. Essentially, Cantor's character was a *nebbish*, literally a "poor thing." Much in Cantor's nebbish characterization can be seen in later comedians such as Jerry Lewis and Woody Allen. The nebbish character was most often used in outlandish situations in which his appearance would provide a humorous juxtaposition.

In the sheik sketch—a satire of romantic film star Rudolph Valentino— after a grand description of the mighty sheik riding his Arabian steed over the desert sands, Eddie peddles on stage riding a bicycle. In order to keep better track of his harem, Eddie makes them punch in on a time clock. When a rival sheik appears, staggering under the weight of his own mustache, he lifts Eddie on the point of his saber. Before he can finish Eddie off, however, he notices a locket around his neck. Upon examination, the other sheik discovers a picture of a woman.

"My wife!" he exclaims.

"My mother, Sophie Tucker!" Eddie replies.

"My child, Sarsaparilla!" he cries embracing Eddie.

"Pop!" the long-lost Eddie sobs.

In the police scene, Eddie again plays the little nebbish who is out of place, this time applying for a job as a policeman. As he enters the station house, Eddie passes a dejected, strapping six-footer. When he asks what's wrong, the giant explains that the force has rejected him for being too puny. Undaunted, Eddie applies to Chief Joe Opp. What follows is again another knockabout reworking of the osteopath-cum-dentist-cum-insurance sketch, with Eddie going through another tortuous physical exam. The sketch ends with Eddie making the squad, but quickly resigning when he learns a local gang is knocking off cops.

Eddie's final comedy turn in *Make It Snappy* did fit his character. In this bit he played a New York cab driver who takes a country bumpkin (Lew Hearn) for a ride, in more ways than one. This sketch gave Eddie the opportunity to sit for a while after the roughhousing of the police sketch, and still deliver a steady stream of one-liners and pearls of wisdom. Cantor would use this character almost thirty years later on the *Colgate Comedy Hour*, under the title "Maxi the Taxi."

*Make It Snappy* opened to strong reviews, with the lion's share of the praise going to Cantor's comedy bits and songs. The audience was also pleased and showed its approval by making the review the number one show on Broadway; it took in over $100,000 in the first four weeks of the run.

Despite predictions of a run through to autumn, after only a few months *Make It Snappy* showed signs of slowing down, not at the box office, but on stage. The hectic pace Cantor had set for himself while framing the show—he was on stage for 75 percent of the two-hour-plus running time—was beginning to take its toll on the frenetic comedian. At first, matinees were trimmed from the schedule, but the onset of summer weather in pre–air-conditioned New York, made it even more difficult to keep the "snap" in *Make It Snappy*. (One particularly sweltering night Nan Halpern collapsed from the heat and had to be carried off stage.)

Cantor appealed to Lee Shubert to close the show for the summer to give everyone a much needed vacation. Without some time off, Eddie was afraid he wouldn't make it through the next season. With the show still pulling in upwards of $18,000 a week, however, Shubert told Cantor, "not to be bothering his head about the weather" and added that *Make It Snappy* was a sure bet for at least another three months.

Soon Cantor was ready to close the show by leaving it himself, with or without the Shuberts' blessing. Before this could happen, however, Lee Shubert went to Atlantic City to check on the progress of one of his out-of-town properties, *Spice of 1922*, which was doing very strong business. Simple mathematics—the top Atlantic City ticket was only $2.50, compared to $3.00 at the Winter Garden—plus the fact that a new show in the Winter Garden would draw better than one almost three months old convinced Shubert that perhaps *Spice of 1922* was just the show to give the worn out *Make It Snappy* troupe a well-earned rest. The benevolent Shubert returned to New York to explain to his star, "Eddie, do you know you are working too hard? I don't want you to break down. You must have a vacation, and I think we'll close July 1 so you can spend the real hot weather away . . . if you want to."

Eddie didn't waste any time recuperating, and soon he was finding other projects to keep him busy while waiting for the road tour of *Make It Snappy* to commence. At one point, Eddie even offered his services to another Broadway show, *The Gingham Girl*. It seems that Eddie's old friend from the *Kid Kabaret*, Eddie Buzzell, was holding out for featured status in *The Gingham Girl*. When the producers balked at his demands, Buzzell threatened to walk out. Cantor immediately volunteered to go on in Buzzell's stead, saying he would even read from the script during performances until he learned the part. It never came to that, and Buzzell was given his sought-after billing by the end of the week.

Eddie Cantor also formed his own corporation during his vacation. In preparation for the day when his Shubert contract would run out, Eddie, along with Ida and business manager/boyhood pal Dan Lipsky, formed the "Eddie Cantor Theatrical Enterprises." The company, which initially capitalized with $50,000, was in business to produce musical shows, though not exclusively shows starring Cantor. The corporation also controlled the Jean Schwartz music publishing business.

In mid–September, *Make It Snappy* went out on the road, starting in Brooklyn and hitting Boston, Detroit, Chicago, and Philadelphia. The show attracted big box office business in all the cities. That Cantor was fast becoming a major star was evident from *Make It Snappy*'s Detroit run at the Garrick Theatre. The Garrick's capacity was 1,200, while across the street Eddie's old *Follies* friend, Ed Wynn, was playing at the Detroit Theatre, which had a capacity of 2,000. Despite being in a theater almost half the size, Cantor easily outgrossed his Broadway rival. To top it off, tickets for *Make It Snappy* were just $2.50 compared to $3.30 for Wynn's show.

Bigger competition awaited Eddie in Chicago, where he wasn't up against just a former Ziegfeld employee, but Ziegfeld himself. When *Make It Snappy* blew into the Windy City, *Sally*, Ziegfeld's smash Broadway musical, starring Marilyn Miller and Leon Errol, arrived the same week. The Ziegfeld show was expected to do record-breaking business. Cantor's was not; but he did. In a pace that even outran the great Jolson's Chicago records, Cantor did $30,000 for his first week at the Apollo Theatre. *Sally* did $40,000 for the same period, but at a price of $4.40 for the best seats. (*Make It Snappy*'s best seat went for only $2.50, with matinees even lower.)

*Variety* took notice of Cantor's feat, writing: "Making allowance of the difference in prices and several other incidents, Cantor's $30,000 gross must be considered a wonder item of the week. It was reckoned that Cantor would hold his own to a profitable extent, but nothing like the demand that was made for Cantor's show was predicted."

The second week was even more remarkable. While *Sally* repeated its $40,000 week, *Make It Snappy* actually went up to just over $31,000. "With shoulders erect to withstand the *Sally* opposition," *Variety* noted, "Eddie Cantor continues to march on for further glory. Cantor is always good for big business for a limited number of weeks here, but this season he's far beyond in records anything he's ever done here. The sympathy that was supposed to be dished out to Cantor for stacking up against Ziegfeld's opposition may now be saved for others."

Overall, *Make It Snappy* grossed over $215,000 for its nine-week Chicago run and set a house record for attendance at the Apollo. The previous record had been held by the Shuberts' number one star, Al Jolson. Despite his achievements under their banner, Cantor was dissatisfied with the Shuberts, however. In mid–March, he officially announced that he would not sign another contract with the brothers when his present contract expired in three months. He accused the Shuberts of cutting corners on his productions and equipping *Make It Snappy* with second-hand costumes and scenery. Tired of plotless reviews, Cantor announced that next season he would produce and star in his own musical production.

Eddie's two years with the Shuberts had only reinforced his desire for the class and polish he had abandoned when he left Ziegfeld. Eddie wanted to go back to Ziegfeld, but all reports indicated that Ziegfeld wasn't interested. Eddie found a way, however, to get through to Ziegfeld. While Eddie was going head-to-head against Ziegfeld's *Sally*, a theatrical writer noted in his column that "Eddie Cantor at $3.30 a seat is better entertainment value than Marilyn Miller and Leon Errol at $4.40." Knowing that such a review would appeal to Ziegfeld's sense of pride, Eddie had the line reprinted in a full-page advertisement in *Variety*.

A few days later Ziegfeld called Eddie from Palm Beach. After exchanging cordial greetings, Ziegfeld asked, "So, what are your plans for next season?" Cantor told his former boss he was interested in starring in his own musical comedy. Ziegfeld was interested in producing such a vehicle and agreed to meet Eddie to work out the details. Neither Ziegfeld or Cantor ever again mentioned the bitter rift that had led to Eddie's two-year Shubert exile. The producer and his star comedian went on to enjoy a long, close, and successful working relationship. By early May, Eddie had signed a three-year contract with Ziegfeld.[1]

By the end of May, *Make It Snappy* "snapped altogether," in Cantor's words, and concluded its run in Philadelphia, the city where it had opened. During the final month in Philly, Eddie introduced one of the biggest song hits of his career. Repeat business had been so good that Eddie was looking for new material for his musical specialty. One afternoon he stopped in at Shapiro, Bernstein and Co. to see if they had anything new he might use in *Make It Snappy*. He picked up a tune so new it hadn't even been printed yet, "Yes, We Have No Bananas," by Frank Silver and Irving Cohn.

Eddie tried out "Yes, We Have No Bananas" at the Wednesday matinee.

Audience response was so tremendous he went back to Shapiro, Bernstein daily for new choruses. From there the song swept the country and became the biggest novelty song of the decade. America was going so bananas over "Bananas" that New York mayor Jimmy Walker returned from a European trip to announce that most foreigners thought the song had become our national anthem. (One observer attributed the success of "Yes, We Have No Bananas" to the fact that it was a pastiche of the "Hallelujah" chorus, "My Bonnie Lies Over the Ocean," and "I Dreamt That I Dwelt in Marble Halls," among other songs.)

## REVIEWS

For those who have been watching [Cantor's] progress, the present piece may disappoint just a trifle, for some of the comedy of last year's show is held over, according to the program, by request, while a couple of other scenes have been improvised, but are basically the same as others with which Cantor has been identified in other seasons.

The gags interspersed are clever, but many miss the mark through the habit of Cantor's adherents finding their seats late, Cantor's songs are all new and just the right ones for him. — Harrison, *Variety*, April 7, 1922, Pittsburgh opening

Eddie Cantor debuts on Broadway as a star in his own name and right with a genuine comedy show and at an opportune time. . . . A big draw on the road, Cantor has kept off Broadway until the ripe moment came around. With the season's musical hits wearing off and nothing of importance in sight for the summer here excepting "The Follies," the Cantor show will breeze along, getting a running start, and it's going to be some summer show that can stop it. When people can find something to laugh at in the hot weather they will forget the heat, and "Make It Snappy" is a laugh. — Sime, *Variety*, April 21, 1922, Broadway opening

## *Note*

1. Information about Cantor's new contract with Ziegfeld is a bit muddled. According to one account in *Variety*, Ziegfeld beat out fellow producer Charles Dillingham for Eddie's services by a mere twenty-four hours. One week later *Variety* reported that Dillingham had in fact signed up Cantor the previous fall, but the term of the Dillingham contract overlapped with the final year of Eddie's Shubert deal and so lapsed at the same time. To make matters even more confused, Ziegfeld spent the week after signing Cantor denying that he had done so, or had any interest in doing so.

# CHAPTER 15

# Kid Boots

At first the new, improved relationship between Eddie Cantor and Flo Ziegfeld seemed suspiciously like their old one. Cantor had an agreement to star in a Ziegfeld musical show of his own, but Ziegfeld had no show in which to put him. As he did in back in 1920, the producer stalled his star while he looked for a suitable property. The longer he stalled, the more anxious Eddie became, as rumors started circulating around Broadway that he would appear in the next edition of the *Follies*. Not wanting to see a repeat of 1920, Cantor (as he had done three years before) vehemently denied the reports.

Loath as he was to return to the review which had made him famous, Eddie nevertheless did work various stints in the *Follies of 1922*. The first took place in early June when he replaced Ziegfeld returnee Will Rogers for a three-week run. Cantor was back in the *Follies* again in August but was careful not to make his appearances too regular and wind up in the show permanently. When the 1923 edition of the *Follies* debuted in October, Eddie did participate, not on stage, but as the author of a skit for Fanny Brice. In addition, he showed up in the audience on opening night with a variety of tools and started removing his theater seat. When an usher tried to stop him, Eddie yelled, "I paid twenty-two dollars for this seat, and I'm going to take it home with me!" It was one of the biggest laughs of the night.

The chances of Eddie becoming a prisoner of his *Follies* successes receded when he was approached by songwriter Joe McCarthy. McCarthy and his partner, Harry Tierney, were hot off their latest success, the score for the hit musical *Irene*. Aside from being a successful composing team, McCarthy and Tierney were members of Siwanoy, a local golf club. Their love for golf gave them the idea to build a show around a country club setting.

Together McCarthy and Tierney had worked out a rough plot revolving around a country club caddymaster who ran a bootlegging business on the side. They based the character of the caddymaster on their own clubhouse attendant, a black fellow named Harry, and christened him "Kid Boots." Knowing that Ziegfeld was looking for a new property, McCarthy thought the role of "Boots" would be a natural for Eddie Cantor (in blackface).

Cantor loved the idea, especially since a country club would give the show a novel setting, thus helping to avoid the conventional boy-meets-girl aspects that had become old hat on Broadway. Ziegfeld liked the idea also and put McCarthy and Tierney to work on the songs, while assigning William Anthony McGuire to do the book. Although McGuire was an up-and-coming writer who had just scored his first success with a play called *Six Cylinder Love*, *Kid Boots* represented his first attempt at working with such a prestigious company and his first try at scripting a musical comedy.

Since McGuire was new to Broadway musicals, Ziegfeld suggested he get together with Cantor and McCarthy to hammer out the details of the plot. This idea was doomed from the start. First the three men couldn't find a day they were all available. When a day was finally agreed upon and a working session scheduled, McGuire never bothered to show up because of an out-of-town appointment. A second meeting a few weeks later managed to bring the three together at McCarthy's home. To celebrate their success at finding themselves in the same place, and in tribute to the "spirit" of *Kid Boots*, the trio enjoyed a few rounds of drinks before getting down to work. After the fourth round of the bootleg booze, none of them, in Cantor's words, "could remember what we had come up there for," and another opportunity was missed.

Finally Cantor, McCarthy, and McGuire got together and decided the following: first, that the show would be called *Kid Boots* and second, that it would be about golf. Having made such incredible progress, they left the play in William Anthony McGuire's hands, with McGuire promising to have a rough draft of the first act in four or five days. A week and a half later not only did they not have the first act, they didn't even have a playwright. McGuire was nowhere to be found. Cantor and McCarthy suspected that he was in hiding working on another play.

In a near panic, Cantor, McCarthy, and Tierney went to Ziegfeld to voice their concerns. Ziegfeld was surprised, especially since he thought the entire play was already finished. The producer managed to track down his missing author, who explained that he needed a few days to work on a few new ideas. As a token of good faith, however, McGuire recited a few samples of dialogue that he had completed. Ziegfeld was satisfied with McGuire's ability as a writer, but suggested that another more experienced playwright, Otto Harbach, come in to help with the actual construction of the plot. McGuire agreed, even though it meant splitting his royalties with Harbach.

With Harbach working with McGuire, the book quickly began to take shape. Cantor himself helped out, making suggestions for various comedy scenes. The first involved a golf lesson routine with Eddie as the caddymaster instructing a behemoth of a woman. Eddie also suggested a revamping of his old standard, the osteopath sketch. This time, however, the sketch would take place in the golf club's locker room. To freshen up the bit, Ziegfeld suggested that they include a new electric chair that his doctor had been using on him during recent back treatments.

Cantor's final suggestion concerned not the show's plot, but rather the race of its title character. Eddie, not wanting to go back to being labeled strictly a blackface comic, insisted that "Boots" be white. As he had first done in the *Follies of 1918*, Cantor proved to Ziegfeld's satisfaction that he could be just as funny without the aid of burnt cork, and "Boots" was made white. Ironically, it was the blackface angle that originally prompted McCarthy to bring the idea for *Kid Boots* to Cantor's attention.

With the script slow in coming, the opening of *Kid Boots* was pushed back several times. Originally, the show had been scheduled to open October 18, but with all the delays, it barely got into rehearsal by that time. By mid–October the first act was finished, and the cast, which included Mary Eaton, Jobyna Howland, Harry Fender, and Harland Dixon, assembled for rehearsals. After three weeks the cast had honed the first act to a rapier edge. Everything was going fine when Cantor realized they still hadn't seen the second act. He rushed to find Ziegfeld, who scrambled to find his authors, and they all hurried together for more story conferences. Finally, after another week, the second act started to evolve.

A few weeks before *Kid Boots* was scheduled to open out-of-town, Ziegfeld approached Cantor and dropped a bombshell. "Eddie, the show's no good," the producer told him. "Let's call it off before we go through the expense of costumes and sets. We'll find something else for you." Ziegfeld, a determined pessimist, was positive he had a flop on his hands. His primary evidence was the fact that the rehearsals were going so well. In Zieggy's mind the better a show was in rehearsal, the bigger flop it would be when it opened. In addition, the great producer knew staging, costumes, and beautiful girls, but was at a loss when it came to comedy, and *Kid Boots* was his first show which was primarily a comedy.

Stunned, Eddie tried to convince Ziegfeld that he was mistaken; *Kid Boots* was going to be a smash. To prove it, Eddie gave a full performance of the show right there in Ziegfeld's office. He sang all the songs, recited the lines, jumped on the furniture, rolled on the floor, laughed, and cried. By the time Eddie was finished, Ziegfeld still had his doubts, but decided to take a chance since the show obviously meant so much to his star. Despite his own pessimism, Ziegfeld went ahead and ordered the sets and costumes. (A few years later when Ziegfeld had four hit shows running simultaneously on Broadway, he sent a telegram to William Anthony McGuire bemoaning his predicament and proclaiming them all flops. McGuire wired back, "Please accept my condolences in this your darkest hour of success.")

*Kid Boots* ran into one last hurdle before its out-of-town opening: the billing of Mary Eaton, the show's female lead. Eaton's lawyer insisted that she get equal billing with Cantor. Both Ziegfeld and Cantor balked at the demand. This was Eaton's first major part in a big show after she had been one of many featured players in the last edition of the *Follies*. Cantor, on the other hand, had two starring vehicles under his belt. "I simply considered it poor business to surrender so lightly the one thing I had surmounted so many difficulties to achieve," Cantor contended. Eddie convinced Mary

Eaton and her lawyer that she should take a lower billing, but equal in size to his own. Thus in the first week of December 1923, *Kid Boots* opened in Detroit with the marquee proclaiming:

EDDIE CANTOR in "KID BOOTS"
With MARY EATON

*Kid Boots* hit the ground running in its out-of-town opening in Detroit and didn't slow down for over two years. Unlike most shows, it required practically no doctoring and aside from a few dances used during encores, it played throughout its run with virtually no changes. The only slight variation came after the first two performances, when a few Detroit critics made some negative comments on some of Cantor's numbers. Eddie had encountered similar criticism the year before when *Make It Snappy* played Detroit. The songs were removed but were later restored to the show at Flo Ziegfeld's insistence, who, after his initial trepidation, evidently liked *Boots* just the way it was.

On opening night, Ziegfeld gathered the cast backstage after the performance and admonished them not to call family and friends back in New York concerning the success of *Kid Boots*. "I don't want anyone to know what kind of a hit we have," the producer told them. "It will only make it harder to live up to expectations. Let's surprise them." Anyone caught breaking Ziegfeld's "gag order" would be fired. For his part, Cantor stayed within the letter of the law when he phoned Ida and told her it was all right now to go ahead and buy the new coat she wanted. Ironically, Ziegfeld himself called all the important New York critics later that night to tell them that *Boots* was a great success. In addition, Zieggy started taking out ads for the show proclaiming it an even greater triumph than *Sally*, his most successful production to date.

After dismissing the cast, Ziegfeld took Eddie for a late supper at a nearby Chinese restaurant. "Well, Mr. Ziegfeld," Eddie said, "you should be pleased with the show."

"Eddie, from now on I'm not Mr. Ziegfeld," he corrected. "I'm Flo. I'm Zieggy." Any awkwardness that remained from their previous rift evaporated in the glow of their current triumph. From that night on, Flo Ziegfeld and Eddie Cantor were close friends.

While they waited for their food, Flo took out a pencil and started writing numbers on the back of the menu. Suddenly, he started to laugh. "Look, Eddie," he chuckled, while showing Cantor the figures, "if we sell out every performance, I'll only lose twelve hundred dollars a week!"

The financial figures for *Kid Boots* were not as dismal as the back of Flo Ziegfeld's menu first indicated. If the show sold out every performance (as it did for more than a year), Ziegfeld (who owned 50 percent of *Boots*) and Leo Feist (who owned the other 50 percent) would turn a profit of around $6,000 a week. Against that, however, were the royalties and production costs, which were estimated at $150,000; *Kid Boots* would not turn an actual profit until the second year of its run.

At first, *Kid Boots* was designed to be a modest musical comedy by Ziegfeld's usual standards. With this in mind, Cantor and Max Hart had originally invested in the production and owned 25 percent of the show. As rehearsals went on, however, Ziegfeld, in spite of his reservations, began to make lavish costume and scenery additions, making the show more and more expensive. Eddie and Max, believing that Ziegfeld was spending too much to ever turn a profit, sold their shares in *Kid Boots* to Ziegfeld.

Aside from spending freely on the production, Ziegfeld also hurt himself financially when he negotiated the theater deal for *Boots*. Instead of paying rent at the Earl Carroll Theatre, where *Kid Boots* would have its Broadway opening, Ziegfeld agreed to a percentage deal, with Carroll calling for a 65-35 split of the box office. The deal wound up a bonanza for Carroll, who received over $10,000 a week for most of the run of *Kid Boots*. Under their original arrangement, Ziegfeld could have originally had the theater for only $5,000 a week. After the successful road opening, Ziegfeld offered to go back to the rental figure, but by that time, buoyed by the out-of-town notices, Carroll had raised the offer to $7,000 a week. Ziegfeld refused, even though he still would have saved $3,000 a week.

After Detroit, *Kid Boots* went on for a week in Cincinnati, one in Washington, D.C., and finally Christmas week in Pittsburgh, prior to the New Year's Eve opening on Broadway. The show did sell-out business in its first three weeks and made front-page news for its week in Pittsburgh. The reason was that *Kid Boots*, at the Nixon Theatre, was going head-to-head against Al Jolson in *Bombo* at the Alvin Theatre. Jolson was the undisputed champ of musical comedy at the time, while Cantor was the up-and-coming challenger. Cantor wound up taking in more money than Jolson, but the top ticket for *Kid Boots* was $4, as opposed to only $3.50 for *Bombo*. Also, the Nixon had almost two hundred more seats. Still, most observers called the week a draw, and while a tie usually goes to the champ, Eddie's showing definitely established him as one of musical comedy's biggest stars.

*Kid Boots* opened on Broadway at the Earl Carroll Theatre on New Year's Eve, 1923. The opening night seats were priced at $16.50 each. In order to make everything just right for the New York opening, Ziegfeld spent over $18,000 replacing costumes that he thought "looked a little smudged" after a month on the road. In addition, he changed Eddie's costume from an oversized cap, a voluminous sweater, and baggy knickers, to tailored golf togs made of cashmere. "You don't need funny clothes," Ziegfeld told his comedian. "You're funny. The words are funny. Don't try to help it."

*Kid Boots* was an unusual musical comedy for its time. In the words of one drama critic, *Boots* was different from its competition in that it had "a plot that wasn't Cinderella." Instead, the show is the story of "Boots," a caddymaster at an exclusive country club in Palm Beach, Florida. "Boots" (played by Eddie Cantor) is so called because in addition to being a caddymaster, he acts as the local distributor of bootleg booze to the members of the club. Boots also gives golf lessons, but the only thing the instructions improve are his own bank balance. Whenever a member shows too much progress, Boots replaces their regular golf ball with a trick ball, invariably leading to a worsening of their game and more lessons.

The romantic plot revolves around Polly Pendleton (Mary Eaton), a club member who is wooed and won by Tom Sterling (Harry Fender), a millionaire who takes a job incognito as the club pro so he can be close to Polly. Plot complications were supplied by Carmen Mendoza (Ethelind Terry), a Spanish beauty who rivals Polly for Tom's affections. Boots acts as Cupid between the two lovers, making everything come out okay for the finale.

The full burden of supplying the show's comedy fell on Cantor. From the first scene, Eddie scored laugh after laugh, keeping the show moving at a quick pace. The opening scene shows Boots confronting the caddies under his charge. At the first words from his mouth, the caddies fall down as one at the authority in his voice.

"Get up!" Boots barks. "I suppose you know I'm the caddymaster here!"

"Yes, ma'am," they reply.

"Yes, ma'am?"

"No, ma'am!"

"No, ma'am?" Boots questions. He then removes his jaunty red necktie and shoves it in his pocket. "Don't let that thing fool you," he tells them. "I'm a pretty tough guy, I am. When I have waffles for breakfast, I throw away the waffles and eat the irons."

Boots then lectures them on the recent rash of missing golf balls around the club. "I don't mind you guys sneaking in a ball now and then," he starts, "but remember, a golf ball is never lost until it stops rolling. Remember, honesty is the best policy. You've either got to be honest . . . or I get half."

After dismissing the caddies, Boots counsels his lovesick friend Tom, the golf pro. Boots tells Tom that all his problems winning Polly will vanish if there's harmony between them.

"Do you know what perfect harmony is?" Boots asks rhetorically. "Perfect harmony is a baseball game between the Ku Klux Klan and the Knights of Columbus, with a Negro umpire, for the benefit of the Jewish War Relief."

Boots advises Tom to forget Polly because she comes from a wealthy family, while he's only a golf pro. When Tom insists that he can't forget her, Boots chides him for his negative attitude.

"Don't say you can't! Look at me. When I was a kid, I promised myself that by the time I was twenty-five I'd own a Rolls-Royce. Well, yesterday I turned twenty-six and I put five dollars down on a Ford."

Cantor's comedy foil was played by Jobyna Howland in the role of Dr. Josephine Fitch, another member of the club. A tall, imposing woman, Howland was a comedy star in her own right whom Ziegfeld hired at $1,500 a week just to play opposite Eddie. Their physical contrast made their scenes together all the more comical.

Their first bit together featured Dr. Fitch as one of Boots' golf pupils. Fitch explained to her tutor that she had played very well the day before.

"Oh, really," Boots asks. "What did you go around in?"

"A blue skirt and a brown sweater," Fitch replies.

"No, no, I don't mean your attire. What was your score?"

"Seventy-one," Fitch proudly proclaims.

"Seventy-one!" Boots exclaims, "Why, that's phenomenal! And the second hole?"

"Seventy," his star student reveals.

Boots then tries to give the doctor a lesson in putting, carefully adjusting her stance, so that by the time she is ready to putt, her form is something akin to a pretzel. When she actually takes a swing, the trick ball naturally makes her shot veer off sharply. In desperation, Fitch swings the club at Boots, who quickly protects himself with the flag stick, and they begin fencing around the stage. Finally, when Dr. Fitch breaks down into tears, Boots puts his arm around her and offers these immortal words of consolation:

"Don't cry, Doctor. Remember Rome wasn't built in a day. You've only been putting two years."

Any discomfort that Boots may have caused Dr. Fitch is paid back in spades a few scenes later. Boots is busy hiding his bootleg liquor in the ladies' locker room when Dr. Fitch enters and catches him by surprise.

"Boots!" she cries out. "What are you doing here?"

"I'm sick," he groans, thinking quickly.

"Where?" the doctor asks.

"In the ladies' locker room."

Dr. Fitch promises Boots a quick cure and throws him on the electric treatment chair. After giving him a few preliminary twists and turns, Fitch secures Boots into the seat and tells him not to get up until he counts to ten.

"Ten!" Boots cries out immediately.

"No, you've got to count slowly," the doctor orders.

"Five and five!"

"Slowly! If you count over fifteen, it might burn you a little."

Fitch then turns on the chair, and it begins to spark and smoke. While Boots counts, Dr. Fitch is called away for a phone call. By the time she returns, Boots, caught in the chair's electrical grip, is screaming numbers in the thousands. When she turns off the contraption, Boots quickly submerges his smoking bottom in the nearest fire bucket.

The electric chair was nothing compared to what comes next. Dr. Fitch lifts Boots onto a massage table and begins to pummel the diminutive caddymaster for the sake of his health. By the time she finishes, Boots staggers off the table, gets back into the electric chair, and motions for her to turn it on, preferring the machine's torture to her own. Although familiar to Broadway audiences as yet another incarnation of the osteopath scene, nevertheless the bit was the hit of the show.

Another comedy highlight was a reworking of the "Joe's Blue Front" bit from *Midnight Rounders* and *Make It Snappy*. In the *Kid Boots* incarnation, the routine is set in the club's pro shop (instead of a clothing store) and the customer is looking for a blue golf sweater (instead of a suit with a belt in the back). As before, Eddie doesn't have what the customer wants, but cajoles and irritates him into taking a totally different item — in this case, a red cap. Cantor had no qualms about reusing previous routines; it was a standard vaudeville practice. "Once a comedian has struck certain styles of comedy that suit him," Cantor explained, "it is interesting to follow the many variations he devises, so that he can use the same idea and yet conceal it." It didn't matter whether you employed the same situation from show to show, as long as you made it seem fresh to the audience.

Aside from his set pieces, Cantor's main contribution to the plot was to help the hero, Tom, get into the climatic golf match. In order to do this, he has to incapacitate the first choice to represent the club, Randolph Valentine (Robert Barrat). Boots accomplishes his mission with the aid of a hammer which he has concealed behind his back. In a comedy-suspense scene, Boots stands chatting with Valentine about the match, all the while waiting for the right moment to hit him on the wrist with the hammer. Cantor milked the scene for all it was worth, each night taking longer and longer to deliver the decisive blow. The longer it was delayed, the more the audience laughed.

Once in the match, however, Tom loses on the final hole when one of Boots' trick balls finds its way into the game. Everything works out in the end, of course, with Boots confessing and Tom winning the match and the girl. The finale takes place at a gala masquerade ball, giving Ziegfeld another excuse to waltz out more exotic costumes. At the ball, Boots arrives in blackface and announces that he is disguised as "Eddie Cantor of the *Ziegfeld Follies*." This not only allowed "Boots/Eddie" to finish the show with a specialty number filled with his growing list of hits, but also to put in a plug for Ziegfeld's other expensive Broadway property.

Aside from the score written by McCarthy and Tierney, Eddie introduced several songs by other writers during his finale specialty. Two of them became standards: "Dinah" and "If You Knew Susie." "Dinah" by Harry Akst, Joe Young, and Sam Lewis, was first played for Eddie by Harry Akst up in his hotelsuite just prior to the show's opening. Eddie recognized the song immediately as a hit and had it put into the show.

"If You Knew Susie," by Buddy DeSylva and Joe Meyer, was given to Cantor by Al Jolson, who had tried it out himself in his current show *Big Boy*. Jolson did not feel comfortable with the song and told Cantor, "Eddie, I think this would fit you better than it does me." When Jolson later heard the applause Cantor was getting with his discarded hit, he told Eddie, "If I'd known it was that good, you dirty dog, you'd never have gotten it!" "If You Knew Susie" became one of Eddie Cantor's biggest hits and one of the songs most closely identified with him.

*Kid Boots* was a tremendous success and garnered rave reviews from all the critics. The show did standing-room-only business, making it one of the hottest tickets on Broadway for most of 1924, a fact that is especially significant because the top ticket to *Boots* went for $5.50 when most other shows at the time were in the $2.75 to $4.40 range. Most weeks *Boots* played to capacity crowds, taking in over $32,000. The only time the box office for *Kid Boots* slowed down was for the Democratic National Convention and the traditionally slow preholiday period. Even during these times *Boots* managed to beat its Broadway competitors. By the time the show's first anniversary rolled around, *Variety* announced it was Ziegfeld's most successful show ever and still the number one musical on Broadway.

The biggest threat to *Kid Boots* came, not from another show, but from Actors' Equity. Embroiled in another dispute with Broadway's producers, the union was threatening to close every show that was not made up entirely of Equity members. Rather than give in to threats, Ziegfeld said he would move the entire production across the Atlantic to London. In addition, the producer announced he would stop selling advance tickets for *Kid Boots* past a certain date in anticipation of the show's closing.

Not wanting a repeat of 1919 (and also wanting to protect his 10 percent of the box office), Eddie Cantor stepped into the breach. A vigorous supporter of Equity, Eddie personally launched a drive to sign up the entire cast and chorus with the union. Ziegfeld, wanting to keep *Boots* on Broadway, where it was doing record business, visited Eddie's dressing room nightly to keep tabs on his star's progress. All parties concerned breathed a collective sigh of relief when Eddie finally announced to Flo, "Okay, boss, it's one hundred percent."

Aside from making Eddie Cantor one of the biggest, if not the biggest, musical comedy star on Broadway, *Kid Boots* also helped make him one of the richest performers on the Great White Way. Although he and Max Hart had sold their 25 percent of the show back to Ziegfeld, Eddie was still in for a piece of the box office. His weekly salary was set at 10 percent of the week's gross. Since the musical averaged over $30,000 a week for its first year, Cantor managed to earn in excess of $150,000 from *Boots* alone. In addition, Eddie's star status made him a desired celebrity for advertising endorsements, raising his income even higher.

In spite of his fame, Eddie still was not a household name, even in theatrical circles. In the middle of *Boots'* New York run, Eddie, as he often did, attended a meeting of the Jewish Theater Guild. At most meetings Cantor was given a seat of honor on the podium. Eddie often interrupted with a joke when discussions looked like they would heat up into arguments. After one such incident, one veteran guild member, Dore Davidson, asked another member why "that young man on the dais was allowed such liberty during meetings." The other man explained that the young man was Eddie Cantor. "Who is Eddie Cantor," Davidson demanded, "and just what is his connection with theatricals?"

Ten weeks after *Kid Boots* opened, a review featuring four brothers opened at the Casino Theatre. The show, the first excursion onto Broadway for the Marx Brothers, was titled *I'll Say She Is*. One day, according to *Variety*, Eddie ran into Groucho (still called Julius by the press) on the street. Groucho told him that he and his brothers had Thursday afternoon off and asked Eddie if he could supply them with four tickets for that afternoon's matinee of *Kid Boots*. Eddie told him he would be delighted to hold four front row tickets for the Marxes.

That Thursday Cantor looked forward to "strutting his stuff before my fellow comedians." When he emerged for his first entrance, Eddie looked in the front row. Instead of the four Marx Brothers he saw four boozy skid row bums with long scruffy beards staring at him. Later Groucho confessed he had paid the quartet $2 each to deadpan Cantor throughout the afternoon's performance.

*Kid Boots* ran at the Earl Carroll Theatre until September 1, 1924, when it moved over to the Selwyn on 42nd Street. Flo Ziegfeld believed that Carroll had taken advantage of him in their lease agreement and determined that Carroll's $10,000 chunk of *Boots'* box office would stop as soon as their contract expired. The announcement shocked Carroll, especially since he believed that Ziegfeld had verbally agreed to extend the show's stay. Two days prior to Ziegfeld's bombshell, Carroll had signed a contract to place his own show the *Vanities* in another theater. Carroll was left in the unenviable position of paying rent to another theater owner for his show while his own theater sat vacant.

Usually when shows change theaters, attendance drops, even when the show was previously a hit. Remarkably, *Kid Boots* actually saw an increase in business at the Selwyn Theatre. In early 1926, after sixty weeks on Broadway, *Boots* finally slid below $27,000 a week, the level at which Ziegfeld had stated that he would be losing money. The announcement of the show's closing managed to boost ticket sales back over $30,000 for the final weeks of the record run.

After a few weeks off, *Kid Boots* went out on tour. Eddie Cantor welcomed the tour and explained to the press that it would give him a chance to relax a little. Cantor estimated that while *Boots* was on Broadway he averaged more than one benefit performance a week, which took up most of his free evenings. Eddie played the benefits despite the fact that his boss frowned on the free performances. Ziegfeld reasoned that the extra work would overtax his star and jeopardize his expensive production.

Once Ziegfeld got wind of another Cantor "freebie" and confronted Eddie. "I understand you're going to appear at the Waldorf Ballroom at midnight tomorrow," Ziegfeld said.

"Don't be silly," Eddie assured him, "I'm going home to bed."

The next night Eddie pranced out on stage at the Waldorf to find Zieggy sitting in the first row with his wife, Billie Burke. The producer sat there with a scowl on his face, while his red-handed star tried every trick in his repertoire to make him laugh. Finally, Eddie got Ziegfeld to smile when he leaned over to him and announced, "It's not me!"

When *Kid Boots* started its road tour in Boston, it did so without the services of one of its featured players, Jobyna Howland. Howland's nightly osteopathic treatments had become a bit too realistic for Eddie Cantor's likings and often left him with actual bruises and muscle strains. As for Howland, she reportedly resented the fact that Cantor got all the laughs. His nightly quips and jokes had become tiresome to her, and she had ceased smiling when he delivered them. Howland was replaced by Cecil Cunningham.

After a strong six weeks in Boston, *Boots* moved on to Newark, Brooklyn, and then Philadelphia. By the end of May, Cantor and the entire company were ready for a vacation. Eddie decided to take Ida to Europe for a second honeymoon. Prior to Eddie's departure, Flo Ziegfeld gave him a gala send-off, proclaiming "Eddie Cantor Night" at the *Follies*. Will Rogers, back with the show, presented Eddie with a platinum watch from Ziegfeld to commemorate the thousandth performance of *Kid Boots*. Eddie then performed a few songs to cap off the proceedings.

Whereas their first honeymoon was one of austerity, Eddie and Ida now pulled out all the stops, sparing no expense on their second honeymoon. "Every morning," Cantor recalled, "we decided on the best place to eat, the nicest place to visit; only once we went back to a humble spot of memory just to marvel at how we were able to endure it." In spite of their spending spree, Ida reminded her husband that "No matter how swell you get, your hat must always fit the head of a little boy on Henry Street."

The couple toured the Continent for almost two months. On their return to New York harbor on the *Rotterdam*, Ziegfeld sent out a yacht to meet them. The yacht, which flew a *Kid Boots* banner from its mast, was packed with *Follies* performers and a band. As the *Rotterdam* neared, the band began to play the song, "Eddie, Behave!"

Back on the road, Eddie and the *Boots* company completed their road tour, taking in some cities they had missed on their two previous trips. The mainstay of the final tour was eighteen weeks in Chicago. The opening at the Woods Theatre was delayed one night, however, when Eddie refused to open on a Jewish holiday. Cantor then confessed to reporters that the delay had more to do with ego than religion. He told them that it had been a lifelong ambition of his to become sufficiently important to postpone a premiere and get away with it.

The marquee of the Woods Theatre was filled with plugs for Ziegfeld and his famous slogan, "glorifying the American girl." When Cantor saw the marquee, according to *Variety*, he called for the manager and told him to dispense with all "the applesauce." "*Kid Boots*," he clarified, "glorified Eddie Cantor and the box office." Cantor made good on his boasts. *Kid Boots* did indeed glorify the box office, setting a record pace for the first ten weeks of its Chicago run, with "absolute capacity" at every performance. *Variety* reported that members of the public were "pleased to get a ticket at any price."

Ziegfeld hadn't come to Chicago with the show, but managed to keep in touch via his favorite form of communication, the telegram. Ziegfeld was legendary in his use of Western Union, often sending pages of telegrams to actors backstage from the theater lobby during rehearsals. During the Chicago run, Ziegfeld sent a twelve-page opus to Eddie. The telegram was filled with suggestions on certain scenes, advice on songs, and questions about everything in the show. Rather than getting embroiled in a lengthy reply, Eddie simply wired back, "Yes." The next day a telegram arrived from Ziegfeld that was longer than the first. "What do you mean, 'yes'?" the producer asked. "Do you mean yes, you will change that song, or yes you will put in the lines, or yes you'll talk to those actors?" Eddie wired back, "No."

The records *Kid Boots* set didn't last very long. Holiday week, three months after *Boots* opened, Al Jolson came to town in his latest show *Big Boy*. Whereas *Kid Boots* did a remarkable $40,000 for the week between Christmas and New Year's, *Big Boy* did an incredible $60,000 for the same period, albeit in a larger house. Still, *Boots* continued to run at capacity, with a huge advance ticket sale.

By late January the hectic pace of performing, coupled with the bitter cold of a Chicago winter, caught up with Eddie, and he developed pleurisy. Because of his rivalry with Jolson, Eddie continued to go out every night. "In my mind's eye I could see the headline," Eddie recalled. "Jolson Drives Cantor Out of Chicago." Every night before he went on stage Eddie had a doctor strap him up with adhesive tape. Still the pain was so sharp he could hardly breathe. The doctor recommended that the fluid on Eddie's chest be drained, but Eddie refused. Ida pleaded with her husband, but to no avail. Finally Jolson, seeing the state of Cantor's health, advised him to close *Boots*.

"Eddie, show business ain't worth it," Jolie told him. "You need some sun, kid. Go to Miami, close the show, and get some rest." Eddie continued, despite Jolson's advice, until one day he couldn't get up from his dressing room chair. *Kid Boots* was closed, and Eddie returned to New York to convalesce. On his arrival, instead of seeing headlines about Jolson driving him from Chicago, Eddie picked up the paper to read: "Jolson Ill, Closes Show." It turned out that Jolson had been as sick as Eddie, but had refused to close first, for the same reasons.

## REVIEW

Eddie Cantor and Mary Eaton make a corking musical combination, Eddie genuinely comic and corkless almost all the way, and Mary sweet enough to be loved by any handsome juvenile, on and off.

Cantor's pace as a comedian of first water is something of a pleasing surprise even to his admirers. He piled up so excellent a laugh score that he should have got the loving cup they gave the golf champ. The references to the pill-chasing game were often funny and never too technical. — Ibee, *Variety*, January 10, 1924

# CHAPTER 16

# *Kid Boots (Film)*

It seems ironic, by today's thinking, that during the silent era Hollywood often sought out hit Broadway musicals for translation to the screen. Nevertheless, the practice did occur. Flo Ziegfeld himself had sold his previous smash hit, *Sally*, to the movies for $60,000. Since the strength of a musical show rested heavily on its score, it was usually the good name that film producers were most interested in capitalizing on. In the first half of the twenties, few Broadway properties had a bigger name on which to capitalize than *Kid Boots*.

In April 1925, *Variety* reported that Ziegfeld had reached an agreement with film producer Lou Christie for a cinematic version of the musical. Under the terms of the contracts, Zieggy would be guaranteed $65,000 for the film rights to *Boots*, along with a piece of the profits once the film had earned a predetermined amount. Included in the deal was the stipulation that Eddie Cantor would repeat the title role before the cameras. For his participation, Eddie would receive a flat fee of $30,000. Ziegfeld agreed to close the highly profitable road version of *Boots* in May 1925 so that production could start in Hollywood on the screen version. After the film was completed, the stage musical would reopen and would be allowed to play for almost another full year before the movie was released in March 1926.

Although the contracts were all written up, the deal was never formalized and soon fell through when Christie's backers, the Motion Picture Capitol Corporation, decided to withdraw from the venture. The primary reason that the MPCC bailed out on *Boots* was its reluctance to finance a picture that would be held from release for ten months, making it close to fifteen months in their estimation before they would begin to realize any profits from their investment.

Almost immediately after the Christie deal fell through, Ziegfeld opened negotiations with First National. The two sides couldn't agree to terms, however, and plans to bring *Kid Boots* to the screen were shelved.

After the various deals and negotiations for a film version of *Boots* failed to reach fruition, Ziegfeld made plans for Cantor's next musical comedy. The producer commissioned William Anthony McGuire, the primary author of

*Kid Boots,* to start work on a Cantor vehicle for the fall 1926 Broadway season. What exactly McGuire may have come up with — based on his work on *Boots* in its formative stages, it probably wasn't more than some short passages of gag dialogue — is unknown, for next season's Cantor stage vehicle quickly became a moot point when it was announced that the star's next project would be a movie version of *Kid Boots.*

In an ironic twist of events, the silent movie of *Kid Boots* became a reality based on Eddie Cantor's performance in an early talking-movie experiment. According to Cantor, Jesse Lasky saw Eddie's Phonofilm short at the Rivoli Theatre in New York and remarked to his manager-in-chief, "There's a screen personality!" Lasky obviously had enough experience in films to make a judgment. After careers as a gold prospector in the Yukon and a vaudeville musician, Lasky took up producing plays. From stage plays, Lasky, along with his director, Cecil B. DeMille, started making films. It was one of their earlier films, *The Squaw Man,* that started Hollywood on the road to becoming the center for motion picture production.

In 1916 Lasky merged his Lasky Feature Play Company with friendly rival Adolph Zukor's Famous Players to form Famous Players–Lasky. A few months after the merger, the new company acquired control of their distributor, W. W. Hodkinson's Paramount Company. Soon Zukor decided that the Paramount name was easier to publicize than the more cumbersome "Famous Players–Lasky." Henceforth, all the company's films were released under the Paramount banner with either "Jesse L. Lasky Presents" (if the picture was made in Hollywood) or "Adolph Zukor Presents" (if it was produced in the East) over the title.

After seeing Cantor singing and cavorting in Phonofilms, Lasky decided that a silent version of *Kid Boots* was just what Paramount needed. In early April 1926, Lasky bought the screen rights for the musical from Ziegfeld for $65,000, with the stipulation that Cantor would play "Boots." For his participation, Eddie would be paid $3,000 a week.

Initially, production on the film was slated to begin at Famous Players' Astoria, Long Island, studios once the current road tour of the stage production closed on May 15. A few weeks later, however, Lasky announced that the film would be shot at the new Famous Players' studio in Hollywood. Ironically, the new Famous Players' studio on Melrose Avenue in Hollywood, to this day home to Paramount Pictures, was the old home of First National, one of the other studios that had bid on the film rights to *Kid Boots.*

June 1, Cantor, along with Ida and their four daughters, left Grand Central Station for the trip to California. A small theatrical contingent including Georgie Jessel, Sophie Tucker, and Walter Houston came down to see the family off. Although his daughters were excited about going to Hollywood, they were, according to Cantor, reluctant to leave their home and friends in Mount Vernon.

Eddie told them that they would have marvelous new friends in California. "I'll have Gloria Swanson play jacks with you," he told them, "and you'll skip rope with Vilma Banky!"

"And I suppose you'll get Norma Shearer to wait on us at table," Marjorie cracked.

Any further objections were quickly dispelled when Cantor explained that the girls would have to leave three weeks before the end of the school term. Once on the West Coast, the Cantors rented a bungalow in Beverly Hills, and Eddie reported to the studio.

Although Eddie's daughters may have been concerned about missing their New York friends, their father had nothing to worry about in that regard. The head of production at Famous Players–Lasky's Hollywood studio was B. P. Schulberg, a transplanted New Yorker who had grown up with Eddie on Henry Street.

A year younger than Cantor, Ben Schulberg had begun his career as a newspaper reporter for the New York *Evening Mail*. From the *Mail* he took a job editing a film trade journal, which led to a job as screenwriter and publicity director for Rex films. In 1912, after a year with Rex, Schulberg accepted an offer to run the publicity for Adolph Zukor's new Famous Players Company. By the early twenties, he had left Zukor to produce his own films independently. Schulberg returned to Paramount in 1925 to become the company's West Coast studio chief.

"Benny" Schulberg made sure his new star felt at home in Hollywood and invited Eddie to his home on numerous occasions to play cards, reminisce about the old days, and talk about the film. Eddie also used the visits to engage Schulberg's twelve-year-old son Budd (a future academy award-winning screenwriter [*On the Waterfront*] and best-selling novelist [*What Makes Sammy Run?*]) in ping-pong matches. Although Cantor was an accomplished player, Budd Schulberg would usually manage to best him, much to his father's amusement.

As the producer for *Kid Boots*, Ben Schulberg assigned Frank Tuttle, a young but experienced and capable director to handle the day-to-day filming. For Eddie's supporting cast, his old Henry Street pal gave him some of Paramount's best, including Billie Dove and Clara Bow. In the summer of 1926, Dove, who played opposite romantic leading man Lawrence Gray, was the bigger star of the two, having just completed *The Black Pirate* with Douglas Fairbanks. Dove had started in show business as a *Ziegfeld Follies* girl and was generally considered one of Hollywood's most beautiful actresses.

While Billie Dove may have been considered more beautiful, when it came to sheer vivacity no one came close to Clara Bow. Bow, who had worked in pictures since the early twenties, was just coming into her own as a major film star, thanks mainly to producer Schulberg's sponsorship. Playing Cantor's love interest, Clara's effervescent personality complimented her leading man perfectly.

Off camera, Clara helped Eddie adapt to the art of performing for the screen. "What rehearsals are to the stage," she counseled Eddie, "spontaneity is to the screen." Clara further advised Eddie to just relax, have fun, and be yourself. In some of their scenes together, instead of delivering lines relevant to the plot, Bow was actually offering her own direction, telling Eddie, "You're doing fine. Just flash those banjo eyes and there's nothing to it."

Aside from reassuring the film's novice star, Clara Bow also managed to have some fun with Cantor, usually at his expense. During love scenes, when the pair was supposed to have been exchanging tender words, Clara was actually trying to break up Eddie with a choice selection of salty language. "She knew all the words," Cantor later noted, "and lip readers must have found those love scenes of ours very funny."

Another time, when they were filming a golf scene one afternoon just after lunch, the script called for Eddie to hit a golf ball. Eddie stepped up and, with his eye on the camera, struck the ball solidly. The "ball" exploded upon impact and showered everyone in the immediate vicinity with a gooey substance. During the lunch break, Clara had substituted an egg for the golf ball.

Although Clara Bow managed to keep the cast and crew relaxed with her practical jokes (with the exception, perhaps of her victims), Eddie Cantor also did his level best to keep the set entertained between takes. Although the films they were making were silent, most studios provided small orchestras to play mood music for their actors while they performed. While the director and technicians were setting up the next shot, Eddie delighted in using the set orchestra for accompaniment for some impromptu versions of his many musical hits.

While Clara Bow was instructing Eddie to "act naturally" and "be himself," director Frank Tuttle was attempting just the opposite. On viewing the preliminary rushes, Tuttle discovered that, while Cantor's frenetic pace wowed live audiences, his usual stage pace was too fast for the slightly speeded-up world of silent movies. Although not exactly a blur, Eddie was still too "hyper" for the sixteen-frames-a-second pace of the hand-cranked camera.[1] Tuttle compensated for the slowness of the camera and the speed of his star by directing Eddie to work at half his usual stage tempo.

Adapting a stage musical comedy into a silent comedy proved to be more involved than just filming the play's plot sans the songs. In the case of *Kid Boots*, not only were the songs thrown out, but just about the entire story too. By the time Luther Reed (who adapted the play) and Tom Gibson (who wrote the script) got done with *Boots*, all that remained were a few of the comedy highlights, some of the characters' names (although their parts were discarded outright), and a vague connection of the story with the game of golf.

Even though *Kid Boots*, the film, bears very little resemblance to the hit stage musical, the deviations from the show's proven plot are not unjustified. Rather the film succeeds very well for what it is, a silent comedy. Any attempts to adhere more closely to the original production would probably have suffocated the film. In the stage version, the musical numbers were integrated into the plot, and thus helped to move it along. Without the score, the plot, though strong for a musical comedy at that time, would show its deficiencies rather glaringly.

In Paramount's *Kid Boots*, Eddie Cantor is a tailor's assistant, not the caddymaster of a country club. In a fairly amusing opening scene, we are treated to yet another rendition of the "Joe's Blue Front" skit—this one all the more interesting since it is played sans dialogue. Aside from starting off the film on familiar territory for Cantor, the bit also serves to introduce both his love interest, Clara McCoy (Clara Bow), and his rival, Big Boyle (Malcome Waite). While running from customer Waite, he runs into Bow. Clara and Boots fall for each other immediately, a fact which only compounds his troubles, since Clara's other boyfriend is Boyle.

Boots finally manages to elude Boyle by ducking into a convenient rumble seat, which also neatly introduces him to the film's hero, Tom Sterling (Lawrence Gray). The film's plot revolves around the attempts of Tom's wife, Carmen, who is about to divorce him, to make a reconciliation with him before their divorce becomes final. The spouse, played by Natalie Kingston, is not motivated by love, but rather by the fact that Tom is soon to inherit $3 million. Her efforts to get Tom alone (and thereby invalidate the final decree) are continually foiled by Boots, who assigns himself the task of never allowing Tom to be alone.

In an attempt to get at least some golf in the film, the story shifts to a golf resort, where Tom goes to work as an instructor. There Tom meets and falls in love with Eleanor (Billie Dove).

With the plot firmly established, *Kid Boots* relaxes into some very strong comedy sequences in which Cantor is allowed free rein to prove his worth as a silent comedian. The first of these is Boots' golf lesson. Tom tries to acquaint his pal with the game, while Boots happily rebuffs any attempts to play it right. As Tom lectures on golf theory, Boots wanders around the course, amazed at all the "lost" balls he is finding. After accumulating at least a dozen, Boots is distracted by the shouts of a nearby foursome. Of course, the golfers are motioning for Boots to replace the lifted balls, but he merely takes their wild gestures to be friendly waves. When the players persist with their waves, Boots resigns to throwing the quartet kisses. Finally, after Tom explains that they want their golf balls replaced, Boots, disgusted that they weren't all that friendly after all, throws down their balls along with at least two dozen more from his pockets.

As amusing as Cantor's cavortings on the course are, they pale in comparison to the tearoom scene. Soon after his arrival at the resort, Boots discovers that Clara is also there, working as a swimming instructor. After an initially happy reunion, their courtship runs into rough seas when Carmen, Tom's estranged wife, tries to make trouble for Boots by coming between him and Clara. With Clara watching from a distance, Carmen sneaks up behind Boots, covers his eyes, and makes a date with him for afternoon tea.

Boots, thinking it's Clara, agrees. When Carmen removes her hands, Boots discovers that not only has he made a date with the wrong girl, but the right girl has been standing there witnessing his unfaithfulness.

Boots tries to explain, but Clara won't listen. She tells Boots that Carmen isn't going to show up for their tea date, but she'll be there to laugh at him when he's stood up. "All right, stick around," Boots tells Clara, "because when I'm full of tea—women can't keep their hands off me."

Tea time comes and goes. While Boots sits and waits for Carmen, Clara watches, giggling from a nearby table. A waiter opens a door in front of Boots' table, obscuring half of the table and setting up the comic highlight of the film. Boots starts to close the door, but gets an idea. While Clara is talking to a waiter, Boots removes his coat halfway, leaving on the side Clara can see, but leaving the other arm bare. He then powders his arm with sugar, adds a few cigar bands (for rings) to his fingers, and wraps his watch chain around his wrist to make a bracelet. With his feminine arm set, Boots carries out a hilarious pantomime deception. Boots kisses the "lady's" hand genteelly, lights her cigarette, and chats amiably with his "guest," all while keeping one eye on Clara, who is shocked by the proceedings.

Boots is so adept at doing two things at once even we, the audience, start to believe there is a woman behind the door. The dainty hand, stirs the iced tea, lifts it to drink, and gestures just like a separate limb. Once the illusion is firmly established, the scene really takes off. Soon the hand is accidentally squirting lemon into Boot's eye, pulling him behind the door for secret kisses (which Boots approximates by smearing jam on his cheek), and even trying to undress him. Boots reacts to "her" advances by threatening to haul off and sock "her." The hand responds by slapping Boots across the face.

Finally Boots gives up the farce when Clara breaks down into tears. While Boots is away from the table comforting her, the real Carmen enters and naturally sits down behind the door. Boots explains that the "femme fatale" was actually him all the time. To prove it, he shuts the door, only to reveal Carmen. Clara rushes out while Boots stares at Carmen in wonder.

The episode, easily the film's comic highpoint, is beautifully mimed by Cantor, who proved that he could put over a routine without his dialects and song stylings. The gag itself was such a hit that it was used in variation not once, but twice in the next year. First, by the wildly popular comedian Harold Lloyd in *The Kid Brother* and second, by Eddie himself in his next Paramount feature, *Special Delivery*.

Following the tearoom tête-à-tête, Tom leaves the resort to avoid any further run-ins with Carmen. Boots stays behind to run interference and manages to get himself into even more trouble. First, he runs afoul of Big Boyle (who also works at the resort). In another version of the osteopath sketch, Boyle is given the opportunity to twist and mangle Eddie to his heart's content. Ironically, the scene, despite its preponderance of physical comedy, does not play nearly as well in pantomime. Most likely this is because the audience is unable to hear Boots' wisecracks between pummelings and his plight thus seems all the more painful. The jokes delivered on stage helped reassure the audience that Boots was still all right. In the film, without these comforting lines, we merely see Cantor grimace and wince in response to his forced contortions. In addition, in the stage version the beating was delivered by Dr. Fitch, a woman, albeit one of Amazon proportions, whereas in the film, with the giant Boyle delivering the beating, the contrast is less comical.

In the style of most silent comedies, *Kid Boots* finishes with a chase scene, and this sequence manages to hold its own with many of its contemporaries. The scene arises because Boots and Clara must get to Tom's divorce hearing before the judge adjourns the case to go fishing. With less than thirty minutes to spare, the pair decide the quickest route is by horseback over the mountain. They set off, followed by Big Boyle. In addition to his rival, Boots manages to encounter prospectors, runaway horses, and even a mountain lion on his journey along the narrow, winding pass.

Finally, the scene climaxes with Boots, Clara, and Boyle all hanging on for dear life to the same rope when they fall off a cliff. Fortunately — since he had originally planned to take an airplane over the mountain — Boots is still wearing a parachute, and they eventually drift safely to the town below, landing coincidentally on the courthouse. Tom is granted his divorce, which allows him to marry Eleanor, and Boots and Clara are hastily wed while chasing after the judge, who is en route to his fishing trip.

*Kid Boots* took six weeks to film. The film could have been done in five weeks, but an extra week was devoted to an elaborate gag in which Boots dives into a pool that Boyle has just emptied. After the scene was completed, Ben Schulberg threw it out, declaring it "too mechanical."

Most of the stunt work on the film, especially the harrowing chase along the mountain pass, was done by stunt doubles. Cantor, new as he was to the movies, decided that he would try doubling for himself in one shot, the one where he was dragged along the dirt road behind the horse. Instead of actually being tied to the horse, Eddie was tied behind a slow-moving car, while the camera truck ran along side.

While Eddie ran, Frank Tuttle shouted for him to "skip gracefully." Eddie tried it, fell, and was dragged along the road while the camera kept grinding. By the time the car came to a halt, Cantor's knees and hands were bleeding from pieces of gravel that had been forced under his skin. From then on, Eddie left the stunt work to the doubles.

After filming on *Kid Boots* was completed, the Cantors returned to New York and awaited news of the finished product. During production, according to *Variety*, word spread that Paramount executives were beginning to express some doubts whether the film would be a success. Cantor agonized for three weeks until he received word from his friend B. P. Schulberg: *Boots* had been previewed and the audience response was positive, both to the film in general and Cantor specifically.

With a successful preview, Paramount got behind *Kid Boots* and promoted it for all it was worth. Eddie was hired to make personal appearances with the film at $7,000 a week plus a percentage of the gross, a record for such appearances up to that time. Jesse Lasky even proclaimed that Cantor was "the most natural picture find I've ever seen." *Variety* went so far as to speculate that Cantor would probably abandon the stage permanently, even though Ziegfeld still held a three-year contract for the comedian's services. Ziegfeld had asked Eddie to return for another season of *Kid Boots*, but Eddie declined unless the producer agreed to give him two weeks off for every four weeks spent with the show.

*Kid Boots* opened at New York's Rialto Theatre on October 16, 1926, to all-around strong reviews. The picture played for a month, though it had originally been scheduled to play for six weeks. (Cantor quit appearing on stage with the film after two weeks and did not go on tour with the film as was initially planned.) Eddie appeared, along with George Olsen's Band, four times daily, for roughly twenty minutes per show. Eddie's turn usually consisted of two songs, with a few minutes of jokes in between.

At one point during the Rialto appearances, Cantor was forced to stop ad-libbing fresh material for every show because a good portion of the audience remained after each performance to see what Eddie would do next. At one evening's late show, Eddie's old *Follies* roommate, W. C. Fields, stopped by to catch "the little fellow with the big eyes," as Fields liked to call Cantor. Fields, also under contract with Paramount, was so taken with Cantor's performance that he got up on stage and kissed Eddie before returning to his seat.

Although he only played two weeks in personal appearances, Eddie Cantor plugged *Kid Boots* to an estimated audience of five million people through the upstart medium of radio. On the evening of November 2, Cantor agreed to appear on the *Eveready Battery Hour* over station WEAF in New York for the unheard of amount of $1,500 for fifteen minutes on the air. The fee was so scandalous that the next day *Variety*'s front-page banner read: "$100 a Minute on Radio!" Even more shocking than Cantor's salary, according to *Variety*, was the fact that he used two of the minutes to plug *Kid Boots*. This was obviously years before radio and television talk shows made the practice of plugging the rule rather than the exception.

Despite *Variety*'s dismay over the broadcast, the appearance was an unqualified success. Eddie received over 1,800 telegrams from cities west of Chicago alone, and the Eveready battery people received over 2,000 requests for pictures of Cantor. At the time, stars from the stage and screen were loath to appear on the radio. (A similar situation occurred twenty or so years later when television started taking off.) The new medium was seen as unwelcome competition. As it was, it took years for show business trade papers to cover radio as a legitimate entertainment channel, instead of a passing fad which took business away from the theater and movies.[2]

Aside from plugging *Boots* on the radio, Eddie Cantor looked ahead and

**Eddie reels from a blow delivered by Malcome Waite while Natalie Kingston (left) and Clara Bow look on in this scene from Cantor's first feature film, *Kid Boots*.**

put in a good word for his next film for Famous Players–Lasky, which was due to start filming in a few weeks on the coast. It was based on an original idea of Eddie's, and he called it *Special Delivery*.

## REVIEWS

That genuinely funny actor, Eddie Cantor, is to be seen at the Rialto in his first screen effort, the film transcription of his successful musical comedy, "Kid Boots." This brisk piece of buffoonery, which contains several of the skits seen and heard in the original Ziegfeld production, achieved its purpose by keeping an audience, at the initial presentation last Saturday evening, interested and merry. Incidentally, Mr. Cantor keeps in touch with the footlights by appearing in a sketch that precedes the photoplay.

Mr. Cantor screens well, and he appears to be just as much at home before the camera as he is on the stage. The fair Clara Bow is captivating in the part of the heart-snatching heroine. — Mordaunt Hall, *The New York Times*, October 11, 1926

Eddie Cantor has arrived on the screen. Jesse Lasky stated that Cantor was a "natural" for the screen before the rank and file in New York had seen the comedian's first screen effort, "Kid Boots." It looks that way.

Cantor is a "natural" in more ways than one, as far as the screen is concerned.

In fact, he has such a sense of natural comedy that those working with him were often broken up and hard put to it as Eddie would improvise a piece of business that was not in the script. As far as pictures are concerned, Eddie need not worry as to his future. He is set if ever a comedian was, and with his first effort.

Cantor is a cinch for the box office on the strength of this one. — Fred., *Variety*, October 13, 1926

# *Notes*

1. While the average silent film was shot at sixteen frames a second, most were projected at twenty to twenty-four frames a second, giving silents, especially the comedies, a certain magical lightness.

2. The advent of nationwide radio networks helped lure stars from other mediums who were eager to take advantage, as Cantor had, of broadcasting's "plugging" potential. Coincidentally, the first big network, NBC, went on the air a few weeks after Cantor's November 2 broadcast. Its flagship station was WEAF.

# CHAPTER 17

# *Special Delivery*

Not long after the release of *Kid Boots*, Eddie Cantor found himself seated next to his boss, Paramount head Adolph Zukor, at a luncheon. At the time one of the studio's hottest properties was the team of Wallace Beery and Raymond Hatton, who had been starring in a string of military comedies.

Between courses Eddie leaned over and told Zukor, "I have an idea how you can make a fortune with comedies like the ones with Beery and Hatton."

Zukor, always interested in a formula for a surefire hit, urged Eddie to continue.

"Start off the picture with some light laughter," Eddie began. "Then as the picture progresses, make the laughs bigger and bigger and at the end," Eddie advised, "give 'em enough boffs to roll 'em in the aisles. Believe me, audiences will go out raving!"

"Why that's wonderful," Zukor exclaimed, "Just wonderful!" After pondering Cantor's rather obvious advice another moment, Zukor did a double take and then asked Eddie, "What did you say?"

"Nothing," Eddie replied, as he started in on the next course.

"That's what I thought," Zukor laughed.

It was soon evident to the public at large, as it was that afternoon to Adolph Zukor, that neither Eddie Cantor, nor anyone else at Paramount possessed a guaranteed formula for making surefire comedies. The proof was his second silent comedy, *Special Delivery*, which, though it is by no means as forgettable as its current reputation would suggest, was still weak enough to send its star back to Broadway.

A second Cantor–Famous Players–Lasky film was announced in mid-July 1926, while *Kid Boots* was still in production, despite the fact that Paramount officials were unimpressed with the early rushes of the first film. The second film, which was also to be shot at the Melrose Avenue studios, was scheduled to go before the cameras right after *Boots* was completed, with Cantor extending his stay on the West Coast. The second feature, initially titled *Love Letters*, was based on an original story by Eddie Cantor himself.

When *Kid Boots* turned out to be better than the Paramount heads anticipated, *Love Letters* was postponed for a few months while Cantor went back East to help promote *Boots*. While Eddie was in New York, *Variety* announced that comedy film veteran, Eddie Sutherland, a former assistant to Charlie Chaplin, was the first choice to direct the film, which was now scheduled to go into production at the end of November.[1]

By the time *Love Letters* got before the cameras in early December 1926, the film's name had been changed to *Special Delivery*, and its director had been changed to William Goodrich, better known as Roscoe "Fatty" Arbuckle. Arbuckle, once one of the most popular film comedians in the world, second perhaps only to Charlie Chaplin, was a victim of one of Hollywood's most infamous scandals. In 1921, at the height of his popularity (Fatty had been one of the first comics to begin production of feature films) Arbuckle was accused of raping and murdering Virginia Rappe during a party held at his hotel suite in San Francisco. After three trials, Arbuckle was acquitted of all charges and received an apology from the jury.

Unfortunately, despite his legal exoneration, Arbuckle was made a scapegoat by the press, church and civic groups, and even the film establishment for all of Hollywood's immoralities. Will Hays, appointed Hollywood's moral guardian in the wake of the scandal, placed a ban on all of Fatty's films, effectively ending his screen career. Arbuckle found plenty of work behind the camera directing films for other comics such as Al St. John (his nephew and former supporting player) and Buster Keaton (whom Fatty had given his start in films), among others. Arbuckle worked under his father's name, William Goodrich, although his old friend Buster often half-joked that he should be billed "Will B. Good," in reference to the scandal.[2]

Cantor had conceived *Special Delivery* as a "more human, less hokey" vehicle only sparsely interspersed with gags. Eddie the screenwriter quickly learned that, more often than not, a writer's original concept rarely makes it to the screen intact. Apparently, Paramount did not have a "less hokey" vehicle in mind. In fact, a full-page advertisement in *Variety*, which ran just as the film was going before the cameras, described Eddie's role in *Special Delivery* as that of "a goofy letter-carrier." So much for humanity.

After writing the original story in Palm Springs, Cantor returned to Hollywood and submitted his script. In an attempt to punch up the movie with more gags, the writers at Paramount managed to excise most of the film's narrative. "Everything between laughs was cut out," Eddie recalled, "giving the hoppy, hiccupy effect of a comic strip or a stale-joke book." To add insult to injury, Eddie was obliged to act out scenes that had been changed from his original treatment. "It was one of those sad cases of authorship where I watched my brain-child get its brains knocked out, and I had to be an accomplice to the crime," Cantor later wrote. Ironically, a little more than six years later, Eddie would be an accomplice to another "gagging-up" of a film script, when Sam Goldwyn brought in writers to add more jokes to George S. Kaufman and Robert Sherwood's screenplay for *Roman Scandals*.

What the rewrite men at Paramount didn't change in Cantor's script for

**Cantor wrote the original story for his second silent feature, *Special Delivery*.**

*Special Delivery*, the United States Post Office did. The film's climax called for a mail robbery in which Eddie's postman character apprehends the culprit, becomes a hero, and wins the hand of the leading lady. After production had already begun, it turned out that the government would not allow the dramatization of a mail robbery, even if it was done in a comical vein.

Cantor later commented that if he had known that the robbery plot would have to be thrown out, he would have scrapped the idea of doing a mailman comedy and chosen an entirely different story. As it was, however, production was already in full swing and had to continue because of the amount of money Paramount had already invested in the picture. A plot involving mail fraud was substituted for the robbery, but this lessened the dramatic impact considerably.

Hindsight is always 20-20, and if Eddie Cantor had any misgivings about his future in films based on *Special Delivery*, he kept them to himself, although he did comment on the set to Morris Gest, producer of the play *The Miracle*: "You might own this production, because if it goes over it's another

'Miracle'!" While privately, Eddie may have been thinking that nothing could save *Special Delivery*, publicly he exuded confidence, even cockiness, that the movies were his future. Cantor's full-page ad in *Variety's* annual holiday issue proclaimed:

HOLIDAY GREETINGS
from the
NEW SCREEN COMEDIAN
EDDIE CANTOR
Famous Players–Lasky
Hollywood, Calif.

The cast for *Special Delivery*, though not containing a single star quite on the magnitude of Clara Bow, was probably on average better than the one assembled for *Kid Boots*. For a leading lady, *Special Delivery* boasted Jobyna Ralston, who for the past four years had served the same function for all of Harold Lloyd's films. Since Lloyd was the most popular comedian of the 1920s, based on box office receipts, Ralston was obviously well known to the film-going public. At roughly the same time she was working on *Special Delivery*, Jobyna was also appearing in Paramount's World War I flying epic, *Wings*. *Wings* was shooting its interiors on sets adjacent to those for *Special Delivery*, and this allowed Ralston quick access to both sets when she was needed. The close proximity of the sets also allowed Jobyna's boyfriend, Richard Arlen, one of the stars of *Wings* (along with Clara Bow and Buddy Rogers), to make frequent visits.

Although Eddie and Jobyna only had one scene that called for kissing, whenever Cantor saw Arlen approaching he would grab his leading lady and rehearse their kiss. "We did it so realistically that Dick Arlen began to get worried," Eddie recalled. "This probably had something to do with their early marriage." (Arlen and Ralston were married in January 1927, while *Special Delivery* was in the midst of production.)

Also included in the cast was William Powell, as Harold Jones, alias "Blackie" Morgan, the film's heavy. Although Powell had been in silent films since the early twenties, he was mainly used as a suave, sophisticated villain. It was not until the talkies came in that Powell became a popular leading man, first in Paramount's Philo Vance mysteries, then as Nick Charles in the *Thin Man* series at MGM. Coincidentally, Powell would go on to play Cantor's former and future boss, Flo Ziegfeld, twice on the screen, first in *The Great Ziegfeld*, then in the review film, *The Ziegfeld Follies*. Oddly enough, Cantor would be portrayed by other performers in both films.

Aside from the problems with the script, filming on *Special Delivery* proceeded uneventfully, except for some difficulties with a bulldog. In one scene, Eddie, playing a postman, was supposed to bait the dog with a string of frankfurters. Evidently the dog was quite impressed with Cantor's performance and took him for a real postman. Instead of leaping for the franks, the dog decided to sink his teeth into Eddie. The wound had to be cauterized, or "cantorized," as the crew wags termed the procedure.

During the filming, Eddie took out an insurance policy to guard against another injury. In the history of Hollywood, many entertainers have insured various parts of their anatomy which were key to their success. Eddie Cantor was no different and took out a $250,000 policy on his eyes to insure them against "klieg eyes," an affliction marked by conjunctivitis and watery eyes that is caused by exposure to the intense klieg lights used in motion picture production. Eddie took the policy with the reasoning that his eyes were his most distinguishable physical asset, especially in silent movies. Prior to this, only one other film star, Ben Turpin, had had his eyes insured. In Turpin's case, however, the policy insured against the straightening out of his famous cross-eyes.

Although *Special Delivery* was a Paramount release, Eddie had opportunities to socialize with celebrities from all of Hollywood's studios. On one such occasion, Eddie attended a dinner party at the home of Harry Rapf, a production executive at Metro-Goldwyn-Mayer. The fete was in celebration of the Rapfs' fifteenth wedding anniversary, and Eddie was called upon to give a speech in honor of the occasion.

In a twenty-minute speech, Eddie waxed eloquent on the virtues of marriage in general and the happiness of the Rapfs' marriage in particular. The speech, which was delivered to a primarily MGM audience, including studio boss Louis B. Mayer, was well received until Eddie's concluding remark. "Finally," Eddie said, wrapping it up, "I must pay my respects to the greatest motion picture producer in the world . . . Mr. Ben Schulberg!"

Although most of the guests were, by *Variety's* account of the affair, "flabbergasted" at Cantor's tribute to his boss, the show business weekly reported that Eddie managed to "remain out of the hospital." It is not known whether Louis Mayer remembered Eddie's little joke thirteen years later when the comedian appeared in *Forty Little Mothers* at Metro-Goldwyn-Mayer.

*Special Delivery* is rare among Eddie Cantor films, and indeed Cantor stage shows, in that it is the only vehicle in which he carries the love interest. (Although *Strike Me Pink*, Eddie's last film for Sam Goldwyn, finds him winning the girl in the end, the picture is for all practical purposes without a romantic plot.) Just why *Special Delivery* carries this distinction can be traced to the fact that Eddie himself wrote the original story, and thereby was in the position to write for himself not only the comic lead, but the romantic one as well. Years later, while working for Sam Goldwyn, Eddie would argue for a repetition of this dual duty, but to no avail. Although some critics pointed out Cantor's deficiencies as a leading man, it must be pointed out, in all fairness to Eddie, that his desire to carry his own plots entirely was not an unusual one.

True, in the world of musical comedy, the love interest was supplied by someone other than the comic, but in the realm of silent comedy the opposite was often the rule, rather than the exception. Keaton, Chaplin, Lloyd, and even Harry Langdon all carried their pictures' love plots. Cantor was thus only attempting something that his contemporaries were doing in almost every film without giving it a second thought. It seems unkind to suggest that Cantor's "funny pan" would bar him from carrying the romantic plot when Charlie Chaplin, with his somewhat grotesque tramp makeup, and Harry Langdon, with his infantile appearance, were doing just that.

That Cantor's involvement in the romantic end of things was even commented on at all is surprising since so little of *Special Delivery* is ever seriously concentrated on anything but gags, and they come fast and furious at the expense of everything else in the film. Again, though the heavy reliance on gags in *Special Delivery* was criticized by reviewers of the day, this too was nothing unusual for a feature-length silent comedy. Both Harold Lloyd, in such films as *Doctor Jack* and *Hot Water*, and Buster Keaton, in his *The Three Ages* and *College*, would designate entire films "gag" pictures, with only a thin narrative to attempt to hold the proceedings together.

The main difference between the "gag" pictures of Keaton and Lloyd and *Special Delivery* is that silent film was the natural venue for Buster and Harold, who had learned their craft over time in numerous gag-filled shorts with a team of gagmen crafting their films around them. Eddie Cantor, on the other hand, was still feeling his way in movies and therefore was less able to carry off such an endeavor on his own.

In addition, a film such as *Special Delivery*, with its reliance on gags over plot, needs a strong character with easily identifiable personality traits upon which to build its gags. With much of his stage persona residing in his ability to be seen and *heard*, Eddie had yet to fashion a unique silent screen personality for himself. Ironically, this was especially true in *Special Delivery*, compared to *Kid Boots*, since the first film had been an adaptation of a stage property. *Special Delivery* is peppered with little self-conscious pieces of physical business such as backwards kicks, delivered by Cantor for no other apparent reason than to give his silent screen character a distinguishable characteristic. Perhaps the suggestion for these physical "tics" came from director Arbuckle or from someone else, since in the film Cantor does not seem to feel at home with them and quickly drops them after the first few reels.

Arbuckle may have been trying to forge a new silent screen clown, as he had helped do a decade earlier with Buster Keaton. At any rate, blame for shifting the tone of the film from a situation comedy to a gag film can probably be placed at Fatty's feet, given his own screen résumé. Arbuckle's films, though immensely popular in their time, cannot be accused of being subtle or low-key affairs. If anything they are gag-packed, anything-for-a-laugh-a-minute, breakneck-paced films, much in the pattern of Arbuckle's former employer, Mack Sennett. More of this style marks *Special Delivery*, rather than the less "hokey" one Cantor first envisioned when writing his original treatment.

In *Special Delivery*, Eddie Cantor plays Eddie Beagle, a new postman attached to the Postal Secret Service. Eddie's father is the head of the Secret

Service, as have been all his ancestors "since the day the scarlet letter was mailed." Unfortunately, Eddie's career in the department is to date less auspicious than the careers of his dutiful forefathers; in fact, as a title tells us, the service's biggest secret is how he ever got in. Eddie's situation is so desperate his father tells him he won't be allowed home until he makes good. Eddie promises him he will succeed and vows to catch the infamous "Blackie" Morgan (William Powell), a con-man who has been using the mails to swindle his victims.

With the authorities beginning to close in on him, Morgan plans to escape to South America, but not before he can persuade Madge (Jobyna Ralston), the film's heroine and Eddie's sweetheart, to go along with him. In a rather unspectacular turn of events, Eddie manages to unmask "Blackie," and after the obligatory closing chase, he captures the villain just as he and the unwitting Madge are sailing to Brazil.

Although he is in the department's Secret Service, Eddie seems to spend most of his time on a normal mail route. Most of the film's gags gravitate around mailman gags. Some of them are old, some fall flat, but a number manage to succeed on their own merit. The best of this group finds Eddie nearing the end of his rounds after a grueling day of deliveries. Walking down the street, Eddie sees a pair of street musicians plying their art on organ and fiddle. He asks them if they know "Bye, Bye, Blackbird." They do and they begin playing while Eddie sings along with gusto. Soon the sidewalk is packed with pedestrians stopping to hear the impromptu recital. After finishing the song, Eddie takes a quick bow and starts calling out names and addresses from his stack of mail. When the parties present respond, he hands them their mail, leaving a bewildered crowd behind when he has exhausted his supply of letters and correspondingly lightened his satchel.

The good parts, what there are of them, in *Special Delivery* only serve to point out just how labored and inconsistent the poorer moments in the film are. Only once in the entire production is Cantor allowed to display the energy which had been the trademark of his stage career. In a scene which takes place in the office where Madge works as a secretary, Eddie asks her to the Postman's Ball. "I'd go anywhere in the world with you, Eddie," Madge beams, sending him reeling in a spontaneous outburst of joyous energy. Eddie jumps up and down, kisses everyone in the office (including a freckled office boy), and launches into his skipping and hand-clapping schtick so familiar to theater audiences. His unbridled glee quickly overflows into the hall, where he jumps into the arms of passing men, dances with a lady, and to top it all off, sweeps a group of passengers disembarking from an elevator into a quick roundelay of ring-around-the-rosie.

The entire episode happens so quickly and is executed so smoothly that it comes as a complete surprise in the context of the rest of the film. It is the only moment of pure Cantor in the movie; though Eddie performs his other duties well, they are not tailor-made to suit his style and could have been performed by any capable comedian. The scene provides probably the best example in his two silent films of Cantor's own peculiar brand of stage personality.

Although *Special Delivery* is crammed with all manner of gags, it still resorts to borrowing from Cantor's previous film for what is evidently designed to be a comic highlight. In the film, Eddie takes Madge to the annual Postman's Ball, only to find himself ignored by her. In an attempt to provoke his date to jealousy, Eddie uses a life-sized doll. Directly inspired by the "lady's arm" bit in *Kid Boots*, Eddie gaily whirls his stuffed partner around the floor, whispering, giggling, and dipping, while Madge becomes increasingly jealous. Eddie turns up the heat on the burning Madge when he and his new "girl" retreat upstairs to a private box in the balcony overlooking the dance floor. With Madge watching, Eddie kisses and caresses the "lady" and orders drinks, while she relaxes by hoisting up her skirts and throwing her legs over the edge.

The charade ultimately ends when the doll falls head first over the rail. Although Eddie manages to catch her, one of her legs falls off in the process. The scene, though funny, is less so than the corresponding routine in *Boots*. The main reason, however, is not because it is copying a previous laugh-getter, though this criticism is valid. Rather the scene here is more mechanical and relies on an inanimate object to play off of, instead of Cantor's own clever use of his own feminized arm. Here we see more of what actually appears to be a real girl, but the illusion is far less satisfying. Also Eddie's motivation to make his girl jealous is not sufficiently established. It seems the only logical reason that Madge will not dance with Eddie is to enable him to perform this bit to make her envious.

It is in this scene — and the one directly following — that the underlying weakness of *Special Delivery* is most evident. The primary motivation behind every character in the film, but especially Cantor's character since he is its principal comedian, seems to be to take the most direct route between gags and let any consideration of a logical story be damned. The jokes are slapped on top of the plot, often against the grain, instead of being interwoven into it. This problem is not often glaring, but it gives the entire film the feeling of a one-reel short, rather than a carefully thought-out feature film. Again, all evidence seems to point to the director, who, though a feature film star at one point, was more thoroughly trained in the school of short subject slapstick.

Coming downstairs alone, Eddie pretends to wipe off lipstick and removes blonde hair from his coat, while Madge agonizes. Even here the action doesn't quite make sense, and the characters behave with mixed motives. While Madge is almost on the point of tears, Eddie laughs behind her back at his clever joke, played at the expense of the girl he supposedly is madly in love with. That Madge's tears and Eddie's mugging are only for comic effect is evident when the entire conflict is dropped when it is time to plough ahead to the next gag sequence.

Much more satisfying than the plethora of mechanical gags at the ball

**Eddie receives a kiss from costar Jobyna Ralston in *Special Delivery* (collection of Brian Gari).**

are the mild, yet relevant bits which occur just before this lengthy scene. Eddie, with the help of his two roommates, is getting ready of the dance. While one shaves Eddie, the other unwraps Eddie's new shirt by removing at least one hundred pins from it. When Eddie discovers that his rented tuxedo has come without all the necessary accessories, the trio improvises the rest of the suit. For a tie, Eddie employs the bow and band from his straw hat; in place of a cummerbund a white towel, accented with black dots of shoe polish for buttons, fills in nicely; and to top off his ensemble, the sink's drain plug and chain make an excellent watch chain. To complete the illusion, the postal Cinderella borrows his father's limousine and chauffeur — without his father's knowledge, of course — to transport him to the ball. Although not inspired, the sequence works nicely because, unlike most of the rest of the film, it fits. One ventures to guess that this was the type of humor Cantor was striving for in his original treatment.

The rest of *Special Delivery* is fast and furious with gags, but even the chase, though exciting at times, is unremarkable for its lack of inspiration and originality. The film's better moments do not suffice to carry the whole, and one is left with the impression that the material included in *Special Delivery* would have been more amusing if mounted in two or three two-reelers, rather than a feature production.

Upon completion of *Special Delivery*, Eddie Cantor rushed back to New York for a benefit performance for the Surprise Lake Camp. After the performance, he took the next train back to Los Angeles for a much needed rest. The frantic pace he had set for himself during the production of the Paramount films left Eddie debilitated physically, and he had started losing weight. He consulted a doctor, who told him his tonsils would have to come out. Eddie returned to New York for the operation. When fellow Paramount star Wallace Beery asked Eddie why he went three thousand miles for an operation they could do just as well in Los Angeles, Eddie replied, "Because they're New York tonsils!"

According to the trade papers, Eddie had very little time to waste recuperating from his tonsillectomy. Throughout the first three months of 1927, Famous Players–Lasky made numerous announcements of new Cantor films. In January, even while *Special Delivery* was filming, the studio reported that Eddie's next project would be a movie entitled *Service Station*, in which he would play a gas station attendant. Filming on *Service Station* was scheduled to begin immediately after the completion of *Special Delivery*.

Less than a month later the studio, perhaps deciding that Cantor did better in adaptations of established stage musical properties (like *Kid Boots*) rather than original screenplays (like *Special Delivery*), announced that they had purchased the rights to the musical *The Girl Friend* for the comedian's next film.

By March, while both Cantor and *Special Delivery* were in the cutting room (Eddie for his tonsils and the film for editing), Famous Players changed their mind again. This time Cantor's next film was to be taken from another original screenplay written by Cantor himself. In this film, Eddie would play a valet to a Spanish toreador.

Eddie Sutherland was named as the film's director, as he had been, incorrectly so, on *Special Delivery*. Although this idea, as the two ones previously announced, never came before the cameras, it was probably the basis for *The Kid from Spain*, made five years later for Sam Goldwyn. Finally, the week that *Special Delivery* was released, Paramount stated that director Gregory LaCava would definitely direct Eddie Cantor's next film — *The Girl Friend*.

*Special Delivery* opened at New York's Paramount Theatre on April 23, 1927. The reviews were generally negative, emphasizing the overabundance of gags and the lack of a strong plot line. There were enough favorable notices, however, for Paramount to run a testimonial advertisement featuring excerpts from critics who liked the film. (The ad went so far as to acclaim Cantor the "New King of Comedy.") Like the reviews, box office business was also mixed at best. *Special Delivery* opened well, but not spectacularly, especially in cities where Cantor had always drawn well during his stage career. Unfortunately, the film had short "legs" and failed to sustain its respectable first week grosses.[3]

After the disappointing public and critical reception for *Special Delivery*, it was not all that difficult for Eddie Cantor to abandon the numerous film projects Paramount had lined up for him. Apparently, it was just as easy for Paramount to say good-bye to Cantor. In mid–May, less than a month after the release of *Special Delivery*, Cantor asked Jessie Lasky for a release from his contract, and Lasky gave it to him.

Cantor and his family packed up and left Hollywood May 30, 1927, almost a year to the day since they had left New York to come west. After two films (one a hit, the other not), Eddie was returning to the venue which had made him a star.[4] Years later, he expressed the opinion that though *Special Delivery* had been a "flop," he was glad that he had made the two silent films, since they exposed him to a wider audience and gave him valuable experience in front of the cameras. As glad as he was for the experience, Cantor went on to say he was just as glad to return to Broadway.

To be fully appreciated, Eddie Cantor had to be seen and heard. His next show would give audiences maximum opportunities to do both.

## REVIEWS

Eddie Cantor's second screen comedy is a fractious, windy affair furnished with old and new gags. It succeeded yesterday afternoon in stirring up plenty of merriment in the Paramount Theatre, but one could never accuse Mr. Cantor or his director of employing any great degree of subtlety in turning out this effort. In fact, there are moments when it seems that Mr. Cantor would have done better to appear in a milder form of amusement, something in which he had more opportunity to prove his ability as an actor.—Mordaunt Hall, *New York Times*, April 24, 1927

Eddie Cantor's second for Paramount is a gag picture with a thread of a story to give its hoke some semblance of coherence. Too much Cantor and a continuous series of practically unconnected comedy scenes makes the picture strain for laughs.

Love interest in this one, with Cantor opposite Jobyna Ralston. It doesn't look as though the popular stage comic can make an amour theme stand up. What pathos he has is not nearly so affective [*sic*] when playing the lover. It should be a happier solution for all concerned if Cantor is isolated from the direct love thing, but is given a hand in its ultimate and proverbial conclusion. In this case, and with that funny "pan" of his, it would be of more value to have him lose the girl, closing out to a laugh in which a "tear" might be embedded. There's nothing romantic about Cantor in celluloid and no use dodging the issue. It will help him to stay away from it.—Sid, *Variety*, April 27, 1927

It's a good thing Eddie Cantor wired his ex-boss, Flo Ziegfeld, the other day and informed Flo that his former stage star comedian intended to stick to the movies forever and ever.

Eddie's second attempt at funny filmery, "Special Delivery," is indeed a special delivery for the Paramount theatre this week. No comedy has revealed itself on that playhouse's screen since the Paramount's premiere, so full of spontaneous gags which make for instantaneous giggles and guffaws.

Eddie's "Kid Boots," movie version might have been a cinema tryout. This one, however, establishes the cantering Cantor as one of filmdom's foremost funsters. It's an absolute riot from start to finish.—New York *Daily News*

# *Notes*

1. In the same article *Variety* also mentioned that Sutherland had directed *Kid Boots*. By all other existing accounts, including press releases, reviews, Cantor's auto-biography, and the film itself, Frank Tuttle was the only director of *Kid Boots*. Sutherland may have assisted Tuttle or done some additional shoots after the primary work had been finished (such was not an uncommon practice at the time), but no evidence exists to substantiate the idea that he was actually the director.

2. According to Arbuckle's second wife, Fatty wrote and directed Keaton's classic *Sherlock Jr.* According to Keaton's autobiography, *My Wonderful World of Slapstick*, Arbuckle was indeed given his first postscandal directing job on *Sherlock Jr.*, but was so temperamental and unsure of himself he had to be replaced. Keaton further claims that Fatty left the picture when he was approached by William Randoph Hearst to direct Marion Davies in *The Red Mill*. To add to the confusion, *The Red Mill*, though directed by Arbuckle, was produced in 1926, while *Sherlock Jr.* was made in 1924.

3. One interesting sidelight, though it probably had little if anything to do with the disappointing returns on *Special Delivery*, was the fact that in some cities the film was shown in an abridged version. It seems that Paul Kelly, listed seventh in the cast, had been convicted of murdering fellow actor Ray Raymond. Kelly reportedly killed Raymond over the affections of actress Dorothy MacKaye, Raymond's ex-wife. Kelly served two years for manslaughter, after which he married MacKaye and continued his career, mostly in B-movies. In silent days, local movie theaters would often censor material from films which they believed might be morally objectionable. Not wishing to condone scandal, some cities cut most of Paul Kelly's part from *Special Delivery*.

4. The *New York Times* reported on May 18, 1927, that Cantor had completed a third picture for Famous Players–Lasky after finishing *Special Delivery*. Since there is no record of another film being completed (or even having been started) and Cantor spent time off for a tonsillectomy and recuperation, it must be concluded that the report was false.

# CHAPTER 18

# Ziegfeld Follies of 1927

While Eddie Cantor was in Hollywood pondering the less than rosy receipts for *Special Delivery*, he received a wire from his former boss, Flo Ziegfeld. The producer asked Eddie to return to Broadway to star in the next edition of the *Follies*, adding that he would not put on another of the extravaganzas unless Cantor was the star. Aside from extending the twenty-year tradition of the *Follies*, Eddie Cantor had numerous reasons for agreeing to go back to the musical stage.

First, his film career had faltered. Thanks to *Special Delivery*, for the first time since he became a star, Eddie Cantor was the recipient of show business's most lethal one-two punch: bad reviews and weak box office. Although his career itself was not the least bit in jeopardy, a return to the safer, more familiar environs of Broadway would likely be a welcome relief after his introduction to Hollywood.

Second, though he had spent a year in the employ of Famous Players-Lasky, Cantor still had three years remaining on his current contract with Ziegfeld. As an added incentive to lure his former star back, Ziegfeld agreed to throw out their existing contract and write a new two-year deal with Eddie, effectively taking a year off Cantor's present obligation. In addition to appearing in the *Follies of 1927*, Cantor would star in a new musical comedy vehicle the following season.

The final inducement, and probably the strongest, was a monetary one. Under the terms of their new agreement, Ziegfeld would pay Eddie Cantor, in the producer's own words, "the largest salary ever paid to a comedian in the world's history." Aside from helping to make Eddie one of the richest entertainers in the world, the record salary implied he was also one of the best. Cantor was earning more than even the great Jolson, the only entertainer considered his superior. Although the details of the contract were not revealed, Cantor was guaranteed a weekly minimum against 10 percent of the show's gross box office.

As with all other Ziegfeld shows, there were no half measures for the *Follies of 1927*. Everything was first class, from the highest paid comedian to the most lavish sets and costumes. The production cost $289,035, including twelve white pianos for one production number and a live ostrich wearing a rhinestone collar for another. Apart from leaving droppings on stage, the ostrich also managed to lose all its feathers prior to opening night. In an attempt to replume the bird, costume designer Jack Harkrider glued feathers originally bought for the girls' costumes on to the ostrich.

The music and lyrics for the show were written entirely by Irving Berlin. Although one number, "Shakin' the Blues Away," managed to become a hit, critics noted that the score, though well crafted and pleasant, was ultimately forgettable. Berlin, not to be bested by Cantor, also earned a record amount for his work on the *Follies of 1927*. The songwriter received an unprecedented 5 percent of the show's gross, the highest royalty ever paid to a composer at that time. Cantor recalled that the percentage even impressed Berlin. One day, while Irving and Eddie were crossing Times Square together, a taxicab grazed Cantor. Berlin yanked the comedian back to the safety of the sidewalk, crying, "For Heaven's sake, Eddie, be careful! Think of my royalties!"

Being the unqualified star of the *Follies* brought added burdens to Eddie Cantor. In past *Follies* from 1917 through 1919, Eddie had always performed in one skit and one specialty set. In the 1927 edition, Eddie Cantor *was* the comedy. Although there were others in the cast who could technically be considered comics, such as Andy Tombes or Cliff Edwards, they played it straight for the most part, serving primarily as foils for Cantor.

As the star of the *Follies*, Eddie Cantor was on stage an average of two hours a night, and that in a two and a half hour show. Aside from his specialty, Cantor appeared in six comedy sketches. Eddie opened the show with a song and routine in memory of his short-lived film career. The song, titled "You've Got to Have It," was full of double entendre and references to Hollywood stars from John Barrymore to Rin-Tin-Tin, and of course the "it" girl herself, Eddie's former costar, Clara Bow. Immediately following the number was a picture spoof, "The Star's Double," in which Eddie plays a movie star who uses doubles for all his love scenes, but draws the line at taking them along on his honeymoon.

"You've Got to Have It," by Irving Berlin, was Cantor's biggest song number in the *Follies of 1927*, although the song had had a rather rocky musical history. It started as an entirely different tune written by none other than Eddie Cantor. Cantor wrote the song after returning from Hollywood, where Clara Bow was the reigning sex symbol. Cantor was performing his version, which he titled "I'm So Brokenhearted 'Cause I Haven't Got It," when Irving Berlin walked in.

"Who wrote that God-awful song?" Berlin interrupted.

"I did," Cantor confessed.

"Do I try to be a comedian?" Berlin snapped, as he sat down at the piano and started rewriting Eddie's musical miscarriage. Soon Irving had transformed the number into something more worthy of Cantor and the *Follies*.

"How can I ever thank you?" a grateful Eddie asked.

"You've done it," Berlin replied passively. "I was in pain, now I'm out of pain."

Aside from "You've Got to Have It," Irving Berlin tried hard to provide another hit specifically for Cantor. Originally, the composer had written a number entitled "It All Belongs to Me" that was loosely based on the song "Ain't She Sweet," which had been a hit for Cantor. Sure that he had another song of the caliber of "You'd Be Surprised," Berlin not only wrote the chorus and verse, but went ahead and penned seven encores for "It All Belongs to Me." When the show tried out in Boston, Eddie performed "It All Belongs to Me," complete with chubby actress Lora Foster to dance along side Cantor as he sang.

Unfortunately, Berlin's seven encore verses weren't necessary, as "It All Belongs to Me" turned out to be an unqualified flop. Mystified at the lack of response to his surefire hit, Irving Berlin shook his head and said, "How're you gonna tell?"[1]

Aside from Irving Berlin's tunes, Cantor, as he had in past shows, frequently substituted other songs into his specialty. One, "My Blue Heaven," by Walter Donaldson, was particularly popular and went on to become a standard.

Two of Cantor's more popular sketches in the show were heavily laced with topical humor. In the first, Cantor parodied the flamboyant New York mayor, Jimmy Walker. As Walker, Eddie stood solemnly on the steps of the city hall, giving out keys to the city to a steady stream of aviators, Channel swimmers, and visiting royalty. Cantor acted bored as he handed out the keys and accompanied each presentation with the same speech, which was essentially the words Walker himself recycled for those occasions. The bit allowed Eddie a chance to use the mimicking skills which had first gotten him into show business almost twenty years before. The audience and critics made it one of the most popular bits in the show. The Mayor Walker impersonation became so popular that for a time almost every musical review in New York included its own version of the routine.

The other topical sketch featured a parody on Charles Lindbergh's recent triumphant solo flight across the Atlantic Ocean. In the bit, Eddie plays Ginsberg, a Jewish aviator who is attempting to duplicate Lucky Lindy's journey. Just prior to takeoff in his plane *Mosquito — The Spirit of New Jersey*, Ginsberg is questioned by the army major in charge of Mitchell Field.

"You don't look like an aviator," the major growls, while looking over the scrawny pilot.

"You don't look like a major," Eddie replies.

"Sit down! You were in the army? Did you get a commission?"

"No, a straight salary!"

"Have you ever flown before," the major asks.

"I had flu during the war."

"Flown! Flown!" the major corrects.

"Flu! Flu!" Eddie insists.

"You must say, 'I have flown,'" the major explains. "You can't say, 'I have flew.'"

"Are you telling me? I was sick in bed with it! I ought to know what I had."

"What's your name," the major continues.

"Ginsberg."

"Your first name?"

"Gregory."

"Gregory Ginsburg. Is that your right name?"

"My right name is Levey," Eddie explains.

"Why did you change it?"

"Well, I was in the South, around Mississippi, during the floods, and I read headlines in the papers that they were going to blow up all the levees."

"I have a few more questions to ask you," says the major, pressing on. "Married?"

"No, sir."

"Children?"

"Major!" Eddie blushes.

"Where were you born?"

"In Chicago. I'll show you the scars."

"Never mind. How do you sleep?"

Eddie folds his hands against his cheek. "Like that."

"I mean, do you sleep well? Are you disturbed at night?"

"Yes," Eddie admits, "I'm terribly disturbed."

"What disturbs you?"

"My brother Morris. I sleep with him."

"How does he sleep?" the major asks.

"Like this." Eddie demonstrates, putting his feet in the major's lap.

"How long can a man live without brains?" the major shouts, shoving away Eddie's feet.

"I don't know," Eddie replies. "How old are you?"

When the examination is finally over, Eddie climbs in his plane, just as Lindbergh did, with only a bottle of water and five sandwiches to sustain him throughout the long flight. The trek is aborted before it begins, however, when the kosher aviator discovers that all five sandwiches are ham.

One night while doing the "Ginsberg the aviator" routine, Eddie noticed that the real Charles Lindbergh was sitting in the audience. In the middle of the skit, Eddie stopped to ask the famous pilot whether he found the "air-pockets too tight while he was flying over Scotland."

Although the familiar osteopath sketch didn't find its way into the *Follies of 1927*, Eddie was careful to include a scene with an opportunity for some similar roughhousing. The "taxicab scene" was a role-reversal bit, with Eddie as a shy suitor, riding in the back of a cab with his forward date. The girl, played by Frances Upton, continually tries to have her way with the bashful Eddie, while he continually fights to preserve his honor.

The Cantors circa 1928. Eddie holds baby Janet while wife Ida and daughters (left to right) Natalie, Marilyn, Marjorie, and Edna look on (collection of Brian Gari).

"You're the coldest proposition," the girl exclaims in disgust.

"I'm sorry," Eddie answers, with dignity, "I'm sorry we're not the same temperature."

Finally, when the struggle becomes too violent, Eddie is kicked out of the cab. The girl gives Eddie a choice: either he can walk the remaining ten miles home by himself or else agree to come back in the taxi and be "mauled with affection."

"I guess I'll 'else'," Eddie cries, climbing back in the cab for a passion-filled return trip.

Other skits included a bit with Eddie as the owner of a dog shop and a serious dramatic sketch. The dramatic sketch was void of any jokes or funny lines, but managed to keep the audience in stitches. The cast delivered their lines in a perfectly straight manner, but all the participants, including Cantor, delivered their serious lines while toe-dancing around the stage dressed as ballerinas.

The dog shop number was probably the weakest of Cantor's numbers, but even Eddie managed to score a big laugh with it during one performance. On the night in question, while Eddie was taking one of the dogs out of its cage, the animal started scratching with its hind leg rhythmically in pursuit of a flea. Cantor saw the the strumming motion and called out, "Ukelele Ike!" ("Ukelele Ike" was the famous nickname for Cliff Edwards, one of the other cast members.) The audience responded with a hearty laugh. Unfortunately, despite Ziegfeld's urging, Eddie could not get the dog to repeat the ad-lib scratch for future performances.

The rest of the cast for the *Ziegfeld Follies of 1927* included singer Ruth Etting (who performed "Shakin' the Blues Away"), dancer Helen Brown, ventriloquist Leo Bill (using his hand for a dummy, à la Señor Wencas), singer Franklyn Baur, Claire Luce (who got to ride the ostrich), the Albertina Rasch Ballet, and of course more than a score of beautiful show girls.

After a little less than a month of rehearsals, the *Follies of 1927* opened in Boston on August 2, 1927. *Variety* described the show's opening night as "the biggest this town has ever seen," with police reserves called in to handle the crowd. The *Follies* did tremendous business, selling out every performance. Ticket sales were helped by slightly lower prices on matinees because it was the summer season. Despite the lines at the ticket office, Ziegfeld, as usual, gloomily estimated that he would lose over $15,000 a week on the show.[2]

In addition to his usual lavish spending on the production, Ziegfeld also spent more than he normally did on the advertising. Prior to the New York opening, Ziegfeld shelled out $7,500 for full-page testimonial ads featuring reprints of the Boston reviews. In addition, the producer reprinted a letter from New York mayor Jimmy Walker praising the show, particularly Cantor's parody of himself. (Walker made a special trip to Boston to see the *Follies* before sailing to Europe just prior to the show's Broadway debut.)

The *Follies* opened at the New Amsterdam August 16. The show played to a top ticket of $6.60 ($3.85 for midweek matinees), giving it a potential weekly gross of $46,150 if every performance sold out. They did, and then some. In the first eleven weeks of its Broadway run, the *Follies of 1927*, with the help of standing-room customers, managed to top its capacity gross. The crowds he helped attract earned Eddie Cantor an average weekly salary of over $4,600.

Any extra money Eddie earned, though not necessarily needed, was welcome, especially since there was another mouth to feed at home. On October 8, in the middle of the *Follies'* New York run, Ida gave birth to Janet, their fifth daughter. When Ziegfeld asked his star why he was having only girls, Eddie quipped, "It's for you Flo, I'm raising my own Albertina Rasch ballet." In commemoration of Janet's birth, an extra verse was added to the lyrics of Eddie's specialty number "My Blue Heaven."

Ida had suffered a particularly difficult delivery and required several blood transfusions and a long rest to restore her health to normal. While she was convalescing, Eddie came home one night with a platinum bracelet encrusted with diamonds. In addition to purchasing the diamond bracelet, Eddie used $80,000 of his *Follies* percentage to buy ten acres of land in fashionable Great Neck, on Long Island. The Cantors rented a home in Great Neck while construction was underway on their own seventeen-room Tudor mansion. Soon after he purchased the property, someone offered Eddie $120,000 for it. Although he turned the offer down, Eddie marveled at the real estate business, commenting, "That's better than working for Ziegfeld."

Although working for Ziegfeld had made Eddie Cantor the world's highest paid comedian, his work load in the *Follies of 1927* made him earn every cent of his cut. As the show's only star, Eddie was on stage for more than 80 percent of the show's running time. "I was on all the time," Cantor recalled years later. "One night I stepped outside to get a breath of air. The doorman looked at me and laughed. 'Don't let Ziegfeld see you, he'll have you selling programs in the lobby!'"

Another time, during a matinee performance, Georgie Jessel stopped at the stage door to see Eddie. When the stage doorman informed Jessel that Eddie was on, Georgie walked right out on the stage in the middle of Cantor's number to talk to his old friend. The two chatted and ad-libbed for about seven minutes. When Jessel left, he said, "Well, goodbye, Eddie. I'll drop in again."

"Do, anytime, George," Cantor replied. "I'm always on."

Cantor's busy schedule may have made for amusing anecdotes, but his hectic pace nearly destroyed his health. Towards the end of the show's twenty-one–week Broadway run, Eddie was forced to miss four performances, closing the *Follies* temporarily. His physician, Dr. Alex Louria, advised Eddie to take a prolonged rest, not only from the *Follies*, but from the many benefits he played on his nights off.[3] Against his doctor's advice, Eddie and the show finished their New York run and then went on to Boston for three weeks. After Boston, the *Follies* was scheduled for a run in Philadelphia.

In between Boston and Philadelphia, Eddie stopped to do some benefits. At one, he had to be strapped up, as he had been during the run of *Kid Boots*, just to get on stage. The next night, in Newark, Eddie nearly collapsed on stage. The diagnosis was again pleurisy. Dr. Louria ordered Eddie back home to Great Neck and prescribed a trip south when the comedian was able to travel.

Cantor's illness forced the *Follies* to close. The review was so entirely built around Eddie that a replacement was impossible. The forced closing left Flo Ziegfeld in a double bind. Not only did the *Follies* close before it could start realizing a profit (it was still $238,000 in the red), but the producer was bound, by Actors' Equity, to pay an additional $39,000 in compensation to the cast.

Ziegfeld filed a formal complaint with Equity, charging that Cantor's illness had cost him and his partner, A. L. Erlanger, $35,000. At the very least, the producer reasoned, Cantor could have given a week's notice, thereby avoiding the necessity for the week's severance pay to the rest of the company. In the complaint, Ziegfeld further charged that Cantor had been seen driving down Broadway, visiting with friends, and taking in shows, all while he was supposedly "sleeping" in Great Neck. In addition, Ziegfeld claimed that the comedian actually planned to go to Hollywood to make more movies.

Feeling that he had already been generous in his exclusive contract with Cantor by allowing Eddie to take a year off to make movies, Ziegfeld's patience was wearing thin. He thought Cantor had over extended himself physically, thereby taking advantage of him. Ziegfeld had always frowned on Cantor's appearances in benefits and vaudeville; now it seemed that those extracurricular activities had finally done the damage he feared they would. The producer stated that if Cantor performed in any medium — including radio, movies, stage, vaudeville, or even benefits — before he returned to complete his contract, Ziegfeld would sue Cantor, not only for the money lost due to the closing, but for the entire production costs of the *Follies*.

In response, Eddie denied any plans to go back to making movies or to do any performing until he was fully recovered, and he insisted that his illness was genuine. "Certainly I would not throw away $4,500 a week for at least six months just to aggravate Mr. Ziegfeld," Cantor told the *New York Times*. He went on to explain that his daily trips to New York were to see Dr. William Bierman, of Park Avenue, for treatments. Furthermore, Eddie volunteered to be examined by Ziegfeld's own doctor in an effort to settle the matter and even offered to post a bond to cover any losses incurred if he were found to be faking his sickness.

On February 9, 1928, a two-hour session that was a combination meeting, examination, and hearing was convened at Equity headquarters on West 47th Street. Those present included Ziegfeld's doctor, lawyer, and business manager; Cantor and his doctor; and a brace of actors from Equity, including George Arliss, who oversaw the proceedings. After a thorough examination, the doctors ruled that Cantor was indeed suffering from pleurisy and should take an extended rest.[4] In addition to his pleurisy, Eddie revealed a large burn on his back, suffered as the result of intense heat lamp treatments he had taken in an effort to keep the *Follies* open. Despite his illness, Eddie was in a jovial mood and denied any plans other than to go to Havana to begin his convalescence.[5] He insisted all his past appearances in films and benefits had been done with Ziegfeld's special permission.

With his rift with Ziegfeld apparently patched up, Eddie Cantor took the next few months off to recuperate. Upon his return, Cantor found that, as in the past, preparations for his next Ziegfeld vehicle were proceeding at a snail's pace. Since Ziegfeld was not yet ready for his services, Eddie accepted an offer of $6,000 a week at Fox's Theatre in Philadelphia. When Zieggy got wind of the plan, he immediately put a stop to the booking and made it clear that any appearances by Cantor, even benefits, would have to be approved by him in advance.

Blocked from performing in vaudeville and picture houses, Eddie Cantor busied himself precisely as he had during a similar dispute with Ziegfeld eleven years earlier — he wrote. Instead of drafting acts for other comedians, as he had done during the *Follies of 1917*, Eddie sat down with gag writer and personal friend David Freedman and penned *My Life Is in Your Hands*, his first autobiography.

By early summer any ill feelings caused by the financial failure of the *Ziegfeld Follies of 1927* had faded, and Flo Ziegfeld and Eddie Cantor set to work on the next show — another musical comedy in the mold of their previous triumph *Kid Boots*. As for the *Follies* itself (which Ziegfeld had christened "a national institution" in referring to the 1927 version), the twenty-first edition was, for all intents and purposes, the last in the series. The Great Ziegfeld would put together one last *Follies* in 1931, but by then the production was mostly a nostalgic grasp at past glories and was devoid of all its former stars who had made the *Follies* as much as the *Follies* had made them.

## REVIEWS

The main interest in every "Follies" first night is what type of entertainment Ziegfeld is attempting. This year's edition is all Eddie Cantor and dancing numbers.

Ziegfeld has most of his eggs in one basket this time in the matter of Eddie Cantor, both as a name and as a comedian, carrying the show on his back. It is this reporter's humble guess that Flo Ziegfeld wishes Eddie Cantor the best of health this season — and means it — and how! — Libbey, *Variety*, Boston, August 10, 1927

Coming fresh from the theatre one finds it easier to write fulsome praise than to report the attractions of the new edition. Mr. Cantor pops around brightly all evening, in one or two wooden numbers, but mostly in skits designed for his eccentric, animated comedy. To see him in blackface again, clapping his white hands and strutting breathlessly across the stage, or to see him in his racial vein of selling maladroit dogs to amazed customers, cracking his straw hat in sheer vexation at an unwilling purchaser, is to see the Eddie Cantor who is justly famous. — J. Brooks Atkinson, *New York Times*, August 17, 1927

The "Follies" has adopted the Paul Ash policy. Take it or leave it, but there it is.

On the comedy end there is Eddie Cantor and nobody else. Andy Tombes doesn't count, for he's doing "straight" all of the time. Others may be in on the comedy scenes, but it's to foil Cantor, and the material Eddie has to work with isn't always funny. The latter is trotting out his usual assortment of songs, starts off with the best of the bunch and never tops it from the lyric angle. Yet, give Cantor credit. He's working his head off with the material weak enough in spots to make him over strive at times. — Sid, *Variety*, August 17, 1927

# *Notes*

1. Although "It All Belongs to Me," was eventually dropped from the *Follies of 1927*, at least one critic thought well of the number. *Variety*'s Boston review of the show made the following observations: "A third number, apparently jammed in during the last day or two of rehearsals and which did not even get in the program was a snappy thing entitled "And She All Belongs to Me." Cantor put it across and built it up by dragging on chubby little Lora Foster who has more curves than a scenic railway and who shook it all up a bit as Cantor sang. The house went a bit goofy over the kid and the number and Cantor had plenty of opportunity for building business."

2. It is quite possible that Ziegfeld lost $15,000 a week during the Boston run, although it is as equally possible that Ziegfeld was also figuring in preproduction and rehearsal costs.

3. It was not uncommon for Cantor to perform in two or three benefits each Sunday night.

4. As to Cantor's reported appearances around town, Ziegfeld's physician, Dr. Jerome Wagner, admitted he found Cantor behaving in the "traditional clown manner — too ill to work, but keeping up a brave painted smile."

5. Although *Variety* and the *New York Times* reported that Cantor went to Havana to recover, earlier reports announced that he would go to either Miami or Palm Springs. In Cantor's own autobiography published the same year (1928), he writes that he went to Palm Springs for six weeks and then to the Battle Creek Sanitarium for another six weeks.

# CHAPTER 19

# *Whoopee*

Eddie Cantor and Flo Ziegfeld, for all their occasional conflicts, knew they made a winning theatrical combination. Once their differences over the *Follies of 1927* had been smoothed out and their friendship had resumed, Ziegfeld signed Cantor to a new three-year contract. As part of the contract, Eddie posted a bond to cover any losses Zieggy might incur if he were unable to perform due to illness.

With their relationship again solid and Cantor's health now guaranteed, Ziegfeld loosened his exclusive hold on his star comedian's services and allowed him to make some personal appearances at picture houses, vaudeville theaters, and benefits. In fact, if Eddie was so eager to put in some extra performances, Ziegfeld decided to oblige him by reopening the New Amsterdam Roof and starting up the *Midnight Frolics* again.

Directly after the demise of the original *Frolics*, which coincided with the advent of prohibition, Ziegfeld had spent over $100,000 remodeling his rooftop nightclub. Unfortunately, the roof theater failed to attract enough patrons to operate, and Zieggy was forced to close it a second time. Although the 18th Amendment still forbad the sale of most alcoholic beverages, the new *Midnight Frolic* would feature a restaurant and dance floor, which, like the original, would continue to cater to the wealthy late-night crowd. The cover charge on the New Amsterdam Roof would be $6 on week nights, $7.50 on weekends.

*Variety* announced that the *Frolics* would feature Eddie Cantor, the George Olson Band, and Ethel Shutta (Mrs. George Olson). Coincidentally, all of the above would be appearing downstairs early in the evening in Cantor's new musical comedy. The *Frolics* were scheduled to open sometime in early 1929, after the musical comedy had premiered.

As for Eddie's early evening schedule, Zieggy announced that he had assigned Edgar McGregor to start writing the book for Cantor's next musical comedy. The show, on Cantor's suggestion, was to be a musical version of Owen Davis' play *The Nervous Wreck*, a Broadway hit from earlier in the twenties, in which the main character, a hypochondriac, goes to the Wild West for his health. The idea of a musical set in the Wild West intrigued

Ziegfeld, who, along with designer Joseph Urban, set about making exotic plans for the show's production numbers. At first, Ziegfeld wondered if the bubbly Cantor would be right playing a hypochondriac, but Eddie, who despite his peppy stage presence possessed what he himself called "a healthy dose of hypochondria," reassured him. "I felt completely qualified to play it," Cantor later wrote. "I'd been rehearsing in doctor's offices and sanitariums for over a year."

Composer Walter Donaldson and lyricist Gus Kahn were brought in to furnish the score. Donaldson, who had just began his own music publishing company, and Kahn were experienced songwriters with an impressive catalog of hits, including "Carolina in the Morning" and "Yes Sir, That's My Baby." Cantor was very pleased with the choice of Donaldson and Kahn, particularly Kahn. Eddie and Gus were good friends who had worked together in the past.

In 1925, according to Cantor, Kahn had written "Yes Sir, That's My Baby" while playing on the Cantor's living room floor with their daughter Marilyn. Marilyn Cantor had a mechanical toy pig which made a distinctive noise as it unwound. Kahn made up words to the toy's unusual rhythm. Later, when the song became a hit, Gus showed Eddie a royalty check and exclaimed, "This is a lot of money for a Jewish boy to make out of a pig's tail."

Eddie Cantor especially appreciated Gus Kahn's talent for quickly turning out funny lyrics. Often if a song was going over well in act one, Kahn would retreat to the men's lounge and come back with a new set of lyrics for a second act encore. In the new musical, one song to which he would add lyrics would be "Makin' Whoopee," which wound up with multiple sets of words based on topical events and persons in the news. Kahn's quickness with a witty lyric complemented Cantor's talent for putting over a humorous song. During the months of work on *Whoopee*, they were, by Cantor's own admission, "inseparable."

While *Whoopee*'s lyricist may have been a fast worker, unfortunately, the same could not be said for its author. Soon after Ziegfeld had given the writing chores to McGregor, he changed his mind, handing the job over to William Anthony McGuire, coauthor of Cantor's earlier hit, *Kid Boots*. *Whoopee* had all the earmarks of following in the footsteps of *Boots*, especially where McGuire was concerned. As with the previous show, McGuire's script for *Whoopee* trickled in scene by scene. By the time the show opened in Pittsburgh in early November 1928, after six weeks of rehearsals, *Whoopee* was still without a finale. McGuire finally came up with an ending with less than two hours to spare on opening night.

The night before the Pittsburgh opening, while McGuire rushed to complete the final scene, Cantor took a long walk in the damp autumn air with two of the show's featured players. Unfortunately, as the trio walked, Eddie did most of the talking, and by the time they arrived back at the Nixon Theatre, Cantor had lost his voice.

After hearing, or rather *not* hearing, his star, Ziegfeld, who was going over some last minute scenery changes (over \$15,000 worth) with designer Joseph Urban, dropped everything and rushed to find the city's leading throat specialist. Ziegfeld finally located the doctor at two in the morning. The doctor, who himself was recuperating from an auto accident, was dragged from his sick bed by Ziegfeld and rushed by ambulance to Cantor's hotel. There he spent the rest of the night painting Eddie's vocal chords and giving the comedian a series of shots. By curtain time the next evening, the problems with Cantor's voice, McGuire's finale, and Urban's scenery had all been solved. *Whoopee* was a smash hit.

During the Pittsburgh run, Flo Ziegfeld was in the audience nightly, usually entertaining friends. Always trying to get the normally stoic Ziegfeld to laugh, the inclusion of the producer's friends added an extra incentive for Eddie to break up his boss. One evening Cantor was going through a scene with foil Spencer Charters in which they compared illnesses. Suddenly, Eddie departed from the script and asked Charters if he'd ever had an operation.

"Yes," Charters replied.

"Where?" Cantor asked.

"Here," said Charters, pulling up his shirt as to reveal a scar.

Not to be outdone, Cantor pulled up his shirt to display his operation wounds.

"I paid a thousand dollars for this operation," Cantor bragged.

"That's nothing," Charters countered. "I paid two thousand for mine."

"Two thousand? Let me see that again." Upon closer examination Cantor nodded, "No wonder, you've got hemstitching . . . and a zipper."

The impromptu bit brought tears to Ziegfeld's eyes. Backstage he confessed, "It's the funniest thing in the show, Eddie. You ought to do more of that."

After that Cantor and Charters expanded the bit to include multiple scars that ran up the chest, around the back, and down the pants leg.

Another impromptu bit of business that amused Ziegfeld occurred during the Pittsburgh run. One night the show's cow (after all, this was supposed to be the Wild West) forgot its dramatic training and deposited a healthy cow chip out on stage in the middle of the performance. Eddie Cantor, waiting in the wings, grabbed a broom and shovel, danced out on stage, swept off the offending chip, and pranced back off, much to the audience's delight. Ziegfeld, also amused, turned to his secretary and said, "Make a note. Keep that in." Unfortunately, the cow never learned to defecate on cue, and as with the dog in the *Follies of 1927*, the animal ad-lib was not repeated.

After a month on the road, *Whoopee* premiered December 4, at Broadway's New Amsterdam. Prior to the New York opening, the cast underwent two revisions. First, Paul Gregory replaced Pietro Gentile in the role of Wanenis, the romantic leading man. Ziegfeld had hired Gregory away from rival producer Arthur Hammerstein specifically for *Whoopee*. When Hammerstein threatened to sue, the two producers came to a cash settlement.[1]

Whatever Ziegfeld paid for Gregory was worth it, as the juvenile garnered high praise from the Broadway critics for his efforts.

The second cast change came about when dancer Ruby Keeler left the show one night in Pittsburgh. Keeler, who had just recently married Al Jolson, departed after receiving a series of telephone calls from Jolson, pleading for her to join him in Hollywood. Without telling Ziegfeld, Keeler boarded the next train to the coast. She did call Ziegfeld from Chicago, however, to inform him of her departure and say that she hoped he wouldn't be too angry. Although she wasn't central to the show, Keeler's tap solo had won her good reviews. Evidently Ziegfeld wasn't too angry, as he went ahead with plans to star Keeler in her own vehicle, *Show Girl*. The fact that she was Mrs. Al Jolson probably helped.[2]

The rest of *Whoopee*'s cast included Frances Upton as the ingenue, Ethel Shutta as Cantor's nurse and love interest, John Rutherford, Spencer Charters, Ruth Etting, and Chief Caupoliean. In all, the entire company numbered over a hundred. (The chorus included a twenty-year-old dancer by the name of Buddy Ebsen.)

*Whoopee*'s songs included two hits: "Makin' Whoopee," sung, of course, by Cantor and "Love Me or Leave Me," sung by Ruth Etting. Eddie was also afforded a specialty number in which he appeared in blackface, as he had in *Kid Boots*. Unlike *Boots*, however, his specialty was integrated into the show's plot. As in the past, Eddie used the specialty to introduce an ever-changing array of tunes (which had nothing to do with the plot, nor did they have to). The songs, by a variety of songwriters, included: "My Blackbirds Are Bluebirds Now," "Ever Since the Movies Learned to Talk," and the Jazz Age lament, "If I Give Up the Saxophone, Will You Come Back to Me?"

Aside from playing a hypochondriac, *Whoopee* found Eddie Cantor playing backstage Cupid again, as he had back in the *Follies of 1918* for Frank Carter and Marilyn Miller. This time the love interest was Ruth Etting and an unnamed actor in the cast. Etting's career had been promoted and sponsored by Chicago mobster (or semigangster as Cantor defined him) "Colonel Gimp" Snyder. Although she didn't love Snyder, Etting married him out of a feeling of debt to the gangster for advancing her career. As Etting's career progressed, Snyder ignored his other "businesses" and devoted himself to Ruth. Intensely jealous, he was a constant backstage fixture, making any extramarital affairs for Etting next to impossible.

When one of the cast members became enamored of Etting, it was Cantor who acted as the go-between. Each night the actor was called upon to shake Eddie's hand onstage in the first act. Cantor used the opportunity to slip him a note from Etting. The actor would slip a response into Eddie's pocket later in the show, which Eddie would deliver to Etting in the backstage elevator after the finale. Unlike Miller and Carter ten years earlier, nothing ever came of this romance, which is just as well for Etting, her lover, and Eddie Cantor. "If the Gimp had ever caught us," Eddie later remarked, "we'd have wound up, in his favorite phrase, 'DSF'—dead stinking fish!" The story of Etting and Snyder was later made into an entertaining film starring Doris Day and James Cagney, which was named after Etting's *Whoopee* hit, "Love Me or Leave Me."

Soon after the Broadway opening of *Whoopee*, Ziegfeld encountered more personnel trouble, this time involving the show's orchestra, the George Olsen Band, and his lead comedienne, Ethel Shutta. Back in Pittsburgh, Ziegfeld had decided to replace the band's conductor and arranger, Eddie Kilfeather, with his own choice, Gus Salzer. To make matters worse, he deducted Salzer's salary from the band's wages.

In protest, Olsen held the curtain up until 9 o'clock one night, refusing to let his band respond to Salzer's baton. Finally, with a standing-room-only audience waiting, Ziegfeld allowed Kilfeather to take over for that performance and the remaining shows that week. That Saturday Olsen and his band quit.

Olsen's departure put his wife, Ethel Shutta, in the awkward position of remaining with a show that her husband had quit. Since she had a run-of-the-play contract, Ziegfeld was loath to release her. (Ziegfeld had displayed Shutta's name prominently in all advertisements for *Whoopee*.) Eddie Cantor, soon stepped into the dispute, trying to act as peacemaker between Ziegfeld and Shutta. In an early example of shuttle diplomacy, Cantor ran back and forth between the warring parties until he secured an amicable release for Shutta. Under the agreement worked out, however, Shutta would not leave until a suitable replacement had been found. This would take some time, since the two leading candidates to take over for her were both out of town with other shows.

Replacing Olsen's band was also easier said than done. While it wasn't hard to find pit musicians, it was hard to find ones who could play the ultramodern jazz orchestrations that the Olsen Band had used. The orchestrations had to be "toned down" and simplified for the more conventional replacements. For a brief time, *Whoopee* had the leading jazz band of the decade, when Paul Whiteman and his orchestra played for *Whoopee* concurrent with their stay on the Roof in the newly reopened *Frolics*.

*Whoopee* was an unqualified smash on Broadway, doing sensational business and winning raves from all the major critics. Although he was on stage for most of each performance, Eddie's health held up.[3] Like Irving Berlin, with the *Follies of 1927*, Gus Kahn did all he could to ensure Cantor's well-being. On opening night, after the performance, Kahn invited Walter Donaldson, William Anthony McGuire, Cantor, and a few others responsible for *Whoopee*'s success, up to his suite for a celebration. When Eddie arrived, Kahn personally fetched him dinner and a drink, got him a comfortable chair, and even provided him with a footstool. When Cantor asked why he was getting the royal treatment, Kahn replied, "You may be Ida's husband, you may be Ziegfeld's star, but to me you just represent 2.5 percent of the gross. What time do you want your massage tomorrow morning?"

Meanwhile, up on the New Amsterdam Roof, the *Midnight Frolics* reopened on December 28, 1928. Although the top price for opening night had been set at $16.50, some tables went for as high as $350. A ticket agency reported that it had been offered as much as $1,000 for a table, but all of the four hundred available seats had long been sold out.

The *Frolic*'s cast included Fanny Brice, comedians Moran and Mack, Paul Gregory (from *Whoopee*), Helen Morgan, Paul Whiteman and his orchestra, and Cantor, as master of ceremonies. Cantor got the biggest laugh of the night when he introduced Morgan, famous for singing while perched on top of the piano, as "the young lady who would do her famous sketch, 'Fannie on the Piano.'"

Despite the first night frenzy, the new *Midnight Frolic* did not live up to expectations. Perhaps the show belonged to another time, one when alcohol could be legally served. After four months, Ziegfeld called it quits and closed the New Amsterdam Roof for the third time in less than ten years. The *Frolics* had lost $75,000 in the cost for talent alone. The expense of refurbishing and decorating the Roof was extra. Fortunately for Ziegfeld, the box office returns for *Whoopee* helped offset his losses on the *Frolics*. In fact, the producer was doing well enough to buy his star a little gift.

One morning a few months after *Whoopee* opened, Eddie Cantor and Flo Ziegfeld were enjoying a massage on adjoining tables. The producer and his star were reflecting on their show, which was the reigning number one hit on Broadway and had been playing to standing-room-only audiences since its debut. Zieggy turned to Cantor and said, "How lucky you are, Eddie. You have a family, you have money. You're the biggest hit in New York, working for the biggest producer in the world. You've got everything."

Eddie smiled, then after thinking a moment, he confessed, "No, Flo, I haven't a Rolls-Royce."

Ziegfeld laughed, but Cantor was serious.

"Remember when I was first working for you on the Roof," Eddie began, "I used to stand downstairs and watch people drive up in their Rolls-Royces. I'd dream of how it would feel to have one."

A few days later, following a matinee, Ziegfeld and Cantor were leaving the New Amsterdam to have dinner together. As they walked up the street, Ziegfeld stopped by a brand new gray Rolls convertible. On the door handle was tied an orchid with a note attached.

Ziegfeld told Eddie to read the card. It said, "Eddie, now you have everything, Flo."

Now, with the gift of the Rolls-Royce, Eddie Cantor apparently did have everything. He was the star of Broadway's biggest hit. At the same time, he was appearing in talking short subjects for Paramount and did a guest spot in a talking feature. He was the newly elected president of Actors' Equity. He was beginning to make occasional appearances on radio at a time when few other Broadway stars did. He was a published author of books and newspaper columns and was working on the script for a Broadway review. He was the second richest actor in the country, with an estimated wealth, according to *Variety*, at between $5 and $6 million.[4] He was on the board of the Manufacturers' Trust Company and was building a seventeen-room Tudor mansion across the street from the home of that institution's president, Nathan S. Jonas.

Having achieved everything the success-oriented go-getter of the twenties was expected to, Eddie Cantor announced that he would retire from show business in June 1930 when his present contract ran out, in order to enjoy the rest of his life. "What does a performer work for?" Cantor asked a reporter rhetorically. "Only two things. If it's money, thanks to Danny Lipsky and Nathan Jonas, they've taken care of that for me. If it's applause—the kick of working—I can always get that from benefits, or if Georgie Jessel, for instance, plays at the Palace, I'll play along with him and not charge the circuit for my services."

For a young man who had just announced his retirement, however, Eddie Cantor was extremely busy. Aside from all the aforementioned projects, Eddie was also planning to do another screen version of *Kid Boots* for Paramount, this one a talkie. Although the silent version was less than three years old, Paramount was going ahead with plans to spend between $750,000 and $1 million on a new *Boots*, this one presumably to be more faithful to the stage musical than was the first film. The production was scheduled to be filmed at Paramount's Astoria studios during the days, with shooting to be worked around Cantor's performances of *Whoopee*. Paramount was following essentially the same plan with the Marx Brothers, who were filming their previous hit *The Cocoanuts* during the day, while performing *Animal Crackers* on stage nightly.

Casting had been practically completed, sets had been designed, and Joseph Santley had been assigned to direct the film when Flo Ziegfeld put a stop to the proceedings. Ziegfeld stated that he would not allow his star to jeopardize his health—and *Whoopee*'s run—by undertaking the additional strain of another project, even though Cantor had posted a bond to offset any losses incurred by another illness.

It is ironic, when one considers the extra projects Cantor was already involved in, that Ziegfeld would draw the line with a talkie version of *Kid Boots*, unless, of course, the producer had other plans for his former hit property. A little more than a month after Ziegfeld nixed the *Boots* talkie, he announced he was entering into a 50-50 partnership with film producer Sam Goldwyn. Although the film version of *Whoopee* was their first announced project, it is more than probable that *Kid Boots* would follow in short order.

Paramount, believing it still held the film rights by virtue of its earlier contract with Ziegfeld, shelved its production until such time as Eddie Cantor would be available. When Cantor and Ziegfeld went west to work with Sam Goldwyn, Paramount announced it would go ahead with a talkie *Kid Boots* starring Jack Oakie instead of Cantor. Although they ran promotional ads for the Oakie *Boots*, the entire production was scrapped permanently when Paramount and Oakie had problems coming to terms on the film.

*Whoopee* ran on Broadway for forty-eight weeks, not including a two-week hiatus in July 1929. During most of its run, the show was the top ticket in New York, averaging well over $40,000 a week in that time. Although it was predicted to run as long as *Kid Boots* had, *Whoopee*'s life was cut short due to events, not on Broadway, but on Wall Street. The great October stock market crash wiped out many fortunes, including those of Eddie Cantor and Flo Ziegfeld. October 29, the day of the crash, found Ziegfeld in court all day for a petty case involving an electric sign. Although his broker had tried to reach the producer all day, Ziegfeld never got the frantic messages. He lost over $2 million.

To make matters worse, Ziegfeld had not had a real money-making hit since *Whoopee* opened almost a full year ago. While most producers would be more than satisfied with one hit a year, especially of the magnitude of a *Whoopee*, most producers were not Ziegfeld, who not only spent more per show, but of late had been producing more vehicles. The large losses for the refurbished *Midnight Frolics* and the disappointing returns for his first film venture, *Glorifying the American Girl*, were cause enough for concern, but when his major production of 1929, *Show Girl*, failed, it made Ziegfeld's market losses that much more devastating.

*Show Girl*, which opened in early July, was the vehicle which Ziegfeld had promised Ruby Keeler the previous autumn when she bolted from *Whoopee*'s cast. Although the show managed to top all competition (including *Whoopee*) in its premiere week, mainly on the strength of Ziegfeld's name, *Show Girl* slumped badly thereafter. By September, Ziegfeld was forced to offer tickets for *Show Girl* at half rates, something he long vowed he would never do on any of his shows. *Show Girl* closed in early October, without even attempting a run on the road.

While *Whoopee* was still packing them in, *Show Girl* represented an embarrassing loss for Ziegfeld. That fall, after a particularly strong week for *Whoopee* where up to one hundred standees were turned away at each performance, Ziegfeld mused over the show's success with Eddie.

"I don't know who's the draw," the producer pondered, "whether it's Cantor or Ziegfeld."

"Well," Eddie offered, "You saw what happened with *Show Girl*."

The Wall Street slump carried over to Broadway, where all shows experienced a downturn in box office, but *Whoopee* was still pulling in over $30,000 a week, a good figure for any other show. Unfortunately, *Whoopee* was not just "any other show." Given the expense of Ziegfeld's productions, the lower receipts made it impossible to turn a profit. Ziegfeld ordered the show on the road, where it would have a chance to pick up the slack.

*Whoopee* played a month in Boston, two weeks in Philadelphia, and six in Chicago before finishing up with brief visits to St. Louis and Cleveland, where the show finally closed. Although it was the biggest attraction in each city it played, the box office for *Whoopee* had to be less than Ziegfeld anticipated and obviously not as much as for previous Ziegfeld shows.

One of the reasons for the less-than-record-breaking business was probably the growth of talking pictures. By late 1929 almost all films were 100 percent talking, with one of the most popular genres being the "all-talking, all-singing, all-dancing" musical. With hard times coming, audiences were reluctant to shell out over $5 a ticket for a Ziegfeld extravaganza, when for a fraction of that they could see a reasonable facsimile from Hollywood.

The night *Whoopee* closed in Cleveland, Eddie Cantor boarded a train bound for the West Coast, where he would take up the next phase of his career, doing exactly what he had just finished doing on the stage.

Since the movie *Whoopee!* is essentially a filmed stage play, the description of *Whoopee*, the stage production, is included in the chapter on the movie.

## REVIEWS

Ziegfeld took this town by the hand this week and led it just where he wanted it to go. By the time "Whoopee" opened Tuesday (election) night he had the dailies and the taxpayers as interested in the premiere as they were in the Smith-Hoover thing.

Eddie Cantor works hard and goes over. He's on and off as often as he was in the last "Follies," more often than anybody else in the company. As the show stands now "I'm Bringing a Red, Red Rose" looks like the best song. The "Whoopee" number isn't so forte on the tune end but gives Cantor, who handles it, a chance to gag. — *Variety*, November 14, 1928, Pittsburgh opening

Mr. Cantor has never been so enjoyable a comedian. From the blackface singer of mammy songs, with a strong dash of Al Jolson in his style and an embarrassing devotion to soiled jesting, he has developed in "Whoopee" into a versatile and completely entertaining comic. — J. Brooks Atkinson, *New York Times*, December 5, 1928

Eddie Cantor in almost anything is worth $5 or $6, and with a glorified musical comedy like "Whoopee" the $6.60 scale is a bargain.

It's a show that has everything and should prove the "Abie's Irish Rose" of musical comedies, at least as far as longevity is concerned, if not plenitude of touring companies. For the show, despite its sterling ingredients, is all to the Cantor. Without that particular satellite it might be something else again. To pursue the parable, it's a musical that should appeal universally. — *Variety*, December 12, 1928

## Notes

1. Although Ziegfeld sent out a press release stating that he had paid Hammerstein $25,000 for Gregory's release, it is likely that the figure was inflated for publicity reasons.

2. Ziegfeld was supposedly also infatuated with Keeler, though his interest never developed into an affair.

3. Cantor did miss a few performances in November 1929 due to laryngitis. *Whoopee* remained open, however, with understudy Buddy Doyle filling in for Cantor.

4. David Warfield was rated as the richest actor, with between $10 and $12 million. Cantor, in second place, topped two veteran musical comedy rivals, Al Jolson ($4 million) and George M. Cohan ($3 million).

# CHAPTER 20

# *Sketch Book*

Since Eddie Cantor had returned to Flo Ziegfeld's employ in late 1923, the pair had enjoyed a close working friendship, although, like many friendships, theirs was tested from time to time by disagreements. In the summer of 1929, the producer and his star were once again at odds; as before, it was over another extracurricular project of Eddie's.

While Eddie Cantor was not restricted from writing material for other performers — a fact established back in 1917 — his latest foray into writing wasn't just an act, but a full review for one of Ziegfeld's rivals. Earl Carroll, the composer/playwright who had given Eddie's career a boost back in 1916 by casting him in *Canary Cottage*, had since added "Broadway producer" to his résumé. With his annual review, *Earl Carroll's Vanities*, Carroll had joined the list of would-be Ziegfelds who emulated the latter producer's *Follies* format. As was the case with his former employee, George White, producer of the *Follies* clone *Scandals*, Ziegfeld never considered Carroll and his *Vanities* serious competition.

In the spring of 1929, Earl Carroll decided to put on another review, this one to be designed as light entertainment for the upcoming summer season. He called it *Sketch Book* and announced the show's author to be none other than Eddie Cantor. Exactly how Cantor became the review's author is another case of two conflicting reports. According to *Variety*'s July 3, 1929, issue, Cantor's contributions to *Sketch Book* were bits he had first submitted to Flo Ziegfeld, presumably for use in an upcoming edition of the *Follies*, which never materialized.[1]

According to Cantor's recollection almost thirty years later in his second autobiography, *Take My Life*, Carroll first approached the comedian with the assignment of writing the review. "I wrote at night," Cantor wrote, "and brought him the show in about ten days." Whichever account is more accurate, it remains that Cantor wrote a good deal of the review, although not all of it. After Eddie submitted roughly five or six skits to Carroll, the producer hired a fleet of writers — although only one, Eddie Welch, was credited — to "punch up" and add "ginger" to Cantor's bits.

Since he was still performing nightly in *Whoopee*, Eddie had been unable to attend the Atlantic City tryouts of *Sketch Book*, although word started filtering back to New York about the review's saucy skits. When *Sketch Book* arrived in New York for its Broadway opening, a special rehearsal was called to allow Cantor to see what his original pieces had evolved into. Apparently Welch and his assistants added too much "ginger," for by the end of the rehearsal Cantor was demanding that Carroll tone down considerably the "blue" or "smut stuff." Carroll promised to clean up the show.

Cantor's concern was well founded, especially since his name was being exploited prominently in the advertising for *Sketch Book*, appearing before the cast and in larger type. In addition, Carroll was using large posters of Cantor outside the theater, another ploy to which Eddie objected.

If Eddie Cantor was upset by some of Earl Carroll's practices, Flo Ziegfeld was downright irate. In an attempt to minimize the effect of Carroll's advertising, Ziegfeld launched a campaign of his own which emphasized that *Whoopee* was the only show in which Eddie Cantor made a personal appearance. This announcement was made necessary due to the inclusion in *Sketch Book* of a Photophone talking short which featured Cantor and Earl Carroll.

The short, which was used at the opening of the show, was particularly irksome to the Great Ziegfeld. Not only did the film use his star—appearing in direct competition with himself in *Whoopee*—but it effectively added insult to injury by lampooning Ziegfeld. In the film, Cantor and Carroll are shown meeting to sign a contract for *Sketch Book*. A photo of Ziegfeld is prominently displayed on the wall of Carroll's office. The photo immediately falls off the wall when Eddie enters the room. After signing the contracts, Eddie shows Carroll the watch which Ziegfeld gave him. Not to be outdone, Carroll presents Cantor with a grandfather's clock. The film ends with Cantor singing "Legs, Legs, Legs," which the chorus picks up as the movie fades out.

The short had purposely been kept out of the Atlantic City tryouts, with Carroll preferring to keep the bit a Broadway surprise for his rival. Relations between Ziegfeld and Carroll had been strained since the previous year, when Carroll came backstage at the New Amsterdam in an attempt to lure some of Ziegfeld's glorified girls over to his own *Vanities*.

Ironically, for a good part of *Sketch Book*'s summer run, it was not in competition with *Whoopee*, since that show closed for the better part of July and the beginning of August. *Sketch Book* opened July 1 and did respectable business for a summer show of its type (light entertainment designed to fill the Broadway void while other shows were on hiatus and before the new fall season opened). Reviews were mixed.

## REVIEWS

There has been much ado about Eddie Cantor, who contributed five or six skits to the revue. Cantor is billed over all the featured players. . . .

"Sketch Book" has a number of rewritten stag stories which will get it talked about, has plenty of pretty girls, with very little on 'em, as little as any show of its type; it has laugh making comedy, playing strength in its cast, speed and stand-out dancing. That's plenty for a revue, even at $6.60.—Ibee, *Variety*, July 3, 1929

Just what Mr. Cantor's services have been in setting the literary tone of "Sketch Book" remains vexatiously obscure. The talking picture, which also includes an excellent photograph of Mr. Carroll's forensic prowess, shows Mr. Cantor reciting a vesper song entitled "Legs, Legs, Legs," whereupon the show picks up the theme and shakes a few. Otherwise the "Sketch Book" does not crackle with the familiar Cantor wit. Surely no one would wantonly ascribe to Mr. Cantor the black-out jests about unfaithful wives and lovers in the closet, which for generations have served the stage in all their besmattered mirthlessness, or the hotel bedroom shockers, or the humor with bathroom proclivities which distinguishes the second act of the show. The humor of the "Sketch Book" sketches is either bankrupt or quagmire. — J. Brooks Atkinson, *New York Times*, July 2, 1929

# *Note*

1. There were no editions of the *Follies* produced between 1927 and 1931.

# CHAPTER 21

# *Caught Short*

The Great Stock Market Crash of October 1929 had far reaching effects, on Broadway as well as on Wall Street. For some years, the fortunes of Manhattan's two most famous streets had been growing more and more intertwined. Not only did the big banks and brokerage houses start investing in, and eventually controlling, show business, but in the dizzying boom market of the late twenties, show people, as well as the rest of the population it seems, began playing the market in a big way.

One of the biggest investors was Eddie Cantor. Thanks to his childhood friend and financial adviser, Dan Lipsky, Cantor had not only built up a substantial investment portfolio, but had been introduced into the inner workings of Wall Street. Lipsky, himself, had worked his way up from stenographer to vice president of Manufacturers' Trust Company. When Dan started to handle Eddie's finances in the late teens, he introduced him to his boss, Nathan S. Jonas, president of Manufacturers' Trust. Together Jonas and Lipsky convinced Cantor to invest his hard-earned money in stocks, particularly those of Manufacturers' Trust.

As Cantor's wealth increased, so did his ties to Jonas. In his 1928 autobiography, Eddie spends long passages praising Jonas. The comedian and the banker had become so close that Cantor stated that Jonas and his wife had "become father and mother to me." Apparently, Mr. and Mrs. Jonas felt the same way about Eddie, calling him "our boy." When Cantor fell ill in Hollywood in 1927, the Jonases rushed across the continent to be near him. And when it came time to build a bigger home, Eddie's Great Neck mansion was built on a ten-acre plot adjoining Nathan Jonas' own fifty-six-acre estate. Jonas, also a philanthropist, advised Eddie on charitable matters as well.

Eventually, Eddie became one of the major stockholders of Manufacturers' Trust, acting as an unofficial adviser to the company on how to increase their business in the entertainment community. Finally, in 1928 Cantor was named to the company's official advisory board. Eddie not only advised Manufacturers' Trust but preached the doctrine of sound investment to his fellow actors, leading them back to the bank. Groucho Marx often told of how Eddie encouraged him to invest in the stock market, especially Goldman-Sachs, which Cantor himself had bought into heavily. On Eddie's urging, Groucho bought $500,000 worth of the stock. When the market crashed, he lost it all.

"I went to see his act one day," Groucho recalled, "and he told me what stock I should buy. It turned out to be the most expensive act I ever saw."[1]

In his 1928 autobiography, *My Life Is in Your Hands*, Cantor expounds on the security of investing in the stock market. In light of the events of the following year, his words now seem bitterly ironic. "A sense of growing security inspired me," Eddie wrote. "I was building my house upon a rock rather than public whim. For the fortunes of my career might vary and the day might come when I'd walk out on the stage and the audience would say, 'Cantor, you're through. Go home.' And I'd answer, 'O.K. We owe each other nothing.' I'd go home, sit in the parlor, and read my clippings, not from newspapers, but from bonds."

It was his substantial portfolio that made Cantor the second wealthiest actor in 1929 and gave him the impetus to announce his retirement from show business. Ironically, Eddie had his prediction backwards. Instead of stocks and bonds being his guarantee against the fickleness of audiences, it was his audience which remained faithful when the financial markets went south during the Depression.

When the market did crash on "Black Friday," October 28, 1929—leading *Variety* to proclaim in its now famous headline, "Wall St. Lays an Egg"—Eddie responded as a true comedian would; he kidded about it. Within days of the crash, Cantor was inserting ad-libs on the market into each performance of *Whoopee*. In less than two weeks, he assembled the jokes into book form, producing a pocket-sized, forty-five page opus entitled *Caught Short*. Written in a scant forty-eight hours, the book was published by Simon and Schuster, who sold *Caught Short*—subtitled *A Saga of Wailing Wall Street*—for $1 a copy.

*Caught Short* was an immediate novelty best-seller. Within a month, Eddie was approached by various studios who wanted a short film of Cantor reciting gags from the book. The best offer, however, came from Metro-Goldwyn-Mayer, which wanted to make a feature-length comedy of *Caught Short*, starring Marie Dressler and Polly Moran. Since *Caught Short* had no plot or characters, MGM was interested only in the rights to the title. Since MGM's offer called for more money and less effort than that of the other bidders, Cantor gladly sold them the rights for $10,000. The film went on to become a box office hit.

If MGM was so quick to part with $10,000 for just a title, perhaps other Hollywood studios would be willing to pay more if there was a plot to go with it. With this end in view, Cantor developed a brief idea for a broad comedy about the stock market crash. It was titled *Selling at Top*, and Eddie did just that when he sold the outline and title to Universal for $25,000. Although the *New York Times* reported that Eddie would write a book to be released concurrent with the motion picture, Universal never developed Cantor's outline into a film, and Eddie never published the book.

While Eddie Cantor managed to squeeze a dividend of jokes out of his stock market losses, as it turned out he survived the crash much better than some have believed. In December 1930, Dan Lipsky told the *New York Times* that although the value of Cantor's stock had declined considerably he was still solvent because he owned all of his stocks outright.[2] Lipsky made his comments in light of rumors that Eddie was selling his new Great Neck estate to shore up his financial situation. The estate was being put up for sale because Eddie and his family were at this point mainly residents of southern California, now that his film career had started to take off.

Although Cantor lost $2 million in the crash, he survived it and went on to become one of show business's prime authorities on finances and the economy throughout the Depression. He wrote many articles that were humorous in tone, but had the purpose of stirring his countrymen out of the economic morass and urging leaders to put aside partisan politics during the crisis. He set them a good example, scraping his plans to retire—made in boom times—and working even harder than before.

"I know that I'm doing three times as much work as I ever did before," Eddie told B. C. Forbes. When Forbes asked him if he was getting paid three times as much, Eddie laughed, "Three times? Half!"

In the same interview, Cantor went on to credit the stock market crash for giving him a renewed outlook on life. According to Eddie, he felt the 1920s prosperity had caused the quality of his work to slip. "If things had kept on going in the up-and-up, I probably would have gone on the down-and-down and been a has-been by now," Cantor said.

All in all, Eddie Cantor emerged from the crash less wealthy, but far wiser. "Understand, though I'm a fleeced lamb, I'm not bleating," he said. "They tell me I'm a better comedian than I was before, and I'm darn well sure that I'm a better philosopher than I was before."

# Notes

1. Three years later Eddie Cantor was among those who brought a stockholder's suit against Goldman-Sachs, charging the brokers with improper handling of funds. Reportedly, stocks that Cantor had paid approximately $330,000 for were now down to around $7,000.

2. Most investors, Flo Ziegfeld included, who were wiped out in the crash had purchased their stocks on as little as 10 percent margin.

# CHAPTER 22

# *Glorifying the American Girl*

Ironically, *Glorifying the American Girl*, Eddie Cantor's first appearance. in a full-length talking picture, albeit as a guest star, started out as a silent film. The project, which was to be Flo Ziegfeld's tribute to his typical *Follies* girl, was first proposed to Paramount back in 1926 and was to be a joint production of Ziegfeld and Jesse Lasky. A teaming of Ziegfeld and Paramount was only natural because they were already sharing the services of Ziegfeld's biggest star, Eddie Cantor, who at the time was at the studio's West Coast facilities making the screen version of Ziegfeld's biggest hit, *Kid Boots*.

As with any production that the Great Ziegfeld had a hand in, *Glorifying* was designed to be a cinematic extravaganza. With that in mind, Lasky announced in August that he had selected one of Paramount's top directors, the legendary Erich Von Stroheim, to bring to the screen the tale of an ordinary chorus girl's rise to Ziegfeldian "glorification." Lasky's announcement was the last concrete progress towards making the picture that would made for the next few years.

What followed was a lengthy process of vacillation over every phase of the film's preparation. First the directorial chores went around the horn from Von Stroheim to Harry D'Arrast to Mal St. Clair to nobody in particular. Then Paramount decided to shelve the project in an across the board move to put all such spectaculars on moratorium for at least six months.

Next, Paramount couldn't decide where to make the film and how large its budget should be. Originally the film was to have been made in New York, using actual theater locations. Paramount then decided it could save $100,000 by making it in Hollywood and faking the New York scenes. (They even considered using an ersatz Ziegfeld for the producer's short cameo.)

Not only the shooting location was undecided, but also the choice for the actress who would play the lead. If the production moved to the West Coast, then Clara Bow would be given the part; if it stayed in New York, then Louise Brooks would have it. Then in the fall of 1927, talkies burst forth, and the decision was made to make *Glorifying* a sound picture. (Ziegfeld wanted to rush the film out on the heels of the partial-talking *The Jazz Singer* and make it the first 100 percent sound film.)

Finally, in June 1928, after the studio had spent over $700,000 on various scripts, sets, and other expenses (including a hefty advance to Ziegfeld), Paramount announced that *Glorifying the American Girl* would be filmed in New York within the next year for release in the 1929-30 studio program. The film, which would be all-talking, would be a duplicate production of the *Ziegfeld Follies of 1928*, thereby keeping further cost to Paramount at a minimum. Such a film, like other early talkies based on Broadway properties which were essentially filmed plays, would be an invaluable document of theatrical history. Unfortunately, no *Follies of 1928* was ever produced, and therefore it could not be filmed. *Glorifying the American Girl* was pulled from Paramount's release schedule — even though advance publicity had been heralding its imminent arrival — and the project was again cast into cinematic limbo.

While Paramount procrastinated and Ziegfeld drew $1,000 a week from the studio for doing nothing (as per his contract), MGM released *The Broadway Melody*, a backstage musical story which took the country by storm and copped the Academy Award for best picture of 1928-29. Practically inventing the genre of the backstage film, *The Broadway Melody* spawned a rash of imitations, effectively taking whatever wind remained from the sails of *Glorifying the American Girl*. Although Ziegfeld had had the concept first, the multitude of production problems, coupled with MGM getting its film out first, had turned his original idea into one that was "old hat" by the time it finally reached the screen. Nevertheless, the success of *The Broadway Melody* probably helped to get *Glorifying* before the cameras, after a three-year wait, in the late spring of 1929.

By the time the film was finally shot, Eddie Cantor had for the past two years again been working for Flo Ziegfeld, who decided to grant Eddie "permission" to appear in the film, even though he was still performing in *Whoopee* on Broadway. Eddie's participation was limited to an onstage appearance in a short sketch. Ironically, after all the sketches Eddie had done over the years for Ziegfeld, the bit that was chosen for the film was "Joe's Blue Front," which he originally performed in Lee and J. J. Shubert's *Midnight Rounders*. Not titled in the credits (but now called the "Cheap Charlie" skit in the film's press releases), the bit included Cantor, along with Lew Hearn reprising his role as the customer. Taking the place of Joe Opp was Louis Sorin as Cantor's partner in the clothing shop.

In addition to his appearance in the sketch, which incidentally was the only comedy in the entire film, Eddie appeared briefly backstage talking to Mary Eaton's character. "They're a great audience," Eddie assures the newcomer. "I've got all my relatives out there . . . and a few gentiles too."

After an interesting opening sequence employing multitudes of girls superimposed over a map of the United States, all flocking to Broadway (supposedly for glorification by Ziegfeld), *Glorifying the American Girl* quickly settles into a rather dull rut. Not wanting to directly copy the plot of *The Broadway Melody*, the authors, J. P. McEvoy and Millard Webb (who also directed), changed the story enough to avoid making it a carbon copy, but not enough to make it interesting.

The plot revolves around Gloria Hughes (Mary Eaton), who is a song plugger at the sheet music counter of a New York department store. Her accompanist, Buddy (Edward Crandall), is in love with Gloria, and while she loves him too, she longs for a career in show business. After a prolonged company picnic scene which only serves to bog down the film even further, Gloria gets a job singing and dancing in vaudeville. On the road, Miller (Dan Healey) her partner/employer in the act, makes advances which Gloria quickly spurns, causing him to fire her. When a talent scout from Ziegfeld comes backstage to offer Gloria a contract, Miller intercepts the offer and signs Gloria to a five-year, 50-50 partnership deal.

Upon arriving back in New York, the team is turned down at their audition, but Gloria is taken. Miller reminds her that he gets half of her earnings. His contract is proven illegal, and Miller, the film's only villain, quickly disappears. On opening night just before the finale, Gloria receives a telegram telling her that Buddy has decided to marry her rival (Olive Shea). Gloria forces back the tears for the opulent closing number, and by the final close-up she smiles, secure in the knowledge that although she has lost her love, she has truly been glorified.

*Glorifying the American Girl* is interesting to watch today, but only for its historical glimpses into the production numbers and specialties of a Ziegfeld show. The film's show-within-a-show is also titled *Glorifying the American Girl* and includes Helen Morgan, singing "What I Wouldn't Do for That Man," Rudy Vallee and his theme song, "Vagabond Lover," Eddie Cantor in the aforementioned bit, and plenty of glorified chorus girls in spectacular costumes and settings. Ziegfeld himself and other dignitaries such as Adolph Zukor and Mayor Jimmy Walker are seen briefly in silent footage entering the theater while radio announcer Norman Brokenshire provides the narration from an obvious lobby mock-up.

Mary Eaton, while garnering good reviews at the time of the film's release, comes across rather stagy today, as does a majority of the cast. Her dancing is fine, but unfortunately much of her singing ability is lost by a combination of poor microphone placement and the marginal quality of early sound recording. Eddie Cantor, on the other hand, is very natural in his brief backstage part and hysterical, along with Lew Hearn, in the clothing store scene. It is no wonder that "Joe's Blue Front" was the hit of both *Midnight Rounders* and *Make It Snappy*, as the bit remains fresh and funny even after repeated viewings.

*Glorifying the American Girl* premiered in New York on January 10, 1930, almost four years after the project had been started. Most of the film's tremendous cost went into preproduction expenses. What was left of the budget can best be seen in the review portion of the film, especially in the lavish production numbers. Consequently, it was this portion of the movie that most reviews praised, while almost unanimously dismissing the story that led up to it. If the film had been released a few years earlier, it probably would have been a success. Released when it was, however, after a flood of similarly plotted musicals, it had little chance of recouping its exorbitant budget.

Prior to *Glorifying the American Girl*, Paramount executive Walter Wagner had been trying to convince Flo Ziegfeld to give up Broadway to become a film producer at the company's Astoria studios, while Universal and Fox were also reported to be after the producer with similar offers. After the disappointing results of *Glorifying*, such offers all but disappeared, leaving it the only film the great Broadway producer would ever supervise.[1]

Although available on video from smaller public domain companies, most available prints of *Glorifying the American Girl* do not include the two-strip Technicolor finale, which shows off Ziegfeld's elaborate costumes and settings to their best advantage. While most of the film is utterly forgettable, the final half hour is worthwhile for those interested in seeing one of the few surviving examples of a Ziegfeld show in the tradition of the *Follies*. For fans of Eddie Cantor, "Joe's Blue Front" alone is well worth the "price of admission."

## REVIEW

> Production values and names rather than plot, narrative, or humor will have to carry this one.... Revue scenes, added after the picture was finished, are highlighted by Eddie Cantor's clothing store skit, a laugh riot.... Promising much, it can hardly be denied that "Glorifying" fails to deliver full weight. Trade judgment would place the blame with the authors and the general confusion of the whole enterprise, with its three year history of change and postponement.
> — *Variety*, January 15, 1930

## *Notes*

1. Although Ziegfeld was listed as coproducer of *Whoopee!* along with Sam Goldwyn, the latter ran the production, leaving Ziegfeld little more than a figurehead.

# CHAPTER 23

# *The Short Subjects*

While it is now a widely accepted piece of Hollywood lore that the first talking picture was *The Jazz Singer*, this could not be further from the truth. That film, which, by the way, was mostly silent with some musical scenes and a few lines of dialogue, opened the floodgates of sound that eventually doomed the silent film, but sound films had been around almost as long as film itself. Thomas Edison, the inventor of the motion picture camera, originally envisioned the moving picture as a companion piece of equipment to his phonograph and thus created movies as an embellishment to recorded sound. Indeed, Edison aside, it was possible throughout the early years of the 1900s to watch sound films—with the soundtrack on a synchronized disc—in France and England. Most of these efforts, however, met with mixed results, due either to difficulties with the synchronization or problems with early attempts at electronic sound amplification.

By 1913, despite the fact that he was already a producer of silent films, Edison returned to his experiments of perfecting talking pictures. This is where Eddie Cantor enters the picture. According to Georgie Jessel, who at that time was appearing with Cantor in *Kid Kabaret*, he and Cantor appeared in Edison's experimental one-reel short, "Widow at the Races." Although he incorrectly remembers the test as having taken place in 1911 (for one thing Cantor was still with Bedin and Arthur then, for another Edison was between sound experiments at that time), Jessel recalls the incident as follows:

> My association with the cinema, talking and silent, goes way back. In 1911 Thomas A. Edison had an idea for talking pictures and the first experiments were tried at an uptown studio. Gus Edwards arranged to have Cantor, Truly Shattuck, a well-known prima donna, and me make the original tests. These tests were tried in a theatre, but were way out of synchronization, and that was the end of that.

That indeed was the end of that. *Variety* dismissed Edison's latest attempt, which included a few other shorts, with the headline "Talkers Flop." Seen today, it is easy to justify *Variety*'s verdict. It is difficult to ascertain whether these shorts are synchronized because they seem to have been filmed and recorded at a speed incompatible with lifelike reproduction. In

157

any event, realizing that their immediate future lay on the live stage, Cantor and Jessel went back to Gus Edwards to continue their success in *Kid Kabaret*. Eddie apparently, purposely or not, forgot the failure — which was more a reflection on Edison than on him and Jessel — while Jessel's recollection of the incident was confined to the four sentences above.

Cantor also neglected his second brush with the motion picture camera, which again was a short subject, and paradoxically, in the midst of the silent era, another experimental sound film. Unlike Eddie's previous foray into sound, this time the process involved the new technique of putting the soundtrack on the film next to the photograph, thus ensuring perfect synchronization. This breakthrough, dubbed "Phonofilms" by its inventor, Lee DeForest, would eventually become the chosen method for talking pictures, even though the talkie revolution would be ushered in by Warner Brothers' "Vitaphone" sound on disc method.

In late 1923 and early 1924, DeForest introduced his new invention via a series of one-reel short subjects starring a variety of stage stars, including the popular vaudeville team of Weber and Fields and, of course, Eddie Cantor. In the short entitled "A Few Moments with Eddie Cantor," Eddie (billed in the credits as the "star of *Kid Boots*") appears in a dimly lit empty set, wearing a normal business suit and a derby. Cantor immediately launches into a series of unrelated jokes, most of them painfully dated by today's standards. After a few minutes of stories, he delivers a rousing rendition of "The Dumber They Come, the Better I Like 'Em," in which he tells of the pleasures of dating slow-witted girls. After this, a few more minutes of yarns eventually leads to the second and closing song, "Oh, Gee Georgie."

The quality of the film is remarkably good, although the same cannot be said of Cantor's gag material. His songs, on the other hand, are delivered with his trademark enthusiasm, which made even the weakest tunes come to life. On the whole, "A Few Moments with Eddie Cantor" provides the earliest glimpse of Cantor on the cusp of the superstardom he would achieve in the mid–1920s. While DeForest's "Phonofilms" were obviously technically feasible, they, for a variety of reasons, never caught on and never progressed past the level of being a novelty.[1]

Although he had appeared in two early "talkers" (as they were then called, not "talkies"), when the medium finally established itself in 1927, Eddie Cantor shied away from it, getting into talking pictures to stay later than most of his contemporaries. By the autumn of 1926, while Cantor was in Hollywood making silents for Paramount, both Al Jolson and Georgie Jessel were appearing in early one-reel "talkers" for Vitaphone. In a way it's ironic that Cantor would wait so long to venture into this new medium, especially since he had appeared in the two earlier abortive sound ventures. Perhaps it was the relative failure of these earlier synchronized films that made Eddie Cantor wary of the medium's future.

In any event in August 1928, a little over a year after he had obtained a release from his previous Paramount contract, Cantor signed an agreement with that studio to do a sound short at their Astoria, Long Island, location. A clause was added to the film contract stating that the deal was "subject to permission of Ziegfeld," with whom Cantor had a new stage contract. Just prior to this, Eddie had been all set to appear in a sound feature for Paramount entitled *Burlesque*. The film, which would have been shot at Astoria while *Whoopee* was in rehearsal, never materialized because Ziegfeld refused to allow Cantor to undertake so large a project while preparing for his new Broadway musical.[2] Less than a year later, in April 1929, Ziegfeld put the kibosh on another proposed Cantor-Paramount feature, *Mister Broadway*.

Apparently Ziegfeld did not mind Cantor exerting the little energy necessary to complete a one-reeler (approximately ten minutes of screen time) because Eddie made one that fall before *Whoopee* left for its out-of-town opening in Pittsburgh. The short, "That Certain Party," opened in early November 1928, about the same time as *Whoopee*'s stage premiere.

Like the Phonofilm one-reeler made five years earlier, and in fact like almost all of the remaining shorts he would complete for Paramount, "That Certain Party" features Eddie Cantor filling nine minutes of screen time with two songs separated by a selection of jokes. The first Paramount short opens with Cantor in a phone booth on the line to the studio. After haggling over his salary, Eddie emerges and sings "Hungry Women," then does four more minutes of gags before closing with "That Certain Party," which he does with the aid of Bobby Arnst, a curvaceous young woman, who helps illustrate the song's lyrics.

Although "That Certain Party" was well received by audiences and critics, apparently Cantor was too busy with *Whoopee* to make an immediate follow-up to his debut short. His next short, this time a two-reeler released in March 1929, was entitled "Midnite Frolics" and was essentially a filmed version of the routine he performed on the New Amsterdam Roof. Unfortunately, the awkwardness of the early sound equipment prevented the short from being shot on the Amsterdam Roof. A set approximating it — complete with an audience of Broadway notables including Richard Dix, Oscar Shaw, and Peggy Hopkins Joyce — was built at the Astoria studios. While not the genuine location, the set was still elaborate enough to recapture the atmosphere of Ziegfeld's famed New Amsterdam Roof.

Cantor's occasional short subjects were heavily promoted by Paramount, but they were not produced on anything even closely resembling a regular schedule. The Astoria studios were available to Eddie any time he had an idea or a desire to produce a one-reeler. Consequently many were done on a whim, based solely on the germ of an idea that the comedian padded out to nine minutes with a few related stories and a couple of songs. Still, while these shorts often have a slapdash appearance, they also have a spontaneous charm and probably give a fairly good example of Cantor's specialty acts in the *Follies* and *Frolics*.

After the film version of "Midnite Frolics," Cantor, busy with *Whoopee*, was a stranger to Paramount's Long Island digs. *Variety* reported in late November 1929 that Eddie had completed a short called "The Vamp," though no subsequent review was printed. (*Variety* regularly reviewed shorts as well as the more important feature films.) Research has also failed to unearth a copy or even a mention of "The Vamp," leading to the conclusion that it was lost or was retitled and issued under another name or was never made, despite the show business bible's assertion to the contrary.

Eddie's next Paramount short surfaced in February 1930. "Getting a Ticket," though only eleven minutes long, is probably the closest any of his shorts get to having a cohesive plot. The skit opens in court, where Cantor and a young lady are accused of necking in a parked car. The case is dismissed when Eddie produces a marriage license proving the woman is his wife. Outside the courtroom the arresting officer apologizes, saying he didn't know the woman was Eddie's wife. "I didn't either," Cantor confesses, "until you flashed the light on her face." Later Eddie is stopped by the same cop, and in an attempt to duck a ticket, sings a peppy version of "My Wife Is on a Diet." Despite having proven himself a celebrity, Eddie is given the summons.

While *Variety* noted that the short was similar to Jimmy Hussey's vaudeville act, the skit, particularly the second half, is based on an incident from more than a decade earlier when Cantor gave an impromptu roadside concert to a traffic cop.

"Insurance," Eddie's next one-reeler released in June 1930, had the distinction of being completed in less than two hours. It is not surprising that the film was completed so quickly since the short was a pastiche of every old doctor joke that Cantor had performed in vaudeville and various reviews down through the years. Eddie enters a physician's office for an insurance exam and quickly frustrates the doctor with a series of mysterious complaints and diseases. "Insurance" closes with the delightful "Now That the Girls Are Wearing Long Dresses," sung by Cantor to the doctor and an attending nurse.

Ironically, since it was originally seen as the first in a series of films, "Cockeyed News," released one month after "Insurance," was Eddie Cantor's final short for Paramount. Written in fifteen minutes by Cantor, the four-minute film was a parody of newsreels. Under the slogan of "Once Monthly ... Sees Nothing ... Hears Nothing ... Knows Nothing," the "Cockeyed News" strove to present absurd jokes as offbeat news items. One of the stories features a farmer winning a loving cup at the county fair for growing the largest corn; the camera then pans down to reveal an oversized bunion on the man's foot. Another item, narrated by Cantor as "Tag Day in Scotland," is illustrated by a shot of a vacant street. The corny material (even for that day), coupled with Eddie's new feature contract with Sam Goldwyn, helped to turn "Cockeyed News" from "once monthly" to "once only."

# REVIEWS

### "That Certain Party"

Seeing Cantor on the screen and watching those eyes, listening to his chatter, song and mimicry, one feels the kid himself is in the flesh. He times his songs, chatter and even his facial movements in such a way that value is gotten out of every inch of film shot. — *Variety*, November 14, 1928

### "Getting a Ticket"

Cantor in whiteface, at ease and at his best. A corking good short. The Cantor name will sell it in the first place and the short will sell itself in the second. — *Variety*, February 5, 1930

### "Insurance"

No vaude house hasn't been hearing for the past three or four years the ones from the coffee and cakers that Eddie pulls in this. Listening to a Rivoli audience laugh every other minute, however, would belie any suggestion of this being a floppo, even though an antique thematically. Apparently Eddie can get as stale as he likes and still they like him.

The insurance doctor does with Eddie all of those things that are so well known, even so well established that folks were giving the answers before Eddie, and then shaking heartily when he substantiated them. — *Variety*, June 25, 1930

### "Cockeyed News"

Means a collection of semi-punning gags with the caption playing the straight to start with.

A derivation of a similar short once employed for some time, long ago, without sound, in vaudeville by Jack Norworth. — *Variety*, July 9, 1930

# *Notes*

1. For a more complete essay on the development of sound films and their ultimate triumph over silents, see the first chapter of *The Silent Clowns*, by Walter Kerr.

2. It was rumored that comedian Joe E. Brown would take over the role slated for Cantor in *Burlesque*, but nothing ever came of it, and the project was dropped.

# CHAPTER 24

# *Whoopee! (Film)*

The stock market crash of 1929 left Florenz Ziegfeld a broke and broken man. Although he had suffered career setbacks in the past, at age sixty-two the Wall Street debacle found him unable to start all over again. To make matters worse for the producer, the world of show business, which he had been so instrumental in forging, was changing rapidly. It was no longer the pinnacle of a performer's career to work on Broadway in a Ziegfeld show.

With the advent of talking pictures, Hollywood was fast replacing Broadway as the mecca for actors and actresses. In the era of the silent film, the movies were fine for performers well versed in pantomime, but the "serious" well-rounded actor and actress (those who could talk as well as mime) usually sought to make his or her mark in New York. After *The Jazz Singer*, and the "talkers" that followed, all bets were off.

All-singing, all-talking productions of hit Broadway musicals flooded the market as Al Jolson, the Marx Brothers, Fanny Brice, Georgie Jessel, and others brought such proven properties as *Big Boy*, *The Cocoanuts*, and *Little Johnny Jones* to the screen. Ziegfeld had already sold the screen rights to *Sally*, *Show Boat*, *Rosalie*, and *Rio Rita*, all to different studios, when he signed a contract with independent producer Sam Goldwyn for the screen rights to the smash Eddie Cantor musical *Whoopee*. Although he had been approached by Paramount in regards to the rights to *Whoopee*, Ziegfeld opted to work with an independent producer, possibly to avoid the difficulties of working with a big studio (like those he had presently been encountering with Paramount over the interminable production of *Glorifying the American Girl*).[1]

Under the terms of their agreement, the film would be a "Ziegfeld-Goldwyn" production, the first, it was reported, of many, including Cantor's other Ziegfeld musical *Kid Boots* and Zieggy's *Simple Simon*, which was currently running on Broadway with Ed Wynn in the title role. While Ziegfeld had previously only sold the rights to his properties, the deal with Goldwyn presented an opportunity to get into films with a partner with whom he felt more comfortable. Working in tandem with Goldwyn, who incidentally was a great admirer of Ziegfeld, would allow the latter to produce films in much the same style he had produced stage shows — first class. For Goldwyn, the deal would link him with the greatest name in show business, one which would instantly add some of the refinement to his productions (and himself) which, though he personally did not possess, he understood, appreciated, and craved.

Goldwyn, born Schmuel Gelbfisz in Poland, had fought his way up the ladder of success in America, first in the glove trade, then in the motion picture business. One of the founders of Famous Players–Lasky — along with Jesse Lasky (who also happened to be his brother-in-law) and director Cecil B. DeMille — Goldwyn found himself edged out of the company when Lasky and Adolph Zukor merged to form what would become Paramount Pictures.

Undaunted, Goldwyn, who was then called Goldfish, formed a partnership with theatrical producers Archie and Edgar Selwyn. The new business, which would produce movies, combined the partners names, creating Goldwyn studios. Goldfish soon took the new company name for his own. Within less than seven years, however, Goldwyn again found himself voted out of a company he had helped to create. Two years later, in 1924, the Goldwyn studios merged with Metro and Louis B. Mayer to become Metro-Goldwyn-Mayer, a company to which Goldwyn contributed nothing but his adopted name. Undeterred, Goldwyn decided to forgo any more partnerships and released the future films he would produce under the simple banner "Samuel Goldwyn Presents."

In the next seven years, Goldwyn built his latest company one film at a time, striving for quality over quantity, lavishing his full attention on each film. Although he was not nearly as polished as Flo Ziegfeld, Goldwyn did possess the necessary showmanship to build a profitable company around his two mainstay stars, Ronald Coleman and Vilma Banky. With the coming of sound, Coleman's rich English voice added to his abilities as a screen actor and his bankability as a star. Banky, on the other hand, with her thick Hungarian accent, did not fare nearly as well and was soon dropped by Goldwyn. In search of another star around whom to build his personal productions, Goldwyn, as many of his fellow film producers had done, looked to Broadway. Specifically, in Goldwyn's case, to Eddie Cantor.

In seeking Cantor's services and the film rights to *Whoopee*, Goldwyn was doubly defying the prevailing Hollywood wisdom. For the first three years of "talkers," the primary product had been musicals. Good or bad (mostly bad, especially by modern standards), the public wanted its entertainment not only to talk, but to sing and dance as well. By late 1929, given the flood of film musicals, the novelty had worn off, and some theaters were actually promoting movies for their lack of music.

Secondly, for various reasons, many in the film industry viewed Eddie Cantor as a stage star only. He had already been tried by Hollywood — in *Kid Boots* and *Special Delivery* — and had been found wanting.[2] True, he had already appeared in numerous talking shorts and in *Glorifying the American Girl*, but these were seen as brief novelty bits and not an indication that

Eddie could carry a talking feature film. In addition, as A. Scott Berg points out in his extensive biography of Samuel Goldwyn, Cantor appealed to the largely Jewish audience of New York, but it was unlikely that the nationwide public would take to "so overtly Jewish a performer," a perceived drawback which would only be amplified when Cantor could be heard in addition to being seen.[3]

Despite these caution signs, Goldwyn saw gold to be mined from the proven story of a hypochondriac out in the hills of the Wild West. The film producer was so convinced that *Whoopee* and Cantor would be a hit that he was willing to pour $1.3 million into the film at a time when the average movie musical cost between $250,000 and $350,000 to produce. Not wanting the typical filmed version of a hit stage production — as the Marx Brothers' *The Cocoanuts* had been — Goldwyn convinced Ziegfeld that the story, set in the West, could be more effectively staged out in Hollywood, where they had "greater experience, top technicians, and the natural scenery (horses and Indians)" than on Long Island. Years later Eddie recalled Goldwyn telling Ziegfeld, "Zieggy, the facilities are so good in Hollywood. For instance, you have that Indian scene. We can get our Indians right from the reservoir!"

Ziegfeld agreed with Goldwyn, especially since his new partner was footing the bill for the production. Under the Ziegfeld and Goldwyn production agreement, the cash-starved Ziegfeld was paid for the rights to *Whoopee*, given a salary under the title of "coproducer," and was cut in for 20 percent of the film's profits.

Eddie Cantor was sold on Sam Goldwyn for other reasons. "He talked with complete confidence and know-how," Cantor remembered in *Take My Life*. "He was Ziegfeld's equal — the first man I'd known who was — a member of United Artists, selling exhibitors Chaplin, Pickford, Fairbanks. A man is known by the company he keeps, also a man is known by the company that keeps him; and I made up my mind that if I was going into talkies, this Goldwyn was for me."

Contracts for *Whoopee!* (the film version was set apart from the stage version by an exclamation point on the end of the title) were signed in December 1929, with production slated to begin in Hollywood the following spring after the completion of the show's road tour. On his departure for the West Coast in March 1930, Eddie wrote a short humorous piece for the *New York Times* explaining his reasons for leaving the stage in favor of films. He cited the stock market crash and the need to accommodate his relatives:

"With the abundance of relatives that I have found in the past few years, it has been a financial impossibility to send them all tickets, and so in putting *Whoopee* on the screen it will solve my problems of relativity."

Ironically, Cantor pointed out, he had always wanted to leave the stage because he didn't care to have anyone be boss over him. Now as a film actor he had two bosses — Ziegfeld and Goldwyn.

Unfortunately, Ziegfeld and Goldwyn did not find any humor in their new partnership. From the start the two master showmen argued over every phase of the production even though each needed the other's expertise, what with Goldwyn being new to musicals, while Ziegfeld had little film experience outside of the debacle of *Glorifying the American Girl*. With the Great Ziegfeld only a shadow of his former self and working in unfamiliar surroundings three thousand miles from his base of operations, Goldwyn managed to prevail in most of their disputes.

The production of *Whoopee!* was divided into five separate units: motion picture, art, dance, music, and costumes, each with its own director. The various directors would meet daily with Goldwyn to discuss the progress and problems of the preproduction schedule. Ziegfeld was allowed little say in the proceedings, and soon many arguments ensued. Eventually the strain of being a fifth wheel was too much for Ziegfeld, who was forced, under doctor's orders, to retreat to Florida for his health. This didn't stop the Ziegfeld-Goldwyn bickering, however; it only forced it to be carried out via Zieggy's favorite form of communication—lengthy telegrams.

One particular area of contention between the coproducers was the script. Goldwyn's writers, used to movies—until recently silent ones at that— tried to make sense out of the often nonsensical plotting of musical comedy. Ziegfeld, on the other hand, was used to wielding musical numbers to showcase gorgeous women in opulent costumes, with little or no regard to the plot. The screenplay writers attempted to make each song flow rationally from their script, an impossible task, especially when one tried to give sane motivation for a group of rough and tumble cowboys to break out into spontaneous song.[4]

The writers' attempts infuriated Ziegfeld, who complained through Western Union to his cinematic partner: "When they get all through, they have motivated everything that was any good in the show right out of it and all they have left is moving picture technique."

The screenplay also left Eddie Cantor with reservations, and he demanded that he too have a hand in the writing of his talking feature debut. In a move that suggested that Goldwyn respected the demands of his star more than those of his partner, the writers were dispatched to Chicago, where Cantor was touring with the stage version. Goldwyn himself even stopped off on his return from Europe to confer with Cantor. Goldwyn's wife Frances, according to Joe Franklin, was quite taken with Cantor's looks, though she was unfamiliar with his work and at first she assumed that her husband's new star had been signed as a leading man (a role which Eddie himself would seek in future pictures made for Goldwyn).

Aside from talking with Cantor, Goldwyn also arranged for his director, Thornton Freeland, to travel with the stage show in order to "get saturated with the material." In addition, Goldwyn ordered Freeland to direct a series of silent screen tests of all the female members of the cast to see which girls would be brought to Hollywood for use in the film version. Evidently, whether or not the men in the show were photogenic was of little concern to the producer or his director.

While Goldwyn may have picked the chorus girls for the film, it was up to a newcomer to Hollywood to choreograph their movements. Young Busby Berkley was hired, at Eddie Cantor's suggestion, to act as dance director on *Whoopee!* Up until this time Berkley, who was born William Enos, had danced in several Broadway shows and directed various other productions. Cantor had seen Berkley's work in a show called *Fine and Dandy* and had decided that his style showed "a great flair for design and a real picture eye."

On the night *Whoopee* concluded its road tour in Cleveland, Cantor took Berkley to a Child's restaurant, where the dance director mapped out his ideas for the film's major musical numbers on the back of a menu. The film's choreography presented unique problems to the stage-experienced Berkley. Whereas a line of chorus girls stretching across a stage could thrill an audience, the same line squeezed into the frame of a motion picture screen would appear almost the same size as a line of match sticks.[5] Berkley rose to the challenge and in the process revolutionized the movie musical.

Soon after *Whoopee*'s closing, Eddie Cantor and his family boarded the train to Hollywood, accompanied by Berkley, Thorton Freeland, and screenwriter William Conselman. Cantor, Berkley, Freeland, and Conselman used their travel time to further adapt and refine *Whoopee* for the screen. Upon their arrival on the West Coast, the Cantors were given a rousing welcome by Sam Goldwyn and members of the George Olsen Band. Eddie took the occasion to announce that, true to his announcement of the previous year, he was indeed retiring—from the legitimate stage.

"This is a permanent retirement," Eddie told the press. "Playing six evenings and two matinees a week is too hard for me. I want more leisure— and more freedom. If *Whoopee* gets across, I'll stay on and make other talkies. Otherwise," he added, "I'll probably go into vaudeville."

Although he would eventually go back to the stage, and even find time to go back into vaudeville, Eddie Cantor's primary concern in the spring of 1930 was "getting across" the film adaptation of *Whoopee*. While he and the various teams of writers and directors had been busily working on the book, one aspect of the hit show, the musical score, was not adapted, rather it was totally discarded. As was the prevailing practice in the thirties for Broadway musicals purchased for the screen, producers often threw away the less important songs—that is, those that weren't big hits—keeping only the bare bones of the original program. In this way a cagey producer could not only avoid paying royalties to the show's original music publishing house, in *Whoopee*'s case Walter Donaldson Music, but produce an new raft of potential hits for their own publishing concern.

For the screen version of *Whoopee*, only the irreplaceable title tune, "Makin' Whoopee," survived the transition from Broadway to Hollywood. The remainder of the score, including the hit "Love Me or Leave Me," was ignored. Ironically, the men Goldwyn hired to create the film's score, Walter Donaldson and Gus Kahn, were the same team whose stage score had just been thrown out.

Donaldson and Kahn arrived in Hollywood in late March 1930 to begin work on the new score, but had a hard time getting together to work. The primary obstacle was Donaldson's mania for golf, which was exacerbated by the abundance of courses in southern California. Once, after filming had already begun, Goldwyn informed his songwriters they needed a new number for Eddie Cantor. After what he considered a reasonable amount of time, the producer asked Kahn for the new song. The lyricist explained that he was waiting on Donaldson to furnish him with the melody.

Finally, after a considerable wait, with a production delay threatening, Goldwyn demanded the song that afternoon. Kahn rushed out and grabbed Donaldson off a local links and dragged him back to their office at the studio. With Goldwyn and Cantor watching, the songwriters banged out a number, improvising as they went.

Goldwyn, naturally looking for a hit, asked if the song was any good for dancing. The pair assured him it was. As Donaldson started playing it again, Goldwyn—in order to test the tune himself—grabbed Kahn in his arms and started dancing around the office with the diminutive lyricist.

"It was quite a picture," Cantor later recounted. "Big six-foot Sam and little Gus bobbing along at chest level."

The song, "My Baby Just Cares for Me," sung by Cantor, turned out to be the best number in the film and a hit.

The interior shooting—which accounts for over 90 percent of *Whoopee!* —was done at the United Artists' studios at Formosa Avenue and Santa Monica Boulevard in Hollywood.[6] Strangely enough, since Sam Goldwyn had boasted of the abundance of western locations, very little of the picture was shot outdoors. What location filming there was, was done in the desert around Palm Springs.

Although the shooting schedule ran smoothly, it did not start out that way. On the first morning in Palm Springs, Eleanor Hunt, who was getting her first starring film role in the part of Sally Morgan, presented Eddie Cantor with a gift. Hunt, as Cantor recalled, "came rushing up with a hundred poppies in her arms and presented them to 'my leading man,'—me! Freeland almost fainted!"

The director's anxiety was well founded. In order to provide a colorful exterior backdrop for the Technicolor process, Thornton Freeland had the stagehands out early in the morning planting hundreds of desert flowers— poppies to be exact. After Hunt presented the flowers to Cantor, Cantor presented them back to Freeland for replanting. Ironically, the number which the poppies had been planted for, "Come West Little Girl," was eventually scrapped.

All exterior work—not just poppy planting—had to be accomplished in the early morning since the Mojave heat made shooting past 11:00 A.M. impossible. Back in Hollywood, conditions for the interior shots were not much better because of the extra lighting required for the early Technicolor film. Powerful arc lights kept the soundstage temperatures hovering around 110 degrees and forced the filming to be completed in segments no longer than a few minutes at a time. It is a testament to all Cantor's claims of being the apostle of pep that his performance contained the vitality it did.

In spite of the difficulties presented him, Freeland managed to complete *Whoopee!* in just forty-three days.[7] Cantor attributes the short filming time to the fact that most of the cast was so familiar with the story. He later recalled that for him personally, recreating the part of Henry Williams seemed an "almost effortless job" and was the role he liked best.

In addition to, and probably because of, wrapping up the filming so quickly, Freeland also managed to bring *Whoopee!* in at $150,000 under the original budget of $1.5 million (up from Goldwyn's original estimate of $1.3 million). Even with Freeland saving 10 percent, *Whoopee!* was one of the most costly productions of its day, much of the expense coming from the use of Technicolor — which not only required more expensive film, but three full-time technicians to act as advisers — and the extravagant tastes of Flo Ziegfeld.

Ziegfeld, though banished from most of the production decisions, still managed to spend extraordinary amounts of money on one of his pet indulgences — women's costumes. Thus, under Ziegfeld's direction, ordinary chorus girls were outfitted with hand-beaded moccasins, and one-of-a-kind dresses, some of which cost as much as $1,200.

Although the hand-beading on the moccasins is not evident, the overall expense lavished on the film is obvious — even sixty years after its initial release. Though filmed three thousand miles from Broadway, *Whoopee!* is probably the best filmed record of the opulence of a Ziegfeld show, even more so than *Glorifying the American Girl*, which Ziegfeld himself produced. Some of the credit for this must go to Sam Goldwyn; after all, it was his money Zieggy was spending. But Goldwyn did more than just open his checkbook to the New York producer, he understood Ziegfeld's style — more so than the heads of Paramount with whom Ziegfeld had had to contend on his previous film venture.

*Whoopee!* opens with Sam Goldwyn's promised desert, complete with cowboys and cowgirls thundering down the range, whooping and waving as they go. This brief exterior soon gives way, however, to one of the interior sets, which, though colorful and full of Western flavor, are obviously inside a soundstage. Although the film is essentially a filmed play, it is not the sets or production values which give this fact away. If anything, the film's staginess is emphasized by the actors and actresses, most veterans of the Broadway production, who deliver their lines in loud stage voices, complete with broad stage gestures. However, this in itself does not ruin the film by any means, especially because many early talkies were hobbled by the same dramatic technique. With this in mind, it is not surprising that the finest moments of *Whoopee!* lie in its musical numbers choreographed by Busby Berkley.

The film's opening number, "The Lassie Who Lassoed Your Heart," shows Berkley hitting the ground running with his first crack at a movie musical routine. The song, delivered by a fifteen-year-old Betty Grable accompanied by the chorus, is a bouncy Donaldson-Kahn creation which features many of the tricks — overhead shots, human geometric patterns, and precision formations — which would soon be recognized as Berkley trademarks.

After being introduced briefly to the plot — the cowboys and girls have converged on a desert mission to attend the wedding of Sally Morgan and Sheriff Bob Wells — we are introduced to the bespectacled Henry Williams (Eddie Cantor), a hypochondriac who has gone west in search of his health. Henry's condition is so acute that his full-time nurse, Miss Custer (Ethel Shutta), explains to one cowboy, "He's so full of pills they can't operate on him — he keeps rolling off the table."

Henry enters with a calf in tow. When his nurse asks what it's for, Henry replies, "Condensed milk."

When Miss Custer urges Henry to give up the calf, he tells her he'd be lonesome without it. Having fallen in love with her patient, she offers to take the bovine's place in his heart. "I'd feel safer with the calf," Henry tells her.

Miss Custer tries to dispel Henry's hypochondria by telling him his maladies are imaginary. "The doctors say your lungs are practically brand new," she states.

"They should be," Henry exclaims, "I never use them. For ten years I've been breathing with my liver."

Hoping to cure Henry with love, Miss Custer starts to make advances on her charge. Putting her arms around him, she coos, "Doesn't this suggest something to you?"

"Yes, it does," he whimpers. "But with my health I better not think about it."

Miss Custer confesses that she has a positive passion for a weak man. "I suppose if I was paralyzed you'd be cuckoo over me," Henry reasons.

Finally, Miss Custer reasons that Henry must really love her after all because he's breathing heavily.

"That's not love, you fool," he wheezes. "That's my asthma!"

Meanwhile, outside, Wanenis, who is half Indian, returns to the mission, accompanied by his father, Chief Black Eagle. Wanenis and Sally had been in love, but Sally's father refused to allow his daughter to marry an Indian. Upon discovering that today is Sally's wedding day, Wanenis rushes to see her. Wanenis sings her the film's love theme, "I'll Still Belong to You," after which they pledge each other their undying love, though Sally will still marry Bob Wells according to her father's wishes.

After a run-in with the sheriff/bridegroom, Wanenis unites with Henry, who cheers him up by telling him his own problems. "Last week I looked so terrible," Henry explains, "two undertakers left deposits on me."

Wanenis contends that his troubles are worse. "I lost the girl I love, and my heart is very heavy today."

"Your heart is heavy?" Henry interrupts. "My heart is five times the normal size."

Wanenis relates that his problems are due to the fact that he is a half-breed. Henry admits that he is a half-breed also because he only breathes through half his nose. Wanenis explains that despite his Indian heritage, he has tried to follow the white man's ways. "For this girl I love," he tells Henry, "I've studied the ways of your race. Why, I gone to your schools."

"An Indian in a Hebrew school," Henry exclaims.

Henry is advising Wanenis not to let a woman push him around when Miss Custer enters and chases Henry away as the scene fades out.

Next, defying the logic of Sam Goldwyn's writers, Henry comes out accompanied by a group of bridesmaids and sings the film's title song, "Makin' Whoopee." Although the song has lived on beyond most people's memory of its show or the star who made it famous, the number remains one of Eddie Cantor's greatest hits. Back in the late twenties and early thirties, the song was so strongly associated with Cantor that once, while visiting England, Eddie was stopped by Winston Churchill and complimented on his many hits, especially "Makin' Whoopee." To prove his admiration of Cantor and the song, the future prime minister insisted on performing some of the song's more obscure choruses right there as Cantor listened.

After "Makin' Whoopee," Henry finds Sally preparing to run away. She asks him to drive her to another town, where she assures him that Bob Wells is waiting for her. Believing Sally's phony elopement story, Henry helps spirit her away.

The wedding begins but quickly comes to a halt when it is discovered that the bride is missing. A note from Sally soon reveals that she has eloped— with Henry. Bob Wells forms a posse and vows to track down Henry and hang him. (In one of the films funniest lines, yet presumably unintentionally so, Bob Wells tells his deputies, "You know what we do to a critter who steals a horse . . . well, this one just stole my woman!")

Meanwhile, Henry's car has broken down on a deserted mountain pass. Sally asks Henry if he has any gas. "Have I got gas?" Henry asks rhetorically. "The way I suffer?"

Henry quickly discovers that while he may have too much gas, his Model T is out of fuel. Sally scolds him for not carrying extra gas, while Henry, feeling faint, sits down on the running board and takes his temperature.

"I haven't any more circulation than a herring," he announces after reading the thermometer. "Here you are bawling me out and my temperature drops to normal."

To make matters worse, Sally confesses that Henry isn't taking her to Sheriff Bob Wells, but away from him. Furthermore, she explains that Wells thinks she and Henry are eloping.

"I wish I were dead," Henry groans. Sally informs him that he'll get his wish as soon as the sheriff catches up with him.

"I don't want to die from Bob Wells," he tells her. "I want to die from my sicknesses. I want to die in bed. And I want doctors, and nurses, and flowers, and a little fruit."

Sally suggests that they run back east and get married.

"We wouldn't have to be man and wife," she tells him. "Secretly we could be just good friends."

"Yeah," Henry says, rolling his eyes, "but I can't keep a secret."

Sally insists that Henry is joking because he's never really been in love. Henry denies this and sings a comical yet bittersweet ballad, "A Girl Friend of a Boy Friend of Mine," about a prior love affair that went awry and supposedly ruined his health, when his best friend stole his girl.

Following Henry's musical confession, Sally suggests they lie down and go to sleep. Any chance for a peaceful night is ruined, however, when a Lincoln touring car comes round the bend. The car's passengers, the rich Mr. Underwood (Spencer Charters), his grown children, and chauffeur demand Henry move his "flivver" so they can continue. Henry explains his predicament and asks to borrow some gas, but Underwood refuses.

Finally, Sally solves the impasse by handing Henry a gun. Now armed, Henry forces the Underwoods out of their car and steals the needed fuel. As a bandit, Henry wavers between bravado and hypochondria, especially when Underwood, who is also a hypochondriac, complains of the toll the incident is taking on him.

The scene is very funny, especially the byplay between Cantor and Charters, who evidently had honed the bit to a fine edge after doing their various routines together for over a year on the stage.

To ensure his captives' compliance, Henry tells them that he has an armed partner, Morris, hidden up on the cliff. When they question his claim, Henry proves Morris' existence by engaging in some small talk, ventriloquistically speaking, with his invisible friend. After emptying the air from the Lincoln's tires, Henry orders Underwood to crank their flivver, and he and Sally make a hasty retreat down the mountain.

The next morning Henry and Sally arrive at a ranch belonging to Underwood. With the ranch in desperate need of a cook, Henry is pressed into service at gun point and is told to fix breakfast. When he asks what to cook, the hand tells him that "a waf-el would hit me right."

"All right," Henry agrees, "I'll hit you with a waf-el."

After the hand exits, Sally emphasizes the trouble they are in, aside from running away from the sheriff.

"We've committed highway robbery," she tells Henry. "We could go to prison."

Henry asks if they have doctors in prison, and when Sally assures him they do, he breathes a sigh of relief, "I'll be all right, I'll get along."

Sally insists they could get twenty years. Henry laughs, "the jokes on them. I can't live more than six months."

Sally exits, leaving Henry to concoct the "waf-els," which he makes from a variety of items in the kitchen, including eggs (with the shells), bananas (skins included), dog biscuits, ketchup, and a box of Epsom salts. Before he can finish his recipe, however, Miss Custer, disguised as a cowboy, enters with a wanted poster offering a $500 reward for Henry.

When she questions Henry, he adopts a thick Mediterranean accent and proclaims, "Me Greek. I fix you up . . . one roast beef . . . one buttered toast . . . one strawberry pie . . . one fried 'hegg."

After Henry reveals his true identity, Miss Custer insists that he ran away because he loved Sally Morgan. When Henry vehemently denies this, Miss Custer, still in her disguise, begins to smother him in kisses. "Hey! What kind of cowboy are you?" Henry wonders before she unmasks herself.

She informs Henry that the sheriff will soon be there, but promises to protect him, that is, until Sally walks in. In a fit of jealous rage Miss Custer lays Henry out with a good right cross and storms out.

Underwood arrives and remarkably fails to recognize that his new cook is the same man who forced him to crank a flivver the night before.

"Where have I seen you before?" Underwood asks Henry.

"In some hospital," he tells him.

"You've been in a hospital?"

"All of them," Henry admits.

Soon the two hypochondriacs sit down to compare their maladies in a rousing and hilarious game of "Can you top this?"

"Every night for nineteen years I've had to take bicarbonate of soda," Henry offers as proof of his nervous stomach.

"That's nothing," Underwood says. "Look at the coat on my tongue."

"Yeah," Henry counters, offering his own. "Look at the pants on mine."

"I've had pneumonia four times," Underwood boasts.

"We're even," Henry replies. "I've had double pneumonia twice."

"Have you ever had the hives?" Underwood asks.

"Brother," Henry admits, "I've had the itch and a broken arm at the same time."

"Are you going to have any more operations?" Underwood asks.

"The doctor said if I have one more operation he's going to put in a zipper."

The duo then begin to compare surgical scars, and they wind up rolling all over the floor, looking up and down each others pants, and measuring with a tape to determine the winner.

Finally, Underwood boasts that his operation cost twelve times what Henry's did. "Oh, no wonder," Henry admits, "You've got hemstitching."

Wanenis arrives, and again he and Sally profess their undying love. Sally tells him she will marry him and live as an Indian, but he refuses her offer and says good-bye.

Henry, hearing the posse approaching, climbs into the kitchen stove to hide. Bob Wells and his deputies enter the kitchen, where he orders them to search the ranch and warns them "not to let a white man get by them." When someone lights the stove, it explodes and Henry emerges in blackface and strolls nonchalantly past the posse. Outside Henry shows his disguise to Sally, who asks how he ever thought of it.

"I didn't," he confesses. "I got in the stove and somebody else thought of it."

While they are trying to get to the garage where their car has been placed, Underwood's son recognizes them. Henry knocks him out and locks him in the garage with Sally, just as the posse enters the courtyard. Bob Wells thinks Henry is acting suspiciously and decides to ask him some questions.

"Where are you from?" the sheriff growls.

"We moved," Henry tells him.

Underwood informs the sheriff that Henry is a cook (although he had previously only seen him in whiteface). Henry adds that he is a singing cook. Wells is unconvinced and demands proof at gun point.

Henry launches into a spirited rendition of "My Baby Just Cares for Me." The number is easily the high point of the film and probably the best film example of the electrifying energy that Eddie Cantor brought to his stage performances. It is not to downgrade in the least the genius of Busby Berkley to say that Cantor's delivery of "My Baby Just Cares for Me," performed with only slight improvised footwork on the part on Cantor in front of a stationary chorus, easily surpasses the vitality of all other musical numbers in the film combined. The piece is certifiable movie magic, especially for fans of Eddie Cantor.

After the number, Underwood's son emerges from the garage and accuses Henry of knocking him out. Henry and two ranch hands are taken back to the kitchen for interrogation. Underwood's son, who has evidently studied enough college psychology to make him dangerous, convinces the sheriff that by using psychology he can read the thoughts of the suspects.

"If you can read my thoughts, you ought to kick me in the face right now," Henry chimes in.

The son has the suspects sit down and places plates on their outstretched fists to serve as crude lie-detectors. He announces that by using word association, he will cause the guilty party to involuntarily drop the plates. Whether or not his method is effective is never found out because Henry continually frustrates his efforts with a steady stream of back talk and nonsense. Henry manages to further implicate his fellow suspects by kicking out their chairs from under them when no one is looking. Finally, Henry is proclaimed innocent because he held his plates steady under the most intense questioning. Of course, Henry, getting wind of the plate plot, put glue on his fists as a precaution.

After Miss Custer leads the cowboys and girls in a snappy number extolling the virtues of the Stetson hat (including the first use of Berkley's ground level, through-the-legs shot), Henry emerges from the cookhouse and nonchalantly waves to the sheriff and his posse. Unfortunately, he has just washed his hands and taken off his black disguise. Discovered, Henry makes his escape by grabbing Bob Wells' gun and driving, with Sally, through the wall of the garage and out across the desert.

They are soon stopped by a party of Indians, one of whom Henry insists is a Jewish traffic cop. The Indians blindfold Henry and take him to their camp. At the camp, Chief Black Eagle asks Henry if he is a friend of the Indians.

"I'm friendly with everybody," Henry admits, adding, "I even like my broker."

To prove his friendship, Henry is forced to smoke the peace pipe, which he surmises is filled with old bicycle tires. Wanenis enters and discovers that Sally is waiting down on the trail. He rushes to her, the lovers again pledge their love, and Wanenis reprises "I'll Still Belong to You."

Meanwhile, Henry notices the chief's surplus of squaws and asks if he gets them wholesale or commits bigamy.

"What mean 'bigamy'?" the chief asks Henry.

"Bigamy," Henry explains, "means you can't marry two or three women."

"Black Eagle no can have two, three women?" the chief replies angrily.

"Who said you no can have," Henry tells him. "I said you can't marry."

"Oh," Black Eagle laughs, "marry!"

"Ah," Henry concludes, "he's a dirty Indian."

Black Eagle is so delighted with Henry's views on love and marriage that he makes Henry an honorary Indian, or as Henry puts it: "Me Big Chief Izzy Horowitz."

Underwood soon arrives and for the third time in a day fails to recognize Henry, who is now sporting an elaborate headdress. In another hilarious scene between Cantor and Spencer Charters, the pair dicker back and forth over the sale of an Indian blanket and doll. When Underwood wants to know why the blanket is so expensive, Henry tells him it has a history and once belonged to Big Chief Spoil-ya-shine.

"Who?" Underwoood asks.

"Spoil-ya-shine! Spoil-ya-shine!" Henry exclaims, while stomping on Underwood's shoes.

The doll, it turns out, also has a history. Its name is "Big Chief Rip-ya-collar." Underwood has never heard of this noble warrior, either, and so has his collar torn off in the process of his education.

Finally, Henry tires of his Indian accent and begins to haggle in a Hebrew accent, substituting Yiddish curses for Indian phrases.

"Look," Henry explains in his thickest Lower East Side accent, "if I sell to you for forty dollars I couldn't make a cent. I should live so long that it costs me thirty-five and a half dollars. Such chutzpa!"

In the end Henry agrees to Underwood's price but manages to steal back half of the merchandise before his customer exits.

Miss Custer enters and immediately recognizes her wandering patient. She notices Henry is acting healthy, a fact which he attributes to the abundance of beautiful squaws. He announces that he would even like to stay with the Indians.

"I tried to get a room here," he tells her. "They didn't have a room so I made a reservation." Under the strain of the pun, Miss Custer picks up a tommyhawk and chases him off.

At this point *Whoopee!* so close to its end, comes grinding to a halt for a long musical number. The sole purpose of the interlude—obviously Ziegfeld designed—is to parade out a steady stream of beautiful girls in expensive ersatz Indian outfits, complete with incredibly elaborate feathered bonnets. While no doubt, given Ziegfeld's long, successful track record on Broadway, these numbers were breathtakingly effective on stage, on film the slow pacing becomes tedious, making what is intended as a finale the low point of the picture.

What follows is little better. The entire plot is resolved when Black Eagle admits to Wanenis, Sally, her father, and Bob Wells that he found Wanenis as a baby in a settler's cabin, and therefore, Wanenis is in reality 100 percent white. What is troublesome here, however, is not the ease with which things are settled—most musical comedies take similar easy outs—but rather the reactions of those involved. Especially by today's sensibilities, it is offensive when Wanenis embraces his foster father and expresses pure joy over the fact that he is in no way related to him or his race. Furthermore, Wanenis is happily rejecting the noble Black Eagle in order to be accepted into a circle which includes the bigoted Bob Wells and Mr. Morgan, who now gladly consents to a wedding.

Despite this ending with its unfortunate prejudice, the film is first and foremost an Eddie Cantor vehicle, and as such it succeeds wildly. With the love story settled, Henry rushes back on, still pursued by the hatchet-wielding Miss Custer. Henry appeals to her sense of romance and speaks tenderly of his need for a companion.

"I'd like to ask you one question," he says, while her eyes light up with anticipation. "What ever became of that calf?"

Before she can bury the hatchet (in his head), Henry kisses her and sings a brief reprise of "My Baby Just Cares for Me." They embrace, but before they can continue their passion, Henry looks at the camera and assures the audience, "That's all there is."

Following filming on *Whoopee!* Eddie Cantor returned to New York in late July to await the film's premiere. Flo Ziegfeld also returned to the East to tend to his declining Broadway enterprises. While seeing to other shows, Ziegfeld still harbored the hope that he would be able to coax Cantor back to Broadway for another smash show like *Kid Boots* or *Whoopee*, despite the comedian's declarations that he was through with the stage.

Cantor had little time for a return to the stage, however. Just before leaving Hollywood, Eddie signed a five-year contract with Sam Goldwyn, under the terms of which he would star in one film a year. Still, Ziegfeld

**A bespectacled Cantor holds Spencer Charters (center) at gunpoint while Eleanor Hunt looks on in this scene from *Whoopee!* (collection of Brian Gari).**

retained some hope. The Broadway producer accompanied Eddie back to California roughly a month later for a preview of *Whoopee!* As Ziegfeld and Cantor rode down to San Diego for the advance screening, Flo urged Eddie to give up Hollywood and return to New York for another show. Cantor was hesitant; before bailing out again on a film career, he would at least like to see the final product of his latest effort.

Eddie told Ziegfeld that if he squeezed his hand during the screening, the producer could go east and begin preparations on another Ziegfeld-Cantor stage show. The squeeze never came. *Whoopee!* was as big a hit on the screen as it had been during its Broadway run. Eddie Cantor was a bona fide movie star.

Initially, an extensive promotional tour to coincide with the opening of *Whoopee!* had been planned for Eddie. Goldwyn changed his mind—perhaps after seeing the initial reviews and audience response—because he decided that the picture would sell itself without its star there in person. The cancellation of personal appearances lost fees for Cantor, who was to have received up to $1,000 a day in some cities. Cantor recouped some of the lost fees via a special radio broadcast which aired on the eve on the film's opening. Heard over the Columbia network (CBS), the hour-long program featured Eddie singing selections from the film, for which the comedian received $7,000.

After numerous delays in its release date, *Whoopee!* finally opened at New York's Rivoli Theatre on September 30, 1930, and was a smash hit with critics and audiences alike. The film managed to gross over $2.5 million — a tremendous box office for that time — in its first three months of release. A large percentage of that figure came from England, where Eddie Cantor was relatively unknown, and further proved his potential as a major screen star. To underscore what the box offices around the world were already saying, United Artists' trade ad for the end of the year featured Eddie as one of the company's biggest stars, the equal of company partners Douglas Fairbanks, Mary Pickford, and Charlie Chaplin.

Flo Ziegfeld, out his biggest star, soured on motion pictures in general and his producing partner Sam Goldwyn specifically. Zieggy returned to the part of show business he had had an integral part in shaping. For the next few years, up until his death in 1932, newspapers would occasionally report rumors that Ziegfeld and Cantor were getting together for another stage musical. But Eddie Cantor was never again to work with the man who had made him the highest paid comedian on Broadway.

Ziegfeld and Goldwyn Productions, after its initial triumph, ceased to be a production entity and remained only as a balance sheet upon which to total the revenues of *Whoopee!* Even then, its two partners could not agree. Well into the next year, Ziegfeld, still smarting from the loss of Cantor, accused Goldwyn of padding the film's financial statement with bogus expenses in an attempt to cheat him out of his share of the profits. Goldwyn countered that Ziegfeld's contribution to the film had been restricted to interfering. "Yes," Ziegfeld replied, "but the only interfering I did was to insist the show reach the screen almost as it was done on the stage and it looks as though I was right."

All hopes of a Ziegfeld-Goldwyn production of *Kid Boots* were lost in the quarreling, if they hadn't already vanished in the ill feeling which developed between the two producers during the filming of *Whoopee!* It is ironic, yet at the same time predictable given the larger than life quality of each man, that the two major producers in Eddie Cantor's career, both consummate showmen in their particular medium, could not work together. Perhaps it is a miracle that they were able to coproduce long enough to complete *Whoopee!* and bring to it enough of their peculiar talent to make the film a success.

## REVIEWS

In this production Mr. Cantor's clowning transcends even Mr. Ziegfeld's shining beauties, the clever direction and the tuneful melodies. And this is saying a great deal, for there is much for the eyes to feast on in the various scenes.

Messrs. Ziegfeld and Goldwyn have had the wisdom to permit humor to hold sway and this results in this film being a swift and wonderfully entertaining offering, a feature that should prove to motion picture chieftains that such attractions are well worth all the trouble taken in producing, despite the subordinating of the popular romantic theme.

It is a picture in which one never tires of Mr. Cantor. Even during those periods of respite, in which the charming showgirls go through their drills and dances, one looks forward to another chance to chuckle and giggle at the ludicrous conduct of the "nervous wreck." — Mordaunt Hall, *New York Times*, October 1, 1930

"Whoopee" is the best musical comedy given to the sheet to date. It is musical and it is comedy, along with a story that does not depend upon a couple of romantic name kids to hold it up.

Cantor never has been funnier on the stage than in this talker. He muffs not a laugh and the timing loses none. — Sime, *Variety*, October 8, 1930

## Notes

1. In all fairness to Paramount, Ziegfeld had been offered a job as a producer at the studio. As the expenses, delays, and problems mounted over *Glorifying the American Girl*, the studio had probably had their fill of working with the producer.

2. The prevailing attitude of 1930s Hollywood towards Eddie Cantor's career in silent pictures is evident by various press clippings printed when he arrived on the coast to make *Whoopee!* Most give only cursory notice that he had made *Kid Boots* at all, and none stated that the film was indeed a box office success. His second film, *Special Delivery*, was totally ignored, as if it had never been made.

3. Apparently the powers that be in Hollywood, although a majority of them were themselves Jewish, forgot that Eddie Cantor played successfully to large portions of Gentile America while he was a vaudeville comedian.

4. To say nothing of the motivation of Henry Williams (Eddie Cantor), a hypochondriac who has emphatically eschewed any notions of romance in a previous scene, to suddenly sing the sexy and savvy commentary on love and marriage "Makin' Whoopee."

5. This problem is evident in the Universal picture *King of Jazz*, also made in 1930. One number in the film employs a chorus line stretched across the screen in just such a manner. Due to the aspect ratio of the film, the girls only fill a thin strip of the frame — approximately 25 percent — the other 75 percent of the frame is blank space. Berkley himself would use a similar chorus line in *Palmy Days* the following year. Berkley avoided the dead space by having the line dance in front of a reflecting pool, which not only filled out the frame but created an interesting effect at the same time.

6. The United Artists studio, where *Whoopee!* and the five subsequent films Cantor did for Goldwyn were shot, started out as the Jesse B. Hampton Studio. In 1922 the studio was bought by United Artists partners Mary Pickford and Douglas Fairbanks, who renamed it the Pickford-Fairbanks Studio. Goldwyn started renting space there in 1924; the studio name was changed to United Artists in 1927, the year after Goldwyn became one of the UA partners. Goldwyn's production output gradually increased, while that of Pickford and Fairbanks decreased until eventually Goldwyn occupied the entire lot. In 1948 the property was renamed the Samuel Goldwyn Studios and remains so today.

7. Almost twenty years later, Cantor would recall in a *Saturday Evening Post* article that *Whoopee!* had been shot in thirty-six days. It is quite possible that Cantor's scenes could have been done in thirty-six days, with an extra week taken for the scenes without him.

# CHAPTER 25

# *Palmy Days*

Finding a film vehicle for Eddie Cantor to follow up the smash hit *Whoopee!* posed a problem for Sam Goldwyn. Since his falling out with Flo Ziegfeld, there was no chance of filming a talking version of *Kid Boots*. (Even if the duo had still been coproducing, a legal battle would probably have ensued with Paramount, which contended that it owned the film rights to *Boots* by virtue of buying the property for the silent screen.) Aside from *Whoopee* and *Kid Boots*, all Eddie's stage successes had been in musical reviews, leaving Goldwyn with the frustrating situation of having one of Broadway's biggest stars with no proven Broadway properties in which to showcase him.

If there were no more ready-made Cantor stage hits to be had, Goldwyn would do the next best thing: hire Broadway's best comedy playwright, George S. Kaufman, to pen the screenplay for Cantor's next film. Soon after the premiere of *Whoopee!* Goldwyn and Cantor approached Kaufman on the project. Initially Kaufman seemed interested and agreed to a royalty percentage on the film's gross against a guaranteed salary figure. After the money was settled, however, the project ran into problems. Although there is no concrete evidence why Kaufman was not signed to write the screenplay, one can guess, given known facts about the writer, why he bowed out from the film.

First, Kaufman, a devout Broadway man, disliked Hollywood and the filmmaking industry based there. His only other screen credit to date had been the adaptation for his own play *The Cocoanuts* (cowritten with Morrie Ryskind), which starred the Marx Brothers. Kaufman had done *The Cocoanuts* because it was filmed in Astoria, only a short ride from Manhattan. Any Goldwyn picture Kaufman might write would be produced at the United Artists Studios in the heart of Hollywood, necessitating a three thousand-mile trip from Broadway.

The second objection Kaufman had was the film's star, Eddie Cantor. A clash between Cantor and Kaufman was inevitable because Kaufman would not tolerate outside interference when he was writing, and Cantor was well known for contributing jokes, dialogue, even whole plots for shows he appeared in.

179

From the outset of negotiations with Kaufman, Eddie was ready with an original story idea for the film which he expected Kaufman to flesh out, with his help, into the screenplay for his second Goldwyn film. Kaufman was not the type of writer who was content to expand on a plot handed to him by a comedian. Unwilling to make the twin concessions of collaborating with an actor on a screenplay which was to be written in Hollywood, Kaufman withdrew from the negotiations.

Ironically, although the second Cantor-Goldwyn film would not spring from these negotiations, the third and fourth films in the series would. Cantor's idea, the one Kaufman refused to work on, would be produced a year later as *The Kid from Spain*, while two years hence Kaufman would agree to write the original screenplay for *Roman Scandals*.

With Kaufman out of the picture, Cantor approached Goldwyn with his idea, which he had dreamed up one night while having coffee with his friend Sidney Franklin. Franklin had grown up in Brooklyn but later moved to Spain, where he became one of the greatest matadors in the world. Eddie thought a picture in which he played a bullfighter would be the perfect follow up to *Whoopee!* He envisioned a hilarious ten-minute pantomime scene for himself in the bullring. Goldwyn doubted, however, that the public would go for "anything Spanish," and the idea was rejected for the time being.

While Goldwyn busied himself trying to find a vehicle and an author for Cantor, Eddie took advantage of the free time to return east for some vaudeville dates, including a standing-room-only appearance at the famous Palace. Upon his return to Hollywood, Eddie reported not to the United Artist Studios, but to Fox, where he had been signed to write a screenplay, along with Edwin Burke, for dialect comedian El Brendel. The script, entitled *Mr. Lemon of Orange*, was a spoof on the current popular gangster film craze. Although *Variety* complimented Eddie's contributions for offering "traces of dynamite in the dialogue," the film as a whole won few raves on its release in the early spring of 1931 and was quickly forgotten.

Meanwhile, back at the studio, Sam Goldwyn decided if he couldn't get George Kaufman to write Eddie Cantor's second talkie, he would do the next best thing: hire Morrie Ryskind, Kaufman's collaborator on *The Cocoanuts* and *Animal Crackers*. In February, Ryskind, along with fellow playwright Guy Bolton, began work on another idea suggested by Cantor. This plot would feature Eddie as the assistant to a phony spiritualist and would be titled *Palmy Days*. Designed as a straight comedy with only two interpolated songs, *Palmy Days* was set to go into production by the end of April, but was delayed when script problems arose — namely, Goldwyn was dissatisfied with the film's gags.

To remedy the deficit of laughs, the producer poured gagwriters galore into the project. Apart from Goldwyn's extra writers, Cantor also jumped into the fray, bringing with him David Freedman, his friend and collaborator. Despite, or rather because of, the combined input of the various teams of jokemen, the script was not ready in time for the scheduled shooting date. As late as mid–May, the *New York Times* reported that Eddie was "prancing through innumerable 'story conferences' that are whipping his second picture into final form as a script."

The *New York Times* was correct in describing Eddie's movement between gag sessions as "prancing," since it would require his boundless energy to shuttle between the small army of writers working on the picture. Sam Goldwyn now had the *Palmy Days* script staff up to a total of nine comedy writers, including Ryskind, Bolton, Freedman, Ray Harris, and what the *New York Times* referred to as "lesser lights." Cantor quipped at one point that they needed only one more gagman to enable them to pick sides for a basketball game.

Despite being short a man, the writers passed jokes and dribbled plot lines as if they indeed were playing a game of hoops, rather than writing a major motion picture. Along with the story and dialogue, musical numbers were also being switched back and forth. The original story called for two songs, but at one point a decision was made that just one number would be used — Con Conrad and Cliff Friend's delightful "Yes, Yes." As time went on, however, the number of tunes ballooned up again until five songs were being considered for the picture — the three finally used and a pair of songs entitled "Goose Pimples" and "Dunk, Dunk, Dunk" not used.

When the dust finally settled on the myriad of script sessions, *Palmy Days* had three songs, a plot about a phony spiritualist trying to infiltrate a bakery, and a series of loosely connected gags and lines of dialogue. With the script in a shambles, casting was understandably difficult, with the only signed members of the cast being the long-limbed comedienne Charlotte Greenwood, brought in to play opposite Cantor, and Spencer Charters, reprising his comic foil duties from *Whoopee!* Interestingly enough, Betty Grable had evidently made enough of an impression with her chorus work in *Whoopee!* to be considered for the part of the ingenue. Betty was fated to remain in the chorus line a little while longer, however, when the part was awarded to Barbara Weeks.

Directing chores on *Palmy Days* fell to veteran comedy director Edward Sutherland. Sutherland began his career in vaudeville, later switching to films, first as a stunt man, then as a comic at Mack Sennett's Keystone Studios. His first chance behind the cameras came in 1923 as an assistant director to Charlie Chaplin on Chaplin's first dramatic film, *A Woman of Paris*. After serving in the same position on Chaplin's classic, *The Gold Rush*, Sutherland was lured away by Paramount in 1926 to direct W. C. Fields' first efforts at that studio. Fields and Sutherland became close friends, and Sutherland was to direct the former Ziegfeld comedian at least five more times through the years, in addition to working with Laurel and Hardy, and Abbott and Costello.

Even a proven director like Sutherland needed a story to work with, but, unfortunately, none seemed forthcoming. Despite such trivial annoyances, filming on *Palmy Days* began, slightly behind schedule and without a complete or even coherent script.

After the smooth, quick shooting schedule of *Whoopee!* — thanks to a veteran cast working with a stage-polished property — progress on *Palmy Days* seemed especially slow to the film's star. "It took forever to make the picture," Cantor later complained of *Palmy Days*, "while the story line was changed while Goldwyn hired writers and fired them." Somehow a serviceable script was finally assembled as filming progressed. In spite of the corps of writers used, final story credit went to Ryskind, Cantor, and Freedman, with a continuity credit going to Keene Thompson.[1]

With the raft of delays and problems, it seemed likely that *Palmy Days* would pale to its predecessor. "People expect too much from pictures these days," Cantor told the *New York Times* during filming, perhaps in an attempt to lower expectations on the film. "Paying 35 cents at the box office doesn't entitle you to the emotional experience of a lifetime, a four-year college course in jungle life and a sun bath."

Eddie soon found out that making a picture for Sam Goldwyn didn't entitle you to any rest or outside pursuits, even after the shooting schedule had been completed. Once filming on *Palmy Days* was seemingly finished in late June, Goldwyn ordered Cantor to stay in Hollywood, even though Eddie had made tentative plans to make some personal appearances back east before touring Europe with an advance print of the film.

A month later, after seeing the rough cut of the film, Goldwyn decided he wasn't satisfied and called select members of the cast, including, of course, Eddie Cantor, back for retakes. While Eddie Cantor had been directed to stay close to the studio, the film's director, Eddie Sutherland, had not. Because Sutherland had since moved on to other projects at other studios, Mervyn LeRoy, on loan from Warner Brothers to direct Goldwyn's production of *Tonight or Never*, was pressed into service.

LeRoy recalls the retakes: "When I went over there, he [Goldwyn] said, 'Mervyn, would you mind doing a couple of retakes on a picture with Eddie Cantor called *Palmy Days?*' I looked at the picture. It wasn't very good, I might say."

According to LeRoy, Goldwyn assured his director that he only wanted what amounted to a few days of retakes on the film's cafeteria scene. "It turned out to be three and a half weeks' worth," LeRoy recalled, "which I wound up doing for nothing."

The cafeteria scene that LeRoy shot included a new song added at the last minute, "There's Nothing Too Good for My Baby," by Eddie Cantor, Benny Davis, and Harry Askt. As originally planned, the song was to be sung by a chorus of girls in waitresses' uniforms, followed by Cantor, who would sing a solo. After trying the song with the chorus, Eddie decided it would go over better with just the solo, and LeRoy agreed. When Sam Goldwyn came down to the set to watch the number, however, he called LeRoy aside.

"Look, Moiphy," (Goldwyn's malapropism of "Mervyn") the producer began. "What's this? Cantor alone? You'd better put a lot of girls behind him."

LeRoy then explained that this was how Cantor wanted to do the number and if Goldwyn didn't like it, he should take it up with Eddie. Goldwyn stomped across the soundstage to argue it out with his star.

"Sam, I was in the *Ziegfeld Follies*," Eddie explained, "and I did solos and they never had to put girls behind me. I can do a number by myself and that's the way I want it."

Goldwyn retreated to his office, where he put in a secret call to Mervyn LeRoy back on the set. "Don't tell Cantor," the producer whispered over the phone to LeRoy, "but in that number when he's singing the song have a few girls whiz by." LeRoy agreed, hung up, and proceeded to ignore Goldwyn's order, and with good reason. Cantor's own animated style more than compensated for any lack of extras in the number and proved that his screen presence was — just as it had been on the stage — more than captivating enough to hold an audience. Mervyn LeRoy later recalled that "There's Nothing Too Good for My Baby" was "the hit of the show."

Speaking of musical numbers, Busby Berkley was back directing the dances. With the musical routines pared down considerably from the number used in *Whoopee!* Berkley was left with only two dances to choreograph. He made the most of the opportunities presented to him though, making the opening, "Bend Down Sister," enjoyable and the finale, "Yes, Yes," quite memorable for the burgeoning "Berkley style" they displayed. In the "Yes, Yes" number, Berkley was particularly innovative in his use of a reflecting pool to help fill the screen when a long shot of the chorus line was used. Berkley's skill and reputation as a choreographer was beginning to attract notice in Hollywood, and the dance director was soon being called upon to repeat his Goldwyn successes at MGM, Universal, RKO, and most notably, Warner Brothers. The latter studio would ultimately succeed in luring him away altogether from Goldwyn and Cantor.

The songs themselves, what there were of them, came from a variety of writers. Most notable and best represented among the songsmiths was Con Conrad, who supplied the music for two numbers: "Yes, Yes" (lyrics by Cliff Friend) and "Bend Down Sister" (lyrics by Ballard MacDonald). Conrad had a proven track record with Cantor; he had provided Eddie with his previous hits "Ma, He's Making Eyes at Me" and "Margie." Conrad was no less successful with his contributions to *Palmy Days*, with "Yes, Yes" becoming a hit and another standard in Eddie Cantor's impressive portfolio ("Bend Down Sister" was sung by the chorus). Together with the aforementioned "There's Nothing Too Good for My Baby," "Yes, Yes" provided *Palmy Days* with probably the two strongest, quintessential Cantor songs to be found in any of the comedian's films. An ironic achievement indeed when one considers that *Palmy Days* was not even designated as a musical by its producer.

*Palmy Days*, as Eddie Cantor's second talkie and a follow-up to the smash hit *Whoopee!* finds itself suffering from the same problems that his second silent film, *Special Delivery*, encountered coming on the heels of *Kid Boots*. Both *Special Delivery* and *Palmy Days* were original screen properties that were conceived to follow soon after screen versions of wildly successful stage shows. Both were produced by people who, though they had worked with Cantor on a previous film, had little idea of how to build a film around his peculiar talents. Both Paramount and Sam Goldwyn knew they had a bankable, proven star but were a little puzzled about what to do with him.

Consequently, as had been the case with *Special Delivery* a scant four years before, *Palmy Days* is a film which relies heavily on gags with only a shred of a story as an excuse upon which to hang them. It is as if Sam Goldwyn, as well as the producers at Paramount, had reasoned to themselves, "Well, we have this comedian, Eddie Cantor, all he needs to make another hit is enough jokes." Comedies, however, like other films, need a workable story to succeed. Goldwyn's mistake with *Palmy Days*, which seems to be a fairly common one among novices in the field of comedy, was to try to cover up an already gag-laden, weak-plotted script with more gags. In such cases more is less, with gags being piled upon gags until the sum is far less than the individual parts and the impact of the comedy is diminished.

The limp plots of *Palmy Days* and *Special Delivery* are even more glaring when one considers that their predecessors, *Whoopee!* and *Kid Boots*, were obviously not *Gone with the Wind*. As it stands, the story of *Palmy Days* is weak at best. Unlike *Special Delivery*, however, *Palmy Days* has the added value of giving the audience the chance to both see and hear Eddie Cantor. Cantor's high energy performance, particularly in his two musical numbers, helps smooth over the film's sparse plot, yet even this does not entirely erase the film's deficiencies. Aside from the musical numbers, which paradoxically rank highly as Cantor's all-time best on film, the film has few assets left to recommend it. The comedy routines, particularly the seance bit and Cantor's impersonations of a French psychic and later a salesgirl, are amusing, but too poorly integrated into the plot to help the film as a whole. Aside from these scenes, however, there are just too many gags and one gets the sense as the film progresses that no one in the film has a true grasp of what's going on. Consequently, the continuity suffers for the most part, along with any sense of pace or timing.

Ironically, not long after the release of *Palmy Days*, Cantor explained to the *New York Times* that the secret of making a successful film musical was careful attention to the story. "I don't know why it is," Cantor said, "but you've got to carry a faster pace in musical stuff on the screen than on the stage, and pay more attention to the narrative of the plot. The audience isn't so willing to take each number as it comes along for what it's worth. They want a unified impression and a lively continuity."

In support of Cantor, the performances of Charlotte Greenwood as Eddie's love interest and Charles Middleton (Ming the Merciless from the Flash Gordon serials) as the fake fakir, Professor Yolando, are sufficiently zany and menacing, respectively. Old foil Spencer Charters as Mr. Clark, the president of the bakery, has precious little to do and is wasted, especially considering the excellent byplay he enjoyed with Eddie in *Whoopee!*

The rest of the cast is utterly forgettable. Barbara Weeks and Stephen

Clayton are stiff and ineffective as the love interest. George Raft is present in one of his earliest roles as Yolando's henchman, Joe the Frog. His few lines give little indication that he was soon to become a major star in similar tough guy roles over at Warner Brothers. Ironically, when the film was reissued in the mid-forties, Raft was listed second in the ads below only Cantor, even though he is a fringe character who appears on screen for less than 5 percent of the film's eighty-minute running time.

*Palmy Days* opens with an exterior view of Clark's Bakery, complete with neon signs proclaiming, "Glorifying the American Donut" (a obvious reference to Cantor's former boss and Goldwyn's erstwhile partner Flo Ziegfeld) and "Eat Our Cake and Have 'It'" ("It," of course, being the then popular euphemism for sex appeal). Inside the bakery, Clark's workers, all of them young, shapely, and female, are meeting in the building's rooftop gymnasium for their daily exercise class conducted by the amazonian Helen Martin (Charlotte Greenwood). After weighing the girls in, Martin gives a musical demonstration of her theories on physical fitness in the catchy number "Bend Down Sister." In the course of the number—imaginatively choreographed, as always, by Busby Berkley—the girls are told if they want to be thin, they need to bend down. After the chorus of the song, the girls follow Martin's advice by bending over in front of the camera enough to reveal an ample dose of pre–production code cleavage.

Having completed her lessons for the morning, Martin rushes off for her weekly seance at the studio of Professor Yolando (Charles Middleton), a local psychic reader. The seance, which is attended by four or five others, is a highly mystic affair indeed, complete with floating horns, elevated tables, and disembodied voices calling from the great beyond. The spirits, it turns out, are not from the great beyond, but rather are all supplied from a well-rigged backroom courtesy of Eddie Simpson (Cantor), one of Yolando's minions.

After the seance, Helen offers Yolando $200 if he can mystically provide her with a husband. He assures her that her dream man will walk into her gym later that morning. She rushes back to work with excited anticipation. When Yolando orders Eddie over to the gym to play the part of her beau, Eddie resists, explaining that he has faithfully carried out his boss's orders until now. "But when you bring marriage into it," Eddie protests, "that's sex!"

Yolando threatens Eddie, which causes him to break into song, a condition which afflicts him every time he gets excited. "You can't make me go," he proclaims defiantly. "Washington wouldn't go! Lincoln wouldn't go! Would Lindbergh go? Lindbergh wouldn't go!"

His bravery escapes him, however, when Yolando's henchman pulls a gun on him. "But after all," Eddie reasons meekly, "I'm not Lindbergh."

Eddie arrives at the gym, where Helen immediately pounces on him with a move that is half hug, half nelson.

"I've waited for this moment all my life," she explains.

"Well, you've had your moment," Eddie tells her, "good-bye."

Helen begs him to stay, explaining that their match was made in heaven.

"Then that's where I'll marry you," Eddie argues.

Suddenly a little man enters carrying a small book and asks if they're ready.

"Not yet, Judge," Helen tells him.

Eddie tries to explain that their romance would be doomed to fail because Helen is so superior to him physically. Determined to make a *man* out of her man, Helen hands Eddie a medicine ball, explaining that it will do him a lot of good.

"Oh," he protests, "you can't swallow a thing like this!"

Next she lifts Eddie on to the mechanical horse. After the motorized steed nearly bucks him to bits, Eddie announces that his posterior is nothing but "pins and needles" and "broken bottles."

From there Helen places him on the massage table and in yet another reworking of the osteopath scene, proceeds to twist Eddie into a human pretzel.[2] With Eddie wrapped up in a tight bundle, Helen asks him if he could learn to love her.

"I'm dying," Eddie screams, "and she's asking me riddles!"

Helen continues the treatment while assuring Eddie that it's good for his diaphragm. "There's nothing wrong with my frying pan," he contends.

Finally, she unfolds her patient and begins to massage him by pounding his chest with her fists.

"Will you marry me now?" Helen asks.

"Keep on hitting me till I say 'yes,'" he replies.

She then puts Eddie in a full nelson and whips his head back and forth, all while confessing the depths of her love. When she finishes, Eddie staggers off the table and climbs back on the mechanical horse.

"Come on," he says, motioning for her to turn it on, "broken bottles."

Meanwhile, back at Yolando's studio, Mr. Clark (Spencer Charters), the president of the bakery, is receiving a reading similar to Helen Martin's. Yolando tells Clark that at noon a man will suddenly appear at his office. Clark is to hire him immediately as an efficiency expert and give him full rein over his affairs. After Clark exits, Yolando tells Joe to go and fill the role of the mysterious efficiency expert so that they can keep a close watch over Clark's fortune.

After a quick obligatory scene introducing the film's love interest (Clark's daughter, Joan, and Steve, a young executive at the bakery), Clark arrives to keep his noontime appointment with the mystery man. Before Joe the Frog can arrive to fill the bill, however, Eddie enters Clark's office through the window after retreating down the fire escape from Helen's rooftop gym.

"Where did you come from?" Clark exclaims.

"Out of the everywhere, into the here," Eddie intones mystically.

When Eddie calls Clark by name, the bakery owner is astonished.

"You know me?" he asks Eddie.

"I saw your picture . . . up there," Eddie says, motioning toward the rooftop gym.

"Up there?" Clark probes, believing Eddie to be heaven sent, then adding, "Not, down there?"

"I haven't been down there yet," Eddie explains.

With Eddie's spiritual credentials verified, Clark hires him on the spot, and the pair get right down to dickering over his salary. Eddie agrees to take only $7,000, less than half what Clark offers, but then insists that Clark cut his own salary from $50,000 to $15,000.

"I'll take fifteen," Clark proclaims getting into the spirit. "What'll you take?" he asks Eddie.

"I'll take twenty!" Eddie announces, giving himself a raise.

When Clark attempts to protest, Eddie cuts him short. "Tut, tut," he admonishes, "can't keep this up all day. This is a business, you've got to go on."

After teaching Clark how to quack like a duck, Eddie goes off in search of an office. He quickly locates one and finds there Clark's daughter Joan, whom he immediately falls in love with and hires as his personal secretary. Eddie overhears Joan talking on the phone about Steve and mistakenly believes that she loves him (Eddie) too.

Eddie soon discovers that his problems are in no way confined to love. Professor Yolando arrives to see who has been hired as efficiency expert over his hand-picked candidate. When Yolando discovers Eddie has taken the position, he is delighted, until Eddie tells Yolando that he's quitting the fortune teller's gang.

"I sent you a letter in the mail today," Eddie begins, informing Yoland of his resignation. "You'll get it tomorrow. Of course there's two cents due on it, but then you owed me a week's salary so we're even."

"You rat!" the enraged mystic shouts at Eddie.

"Mr. Rat, to you," Eddie corrects, reminding him of his new prestige.

Yolando storms out, but not before threatening to get even with Eddie, even if he must murder his former peon.

Eddie is frantically searching for a way to handle Yolando when he notices a newspaper story about Professor Ledoux, a renowned French psychic who is visiting the city.

"Now where can I get some whiskers," he asks himself while studying the photograph of the bearded Ledoux.

Back at his studio, a few hours later, Yolando is delighted to learn that the famous Professor Ledoux has come to call.

"We can learn a lot from Ledoux," Yolando tells his henchmen, adding, "He's no phony."

Ledoux may be no phony, but the man who is ushered in certainly is. Eddie, complete with goatee and cutaway coat, strides into the room, spouts some high school French, and kisses Yolando on both cheeks. Eddie then proceeds to denigrate Yolando's methods.

"Passé! Passé!" Eddie cries, while smashing Yolando's expensive crystal ball. "It's worthless. Poo-poo! Poo-poo-a-doo!"

He then moves on to Yolando's palm chart, which he tears off the wall and rips to shreds. "Coney Island," Eddie remarks disdainfully.

Yolando asks Eddie to show him the modern method. Eddie is glad to oblige, especially since Eddie's "modern method" consists of Yolando lying prone on the couch while Eddie slaps him silly.

"That hurts," Yolando protests.

"But only for the first half hour," Eddie reassures him. Having given his face a good pummeling, Eddie starts to pound Yolando's Adam's apple with karate chops.

"You're choking me," Yolando cries.

"Oh," Eddie tells him, "but it is the latest French method."

"It's painful!"

"But it will feel so good when I stop."

After sprinkling his victim with water and growling at him like a dog, Eddie looks into Yolando's eyes and starts his reading.

"I feel you are an honest man," Eddie begins. "You only take things beginning with an 'a,' like 'a' thousand dollars, 'a' diamond bracelet, 'a' pearl necklace."

"Those things never came to my mind," Yolando tells him.

"It does not come to your mind, but it comes to your hands," Eddie scolds.

Eddie then gets up on top of the reclining Yolando and begins pacing back and forth on top of him. He tells Yolando that there is a young man in the mystic's service (who amazingly fits Eddie's description) whom the spirits are "crazy for." If Yolando does not set Eddie free, he tells him, then the spirits will do Yolando harm.

"I see the number thirteen," he tells Yolando. Yolando is delighted, explaining that is his lucky number.

"Not this time," Eddie interrupts, "it is your unlucky number. Thirteen — twelve men and a judge." Eddie then describes Yolando in the electric chair, complete with steam coming out of his ears.

Browbeaten, pummeled, and walked over, Yolando agrees. Eddie is so happy that he forgets his disguise and starts to sing. Yolando immediately recognizes him, tears off his phony whiskers, and starts to treat Eddie to some of those latest methods from France.

Just then Clark arrives for his afternoon reading. Eddie tells Clark that he has just had his reading for him to save time.

"Boy," he tells Clark as they exit, effecting his escape, "you've got an efficiency expert."

Back at the bakery, Clark and Eddie are on an inspection tour of the plant's public restaurant. Clark explains business has been bad lately and leaves it to Eddie to find out why. After a quick investigation, Eddie concludes that the cafe is not doing the business it should because it lacks entertainment. He promises Clark to transform the cafe into the talk of the town.

The scene shifts to the cafe, now bulging with patrons, with more standing outside waiting to get in. On one side of the room now sits a small orchestra, all its musicians dressed like bakers. After a fanfare, Eddie emerges in blackface to sing "There's Nothing Too Good for My Baby," a delightful, typically "Cantoresque" tune complete with bouncy melody and witty lyrics all about "his Baby"—most of Cantor's songs seem to be about this "Baby"—who wants only the finest things life has to offer, but somehow winds up with less.

The song, an afterthought to the completed film, is easily one of the high points of *Palmy Days*, showing Cantor at the top of his form. The number ranks in the top examples of Eddie Cantor's unique song styling on film, along with "My Baby Just Cares for Me" from *Whoopee!* "Yes, Yes," also in *Palmy Days*, and "Okay, Toots," from *Kid Millions*.

Later, in his office, Eddie sees Joan typing a love note to Steve, but mistakenly thinks it is to him. Eddie's suspicions are further reinforced when Clark tells him he is going to announce Joan's engagement that night at a party at his home. Eddie is shocked, but delighted, still thinking he is the intended fiancé.

Clark also plans to distribute the bakery bonuses at the party—$25,000 worth. He is giving the money to Eddie for safekeeping when Yolando enters. Eddie insists the money be put back in the office safe. Clark agrees and gives him the combination.

Eddie leaves Clark's office, but Yolando follows, ordering two of his henchmen to find Eddie and get the combination. With the two goons closing in on him, Eddie ducks into a laundry bin, reemerging moments later dressed as one of the girl bakery workers, complete with a blonde wig. His pursuers eye him suspiciously while he retreats through the cafe, picking up unfinished meals from one table and delivering the half-eaten fare to other tables as he hurries by.

Seeing a group of the waitresses marching in formation down the hall, Eddie falls in line, only to discover their destination is the girls' locker room. Inside Helen spots the "new girl."

"What's your name?" she asks.

"Daisy," Eddie replies, "Daisy Crumb."

"Oh, one of the Virginia Crumbs?"

"No," Eddie admits, "just a New York crumb."

Helen tells "Daisy" to get ready for her swim—a skinny dip—with the other girls and points her to a locker. Eddie tries to escape, but Yolando's men have the exits covered.

Eddie finds a large Turkish towel in which to mask his masculinity and proceeds to the shower room. All the showers are occupied (by bare girls, barely concealed), and Eddie delights in the fact that he will have to skip his. Helen leads him to a small shower in the corner, shoves Eddie in, and grabs his towel.

"Oh," Eddie cries, "I'm ruined! I'm going to be here for life."

Eddie calls for a towel. An attendant brings one no bigger than a face cloth. Undaunted, he removes the entire shower curtain, complete with its circular rod, which he wears around his neck like an oversized collar.

"I was engaged to be married last week," he explains to the other bemused bathers, "and the girls gave me a shower."

Eddie finds another large towel just in time to take his place at the edge of the pool where a line of girls are waiting for their dip. At Helen's direction, the girls shed their towels one by one and dive naked (and off camera) into the pool, while Eddie stands witness half-embarrassed, half-enthralled at his once in a lifetime opportunity.

When his turn comes to throw in the towel, Eddie refuses to go. Helen grabs the towel and pushes him in. When Eddie fails to surface after a minute, Helen dives in. Eddie soon emerges from the other end of the pool wearing her bathing suit and strides off.

In the meantime the thugs have found the combination in Eddie's discarded clothes and proceed to Clark's safe. Upon opening it, however, they discover it is empty. Eddie has gotten there first, removed the money, and baked it into a loaf of bread. With the bread in hand, he leaves for the party.

At the party, Eddie tries to tell Clark about Yolando's plot, but Clark keeps putting him off. While waiting to talk to her father, Eddie dances with Joan. She tells him how happy she is about her upcoming engagement. Eddie, unable to contain himself, bursts into song, singing "Yes, Yes."

Following the number, which included some of the best examples of Busby Berkley's early work, Clark starts to announce his daughter's engagement. Before he can, however, one of his workers rushes in to announce that the safe has been broken into and the bonus money is missing. Eddie is immediately the prime suspect, and Clark's security man takes him into the parlor for interrogation.

"Where's the dough?" the detective asks repeatedly.

"The dough is in the bread," Eddie keeps telling him matter-of-factly.

The security man decides hypnosis will loosen Eddie's tongue.

"Stare at me," the detective commands, while moving his hand around in a circular pattern. Eddie follows intently, but soon his large, rolling eyes put his interrogator into a hypnotic trance instead.

Outside, Eddie tells Clark he has the money hidden safely in the loaf of bread. When he tears the loaf open, however, there's nothing but bread inside. Clark expresses his disappointment in Eddie and has a policeman take him away. Helen tags along, telling the cop she can attest to Eddie's crookedness. Yolando and his gang, figuring Eddie has taken the wrong loaf, rush back to the bakery in search of the money.

On the way to the police station, Eddie throws his hat away and then has the cop stop the car so he can retrieve it. The cop, reasoning that Eddie will run away, decides he better go and get the hat. When he does, Eddie and Helen speed away to the bakery, arriving ahead of the crooks.

**Long-legged costar Charlotte Greenwood keeps Eddie's admirers at bay in this still from *Palmy Days*.**

They rush into the storeroom, where hundreds of thousands of loafs await them. Helen urges Eddie to start looking, but Eddie confesses it's hopeless. While attempting to prove his point, Eddie grabs a loaf at random, rips it open, and immediately discovers the $25,000. Just then Yolando and his gang rush in. A game of keep-away ensues, before Eddie and Helen lock themselves in a storeroom. There they call Clark and succeed in getting Yolando to unwittingly confess through the door.

The crooks break in, leading to a clumsily staged fight, complete with a mechanical bread slicer and oven thrown in to add a degree of stagey suspense. Clark and police soon arrive to mop up the crooks.

Back at the party, Eddie tells Clark he's discovered that it is Helen that he truly loves. He asks Clark to break the news to Joan. Mystified, Clark just shrugs his shoulders and walks away laughing. Eddie finds Helen and proposes. Helen quickly pulls out a judge—who apparently has been waiting around since the scene in the gym—from behind a bush. He marries them as they sing a reprise of "Yes, Yes."

*Palmy Days* had its grand premiere at New York's Rialto Theatre on September 22, 1931, before an invitation-only crowd. After the film, Cantor got up on stage and told the audience, "I hope you liked 'Palmy Days,' but it wasn't made for you; it was made for the masses." At least one critic agreed with Eddie's assessment, saying that the film was aimed at the average audience, including children.

*Palmy Days* performed well in its opening weeks in major cities throughout the country, even though first-run prices often were as high as $2 a ticket. The opening week in New York was aided by a vigorous ad campaign, including several appearances by Cantor himself. Eddie judged a prettiest waitress contest at Child's, decided the winner of a "newsboy with the biggest eyes" competition, and spent an hour making doughnuts in the window of a Broadway bakery. The week of events was topped off with a parade of 200 trucks from the Continental Baking Company.

A curious display card promoting the movie was distributed to well over one hundred Manhattan shops. The board featured Cantor's picture along with the slogan: "Eddie Cantor says enjoy 'Palmy Days'—Buy Now!" This campaign was used not only to tie in with *Palmy Days*, but also with Eddie's latest slim volume of jokes on the depression (à la *Caught Short*) entitled *Yoo Hoo Prosperity*.

Although the United Artists' ads proclaimed *Palmy Days* "A Surging Niagara of Laughs," adding that it "Positively Out-Whoops 'Whoopee'!" the film failed to repeat the business of its predecessor. Reviews were almost unanimously favorable, but almost all critics made unfavorable comparisons between *Palmy Days* and *Whoopee!*

After a vigorous, yet below expectations, first week *Palmy Days* dropped off quickly at the box office. Unfortunately, the film was released almost simultaneously with the Marx Brothers' latest, *Monkey Business*, and Laurel and Hardy's first starring feature, *Pardon Us*, bringing stiff competition for the comedy dollar. Still the film managed to turn a healthy profit (over $1 million) and was listed as one of United Artists' top three films of 1931, along with Charlie Chaplin's *City Lights* and *Street Scene*, another of Sam Goldwyn's productions.

## REVIEWS

It is quite good entertainment, this "Palmy Days." It is a more or less funny diatribe written by Mr. Cantor, Morrie Ryskind and David Freedman. There are two or three inconsequential melodies and a great deal to gaze, including pretty damsels from the Pacific Coast and effectively photographed groups of dancers.

The wit may not be as nimble as Mr. Cantor's image, but it is good enough to make one laugh heartily several times and not really tedious when the crystal gazer is plotting.—Mordaunt Hall, *New York Times*, September 24, 1931

It's going to bring the laughs it was made for in the regular picture houses, with the kids not the least amused among any audience.

Comedy is plainly gagged at times but surely nearly always. It's not a continuous laugh, but most of the gags will find the laughs they are going after by those who pay to be entertained. That's the kind of a picture it is all the way.

"Palmy Days" is not a "Whoopee" but it's a laugh, and that's what Cantor in a theatre guarantees. — Sime, *Variety*, September 29, 1931

Eddie Cantor wistfully tearing through a mad, exaggeratedly lavish production that has speed, gay absurdity, naturally introduced numbers, and gags which have never failed. All combined in shrewdly paced entertainment to overcome the usual unwieldiness of picture musicals, thereby making a film important on the ladies' lists. — "The Woman's Angle," *Variety*, September 29, 1931

## *Notes*

1. Sheet music from *Palmy Days* released concurrently with the film, however, gave full story and dialogue credit to just Cantor, Ryskind, and Freedman, in that order.

2. At one point in the scene, it would appear that Eddie's legs are locked behind his neck. Since the camera never actually shows his face while in this position, it is likely that a contortionist was used for the shot.

# CHAPTER 26

# *The Cantor-Jessel Vaudeville Show*

By mid–1931, while shooting *Palmy Days*, Eddie Cantor was starting to enjoy film stardom. So much so, in fact, that he announced to *Variety* that he intended to do two films a year in order to "retain his hold on the public." With one smash hit under his belt and another promising film before the cameras, Cantor decided that he would take advantage of his current popularity while the timing was right.

Sam Goldwyn, on the other hand, was content to produce one Cantor film a year, despite the fact that so far the banjo-eyed comedian had proved a gold mine for his small studio. Goldwyn's personal attention to each of his films prohibited his getting involved in more than one Cantor musical comedy extravaganza a year—no matter how popular and profitable they were. Eddie was not the only star in the Goldwyn stables. There was the equally, if not more, successful series of films starring Ronald Coleman, a Goldwyn star since the silent days. Apart from films involving these two stars, Goldwyn produced other films, each stressing a standard of quality that only came from painstaking, time-consuming attention from the producer. If Eddie Cantor wanted to do more than one film annually, it would seem that he would have to do them somewhere else.

In keeping with his newfound film stardom, Eddie planned to do a personal appearance tour of Europe in the fall of 1931 to coincide with the opening of *Palmy Days* on the Continent. Stage appearances were tentatively scheduled in London, Berlin, Vienna, Paris, and Rome. A funny thing happened on the way to Europe, however; Eddie never got there. Neither did he parlay his current picture popularity into a second film contract with another Hollywood studio. Instead, upon arriving in New York in September for the opening of *Palmy Days*, he took two different career paths altogether—one old, one new.

First, Eddie decided to spend the winter in New York, where he signed a contract to broadcast over the NBC Radio Network with a weekly radio program. The hour-long show, sponsored by Chase and Sanborn Coffee,

**Producer Sam Goldwyn and one of his biggest money-makers in the thirties (collection of Brian Gari).**

would run until the spring, when Eddie was due back in Hollywood for his next film.

Second, as long as he had to stay close to New York for the radio program, Cantor decided, along with his close friend from the *Kid Kabaret*, Georgie Jessel, to play vaudeville again. The idea sprang from a recent number of benefits the pair had played together. Eddie reasoned that they could get together a few acts built around the two of them and produce a full bill. This wouldn't be just any vaudeville appearance, however, but an extended run at the Palace Theatre, with Cantor receiving $8,800 per week. Jessel, a name, but still a considerably lesser one than his good pal, received $3,500. The total salary for the bill would reach between $15,000 and $16,000 per week, a record for the Palace. Still the Palace stood to make a good profit, especially with Eddie heading the bill, since his previous appearances had also set the house record of $35,000 at the box office.

Sharing the bill with Cantor and Jessel were Ben Meroff's Orchestra, a popular Chicago band brought to Broadway for the first time by Cantor's request, singer Janet Reade, the 3 Rhythm Dancers, and the team of George Burns and Gracie Allen. Burns and Allen, then a big-time vaudeville act, almost didn't make the cut. According to George Jessel, the booking office thought the act "too cute" for the type of dynamic show Cantor and he were putting together. Jessel convinced the management that George and Gracie had a new act—even though he had no knowledge that they did—and the team scored a huge success, not only in their own routine, but in skits with Eddie and George.

Cantor was so impressed with Allen that he asked Gracie to be a guest on his Chase and Sanborn show. Although he was not included in the offer,

George Burns agreed to let Gracie go on alone, provided he write the material. Burns made some slight revisions to a few of their routines, but the basic premise was the same, with Gracie getting all the laughs and Cantor filling in Burns' straight lines. Gracie's appearance was a hit, and within a week Burns and Allen had a steady spot on Rudy Valle's program, which soon led to their own show on CBS.

Opening October 31, 1931, the Cantor-Jessel show at the Palace was a tremendous hit. What they originally thought might be good for a two-week run, ran to a nine-week engagement, setting Palace records for length of engagement and highest box office receipts.

According to George Burns, the Palace show also set a record for the biggest laugh he ever heard in vaudeville. At one performance, while Cantor and Jessel were trading ad-lib insults to the delight of the audience, George topped Eddie. Eddie, unable to think of a better comeback line, took off his shoe and hit Jessel on the head with it. The audience roared.

Jessel stepped up to the footlights and proceeded to deliver a speech on Cantor and the nature of comedy. In it, he expressed sadness at the discovery that his friend and partner was an idiot. "Mr. Cantor couldn't think of anything intelligent enough to say," he explained to the audience, "so he resorted to the lowest form of humor, he hit me on the head with his shoe."

George continued to say how sorry he was that Cantor, whom he considered a great comedian, would stoop so low. All during Jessel's lecture Eddie stood silently by, listening to every word. Finally, after fully expressing his disappointment, George turned to Eddie and asked, "Now, what do you have to say for yourself?" Eddie looked at him for a moment, then hit him on the head again with his shoe, eliciting an even bigger laugh.

Even though their *Kid Kabaret* days were almost twenty years behind them, Eddie and Georgie behaved basically the same as they had when they were working for Gus Edwards. Georgie still ran around till all hours of the night and spent freely, which irritated the much more sober-living Eddie.

"Despite the fact that I found little time for sleep," Jessel later wrote, "I was in the best of health. Cantor, meanwhile, was going right to bed after the show each night. He took all kinds of medicines and was on three different diets—all of them consisting principally of milk."

Unlike their earlier days in vaudeville, however, now it was Jessel who was giving Cantor lectures on how to live. Georgie would tell his longtime and hypochondriac friend to throw out his diet and prescriptions and go on a spree. To illustrate his point, Jessel would mix drinks consisting of gin, ketchup, cigar ashes, and anything else handy. While Eddie would sip his milk, Georgie would gulp down these ghastly concoctions.

"I never became ill," Jessel bragged. "He would have some graham crackers and milk, and get a bellyache."

After the Palace, Eddie and George took their part of the show to Chicago, where they managed to take in $59,000 in a week, despite playing only four shows a day at a movie house. A year later, again in Eddie's off-season from his picture work, the duo decided to take an entire show on a extended road tour.

Playing at $2 top (the highest priced ticket for the best seats in the house), this tour consisted of Cantor, Jessel, Meroff's band, and five other acts, none as noteworthy as Burns and Allen but still strong vaudeville acts. The tour, which began in Springfield, Massachusetts, in late January 1933, played one-nighters up and down the East Coast, including stops in Albany, Rochester, Buffalo, Pittsburgh, Reading, and Richmond. In one week the show took in over $45,000, with its biggest night coming in Richmond despite a heavy snowstorm.

The show moved down to Palm Beach for a brief working vacation, before moving on to other southern dates. All told, their tour took in thirty-five cities in thirty-six nights, setting many house records along the way. The extra night was made necessary in Miami when their first performance was cut short by an attempted assassination of President-elect Franklin Roosevelt just a few blocks from the theater.

As they had in the past, the two close friends often squabbled, mostly on matters of a personal nature. Cantor, for instance, couldn't stand Jessel drinking in his dressing room and claimed the smell bothered him. "The only alcoholic beverage Cantor ever drank was a little sherry," Jessel explained, "and this only when Ida gave birth to a baby. In other words, Cantor has had five drinks."

Eddie was still bothered by his pal's total lack of frugality. One night in Houston, Jessel overheard Cantor in his dressing room telling his valet that if Georgie would stop calling glamour girls on the telephone all the time, he might have something to eat in his old age. Jessel held his tongue — but only till he was out on stage during his monologue.

Across the street from the auditorium was a large church with a huge neon sign which read: "Jesus Saves." "That's an inspiring electric sign across the street," Jessel told the audience, "but it should have added to it, 'But not like Cantor!'"

The tour was cut short when it reached New Orleans, and again, Franklin Roosevelt was responsible. In an effort to stem the tide of the nation's financial panic, the newly inaugurated president imposed an extended bank holiday that brought many businesses to a standstill. Instead of breaking up the acts, Cantor, in conjunction with the William Morris Agency, which booked the tour, decided to perform for a week in Washington, D.C., before resuming the planned schedule after the bank emergency. Jessel balked at the suggestion.

"Why knock ourselves out playing five shows a day for a couple of lousy thousand dollars?" Jessel argued. "I'm going to Palm Beach and enjoy myself." With that statement, he left Eddie and the rest of the bill in the capital.

A few days later, while hard at work in D.C., Eddie received a letter from Georgie, along with a photograph of Jessel on his yacht decked out in swanky yachting togs. On the picture Jessel wrote, "Sucker! Why aren't you doing this?"

Three days after that, however, Cantor received an emergency telegram from his truant friend. It read simply: "Please wire a hundred bucks. Need gasoline for the boat. Georgie."

# CHAPTER 27

# *The Kid from Spain*

In the spring of 1932, after a profitable winter of radio and vaudeville, Eddie Cantor returned to Hollywood to start work on his third picture for producer Sam Goldwyn. Just what that picture would be was a bit uncertain.

Originally, after the success of *Palmy Days*, Goldwyn had reconsidered Eddie's idea from the previous year for a comic bullfighting picture. "Let's see that Spanish thing, Eddie," he told his star comedian. Goldwyn decided that perhaps Eddie had been right after all, and it was announced that this year's Cantor extravaganza would be *The Kid from Spain*.

Because of the success of *Whoopee!* and *Palmy Days*, Goldwyn also decided that perhaps the public would flock to two Eddie Cantor films a year instead of just one. Ironically, it was Eddie himself who had decided the previous June that *he* would like to appear in two movies a year in order to "retain his hold on the public." At the time, however, Goldwyn had thought two Cantor musicals a year would be excessive.

With a slate of two films planned for his banjo-eyed gold mine, Goldwyn revealed that he was setting aside *The Kid from Spain* for the time being, but added that it could well be the second Cantor film later that year. In its place, according to an item in *Variety*, it was announced that Eddie Cantor's next film, and the first on the Goldwyn Studio calendar for 1932, would be something called *Ballyhoo*. What exactly *Ballyhoo* was — aside from the title of a sarcastic Depression song which Eddie had recently recorded — is unknown, for soon after the plans for it were announced, they were quickly dropped and preparation resumed on *The Kid from Spain*, for the third time since Cantor had first conceived of the project.

Giving the excuse that the United Artists Studio lot was too small, Eddie decided that the set of *The Kid from Spain* would not be cluttered up, as *Palmy Days* had been, with a battalion of gagmen. Instead the songwriting team of Bert Kalmar and Harry Ruby was picked to flesh out Eddie's original story. Aside from their composing successes, Kalmar and Ruby had also written a number of comedies prior to this along with Guy Bolton, who, incidentally, had worked on the early drafts of *Palmy Days*.

Kalmar and Ruby, friends of Eddie's from back in New York,[1] would have been glad to work on his latest picture, but they were under contract over at Paramount to write the Marx Brothers' latest film, *Horse Feathers*. With Kalmar and Ruby tied up until the middle of March, the writing assignment fell to William Anthony McGuire, author of *Kid Boots* and *Whoopee!* Given McGuire's lingering work habits, which matched the overall leisurely pace of the production, Kalmar and Ruby wound up working on the script after all, once they had finished *Horse Feathers*.

In early March, Eddie joined Kalmar and Ruby for a working vacation in Palm Springs, where the writers were already conferring with the Marx Brothers on the finishing touches for *Horse Feathers*. Also staying there at the El Mirador Hotel was Jimmy Durante, Eddie's old Coney Island pal now under contract at MGM. For four days the comedians and the comedy writers played and worked leisurely around the hotel's pool in their bathing suits.

Upon returning to Hollywood, Cantor announced that he would build selected scenes from *The Kid from Spain* into a stage production to try out the material. Since he had his favorite stage writer, McGuire, working on the film's script, Eddie reasoned that a short test run in front of a live audience would be beneficial to set the timing and sharpen the gags. Originally he envisioned a six-week tour to commence with a fortnight in San Francisco.

Initially, however, Sam Goldwyn balked at the idea, stating that previewing the film's script before a live audience would make the jokes stale and present an opportunity for other comedians to steal the picture's best gags before it could even be filmed. In addition, like Cantor's previous producer, Flo Ziegfeld, Goldwyn was loath to allow his star to appear in other mediums, because he thought that the extra exposure would be overexposure that would lessen Eddie's success in Goldwyn vehicles. Unfortunately for Goldwyn, as for Ziegfeld before him, the producer was dealing with a star who thrived on performing not only in vaudeville, picture house appearances, and benefits, but now on coast-to-coast radio in the off-season.

In spite of his objections, Goldwyn allowed Cantor, accompanied by Kalmar, Ruby and musical director Alfred Newman, to tryout various gags and songs in a week of four-a-day shows at San Francisco's Fox Theatre. The extra effort seemed to do the trick and gave the script of *The Kid from Spain* the polish that a proven stage property like *Whoopee* possessed and the static, overloaded *Palmy Days* sorely lacked. Although he is often credited with pioneering the testing of film material before a live audience, producer Irving Thalberg first used the device a full three years after *The Kid from Spain* tryouts for his production of the Marx Brothers film, *A Night at the Opera*.

In addition to traveling north to San Francisco, the trio of Cantor, Kalmar, and Ruby also ventured south of the border to Mexico City in search of "local color." Although he had been pitching the idea of a bullfight picture to Sam Goldwyn for over a year, Eddie Cantor confessed he had never actually seen a bullfight. A special fight (including a display of some of Mexico's finest bulls) was arranged on April 3 for the visitors from Hollywood.

**The Cantors in Hollywood in the early 1930s. Ida and Eddie with daughters Marjorie, Natalie, Edna, Marilyn, and Janet (collection of Brian Gari).**

"Some grade A bulls have been engaged for the fight," Eddie told the *New York Times*. "I'm prejudiced against any but grade A bulls—whatever they are," he added, admitting his ignorance of the sport.

After three months of preproduction work, filming was set to begin in mid–June 1932, a month and a half behind schedule—that is until the project's director quit. Two days before the cameras were to have rolled, Al Rogell left the picture over a dispute with Sam Goldwyn. Press reports were vague, saying only that the producer and his director "couldn't agree on certain story points, and rather than go on with a subject he did not believe, Rogell resigned." Rogell's abrupt departure, though setting the picture into further delays, was indeed a blessing for *The Kid from Spain*. For the most part, Rogell was strictly a "B" picture director and made mainly low-budget

Westerns. It is hard to imagine why Goldwyn would entrust such a high-budget picture to a director like Rogell in the first place, and why Rogell, given such an opportunity, would walk away from it to return to a career of second features.

For a time, comedy directors Eddie Cline and Eddie Sutherland were both considered to guide Cantor's latest film, but the chore eventually fell to Leo McCarey. McCarey would go on to win two Academy Awards, along with a reputation as one of Hollywood's top directors—especially in the realm of comedy—but in the summer of 1932, when he directed *The Kid from Spain*, Leo McCarey was still regarded as somewhat of a "kid" himself when it came to feature films.

Originally a graduate of USC law school, McCarey broke into films in 1918 at the age of twenty, as an assistant to director Tod Browning. After five years in a variety of film jobs, he joined Hal Roach Studios as a gagman and director of short comedies, supervising such stars as Charley Chase and Laurel and Hardy (whom he was also instrumental in teaming). McCarey started directing features in 1929, with *The Kid from Spain* being his first big hit among a string of many. In the next few years, McCarey would direct the Marx Brothers' *Duck Soup*,[2] W. C. Fields' *Six of a Kind*, Harold Lloyd's *The Milky Way*, and the delightful *Ruggles of Red Gap*, with Charles Laughton.

With a new director at the helm, an additional six weeks went by before production began while McCarey rewrote and fine-tuned the script. Although Goldwyn used the time to recruit extra members for his sixty-girl chorus, the producer still grew impatient, especially with McCarey, to get the $1.4 million production under way.

Cast selections were finally made the second week of July—up to this point only Cantor and comedienne Lyda Roberti had been cast—with rehearsals to begin July 18, and the actual five-week filming schedule to commence three days later. Sam Goldwyn ordered a closed set on the picture, primarily to conceal the fact that the majority of his hand-picked chorus girls had no previous stage or screen experience.

In mid–July, after four and a half months of preproduction delays, the project was pushed back yet again. This current delay was supposedly caused by Eddie Cantor's need for a two-week vacation at Arrowhead Springs, but it was more likely that McCarey wanted another two weeks to further refine the script. Production finally began on August 1, 1932, and lasted roughly eight weeks, three weeks beyond the original schedule.

One Saturday after shooting had begun, McCarey was again dissatisfied with a scene that wasn't living up to its comic potential. He approached Cantor for help.

"Eddie," the director asked, "why don't you get sick? We'll go to Santa Barbara, rewrite the scene, and shoot it Monday morning."

"I'm not only sick," cried the abetting Eddie, "I'm almost blind." Eddie immediately came down with a blinding headache, and within the hour the pair was on their way up the coast. The new scene, according to Cantor, turned out to be one of the best in the picture, although Sam Goldwyn never did quite figure out where it came from.

McCarey displayed the utmost patience in crafting *The Kid from Spain*, laboring until each scene was exactly what he wanted. Unfortunately, the more care the director took, the shorter Sam Goldwyn's fuse became. While Goldwyn was accustomed to holding up production for numerous rewrites, he was not used to such delays when a film was before the cameras.

"Goldwyn wasn't too happy with McCarey," Cantor recalled years later, "and for a while wanted to take his name off the picture. But McCarey had written half the picture or rewritten it, as well as directing."

Most of the delays on the set of *The Kid from Spain* came from an area in which neither Goldwyn, McCarey, or Cantor had any experience — bulls. Goldwyn had built a large bullring which he stocked with four or five of the best bulls he could find in Mexico. He also hired Cantor's friend and inspiration for the film, bullfighter Sidney Franklin. Franklin appeared as himself in the final bullfight scene in addition to providing technical advice.

At one point, filming was held up almost a week while McCarey attempted to get a bull to jump over the fence which encircled the bullring. With the arena filled with extras, the bull, for whatever reason, resolved to be bullheaded and refused to make the leap. Finally an irate Sam Goldwyn arrived on the set to order things along.

"Leo," the producer asked, "why doesn't that bull jump?"

"I'm trying to get him to jump," McCarey argued.

"Well," Goldwyn reasoned, "you're the director, aren't you?"

"Yes," McCarey admitted, "but the bull isn't a member of the actors' union. You're the boss, Sam, you tell him!"

The first day of the bullfight scenes featured Franklin fighting the bull while a stadium full of extras, including well-disguised stars such as Mary Pickford, Charlie Chaplin, and Harold Lloyd, cheered him on. After watching his friend Sidney come close to getting gored — Franklin had personally advised Goldwyn to get the most ferocious bulls to add to the scene's authenticity — the following day it was Eddie's turn. Although he was separated from the bull at all times by an electrified wire, and many of the shots finally used in the picture were achieved by the obvious use of rear screen projection, Cantor still had to get into the ring with the killer bulls.

"The wire was always there between me and the bull," he later confessed, "but I was a happy toreador when that part of the picture was finished."

Ironically, just when he thought he had seen the last of the bull, Eddie was thrown back into the ring. At a preview of the finished film in San Diego, Goldwyn expressed dissatisfaction with the bullfight scene and ordered retakes. McCarey argued that he could allay Goldwyn's qualms with additional editing. Cantor, not wanting to go back with the bulls, backed his director's opinion vehemently, but to no avail. Retakes were done at a cost of over $60,000 until Goldwyn was satisfied and Eddie could retire at last from bullfighting.

The delays in filming *The Kid from Spain*, whatever their source—the writers, McCarey, or the bulls—seem to have paid off. The film is a quick paced, consistently entertaining extravaganza of comedy and music, and thus is arguably Eddie Cantor's finest film. In addition, after the disappointments of *Palmy Days* and *Special Delivery*, *The Kid from Spain*, Eddie's fifth feature, succeeds on its own cinematic merits, and not as a film adaptation of a previous Broadway vehicle.

The comedy is well integrated into the plot, and while not every joke hits the mark, the small percentage of those that don't are not detrimental to the film as a whole. The songs by Kalmar and Ruby are pleasant, often clever, and one, "What a Perfect Combination," is just as good as any in the Cantor canon. Busby Berkley, although restricted to only two production numbers, makes the most of his opportunities. He is aided in both numbers, the "College" number and "What a Perfect Combination," by lavish sets, which he employs to their full effect. The sets in general are quite impressive, displaying plenty of Mexican style and flavor.

One of the most impressive sets, especially considering that it was only used for the opening five minutes of the film, is the girl's dormitory where the film begins. A pretty young coed awakes from her slumber to announce to the camera, in verse, that the film will start with a "peek inside a dormitory where all the pretty coeds sleep."

After a dazzling Berkley number in which the girls not only awake to dance in formation, but enjoy a synchronized swim in their private Olympic-sized indoor pool, the coed's song is brought to an abrupt halt when the dorm matron enters. The matron awakens some late sleepers, whom she punishes by making them recite: "I'm a naughty girl" twenty times. When she comes to one especially stubbornly slumbering girl hiding under the covers, the matron is forced to yank away the sheets. Instead of a pretty young coed, she finds Eddie Williams (Cantor) in his pajamas.

"I'm a naughty girl. I'm a naughty girl," Eddie begins to cry, already resigning himself to the punishment for oversleeping.

"How is it, young man, that I find you in the girls' dormitory?" the matron demands. "How is it?"

After getting an eyeful of his surroundings, Eddie pronounces judgment: "'Tain't bad!"

The matron leads Eddie into her office in an attempt to get to the bottom of the incident. She reasons that Eddie, a student who is just about to graduate after working his way through college as a waiter, would not jeopardize his degree so carelessly. She questions Eddie's mental and emotional stability. Eddie admits he has an affliction. Every time he hears a whistle he involuntarily starts hitting the nearest person, while jumping up and down. To test the veracity of this, the matron blows a whistle. True to his word Eddie has a fit, knocking himself and the matron to the floor. Just then the dean enters to question Eddie further.

"There's nothing to tell," Eddie pleads. "I just grew tired of sleeping with the fellows and thought I'd try the girls' dormitory . . . for a change."

Unconvinced, the dean ushers in Ricardo (Robert Young), Eddie's best friend and roommate, who is an exchange student from Mexico. Ricardo has confessed to placing the sleeping Eddie in the girls' dorm as a practical joke and is summarily expelled. Eddie, on the other hand, is commended by the dean for attempting to protect his errant roomie. The dean's praise is interrupted, however, by a nearby steam whistle, which causes Eddie to shower the dean with punches, leading to his expulsion as well.

From their dorm room, Ricky and Eddie sadly watch the graduates parade by in their caps and gowns while they pack. Ricky apologizes for getting Eddie expelled, but Eddie insists he doesn't mind.

"I'm glad I'm not graduating," Eddie says, in a valiant attempt to hide his disappointment. "Say, I'd look terrible in one of those black kimonos. Besides," he adds, "you've got to buy a frame for the diploma. You've got to run up to the attic every time you want to look at it. What's a diploma anyway? It's only a license to look for a job."

Changing the subject, Ricardo invites Eddie to Mexico, where he assures his roommate that every man becomes a great lover. Ricky attributes this to the combined effects of the Mexican sun by day and the moon by night.

"What do you do when it rains?" Eddie asks, before withdrawing his question. "Wait," he cries, rolling his eyes, "don't tell me. It's the same the world over — Poop-oop-a-doop! Poop-oop-a-doop!"

Meanwhile, outside a nearby bank, a carload of bank robbers pull up. While the robbers are inside, a policeman comes by and tells their driver to move along because he's in a no-parking zone. As soon as he pulls away, Eddie and Rickie pull up. Rickie goes into the bank while Eddie waits. The robbers run out of the bank into Eddie's car and order him at gunpoint to drive them away.

On the way to the hideout, Eddie hits a traffic cop on purpose and begins to insult the officer in the hope of getting them all arrested.

"Where do you think you're going?" the cop asks.

"Why, who wants to know?" Eddie cracks back.

"You know," the cop tells him, "I got half a mind to give you a ticket."

"What's stopping you?" Eddie answers. "Whether you give me a ticket or not, you've got half a mind."

Unfortunately, the cop admires Eddie's bravado and offers to let him go with just a warning. Eddie continues his barrage of wisecracks, finishing off by calling the officer a "yellow bohunk." Having reached his breaking point, the cop jumps on the running board and tells Eddie to drive down to the station.

Eddie begins to tell the cop that he's got a carload of crooks, but before he can, the robbers push the cop off. Eddie goes on describing his ruthless captors until he realizes his savior is curiously absent. He sheepishly smiles at the bandits and asks, "Where to, please?"

At the hideout, Eddie grabs the gun of one of the bandit and orders the gang to put their hands up. In his best Jimmy Cagney tough guy accent, Eddie lectures the crooks while he picks up the candlestick phone to call the police.

"Thought I was some kind of sap, eh?" Eddie growls. "Ya' bunch of criminals! You'll find out that crime doesn't pay." Unfortunately, Eddie points the phone receiver at the crooks, while putting the barrel of the gun to his ear. He soon realizes his error and meekly hands the gun back, resigned to the fact that he's out of his element with firearms.

The gang leader informs Eddie that he's going to Mexico because he was a witness to the robbery. When Eddie refuses, the boss reminds him that he drove the getaway car and thus is an accomplice to the crime. To make sure he gets across the border, the gangster escorts Eddie there personally.

In Mexico, Rosalie (Lyda Roberti) bursts into the bedroom of her best friend, Anita (Ruth Hall), to inform her that Ricardo has returned. While Ricardo waits for Anita in the courtyard, Anita's father, Señor Gomez (Noah Beery), entertains Pancho (John Miljan) in the living room. It seems that Señor Gomez has already arranged for his daughter to marry Pancho, who is one of Mexico's greatest bullfighters. He tells Ricardo that he must no longer call on Anita. Ricardo states that he will go away rather than see Anita married to someone else.

The next day at the border a long line of people, including Eddie, wait to get into Mexico. News of the bank robbery has already reached the border.

"Imagine," one man in line says, "another bank robbery in broad daylight."

"Believe me," a stout woman announces, "I take no chances. I bank my money right here," she says, patting her bosom.

"You're right, Lady," Eddie agrees. "now-a-days you can't tell which bank is a bust."

When Eddie absentmindedly falls out of line, he is called to the front by the Mexican border guard, Gonzales (Paul Porcasi), who questions him.

"Are you going to Mexico to live?" Gonzales asks.

"I was told I couldn't live in the United States," Eddie answers, looking over his shoulder at the gang leader.

"Who told you? A doctor?"

"No," Eddie replies, "A specialist . . . a big shot."

"You sick?" Gonzales continues, singling out Eddie's most prominent feature. "What's wrong with you? Your eyes? You need glasses?"

"Yeah," a prohibition-weary Eddie admits, "with beer in them."

Not in the mood for jokes, Gonzales sends Eddie back to the end of the line. When his turn comes again, Gonzales makes Eddie promise he won't tell any more jokes and then asks for some identification. Eddie explains that he comes from a farm and for proof produces a photograph of his cow eating corn. The picture, however, shows only an barren field.

"Where's the corn?" Gonzales asks.

"The cow ate it," Eddie says.

"Where's the cow?"

"Well," Eddie says, "after she ate up the corn there was no use in her hanging around."

Gonzales again banishes Eddie to the rear.

"You'll never get any customers for Mexico that way," Eddie cries, as he retreats. "I'm surprised you do any business at all."

Eddie finally gets across the border dressed as an erzatz Mexican after swapping clothes with a mannequin in a nearby shop. Grover, a detective investigating the bank robbery, is waiting at the border armed with a good description of the gang's driver. Eddie raises his suspicions, especially after responding to Gonzales' "adios" with an "adios and pastafazool."

Luckily, Eddie runs into Ricardo just over the border and explains his predicament just as Grover comes over to interrogate him. When the detective asks who Eddie is, Ricardo tells him that his friend is Don Sebastian the Second, a bullfighter and son of the great Don Sebastian, a world-famous matador killed in the bullring. He goes on to explain that Don Sebastian the Second is in town to perform in next Sunday's bullfight. Grover suspiciously eyes Eddie and promises that he'll be at the bullfight to see him perform.

That night Eddie and Ricky crash a party at Señor Gomez's beautiful hacienda. "Say," Eddie remarks, "isn't this a nice place . . . to get kicked out of."

While they wait in the garden to catch a glimpse of Anita, Ricardo tells Eddie that he has nothing to worry about concerning the bullfight.

"Oh," Eddie says, breathing a sigh of relief. "You'll get me out of it?"

"No," say Ricardo, "I'll get you into it."

"Who's side are you on?" Eddie asks. "Mine or the detective's? Or maybe you're working for a bull."

Ricardo comments that Eddie's problems are minor compared to the sorry state of his own love life. To prove that love is the common problem of most people, Eddie sings "In the Moonlight." In this clever little tune, he explains that most difficulties throughout history have been caused by lovers walking in the moonlight.

As Eddie finishes the number, Grover arrives to question him further. Eddie escapes into the house, where Señor Gomez is telling Ricardo that Anita will marry Pancho because he once saved Anita's mother from a band of kidnapers, even though the incident proved fatal to her. Before exiting, Ricardo introduces Eddie as Don Sebastian the Second. As luck would have it, Señor Gomez was best friends with the first Don Sebastian and even raised bulls for him. He welcomes Eddie with a tearful embrace which is repeated often while the pair discuss "Papa" and bulls.

Eddie regales his host with a colorful tale of how he once fought four bulls at one time in Barcelona.

"The bulls get into a huddle," Eddie begins. "They get out of a huddle. They charge. I charge . . ."

"You charge?" Señor Gomez interrupts.

"Yeah, twenty cents for the first mile, five cents for each quarter mile and ten cents for waiting."

"Waiting?"

"If the bulls make me wait, I charge," Eddie insists.

"You killed them?" Señor Gomez asks breathlessly.

"Four bulls . . . Don Sebastian . . . Roast Beef," Eddie brags matter-of-factly.

"Well done!" cries Señor Gomez.

Señor Gomez proceeds to show Eddie his collection of bull heads mounted on the wall.

"This bull," he begins, "killed ten horses and two matadors in one afternoon. I have his son. You want to fight him?"

"No, I would rather fight him," Eddie admits, pointing to the stuffed head.

Before he can describe his last trophy, Señor Gomez breaks down into a flood of tears. It seems this last bull was the one which killed Don Sebastian the First.

Fighting back mock tears, Eddie slaps the beast's nose and chides, "Naughty bull!"

Regaining his composure, Señor Gomez points to a large chest. "And here I have . . ."

"My father?" Eddie asks.

Señor Gomez opens the trunk and produces the suit Don Sebastian was wearing when he was killed. Closer inspection reveals a hole in the seat of the pants where he was gored, but Eddie insists the bull got him through the heart. "He was a very short man," Eddie explains.

Señor Gomez asks Eddie if a bull ever got him.

"Yes," he admits, "but I was not killed." He goes on to describe how a bull ripped his cheek off, but a doctor grafted skin from another part of his body to reconstruct his face. Señor Gomez feels Eddie's cheek and asks him what part of the body they took the patch from.

"I don't know," Eddie admits, "but every time when I get tired, my face, it wants to sit down."

Outside in the courtyard Pancho catches Ricardo talking to Anita. The two men start to fight, and the local police come and arrest Ricardo. When Eddie tries to intervene on behalf of his friend, a policeman blows his whistle, sending Eddie into a fit. He too is taken into custody.

In prison, Ricardo makes Eddie promise to spirit Anita away after he is released, since he is most likely to be freed first. When Eddie confesses that he doesn't know what Anita looks like, Ricardo tells him to serenade beneath her balcony until she comes out. Eddie begins to practice his serenading, when the prisoner in the next cell, a tough-looking bandit named Dalmores (Julian Rivero), joins in. After making sure the bars between them are quite strong, Eddie tells his grisly accompanist to shut up. This only makes Dalmores angry. Eddie continues to taunt Dalmores—even calling him a "palooka"—until the bandit is beside himself with rage.

Just then the jailer comes with instructions to put Eddie in cell three—with Dalmores. Dalmores jumps up and down with glee, while Eddie meekly tries to explain to the jailer that "He don't like me." With the transfer completed, Dalmores dives on top of Eddie, wrestling him to the ground for calling him a "palooka." Eddie discovers, however, that Dalmores doesn't even know what a palooka is.

"'Palooka,'" Eddie tells him, "means 'gentleman.' Dalmores is the biggest palooka what can be."

Dalmores warms to this new definition, until Eddie adds that his father was also a palooka. Obviously, Dalmores has a different opinion of his father and resumes his beating of Eddie.

In the prison yard, a firing squad is falling in, with Dalmores its next victim. Back in their cell, Eddie tells Dalmores he has to get out to help a señorita and will do anything to escape. Dalmores explains he will be leaving soon and offers to switch clothes with Eddie. Eddie express his gratitude, but Dalmores insists the pleasure is all his.

After they exchange outfits, the firing squad comes for their prisoner. Eddie, thinking it's a honor guard to escort him out, follows happily. Out in the courtyard Eddie begins to say good-bye, when the guard offers him a blindfold.

"Oh, excuse me, I didn't know," Eddie apologizes, taking the cloth and wiping his nose with it. "I'll let you borrow one of my handkerchiefs when they come back from the cleaner," he adds.

The sergeant positions Eddie against the wall, presumably, Eddie believes, for a picture. As he takes out his comb to fix his hair for the "shot," Eddie realizes that his "photographers" are all toting rifles.

"Wait a minute," he cries. "They're aiming at me. You want to kill me?"

"Si," the sergeant answers.

Eddie starts dancing back and forth while the confused firing squad tries to follow him. At the last minute, Señor Gomez arrives with the warden to save Eddie. Gomez explains the mistake they've made and goes on to praise "Don Sebastian the Second" as the bravest and most courageous man in Mexico. When the soldiers fire their rifles in salute, the most courageous man in Mexico faints.

That night Eddie comes, underneath a six-foot sombrero, to serenade Anita. Pancho hears him and shoots at him from the balcony. When Pancho runs downstairs, Eddie scrambles up the trellis and enters Rosalie's bedroom by mistake.

"Do you realize this is my bedroom and I'm undressed?" Rosalie asks.

"I'm here on business. Take off that nightgown," Eddie demands, before adding, "and get dressed."

When Rosalie refuses to go with him, Eddie pulls out a pistol and holds it shakily while she climbs out of bed.

"Don't look at me," she cries. "I'm half undressed."

"That's okay," Eddie insists. "I keep one eye closed!"

After Rosalie gets dressed, she leads her unsure kidnapper to their escape route. As Eddie and Rosalie drive away in a borrowed car, Pancho and Pedro watch from the balcony, too late to stop them.

Pedro vows that he will "keel" Don Sebastian the Second for stealing his girlfriend.

Out in the country, Rosalie makes Eddie stop the car so they can neck. Eddie, still thinking he has Anita, insists that Ricardo won't like it. Rosalie says she doesn't care, adding: "I do not love Ricardo, I love you."

Eddie demands that "Anita" stop carrying on and think of Ricardo. Rosalie tells him that she isn't Anita.

"I took the wrong girl," Eddie realizes. "What have I done?"

"Nothing," the boy-crazy Rosalie answers, "but I'm waiting."

Eddie insists they drive back and get Anita, but Rosalie takes the car keys, putting them down her décolletage until Eddie ransoms them with a kiss. Eddie quickly gives her a peck on the cheek, but Rosalie insists that he kiss her like "a hawk or an eagle."

"How 'bout like an ostrich?" he offers.

Finally Eddie obliges with a long, sensuous kiss. Breathlessly, Rosalie hands the keys over to Eddie, who, having enjoyed the process so much, drops them back down her dress.

"Give me the keys," Eddie then demands, while embracing her for another round. After a few more lengthy kisses, Rosalie, finally having found a man who can satisfy her passions, insists she will give him the keys.

"I already got them," he announces.

"My Don!" Rosalie cries with delight.

To emphasize the fact that they've fallen for each other, the couple sings "Look What You've Done." Just as the song ends and the two new lovers fall into each other's arms, Pedro, Rosalie's former boyfriend, arrives on horseback accompanied by his gang of bandits. Pedro slings Eddie over the back of a horse and instructs Jose (Stanley Fields) to take him for a ride — Mexican style. Jose rides away with Eddie while Pedro takes Rosalie back to town.

Meanwhile, now out of prison, Ricardo reads a letter from Anita telling him that he must go away, even though she loves him more than ever. At Señor Gomez's home, Anita and Rosalie cry over their lost loves.

Somewhere out in the jungle at Pedro's hideout, Jose, after a number of farewell drinks, proceeds with his orders to kill Eddie. He tells Eddie how lucky he is to be killed by the greatest bandits in Mexico.

"That's nice," Eddie agrees. "If I should be killed by some cheap, small bandits I would never get over it."

Jose decides to kill Eddie with a gun, but Eddie calls for one last drink. The already tipsy Jose agrees and quickly belts down a healthy slug of tequila. Eddie then doubts whether or not Jose is in any condition to shoot him. He stands nose to nose with the bandit, so Jose won't miss. Jose insists he could still shoot Eddie with "one eye closed" and orders him to move back. Eddie obliges and steps back a few paces.

"Could you shoot me from here?" Eddie asks.

"Oh, without the gun!" Jose brags. Eddie moves back.

"How about from here?" Eddie calls from a few yards further.

"Go back a little more," Jose commands, until Eddie is far down the path.

"How about now?" he cries from the distance.

"No," Jose admits, "you're too far."

"That's all I want to know," Eddie shouts, disappearing into the jungle.

Back at Ricardo's, he and Rosalie are discussing Eddie's whereabouts when Eddie staggers out of the jungle, his clothes in tatters. Eddie begins to tell of his harrowing escape from the bandits when Grover walks in to remind Eddie of his upcoming bullfight.

"I'll be in a box on Sunday," the detective proclaims, waving his tickets.

"He'll be in a box on Sunday," Eddie moans after Grover exits, "and I'll be in a box on Monday."

Eddie asks Ricardo if he can find a gentle bull for him to fight. Ricardo replies there are none.

"There must be," Eddie insists. "There are contented cows aren't there? Well," he adds rolling his eyes, "for every contented cow there must be a contented bull."

Ricardo manages to find a trained bull named "Max." Max's trainer demonstrates that his bull will respond to hand signals and other directions. The trainer goes on to explain that if Max charges, he can be brought to a halt by saying "Popocatepetl." Eddie can't remember the magic word, little more say it, so the trainer writes it out for him.

Lurking in the shadows, Pedro and Pancho witness the fix and determine to replace the passive Max with a mankiller named "Diablo."

That night at a nearby cafe, complete with a huge, multitiered, revolving dance floor, a party is held in honor of the next day's bullfight. Eddie manages to get Ricardo and Anita together. While the lovers talk, Eddie runs interference for them, luring Pancho and Pedro away. The pair pursue Eddie, who finally manages to elude them by ducking under a nearby table.

Pancho and Pedro soon give up their search and sit down at the table Eddie is hiding under. The villains get into an argument over whom they will kill first, Ricardo or Don Sebastian the Second (Eddie). They give action to their rage by kicking each under the table, but, naturally, it is Eddie who must silently accept the blows and then pass them on to their intended receiver so as not to arouse suspicion.

The disagreement intensifies when Pedro threatens to tell Señor Gomez that it was Pancho who arranged the kidnapping and death of his wife. Pancho pulls out a gun and points it under the table. Pedro also draws, and Eddie thus has a barrel in each of his ears. While Eddie closes his eyes in anticipation of the shots, a nearby waiter pops open a bottle of champagne. The cork hits Eddie, giving him an idea.

While the bandits calm down and put away their weapons, Eddie burns the cork and uses it to black up. In order to facilitate his escape, Eddie reignites the villains' argument by hitting them both in the shins. When they start bickering again, Eddie crawls away. Pedro spots this "black" man, and he and Pancho pull Eddie off the floor.

"What were you doing under that table," Pancho demands to know.

"Oh, nothing, sir," Eddie drawls, "I'm just a table-looker-under."

Before Pancho can interrogate him further, however, Eddie excuses himself to join a blackface dance act already in progress on the stage. Bewildered, the other two dancers try to push Eddie off, but he follows them until they start off the stage. Rather than retreat to the wings where Pedro and Pancho are waiting, Eddie remains onstage to sing "What a Perfect Combination," another tune tailor-made to his particular style.

As he finishes the chorus, a bevy of Goldwyn Girls—though they wouldn't officially be called such until the following year—rise on elevators out of the surrounding tables, clad in skintight toreador pants and almost nonexistent tops, to perform the geometric patterns of yet another meticulously produced Busby Berkley routine.

Evidently Pancho and Pedro grow tired of waiting for the number to conclude, because the next scene takes place at Sunday's bullfight. While Sydney Franklin fights the preliminary bout, back in his dressing room, Eddie tells Ricardo that Señora Gomez's kidnapping was all Pancho's doing. With his problem resolved, Ricardo relaxes.

"Listen to those castanets," he tells Eddie, enjoying the band.

"Castanets!" Eddie cries. "Those are my knees shaking."

Ricardo insists that Eddie has nothing to worry about since he has Max and "Popocatepetl" to fall back on. Unfortunately, Eddie still hasn't memorized the word, though it would be of little use since Pancho and Pedro have succeeded in substituting Diablo for Max.

Acknowledging the cheers of the crowd, Eddie strides into the bullring and throws back his cape to reveal that he's forgotten his pants. The other bullfighters flock around him while he borrows trousers from one of them.

"Gracias, and thanks for the knickers, Señor," Eddie tells the donor, before getting down to business. The bull is released, and Eddie gets set to give Max the prearranged signals. When the bull fails to respond to Eddie's commands, preferring instead to charge at will, Eddie scolds him. Ricardo, watching from the sidelines, quickly realizes that Eddie is in the ring with a killer, but Eddie keeps trying to put "Max" through the routines.

Eddie realizes that Max has been switched when the bull gives him a quick ride around the ring on his horns. Eddie tries in vain to say "Popocatapatel" and finally puts the paper in front of the bull and tells him, "Here, you read it!"

Instead of reading, Diablo throws Eddie aside and charges, landing on top of him. In retaliation, Eddie bites the bull's tail, sending him fleeing.

Eddie seeks refuge from Diablo behind the various barriers around the edge of the ring, but each time he tries to get behind one, the other bullfighters push him out and back into the ring.

Finally, Eddie jumps over the wall altogether, but Diablo follows suit and chases him down the narrow inner ring. (Although most of Cantor's close-ups in the scene are rear screen shots, only this sequence is rather poorly matched and thus obviously fake.) When Eddie tries to get back into the ring, the bull again pursues him.

Reinforcements rush in to give Eddie a respite, but even these professionals are little match for this bull, and one is carried off on a stretcher. A doctor administers chloroform to the injured matador and then throws the drug-laced towel over the fence of the arena. Eddie pauses to mop his brow with the cloth and immediately starts to swoon. Recovering, he realizes what's in the towel and rushes back into the center of the ring. There Eddie takes a few passes from Diablo before he succeeds in draping the chloroform-soaked towel over the bull's horns.

Soon Diablo lapses into a slow motion lope and falls asleep. Eddie places his foot on the bull's neck while the crowd showers him with their sombreros. Eddie carefully looks around the ring till he finds one the right size and puts it on as he rushes off.

Señor Gomez proclaims Don Sebastian the Second the greatest bullfighter in all of Mexico and announces that he will arrange for him to fight every week. Rosalie insists that Eddie must retire from the ring, and he promises he will do so, adding that he will never leave her side again. Just then Grover enters the box, and Eddie tells Rosalie he will be back in twenty years.

Grover assures Eddie that they have caught the bank robbers and that his named was cleared days ago; he just wanted to see Eddie fight the bull. The detective asks Eddie why he did it.

"I did it for the wife and kids," Eddie proclaims.

"Have you got a wife and kids?" a stunned Rosalie asks.

"No," Eddie grins, "but I'm going to have."

The 76 chorus girls used in *The Kid from Spain* were chosen from a field of 8,855 girls, 648 of whom were tested on film at a cost of over $18,000. The total cost for assembling the chorus reached $90,000. After going through the trouble of personally selecting the 76 chorus girls, Sam Goldwyn decided to get the most out of his investment. The producer planned to send 16 of the 76 on tour with the film under the appellation "Goldwyn's Girls," which would soon be shortened to the now familiar "Goldwyn Girls." While the picture was in postproduction, however, Goldwyn decided—as he had two years earlier with the aborted promotional tour for *Whoopee!*—that the film would be an expensive enough draw on its own and released the girls.

Even without a live chorus line to accompany *The Kid from Spain* around

**Eddie and Lyda Roberti in *The Kid from Spain*.**

the country, Sam Goldwyn released the film as a road show, charging $2.20 a ticket for the initial release. The plan drew criticism, especially from United Artists, since Goldwyn refused to let the releasing company sell *The Kid from Spain* for its premiere engagements, deciding instead to book the film himself.

Opening at New York's Palace Theatre (recently converted from a vaudeville house to a movie theater) and Hollywood's Warner Western Theatre, Goldwyn demanded and got a straight 50 percent of each ticket sold. Prior to this, only one film, Charlie Chaplin's *City Lights*, had received such terms.

The exorbitant ticket price—the country was after all in the depths of the Great Depression—was one of the few things *Variety* could find fault with in *The Kid from Spain*. The show business paper commented that the film was "a swell flicker. . . . But it's not two bucks' worth." Even Eddie Cantor was overheard complaining about the high ticket cost to a United Artists bigwig at the film's New York opening.

"I'd be happier if this were in the Rivoli at seventy-five cents," Cantor told the executive. "Believe me! A guy making a small salary must give up 10 percent of his income to see me in a picture. That's too tough nowadays."

For their $2, however, the road show public did get to see more *Kid from Spain* than the general release audience would. The film's original running time for the New York and Hollywood release was just shy of two hours

(118 minutes to be exact), quite long, especially for a musical comedy film. One reviewer commented that although he enjoyed *The Kid from Spain*, cutting would only improve the film. Indeed, by early January 1933, when it went into general release, *The Kid from Spain* clocked in at ninety-six minutes, which is how it stands today.

As it turned out, Eddie and United Artists were right. After a strong week following the November 17 opening, *The Kid from Spain* took a steady decline at the box office. This slump was no reflection on the quality of the film, but rather a case of simple economics — very few people could afford to see anything at $2.20 a pop. The truth of this was evident when the film went into general release at "popular prices" and did record business around the country. Playing to standing room only and held over extra weeks in most cities, *The Kid from Spain* went on to become one of the highest grossing films of 1933. This was particularly remarkable because at the time, musicals had fallen out of favor with the public. (This was a trend which would begin to turn around in the coming year with the Busby Berkley films produced by Warner Brothers.) Thanks to the success of *The Kid from Spain*, Eddie Cantor was proclaimed United Artists' hottest star.

Not everyone loved *The Kid from Spain*, however. Mexico banned the film outright, refusing to allow it to be exhibited or even brought into the country. The government asserted that the picture slighted Spanish, as well as Mexican, customs (not to mention that most of the characters speak broken English laced with horrendous grammar). A few years later, *The Kid from Spain* was also banned in Germany. Not because of any German slight — there are none in the film — but rather because of the Nazis' refusal to continue to exhibit a film with a Jewish protagonist. The Nazis' snub was just fine with Eddie Cantor, who commented that he had "no desire to make those people laugh, because they had made my people cry."

During the filming of *The Kid from Spain*, Eddie signed a new contract with Sam Goldwyn calling for five more films, one each year for the next five years, following the completion of the one under production. Given the cost of *The Kid from Spain*, coupled with the fact that it would take the better part of a year to complete, Goldwyn apparently dropped his idea of producing two Cantor films a year. The new arrangement was fine with Eddie, who was still under contract to resume his weekly radio program in New York once picture production was wrapped up for the year. In addition, Eddie planned another series of vaudeville and picture house appearances, along with a weekly magazine serialization, with collaborator David Freedman, on the life of Flo Ziegfeld.

The Great Ziegfeld had died July 22, at Cedars of Lebanon Hospital, not long after coming west to rest from a bout with pleurisy. Eddie, along with another Ziegfeld star who had since made it big in movies, Will Rogers, helped Billie Burke with the funeral arrangements. Less than a month before his death, Ziegfeld had written one final note to the star he had been so instrumental in making. In this note he talked of his current revival of *Show*

*Boat* on Broadway and his plans to come to California for his health. Finally, he asked Eddie what his plans were, closing with: "Would love to do another show with you before I pass on. Love to all, Flo."

## REVIEWS

That nimble little comedian, Eddie Cantor, is the leading light in Samuel Goldwyn's latest picture, "The Kid From Spain," which was offered last night at the Palace. It is an astutely arranged combination of fun and beauty, with such effective groupings of dancing girls that these scenes themselves aroused applause. The film keeps Mr. Cantor busy most of the time and there is no objection to this, for he makes the most of his painful experiences, especially those in the closing episode. — Mordaunt Hall, *New York Times*, November 18, 1932

[The] Picture has everything for the popular gate. There's romance, action and comedy — what's more to be desired for an evening's entertainment?

The songs are well-fitting to Cantor although they're not particularly "commercial" as pop songs go.

The picture is all Cantor's. Almost every scene, save the opening co-ed stuff, has Cantor in it and to his credit, he more than sustains the tempo. — Abel, *Variety*, November 22, 1932

## *Notes*

1. Cantor had introduced one of Kalmar and Ruby's earliest hits, "My Sunny Tennessee," in *Midnight Rounders* eleven years earlier.

2. Based on his success with *The Kid from Spain*, Leo McCarey supposedly was hired to direct *Duck Soup*, in which he created the classic "mirror scene."

# CHAPTER 28

# *Roman Scandals*

After having discovered with *The Kid from Spain* the formula for a successful Eddie Cantor picture, Sam Goldwyn approached his star's next picture with confident enthusiasm. First indications were that Goldwyn had finally wooed the legendary playwright George Bernard Shaw into agreeing to a film version of *Androcles and the Lion*. With his hot star in the title role, Goldwyn envisioned, no doubt, a flashy period picture with high production values and plenty of opportunity to show off his newly christened "Goldwyn Girls" in revealing "classic" garb. Goldwyn went so far as to announce the picture, along with its proposed director, Frank Tuttle, who had guided Cantor's first feature film, the silent *Kid Boots*. Unfortunately, the project was not to be, for once again Shaw turned down Goldwyn's proposal (Goldwyn had previously tried to secure the rights to *Arms and the Man* as a Ronald Coleman vehicle).[1]

Although he could not use Shaw's story, Goldwyn was convinced that the exotic surroundings of ancient Rome were the perfect setting for Cantor and the Goldwyn Girls. Envisioning even more sumptuous production values than in *The Kid from Spain*, the producer sought out another playwright, Broadway's Robert Sherwood, to furnish a plot to match the chosen locale. Goldwyn selected Sherwood because his play *The Road to Rome*, which was about Hannibal, was set in the ancient city. Goldwyn also wanted the services of Sherwood's occasional collaborator, George S. Kaufman. Goldwyn had long sought to produce a picture written by Kaufman. They had come close to making a film together—Kaufman almost wrote Cantor's follow-up picture to *Whoopee!*—but as had Shaw, Kaufman always managed to resist the producer's advances.

In order to sign Kaufman and Sherwood, Goldwyn agreed to two concessions to avoid the problems that had doomed their previous attempt to work together: first, the pair could write the script in New York, and second, Kaufman would not have to accept any interference from the picture's star, Eddie Cantor. The terms of the contract called for Sherwood and Kaufman to receive $25,000 each for their services, payable in three installments which would coincide with the three drafts of the screenplay.

217

Unfortunately, the writers were not as cloistered in New York as they may have hoped. After the first draft of their screenplay, which they titled *Roman Scandals*, was completed, Kaufman and Sherwood were greeted by a visitation which must have seemed to them like Hannibal's invasion of Rome. Sam Goldwyn and his staff arrived for a story conference on the first draft, along with Eddie Cantor. Thus in one fell swoop, George Kaufman had to deal with two factors he had sought so hard to avoid—long conferences and Cantor.

Goldwyn had allowed Eddie to sit in on the session on the condition that he sit still and keep quiet. Wary of this uninvited guest, Kaufman proceeded to read the rough draft of *Roman Scandals*. When he finished reading the film's basic story—the gags were to be added later—Eddie asked Goldwyn if he might make a comment. The producer agreed to his star's request, though three hours later, when Cantor finally stopped talking, Goldwyn regretted it. After Eddie turned the conference into a marathon and Kaufman and Sherwood's plot into an entirely different story, the writers had had more than enough. They informed Goldwyn that they were quitting and walked out, arranging for George Oppenheimer to complete the screenplay.

Ironically, twenty-four years later, Cantor in his autobiography had nothing but praise for the two authors he personally had a hand in alienating. "The lack of material on our early efforts drove me wild," Cantor recalled in *Take My Life*. "I hollered loudly enough so that by the time we got to *Roman Scandals* we had a real book. The writers were Robert Sherwood and George S. Kaufman. They gave us a script that *was* a script."

With the desertion of Kaufman and Sherwood, however, Sam Goldwyn had a script that *wasn't* a script. The producer handed the story over to his staff of writers and gagmen, including William Anthony McGuire, Arthur Sheekman, and Nat Perrin, for completion. Although Goldwyn used Kaufman and Sherwood's story, the producer refused to pay them any of their $25,000, and the pair wound up suing Goldwyn for that amount. They blamed Goldwyn for allowing outsiders to interfere with their work, while the producer claimed Kaufman and Sherwood had left him high and dry with only a rough draft, although they had given the script to Oppenheimer for completion. Three years later, in August 1936, Kaufman and Sherwood settled out of court for $20,000 each, most of which reportedly went towards attorneys' fees. Despite the imbroglio, Goldwyn remained a fan of Kaufman's and continued a laudatory correspondence with the playwright that only served to puzzle the writer. Goldwyn's admiration for Sherwood was also evident because that author went on to write two of Goldwyn's greatest and best-loved films: *The Best Years of Our Lives* and *The Bishop's Wife*.

Sam Goldwyn's legal problems on *Roman Scandals* didn't end with his writers, but extended to his dance director, Busby Berkley. Thanks partially to the success of *The Kid from Spain*, movie musicals—after spending a few years as the pariah of film genres—were enjoying a renewed popularity. In response to this revival, in early 1933 Warner Brothers were beginning a series of musicals and signed Berkley to an exclusive seven-year contract to design and direct their production numbers. Since he only produced one musical a year, the annual Cantor picture, Sam Goldwyn never saw the need for an exclusive contract for the choreographer's services and thus only signed individual picture deals. In between the Cantor musicals, Goldwyn loaned Berkley out to MGM, Universal, RKO, and Warners, going so far as to negotiate salaries for the dance director.

Under his new contract, however, Busby Berkley's primary concern was his work for Jack Warner. Berkley was hard at work on Warner's *Footlight Parade* when Goldwyn called for him to start immediately on *Roman Scandals*. Berkley told Goldwyn he had at least a few weeks work left at Warners before he could start on *Roman Scandals*. Goldwyn responded by bringing Jack Warner before the Association of Motion Picture Producers. Eventually, the matter was settled, with Berkley returning to Goldwyn for one last picture before moving over to Warners exclusively.[2]

The effects of the battle over Berkley's services were evident in *Roman Scandals*. For while Busby Berkley was supposed to be focusing his full attention on *Roman Scandals*, at night he was secretly sneaking over to Warners for clandestine work on *Footlight Parade*. During much of his final Cantor picture, the dance director was sustaining himself on short naps caught between his two full-time productions. As a result, the dances in *Roman Scandals* are, on average, uninspired, and half-thought out; they have an overall hastily prepared look about them. Still, while not up to the standard he set in the three previous Cantor films, second-rate Busby Berkley was still head and shoulders above the work of most of his contemporaries, a fact which would be sorely evident in *Kid Millions* and *Strike Me Pink*, the next two Cantor musicals following *Roman Scandals*.

If Busby Berkley lacked inspiration for the dance numbers in *Roman Scandals*, it obviously wasn't because of a shortage of strong tunes. The film's songs were provided by the team of Al Dubin and Harry Warren. While relatively new to films in 1933, within two years the duo would go on to win the Academy Award for best song ("Lullaby of Broadway"). Ironically, Dubin and Warren had also written the score for Warner's *Footlight Parade*, and after completing their work on *Roman Scandals*, they would spend the next handful of years supplying the music (whole or in part) for no less than nine Berkley musicals at Warners. For Goldwyn and Cantor, the team furnished four very good numbers: "Build a Little Home," "No More Love," "Keep Young and Beautiful," and "Put a Tax on Love." While none were "showstoppers," all were pleasant and integrated nicely into the film, eliminating the need for the plot to grind to a halt while a musical number passed through.

The cast of *Roman Scandals* was particularly fine, and provided Eddie Cantor with an assortment of funny foils, including Verree Teasdale, as the Empress Agrippa, Alan Mowbray, as the emperor's majordomo, and Edward Arnold, as the Emperor Valerius. Arnold, a product of Manhattan's lower East Side, as was Cantor, had recently come to Hollywood following a long stage career. After numerous dramas and Shakespearean roles, the low comedy of *Roman Scandals* presented quite a departure for Arnold. In his autobiography, "Lorenzo Goes to Hollywood," Arnold fondly recalled his portrayal of the corrupt emperor: "In this [*Roman Scandals*], the broader gestures, the strutting and the stamping around all contributed to making the part swashbuckling and 'hammy.'"

When Cantor saw his distinguished costar in his imperial toga, he knew immediately that Arnold was perfect for the part, despite his lack of comedy experience. "I don't know of any actor who is more natural on the screen than you," Eddie began. "But when you dress up in this regalia, all the 'ham' that was ever in you will come out. It's bound to." It did, and as Arnold himself later commented, "A hilarious time was had by all."

Among the others in the cast having a "hilarious time" was Ruth Etting, the popular songstress who had worked with Eddie back on Broadway in *Whoopee*. *Roman Scandals* marked her first feature film appearance, and though her part was relatively small, she did receive second billing, along with the opportunity to sing the torchy "No More Love." David Manners and Gloria Stuart (writer Sheekman's wife) rounded out the cast as the film's love interest, doing a fine job in roles which offered relatively little. In addition to playing the hero, Manners also gave Cantor lessons on how to drive a chariot for the film's climatic chase scene, which, incidentally, was shot first when filming began in late July 1933.

Paradoxically, since he had always urged Sam Goldwyn to let him carry the primary romantic plot, for the first time in his film career, Eddie Cantor was without any love interest. Aside from an unrequited attraction to Stuart's character (which he nobly sets aside when her love for another is made evident), Eddie passes through the film unattached and unloved.

This absence of a love interest, coupled with the character roughed out for him by Sherwood and Kaufman, gives Eddie a new shading, making him slightly less comic and more sympathetic. His energetic, aggressive enthusiasm of the past is toned down, leaving him more passive, more likely to be acted upon than to act himself. He is still the little nebbish, ever ready with a wisecrack, but now the jokes are employed where the situation calls for them, not just for the sake of delivering a funny line. The result is that in *Roman Scandals*, Eddie is closer to being a comic actor, and a very good one, than in his previous films, where he was a comic thrust into dramatic situations. The credit for this change must go to Kaufman, who frequently created reactive characters. A similar development occurred two years later when the Marx Brothers experienced a like shift in style for *A Night at the Opera*, also written by Kaufman.

Although this character change would be duplicated to some extent in the following year's *Kid Millions*, it was not permanent. *Strike Me Pink* finds Eddie shifting back to his more aggressive persona, and the cycle came around fully by the 1937 *Ali Baba Goes to Town*. Unlike Cantor, however, the Marxes would be forced (by MGM) into carbon copies of similar parts, which, without the benefit of a top writer like Kaufman, would succeed in turning their manic style into mush in less than five years.

It is unlikely that Eddie Cantor or his gagmen were cognizant of these subtle swings in the comedian's film roles. Rather, they were just trying to make the funniest movies possible. *Roman Scandals* is not a typical Cantor comedy, although many critics and historians consider the movie the quintessential Eddie Cantor film. Without question, it is one of Cantor's finest, but not wholly representative of his work.

*Roman Scandals* is a fantasy, made up of a mix between Twain's *A Connecticut Yankee in King Arthur's Court* (filmed two years earlier with Eddie's old Ziegfeld pal, Will Rogers) and Baum's *The Wizard of Oz*. As in both stories, the protagonist, Eddie, is somehow transported to another place and time, where, as in *A Connecticut Yankee*, he cavorts through an ancient time in modern fashion and returns to discover that, as in *Oz*, the best place for him after all is where he started.

The film opens with the dedication of a Roman museum in the small middle American town of West Rome. The building and its contents have been generously donated to the community by leading citizen Warren Fenwick Cooper, who, by the looks of the rest of the town, either owns or has built the entire city.

As Cooper proudly shows the opening-day crowd the museum, he runs across an odd assortment of "artifacts," including shoes on a statue of Mercury, a clothesline between two marble warriors, and a hot water bottle. The source of these new exhibits is soon made clear when an alarm clock sounds, drawing attention to Eddie (Eddie Cantor) dressed in his nightshirt, awaking from a good night's sleep atop the statue of the Empress Agrippa.

Cooper angrily demands to know why Eddie has been making a bed of the Empress.

"It's the only statue lying down," Eddie explains sleepily. "You see I can't sleep standing up."

The mayor, an ineffectual little man, explains that Eddie is harmless and urges Cooper not to have him arrested. Cooper manages to control his temper until Eddie, an expert on Roman history, continually contradicts Cooper's commentary on the subject. Cooper finally has Eddie forcibly ejected.

Eddie, a victim of the depression, supports himself by doing odd jobs for a variety of local merchants. Unfortunately, he is not a very good businessman and often gives the shopkeepers' goods away to the needy. Consequently, he has been fired at one time or another by everyone in town. Still his practical charity, unlike Cooper's which consists of museums and cemeteries, makes him one of the most popular figures among the townsfolk.

His latest employer, the grocer, complains that Eddie has given away $14.50 in food during the last week, while his salary is a mere $2. "What are you going to do about it?" the grocer demands.

"Couldn't you raise my salary?" Eddie suggests.

Meanwhile, Cooper, the mayor, and the chief of police are riding through a residential neighborhood which has been selected as the site of the West Rome jail, despite the fact that scores of poor people will be thrown out of their homes. It seems that Cooper's generosity towards the town is actually a series of graft-laden projects at the public's expense. After describing his latest scheme, Cooper hands the mayor and the police chief their cut from the museum scam.

While on his rounds, Eddie's delivery wagon is broadsided by Cooper's limousine. Cooper angrily threatens to have Eddie run out of town, but again the mayor intercedes on his behalf. The trio drive off, but the chief's bribe check is left behind. Eddie picks up the envelope and stuffs it into his shirt.

Later, Eddie comes upon the evicted tenants sitting on their furniture in the streets. He tells them that since the city put them in the streets they ought to set up housekeeping there until the city finds other homes for them. To illustrate his plan, Eddie sings "Build a Little Home," a delightful little song whose impact is diminished by what is probably some of Busby Berkley's most uninspired staging ever. After numerous choruses, in which the people and even the police participate, the number is broken up by the arrival of Cooper, who tries to placate the crowd by explaining their homes are being given up to build a magnificent new jail.

"Say," Eddie tells him, "the old jail was good enough for your father. It ought to be good enough for you."

Finally, Cooper's patience with Eddie reaches an end. He orders the police to escort Eddie to the city limits and throw him out of town. Eddie asks the cops where he should go. They tell him to go back to ancient Rome, since he's always talking about it.

"I wish I could," Eddie wishes, adding, "they knew how to treat people there!"

As Eddie trods along the dusty road, he starts chanting, "Rome, Rome, Rome." Then, in a close-up of his feet, Eddie's shoes dissolve into sandals. A long shot reveals Eddie in a toga, attempting to hitch a ride in a passing chariot. Eddie does a double take as the chariot speeds past. He looks up to see three Roman centurions standing beside him.

"Hail, citizen," the trio greets Eddie.

"Hello, fellows," Eddie answers. Then in an attempt to make sense out of what he's seeing, he adds, "Where's the circus?"

The soldiers inform Eddie that the Circus Maximus is straight down the road.

"Maximus?" Eddie questions. "Not Ringling Brothers?"

The centurions are returning from their victory over the Britons. "They lost their shirts," one soldier explains.

"Yeah, but they got your pants," Eddie observes, pointing out their togas. "Why don't you boys go back into the dressing room and put them on?"

Unaccustomed to such disrespect, the soldiers become suspicious of Eddie.

"Me thinks thou art a spy," one of them accuses.

"Me thinks thou art nuts," Eddie counters.

"Nuts?" the soldier asks.

"Yeah," Eddie explains. "I'm giving you the raspberry."

"Nuts? Raspberry? Perhaps he is a food vendor," they reason.

Eddie confirms the centurions' suspicions that he is a dangerous character when he brags that he sleeps with the Empress Agrippa.

This is blasphemy to the soldiers. They draw their swords, but Eddie, still thinking they're actors, refuses to take them seriously. Since Eddie won't "die like a Roman," the soldiers discuss other methods of dealing with the infidel.

"Boil him in oil," one suggests.

"Cut his heart out," another intones.

"Let him go," a third gravely voice, which turns out to be Eddie's, demands.

Finally, they tie Eddie to a stake and use him for bow and arrow practice. When one of their bowstrings snaps, Eddie offers to replace it with some string which he has in his pocket. Only then does Eddie realize his pockets are gone, along with his pants, which have been replaced with a toga.

"Good heavens!" Eddie cries. "Then I'm really living in ancient Rome?"

"Not for long," one centurion assures him.

"If this is really Rome, you can't kill me," Eddie argues with faultless logic. "I haven't been born yet. It wouldn't only be murder. It would be birth control."

Before the centurions can execute him, however, Eddie pulls the stake out the ground and runs away with it. The centurions pursue in order to resume their torture, only to be stopped when Josephus (David Manners), an influential citizen, rides up in his chariot. After hearing the charges against Eddie, Josephus decides that death is too good for the blasphemer and orders Eddie sold at the slave market.

"Perhaps I'll buy you myself," Josephus threatens. "if only to let you feel my whip."

"Save your money," Eddie whimpers, while reaching out to touch the whip. "I can feel it here."

Eddie is dragged off to the slave market, where he succeeds in discouraging prospective buyers until he learns that unsold slaves are thrown to the lions. Immediately he acts as a shill for the auctioneer (Stanley Fields) by reciting his résumé.

"I can cook a little," he tells the throng. "I can take care of the children. If there are no children, I can take care of that . . . by being a son to you."

Finally, after he displays his imported skin ("all the way from Russia"), someone bids 100 piffix, the equivalent of ten cents.

"What do you think this is?" Eddie asks, "Woolworth's?"

The bid is raised by Josephus, who glares angrily at Eddie, while ominously stroking his whip. Eddie pleads with the crowd to buy him away from Josephus. At last an ugly woman tops Josephus' bid.

"I'm weak. I can't do any work," Eddie tells his prospective mistress.

"I'm not buying you for work," the matron leers.

"That's what I was afraid of," Eddie sighs.

Figuring that he's in for a fate worse than beating, Eddie changes his tune and begs for Josephus to buy him. "You can even whip me on my day off," Eddie promises. Josephus agrees and purchases Eddie.

Nearby in the slave market, Olga (Ruth Etting), the emperor's concubine, is also being sold. She laments the state of disfavor she has fallen into in a torch song entitled "No More Love." As she sings, another slave girl (presumably one of her handmaidens) is also put up for sale before a lascivious, drooling rabble of men.

Despite Berkley's lackluster effort (lackluster for Busby Berkley, that is) on *Roman Scandals*, there was one musical number which managed to attract attention, if not for its ingenuity, then for its daring. The slave auction number took Berkley's previous reputation for tight outfits and plenty of cleavage one giant step better—a substantial portion of the Goldwyn Girls performed the number in the nude.

In one of the most decadent musical numbers ever released by mainstream Hollywood, Sam Goldwyn and Busby Berkley pull out all the stops in a scene complete with naked girls (their breasts and genitals covered by long blonde wigs) and enough sadomasochism to last the audience for some time to come. The number, which was filmed at night on a closed set, is a final slap against the powers who had just pushed a new, much stricter production code on the Motion Picture Producers Association. Although future Cantor-Goldwyn musicals would feature plenty of pretty Goldwyn Girls there would be no more of the scanty costumes, cleavage, and strong sexual overtones that came to their zenith in the slave girl number. The new production code was approved in the middle of filming on *Roman Scandals*, so the film was unaffected by the purer rules.

One would like to say that Berkley used this last bit of freedom to produce a dazzling number. Unfortunately, the main attraction here is sex, and pretty deviant sex at that (for the time), with little of the style which helped make Busby Berkley famous. Again, another number in *Roman Scandals* fell prey to Berkley's double schedule.

Despite any outrage which the slave girl number might have provoked from the guardians of film morality, the bit was evidently a tremendous hit with other segments of the population. After the film's release, Sam Goldwyn's secretary was deluged with requests for the identities of the Goldwyn Girls. Most of the letters cited specific girls by their position in a particular scene or shot.

After the scandalous slave girl number (which ends with the shocking death of a girl), the film slams back into the lighthearted mode. Josephus and his new slave, Eddie, get acquainted.

"Have you ever been lashed before, slave?" asks Josephus.

"Oh, yes," Eddie replies, "when I was a kid."

"Where was that?"

"In the usual place," Eddie sighs, rubbing his posterior.

Josephus informs Eddie that he isn't going to be beaten, and that the whip is only used for his chariot. Josephus gives his whip a mighty crack and hands it to Eddie so he can try. On the backswing, however, Eddie manages to wind the whip around the neck of the emperor's majordomo (Alan Mowbray), pulling him to the ground. The majordomo insists Eddie be arrested, but Josephus intervenes. Eddie reasons that he couldn't repeat the whip trick if he tried, but of course when he cracks the whip, he again succeeds in pulling down the majordomo. Eddie and Josephus flee.

Josephus tells Eddie the only reason he bought him was to set him free. He removes the slave marker from around Eddie's neck, but Eddie protests.

"Don't throw away the price tag," he advises Josephus. "You won't be able to get a refund."

The former slave and master become fast friends, with Eddie calling Josephus "Joe" and Josephus referring to Eddie as "Oedipus." Before the two friends can become better acquainted, however, the Emperor Valerius (Edward Arnold) and his legions parade by, fresh from their victory over the Britons. Included among the emperor's plunder is the beautiful Princess Sylvia (Gloria Stuart). As she passes, the princess and Josephus catch a glimpse of each other and fall in love. Eddie, standing next to Josephus, misinterprets Sylvia's glance and believes that the princess has fallen for him. In an attempt to free the princess, Eddie runs out into the parade. He is immediately arrested by the centurions.

Eddie is placed in a dungeon with another man, who, from the looks of him, appears to be a long-term tenant of the prison.

"I know you," the man cackles.

"You do?" Eddie asks.

"You're the man I just saw the soldiers bring in here," the man continues. "I know you very well."

"Too bad you didn't see them arrest me," Eddie cracks. "We might have been relatives."

"Those are the emperor's torturers," the prisoner informs Eddie, motioning to a burly pair of guards. "They twist your spine and bend your bones."

"Oh," Eddie nods, "chiropractors."

Despite his misery, Eddie's cellmate tells him that he has found the secret of eternal laughter—lava gas. One whiff of this gas and the most intense suffering is turned to uproarious laughter. The prisoner soon makes good his claims when the jailers come and take him away for a torture session, bringing the Princess Sylvia to take his place in the cell. The princess has been banished to the dungeon for refusing the advances of Valerius. In the cell, Eddie starts to confess his love for her. Before he can, however,

Josephus comes to set them free, having bribed the jailer. Their escape is thwarted, however, when Valerius arrives. The emperor warns Josephus, takes Sylvia, and orders Eddie tortured for wisecracking.

As the two torturers begin their work, Eddie accidentally knocks over the lava gas and is soon in fits of laughter brought on by the prospects of being tortured. The jailers soon join with Eddie in the uncontrolled chuckling (one after sitting on a hot stove, the other while thinking about his dead brother). When Valerius enters, he is greeted with howls of merriment instead of screams of agony. The emperor soon enters into the jolly spirit when he too sits on the hot stove. He orders the torture to stop and makes Eddie his imperial jester—provided he can continue to make him laugh.

"Hold on fellows," Eddie tells the torturers, as he strides off arm in arm with the emperor. "I may be right back."

Back in the palace, Valerius pauses for a drink with his wife, the Empress Agrippa (Verree Teasdale). Agrippa has long been attempting to poison her husband so that she may take control of the empire. Before enjoying his wine, Valerius gives the cup to his food taster to sample. The man immediately falls down dead. Valerius assuages his wife's mock concern by telling her that she may have better luck with her next attempt.

Eddie is escorted into the throne room by the majordomo and proceeds to entertain the imperial couple with a very amusing monologue on the American traffic system (traffic safety was one of Cantor's pet crusades at the time, particularly on his weekly radio show).

As Eddie concludes his talk with an explanation of Mickey Mouse and "Minnie the Moocher," a pair of dice fall out of his toga. The emperor confesses he's never seen such "cubes" before, so Eddie proceeds to teach Valerius how to shoot craps.

"Oh, Emperor," Eddie begins, "are we going to have fun."

"If I win, that's a good sign?" Valerius asks, trying to grasp the concept of the game.

"If you win, that's a miracle," Eddie admits.

In short order Eddie wins all the emperor's ready cash, along with the forum, the colosseum, and the majordomo. Not knowing of the emperor's interest in her, Eddie offers to trade it all back in exchange for the Princess Sylvia. Wanting to eliminate all competition, Valerius instead offers Eddie a job as his food taster, explaining that all he has to do all day is eat. Although he knows nothing of the attempts on Valerius's life, Eddie is hesitant to accept the job.

"There's just one thing," Eddie begins. "Do you like spinach?"

"No," Valerius assures him.

"Well," Eddie says, breathing a sigh of relief, "in that case I can go to work right away."

Presently a servant brings in a goblet containing the last portion of the emperor's favorite wine. The cup is handed to Eddie, who takes a tentative sip.

"I might be right . . . hic." Eddie starts, then takes another sip. "And then I might be wrong . . . hic." As the emperor nervously awaits the results, Eddie takes yet another gulp, draining the cup, before he announces with a smack of his lips: "I was wrong. It's good stuff."

After a brief obligatory love scene to further the plot, we see the empress calling Eddie to her bedchamber. Agrippa plans to make yet another attempt on Valerius' life, this time with the help of his food taster, Eddie. In a very funny reversal of roles, Eddie enters Agrippa's suite in the manner of a naive young maiden who is about to be seduced. Skipping coyly around the room, swaying his toga, Eddie pauses to bat his eyes, while Agrippa beckons him to sit beside her on the bed. He finally lights on the opposite end of the bed.

"Let me hold your hand," Agrippa says, pulling him towards her.

"No," Eddie resists, "you'll start out holding my hand and pretty soon you'll want to shuffle the whole deck."

Eddie moves further away, but again Agrippa slides over.

"You'll wear something out doing that," Eddie warns.

"Have you ever been fired by passion?" the empress asks in a sultry tone.

"No," Eddie admits, "but I've been fired by everyone else."

"Tell me about your country. What do they know about love?"

"Well, enough to keep things going," Eddie confesses, with a roll of his eyes. "We're still building schools!"

Agrippa's attempts to seduce Eddie are foiled by his recurrence of the hiccups. He suggests that she scare them out of him. Agrippa tells Eddie of her plot to kill the emperor, a plot in which he is to take a major part. At first Eddie thinks this is only an attempt to cure his hiccups, but when he realizes she is serious, he protests.

"Listen, Mrs. Valerius," Eddie begins, "it isn't any of my business, but you're not being a very good wife. Your husband works hard all day to give you a nice home and fine clothes. He comes home tired and hungry, and what does he get—poison."

Agrippa threatens to kill Eddie if he does not join the plot. Reluctantly he agrees.

Meanwhile, the emperor is planning a similar fate for Josephus, whom he orders to leave Rome or incur his wrath. Josephus encounters Eddie, who tells him of Agrippa's plot to poison the emperor at a banquet. Josephus asks Eddie to warn Sylvia (who will be attending the feast) and tell her he will rescue her and take her with him into exile. Josephus then confesses his great love for her, and Eddie realizes that she must have loved Josephus all along. Eddie vows to help the lovers and goes off to find Sylvia.

After scaling the wall of the harem, Eddie manages to elude detection by covering himself with mud pack and posing as an Ethiopian beauty expert. Finding Sylvia, Eddie tells her to be ready to flee with Josephus. Before he can sneak back out, however, Eddie is called upon to share his beauty secrets with the girls. This he does musically in the number "Keep Young and Beautiful," which despite its melodiousness, is somewhat offensive by modern sensibilities not only in the use of blackface, but in its lyrics which preach that a woman's value is only in her beauty.

The number affords the Goldwyn Girls ample opportunity to preen before the camera (some of the girls demonstrate the lyrics by brushing their teeth while singing), but aside from this the direction is again half-conceived and halfhearted in its execution. This is unfortunate because visually the potential for a classic Berkley number is there. The sets and indeed the girls themselves are contrasts of white and black (the platinum blonde harem girls are assisted by ebony servant girls). Instead of using this material as he would in similar instances at Warners, Berkley fails to capitalize on what has been given him, and the number suffers.

After Eddie escapes from the harem (the girls discover his racial charade and in effect chase him out), he literally bumps into a pair of crooked senators just emerging from a graft session with the emperor. In their haste the senators have dropped the proof of Valerius' corrupt dealings. Eddie tries to call after them, but is ignored.

"Just like all senators," he concludes, pocketing the evidence for future use, "never listen to the people."

Further down the hall, the empress pulls Eddie into the kitchen where Valerius' poison dinner is being prepared. Agrippa explains that although a pair of nightingales will be served, only one will be poisoned.

"Thank you," Eddie interrupts, "but I'm on a diet. My doctor has forbidden me any poison."

Agrippa ignores him and goes on to explain that he will know the poisoned bird by the sprig of parsley which garnishes it. The safe squab will be bare. In a bit which Danny Kaye would expand even further in *The Court Jester* ("The chalice from the palace has the brew that is true"), Eddie is told that "the one without the parsley is the one without the poison." Try as he might, however, Eddie has trouble keeping the incantation straight. Agrippa urges him not to waiver and reminds him of the rewards the death of the emperor will bring to them both.

"I shall be supreme ruler of Rome," she tells Eddie. "And you, Oedipus, will be the most popular man . . ."

"In the cemetery," Eddie nervously concludes.

A wrench is thrown into Agrippa's plot, however, when a piece of parsley is accidentally placed on the bare nightingale, leaving Eddie without a clue. Eddie tries to forestall his tasting duties, first by bringing along his own lunch (a hot dog and a pickle), then by trying to replace the scheduled meal with cheese blintzes.

"Deviled nightingale is my favorite dish," Valerius tells Eddie. "I never seem to get enough of them."

"You'll get enough of them," Eddie promises.

Eddie tells Valerius that he doesn't need food for the stomach, but food for the soul — music. To illustrate, he sings the snappy little "Put a Tax on

**Eddie sneaks into a ancient harem in *Roman Scandals*.**

Love," probably the most typically Cantoresque song in the film. As the song ends, Valerius grows impatient with Eddie's stall tactics and orders him to taste the nightingales. The reluctant food taster tears off a bit of the bird and throws it to Cleo, the royal crocodile. Eddie jokes that just as he is Valerius' food taster, Cleo is his.

"Don't you realize that might be poisoned?" the emperor scolds.

"Don't I realize?" Eddie asks rhetorically. "It's an even bet."

Sure enough, Cleo soon flips over dead. Agrippa comes forward and warns Valerius of the plot, implicating Eddie and Sylvia as the conspirators. Valerius orders Olga to take Sylvia away. Before Eddie is taken away, Valerius tells him that he has ordered that Josephus be killed when he boards the ship which will take him away to exile.

Olga manages to spirit Sylvia away down a secret stairway hidden underneath the floor, which leads to the chariot stable where Josephus is waiting. Eddie is also taken away, but by an armed guard, who just happens to march him down the same hallway with the secret stairs. As Eddie walks between the two columns of guards, he absentmindedly descends the staircase, unnoticed by his captors.

Unfortunately, Eddie arrives at the stable too late to warn Josephus and Sylvia of the emperor's trap. Eddie hops a chariot to follow them, but quickly falls off. To remedy this, the driver nails Eddie's sandals to the floor of the vehicle, and they speed off. The majordomo, along with a dozen men, soon joins in the pursuit.

What follows is an exciting, very funny chase, complete with excellent photography and special effects. It is probably the finest finale of any Cantor film. Eddie manages to catch up to the lovers and warn them, while at the same time drawing the pursuing chariots after himself. When Eddie's driver is shot by a pursuer's arrow, Eddie must take the reins while still nailed down to the rear of the chariot. The majordomo soon gets close enough to crack his whip at Eddie. The whip gets wound around his neck, but, of course, Eddie cannot fall off and so it is the major who is pulled from his chariot.

As Eddie's chariot careens around mountain roads, the majordomo is whipped around, over, and off of the road, before he finally lets go just as he is over a cliff. Eddie's troubles don't end here. Soon his chariot starts falling apart, and Eddie is pulled on two planks like a water skier. When the reins snap, Eddie too is propelled over a cliff. Unlike the majordomo, however, Eddie manages to do a ski jump before falling to the valley below.

In a daze, Eddie looks up to see a Roman soldier standing over him, but the stern face soon fades into that of his boss from the West Rome grocery store. It seems that Eddie has been lying unconscious after being struck by the grocery wagon. Eddie starts to tell about his adventure in ancient Rome and offers the emperor's bribe to the senators as proof. When he reaches inside his shirt, however, he pulls out Cooper's bribe to the chief of police.

Cooper is quickly indicted, and Eddie becomes the town's hero. He strides down the residential street—yes, the people have been given their homes back—singing "Build a Little Home," as the townsfolk come out to shower him with their adulation and confetti.

*Roman Scandals* was scheduled to premiere at Grauman's Chinese Theatre on November 24, 1933, a little more than a month after the completion of shooting. The picture's opening was delayed, however, not because of the extremely short postproduction schedule, but because of the big Stanford–University of California football game on November 25, which most of Hollywood's more important stars were leaving town to attend. At the suggestion of Sid Grauman, who evidently was also going to the game, the premiere was pushed back to November 28. After three strong weeks at premium prices, the picture went into release around the country just in time for the holidays.

*Roman Scandals* did top business in every city it played in and turned out to be quite a Christmas present for Sam Goldwyn and Eddie Cantor (who received 10 percent of the gross, making him one of Hollywood's highest paid performers). The film, which opened in the last week of 1933, ran for months into the new year around the nation, making it one of the fifteen most popular films of 1934, and United Artists' top money-maker for the year. In addition, Eddie Cantor was again United Artists' number one star and producer Goldwyn's number one cash cow. Reviews were strong also, but not as enthusiastic as for some of Cantor's previous films.

Just as the history of *Roman Scandals* had begun with a lawsuit, not surprisingly it ended with legal action. More than a year after the film had become a huge hit, at least two additional suits were filed. The first was by a writer named Eisman, who claimed the film was a "deliberate piracy and infringement" on a drama he had written back in 1929. The second was a $100,000 suit against Eddie Cantor by scenarist Eddie Conrad, who claimed that he was owed the money for work on the film's script. Both cases were eventually dropped.

## REVIEWS

Mr. Cantor does as well as possible in his role and he is exceptionally good in the episodes in which he sings. In a modern incident he excels with his singing and renders a number entitled "Build a Little Home."

Some of the fun is effective without being especially keen wit.... Such as one might expect from either Mr. Kaufman or Mr. Sherwood.—Mordaunt Hall, *New York Times*, December 25, 1933

Comedy high spots and moments of exotic beauty in production qualify this Cantor release for box-office. These two elements of entertainment retrieve a sometimes ineffective vehicle. Subject matter is the hokiest kind of hoke, but it has the virtue of being vigorous low comedy conveyed in terms of travesty, and the device is almost foolproof.—*Variety*, December 26, 1933

## *Notes*

1. In refusing Goldwyn's previous overture, Shaw had commented that he was only interested in money, while Goldwyn was interested in art. *Androcles and the Lion* was finally made into a film in 1952 with Alan Young in the part of Androcles (he would later find fame with another animal companion on TV's "Mr. Ed").

2. The defection of Busby Berkley to Warners could not have been as great a surprise to Sam Goldwyn as some suggest because in February 1933, while *Roman Scandals* was in the early stages of preproduction, Goldwyn announced that Bobby Connolly would stage the dances for the picture. This was months before his battle with Jack Warner for the rights to Berkley's services.

# CHAPTER 29

# *Kid Millions*

After two unqualified smash hits and four highly profitable films in a row, Sam Goldwyn, in planning his annual Eddie Cantor picture, had been smitten by a frequent by-product of success—complacency. According to Cantor in his 1957 autobiography, Goldwyn was content to coast after *The Kid from Spain* and *Roman Scandals*, turning the annual Cantor vehicles into formula pictures, albeit expensive ones. "I felt Sam selfish, I felt him spoiled," Cantor recalled. "*Roman Scandals* had been such a hit he thought we could keep rolling along on the strength of it. I told him, 'It's like Babe Ruth up at bat. The fact that he made a hit yesterday has nothing to do with today.'"

In addition, Goldwyn's attention at the time was being drawn away from the yearly Cantor musicals towards more prestigious projects. Goldwyn was no longer content to merely turn out money-makers, he wanted respect, he wanted to make "art," he wanted to win Academy Awards. For all their profits, extravagance, and entertainment value, no one would ever expect Eddie Cantor's films to win any Oscars. Having achieved a workable format for the musicals, Goldwyn was content to let the films continue to earn the studio profits, while he focused on "important" pictures like *We Live Again* (based on Tolstoy's "Resurrection") and *These Three* (from the provocative Broadway drama *The Children's Hour*).

Upon completion of the script for *Roman Scandals*, Goldwyn assigned Arthur Sheekman and Nat Perrin, two of the writers who had fleshed out Kaufman and Sherwood's story, to come up with a workable story for Cantor's 1934 release. While the pair worked on various plot possibilities, the producer purchased another property in which to place Eddie—*The Wizard of Oz*. Filmed as a silent feature in 1925 (with Larry Semon as the Scarecrow and still Laurel-less Oliver Hardy as the Tin Man), *Oz* was an ideal subject for a musical, especially now that Technicolor had perfected its three-strip color film process. For a time Goldwyn considered bringing *The Wizard of Oz* to the screen as a Cantor extravaganza, with Eddie as the Scarecrow, but the project never progressed past the discussion phase. Five years later MGM bought the rights from Goldwyn, and it produced its classic version the following year.[1]

With plans for *The Wizard of Oz* shelved, Eddie's next picture was in the hands of Sheekman and Perrin. After eight months of work, in which time Goldwyn rejected numerous story ideas, the pair finally submitted a plot to the producer's liking in early April 1934. Entitled *Treasure Hunt*, the project was tailored to the talents of Cantor and Ethel Merman, who had recently been signed to play opposite Eddie. George Oppenheimer, who had worked with Sheekman and Perrin on *Roman Scandals*, was brought in, as was Nunnally Johnson, to help work on the film's screenplay, though only Sheekman, Perrin, and Johnson would receive on-screen credit.

By the time Cantor had concluded his current radio season for Chase and Sanborn on NBC, Ann Sothern and George Murphy had been signed to play the love interest in *Treasure Hunt*. Sothern, who had previously worked under her given name, Harriet Lake, had appeared in a variety of bit parts in films before leaving Hollywood for Broadway; there she worked her way up to more substantial roles. Murphy, on the other hand, was fresh from the East Coast, where he had gained a reputation as a dancer with his partner, and wife, Julie Johnson. *Treasure Hunt* would mark Murphy's debut in front of the cameras. Coincidentally, both Sothern and Murphy were under contract to Columbia, with Sothern being on loan, while Murphy's first Columbia project would start upon completion of his work for Sam Goldwyn.

Murphy had been signed for the picture in New York by Goldwyn scout, assistant, and future producer, Fred Kohlmar. Having completed a New York talent search, Kohlmar accompanied Cantor, his two oldest daughters (Marjorie and Natalie), and Jack Robbins (the music publisher who was coming west to help select the songs for the film) back to Hollywood in mid-April.

Charlie Tobias, Cantor's cousin by marriage, and Murray Mencher were originally slated to write the film's musical numbers, but were replaced at Robbin's suggestion by the teams of Walter Donaldson and Gus Kahn, and Burton Lane and Harold Adamson. In addition, Irving Berlin's standard "Mandy" was trotted out again for the film's minstrel show number. With so many songsmiths working on the film, it is little wonder that it turned out to be the most musical Cantor musical since *Whoopee!* and employed seven tunes altogether.

Unfortunately, considering the raft of songs being poured into the picture, Busby Berkley would not be directing the film's musical numbers, although it was not for lack of trying to secure the dance director's services. Although Berkley was under long-term contract at Warners, Goldwyn had reached an agreement with the rival studio to borrow him for two films a year. The contract stipulated, however, that Berkley would only be loaned when he wasn't busy directing at Warners. When Goldwyn called for Berkley in the spring of 1934, Jack Warner balked, refusing to release his hot talent.

The matter wound up in superior court, with a parade of Hollywood luminaries, including producers, directors, actors, and songwriters, appearing for both sides. Cantor appeared, for Goldwyn of course, and testified that Berkley's absence had held up the film's production and resulted in him "marking time," waiting for shooting to get under way.[2] The main point of contention seemed to be what constituted "rehearsal," since Warners argued that Berkley was perpetually in a state of rehearsal when not actually behind the cameras. Ultimately, the court invalidated the contract, forcing Sam Goldwyn to produce his first musical without Berkley directing the numbers.

Despite the fact that the Busby Berkley matter was settled by the end of May, production on the project, which was now called *Kid Millions*, did not get under way until the latter part of July. Although delays on Cantor's films for Sam Goldwyn had become routine, the delay on *Kid Millions* had come from an entirely new source—Technicolor. Goldwyn, forgoing a full-color version of *The Wizard of Oz* for his number one star, had nevertheless decided to use the new three-color process for the film's finale.

With the number set in an ice cream factory, Goldwyn was very particular concerning the colors used, especially on the ice cream. "The vanilla must look like vanilla, the chocolate must look like chocolate, and the strawberry must look like strawberry," Goldwyn repeatedly told Dr. Herbert Kalmus, the inventor of the process and color consultant on *Kid Millions*. George Oppenheimer, working as the film's story editor, recalled that Goldwyn had developed an absolute obsession over the color of ice cream, agonizing over it for more than a month. Finally, Goldwyn saw a Technicolor test of the frozen dessert.

According to Oppenheimer, "The lights went out, and on the screen, against a white background, there appeared a large and luscious Technicolor plate of chocolate ice cream. There was a moment's appreciative silence, broken by the smacking of Goldwyn's lips and his comment, 'Mmmmm, strawberry.'"

Unfortunately, Goldwyn should have spent less time on the ice cream and more on the Technicolor appearance of the actors, particularly his star. While the vanilla looks like vanilla and the chocolate looks like chocolate, Eddie Cantor survived the experience looking like a teenage girl after her first experiments applying her older sister's makeup—complete with brightly rouged red cheeks and overly made-up lips.

If nothing else, *Kid Millions* is probably the most mobile of all of Eddie Cantor's films, with the action bouncing from the docks of Manhattan to a luxury liner to Egypt and finally back across the Atlantic via biplane to an ice cream factory. Most of these locations were handled within the United Artists' soundstages, all except the Egyptian exteriors, which were shot in Calabasas, California. Never a piker with his budgets, Sam Goldwyn pulled out all the stops recreating the streets of Cairo, right down to the camels.

On the first day on location, Ethel Merman had an encounter with one of the dromedaries, which was much closer than she would have liked. "You must never get in the way when a camel expectorates," Cantor later recalled. "It's as unwise as getting chummy with a skunk." Unfortunately, Miss Merman was uninformed on her camel facts and was doused with a generous portion of camel spit. The next day, however, when she arrived on the set, Ethel walked right up to the offending animal and returned the compliment, telling the beast: "I'm gonna get you first today."

For all its different locales, numerous musical numbers, and pioneer Technicolor work, *Kid Millions*, once it finally got before the cameras, stayed close to schedule, thanks to director Roy Del Ruth. Originally a gagwriter for Mack Sennett, Del Ruth soon worked his way up to directing two-reel shorts and, by the mid–1920s, features, earning a reputation for being a thoroughly professional, if somewhat uninspired, director. *Kid Millions* is representative of Del Ruth's work—he completed it efficiently, with a certain amount of craft, but lacked the skill that a McCarey or Tuttle had infused into earlier Cantor pictures.

In all fairness to the director, however, the script of *Kid Millions* leaves much to be desired. On the whole it is a fractious work, rushing headlong from comedy bit to musical number with very little cohesiveness to keep it from flying off in divergent directions. Sam Goldwyn, no doubt, thought he was laying the foundation for a repeat success when he assigned the screenplay chores to the team that had fleshed out the script for *Roman Scandals*. While Sheekman and Perrin might have been adept at hanging gags on a furnished framework, the plot of *Kid Millions* found them woefully out of their league when they were asked to supply a story as sturdy as the one Kaufman and Sherwood had concocted a year earlier. Instead of repeating the formula of *The Kid from Spain* or *Roman Scandals*, *Kid Millions* is a return to the style of the gag-packed *Palmy Days*.

One criticism leveled at *Roman Scandals* was that Eddie Cantor had too much screen time—approximately 90 percent of the picture. This was remedied in spades for *Kid Millions*, in which the comedian's screen time is not only curtailed drastically, but the time taken from him is given to a plethora of "funny" characters. As a result, Cantor is often forced to play the straightman in a film where he is not only the star but presumably the principal comedian. Again, it is a 180-degree switch from *Roman Scandals* (and most of Cantor's other vehicles in his career), where much of the laughs came from the fact that wisecracking Eddie was surrounded by a cast who played their parts absolutely straight. It is a case of subtraction by addition. There are simply too many comedians spouting too many gags, many of them worn in their familiarity, and too little story.

Another glaring fault of *Kid Millions* is the problem of Eddie Cantor's character. At first viewing, it would seem that the screenwriters have scripted him to be a schizophrenic. For the first two reels of the film (actually he doesn't even make his entrance until about fifteen minutes into the picture), Cantor plays the same appealing little guy who film audiences became familiar with over the course of his four previous talkies. When the action shifts to the ocean liner, however, Eddie turns into an infantile simpleton who believes that Ethel Merman is his mother and fails to see the snare she has set for him. Instead of being the wisecracking nebbish, Eddie becomes, in voice and manner as well as action, something akin to the persona Lou Costello would bring to the screen in another six years. What makes this change even more jarring is the fact that Eddie reverts to a "normal adult" when not around Merman and her henchman/boyfriend played by Warren Hymer. Later in the picture, during his scenes with the sheik, Eddie drops the baby talk and reverts to form for the final two reels.

With these burdens to bear, one would expect *Kid Millions* to fail totally. It does not, nor does it succeed. Rather it is a film containing moments that are as entertaining and delightful as any in Eddie Cantor's career, balanced out with others that simply do not work.

*Kid Millions* opens with Dot (Merman), a song plugger, hard at work in a Times Square music store, singing "An Earful of Music" (Kahn and Donaldson). After the number, Dot is told by her boyfriend, Louie the Lug (Warren Hymer), that she is rightful heir to a fortune of $77 million left behind by archaeologist Edward Wilson (Cantor, shown bewhiskered in a newspaper photo). Louie reasons that because Dot once strolled on the boardwalk in Atlantic City with Wilson, she is his common-law wife and thus entitled to the treasure. The two start making plans to travel to Egypt (which Louie in his "colorful" Brooklynese pronounces "Egg-yipt") to retrieve the treasure.

Unbeknownst to Louie, however, the lawyers for the Wilson estate have located the rightful heir, a son named Edward Grant Wilson, Jr. (Cantor). It appears that Eddie has been living on a barge in the East River with an old stevedore and his three sons since his father disappeared twenty-three years ago. (It is never explained how Professor Wilson disappeared into Egypt twenty-three years ago, but recently managed to spend a weekend in Atlantic City.) A lawyer is dispatched to the docks to find Eddie and put him on the next boat to Egypt.

Searching for Eddie, the attorney stops at the barge next door, where Toots (Doris Davenport), Eddie's girlfriend, lives. After he is sent away, it turns out that Eddie is hiding inside Toots' home, along with a dozen of the neighborhood kids (many of them borrowed from Hal Roach's "Our Gang"). Eddie is trying to avoid the stevedore's sons.

"They ain't your real brothers, are they Eddie?" one of the gang asks.

"No," Toots explains, "they're his stepbrothers."

"Yeah," Eddie adds, "and every chance they get they step on me."

In the barge next door, it is soon clear why Eddie is hiding from his stepbrothers: they are three of the biggest, roughest, thugs ever to hang out on a wharf (played with gusto by Edgar Kennedy, Stanley Fields, and John Kelly). The trio are engaged in their favorite pastime — a brawl in which they knock each other unconscious — when the lawyer enters in search of Eddie. Their father (Jack Kennedy), disavows any responsibility for Eddie, until he learns that Eddie has fallen heir to a treasure worth $77 million. Father and sons then all rush off in search of their bargemate.

Back at Toots', Eddie is conducting the gang's band practice. As they play, he notices a cargo ship passing and tells in a delightful song what he will do "When My Ship Comes In." As the song ends, Eddie's stepbrothers rush aboard and take him back home, where they come close to killing him with their version of kindness. Their battle over who can treat Eddie the nicest is interrupted when the lawyer reappears and informs Eddie of his inheritance. Eddie faints.

The action shifts to a luxury liner bound for Egypt. Aside from Eddie, the ship is also carrying Colonel Larrabee (a particularly annoying character played by Burton Churchill), the head of the Virginia Egyptological Society; Joan Larrabee (Ann Sothern), his niece; Dot; and Louie. The colonel is also going to Egypt to claim the treasure because his organization had funded Professor Wilson's expedition. Joan is along to meet her beau, Jerry Lane (George Murphy), the Wilson estate representative, who will be boarding in Gibraltar. Eddie meets Joan when she agrees to take his picture.

Dot discovers Eddie's name on the passenger list and tells Louie that their claim will be disallowed because Professor Wilson has left a blood relation as heir. Louie, forgetting he is on a ship, offers to "bump off" Eddie and make an easy getaway in a taxi. Dot has a better plan and soon presents herself at the door of Eddie's cabin as his long-lost mother.

After a tearful reunion, Dot gives Eddie a more than motherly kiss.

"Now I know what killed father," Eddie exclaims breathlessly.

Eddie is taken with her youthful appearance and asks her age.

"I'm nineteen," she informs him.

"And I'm twenty-five. Twenty-five . . . nineteen. Say," Eddie adds after a moment's thought, "maybe I'm your mother."

For some odd reason (perhaps Eddie has left the common sense he possessed in the first reel back in New York), Eddie accepts Dot as his mother, and the pair start to catch up on family news. Dot tells Eddie that he is just like his father.

"You look like him, you talk like him, I bet you even write like him." To prove it, Momma asks Eddie for a sample of his handwriting—preferably his signature—on the bottom of a legal form releasing all claims to the treasure. When Eddie complains he has no pen or paper, Momma produces the necessary items from down in her ample cleavage, along with a blotter to finish the job with.

"Momma," Eddie asks in wide-eyed wonderment, "you don't happen to have a writing desk handy?"

Eddie unwittingly signs the document but puts it into his pocket when a knock comes from the door. It is Louie, checking on Dot's progress. Momma explains to Eddie that this is his "Uncle Louie" and insists that uncle and nephew kiss.

After a reluctant exchange, Eddie admits, "Uncle Louie, you don't kiss like Momma."

Momma ushers Uncle Louie out and resumes her attempt to get the signed paper. Eddie doesn't want to talk about papers, however, he wants to hear more about his newfound family. Momma tells Eddie about the wonderful times that Eddie, his father, she, and Uncle Louie used to have.

"I don't remember," Eddie confesses.

"That's because you were an itsy bitsy baby," Momma reasons.

"And you weren't born yet," Eddie concludes. "I'm all mixed up."

Momma tells Eddie about a game they used to play called "tickle me, tickle me, more" and demonstrates it in another failed attempt to wrest the document from Eddie. Finally, Momma suggests a game of leap-frog, during which she tackles Eddie to the ground. While the pair are wrestling on the floor, Joan enters. Eddie tries to explain that the woman is in fact his mother, but Joan exits. Eddie starts to follow, when Momma reminds him of the signature. Eddie agrees, takes out the paper, rips the corner with his signature off, and hands it to her as he walks out.

The ship makes a brief stopover at Gibraltar, where Jerry Lane boards. In the ship's bar, Colonel Larrabee and Uncle Louie meet and soon discover they are rivals for the same fortune. An argument ensues, which is broken up when Jerry enters and tells them both, as the estate's representative, that neither has any claim to the money. Jerry goes on to all but accuse the colonel of embezzlement, when he explains that Professor Wilson never received any of the money which the colonel was supposed to have sent. Joan overhears this accusation against her uncle and refuses to speak to Jerry.

In the meantime, Uncle Louie has grown tired of the charade he is playing with Eddie, whom he calls "Junior." He tells Dot that he is going out to kill Eddie. Under the pretense of playing with his "nephew," Louie blindfolds Eddie and places him in a wheelchair.

"Uncle Louie," Eddie asks, "are you taking me for a ride?"

"You took the words right out of my mouth," Louie admits.

Louie takes Eddie to the edge of the ship, removes the guard rail, and attempts to push the wheelchair overboard. Each time he pushes, however, the roll of the ship brings the chair safely back from the edge. Blindfolded, Eddie thoroughly enjoys the ride and squeals with delight. He soon grows tired of the game, however, removes his blindfold, and asks Uncle Louie to take his picture. Louie agrees and urges Eddie to keep moving backwards, until at last Eddie and the wheelchair disappear backwards over the side. Dot runs up, and Louie happily informs her that "Junior is playing with the mermaids." Just then, however, Eddie's voice is heard calling for Uncle Louie from over the side. Dot and Louie look down and discover to their amazement that Eddie, chair and all, has landed safely on a spar.

As he hangs on the side of the ship, Eddie asks, "Did you get my picture before I moved?"

In a brief return to his adult persona, Eddie tries to reconcile Joan and Jerry by teaming them in the ship's concert to be held the following night. Although Joan shows signs of melting as the couple practices "Head on My Shoulders," she resumes her hostile outlook as soon as the rehearsal is over.

The next night the ship presents its gala minstrel show. In a prolonged but entertaining interlude, Eddie (in blackface), Dot, Joan, Jerry, the Nicolas Brothers (supplying an outstanding tap specialty), and of course the Goldwyn Girls, perform Irving Berlin's "Mandy" and Adamson and Lane's "I Want to Be a Minstrel Man."[3] Joan and Jerry reprise "Head on My Shoulder" in something of a dream sequence in period costume which is sandwiched in between choruses of "Mandy." The energy of the various performers helps put the number over because the dance direction by Seymore Felix only serves to illustrate how sorely Busby Berkley's touch is missed. Interestingly enough, Joan again starts to warm to Jerry's overtures during their duet, but she freezes up again later. Perhaps it is not Jerry, but the Lane-Adamson song with which she is in love.

Soon the liner arrives in Egypt and *Kid Millions* takes a marked turn for the better. Uncle Louie pays a group of street toughs to kill Eddie, but winds up being beaten himself when he runs afoul of a local street magician. The magician, whom Louie has called a fake, lures him through his trap door and replaces him with a dog. The dog runs off, pursued by Eddie, who, in his last display of dementia, believes the mutt to be Louie.

The dog jumps up onto a camel and into the lap of Fanya (Eve Sully of the vaudeville team of Block and Sully), the daughter of the local sheik. Fanya screams for help (she believes the dog is a bear), and Eddie comes to her rescue. She explains that she is royalty and that her father the sheik will reward Eddie handsomely.

"A sheik's daughter," Eddie exclaims. "I thought there was something distinctive about you."

"Oh, that's probably from hanging around these camels," Fanya explains in her New York accent.

Fanya, who is not only a little dizzy, but boy-crazy to boot, insists on showing her appreciation to Eddie in the form of kisses. She tells Eddie that he must stay with her family at the palace.

"What would I do at the palace?" Eddie asks.

"Oh, we play games and . . ."

"What kind of games?" Eddie inquires suspiciously.

"Hoola-Goola," Fanya squeals.

"What's Hoola-Goola?"

"That's something like your American ping-pong," Fanya begins, "and it's some fun I'll say. You hit a little ball and it goes under the table. Then you hit it again and it goes under the table. Then you pick it up . . ."

"Yeah," Eddie interrupts, "but where does the fun come in."

"Under the table," Fanya exclaims, with a nudge.

At the palace, the sheik (Paul Harvey, in a wonderfully amusing performance) examines the treasure and swears to kill the heir of Professor Wilson, who has defiled the tombs of his ancestors. Just then Fanya and Eddie are carried in on a sedan chair. Fanya introduces Eddie (whom the sheik calls Eddie-bay) to her father and Ben Ali (Jessie Block), her fiancé. Fanya spins an incredible yarn about how Eddie rescued her from not only a bear, but a lion as well. Eddie keeps insisting that it was only "a small dog." The sheik decides to make Eddie his honored guest.

Later the sheik and Eddie are relaxing while the Goldwyn Girls dance before them. Eddie remarks on the quality of the entertainment, but the sheik informs him that these are just his 125 wives. Eddie is amazed at the number, but the sheik tells him that he used to have over two hundred spouses.

"I know," Eddie sympathizes, "everyone cut down during the depression."

When a second group of girls punch in (the sheik has them on a time clock), the sheik complains that they are late and singles out one girl in particular, who is chronically tardy.

"I traded a very fine camel for her," he laments. "I certainly got cheated."

"You mean you prefer a camel to . . ." Eddie asks, pointing to the girl.

"Oh, Eddie-bay," the sheik continues, "she won't even kiss me."

"Did the camel kiss you?" Eddie inquires.

"Of course not."

"Then what are you complaining about?" Eddie reasons.

"Oh," the sheik nods. "Thou speaketh wisdom, sahib."

Eddie wonders how much alimony the sheik would have to pay to get rid of his wives, but the word is unfamiliar to his highness.

"What is alimony?" he asks.

"In America," Eddie explains, "when you get rid of a wife you have to keep paying her money."

"But is that not like buying oats for a dead horse?" the sheik wonders.

"Thou speaketh a hunk of wisdom yourself, Sheiky," Eddie admits.

The sheik decides to sneak out to see one of his girlfriends in town. He asks Eddie not to tell his wives, but then wonders if his harem will be safe with Eddie. Eddie assures him that he has his own girlfriend and shows him a picture of Toots. The sheik is impressed with her beauty and offers to trade Eddie a horse for her.

"How would it look? Me sitting in the movies holding hands with a horse?" Eddie asks indignantly.

The sheik exits. With their husband absent, the girls swarm around Eddie. On the verge of being overwhelmed, Eddie orders the girls back into line and proceeds to tell them, by way of the marvelous song "Okay, Toots" (Kahn and Donaldson), of his fidelity to his sweetheart back in America.

The following day one of the sheik's advisers enters to announce that a claimant has come for the treasures. Dot and Louie are ushered in, but before they can stake their claim, Colonel Larrabee and Joan enter, followed in short order by Jerry. As the Americans bog down in quarreling, the sheik announces that the rightful heir will be "boiled in castor oil." In the face of this addition to the inheritance, all the parties immediately drop their claims.

Seeking to avenge his ancestors, the sheik bellows, "Bring me the heir of Edward Grant Wilson!"

Eddie merrily skips in, asking, "Did someone call me?"

The sheik, never knowing Eddie as more than "Eddie-bay," is astonished to learn of his last name. Eddie happily insists that he is indeed Edward Grant Wilson, Jr. Everyone, including the sheik, who has grown fond of Eddie, tries to convince him that he is not *the* Eddie Wilson, heir to the treasure. Eddie refuses to be dissuaded, however, producing a family mole and his birth certificate as proof positive. The sheik regretfully announces that Eddie must be put to death.

"I'm sorry, Eddie-bay," the sheik explains, "but an oath has been taken."

"But I didn't take it," Eddie pleads. "Search me!"

While the others are imprisoned, Eddie is led away to a dungeon complete with an oversized cauldron. There he will be made into soup for the sheik's camels. Eddie's robe is pulled off, leaving him naked, save for an oversized diaper.

"What is this?" the sheik asks.

"This is the way I came into the world," Eddie states matter-of-factly, "and this is the way I'm going out."

Attendants begin to season Eddie prior to his going into the pot. "I'm going out for some vegetables," Eddie announces and starts to leave.

"Wait," one of the attendants says, "I'm the chef."

"Sure, you're the chef," Eddie concedes, "but I'm the soup."

Before Eddie can be made into soup, Fanya enters to whisper a urgent message in her father's ear.

"What?" the sheik roars. "He has committed tramofats!"

The others are all similarly surprised. When Eddie asks what tramofats is, he is told that it is a very serious offense which occurs when a boy kisses a girl while on a camel. The only recourse when tramofats has been committed is marriage.

Faced with the prospect of marrying Fanya or boiling in camel soup, Eddie makes his decision. "That settles it, boys," he tells his captors. "Drop me in."

Eddie is taken away and placed in one of the palace's more comfortable rooms, except, that is, for the leash he is placed on to prevent him from running away. The jealous Ben Ali enters stealthily.

"Are you alone?" he says in a hushed voice.

"No," Eddie admits.

"You're not alone?"

"No, you're here."

"So," Ben Ali begins, "you're going to marry Fanya? Do you know what a wedding means?"

"Sure," Eddie replies, "a wedding is a funeral where you smell your own flowers."

Ben Ali confesses that he has come to kill Eddie. Ben Ali shoots but narrowly misses. Eddie tells him that he doesn't want to marry Fanya, all he wants to do is go back to America. Ben Ali promises to help Eddie escape.

Leading him down to a crypt full of ancient sarcophagi Ben Ali orders Eddie to hide in one of the coffins while he goes to arrange the escape. Before he climbs in with a mummy, however, Eddie discovers the chest containing the treasure. As he gazes at the jewels, Eddie is being watched by the other Americans, who have also escaped and are hiding out in the other coffins.

The sheik comes down to the crypt to commune with his ancestors. Eddie, speaking from the coffin, tells the sheik he must free all the Americans or he will be haunted by his forefathers. The others join in with Eddie, ending their demands with a spirited rendition of "Let My People Go." The sheik calls for his minions and orders them to release the Americans and bring the casket containing Eddie up to the throne room so he may continue the conversation. The sheik exits while his servants start to remove the mummy case. When Eddie cautions them to be careful, the bearers drop the sarcophagus down a flight of stairs, smashing it to pieces.

Meanwhile Louie goes back to the crypt, empties the treasure into a sheet, and places it into a biplane waiting outside the palace. Before he can take off, however, he is captured by guards and taken away.

Ben Ali finds Eddie and leads him to the waiting plane. He orders Eddie to fly away. When Eddie admits he can't fly a plane, Ben Ali threatens to shoot him. Eddie takes off, bouncing the plane up and down and around the desert before finally leaving the ground for good. Eddie discovers the bundle of treasure, which he first believes to be someone's laundry, and flies off for America. After a ride complete with numerous tail spins and near crashes, Eddie's plane soars over the Manhattan skyline.

The film switches to Technicolor for the finale, with the transition made smooth by the use of a black-and-white newspaper for the first shot appearing in color. The paper's headline announces that Eddie's free ice cream factory is opening today, in keeping with the promise he made to local children (the promise was contained in the lyrics to "When My Ship Comes In").

In a sequence which is nothing less than dazzling—especially, one would assume to the audiences of 1934, most of them experiencing full Technicolor for the first time in a live action film—hundreds of children converge on "Eddie Wilson, Jr.'s Free Ice Cream Factory." The factory, which is equipped with oversized everything, from giant cows to enormous strawberries ("Mmmm, chocolate"), is staffed by Eddie, Toots, Dot, and Uncle Louie, along with help from the Goldwyn Girls. In a clever sequence, the Goldwyn Girls carry the giant ingredients up a spiral staircase to the top of an old-fashioned ice cream freezer that is two stories high. After the flavorings are dropped in, the Goldwyn Girls, now on ice skates, crank the freezer by skating in formation around the top of it. Soon, down below, huge blocks of spumoni shoot out of double doors at the base of the freezer, each with its own Goldwyn Girl sitting atop it.

The children, who have been patiently watching all this from outside, can wait no longer. They break down the door (with Eddie under it) and flood into the factory, taking their places at the fifty-yard-long tables or atop

**Eddie in blackface with Ethel Merman in a production number from *Kid Millions*.**

the ten-foot-high hydraulic stools which whisk them to the top of giant ice cream sodas. Eddie and Toots ride down the aisles in their automatic ice cream dispensing wagon, while Dot and Uncle Louie follow in a roadster complete with a machine gun that shoots maraschino cherries. This scene must be seen to be believed.

Soon the kids are bloated to roughly twice their normal size, but happy. Eddie tells them in song that next time they visit they should wear a tent. He and Toots kiss for the final shot.

Upon completion of *Kid Millions*, Eddie Cantor returned to the East Coast to make a number of personal appearances with his radio sidekick, Dave Rubinoff, and wait for the film's premiere. The film opened November 10, 1934, at New York's Rivoli Theatre, with its national release three days later. Reviewers soft-pedaled the film's short comings and almost unanimously praised *Kid Millions* as a first-rate entertainment extravaganza.

*Kid Millions* opened to strong business in New York, where it played well for four weeks, and in all the major cities throughout the country. The New York run was helped by the inclusion in the Macy's Thanksgiving Day Parade of an enormous Eddie Cantor balloon. In some other cities, free ice cream cones were given away to child patrons in a cross-promotion with local dairies (in Baltimore the mayor proclaimed the first seven days of the opening of *Kid Millions* "Ice Cream Week" at Cantor's suggestion). *Kid Millions* continued to draw well — in some theaters the film delivered the best grosses they had seen in years — making Sam Goldwyn a lot of money and giving Eddie Cantor another year as United Artists' top star.

Changing his pattern of the previous three winters, Eddie Cantor did not play a full season on the radio. Instead, a few weeks after the opening of *Kid Millions*, he took Ida and some of his daughters on a cruise to Europe until after the New Year, thanks to Sam Goldwyn. One of Goldwyn's managers had handed Eddie a $25,000 letter of credit from the producer, along with a note expressing his appreciation for his work. Goldwyn concluded by saying: "Take Ida and the girls to Europe and have fun."[4]

Despite Sam Goldwyn's generous token of appreciation, elicited no doubt by the strong box office returns on *Kid Millions*, relations between the producer and his top star had grown increasingly strained. The problems that had peppered their successful collaboration were intensifying and would only be exacerbated by their next project together.

## REVIEWS

Another Goldwyn-Cantor musical comedy extravaganza and again strong entertainment and strong box office. Follows more or less the comedy lines of all Cantor pictures. . . . "Kid Millions" is up to standard. And that's good enough.
There are possibly six or seven of the oldest gags that ever escaped the scissors in a major film production, but outside of these wheezes the situations and lines are funny. — Land, *Variety*, November 13, 1934

Samuel Goldwyn, the Ziegfeld of the Pacific, has mounted the million-dollar orbs of his favorite comedian in a rich and merry setting for the annual Eddie Cantor show. "Kid Millions," though it erects its pennant at a shade this side of inspiration, is a superior screen comedy into which the generous Mr. Goldwyn has poured almost everything that seems helpful to the cause of pleasure.
Not all of "Kid Millions" is as good as its best, but it is invariably diverting, a continuously reliable bazaar of gaiety and music.
The lavish ice-cream factory scene, filmed in the new Technicolor process, is the most successful example of fantasy in color that Broadway has seen outside of the Disney cartoons. — A. Sennwald, *New York Times*, November 12, 1934

## *Notes*

1. An Eddie Cantor version of the *Wizard of Oz* could have been very interesting indeed. Aside from Cantor as the Scarecrow, one could easily imagine W. C. Fields in the title role (which he almost played in the MGM version) and Will Rogers as the Tin Man, reuniting in one film Ziegfeld's "three musketeers."

2. Ironically, no Eddie Cantor musical produced by Sam Goldwyn had ever gotten before the cameras on schedule, a fact which was increasingly irritating to Cantor and for which Goldwyn himself was ultimately responsible.

3. Fans of film musicals will probably recognize the Burton Lane tune to "I Want to Be a Minstrel Man." The songwriter used the melody seventeen years later, coupled with new lyrics by Alan Jay Lerner, in MGM's *Royal Wedding* under the title "You're All the World to Me."

4. In his 1957 autobiography, Eddie Cantor remembers this note from Goldwyn as following the completion of *Roman Scandals*. Press accounts, however, show no evidence of a vacation to Europe by Cantor in late 1933, but rather place the trip in late 1934, following *Kid Millions*.

# CHAPTER 30

# *Strike Me Pink*

By the spring of 1935, the strained relationship between Eddie Cantor and Sam Goldwyn had neared its breaking point. Ironically, each felt that the other was remiss in the amount of attention being paid to their joint film projects. On the one hand, producer Goldwyn could never understand why Eddie would want to bother with any other venue of entertainment when he could devote himself wholly to being a star in Goldwyn pictures. Cantor, in a similar vein, had taken to complaining that Goldwyn was not working hard enough to find the best possible stories for his annual film and was instead paying closer attention to more prestigious pictures.

Goldwyn, like Flo Ziegfeld before him, resented Cantor's numerous public appearances, benefit performances, and radio broadcasts—especially radio. Unlike Ziegfeld, however, Goldwyn did not hold an exclusive contract to his star comedian's services. Whereas Ziegfeld could keep Eddie busy nightly on stage, Goldwyn's one picture a year barely kept Cantor before the cameras three months out of twelve, leaving ample time for the hyperactive Eddie to pursue other projects.

It was Cantor's broadcasts, however, that seemed to rankle the producer the most. Often Goldwyn would call Cantor back to Hollywood to begin work on a picture weeks earlier than scheduled. When Eddie arrived, he would be left cooling his heels while stories were thrown out and scripts revised. In the meantime, Cantor would be losing as much as $10,000 a week for each broadcast he missed.

According to Cantor, Goldwyn never realized the importance of radio to the success of the Goldwyn-Cantor pictures, especially in towns where he had never appeared in his Ziegfeld shows. "I'd plug the hell out of our movies on the air," Cantor recalled. "Our pictures had a big opening in these small towns because the people were radio fans. If you play to forty million people on Sunday night and tell them about *The Kid from Spain*, you're bound to have a Monday opening in Des Moines."

Goldwyn still refused to believe that Cantor's broadcasts helped ticket sales for his films; in fact, he used every opportunity to knock Eddie's radio career. Once Goldwyn and Cantor were at a party and ran into William

Paley, the founder of CBS. "Bill," Goldwyn asked Paley, "what do you think of this Eddie Cantor? I can't get him off the air."

"Try to get him off NBC, Sam," Paley replied. "We could use him."

As Goldwyn's antiradio comments continued, it was becoming evident that films were not necessarily Eddie's number one priority. In November 1934, while he was in New York to promote *Kid Millions*, a reporter for the *New York Times* asked Cantor which entertainment medium he liked the most: stage, screen, or radio. "He admitted," the piece continued, "'getting a kick' out of all three, but his manner implied that at the particular moment his chief interest was with the radio. This being treason to the cinema, the subject was dropped — which seemed to suit the comedian, too." No doubt this sort of attitude rankled Goldwyn to no end.

Although Eddie was one of the top broadcasting stars in the nation, Goldwyn felt that his radio appearances were competition, not promotion, for his own movies and therefore counterproductive. Often Goldwyn would greet his star with the rhetorical question: "You're still on the air, huh?" In reply, Cantor would tell his boss of his latest high radio rating. In the end neither would convince the other.

Cantor, on the other hand, believed that Goldwyn was ignoring the quality of the scripts in the comedian's films and relying instead on production values and the Goldwyn Girls to carry the show. "People expect big pictures from us," Eddie wrote to the producer. "True — but girls don't make them bigger. Neither do the goddamned juvenile and ingenue. Big sets, interesting personalities, good songs, interesting story, new situations are what we need. Half of our time is usually spent on the 'girl' lead. Let us concentrate on a story that gives us great excitement."

One project in particular excited Eddie — a new Broadway play entitled *Three Men on a Horse*. The play first came to Cantor's attention through Fred Kohlmar, one of Goldwyn's managers who had been east scouting for suitable material for their star comedian. Kohlmar told Goldwyn that for only $25,000 he could buy 25 percent of the stage show, including the first crack at the picture rights. The script was sent out to Goldwyn, who never read it but gave it to a staffer to read. When the staffer turned it down, Cantor, who had lobbied heavily for the play, was furious. Cantor thought the story, which revolves around a timid greeting card author who has a gift for picking winning horses, was a natural vehicle for him, despite the lack of songs.

Later, when Goldwyn actually saw the show on Broadway, he agreed with Cantor's assessment of the play. Goldwyn offered $90,000 for the film rights to a play which he could have had earlier for less than a third of that price. Unfortunately, it was a case of too little, too late. By the time Goldwyn made his offer, the play was the hit of Broadway, and he was outbid by the Warner Brothers' offer of $100,000. With Goldwyn failing to land *Three Men on a Horse*, Eddie asked Goldwyn to loan him out to Warners so he could still play the lead. With the memory of how the loan of Busby Berkley eventually led to the talented dance director's outright defection to Warner

Brothers still fresh in his mind, Goldwyn refused. The Warners made the picture with character actor Frank McHugh in the role which Cantor had coveted. The incident only served to strain the Goldwyn-Cantor partnership even further.

In lieu of *Three Men on a Horse*, Sam Goldwyn searched for a new vehicle for the next Eddie Cantor film. Instead of something "new," however, the producer kept coming up with more of the same old stories. First he announced that the next Cantor project would be a film based on *Sweetheart Time*, a somewhat routine Broadway musical of a few years back, which was based on *Never Say Die*, a play from even more years back. A few months later it was reported that Eddie's next film was to be something called *Waiting at the Church*. What exactly this one was about is unknown since no story or cast was ever revealed, and the project itself was soon scrapped.

Another two months went by before Sam Goldwyn announced that he was borrowing screenwriter Frank Butler from producer Hal Roach to work on Cantor's next film. Butler, a former actor on the stage and in silents, had scripted a number of films for Laurel and Hardy. At the same time, Goldwyn was also negotiating with English novelist Joseph Fairlie to develop a story suitable for Cantor. One can only imagine what kind of plot Fairlie would have submitted because the author had no background in comedy and specialized instead in detective stories.

Fairlie was not hired for the next Cantor film, but it seems that just about everyone else in Hollywood who had ever pounded a typewriter was. In mid–February 1935, about the same time Frank Butler signed on the project, Arthur Sheekman and Nat Perrin (veterans of Cantor's last two films) were piped aboard, along with Lawrence Riley. After a few weeks of fruitless attempts, Butler was temporarily returned to the Roach lot, where he was immediately loaned out once again to work on the screenplay for Harold Lloyd's film *The Milky Way*.

Ironically, while Frank Butler was leaving an Eddie Cantor script to work on one for Harold Lloyd, a story that had originally been written with Lloyd in mind was purchased by Sam Goldwyn for the next Cantor film. The previous summer, writer Clarence Buddington Kelland had conferred with Lloyd on a story titled *Dreamland*. After working out an rough outline of the plot with the bespectacled comedian, Kelland then serialized the story for publication in the *Saturday Evening Post*. Lloyd then decided that *Dreamland* wasn't exactly what he had in mind and dropped his plans for bringing the story to the screen. Still searching for a suitable subject for his annual Cantor release, producer Goldwyn purchased the story in late March, prior to its publication in the *Post*.

*Dreamland*, a story about a timid fellow who winds up running an amusement park and thwarts the local underworld in the process, was originally announced by Goldwyn as a departure from the usual Cantor fare. Goldwyn told the press that he planned the film to be more of a farce with songs and less of a musical extravaganza. Moreover, the producer did not intend to use the Goldwyn Girls in any production numbers. Perhaps Goldwyn's decision, coming as it did as *Kid Millions* was winding down, was predicated on the returns of that costly production, which although it made money, was not the top-ten hit that *Roman Scandals* or *The Kid from Spain* had been.

What Sam Goldwyn planned to save on production numbers, he was quickly spending on more writers. In April, while Eddie Cantor was still in New York doing his radio show, Goldwyn dispatched writer William Conselman (on loan from Fox) to the Big Apple to confer with Cantor and an additional two writers (Howard Lindsay and Russel Crouse) on the script for *Dreamland*. Unwilling to split the preparation for *Dreamland* between two coasts, Goldwyn urged Cantor to rush to Hollywood as soon as possible to get to work on the picture. Eddie, having just finished his first thirteen weeks for Pebeco on CBS, heeded the producer's call, forgoing a lucrative option for another eight weeks. It was a decision the comedian would have plenty of time to regret.

Cantor left for Hollywood in early May. Also taking the trek west were yet another two writers, Phil Rapp and Nick Parks, from his radio show (the writing staff was now nine and growing), and Parkyakarkus (Harry Einstein), Eddie's second banana on radio, who was slated to play a supporting part in *Dreamland*. Much to his chagrin, however, when Cantor arrived, he found he had once again been a victim of Sam Goldwyn's "hurry up and wait" scheduling. *Dreamland*, which was now going under the new title of *Shoot the Chutes*, was nowhere close to going before the cameras. In fact, the script was still being worked over by what was now rumored to be close to fourteen writers. It was starting to look like *Palmy Days* all over again.

After two months of waiting, Cantor began to vent his frustrations with his boss in public. Once in late June, after going to the hospital for a digestive problem, Eddie told a reporter he had gallstones, then added: "What d'ye expect from Goldwyn, pearls?" Cantor's fuse finally ran out. One day at the studio Eddie blew up and told Goldwyn and his staff that he was having his local attorney and two of his East Coast lawyers try to find a way out of the remainder of his contract. In addition his loss of extra weeks of radio work, the comedian cited Goldwyn's tendency to disregard his story ideas.

Goldwyn quickly calmed his star down, and in a "peace conference" between the warring parties, Cantor's grievances were addressed. The producer agreed to include a couple of Eddie's ideas into the script of *Shoot the Chutes*, in addition to reimbursing him for the greater part of Rapp and Parks' salaries, which Cantor had been paying since they accompanied him to Hollywood. Despite Sam Goldwyn's concessions, however, both employer and employee remained at odds with one another.

With their difficulties ironed out for the time being, Sam Goldwyn announced that *Shoot the Chutes* would start filming July 22. When the scheduled production date arrived, however, the script was far from resembling anything workable. Instead of stewing further in his Goldwyn studio juices, Eddie took Parkyakarkus, along with Rubinoff, up to San Francisco to try out lines from the film during a week of shows at the Fox Theatre. Also accompanying them was Eddie's eldest daughter, Marjorie, who was now serving as a secretary for her father. One of Marjorie's tasks during the shows was to clock the audience reaction to the various gags. After San Francisco, the trio returned to Los Angeles for a five-show-per-day engagement at the Paramount. (The schedule was pared down to four a day after the pace began to drive Eddie to the point of exhaustion.)

In mid–August, while still waiting for production to get underway, Eddie received the shocking news that his good friend Will Rogers had died in a plane crash, along with aviator Wiley Post. Eddie had just seen Will recently in San Francisco, where the cowboy from Oklahoma—now the nation's top film star—was performing in the Eugene O'Neil play *Ah, Wilderness!* According to Cantor, during the run of the play Rogers received a letter from a clergyman complaining about what he considered some off-color material. Rogers was so upset by the criticism that he dropped out of the play, and the subsequent MGM film version. In lieu of *Ah, Wilderness!* Rogers promised to make another film for MGM and left on the ill-fated round-the-world flight.

Rogers' death affected Eddie Cantor deeply. Years later Cantor confessed that Will was still as much a personal role model for him as he had been back when Eddie was in the *Kid Kabaret* and Will was a vaudeville rope-trick artist. "To this day," Cantor wrote in 1957, "I so often stop and think, 'What would Bill do in this situation?'" With production on *Shoot the Chutes* still on hold, Cantor traveled to Tulsa on the invitation of Oklahoma's governor to fill in for Rogers at the state's citizenship day rally.

While Rogers' passing may have stirred memories for Eddie Cantor of their days together in the *Follies*, across town at MGM those days were being recreated on film. *The Great Ziegfeld*, the long awaited film biography of the legendary producer, was going into production. Ironically, even though the delays at Goldwyn's would have given Cantor plenty of time to play himself in the film, Goldwyn's no-loan policy made the guest appearance impossible. In fact, few of Ziegfeld's former stars were set to play themselves because of other contracts, commitments, or death (from the earlier *Follies* only Fanny Brice represented herself). This left Metro with the headache of seeking doubles for not only Cantor, but W. C. Fields, Bert Williams, Will Rogers, Marilyn Miller, and Van and Schenck. After an exhaustive search, only Rogers and Cantor were doubled—the other stars were simply omitted from the story. Buddy Doyle, Eddie's understudy from the stage version of *Whoopee*, wound up imitating Cantor. Although Eddie was not mentioned by name, Doyle's version of "If You Knew Susie," complete with blackface, left little doubt in anyone's mind who he was supposed to be.

After a summer fraught with frustration and sorrow, Cantor's next film finally got underway in the first week of October. Despite the late start (*Variety* reported that the script alone took more than forty weeks work), Sam Goldwyn announced that as in previous years he hoped to have the annual

Cantor offering in the theaters for the Christmas holidays. At the helm of *Shoot the Chutes* was veteran comedy director Norman Taurog. Taurog had begun his career in the late teens directing Larry Semon shorts before graduating to features almost ten years later. The Academy Award winner for best director in 1931 (for *Skippy*), Taurog was a craftsman who was capable of turning almost every film he worked on into an appealing, well-mounted piece of entertainment.

Back again in support of Cantor was Ethel Merman, who was hot off the lead in Paramount's first screen version of Cole Porter's *Anything Goes*. Goldwyn rewarded Merman's work in *Kid Millions* by handing her three of the new film's four songs. Cantor on the other hand only had two songs; one a duet with Merman, and the other half of a production number. Despite his announced intentions otherwise, the producer had decided to build three rather elaborate numbers into *Shoot the Chutes*. While none were as elaborate as the Berkley numbers of a few films back, all were slick and well executed. In view of the Goldwyn-Cantor feud, it may not have been a coincidence that the more elaborate production numbers were mounted behind Merman's songs, not Cantor's. The songs, by Harold Arlen and Lew Brown, were pleasant but ultimately forgettable, making the film one of the weakest entries musically in the Cantor canon. For the dance direction, Goldwyn, perhaps hoping to find another Busby Berkley, imported Broadway choreographer Robert Alton.

*Shoot the Chutes* dispensed with a love interest (probably one of the concessions Goldwyn made to Cantor at the time of the comedian's threatened walk-out) and gave what little romantic story there was to Cantor and actress Sally Eilers. Rounding out the cast were Parkyakarkus, Helen Lowell, William Frawley, Gordon Jones, Edward Brophy, Rita Rio (in a dance specialty), Brian Donlevy, and Sidney Fields. Fields was an excellent burlesque and vaudeville straight man whom Cantor had just signed to a two-year personal contract.

Although director Taurog kept the filming moving along at a brisk pace, the set of *Shoot the Chutes* was not a particularly happy one, mainly because of the friction which still existed between the producer and the star. At one point, Goldwyn dropped by to see how the production was going. Cantor immediately stopped working in midscene and informed Norman Taurog he wouldn't continue until "that man left the set."

Filming was not completed until early December, eliminating any chance for a Christmas release for *Shoot the Chutes*. Just as shooting was in its final days, however, Goldwyn announced that he was changing the title to *Strike Me Pink*. Goldwyn bought the title — *Strike Me Pink* had been the title of a Broadway production of a few years back — from Ray Henderson and Lew Brown, the play's producers, who coincidentally or not had also worked on the current film. Goldwyn's reason for the title change was two-fold: first, Cantor's character in the film was named "Eddie Pink," and second, the title was also a popular phrase in England, where Cantor had always been a favorite box office star.

It is doubtful whether even Eddie Cantor's loyal British fans enjoyed him very much in *Strike Me Pink*. The film, which is fraught with weaknesses, is undoubtedly the least successful of the comedian's films for Sam Goldwyn. The main problem lies with the script, which, with its legion of writers (screen credit ultimately went to Walter DeLeon, Francis Martin, and Frank Butler, with additional dialogue by Philip Rapp), proved the old adage: "Too many cooks spoil the broth." Speaking of old adages, the script is also heavily laced with them. In place of jokes, many of Cantor's lines are clumsy platitudes, supposedly used to help define his character. They define it, or rather over define it, making the film's lead comedian a well-drawn, but woefully unfunny, person.

One of the difficulties with Cantor's character in the film is that it is not Cantor's character — rather it is Harold Lloyd's. The raft of writers never bothered to adapt *Dreamland*'s original protagonist (which was written specifically for Lloyd) to fit the screen persona of Eddie Cantor. Throughout the film Cantor struggles to be another comedian. Some places in *Strike Me Pink*, Eddie succeeds in squeezing into Lloyd's shoes (after all, there are some similarities between Cantor's nebbish and the timid young man who ultimately overcomes himself that Lloyd often played), but these are too few and far between to sustain the picture. For the most part, Cantor's few good moments in the film come with radio sidekick Parkyakarkus, when they deliver their typically hokey, yet still amusing jokes. (These routines were probably the additional dialogue supplied by Phil Rapp, their radio gagman.)

Aside from the problems involving the character Cantor plays, the rest of the script suffers from an acute lack of cohesion. Lines are slapped into the screenplay without any regard to how they fit the ones proceeding and following them — just as you would expect when fourteen (or more) writers are rewriting each other's work. Each gag line and joke struggles for a life of its own without seeking support from the basic framework of the story. Consequently, most die, and in their death throes take the rest of the script with them.

The basic premise of *Strike Me Pink* isn't that bad. Cantor is Eddie Pink, the timid proprietor of Pink's Super Service, a odd-job emporium situated near the campus of Millwood University. Pink's services include tailoring, laundering, breaking in shoes and pipes (with the use of some cleverly conceived machines), and other odd jobs. Eddie is wrapping a pair of trousers in some newspaper when he discovers a picture of nightclub singer Joyce Lennox (Ethel Merman). He cuts out the picture, destroying the underlying pants in the process, and hangs it up in the closet along with five hundred other pictures of the chanteuse.

Eddie's reverie is shattered, however, when a gang of students from the college enter and lock him in the closet. (It seems that milquetoast Pink is the favorite butt of their practical jokes.) After the students exit, Eddie breaks out of the closet as Butch (Gordon Jones) enters. The burly Butch

Carson is Eddie's only defender and friend; their friendship has had plenty of time to grow, since Butch has been attending Millwood for the past seven years. The boys' pranks anger Butch.

"Why don't you send for me when you're in trouble?" Butch asks his weakling pal.

"Oh, Butch," Eddie explains, "I can't be sending for you thirty or forty times a day."

Butch goes off to study while Eddie receives a long awaited package with the day's mail. "This is the courage you sent for," the bold print on the parcel proclaims. Eddie quickly unwraps the self-help manual, *Man or Mouse—What Are You?* along with its companion phonograph record. Eddie immediately puts the record on.

"Stand up!" The deep, assertive voice on the record commands. "Look at yourself in the mirror."

Eddie peers at himself in the full-length shop mirror.

"What do you see there?" the disembodied voice asks. "A man or a mouse?"

"A man . . ." Eddie squeaks.

"A mouse," the voice corrects. "Sit down!"

Eddie quickly devours the material presented in the course, which consists mainly of platitudes on assertiveness. Also included is a coin, one side of which is engraved with a man, the obverse side with a mouse. When confronted with a situation that demands courage, Eddie is instructed to flip the coin. If the side with the man comes up, he is to proceed forcefully; if the mouse comes up, then he is to continue flipping the coin until the man comes up.

The book also teaches Eddie the use of "the magnetic finger, the magnetic eye, and the magnetic stance," which, when used in conjunction with one another, are supposed to render an opponent helpless to the user's will. As practiced by Eddie, with one eye closed, the other bulging, and index finger thrust out "forcefully," they look rather ridiculous.

The scene shifts to Dreamland amusement park, where Butch's mother, Ma Carson (Helen Lowell), is having a tough time running the park which her late husband founded. Although she has the able assistance of Claribel (Sally Eilers), Ma is having difficulty keeping a manager at the park. It seems they all meet with mysterious accidents which Claribel believes to be the work of Vance (Brian Donlevy), a local gangster who is trying to force Ma into filling the park with his crooked slot machines. Ma wishes aloud that they could find a "hard fighting manager."

Back at school, Eddie has arranged for Butch to take a oral exam, which, if he passes, will finally allow him to graduate. To ensure Butch's success, Eddie has wired his pal with a secret microphone and an earphone through which he can feed the right answers. In an amusing, yet somewhat predictable sequence, Eddie is continually interrupted by phone calls and other disturbances while trying to give Butch the answers. When the trio of professors ask Butch what the connecting link between the animal and vegetable kingdom is, Butch relays Eddie's lunch order and responds, "Hash."

To a question on the national debt, Butch responds that it consists of "three shirts, three drawers, four pair of socks and one pair of pajamas with the top missing" (Eddie's answer to a customer's laundry inquiry). Ultimately, the stream of incongruous answers serves to totally befuddle the panel, and Butch is graduated by default.

Ma and Claribel come to see Butch and offer him the job as Dreamland's manager. Butch agrees, but only if Eddie can come along too. Eddie impresses Ma with his stream of assertive adages, but Claribel only makes wisecracks about him. Butch and Eddie promise to report to the park tomorrow. Butch must first go and tell a man that he cannot take a cruise with him, as he had previously promised.

That evening Butch and Eddie go out on the town, which, at Eddie's insistence means going to see Joyce Lennox perform at the swank Club Lido. Joyce performs "First You Have Me High, Then You Have Me Low," in an elaborate production number complete with the Goldwyn Girls and, for the first time in the Cantor musicals, male choristers. When the number is over, Eddie gives Joyce a standing ovation, then absentmindedly tucks a pancake under his chin and eats a syrup-covered napkin. Joyce joins Vance and his thugs at their table as they plot a way to put their slots in Dreamland.

The next day Eddie reports to his office at Dreamland. Claribel, his skeptical secretary, explains that all four of his predecessors met with untimely, and presumably fatal, accidents. Eddie tries to allay her fears by spouting his slogans, but she tells him he's nothing but a "big wind."

Presently, Copple (William Frawley), Vance's henchman, and three of his thugs pay a visit to Eddie. Copple explains that they want to place 150 "amusement machines to educate the public" in the park.

"Are they games of chance?" Eddie asks.

"Chance?" Copple laughs. "Not a chance!"

Claribel rushes in and hands Eddie a note reading: "These mugs are crooks. Tell them no!" She then exits.

Eddie follows Claribel's advice, turning down Copple's demands. The thugs start to threaten Eddie, when Claribel enters with another message: "Get Tough! P.S. Watch the thin guy. He's got a gun!" Eddie quickly flips his coin and decides to take drastic action. Using the magnetic eye, finger, and stance, he orders the mobsters out. Before they can react, Claribel delivers yet another note: "You're doing swell! P.S. I've just put a gun in your pocket." Eddie starts to swoon, but recovers enough to repeat his order to the gangsters. As they start to exit, one of the thugs begins to reach for his gun. Reaching into Eddie's pocket, Claribel shoots first, but only succeeds in shooting the cigar out of Copple's mouth. Copple warns Eddie that they'll be back, and they exit. Ma enters and kisses Eddie.

"Eddie, you've got something!" she beams.

"Yeah," Eddie whines, "a hole in my coat."

Fortunately for Ma Carson, Eddie has shown some promise, since Butch will be of no help at all. The cruise Butch has promised to go on turns out to be an enlistment in the navy, which leaves Eddie to manage Dreamland by himself.

The next day Vance sends a hired gun (perennial dumb-guy Edward Brophy in a marvelous bit) to kill Eddie. The killer sneaks into Eddie's office, pulls a gun on Eddie, and orders him to put up his hands. Eddie responds by spouting some more adages on courage. The killer is confused and asks Eddie to repeat himself. Eddie obliges.

"That's what I'm supposed to say," the killer exclaims. By coincidence it turns out that both men have enrolled in the same mail-order course. Simultaneously, they leaf through their respective copies looking for an advantage over the other.

"Did you read the chapter about 'might is right?'" Eddie asks.

"No," the killer confesses, "I only got as far as page forty-five."

"Then you haven't a chance," Eddie beams. "I've read the entire book. I'm the one who's dominating the situation." Happily Eddie demonstrates: "The magnetic eye . . . the magnetic finger . . . the magnetic stance."

Eddie orders his would-be assassin to drop his weapon. Helplessly, the killer obeys, but quickly picks it up again when Eddie turns his back.

"In an extreme emergency," Eddie reads, "use the super magnetic eye, both magnetic fingers, and the super triple magnetic stance." Leaning over his victim at a 45-degree angle, Eddie forces the killer to relinquish his pistol and then decides to further exploit his powers.

"Now, dance slave." Eddie orders, "Your king commands you."

The stocky hitman begins to prance around the office performing a mock ballet to "The Dance of the Hours." Next, Eddie commands the killer to strew flowers before his path. He picks up a wastebasket and starts tossing bits of paper as if they were rose petals. Finally, the mesmerized thug skips helplessly out of the office and into the park, to the amusement of the customers and the bemusement of Copple and his gangsters.

Ma and Claribel decide to hire a bodyguard to protect Eddie, especially since Claribel is starting to fall for her boss. Claribel explains to Eddie that the guard must be big, strong, and fearless.

"Yes," Eddie agrees, "a man with the courage of a lion and the strength of Hercules."

"Here I am," an offscreen voice proclaims in a Mediterranean accent. Eddie and Claribel turn to see an odd-looking man standing in the doorway. Enter Parkyakarkus, who tells them he is the perfect man for the job.

"I'm a G-man," Parkyakarkus boasts.

"A G-man?" Eddie asks. "You mean a government man?"

"No, a Greek," he admits.

Parkyakarkus tells Eddie he has been sent by Butch to help Eddie out at Dreamland. When Eddie says he's never heard Butch talk about him, Parkyakarkus gives a written reference.

"It says right in the letter," the Greek explains, "I've been a brother to him, and I'm gonna be a brother to you too!"

"Dear Eddie," Pink reads, "this fellow has been a bother to me, and he'll be a bother to you too!"

Eddie asks if Parkyakarkus has had any previous experience in the field. Parky tells him that he was bodyguard to one man for six years. Eddie is impressed until the Greek continues the tale.

"I could even still have that job today."

"But what?" Eddie asks.

"He was killed," Parkyakarkus confesses.

"You must be a fine bodyguard," Eddie says sarcastically.

"Sure," Parky admits, "they didn't get me!"

Parkyakarkus boasts that he can rip a phone book in half. Insisting he must see this, Eddie hands the Greek a directory, which Parkyarkarkus starts right in on.

"Wait a minute," Eddie interrupts, "you're tearing one page at a time."

"I ain't in a hurry," Parky replies.

After giving Eddie a gun loaded with blanks (to scare away any more potential assassins), Parkyakarkus demonstrates his skill with handcuffs by swiftly slipping a pair on Eddie.

"Say that's all right," Eddie says admiringly, "you're pretty slick. Now, take them off. Where's the key?"

"What?" Parkyakarkus replies with genuine surprise. "You don't got the key either?"

"Either?" Eddie cries.

Excusing himself for a coffee break, Parkyakarkus leaves Eddie alone with his wrists shackled together. Eddie crosses to his desk, takes out a box of jujubes candy, places them all in his mouth, and sits down. One of Copple's thugs enters. Seeing him, Eddie grabs for the pistol Parkyakarkus has left on the desk, but the hitman reaches it first, and points the gun — still loaded with blanks — at Eddie.

"Now it's self-defense," he grins and fires point-blank. As he shoots, Eddie spits one of the jujubes out at the metal desk lamp to approximate the bullet's ricochet. The thug is amazed and fires again and yet again. Each time the bullets seem to bounce harmlessly off Eddie. Terrified by the superhuman Mr. Pink, the gunman flees.

Later, that evening, Claribel tells Eddie that his management has brought an increase in business to Dreamland. Not everyone is as pleased with Eddie's performance, however. At his hideout, Vance and his "associates" are trying to figure out some way to eliminate Pink. Copple complains that Eddie is indestructible, but Vance decides to try a different approach. Learning that Eddie has a weakness for Joyce Lennox, Vance arranges to use the songstress (who evidently owes the mobster a few favors) to get to Pink.

Back at Dreamland, Ma and Eddie witness a barker who is drunk on the job, and Ma urges Eddie to take his place. After a quick consultation with his Man/Mouse coin, Eddie jumps up on the stage and pitches the virtues of Rita Rio's tap dance review in the number "The Lady Dances." After an opening chorus by Eddie in a song which is okay, but not really suited to his style, the number moves indoors for an elaborate specialty that includes Rio, the Goldwyn Girls, and Eddie for the sequence's finale. Cantor is relegated to a supporting role, serving as little more than a framing device in this scene, which is the only production number in which he appears, even though he is the star of the picture. Quite a comedown for a performer who was once the most energetic musical performer on Broadway.

After the number, Eddie is handed a note from Joyce that urges him to meet her backstage at the Club Lido. After ditching his vigilant bodyguard, Eddie hurries to the Lido. Inside the club, Vance has arranged a frame-up for the unsuspecting Pink. Joyce's brother Charley (Sidney Fields) will pretend to be a murder victim, with the obvious suspect being Joyce herself. As Eddie reaches the Lido's back door, a shot rings out. Joyce comes out carrying a smoking pistol, describes the murder, and pleads for Eddie's help. True to form, her hero faints into her arms. After reviving Eddie, Joyce sends him inside to retrieve her purse, which is lying under the "corpse." Eddie then escorts his lady in distress back to her apartment. Vance and some of his thugs follow them up to the apartment and force their way in. Vance accuses Joyce of murder. To protect the woman he loves, Eddie confesses that he committed the crime. Given Eddie's mousy demeanor, Vance finds this hard to believe. Eddie tries to convince him of his killer nature.

"Last week," Eddie brags, "I killed three men! No, four! No, three . . . you can't count that last one, he was a kid."

Vance offers to get Joyce off the hook for Charley's murder if Eddie agrees to put 150 slot machines in Dreamland. Eddie hesitates saying the machines are crooked. Vance produces a rigged machine for a demonstration. Eddie tries the machine and hits the jackpot each time; on the final try, the machine even sprouts tiny flags and plays "Yankee Doodle." Vance tells him that not only are the slot machines not crooked, they're patriotic.

"What this country needs are more of these machines," Eddie agrees, while signing the contract.

In return for rescuing her, Joyce meets Eddie the next day for a date at Dreamland. Eddie takes her on a ride through the tunnel of love. In the darkness the sound of kisses can be heard. Joyce expresses surprise at Eddie's outburst of romance. When Eddie lights a match, however, it turns out that Parkyakarkus has been providing the passion. Determined to get away from the pesky Greek, Eddie takes Joyce on the ferris wheel. When it stops at the top, Eddie confesses his love for Joyce. The two sing "Calabash Pipe," a pleasant little song about giving up the bustle of the city for a simpler life in the country. For the second verse, Eddie and Joyce illustrate the lyrics by dissolving into a horse and buggy, where they are made-up as two senior citizens. Brief, but cute, the number is the best of the two songs that Cantor is allotted in the film.

Eddie's own private dreamland is shattered the next day when the slot machines are delivered. Eddie tries to explain to an outraged Ma and Claribel that the machines always pay out more than is deposited in them. When he tries to prove it, the slots fail to deliver, and Eddie realizes he's been duped. He promises to have the slots taken out of the park, but first he must spirit Joyce out of town.

Eddie rushes to the Club Lido. While he waits at the stage door, Joyce performs "Shake It Off with Rhythm" on stage, accompanied by Rito Rio, the Goldwyn Girls, and a company of male dancers. The number, coming where it does, disrupts the pacing of the film, but judged on its own merits, it is the slickest number of the film.

After the number, Eddie is informed that Joyce has left the club by the front door. Rushing to her apartment, Eddie arrives ahead of Joyce and is let in by a maid. Charley, supposedly dead, is also in the flat and calls Vance to warn of possible trouble. Dressed in a long white bathrobe, Charley is accidentally seen by Eddie. Charley quickly adopts a ghoulish demeanor and tells Eddie he is in fact a ghost. In a variation on a proven burlesque routine (Cantor signed up Sidney Fields out of the review *Life Begins at Minsky's*), Charley compels Eddie to play a friendly game of poker with two other (invisible) ghosts. The game is continually interrupted by threats of violence from the imaginary players, which are conveyed quite convincingly by Charley, so much so, that by the end of the game Eddie can almost see and hear them too. Eddie winds up losing real money, while the ghosts naturally pay their gambling debts in invisible specie. The ruse is broken, however, when Eddie finally sees through Charley's deception because in Eddie's opinion "deadmen don't hiccup."

Eddie runs out into the living room and ducks behind the radio set when he hears Vance and his men entering. Eddie discovers that the radio also contains a home recording unit. Setting a fresh disc on the turntable, he manages to record Vance giving a complete rundown of his extortion, racketeering, and gambling enterprises. Eddie takes the record and slips out the balcony and down the fire escape before the villains realize they've just given a complete confession. They shoot at Eddie as he flees down the side of the building, but he manages to escape.

Meanwhile, at the park, Parkyakarkus has somehow managed to rerig all the slot machines so they hit the jackpot every time. Needless to say, this makes the machines extremely popular the following day and draws huge crowds eager to cash in on them. Also at the park are Vance and his men, eager to destroy the recorded confession and silence Eddie for good. Disguised as cops, they almost succeed in getting Eddie to hand over the evidence. Eddie discovers their ploy, however, and a prolonged chase around Dreamland ensues. Most of the credit for this finale must be given to the stunt men (especially two who broke their legs) and special effects people. The stunts in this scene are particularly well done and not at all phony looking.

When the record rolls away from Eddie, he pursues it up onto a roller coaster, sliding up and down the steep incline several times before the chain drive carries him to the top. In a fast and furious sequence, Eddie scrambles around the roller coaster, then around the park on a midget racer, before he finally ends up adrift in a hot air balloon with Parkyakarkus.

The villains soon discover Eddie's location and begin jerking the guide wire in hopes of upsetting the basket. After almost falling out, Eddie and Parkyakarkus throw ballast down on the thugs, scoring several direct hits. With the extra weight gone, however, the balloon begins a rapid ascent, which continues unchecked until it reaches the end of the wire. At that point, the balloon is brought to such an abrupt halt that Eddie falls through the bottom of the gondola and hangs on by only his hands. Parkyakarkus looks around for his boss but cannot find him, mainly because he is standing on top of Eddie's head. Once he gets the Greek off him, Eddie manages to climb back in the basket.

The pair discover some flares and try to signal for help, but only succeed in poking a hole in the balloon. They tumble out of the balloon, but their fall is broken by the parachute which Parkyakarkus has had the forethought to wear. They float downward, with Eddie holding on to the Greek's feet. When Parky's shoe buttons pop off, Eddie loses his grip and falls into the middle of an outdoor trapeze act, quickly becoming part of the act. The mobsters try to catch Eddie by climbing onto the safety net, but they are bounced off when Eddie drops onto it. At that moment the real police show up to arrest the entire gang and take the recorded confession as evidence.

Ma and Claribel rush to Eddie's side, but Eddie runs off in search of clothes (he lost all but his long johns in the trapeze act). Claribel follows and catches up to him while he's donning some sort of Chinese costume. Claribel proposes, and Eddie, realizing that Joyce Lennox was making a fool out of him, accepts. Claribel asks for a kiss, but the timid Pink demurs. She then adopts the magnetic stance and makes the request a command, and he complies passionately.

"Where did you ever learn to kiss like that?" Claribel pants breathlessly.

"I used to blow a bugle for the Boy Scouts," Eddie explains as the film fades out.

Despite the inordinate amount of time in took to produce, *Strike Me Pink* had its world premiere at Radio City Music Hall on January 16, 1936, just three weeks after its targeted Christmas release. The film managed to garner some good reviews, although most notices were mixed on the picture. As with *Kid Millions* a little more than a year earlier, *Strike Me Pink* managed to do good box office business in its first week, but dropped off even more quickly than its predecessor in subsequent weeks. Still, *Strike Me Pink*, as all the Cantor films, wound up being a money-maker for Sam Goldwyn, and Eddie was once again among United Artists' top grossing stars for

**Eddie's crown of calabash pipes fails to impress Sally Eilers and Helen Lowell in this scene deleted from *Strike Me Pink*.**

the year, second only to Charlie Chaplin (appearing for the first time in five years in *Modern Times*).

Prior to the release of the picture, Eddie Cantor rushed back to New York to continue his radio series, and Sam Goldwyn started looking for the next property in which to showcase his star comedian. At first, by all accounts, it would seem that the producer and star were back to business as usual, but the harmonious veneer would soon crack.

Sam Goldwyn's first move was to offer $200,000 — at the time one of the costliest bids for a stage property — to Billy Rose for the screen rights to his production of *Jumbo*. Envisioning Cantor in the role created on stage by Jimmy Durante, Goldwyn announced that he would lavish a million dollars on the production. In less than a week, however, the producer withdrew his offer, not only because Rose reportedly wanted $250,000, along with a two-year wait before the film could be released, but also because Ben Hecht, *Jumbo*'s coauthor with Charles MacArthur, advised Goldwyn that he would be "a sucker to pay over $5,000" for the rights. Hecht further advised that the producer go to Budapest, where a similar circus-theme play was running, buy the rights for $15,000, and "then pick your own title." Goldwyn ignored the suggestion and soon put a team of writers on a script for Cantor entitled *Pony Boy*.

In the meantime, Eddie Cantor was still talking to the press about the possibility of a loan-out to Warner Brothers to do *Three Men on a Horse*. Despite Cantor's intense desire to do the film version of the play, Goldwyn again refused his star's request. (This didn't prevent Eddie from seeking to play the part in a radio version of the play done as part of the *Lux Radio Theater* series.) As before, Cantor fumed.

The rocky Cantor-Goldwyn partnership finally reached its breaking point on July 27, 1936, when Eddie removed his personal effects from the United Artists lot. Two days earlier Goldwyn had ordered Cantor back to the studio to begin work on the script for a film version of *Never Say Die*. Cantor refused, referring to the property as "an old chestnut" and adding that the producer was submitting the story in an attempt to stall for time until a real script was found. As proof that Goldwyn was wasting his time, Cantor noted that the same story had been submitted to him a year earlier, at which time it was summarily rejected.

Cantor then announced that he wanted out of his current contract with Goldwyn and would, if necessary, sue the producer—on the "reasonable time" clause in the contract—to accomplish his release. Cantor's attorneys next met with Goldwyn's lawyers and a settlement was reached whereby Cantor was allowed to buy his way out of the contract for an undisclosed sum (later estimated at approximately $25,000) which would go to reimburse the producer for unused properties he had purchased with the comedian in mind.

Eddie Cantor's walkout at Goldwyn also affected his friend George Jessel. At the time Jessel had been working at the United Artists Studios on a screenplay based on the life of Cantor, presumably for production by Sam Goldwyn. When Eddie left, Georgie was taken off the producer's payroll and moved off the lot. Jessel soon landed at Universal, where he was hired as a producer.

Although Goldwyn and Cantor didn't speak to each other for a long while after their bitter parting of the ways, in time the two again became cordial friends and admirers of one another's talent. More than twenty years later, in his second autobiography, Eddie Cantor paid Goldwyn the highest tribute he knew, comparing the film producer to a man they had both looked up to as the hallmark of the entertainment industry—Flo Ziegfeld.

"I was eager to leave him [Goldwyn]," Cantor wrote, "eager to make pictures on my own, and I did. But they never came up to the caliber of the Goldwyn pictures. If Sam gave me nervous indigestion while I waited for a script, he also eventually brought out something that *sold* and that established me in pictures as Ziegfeld had established me in the theater."

## REVIEWS

Many and varied gags, majority of which land, combine with a set of good songs and individual performances to make Eddie Cantor's latest good entertainment. Picture doesn't look the cost of previous Cantor starrers. It is a little less lavish. At the box office both here and abroad the take will be big.

Cantor is hard at work at all times, eating up a lot of footage. . . . Cantor is aces all the way. — Char, *Variety*, January 22, 1936

Eddie Cantor Week — the song, dance and slapstick festival which Samuel Goldwyn arranges for the multitudes each year — began yesterday at the Radio City Music Hall with considerably less hilarity than we have come to expect of the annual Goldwyn-Cantor shows. "Strike Me Pink," the latest gift from the Ziegfeld of the Pacific, appears to lack some of his customary expansiveness and much of the comic invention that has made the well-known father of five one of the screen's most likable funny men. — Frank S. Nugent, *New York Times*, January 17, 1936

# CHAPTER 31

# *Ali Baba Goes to Town*

If Eddie Cantor compared his relationship in film with Sam Goldwyn to his stage relationship with Flo Ziegfeld, then in many ways his film career after 1936 paralleled his stage work for the Shubert brothers after his initial feud with Ziegfeld—just show business without the class. However, while 20th Century–Fox head Darryl Zanuck may have not lavished the detailed individual attention on each of his pictures that Sam Goldwyn could afford to, nevertheless, he would come closer to the mark set in the Goldwyn films than any of Eddie Cantor's subsequent producers (including Cantor himself). Zanuck and Cantor's only collaboration, *Ali Baba Goes to Town*, is a consistently entertaining and opulent production which comes within a hairsbreadth of duplicating the gloss of the Goldwyn productions.

From the first reports of Cantor's walkout from the Goldwyn lot, newspaper and trade accounts gave his likely destination as being a few miles west down Santa Monica Boulevard to 20th Century–Fox. Not wanting to go public in his pursuit of Cantor until his release from Goldwyn was a done deal, studio chief Zanuck denied the stories which had Fox and the comedian close to a deal. However, the day of Cantor's release, August 1, 1936, contracts were already being drawn up at Fox, although it took over a month for all the details to be hammered out. When a deal was finally made between Eddie and his new studio home, it was for a then record-breaking $333,333 per picture in a three-picture contract—a million dollar contract. The exact figures called for a base salary of $200,000, with the balance to be made up via percentages of the gross. Another important facet of the 20th Century–Fox contract was the understanding that Eddie was to be given full permission to continue his work in radio without the undue interference which the comedian had encountered from Sam Goldwyn. The contract, negotiated by Cantor's personal representative, Benjamin Holtzman, and his New York attorney, A. L. Berman, was also witnessed by Abe Lastfogel, general manager of the William Morris Agency, who henceforth would represent Eddie.

Under the terms of his Fox contract, Eddie Cantor was now making more money than he had with Goldwyn, and he had the freedom to pursue other entertainment venues without interference. But ironically the one issue he had stressed during the Goldwyn break still haunted him at the new studio—waiting for a story. Two months after signing Cantor, Darryl Zanuck announced that the star's first project at Fox would be *Saratoga Chips*, an unproduced play set at a horse track. Written by Damon Runyon and Irving Caesar, the story fetched a record, but unreported, figure for an unpublished scenario. Leonard Parskins was set to work on the story adaptation, which coincidentally or not featured the same locales as Cantor's much sought after *Three Men on a Horse*. The studio also announced that Lawrence Schwab had been assigned to the picture as associate producer, with production scheduled to begin in January 1937.

Fortunately for Eddie Cantor, his new boss had no qualms about him doing outside work, for while Eddie waited for his premiere Fox film to go before the cameras, instead of fuming as he had done in a similar situation the previous year, he busied himself with extra-curricular activities. Aside from his regular weekly radio show, Cantor kept up an exhausting schedule of personal appearances throughout the entire country, including many benefits for various charities. One cause which had caught the comedian's eye of late was the Youth Alyiah Movement, an anti–Nazi organization devoted to bringing Jewish children out of Hitler's Germany and relocating them to Palestine and the United States. While many in America turned a deaf ear to the reports of anti–Semitic atrocities filtering out of Germany, Cantor toured the country warning of the Nazi menace, despite the fact that his efforts were unpopular in some circles and even provoked threats against him and his family.

By early 1937, instead of starting production on *Saratoga Chips*, 20th Century–Fox announced a entirely new project. Titled *His Arabian Nights*, the film, from an original story by Gene Fowler, C. Graham Baker, and Gene Towne, was an elaborate musical parody of *A Thousand and One Arabian Nights*, with Eddie in the role of Ali Baba. The Runyon-Caesar racetrack story was pushed back on the schedule to be filmed after *His Arabian Nights*. Although a projected starting date of March 1 was announced, the film, which was soon retitled *Ali Baba Goes to Town*, wouldn't actually begin filming until the middle of June. The change in title was a spoof on Frank Capra's popular film of the previous year, *Mr. Deeds Goes to Town*.

David Butler, who was to have directed *Chips*, was assigned the helm on the new project. Butler, the son of a stage director, first worked as an actor before becoming a director at Fox in the late twenties he was one of the studio's best. An efficient worker who turned out films of consistently high quality, Butler was more than qualified to handle the needs of a musical comedy like *Ali Baba Goes to Town*, having of late directed two of Fox's most important stars, Shirley Temple and Eddie's pal, the late Will Rogers.

The cast Zanuck assembled in support of Cantor was first-rate also. Unlike Eddie's two previous Goldwyn films, his costars provided the star with excellent backing without upstaging him. Other cast members included singer Tony Martin, in the romantic lead; Roland Young as the sultan in a marvelously befuddled performance; June Lang as his daughter, the other romantic lead; Louise Hovick (better known as Gypsy Rose Lee) as the villainous sultana; and the ever-menacing John Carradine and Douglas Dumbrille as her co-conspirators.

The songs for *Ali Baba* were provided by Mack Gordon and Harry Revel, who turned out one of the best overall scores Cantor had worked with since *Roman Scandals*. Although none of the tunes became standards, there was a consistently pleasant variety of numbers, with particularly good songs reserved for Cantor's unique style.

The film's screenplay, by Harry Tugend and Jack Yellen, is in many ways a return to territory covered by Cantor in *Roman Scandals* four years earlier.[1] Again Eddie's twentieth century character is transported to an early civilization. Rather than being a tired rehash of former triumphs, however, *Ali Baba Goes to Town* manages to follow the same general path of its predecessor without resorting to treading in its exact footsteps. Instead, where *Roman Scandals* could be classified a historical fantasy, *Ali Baba* utilizes the time travel for a topical satire of the thirties — specifically Franklin Roosevelt's New Deal.

While the topical parody is one of the film's strong suits, at the same time it is to modern audiences one of its downfalls. Many of the jokes and barbs hurled in *Ali Baba* fail to connect with contemporary viewers unless they have a background in depression policies and politics. There are references which range from things as familiar as welfare programs to some as obscure as Roosevelt's attempt to add associate justices to the Supreme Court.[2] Even without a history primer, however, the film is energetic and immensely enjoyable from start to finish.

The film (which opens to the strains of "Makin' Whoopee," perhaps as a reminder of the star's earlier triumph) begins with Aloysius Babson (Cantor), a movie-crazy young man, riding across the country in a boxcar to Hollywood. Once there, Aloysius plans to spend his vacation adding to his already extensive collection of stars' autographs. Aloysius is just preparing his morning coffee when the train slows down and two tramps (Stanley Fields and Warren Hymer) climb aboard. Aloysius offers the pair coffee, giving them both pictures of movies queens to use as napkins. He shows them his autograph book, which coincidentally is loaded with signatures of 20th Century–Fox stars, among a few others. When Aloysius gets to Bing Crosby's autograph, he does a little imitation of the crooner, which the tramps enjoy. Stating that they enjoy singing with their coffee, the tramps order Aloysius to favor them with a song. He obliges with an energetic rendition of "Laugh Your Way Through Life," a rousing, peppy number in the best Cantor tradition. Unfortunately, however, Aloysius gets carried away with his performance, literally, when he falls through the door of the moving boxcar and subsequently tumbles backwards into the surrounding desert.

The train speeds off, leaving Aloysius to cross the desert on foot. Before long, he sees what appears to be an Arabian city in the distance. As he approaches the city, however, a band of horsemen come upon him from the rear. Aloysius attempts to escape from them, but they follow him into the city, where one of the horses runs him over. We soon see that the entire city is an elaborate 20th Century–Fox movie location. The director (Alan Dinehart) yells "cut" and orders the crew to take the unconscious Aloysius to the first aid tent.

Inside the tent Nurse Dinah (Virginia Field) is attending to Aloysius as he comes to.

"How do you feel?" Dinah asks.

"I don't know," Aloysius begins. "If I'm alive, I feel fine. If I'm dead, I feel rotten."

Dinah explains that he is very much alive and is in the hospital tent of the production of *Ali Baba*. Movie-crazy Aloysius becomes excited when he learns that on the set are Roland Young, Tony Martin, and June Lang. He starts out with his autograph book, when the doctor (Charles Lane) enters along with one of the studio representatives (John Carradine). The doctor pronounces the patient healthy, and the studio man tries to get Aloysius to sign a liability release. Aloysius at first is willing to sign, but starts to moan when Dinah motions him not to.

"What hurts you," the doctor asks.

"I can't tell, 'till I see my lawyer," Aloysius groans.

The studio rep offers Aloysius a job as an extra on the film, along with all the autographs he can collect in return for the release. Aloysius eagerly signs the paper. The doctor instructs Dinah to give Aloysius some pills for any residual pain he may suffer. Dinah helps Aloysius into his Arabian costume and sends him off to the set, not before giving him a bottle of pain killers, along with the instructions to take two pills at 12 o'clock.

On the set Aloysius is given a part as one of the forty thieves. The director explains that the thieves are to be carried into the sultan's banquet hidden inside huge pots. At the signal they are to jump out and rush the sultan and his daughter, all except Aloysius, who is to cry "Death to traitors" and stab the villain, Prince Musah, who has arranged this plot. The director goes on to explain that the sultan has over 300 wives and one daughter.

"Three hundred wives? And only one daughter?" Aloysius asks, rolling his eyes in a reference to his real-life family.

As Aloysius climbs into his pot, the director bewails the fact that it's 2 o'clock and they haven't shot the scene yet.

"Two o'clock," Aloysius says to himself, taking out the pain killers. "Twelve pills at two o'clock."

After gulping down the pills, Aloysius falls fast asleep in the huge jar and dreams of ancient Baghdad. As he sleeps, Princess Miriam (June Lang) dances for her father, Sultan Abdullah (Roland Young), her stepmother, the sultana (Louise Hovick), and the sultana's brother, Prince Musah (Douglas Dumbrille). Musah is visiting with hopes of marrying Miriam and thus eventually seizing power in Baghdad. He comes bearing gifts — forty jars filled with precious gems and treasure. Musah describes the contents of each jar, while his slaves display the rare jewels. When they come to the pot which is supposed to contain pearls, however, the servants can only pull out the sleeping Aloysius. Musah calls for the guards and a gong is rung. Aloysius, hearing his cue, awakes and rushes Musah, crying, "Death to traitors." The guards grab him.

Aloysius chides the guards for ruining the scene. While the others debate who he is, Aloysius complains that they aren't sticking to the script and asks to see the director. Musah explains that in his country an assassin is customarily put to death with his own knife. The sultan is hesitant.

"Here? Before lunch? Try not to stain this rug," he adds. "It's rather expensive."

Musah grabs Aloysius' collapsible prop dagger and lunges at him. After repeated attempts which only tickle Aloysius, Musah drops the weapon and recoils in astonishment.

"A sorcerer," he concludes. "Black magic!"

Having had enough, Aloysius announces he's leaving and reaches under his robe to get his book for a few final autographs. In a scene using the same device as in *Roman Scandals*, Aloysius discovers that he is not only missing his autograph book, but also his pants. He quickly realizes that he has somehow been transported to ancient Baghdad.

"Who are you?" the sultan inquires.

"Me? I'm Al Babson," he replies.

"Ali Baba's son!" the sultan cries with delight and invites Aloysius to lunch.

Meanwhile, outside, a hungry mob presses the palace gate, clamoring for food. Their leader, Yusuf (Tony Martin), appeals for calm and promises to talk to the sultan. Princess Miriam hears his case instead and promises to speak to her father about it.

Inside, the sultan leads Ali Baba into the banquet room. The sultan apologizes for the meager menu, when in actuality the tables are heaped high with delicacies.

"You know," Ali comments, "a fellow with a drugstore here could make a fortune just from bicarbonate of soda."

Miriam enters to plead the case of the starving citizens waiting at the gates. When Musah advises the sultan to shoot them down, Ali Baba calls him "a heel."

"Heel?" Prince Musah asks.

"In my country a heel means something," Ali explains.

"Ah!" the prince beams, "I'm a heel."

Ali Baba advises the sultan to solve the local poverty problem by taxing the rich to help the poor. He explains that in America they call this "relief."

"It relieves everybody," Ali continues, "the poor of their hunger, and the rich of their money."

Ali goes on to describe the American system of taxation to the sultan, explaining that the rich are taxed to give to the poor, who spend this money and increase profits, which in turn are taxed.

"If they go on taxing and taxing, where will it all end?" the sultan asks, trying to make sense of it all.

"That's just what they were worrying about when I left," Ali Baba confesses.

The crowd outside becomes more vocal, demanding the sultan's attention. Musah again advises for a violent slaughter of the protestors.

"Why kill them with cannon balls?" Ali reasons. "Keep them alive with meatballs. Nobody ever started a revolution on a full stomach."

The sultan agrees to Ali Baba's plan and orders the crowd fed. As he watches them fill their empty bellies, the sultan has compassion on them.

"My poor subjects," he sighs.

"Your subjects?" Ali comments. "They eat like they were your relatives."

Ali Baba urges the sultan to adopt a Baghdad version of the New Deal, complete with works projects to build theaters, dams, bridges, and roads. He suggests they send crews out to work chopping down trees. The sultan confesses that they have no trees in the desert.

"Plant the trees, then chop 'em down," Ali tells him.

When the sultan asks how to pay for all this, Ali tells him with taxes.

"Why a tax on wives alone would balance the budget," he reasons.

"You'll ruin me," the sultan complains. "I've got 365 wives."

"Three hundred sixty-five? What do you do on leap year?" Ali asks.

The sultan appoints Ali Baba his prime minister and then takes him out to address the crowd. As Ali Baba speaks to the throng (in his best imitation of FDR), Musah, the sultana, and their henchman Ishak (John Carradine) plot from a nearby balcony. Musah has a soldier poised to kill Ali with a spear, until he hears him tell the crowd that he plans to disband the army. With Baghdad undefended, Musah reasons he can take over the city easily. He decides to let Ali Baba alone for the time being.

As Ali Baba regales the citizenry with his speech, he notices one group of people sitting by the wayside ignoring him. The sultan explains that they are his new musicians from "Afrika," who don't understand the language. Ali tries to talk to them in French, Spanish, Italian, and even Yiddish, before he tries the Cab Calloway dialect.

"Heidi Heidi Ho!" Ali calls to them. They immediately respond in kind. Ali takes a coal and starts to black-up, while continuing his repertoire of contemporary Harlemese. He joins them on the bandstand, telling them in song of the great day coming "a thousand years from today," when the world will flock to their music and call it "swing." Ali Baba and the band break into the highly infectious "Swing Is Here to Sway." The prolonged number, which includes a dance specialty by Jeni Le Gon and a musical reprise by the Peters Sisters, soon manages to have the entire city "truckin'" to the music, including the sultan and the villains.

Within a few days the effects of Ali Baba's programs are evident throughout Baghdad: camels now have license plates and are serviced at W.P.A.-sponsored filling stations, workers have been unionized (one group pickets a harem, claiming it is "unfair to organized attendants"), and dance parlors have opened to teach the latest swing steps. Musah decides to take advantage of the city's preoccupation by attacking. He leaves to join his army.

Meanwhile, in the street, Ali Baba thinks he sees the nurse he met back in the film company's first-aid tent. He excuses himself to the sultan and follows her. He calls her "Dinah," but the girls tell Ali her name is "Deenah."

"That's ridiculous," he tells her. "How could you sing, 'Deenah is there anyone feener?'"

Ali walks Deenah home, where she lives with her grandfather, Omar the rugmaker (Maurice Cass). Omar has been working on a magic carpet.

"Magic carpet?" Ali asks. "What does it do, beat itself?"

Omar explains that it should fly, but as of yet he hasn't been able to find the magic word which will make it take off. Deenah introduces her grandfather to the illustrious Ali Baba.

"May a bountiful Allah bless you with many sons!" the old man exclaims.

"Me," Ali smirks, in another reference to his real life family. "Many sons? You know me, Al!" The scene fades out.

That night in the palace garden Yusuf serenades Princess Miriam with the song "I've Got My Heart Set on You," a pleasant enough ballad, the full effect of which is diminished somewhat by June Lang's silly attempts at approximating an Arabic dance as Tony Martin sings. His singing and her gyrations are a sure sign that the couple has fallen in love. Unfortunately, since Miriam is royalty and Yusuf a commoner, they cannot marry. The next day Miriam complains to the sultan, who offers no solution to the lovers' dilemma. Ali Baba, on the other hand, suggests that the sultan resign so Miriam and Yusuf can wed. The sultan objects, but Ali explains that he can still be the ruler, but of a different kind of government.

"You can be a president, like in America," Ali tells the sultan.

"Does he rule the country?" the sultan asks.

"Does he rule the country?" Ali repeats. "Ask the Republicans."

Soon all of Baghdad is caught up in the fervor of an American-style presidential campaign, with one difference, the only candidate is Sultan Abdullah, whom Ali has christened "Honest Abe." The citizens parade through the streets carrying campaign plaques sporting such slogans as "Every man a sultan! Every home a harem!" (a reference to Huey Long's "Every man a king"). Ali Baba and Yusuf punctuate the rally with the campaign song "Vote for Honest Abe," a clever little lyric set to the tune of "Laugh Your Way Through Life." The song, which includes plenty of mugging by Cantor, is interrupted at intervals for the sultan's befuddled attempts at speech making, all of which come out wrong.

The night before the election Ali Baba is mapping out the final day's campaign strategy with Abdullah when they are interrupted by a campaign parade outside in the street. Instead of being a well-planned rally for the sultan, however, the ruckus is a spontaneous demonstration in support of Ali Baba for president (the crowd even chants, "We Want Ali," to the tune that Eddie's radio audiences sang the familiar catch phrase "We Want Cantor," and plays his radio theme "Now's the Time to Fall in Love"). Despite Ali's pleas of innocence, the sultana accuses him of treason.

"Me? President?" Ali cries in his defense. "Why back home they wouldn't even let me in the Elks."

The sultana convinces her husband that if Ali Baba wins the election, he should be boiled in oil. The next day Ali campaigns vigorously against himself, going so far as to hand out exploding cigars. His popularity is so pervasive, however, that the citizens praise him for his great sense of humor.

On election night the sultan and his family listen to the returns announced by a radio-style announcer speaking through an elaborate series of rams' horns (the program includes commercials from the Sahara Finance Company offering loans for used camels). Ali Baba listens with the royal family, but he is in chains to prevent his escape. As the oil boils, the country goes overwhelmingly for Ali—he even carries the sultan's own harem by a 364 to 1 plurality. Before the president-elect can be executed, however, he is freed by Yusef and escapes. The next day the sultan's nine counselors (a parody of the Supreme Court) declare the election void and orders Ali Baba captured and killed.

With all of Baghdad looking for him, Ali, with the aid of Deenah, manages to sneak out of the city dressed as a harem girl. Outside the gates, he mounts a waiting donkey and bids Deenah farewell.

"Funny," he tells her, "a little while ago I was running for president. Now, I'm just running!"

That night, still in drag, Ali rides into Muzah's army camp. He overhears the soldiers talking about their plan to attack Baghdad the following morning. When one soldier tries to flirt with him, Ali knocks him out and flees into a nearby tent. In another tent, Musah and his generals are enjoying the performance of a pair of harem girls (the Pearl Twins), who are dancing to "Twilight in Turkey," as played by the Raymond Scott Quintet (the group, decked out in Arab costumes and beards, are obviously having the time of their lives). After the specialty, another group of dancing girls enter with Ali Baba along with them. Although he/she is comically out of step, Ali manages to catch the fancy of Muzah. At the conclusion of the dance, Muzah takes Ali away to his private tent, where Ali pretends to be a shy harem girl.

"There's nothing to be afraid of," Muzah reassures his prey.

"I know," Ali squeaks, "but there's no one here."

"Not a soul ever comes here," the prince admits.

"Why don't you put in Bank Night?" Ali advises, recommending the popular movie theater promotion of the day.

Muzah begs for a kiss, but only receives solid, but playful, slaps. Finally, he asks Ali to dance for him. In return for the dance, Muzah promises to deliver Ali Baba's head on a platter. Ali begins to dance the dance of the seven veils, but actually uses the layers of silk to bind Muzah to the tent's center pole. He unmasks himself before delivering a head butt to Musah's stomach that knocks the villain out. Ali then rushes off to warn Baghdad.

By the next morning when Ali Baba arrives back at the city, Musah's army is already visible out across the plains. Ali rushes to the shop of Omar, where the rugmaker and his granddaughter are waiting.

"There's a reward of two thousand dirums for you," Deenah warns him.

"Two thousand!" Ali exclaims. "I've a good mind to kill myself and collect the reward."

Omar comments that they could save Baghdad with the flying carpet. Unfortunately, the rugmaker still hasn't discovered the magic word which will make the broadloom go. While standing on it, Ali explains that in America there's a word that makes everything go up: *inflation*. As he speaks, the carpet magically rises to the ceiling, causing Ali Baba to hit his head. Omar and Deenah marvel and wonder what made it go up.

"All I said was 'inflation,'" Ali admits, and by his use of the word receives another knock on the noggin.

Both Omar and Deenah keep repeating the strange magic word, much to Ali Baba's protests, until his skull is almost caved in. Ali quickly realizes that *deflation* is the corresponding command which makes the rug return to the ground. With the basic controls figured out, Ali instructs Deenah to give him a rope soaked in oil. Armed with his unorthodox ammunition, Ali orders the doors opened and glides out atop the flying carpet.

In a fairly convincing long-range camera shot, Ali Baba soars over the city on his magic carpet (aside from this establishing shot, the rest of the carpet effects are accomplished by use of rear screen projection). Ali then rides out to meet Musah's army, which is approaching on horseback. After setting the oil-soaked rope aflame, Ali dangles it over the edge. The burning rope, which is hanging at the horsemen's eye level, creates a panic among the soldiers and their steeds, causing them to scatter. When Ali chases Musah, at first the prince is also thrown into confusion. He quickly regains his composure, however, and grabs onto the rope, climbing to the top.

With the entire city watching and rooting for Ali Baba, the pair engage in a life or death struggle. At one point Musah has Ali in a choke hold.

"Stop!" Ali Baba cries. "Why are you so mad?"

"I just found out what a heel is," Musah tells him.

Finally, Ali succeeds in pushing Musah off (presumably to his death), and he rides over the city to receive the cheers of its citizens. Unbeknownst to Ali, however, the flaming rope has set his carpet on fire, and soon only a tiny edge is left uncharred. Ali turns to see the flames and quickly tumbles off.

Instead of crashing to his death, however, Ali Baba awakens back in the twentieth century. As the film's director is screaming at him for missing his cue, he realizes he's just plain Aloysius Babson again. Thrown off the set, he continues to Hollywood.

In what is either a record for the fastest postproduction work on a film or the slowest walk to Hollywood, Aloyisus arrives just in time to attend the world premiere of *Ali Baba* at the Carthay Circle. There, waiting to collect more autographs, he meets Dinah again. As Tony Martin acts as master of ceremonies, Al watches the stars go by, including Douglas Fairbanks, the Ritz Brothers, Sonja Henie, Ann Sothern (appearing in her second Cantor film), Tyrone Power, and "the biggest star in pictures—Shirley Temple." Aloysius is thrilled until the final star appears—Eddie Cantor.

Dinah feels Mr. Cantor is wonderful, but Aloysius only expresses disgust with the comedian, especially when he is called to the microphone to say a few words or "perhaps sing."

"Sing?" Cantor asks, before immediately answering, "All right, I don't mind."

"He certainly has to be coaxed," Al sneers sarcastically.

Cantor launches into a crowd-pleasing reprise of "Laugh Your Way Through Life." Cantor finishes his song and exits into the theater, but not before smiling and waving at Dinah. Aloysius is revolted.

"I ought to sock him in the nose," Aloysius threatens.

"Oh," Dinah sighs, "I think he's awfully nice. Don't you?"

"What's he got that I haven't got?" Al asks, while rolling his eyes as the picture fades out.

Filming on *Ali Baba Goes to Town* began in late June 1937 and ran through early September. Although the first few months of production proceeded smoothly, tragedy struck the set in late August when two studio property men (Philo Goodfriend and Harry Harsha) were killed when the magic carpet collapsed. The accident, which was caused when a faulty guy wire snapped, also injured two other stagehands. Despite the tragedy, which held up the completion of the filming for a few days, a few weeks later Cantor, in a publicity stunt for the film, was made an honorary member of the Hollywood Stunt Men's Club. The club cited Eddie for his cooperation with stunt performers and his willingness to often perform his own stunts, "particularly in *Ali Baba Goes to Town*."[3]

*Ali Baba* previewed on October 13, 1937, at Grauman's Chinese, in a gala opening reminiscent of the one staged in the film. Demonstrating that life imitated art, 20th Century–Fox used clips of the film's premiere in their Movietone News. Cantor appears in the newsreel, along with Ida, expressing his interest in "seeing this fellow Cantor" after hearing from others how wonderful he is. Ida, on the other hand, reveals that her favorite actor is Paul Muni, to which comment Eddie replies that Muni can buy her her next fur coat.

*Ali Baba Goes to Town* went into nationwide release October 29, 1937, at the end of "Eddie Cantor Week," a seven-day celebration of the comedian's silver anniversary in show business. The celebration was an obvious 20th Century–Fox publicity extravaganza, especially given that fact that

The sultan (Roland Young) enlightens Ali Baba/Al Babson (Cantor) in the topical satire *Ali Baba Goes to Town*.

twenty-five years earlier (1912) Cantor had already been in show biz for at least three years. Still no one brought up the fact that the dates were wrong, either out of politeness or forgetfulness, and the "mammoth" celebration went on as planned. Joseph Schenck, chairman of the gala's executive committee, was backed up by an honorary committee of 100 of America's most influential business, entertainment, sports, and political leaders.

The week climaxed in a testimonial dinner at the Hotel Ambassador in Los Angeles. The dinner, hosted by Georgie Jessel, was broadcast from coast to coast and the who's who of Hollywood attending included Jack Benny, Louis B. Mayer, Darryl F. Zanuck, Deanna Dubin, and Jimmy Durante, to name but a few. The program featured sixty-six of the hit songs Eddie had introduced. When Eddie was finally called upon to speak, he found himself, as *Variety* reported, "on one of the few occasions of his life groping for words." In addition, a similar banquet was staged concurrently with the West Coast fete on the site of 47 Henry Street, where Eddie had lived with Grandma Esther. By 1937, however, the address was a vacant lot.

After the extravaganza of Cantor week, which also included extensive coverage in newspapers and magazines, almost anything would be anticlimactic, including the opening of the film the event was designed to promote.

Despite the media blitz (including an ad campaign which boasted that *Ali Baba* was a "Cantornado of laughs") and the almost unanimously favorable reviews, the film failed to meet Fox's expectations. As did Cantor's two previous Goldwyn releases, *Ali Baba Goes to Town* opened well, but then quickly faded. Although the film made money, it failed to keep pace with *The Awful Truth* (directed by Leo McCarey) and Ronald Coleman in *The Prisoner of Zenda*, both of which were released the same week as *Ali Baba*.

Although Eddie Cantor would continue performing well into the 1950s, *Ali Baba Goes to Town* would mark a milestone in the comedian's career, but it was not evident at the time. *Ali Baba* was the last of a long line of Cantor star vehicles reaching back to the stage version of *Kid Boots* in which Eddie was the youthful little apostle of pep who would carry an entire show on his own energetic shoulders. It is fitting that a testimonial gala was thrown at this time, for aside from saluting Eddie for a spectacular career, it also looked back nostalgically on those accomplishments, something which Cantor himself would do more and more in his future projects.

Although he was still extremely popular, Cantor's popularity would come more and more from his audience's fond remembrances of the spritely comic of an era when both he and they were younger. By 1937, Cantor was forty-five, though he looked younger. Like most comedians, however, Cantor's character was firmly based in youth. Cantor, like Harold Lloyd, depended on that youthful zest and energy, while others, like Stan Laurel and Harry Langdon, needed their baby faces to compliment their aura of childlike innocence. With the addition of a few lines or a bit more jowl, the illusion these clowns created was distorted.

Fortunately for Eddie Cantor, he did not continue to put himself in the same roles which had comprised his first "twenty-five years" of show business. Rather, unlike some other clowns, he had either the wisdom or the luck to move on to other roles. In his subsequent movies, Cantor would play a scholarly professor, a cabbie, a retired vaudevillian, and even himself (in three films). Only once, in the nostalgically autobiographic *Show Business* (1943), would his actual age intrude on the believability of the part he was playing. Although his supposed age is never mentioned in the film, it is strongly suggested that he is something of "a kid" at the film's start; the character's believability suffers as a result.

None of this was evident, however, in 1937, and preparation for the next Cantor musical went ahead as planned at 20th Century–Fox. Although *Ali Baba*'s follow-up was to have been *Saratoga Chips*, originally slated as its predecessor, a variety of alternate stories soon pushed *Chips* off the production schedule. The first proposed change was to a property entitled *Sing While You Sleep*, which was sold to the studio by none other than Eddie Cantor. Originally conceived by one of Cantor's radio writers, Eddie Davis, *Sing While You Sleep* centered around a songwriter who received his inspiration while slumbering. The story by Cantor offered the opportunity for plenty of musical numbers.[4]

By the spring of 1938, a full five months after *Ali Baba*'s release, Darryl F. Zanuck had dropped *Sing While You Sleep* in favor of one of two stage properties, both musicals. The producer was considering *White Horse Inn* (a Broadway extravaganza which had also, partly due to its expense, been a resounding flop) and *Pins and Needles*, a semiprofessional Off Broadway show put on by the members of the International Ladies Garment Workers Union. The rights to the former show had already been purchased by Harry M. Warner, but Zanuck was willing to pay up to $100,000 if Cantor was interested in the vehicle. Eddie, on the other hand, was more interested in *Pins*, in which he envisioned playing the dress firm foreman who becomes stagestruck. While Zanuck deliberated which to buy—he eventually decided on neither—Cantor stayed on the East Coast, exercising the option on his radio show, performing at benefits and personal appearances, and even lecturing to a class at Columbia on the future of radio.

With the issuance of the Fox announcement book (which gave a rundown of the upcoming films by the studio's biggest stars), it was revealed that Eddie Cantor was to appear "in one laugh smash" that was as yet untitled. The copy went on to promise:

> Eddie's most hilarious and by far most original role . . . Eddie wins a contest as "The Average Man" but in doing so becomes a human guinea pig . . . with spies watching every intimate detail of his life. A screaming situation . . . and what Eddie does with it makes laugh history. Spectacularly produced . . . with a flock of beautiful gals . . . a whopping all-star cast of swingsters, funsters . . . and the grandest songs that ever topped a Hit Parade!

As is often the case in Hollywood, all the studio had compiled on the project was the idea and the advertising copy.

While the studio went to work on the "screaming situation" and "the grandest songs," Eddie Cantor made plans for another trip to Europe. Unlike his vacation of a few years earlier, this voyage was definitely of a more serious nature: it involved the rescuing of children from Nazi Germany. Sailing from New York in early July, Eddie, along with Ida, spent three weeks in England raising additional funds for the refugee work. Although Cantor had originally hoped to raise $150,000 for the cause, after a whirlwind tour of the major cities of England, the final tally came closer to $250,000, proving that he was still immensely popular in Great Britain.

Cantor spent the final day of the English tour saying thank you by way of a special radio appearance on the BBC's *Saturday Sing-Song* program. In a twenty-minute spot, Eddie joked about his impressions of England, told a few stories, sang (by request) "Making the Most of Each Day," and the local standard "The Lambeth Walk." As was typical of his American network broadcasts, Eddie concluded the program with a serious appeal for another of his pet projects, traffic safety.

The next day, July 27, Cantor sailed on the *Normandie*, accompanied by Darryl Zanuck and a few other executives from the studio. On the return trip, Cantor and Zanuck conferred on the comedian's next film. The script, which was first called *The People's Choice* and then switched to *Mr. Average Man*, was set to go into production by the end of August. After a week's stopover in New York, Eddie and Ida returned to Hollywood just in time for the marriage of their daughter Edna to Jimmy McHugh, Jr., son of the songwriter.

With less then a month to go before work was scheduled to begin on *Mr. Average Man*, Eddie Cantor was still not satisfied with the film's screenplay. The main disagreement lay in the proposed character the comedian was to play. While Zanuck wanted Cantor to continue in the formula which he had perfected in more than a half-dozen films, Eddie wanted no part of his now familiar screen persona.

In a prepared statement, Eddie explained his dissatisfaction with the roles he had been playing: "It is important at this time to make a big musical, where I can play 'Eddie Cantor' for a change. I want to sing, and I want to play something else besides an insipid character which the audience does not believe."

Unable to come to an agreement on the future course of his career, Eddie Cantor and 20th Century–Fox parted ways in early September 1938. The disagreement with Darryl Zanuck was, according to Cantor, a friendly one, though the *New York Times* reported that Fox executives accommodated Cantor's request for a release "with alarming speed," suggesting that they were just as eager to be rid of him as he of them. Contrary to Eddie's own account of his rift with Zanuck, the *New York Times* also reported that the trouble stemmed from Cantor wanting to do a minstrel-type show with him in the limelight, whereas the studio wanted a strong plot with strong supporting players. One would tend to believe the comedian's version, not only on the strength of Cantor's own statements, but because of the course of action he eventually took.

Although he did not want to abandon the genre in which he had thrived, Cantor obviously was looking for a change. It would seem that he was seeking to mature his screen character before he outgrew it. Perhaps this shift to a more believable, more serious screen persona was a reflection of a similar shift in Cantor's personal life, especially in light of his recent work on behalf of Jewish refugees. Whereas before Cantor's many pet charities had been for such worthy appeals as summer camps, of late he had become deeply involved in such life or death causes as the Aliyah and the March of Dimes. Understandably, like many comics, Cantor found that sheer laughter was no longer enough. After years as a top comedian, he wanted to be appreciated for himself—not for his alter ego, no matter how appealing that character might be. His next film would reflect this more serious outlook.

## REVIEWS

A gay and quippish musical, topical as a fireside chat and lighter than a magic carpet, Eddie Cantor's "Ali Baba Goes to Town" emerged yesterday at the Roxy as one of the better entertainment risks of the season.

It is, as any one can see, a fresh and fertile field for musical extravaganza, and Mr. Cantor and his aides have tilled it well, taking time out now and again to bring on the dancing girls of Twentieth Century-Fox to celebrate—in song—the fact that "Swing Is Here to Sway,"[5] to hint briefly at the romance between the Sultan's daughter (June Lang) and the crooning commoner (Tony Martin). Mr. Cantor doesn't need their help, though; Ali Baba's trip to town is pretty much of a solo hop, skip and jump.—Frank S. Nugent, *New York Times*, October 23, 1937

Assuming that the mass population of America which patronizes the picture theatres is ready to laugh at recent and current nipups in Washington, then "Ali Baba" is due for a smashing domestic boxoffice career. If Darryl F. Zanuck has overshot the mark of timeliness, the attraction still possesses appealing and popular assets. . . .

It has been more than two years [closer to 18 months] since Cantor last appeared in films but he has been out front among radio favorites during that time. "Ali Baba" presents him more to his character as a one-time musical comedy star than any of his previous films.—Flin, *Variety*, October 10, 1937

# *Notes*

1. Ironically, *Ali Baba*, like *Roman Scandals*, was also the subject of a plagiarism suit. In a court deposition over the *Ali Baba* suit in 1939, Cantor contended that he was just a "yes-man" when it came to story conferences, adding that Darryl Zanuck was "the dominant figure in all this stuff."

Strangely enough, however, while various authors tried to sue over the two films, no one pointed out the obvious source of inspiration of both vehicles—Mark Twain's *A Connecticut Yankee in King Arthur's Court*.

2. One gag, which was well received during the film's initial release but is seldom understood today, is a reference to the 1936 presidential election in which FDR carried all the states except Maine and Vermont.

3. Regardless of the stunt men's commendation, it is unlikely that even if he had been willing, 20th Century–Fox would have allowed Eddie Cantor to perform such dangerous stunts as falling backwards from a moving train or getting run over by a horse. However, the one long shot of the magic carpet flying over the Baghdad set does appear to use Cantor.

4. At first glance the premise of *Sing While You Sleep* would seem to bear more than a passing resemblance to the Cantor-coveted *Three Men on a Horse*, in which the protagonist also possesses a similar unconscious ability, not to write tunes, but to pick horses.

5. It is uncertain what "dancing girls" Frank Nugent may have seen in the film, especially in the "Swing Is Here to Sway" number, where the only girls dancing are the seriously overweight Peters Sisters. The only other chorines in the film are shown briefly in the film-within-a-film portion of the show.

# CHAPTER 32

# Forty Little Mothers

More than two and a half years elapsed between the release of *Ali Baba Goes to Town* and Eddie Cantor's next film, *Forty Little Mothers*. The lengthy span between pictures does not reflect, however, a similarly long vacation on the comedian's part. Rather, if anything Eddie was busier in the preparation of his next film project than he had been for any of its predecessors. The delay involved not only what exactly that film would be, but where in fact he would make it. As typical as it had become to expect production delays and changes in scripts on Cantor films (though not necessarily through any fault of Cantor's), the period from 1938 to 1940 saw what seemed to be a record for the most activity resulting in the least amount of product.

As had been the case when he split with Sam Goldwyn, Eddie Cantor already had other film offers lined up when he parted ways with 20th Century–Fox in early September 1938. Within a week, Cantor was negotiating with two studios, RKO and MGM, for the rights to a vehicle, which, of course, he himself would star in. The screenplay in question was one being written by Izzy Ellison and Joe Quillan, two of Cantor's radio writers. The title and the plot of this script are unknown, but according to *Variety*, it was to be completed by the time any deal was made. When a deal was struck by the end of the month, however, no more mention was ever made of the Ellison-Quillan collaboration.

Eddie Cantor made headlines with his signings that week, not because they were for record amounts (as had been the case with the 20th Century-Fox deal), but because he inked two contracts with two separate studios in the space of one week. The agreements, negotiated by Abe Lastfogel of the Morris Agency, called for the comedian to make two pictures in the upcoming year. The first, for RKO, was to go before the cameras within five months, while the other, for Metro-Goldwyn-Mayer, was to start within twelve months. The RKO deal called for an undisclosed amount of money plus a percentage of the gross. The MGM contract called for only a flat fee.

The *New York Times* heralded the signings in an article titled "Upturn for Hollywood Comics," which was subtitled "Do Eddie Cantor's MGM-RKO Contracts Presage Another Slapstick Cycle?" Despite the wishes of the piece's author, Douglas W. Churchill, that Cantor's new films would some-how stir the great film clowns of the early thirties into a new golden age of Hollywood high jinks, it was simply not to be. The story went on to report that the RKO film was shrouded in mystery, though it would probably not have any music in it, while the MGM vehicle would most likely be a splashy "minstrel type of show."

Despite Cantor's desires to play a character who was less "insipid" and to do more believable stories, the comedian was hesitant to abandon musi-cals all together, a position which brought him into conflict with his new bosses at RKO. The studio executives thought that there had been a down-turn in the popularity of musicals of late; even RKO's phenomenally popular Astaire-Rogers series was in a down cycle and would be brought to a close the following year. Cantor, on the other hand, confidently stated that musi-cals had been in a similar slump when he was working at Goldwyn's earlier in the decade, but he had succeeded in bucking the tide.

Cantor's idea (which was eventually produced by RKO in 1944 as *Show Business*) was for a cavalcade type of film, spanning the entire careers of a group of show people. The studio and the comedian compromised. Cantor's first RKO film would be *The Flying Yorkshireman*, based on the British novel by Eric Knight. With a screenplay by Jack Yellen (coscripter of *Ali Baba Goes to Town*), the film would be a straight play with no musical interludes. In return for his dramatic debut, the studio promised Cantor that his next project for them would be the cavalcade film.

Although Cantor left New York (where he had been broadcasting his weekly radio show for Camel cigarettes) for Hollywood in January 1939, pre-sumably to start work at RKO, no film was forthcoming. Even though the studio had listed Eddie as one of their top stars in *Variety*'s year-end issue, all plans, dramatic or musical, were put on indefinite hold. Instead, Eddie turned up in Culver City at Metro, which evidently was willing to go RKO's compromise with the comedian one better. In their spring book of upcoming productions, MGM announced that Cantor would soon star in a "comedy-drama with music." The film would be called *Banjo Eyes*, after Eddie's oft-used anatomically correct nickname. *Banjo Eyes* would not be produced, however, not at MGM at least, and not as a film. The title, too good to go to waste, would be attached to the Broadway musical comedy in which Can-tor would star the following year. By mid–August, Metro would reveal differ-ent plans for Eddie.

MGM announced that Cantor's first project would be a remake of *Girl Crazy*, the Gershwin Broadway musical which had first been filmed in 1932 with the comedy team of Wheeler and Woolsey. Ironically, the entire proj-ect was filled with refugees from the RKO lot. First, the original celluloid version had been an RKO film to which Metro purchased the rights. Next, two of its three scheduled stars, Cantor and Fred Astaire, had recently been under RKO contracts (Astaire was just completing his first film for MGM, *Broadway Melody of 1940*, after a lengthy stay at the other studio). The only

**Crowds stretch around the block at Loew's State in Manhattan for tickets to a Cantor performance in 1939 (collection of Brian Gari).**

homegrown MGM part of the production was Eleanor Powell, also in *Broadway Melody of 1940*.

Although it was never filmed—perhaps the disappointing returns of *Broadway Melody of 1940* were part of the reason—*Girl Crazy* (along with a sound version of *Kid Boots* and a film version of the stage show *Banjo Eyes*) must rank high on the list of proposed Cantor films which never made it to the screen. Although the Astaire-Powell dance team had failed to "click," *Girl Crazy* starring Astaire, Powell, and Cantor would have been at the very least an interesting film to watch. What makes the "what if" all the more tantalizing is that Bert Kalmar and Harry Ruby, coauthors of *The Kid from Spain*, had been assigned to write the screenplay along with Jack McGowan.

Ironically, Cantor's first MGM film wound up being a nonmusical directed by a genius of the musical genre. Busby Berkley, who had cut his film teeth directing the numbers in Eddie's first four Goldwyn films, was assigned the task of bringing the story of *Forty Little Mothers* to the screen. Actually, the story had already been on the screen once before under the title *La Mioche*. A little more than a year earlier, Cantor and his wife had wandered into a New York theater where the French film was playing. The story of a bachelor who must suddenly care for an abandoned infant, *La Mioche* won over Cantor immediately.

"First thing I knew," Cantor later told a reporter as he recalled the film's lead, "there I was crying, really crying, about this poor fellow. I felt sorry for him, that he had this baby and loved it and took care of it and didn't know what to do."

Eddie Cantor recommended the film to Nicholas Schenck, president of Lowe's, MGM's parent company. Schenck, along with other decision makers at the studio, thought the story had merit, and the rights were obtained.

With a screenplay by Ernest Pagano and Dorothy Yost, adapted from the original story *Monsieur Petiot*, by Jean Guitton (upon which *La Mioche* had been based), *Forty Little Mothers* offered Cantor the opportunity to step out from behind his usual screen character and act. Although Eddie did get to sing one song in the proceedings—a lullaby, "Little Curly Hair in a High Chair"—the rest of the film offered scant opportunity for hand clapping, the rolling of eyes, or any other components of the standard Cantor schtick.

Described as a comedy-drama, the story, which casts Eddie as a professor teaching at an all-girls' school, was more of a drama, especially when it came to Cantor's part. For the first time in his career, Eddie played it relatively straight, with most of the film's comedy going to the girls of the school, along with Nydia Westman in the part of the flighty Mademoiselle Cliche. In addition to farming out the majority of the laughs, Cantor also had the thankless task of playing a majority of his scenes one-on-one with an infant.

It is a tribute to Cantor's acting ability in a straight role that unlike most performers thrust into such partnerships, he is rarely upstaged by Baby Quintanilla. Despite MGM's ad campaign for the movie—a series of cartoons featuring caricatures of Cantor and the baby, many of which referred to the tot's stealing the picture from its star—Cantor and Quintanilla made a believable and engaging team. Eddie's rapport with the infant was probably enhanced because he had recently become a grandfather himself and thus had plenty of opportunity for practice.

While Eddie Cantor may have had some previous experience with babies, his part in *Forty Little Mothers* presented a definite departure for him in other respects. The role wasn't a straight dramatic one, but it was totally different from all the parts—or to be specific, the one part—the comedian had played before. "It's not Eddie Cantor," Cantor told Eileen Creelman, contradicting comments he made a few years earlier upon his departure from Fox. "That's something I've never done before, not play Eddie Cantor. That's what I've always done, for Ziegfeld, for Goldwyn, for everyone. Now, that's all right for a while. But you can't go on playing yourself always. Some day they won't believe you. When you're old, they won't believe you. It has to stop. Imagine when I'm sixty, playing Eddie Cantor. They'd never believe me at sixty."[1]

Although all this may have been a new experience for Eddie, for Berkley, now working behind the cameras at Metro after a lengthy stay at Warners, working on a drama was nothing new. As early as 1933, with *She Had to Say Yes*, codirected by Berkley and George Amy, Berkley had branched out into other films, anticipating the day when musicals would again fall out of favor with the cinema-going public. That Berkley was capable of handling drama was proven in the 1939 *They Made Me a Criminal*, the director's last film at Warners and the vehicle which made John Garfield a star.

It was quite a switch, however, from guiding Garfield's tough guy character to the direction of a baby. Berkley rose to the challenge, taking charge of the infant from casting to camera. "It was my idea," Berkley explained, "that we should get a baby young enough to be cute but helpless. I wanted the sort of a baby that because of his helplessness, anyone in the audience would want to adopt, as Cantor does in the story."

As it turned out, a baby girl was chosen to play the part of the film's baby boy.[2] Finding the eight-month-old Baby Quintanilla, was one thing. Directing the child was an altogether different situation, as Berkley would soon find out. "We found the baby," Berkely recalled, "and I found a problem I hadn't bargained for: how to get this baby to register expressions called for in the script." Berkley solved the problem by becoming Quintanilla's unofficial nurse, playing with the child, quieting her when she cried, and becoming almost an extra parent. The director's efforts were rewarded when the baby, won over by Berkley, became a willing mimic of his facial expressions. If Berkley had a sad look on his face, the baby would copy it. Conversely, if a happy look was required from the young trouper, the director would adopt an appropriate giddy visage. The technique worked, although it sometimes took as long as three-quarters of an hour for Berkley to get (and keep) the right expression on Baby Quintanilla long enough to film it.

Throughout the filming of Baby Quintanilla's scenes, director Berkley went to extraordinary lengths to capture the necessary moods from the young star. In one scene, where a sad look was called for, Berkley tried every trick he knew, to no avail. Finally, he picked up the tot and bawled her out just as if she was a temperamental starlet. It worked. Quintanilla's puzzled reaction fit the situation perfectly, and it was captured on film.

Another time Berkley, trying to get the baby to cock her head to one side, gave himself a stiff neck before she would imitate the precise movement needed. Other Berkley stunts included hanging upside down from a parallel beam, standing on his head, and blowing slide whistles. In one scene, Quintanilla was to lie next to Cantor in bed and hit the comedian with a shaving brush while he tried to sleep. The infant performed the bit perfectly, but only after Berkley climbed into bed with Cantor and showed her how it was to be done—for ten minutes. The director admitted that his numerous histrionics made the crew and visitors to the set believe he had gone insane. "But I hadn't," Berkley confessed. "Only half insane."

Half insane or not, Busby Berkley managed to extract the necessary performances from Baby Quintanilla, along with the rest of the actors and actresses, and somehow completed production by the late winter of 1940. The cast also included Judith Anderson, fresh from her greatest role in Alfred Hitchcock's *Rebecca*, as the headmistress of the girls' school; Nydia

Westman as her delightfully skittish assistant, who despite her spinsterish appearance was only thirty-eight at the time; veteran character actor Ralph Morgan (brother of fellow MGM player Frank); and popular teenage actress Bonita Granville, as the school's student leader.

The film itself has that distinctively rich MGM gloss about it, even in the scenes set in Cantor's tiny boardinghouse room. Berkley's direction is crisp and keeps the proceedings moving along at a pleasant pace (the film is only eighty-nine minutes long). He manages to keep the tale from becoming too saccharine most of the time, no small feat given the potentially maudlin nature of the story. Cantor's performance, especially when viewed against his usual roles, is remarkably restrained. Often comedians are criticized for the occasional itch to "play Hamlet," but Cantor acquits himself nicely in his part, showing an acting ability beyond musical-comedy. He is particularly believable in his many scenes alone with Baby Quintanilla.

*Forty Little Mothers* begins with a gala reunion banquet for Camford University's class of 1916. In an amusing vignette, those who had earlier won the various class superlatives are called up to the stage, where they are matched against enlarged photos of their former selves. Ironically, the school's great track star is now grossly overweight, while the class Casanova is a withered fellow who employs a ratty toupee to cover his bald pate. Unbeknownst to his fellow classmates, a similar fate has befallen the "most likely to succeed"—the absent Gilbert Thompson. While his classmates toast him and sing "Auld Lang Syne" in tribute to him and his success, Gilbert Thompson (Cantor) is down at the city docks waiting to apply for a job as a deckhand. A former professor, Gilbert is the victim of an oversupply of teachers and is thus forced to find whatever employment he can scrounge up.

In a nearby ferry waiting room, a young mother (Rita Johnson) kisses her eight-month-old baby boy (Baby Quintanilla) goodbye and exits, abandoning the infant while she goes out to commit suicide. As she nears the edge of the pier, Gilbert sees her, surmises her intent, and rushes to stop her. He asks for a match, then explains that he doesn't really need one because he's just found the willpower to give up smoking.

"Funny thing, willpower," he tells her. "You never know you have it till you try and use it, then you find you have more than you need."

Gilbert takes the woman to a nearby cafe. There he buys her coffee, encourages her, and even manages to find her a job as a waitress. Unfortunately, while Gilbert was saving a life, he was also losing his chance for a job. He wanders into the waiting room, where he finds the abandoned baby. As the waiting room empties, Gilbert realizes that the child is alone. He tries to find the infant's mother, but no one claims the baby.

"People certainly are careless these days," Gilbert comments to the baby.

Upon closer examination, Gilbert discovers a note in the basket, asking the finder to give a good home to the child.

"That's funny," Gilbert tells the baby, "I wish I had a good home to take you to." After thinking a moment he adds, "I wish I had a good home to take me to."

It starts to rain, so Gilbert decides to take the child back to his meager room in a nearby boardinghouse. As soon as he exits, however, the mother returns, searching for her baby. After a fruitless search of the area, she rushes to the police station.

In his room, Gilbert unpacks the baby's basket. "Oh," he remarks upon finding extra diapers, "spare parts."

"You know," he tells the infant, "I've had no experience with baby boys." (This is the film's only reference to one of Cantor's favorite joke subjects.)

Gilbert starts getting the bed ready for his small guest, whom he has christened "Chum." After putting Chum in a makeshift high chair, Gilbert spreads some newspapers on top of the mattress.

"Just in case," he grins, adding, "in case you want to read at night."

As Gilbert dresses Chum for bed, he sings the delightful little lullaby "Little Curly Hair in a High Chair" (by Charlie Tobias and Nat Simon). By song's end, Gilbert and Chum are tucked in and ready for sleep, only Chum decides he would rather hit his bedfellow with a shaving brush than slumber. Gilbert decides that his tiny charge must be hungry and goes out to get the baby something to eat. Having spent his last dime for coffee earlier in the evening, Gilbert asks his landlady for some milk, but she has none. He asks her to watch Chum while he goes out.

The scene shifts to a courtroom where Gilbert is awaiting trial on the charge of "milk stealing." The judge (Ralph Morgan), a fellow member of the class of '16, recognizes Gilbert and takes him into his chambers. Gilbert tries to explain the incident as a prank done on a dare. Gilbert goes on to explain that the college he had been teaching at lost its endowment and was forced to close. Excusing himself, the judge places a call to Madame Granville's School for Girls, an upstate private school in need of a professor. The judge then informs Gilbert that the job is his if he wants it.

"Judge," a choked-up Gilbert tells him, "that's about the nicest sentence you've ever given anyone."

To seal the bargain, the judge then gives Gilbert an advance on his salary and sees him off. As Gilbert leaves the courthouse, he passes the missing persons department, where, unbeknownst to him, the young mother is filing a report on her lost baby.

Gilbert arrives back at the roominghouse weighed down with packages containing new wardrobes for both Chum and himself. Gilbert sheepishly asks the infant to go along with him to the school.

"I was just wondering," he begins hesitantly, "how you'd like me for a father . . ."

Before he can continue, however, Chum "razzes" him. Gilbert is taken aback.

"You want to think it over?" Gilbert asks. "Well, that's all right."

Chum laughs, which Gilbert takes as a yes. He packs up their belongings while singing the film's lullaby and leaves with the baby.

At Madame Granville's School for Girls, the teenage student body is climbing the walls, literally, to get one last glimpse at Professor Lang, a handsome young professor, who has been discharged because all his students have fallen in love with him. As they wave good-bye, the dithery Mlle. Cliche (Nydia Westman) comes by to pull the girls down from the wall and escort them back to class. She tells the girls that Lang's replacement, Gilbert Thompson, is arriving that day. The girls, led by Doris (Bonita Granville), decide they want no part of the new professor, whom they deride with the nickname "Gilly."

Soon Gilbert arrives alone (he has left Chum at a boardinghouse in the town), and he is ushered in to meet Madame Granville (Judith Anderson). In light of Professor Lang's dismissal, she informs Gilbert that he must not only teach, but help mold the students' characters. In addition, he is to teach philosophy, history, science, and gymnastics. Gilbert confesses that he has never taught gym before.

"In gymnastics," Madame Granville explains, "you'll instruct the girls in the control and development of the body beautiful."

The bachelor professor does a double take, prompting the Madame to add: "Theoretically . . . of course!"

Gilbert is then informed that he, like all faculty members, must live on campus; his quarters are directly above Madame Granville's office. In addition, he is told, no children are allowed. Granville exits, and Gilbert calls Mama Lupini, the Italian landlady with whom he has left Chum. He arranges for Chum to stay with Mama, who, having a large brood of her own, is glad to take care of an extra baby. She puts Chum on to speak with Gilbert, and the new "father" starts conversing with the tyke in a stream of baby talk. As he babbles, Mlle. Cliche enters and stares at him with puzzlement. When Gilbert finally notices her, he adapts the "goo-gooing" slightly, hangs up, and explains that he's been speaking "Hungarian."

Gilbert is soon introduced to the faculty and the girls. The rest of the faculty, which is all female, ignores him, and the girls give him the cold shoulder. Back in their dorm room, the girls plot Gilbert's downfall. The next morning in class the girls disrupt Gilbert's history lesson by singing repeated choruses of "Good Morning to You," refusing to sit while he is standing, taking pointless ballots over trivial subjects, and breaking out into dueling choruses of "Columbia, the Gem of the Ocean" and "Dixie." The last straw comes when Gilbert pulls down what is supposed to be a map of ancient Greece and finds a wall-sized cartoon of a jackass instead. Gilbert decides that since they've had their fun in class, they can write a two thousand–word theme for homework.

The extra assignment only strengthens the girls' resolve to get rid of "Gilly." They decide that they will intentionally get Gilbert fired the same way they unintentionally lost Professor Lang—by falling in love with him.

To this end they leave passionate love notes to Gilbert strewn around the campus. The notes are quickly discovered, and Gilbert is summoned to Madame Granville's office for an informal hearing to determine if "lightning has struck twice."

Gilbert enters, unaware of the love letters and uninformed about his reason for being there. Madame Granville orders Gilbert to turn around slowly while she and Mlle. Cliche examine him for any clues as to what might make him attractive to the student body. Gilbert spins until he becomes dizzy, but the ladies still are baffled. Granville next commands him to remove his jacket and flex his muscles. While Gilbert stands mystified, the two women proceed to feel his biceps; Mlle. Cliche especially enjoys this part of the hearing and helps herself to a few extra squeezes on the side.

Next, in a test of his emotional responses, Granville orders Gilbert to have a seat with his back towards her. While Cliche studies Gilbert's expressions, Granville reads excerpts from the mash notes.

"This may surprise you, Gilly," she begins reading, "but I desperately love you. You are the most adorable man I have ever known."

Gilbert, unaware that she is reading, squirms uneasily while he listens to Granville's outpourings of passion. He soon falls out of the chair, overwhelmed by what he believes are Granville's unbridled emotions.

"Now," she asks Gilbert, "what do you think of that?"

"Well," Gilbert begins, his voice raised an octave by the strain of the moment, "it's very flattering, of course, but do you think we're suited to each other?"

"What's that got to do with it?" Granville asks.

Unable to think of a comeback, Gilbert excuses himself, but not before Granville tells him, "Hold yourself in readiness. I may call upon you later."

"I see . . ." Gilbert starts, adding in shock, "You mean tonight?"

"It's possible," Granville states matter-of-factly.

"Ohhh," Gilbert groans as he stumbles out the door.

To complicate Gilbert's precarious situation, Mama Lupini arrives with Chum. She explains that her children have come down with the mumps, and, consequently, Chum must stay with Gilbert until they recover. Gilbert sneaks Chum up to his room.

That night, the girls decide to intensify their anti–Gilly campaign, going from the written word to overt acts of love. They draw lots to decide who will do what and where to the unsuspecting professor. One of the girls, a Southern belle named Eleanor (Margaret Early), is assigned to lure Gilly to the gazebo and kiss him. She calls up Gilbert and implores him to meet her there to discuss an urgent problem. Reluctantly, Gilbert leaves Chum after pinning him in bed and goes off. At the gazebo, Eleanor tells the professor she has fallen in love and needs advice. At first Gilbert responds with a compassionate discourse on young love, but soon he discovers that he is the object of Eleanor's affections. Eleanor grabs Gilbert and begins to kiss him wildly, just as Cliche happens by.

"Oh, Gilly!" Eleanor cries.

"Wait a minute, Eleanor," Gilbert pleads. "I'm old enough to be your father!"

"Oh, Daddy!" she corrects herself, while continuing the kiss barrage.

Gilbert runs away to his room, but not before a swarm of girls encircle him, leaving his face covered with lipstick. Cliche hurries to inform Madame Granville of this latest incident. When Gilbert finally manages to return to his apartment, he is met there by Marcia (Diana Lewis), who chases him around the room, trying to seduce the hapless professor. While the rest of the girls sing a serenade on the porch, Doris climbs up a trestle into Gilbert's bedroom, where she discovers Chum. She quickly climbs down, orders the other girls to disperse, and calls off Marcia. The students manage to flee just as Granville and Cliche are arriving to see what is going on. They enter the apartment to find Gilbert sprawled out on the floor, his hair mussed and his face red with rouge. Madame Granville expresses her shock, puts Gilbert on probation, and exits.

Meanwhile, back in the city, the police have discovered that Gilbert has Chum, but since his friend the judge is out of town, they have no way of contacting him. They tell the frantic mother they will soon find out where he is, however, and reunite her with her child.

The next day Gilbert, still believing the girls' show of affection to be sincere, kindly lectures them on love. He relates a very personal story about a crush he once had and concludes by telling them not to "mistake friendship for love." His compassionate talk is brought to an abrupt halt, however, when he turns to the blackboard and discovers a cartoon of a wailing baby along with the caption "Gilly, Jr." The girls break out into uproarious laughter. As Gilbert stands stunned, they sing their own version of "Rock-a-bye Baby," complete with references to how he will be fired as soon as they tell Madame Granville about Chum.

Furious, Gilbert tells the girls that his love for Chum means more than any job ever could. He asks them why they went through so much trouble to make him feel liked. The girls sit in ashamed silence. Gilbert exits to hand in his resignation, telling the students that they needn't bother to let Madame Granville know about Chum.

"I wouldn't want her to think that any of her girls would stoop so low to take advantage of a baby just to get me fired," Gilbert explains as he storms out.

After Gilbert returns to his room to collect Chum, the girls enter. Tearfully they apologize to Gilbert and beg him to stay. They promise not to tell Granville about Chum and even offer to help him care for the baby. Gilbert happily agrees to the new arrangement.

Soon the entire student body is busy taking care of Chum, knitting him clothes while out rowing, washing them while swimming, and even doing the mending behind the targets on the archery range. Despite their efforts to keep their newfound activities a secret, faculty members soon find out about the motherly chores. With Granville out on her day off, the teachers anxiously await her return that night.

Meanwhile, Gilbert and the forty little mothers, unaware that they have been found out, go about their normal routine. That evening they meet in Gilbert's apartment to give Chum his bath. When Granville arrives back early, the girls are trapped in the apartment. After hearing the testimony of the other teachers, Granville decides to question the only absent member of the faculty—Gilbert. After Granville enters his apartment, it is soon obvious that the tiny room is loaded with girls attempting to hide. One by one, the girls flee as quickly as they are discovered. Granville is shocked.

"It's a lie!" Gilbert proclaims, in a voluntary response to an unasked question.

"You bluebeard!" Granville accuses.

Finally, Granville reaches Gilbert's bedroom closet, where she discovers Doris holding Chum. She faints. Gilbert tries to revive her with milk from a baby bottle.

The next day Granville announces to the students that Gilbert has been fired for violating the school rules. As soon as she exits, the girls decide they will mutiny until Gilbert is rehired. They raid the kitchen for supplies and then barricade themselves in their dorm. After hearing of the mutiny, Mlle. Cliche rushes after Gilbert, who is just leaving the campus with Chum. She implores him to talk to the girls. Outside the dorm he tries to talk to the girls, but they insist they will burn the dorm down. Handing Chum to Cliche, Gilbert climbs a ladder to the girls' second-story fortress. They quickly pull him inside.

Cliche, with Chum in her arms, bursts into Granville's office to notify her of the situation. Chum quickly wins over the normally stern headmistress. Back in the dorm, Gilbert has convinced the girls to give up their mutiny and return to class. He promises to come back, along with Chum, for visits.

While Gilbert is talking with the girls, Chum's mother enters Granville's office looking for her baby. She informs Granville that she had been abandoned by her husband, whom Granville assumes to be Gilbert. Granville takes the mother and Chum to meet the girls, who are now back in class. Believing Gilbert to be a wife deserter, Granville tells the girls what kind of a man they have been defending. The girls vehemently stick up for Gilbert.

The confusion is sorted out when Gilbert enters. He and the mother immediately recognize each other from their meeting on the pier. She then realizes that the man who saved her from suicide is also the stranger who has been taking care of her baby.

"He had the best care in the world," Gilbert explains, "and the love of forty little mothers."

As the girls surround Chum and his mother, Gilbert quietly slips out of the room. Outside, in the film's most touching moment, Gilbert carefully separates Chum's belongings from his suitcase, but not before keeping a pair of the baby's shoes to remember him by. Chum and his mother soon join him, and he bids them farewell before walking off alone.

As he turns the corner outside the school's gate, the entire student body scales the brick wall of the campus—just as they had for professor Lang—only now they are joined by Granville and Cliche. Granville tosses a note to Gilbert, then whistles to get his attention. Gilbert picks up the message, reads it, and smiles. Evidently the note informs Gilbert that he had been re-hired, along with Chum's mother in some capacity.

The final scene shows Gilbert, Granville, Cliche, and Chum's mother all standing by the side of the lake, singing "Little Curly Hair in a Highchair" (complete with Cantor clapping his hands in his familiar style), while watching a crew race through binoculars. Chum is absent, but in the film's final shot, the baby is seen in the crew scull, acting as the school's coxswain.

Continuing a trend which had begun with *Ali Baba Goes to Town*, the promotion of *Forty Little Mothers* was steeped in nostalgia designed to capitalize on Eddie Cantor's long and popular career. The film, which had its opening at New York's Capitol Theatre on April 18, 1940, had its world premiere a day earlier at Loew's Canal Theatre on Manhattan's Lower East Side in Eddie's boyhood neighborhood. The showing of the film that evening, with the proceeds going to local charities, was just the culmination of an entire Eddie Cantor day in the comedian's old stomping grounds. A full slate of activities, which included the unveiling of a commemorative plaque on Henry Street, a testimonial luncheon, various appearances, and a parade, were well orchestrated to insure the optimum amount of publicity for *Forty Little Mothers*.

As if lionization of one the Lower East Side's favorite sons wasn't enough, MGM pulled out all the stops for the film's run at the Capitol, putting together a live stage show which not only included Cantor, but also his longtime pal, Georgie Jessel. Reunited for the first time since their successful 1933 tour, the two comedians were accompanied on the bill by Don Albert's orchestra, along with Gracie Barrie, Buster Shaver, and Oliver and George. The headliners went through a nostalgic pastiche of songs and routines, punctuated, as always, with a healthy dose of mutual ribbing and one-upmanship.

Despite the best efforts of MGM, Cantor, and Jessel, *Forty Little Mothers* was in *Variety*'s estimation a "severe disappointment." Opening week grosses failed to hit $35,000. With Cantor's salary alone for the week being $15,000 (Jessel and the rest of the cast and crew divided up close to $20,000), a tentatively scheduled second and third weeks were canceled. Cantor's solo tour with the film was also curtailed after a similarly subpar week in Washington, D.C. Without Cantor in person, the film did even worse, winding up on the lower end of double features a scant two months after its release. Quite a come down for a performer whose pictures used to be road show events.

**Professor Gilbert Thompson (Cantor) and "Chum" (Baby Quintanilla) in *Forty Little Mothers*.**

Reviewers also received *Forty Little Mothers* lukewarmly, giving the film mixed reviews. Few placed the film's failure at Cantor's feet, however; most cited the weakness of the plot. The film's title probably didn't help draw patrons into the theaters either, because it drew attention to the film's sentimental slant. As stated previously, ads for the movie heavily featured cartoons of Cantor and his infant costar, a stark contrast for the comedian whose previous ad campaigns had surrounded him with beautiful chorus girls.

Viewed today, the film holds up fairly well as a flawed experiment. Had the audiences of 1940 been inclined to take their Cantor in straight roles it is likely that more films in the same vein would have been produced. As it was, however, they apparently liked their Eddie with more vigor and corn. This fact was not lost on Cantor, who would in the future stick to more typical vehicles.

With the failure of *Forty Little Mothers*, Eddie Cantor would return to entertaining audiences in the manner which had made him one of America's top entertainers for over twenty years, though his future films would be more nostalgic remembrances than portraits of a star in his prime. It is not surprising then that Eddie Cantor's next vehicle would mark a return to the venue which had first made him a star — the Broadway stage.

## REVIEWS

That presumably vast public which interests itself in the family affairs of Eddie Cantor will be enchanted, in "Forty Little Mothers" (at the Capitol), by the spectacle of Mr. Cantor as a sort of forty-first little mother, and a rather amusing one at that. Mr. Cantor is shrewd: instead of trying to be funny himself he keeps bringing up reinforcements of young proteges to steal the show from him, assuming that there is a moiety of show to steal. In this case there is, and the young thief to whom the picture owes grateful acknowledgement this time is Baby Quintanilla, who disrupts a young ladies' seminary when he is introduced by big-hearted Professor Cantor into Faculty Row. — B. R. Crisler, *New York Times*, April 19, 1940

Eddie Cantor's first starrer for Metro-Goldwyn-Mayer provides him with a straight dramatic role — and without the filmusical trimmings that have been present in all of his former talkers.

"Forty Little Mothers" is decidedly reminiscent of "The Charm School" of two decades ago in basic formula. But it carries handicap of dated scripting and erratic direction. Overcoming these deficiencies to some extent is the inclusion of a waif who gets plenty of attention with its cuteness, spontaneous antics and baby gibberish. — Walt, *Variety*, April 17, 1940

# *Notes*

1. Paradoxically, in his next film Cantor would literally play himself. In fact, the majority of Cantor's remaining screen appearances would be either guest appearances as himself or as characters based on himself. Perhaps the relatively disappointing box office returns would help the comedian realize that his greatest success in show business came from the unique personality of Eddie Cantor.

2. Although only billed as "Baby Quintanilla," the young performer's first name was actually Barbara. MGM most likely kept the child's sex a mystery because she was playing a boy. The studio was used to such gender bending, beginning the tradition with one of its greatest stars — Lassie.

# CHAPTER 33

# *Banjo Eyes*

With the failure of *Forty Little Mothers* at America's box offices, the film career of Eddie Cantor cooled considerably. MGM, which had planned to star Eddie in a review film to be called *Ziegfeld Follies*, shelved the idea indefinitely.[1] (The studio's acquisition of the rights to Ziegfeld's life story also left it with the privilege of using the producer's name in the title of other film projects.)

Although Cantor in a film version of the *Follies* would have been an invaluable record of the comedian in the venue which had made him famous, this MGM-Cantor film which never made it to the screen is yet another tantalizing case of "what might have been." After the completion of *Forty Little Mothers*, Cantor and famed director Ernst Lubitsch considered working together on a comedy tentatively titled *The Wedding Crasher*. The film, which would have been produced in late 1940, was to star Eddie as a professional interloper at weddings, a role which the comedian had played in real life during his lean teenage years on Manhattan's lower East Side.

"This fellow does nothing but crash gates," Cantor told interviewer Eileen Creelman one afternoon at Lindy's, "just goes from one wedding after another. That's one thing I know all about. Didn't I do it all the time when I was a boy? Didn't matter what kind of a wedding, Jewish wedding, Polish, Italian, any kind. When you're hungry you don't care."

Unfortunately—especially since *The Wedding Crasher* would have teamed Cantor with the most talented director he had worked with since Leo McCarey—the project never advanced beyond the negotiation stage. While Eddie's prospects at Metro were fading away, an unusual offer arose at roughly the same time. In the spring of 1940, almost four years after their bitter split, Cantor was talking to Sam Goldwyn about a proposed remake of their first great success, *Whoopee!* The idea, which initially was Cantor's, was to produce the story again as a straight comedy, without the musical numbers and preponderance of chorus girls. What in effect would be a film version of *The Nervous Wreck*, the play upon which *Whoopee!* had been based, was another project which was evidently not to be. Although Cantor would not star in a remake of *Whoopee!* apparently Goldwyn thought the idea good

292

enough to adapt the vehicle four years later for his first film with Danny Kaye, *Up in Arms*.[2]

With no immediate film projects in the works, Eddie Cantor was free to return to the stage. Although it would make a very tidy tale to explain Cantor's move back to the legitimate theater as a retreat following on the heels of a declining movie career, this is simply not so. While it is true that he was no longer one of the top-ten box office draws he had been during his Goldwyn years, Eddie was still considered a major star, a fact to which the various offers and projects he fielded in the early forties would attest.

While Cantor's reappearance on Broadway would culminate a year and a half later in his starring role in *Banjo Eyes*, initially he set out not to perform, but to produce and possibly even direct, stage properties. Describing his latest theatrical work as simply a way of working off some of his "excess energy," Cantor chose for his first effort the production of an all-black musical entitled *Sweet Land of Liberty*. Described as both a fantasy and a "political 'Green Pastures,'" *Sweet Land of Liberty* was to include a book by Cantor and John Hymer, with Ira Gershwin and Yip Harburg supplying the lyrics to Harold Arlen's music. For his leads, producer Cantor sought none less than Ethel Waters, Bill Robinson, and Paul Robeson.

Preceding *Sweet Land of Liberty* onto Broadway was another musical in the political vein, *For the Rich They Sing*. While *Liberty* was designed to poke fun at Washington and the current administration, *For the Rich They Sing* was a farce aimed at Communism. Written by Bud Pearson and Lester White, the show was not only to be produced, but also directed by Cantor, who wanted Eve Arden for the lead. Ultimately, neither show was produced. *For the Rich They Sing* was simply dropped, while Cantor explained that producing a musical like *Sweet Land of Liberty*, which satirized the White House, was, "in this hour of danger . . . sacreligious." (World War II was raging in Europe, though the United States was not yet involved.)

His plans to emulate his former boss, Flo Ziegfeld, gone awry, Eddie Cantor still entertained thoughts of a Broadway show, not as a producer, necessarily, but before the footlights. In the year between mid–1940 and mid–1941, the comedian considered no fewer than five different stage shows. First Cantor contemplated an autobiographical play in which he would appear if George S. Kaufman and Moss Hart could be persuaded to shape his rough outline into a workable script. The play never materialized, quite possibly due to Kaufman's reluctance to work with Cantor following the sour experience of *Roman Scandals* seven years earlier. Eddie would have to wait until 1944 to bring the idea to life—on the screen, not on the stage—in the film *Show Business*.

In the fall of 1940, Eddie met with his former employer Lee Shubert and briefly entertained a notion of a return to the stage under the Shubert aegis. Shubert offered Cantor two possible vehicles, both musical comedies. The first, entitled *The Glamour Boy* (formerly *The Sky's the Limit*), was written by Edward Hope, Russel M. Crouse, E. Y. Harburg, and Arthur Schwartz, while the other was a Guy Bolton–Eddie Davis opus called *Not Tonight, Josephine*, which reportedly was "streamlined hoke" in the tradition of *Kid Boots* and *Whoopee*.

Next, Eddie considered coproducing with Al Lewis (producer of *The Nervous Wreck*) an untitled play which was written by three novices: two college students and "a youngster employed by the city of New York." The script, the plot of which was undisclosed, was a comedy without songs, although Cantor mentioned plans to insert three or four musical specialties into the proceedings. Announced in late July, the show was to have tried out in Boston in mid–September, with a Broadway opening to follow a fortnight later. Autumn came and went without any further mention of the show.

In January 1941, *Variety* reported that Cantor would return to Broadway the following fall in a stage musical, *Christopher Columbus, Jr.* The show, which would be coproduced with Al Lewis, was to be financed by Cantor. Aside from the one item report in *Variety, Columbus, Jr.* would quickly join the growing list of announced but unproduced Cantor vehicles. Oddly enough, the next Cantor project was announced in the same issue of the show business bible, just a few inches above the item on *Christopher Columbus, Jr.* Al Jolson's Broadway comeback musical, *Hold on to Your Hats*, had recently been closed down by its star's illness. Jolson, wanting to get away for a Florida vacation, suggested that either Cantor or Jessel could easily take over his role. Although Jolson returned to the show a little more than a month later, Hollywood producer Jules Levey announced plans to star Eddie Cantor in a film version of *Hats*. Along with comedienne Martha Raye, who had been in the stage show, Levey also hoped to land the up-and-coming comedy team of Abbott and Costello for support. Levey, who was producing independently under the banner of Mayfair Productions, hoped to release the film through Universal, which coincidentally or not, had Abbott and Costello under contract.

Filming was scheduled to begin on the West Coast in late April, with Roy Del Ruth, who had directed Eddie in *Kid Millions*, slated to bring *Hold on to Your Hats* to the screen. Problems soon began to crop up, however, with other stars — old and new. First, Jolson, who had initially suggested that Cantor take the part, decided that he would like to take the show on a road tour. Not wanting concurrent competition from a film version of the same show he was appearing in onstage, Jolson asked Jules Levey to hold the film back from cities he was planning to tour. Levey and his financial backer, former RKO president Leo Spitz, agreed to try to accommodate Jolson's road schedule, which was to begin in Atlantic City in late August.

Jolson's request was a minor inconvenience at best; it was Abbott and Costello who brought plans to a halt. Riding the crest of the wave of their first starring feature, *Buck Privates*, the boys were suddenly the hottest comedians in Hollywood and evidently felt that they were no longer supporting players. Before the year was up, Abbott and Costello would rank third in popularity among film stars. In keeping with his newfound stardom, Lou

Costello demanded and got Jolson's role in *Hold on to Your Hats*. Producer Levey apparently had no qualms about replacing the "old hat" Eddie Cantor, with the chubby comedian. The question of just who would star in the film was a moot point, however, since the film was never made.

If Eddie Cantor was nonplussed over being dropped from *Hold on to Your Hats*, he didn't remain so for long. Within a week, the comedian was finalizing a deal with United Artists to become an independent producer and star for the releasing company. Under the terms of the agreement, Cantor would produce three films in three years, all starring himself, with an option for two additional films each year, with or without him on screen. United Artists, which had released all of Eddie's Goldwyn films, offered to aid in the financing of the pictures, but was told by Cantor that he, along with some personal friends, would supply all the necessary funds. Although he had no particular story in mind, Cantor announced that his first UA film would be a big musical, à la the Goldwyn vehicles, with big-name star support. The comedian/producer anticipated getting before the cameras by July, with a Christmas release planned.

Less than a month later, Eddie announced that his first production might be Latin-American in theme. With war raging in Europe, effectively closing many Hollywood markets, the film industry was producing a wide range of films with South American settings, stories, and music in an attempt to please the Latin audiences. The Roosevelt administration, with its Office of Inter-American Affairs, sought to further its Good Neighbor Policy in Hollywood through Jock Whitney, the office's film liaison.

Cantor sought Whitney's help, along with some of the agency's capital, to put together a film musical which would present a medley of Latin musical flavors, from the conga to the samba to the tango. With the prospect of touring and perhaps even filming in South America, Eddie began taking lessons in Spanish and Portuguese. He explained that he not only wanted to be able to represent democracy to the neighbors south of the border, but to do so in his own style.

"I want to have a good enough understanding of the words so that I can put some humor into my answers," Cantor told *Variety*. "That's always the most effective way of creating good will."

Unfortunately, Eddie's trilingual efforts would not be needed. By early June it was his deal with United Artists, not Eddie Cantor, that was going south. After some difficulties with United Artists over the particulars in their agreement, Cantor decided to put on hold his plans for producing and starring in any UA releases. Citing the unsettled state of affairs at UA—with a revolving door of producers the company was almost always unsettled—Cantor, for the eleventh or twelfth time (depending on how you keep score) in the last fifteen months abandoned an announced project.

In early July 1941, after a tour of army camps, Cantor once again heralded his return to the legitimate stage, this time in a show which would blend elements of at least two of the aborted ventures of the past year and

**A handsome formal portrait of Eddie and Ida Cantor (collection of Brian Gari).**

a half. The musical, which would be titled *Banjo Eyes* (once listed by MGM as an upcoming Cantor film), was to be a dramatization of Eddie's show business career (an idea which also had been explored as a possible film vehicle). With Al Lewis coproducing, Cantor hoped to get Gene Fowler to write the book. Initial plans called for a fall opening on Broadway, followed by a six-month run, after which the show would shift to Hollywood for a scheduled spring production as a United Artist film.

Although *Banjo Eyes* would eventually make it to Broadway, it would not arrive as a biography of its star. Rather, somewhere between July and late August the show metamorphosed into a musical version of yet another Cantor pet project from five years earlier—*Three Men on a Horse*. Since the rights to *Three Men* were held by Warner Brothers, Eddie had to go see Jack Warner before any definite plans could be made. Instead of going with just the germ of an idea, Cantor worked out the entire show, including new situations and bits of potential business. With a blueprint for *Banjo Eyes* firmly drawn in his mind, Cantor met with Warner to pitch the idea. After hearing the initial concept, the producer asked what producers will invariably ask: "How are you going to do it?" For fifteen minutes Eddie gave Jack Warner a dry run of the show that secured him the rights to *Three Men on a Horse*.

Eddie worked out a deal with Warner Brothers whereby the studio would provide the rights to the stage play, along with 50 percent of the costs of a stage production of *Banjo Eyes*, which was to serve as a prelude to making the film version of the musical. Cantor would pay the other half of the expenses in addition to playing the role which he had coveted since he first saw it played on Broadway. Al Lewis would act as producer for Warners.

Joe Quillan and Izzy Ellinson, two of Cantor's radio writers, were assigned to adapt the John Cecil Holm–George Abbott original to fit the peculiar style of their boss. Although neither Quillan or Ellinson had written the book for a musical before, not much work was called for, aside from providing some new gags and a handful of new scenes, because the plot from *Three Men on a Horse* survived the transition to a musical intact. As in the original, the plot of *Banjo Eyes* centered around the milquetoasty Erwin Trowbridge, a greeting card writer from Jackson Heights who has an uncanny knack for picking horses. This talent eventually involves Erwin with some criminals frequenting racing circles, who attempt to use his talent for their own crooked schemes.

A number of comedy scenes were added to the show, most of which were blended into the plot. The only skit which digressed from the show's horse racing theme involved a short stint in which Erwin was drafted into the army. Inspired by the United States Army's recent peacetime draft, the bit became even more topical when the nation was plunged into World War II during the pre–Broadway tryouts of *Banjo Eyes*. (The show was in Philadelphia when Pearl Harbor was attacked.) Other standout routines in the musical included a burlesque of the Clark Gable–Lana Turner love scene from *Honky Tonk* perpetrated by Cantor and Audrey Christie (as Mable, the gangster's moll), a drunk bit by Cantor in the first act, Cantor's dream sequence conversation with "Banjo Eyes" the horse, and Cantor's various chores at the greeting card company.

The highlight of *Banjo Eyes*, according to most reviewers, came in the show's finale. Set at the grandstand of Belmont Park, the conclusion featured Cantor in his trademark blackface and white rimmed glasses stopping the show with a lengthy medley of his standards. The nostalgic pastiche included such hits as "That's the Kind of Baby for Me," "Margie," "Ida," "If You Knew Susie," "Makin' Whoopee," and "Now's the Time to Fall in Love" (Cantor's radio theme). The medley always proved a greater hit with the audience than the show's original score (provided by John Latouche and Vernon Duke, who also wrote classical music under the name "Vladimir Dukelsky") and helped to underscore that the greatest attraction of *Banjo Eyes* was not the plot, the score, the girls, or the opulent sets and costumes, but Eddie Cantor.

With the outline of *Banjo Eyes* already worked out by Cantor and his writers, even before they had the rights to the show upon which they were basing it, the production went fairly quickly and smoothly. Unlike most stage shows, particularly the previous ones that Cantor had worked on, *Banjo Eyes* started in rehearsals in roughly the same form in which it would reach Broadway. Still, there was plenty of ad-libbing by Eddie in rehearsals, with many of his off-the-cuff lines being placed permanently in the script. Many of the lyrics in the songs in *Banjo Eyes* came about in the same way, supplementing those already written by the twenty-four-year-old Latouche.

In addition to the aforementioned Audrey Christie (in the role of Mable), *Banjo Eyes* boasted a good supporting cast, with Lionel Stander (who had briefly provided the voice of Rubinoff on Cantor's radio shows) and Romo Vincent winning praise and laughs as Patsy and Frankie, the two racetrack touts. June Clyde played Erwin's wife, and the dance team of Sally and Tony DeMarco supplied three specialty numbers. In addition, the show carried a bevy of twenty-six chorus girls.

Although it was clearly a Cantor show, Eddie was not stingy with the material; he handed out a good portion of the laughs, as well as the musical numbers, to his fellow actors and actresses. Aside from Cantor's medley at the finale, however, what songs he had to share were generally rather weak, with only two numbers — Romo Vincent's "I Gotta Be Rollin'" and Eddie's "That Can Only Happen in the Movies" — being singled out during the show's out-of-town tryouts.

*Banjo Eyes* had almost two months on the road to whip it into shape, and apparently the musical needed all the time it could get. Originally the show was scheduled to play a few days at New Haven's Shubert Theatre in early November before moving on for three weeks at the Colonial in Boston prior to a scheduled Broadway debut around December 4. Opening night notices from New Haven, however, found *Banjo Eyes* lacking. *Variety* noted that when the curtain went up S.R.O. (standing room only) was in evidence, but by the time the curtain rang down those letters were changed to "S.O.S." While reviewers complained that the book had not retained the laughs of the original — many of the "new" gags were tired and old — the main problem appeared to be with the score. Extra weeks in Philadelphia were added to the pre–Broadway run, with Cantor promising that he would not bring *Banjo Eyes* to New York until the show was 100 percent ready. He considered adding additional weeks in Pittsburgh and Cleveland to further work out the rough spots, but he later deemed this unnecessary.

In an attempt to punch up the Latouche-Duke score, a pair of outside songs were inserted into the show. They instantly became two of the strongest numbers in *Banjo Eyes*. The first, "We're Having a Baby (My Baby and Me)," by Duke and Harold Adamson, was performed by Cantor and June Clyde. The other number was added during the show's run at Philadelphia's Forrest Theatre. Introduced a mere two days after the sneak attack on Pearl Harbor was the determinedly patriotic "We Did It Before and We Can Do It Again," by Cliff Friend and Charlie Tobias. Added to the second act's army routine, the tune became one of America's first hits of World War II.

Along with a shuffling of the score, several cast changes were made before the Christmas Day Broadway premiere. Romo Vincent was replaced, along with dance specialty Bill Bailey. Also let go was dance director Charles Walters — a move that reportedly caused some friction between Cantor and Al Lewis. Another substitution made for New York was twenty-one-year-old Virginia Mayo in the relatively minor part of Ginger. Contrary to some popular legends, Mayo did not play the tail end of "Banjo Eyes" the horse. That equine impersonation was perpetrated by the team of Andrew Mayo and Nonnie Morton, who had perfected their craft in the "Pansy the Horse" vaudeville routine.

*Banjo Eyes*, despite being in an almost constant state of flux during its six weeks plus on the road, managed to do top box office business in each of the three cities it played. Although in each town the local critics cited the show's various weaknesses, almost all of them highly recommended *Banjo Eyes* because it marked the triumphal return of Eddie Cantor to the legitimate stage.

Most reviewers also gave high marks to the lavish costumes by Irene Sharaff and the fanciful settings by Harry Horner, many drew parallels between the opulent trappings of *Banjo Eyes* and those provided by the Great Flo Ziegfeld. Indeed, Ziegfeld would have been impressed by his protégé's attempts at coproducing a musical show, especially when it came to spending money freely. *Banjo Eyes* cost Cantor and Warner Brothers the then astronomical sum of $160,000 — a princely amount to recoup, especially when taking into account that the top ticket for the show went for $4.40.

*Banjo Eyes* galloped into Warner's Hollywood Theatre on December 25, 1941. Initially, Cantor had opted for the 46th Street Theatre, citing that the Hollywood, which was frequently used as a movie house, was often a jinx to legitimate attractions. The switch was made necessary when it became clear that Cole Porter's hit, *Panama Hattie*, would extend its run at the 46th Street Theatre, leaving *Banjo Eyes* without a house to open in. Unfortunately, an additional $10,000 had already been wasted on scaling down the already expensive sets for *Banjo Eyes* to fit the smaller 46th Street stage (ironically, the scenery had originally been designed to fit the Hollywood Theatre).

First night reviews unanimously praised Cantor's return to Broadway, although, as with the out-of-town notices, the universal plaudits did not extend to every phase of the by now heavily doctored show. The less than favorable comparisons with *Three Men on a Horse* didn't seem to bother the public, however, for *Banjo Eyes* was one of the top tickets in a strong field. *Banjo Eyes* had all the markings of being a smash hit. It was helped along by a flood of free publicity in most of the New York newspapers and magazines, which in general hailed the show for bringing Cantor back to Broadway after a twelve-year absence, and it was also aided by several advertising tie-ins. In its first full week of business, the turnstiles clicked to the tune of over $38,000. For the first ten weeks of its run, *Banjo Eyes* managed to play at or near capacity, consistently bringing in over $30,000 a week, even though there were no Wednesday performances because of Cantor's weekly radio show.[3]

One of the other musicals on Broadway that season was Georgie Jessel's review *High Kickers*, which starred Jessel along with Red Hot Mama, Sophie Tucker. Like Cantor with *Banjo Eyes*, Jessel had his own money invested in *High Kickers*, so the longtime friends were rivals not only on the stage, but behind the scenes also. Again, as in their past competitions, Cantor came out on top, proving himself not only a bigger audience draw, but a more successful producer. Back when both shows were in the casting stages, Jessel had coveted several performers, most notably the dance team of the DeMarcos, who wound up signing with Cantor.

Another comic in competition with Cantor was Danny Kaye, who was appearing in *Let's Face It*. During one matinee performance, Kaye made an unannounced onstage visit to Cantor at the Hollywood Theatre, showing up in the middle of the army scene. The bit, which included Cantor along with sixteen chorus boys dressed as soldiers in support, revolved around Eddie's character falling out late for formation. Consequently, as the other soldiers stood neatly in line, Eddie appeared in his long underwear with various parts of his outer uniform draped haphazardly around his shoulders. In addition, because he had not eaten breakfast yet, Eddie would attempt to gulp down hard-boiled eggs while avoiding detection from a general carrying out an inspection.

With America's involvement in World War II just getting underway, there was a constant stream of chorus boys in the show, with new ones appearing almost nightly to replace those gone into the service. Although Cantor was used to seeing new faces in the routine, one Thursday afternoon he rushed on to the stage for the army bit to find a new face that was familiar at the same time. It looked like Danny Kaye. Cantor sidled over next to the new recruit and sure enough it was Danny Kaye. (Kaye had Thursday afternoons off because *Let's Face It* presented its matinees on Wednesday.) Instead of carrying on with the routine as usual, Eddie made a few changes for his guest.

"I took out my hard-boiled egg," Cantor recalled, "cracked it on my knee, salted it daintily, and took a bite. Then I shoved the rest of it in Danny's mouth. While his mouth was still wide open I shook salt in it too. Then a banana. I took a bite of the banana and fed Danny. By now the audience had recognized him and as I fed him, they roared." According to Cantor, the show came to a halt for fifteen minutes as Eddie fed Danny Kaye whatever digestibles were handy. The next day, Eddie returned the joke by sending Danny a bill for the overtime paid to the stagehands made necessary by Kaye's appearance. Kaye had the last laugh, however, when he had his agent send a note explaining that "Mr. Kaye" would be happy to pay the bill as soon as "Mr. Cantor" paid "Mr. Kaye" for one afternoon's performance.

Even without the regular inclusion of Danny Kaye, *Banjo Eyes* pleased audiences enough to run strongly for sixteen weeks, only dropping below $30,000 twice during that period. The show seemed fairly certain of running through the summer when suddenly it closed in mid–April following the hospitalization of Eddie Cantor. Cantor underwent an undisclosed, but "slight" operation—rumored by some to be a severe case of hemorrhoids—on Monday, April 13, in the office of his physician, Dr. Joseph S. Diamond. Still, that night, theatergoers holding tickets to *Banjo Eyes* were either given a refund or an exchange, and the press was notified that Cantor would be back bounding about the stage of the Hollywood in time for Thursday night's performance. Although he was initially sent back to his suite at the Essex House for convalescence, the following day (Tuesday) Cantor checked into Sydenham Hospital to recuperate.

Thursday, however, found Eddie still in the hospital, and the show's re-opening was postponed until Sunday. As the week went on, it was becoming evident that Cantor would not be returning to *Banjo Eyes* in the near future, and perhaps he would never go back. Dr. Diamond told reporters that the comedian's treatment would have to continue for at least several more weeks. He further cited that the nature of the operation necessitated that Cantor should stay off his feet. With Eddie running an estimated mile each night on the stage, his removal from *Banjo Eyes* amounted to doctor's orders.

Although Eddie Cantor was still in the hospital, he had little trouble fulfilling his weekly radio obligation. Bell Telephone spent most of Wednesday running special wires into Cantor's sick room, at a cost of over $1,000, so that the comedian could do his regularly scheduled broadcast from bed. That week's radio show made light of Eddie's hospital stay, but the closing of *Banjo Eyes* was no laughing matter to many of its cast members.

Soon it was clear that Cantor was not going to return to *Banjo Eyes*, and the show was officially closed, throwing more than two hundred people out of work. (The show had not only carried a larger than normal chorus, but also a bigger orchestra and stage crew.) There had been hopes that Jack Haley might step in to replace Cantor, but after considering it, Haley begged off, citing previous commitments. With the closing of the show, rumors started circulating that perhaps Cantor was not as sick has he had been portrayed. While some around the theater reported that the comedian had been happy with the show, others cited that there had been increasing friction between Cantor's personal representative, Jack Kreindel, and the show's management.

The premature demise of *Banjo Eyes* left not only the show's cast and crew in a financial lurch but also the musical's backers. *Banjo Eyes* cost an estimated $160,000 to produce. Although it was one of the top three money-makers on Broadway, it had only returned $60,000 by the time of Cantor's illness, leaving a $100,000 loss.[4] Cantor had initially provided 50 percent of the show's backing, but *Variety* reported that he had recently sold a portion of his interest to a New York businessman. This, coupled with the weekly salary he was drawing as the star of the show, probably allowed Cantor to escape from this financial morass relatively, if not totally, unharmed, which made Cantor's continued claims of ill health even more suspicious.

By the end of the month, following one last New York radio broadcast, Eddie Cantor had left for Hollywood, where he would continue making an occasional film and doing his radio shows. Perhaps at fifty the grueling demands of carrying a Broadway show — especially given Cantor's frenetic performing style — were physically overwhelming. The same duties had ruined his health during the *Follies of 1927*, and he was fifteen years younger then. Still, as with Al Jolson's comeback show the previous year, it's possible that Cantor's illness was a mixture of physical symptoms and simple ennui. It seems likely that both performers, after proving that they could return to the scene of some of their greatest triumphs and duplicate them, grew tired (and bored) once they had accomplished what they had set out to do and walked away, leaving backers, casts, and crews holding the bag.

In any event, *Banjo Eyes* marked the end of Eddie Cantor's career in Broadway musicals. Aside from some one-man shows — which were more of a stroll down memory lane than Cantor's usual bouncing around the stage — the comedian, having proven that he could come back and recapture Broadway, never would attempt it again.

## REVIEWS

Show brings Cantor back to the boards after a lengthy layoff. Although comedian does yeoman duty throughout, and registers personally, his efforts are not enough to swing "Banjo" into the hit class under present conditions. — Bone, *Variety*, November 12, 1941, New Haven Opening

Grandpa (It's a boy) Cantor continues on his merry way at the Colonial, where "Banjo Eyes" is stepping into line as one of the most lavish shows of the spanking good season.

Eddie, from a pair of tired old eyes, is the show. For although there are revolving stages, and the De Marcos, and the most gorgeous gals and costumes and sets and what-not you've ever seen, the big moment is when the Cantor dons his alpaca suit, his string tie, his lamp-black and his straw benny, and goes into "Ida," and "Whoopee," just to mention a couple. — *Boston Sunday Advertiser*, November 16, 1941

Eddie Cantor got around to coming back to Broadway last evening, showing up at the Hollywood Theater in the middle of a large musical called "Banjo Eyes." This makes a pleasant Christmas gift for Mr. Cantor's admirers, a select group numbering hundreds of thousands and including this reviewer, and is also an extremely lucky break for the producer to say nothing of the authors and composer, of "Banjo Eyes." "Banjo Eyes" is most easily described as a musical which needs Eddie Cantor. — Richard Lockridge, *New York Sun*, December 26, 1941

"Banjo Eyes" is as opulent a musical as has reached Broadway since the Ziegfeld era. Its production is magnificently lavish; the Irene Sharaff costuming is gorgeous and worn by girls who appear hand-picked for the ultra physical attractiveness; Hassard Short's lighting job is completely eye-arresting. All this, and Eddie Cantor too should be sufficient to fashion a hit, but militating against it is a book so familiar that many of the comedy punches are telegraphed and a musical score that's mediocre at best. — Scho, *Variety*, December 31, 1941

In a swiftly changing world it is pleasant to find Mr. Cantor unchanged. It was particularly pleasant last night at the Hollywood to have him brush aside the book of Banjo Eyes near the evening's end; to see him in blackface once again, and to hear him singing such of his old favorites as Margie, Ida and If You Knew Susie.

These songs are all of them memories one is happy to revive. But I doubt if, in a similar mood of retrospection a decade hence, Mr. Cantor will find anything he will want to sing from his newest vehicle. I know I did not find much in it that I will desire or bother to remember after tonight, except for the fortunately unchanging Mr. Cantor, and I look forward to seeing him in a gayer, hence worthier, musical. — John Mason Brown, *The New York World-Telegram*, Dec. 26, 1941

# Notes

1. *Ziegfeld Follies* was eventually filmed in 1944, but because of various problems, it was not released until 1946. William Powell reprised his role as the great producer, this time looking down from heaven to arrange MGM's top stars for one last *Follies*. The film does make a brief reference to Eddie Cantor in the opening sequence, where Powell reviews his former success via a series of vignettes performed by animated puppets. A Cantor puppet, in blackface, does a brief rendition of "If You Knew Susie," again sung by Cantor's one-time stand-in, Buddy Doyle.

2. Unfortunately for Danny Kaye, Goldwyn's attempts to recreate his earlier successes with Cantor were not limited to casting Kaye in *Up in Arms*, a film inspired by Eddie Cantor's highly successful *Whoopee!* According to A. Scott Berg's excellent biography of Goldwyn, the producer was constantly trying to push Kaye, a unique talent in his own right, into being a second-coming of Eddie Cantor. Goldwyn's efforts were so single-minded that he would often greet Kaye with a cheery "Hello, Eddie!"

3. An extra performance was added Sunday night in an attempt to make up for Wednesday's lost business. At the time, however, Sunday was generally regarded as a weak theater night — especially since most shows had only gone to Sunday performances the previous year, usually at discounted prices. *Banjo Eyes* kept its top ticket price at $4.40, even on Sundays, without a noticeable drop at the box office, a further testament to the show's draw.

4. To make financial matters worse, at the time of its closing *Banjo Eyes* had advance ticket sales of around $35,000, all of which had to be refunded.

# CHAPTER 34

# *Thank Your Lucky Stars*

After the abrupt closing of *Banjo Eyes*, it would seem that Warner Brothers, left holding half of the show's financial loss, would have been cool to any more projects with Eddie Cantor; however, this was apparently not the case. As soon as Cantor arrived back in Hollywood in early May 1942, Warners announced that they were busy preparing an all-star extravaganza in which Eddie would have the central role. Planned as Cantor's first feature at the Burbank studio, to which a filmed version of *Banjo Eyes* would be a follow-up, the film was to include as many of the studio's stars as possible. Under the aegis of producer Mark Hellinger, Arthur Schwartz and Everett Freeman were assigned the task of developing a workable story to hold together the numerous cameos that would be the film's major selling point.

The project, which was soon given the title of *Thank Your Lucky Stars*, was one of the first in a series of lavish, star-studded musicals that Hollywood turned out during the war years. Like Paramount's *Star-Spangled Rhythm*, United Artists' *Stage Door Canteen*, MGM's *Thousands Cheer*, Universal's *Follow the Boys*, and Warners' own *Hollywood Canteen*, *Thank Your Lucky Stars*, aside from including almost every contract player on the lot, was designed as patriotic entertainment for America's servicemen and the families they left behind. A similar wave of reviews had swept over Hollywood in the late twenties and early thirties, but these were fashioned as a showcase of studio's stars in a talkie setting, rather than a show business call-to-arms.

Considering the scope of the project, preproduction work on *Thank Your Lucky Stars* proceeded relatively smoothly. Norman Panama, Melvin Frank, and James V. Kern made a serviceable screenplay from Schwartz and Freeman's original story, no small task considering that more than a dozen musical numbers had to be worked into and around the plot along with appearances by an even greater number of stars. The song numbers were supplied almost exclusively by Arthur Schwartz, working with Frank Loesser, whose contributions ranged from the ridiculous to the sublime. Fortunately, however, the score contained more hits than misses. David Butler, who had directed Cantor so well in *Ali Baba Goes to Town*, was again behind the camera.

Joining Cantor in the cast of *Thank Your Lucky Stars* was his radio protégé, Dinah Shore. Although Shore had been previously sought by other
studios, *Thank Your Lucky Stars* marked the singer's film debut. Also in the
cast, aside from those "lucky stars" who appeared as themselves in cameo
roles, were Warners' regulars Dennis Morgan and Joan Leslie (as the film's
love interest), with veteran character actors Edward Everett Horton and S. Z.
"Cuddles" Sakall providing strong comedy support.

Although he was listed in the cast alphabetically, it was Eddie Cantor
who was the glue that made *Thank Your Lucky Stars* more than just a hodge-
podge of Warners' luminaries. In fact, not only was Cantor given more
screen time than any of the other stars, he was given a double role as himself
and a bus-driving actor named "Joe Simpson." Oddly enough, in his double
role, Cantor is given the double duty of being both the film's protagonist and
villain. As Joe Simpson, Eddie is essentially the same lovable fellow that audiences had come to expect; while as himself, Cantor is a pushy, egotistical,
and hammy star who is despised by just about everyone else in the film.

Cantor plays himself with a good-natured dose of self-kidding, and indeed he seems to enjoy painting himself with a wide, unflattering brush
much more than playing his other, good-natured part. To make matters even
more interesting, at one point in the plot Eddie, as "Joe," gets to impersonate
"Cantor," which gives him the opportunity of playing another character who
plays himself, playing himself. While some fans of the comedian may be uncomfortable seeing Cantor portraying himself in such an unflattering light,
the situation allows for a great deal of humor and helps to make *Thank Your
Lucky Stars* a lot of fun.

The film opens at a Hollywood radio studio, where Eddie Cantor's *Time
to Smile* radio show is being broadcast. As Dinah Shore sings the film's title
tune, Cantor is backstage discussing the broadcast with his guest star, tough
guy John Garfield. True to his screen persona, Garfield roughs up Cantor
while warning the comedian not to interfere with his lines.

"I never interfere with anything," Cantor explains while combing Garfield's hair and straightening his tie. "With me it's live and let live."

Cantor and Garfield go out on stage, where John performs a comic rendition of "Blues in the Night." In between verses, Garfield takes time to
strangle Cantor, whom he mistakes for someone named "Fisheyed Louie"
in a variation on the old "Niagara Falls" burlesque routine. After Garfield's
number, Cantor signs off the program with "Now's the Time to Fall in Love."
As Cantor sings, the scene shifts to a nearby street corner, where Joe Simpson (Cantor, but with longer hair and Harold Lloyd glasses) attempts to fill
his tour bus. Joe's attempts are interrupted by Cantor's singing over the
radio. Joe, who detests Cantor—calling him a "pop-eyed baboon"—pleads
with the owner of the radio to turn it down.

While drumming up customers, Joe runs into David Butler and Mark
Hellinger (the real director and producer of the film). Joe asks the pair if

there are any parts for him in their upcoming film, but he is not encouraged by their response. After walking away, Hellinger remarks on the uncanny resemblance between Joe and Eddie Cantor. Butler tells him that Joe is actually a fine dramatic actor whose career has been ruined because he is the exact double of the comedian.

Back at the radio studio, the show's stars sign autographs for the studio audience. Mobs clamor around Garfield and Dinah Shore, while Cantor is all but ignored. One of his few autographs goes to a small boy who asks him: "Can we go home now, Uncle Eddie?" While the audience files out, two producers, Farnsworth (Edward Everett Horton) and Dr. Schlenna (S. Z. Sakall), discuss their upcoming benefit for Allied War Charities — the Cavalcade of Stars. Schlenna insists that they must have Dinah Shore for the benefit, but Farnsworth explains that to secure her services they must first go through the difficult Cantor.

Also in the audience is Barney Jackson, a con-man who tricks the egotistical Cantor into signing his name on the bottom of a radio contract. The con-man then takes the contract out to the waiting Tommy Randolph (Dennis Morgan), who pays him a $60 agent's commission for the document, which will ensure him a job on the Cantor radio show. Jackson also runs into Pat Dixon (Joan Leslie), a young songwriter whom he has promised to manage, also for a fee. Pat complains that Jackson has done nothing to earn his fee, to which Jackson replies with a fast line of double talk, before beating a hasty retreat. Pat tries to follow him, but hops into Joe's tour bus instead of a taxi, and Jackson gets away.

Joe takes Pat along on the tour and tries to comfort her between descriptions of the stars' homes (most of whom seem to work at Warner Brothers). Pat explains she is a writer of beautiful sentimental ballads, like her latest, "Moondust."

"That'll be refreshing," Joe says, commenting on the popular music of the day. "Today all you hear is 'Scrub Me Momma with a Salad Fork' or 'Beat Me Baby with a Boiled Potato.'"

After the tour, Joe takes Pat back to Gower Gulch, a makeshift community built from discarded film sets by out-of-work actors. The residents sit around a campfire while some of them, who happen to be Spike Jones and His City Slickers, entertain the group with a rendition of "Hotcha Cornea."

Joe introduces Pat to his best friend, Tommy. Tommy explains that he and his friends are celebrating his new radio contract. Joe congratulates him, but faints dead away when he discovers the deal is with the hated Eddie Cantor. Tommy shows Pat around the Gulch, while she tries to audition "Moondust," doing imitations of Ida Lupino and James Cagney (one of the few Warners' stars not in the film). Before she can recite her lyrics, however, Tommy is called upon to sing the Western-style "I'm Ridin' for a Fall."

The next day Joe drives Tommy and Pat over to Eddie Cantor's house for the singer's first meeting with his new boss. En route Pat reads the lyrics to "Moondust," which she wrote under the nom de plume of "Irving Dixon."

"Irving?" Joe asks.

"Well," Pat explains, "Berlin did all right with it."

"Yes, he did all right," Joe deadpans.

Tommy and Joe grimace at the banality of the "Moondust" lyrics Pat reads to them. The number probably has the worst lyrics in songwriting history (rivaled only perhaps by "No You, No Me" or "Good Night, Good Neighbor," both of which are featured later in the film).

"Do you think this song is right for Mr. Cantor?" Pat asks.

"Nobody else should ever have that number," Joe assures her.

Meanwhile, Cantor is entertaining Farnsworth and Schlenna by his pool, while his flunky Olaf (Mike Mizurki) does exercises nearby, presumably for Cantor's benefit. The producers explain they would like Dinah Shore for their upcoming show; however, when Cantor discovers it's the *Cavalcade of Stars*, he immediately tries to make himself the star of the show. He assures them that he only wants to do a few numbers amounting to a half hour of stage time; "forty-five minutes with applause," he adds.

When Farnsworth and Schlenna balk at having Cantor in the show, he offers to give them a sample of some of his new material. Before he can begin, however, Cantor summons his household staff in order to give the hired help a "treat." The staff members, who evidently are dragged out often for such "treats," grumble as they are called away from their work.

"Here we go again," the chef complains.

"What about the roast beef?" his assistant asks.

"Never mind the roast beef," the chef explains. "We gotta watch the ham."

The help gather around the poolside while Olaf limbers up on the nearby piano.

"I always try out my songs on the household staff," Cantor explains to the producers. "If they laugh, I use the new song. If they don't . . ."

"We get a new staff," Olaf interrupts.

Cantor goes into a spirited interpretation of "We're Staying Home Tonight," an amusing song in the typical Cantor style, which reflects the limitations of Home Front America. After the song, the well-trained staff delivers a polite round of applause.

"What? Only one bow?" Cantor asks after they've stopped clapping. They immediately resume their forced adulation. "They love me," Cantor beams.

Cantor begins arguing with the producers, who claim he has a reputation for taking over every production in which he is involved. Cantor is adamant, however, insisting that unless he is made chairman of the benefit committee, Dinah will not appear in the show. Tommy soon arrives and pleads Cantor's case. The comedian wonders who his defender is. Tommy shows Cantor his contract, which Cantor honors by having Olaf throw Tommy out. Finally, Farnsworth and Schlenna agree to make Cantor chairman, with the stipulation that it is a purely honorary position. Cantor promises that he won't even come to rehearsals.

The scene quickly segues to the next day's rehearsal, with Cantor not only in attendance, but in danger of ruining the entire show. Having re-scored Schlenna's music, Cantor has moved on to reworking Farnsworth's dance direction. The pair watch in agony, before coming up with a plan to get rid of the pesky comedian. Adopting a Dixie accent, Farnsworth calls Cantor and explains that he represents a Deep South newspaper in search of the star's life story. The egotistic Cantor obliges with a prolonged, windy yarn, covering his family history in minute detail. While Cantor is on the phone, Schlenna continues rehearsals, beginning with Jack Carson and Alan Hale, Sr., in a hokey vaudeville bit entitled "I'm Going North."

Back at Gower Gulch, Tommy, still smarting over what he believes to be a double cross from Cantor, is considering his next career move. Pat comes up with an idea to get Tommy in *Cavalcade of Stars*, reasoning that some producer will surely spot him in the show and give him a contract. Joe announces that he knows the stage doorman at the Cavalcade's theater, and the trio depart.

After Ann Sheridan's specialty, "Love Isn't Born," they arrive outside the theater, but Joe's pal isn't on duty. Tommy tries to storm the entrance anyway, only to be stopped by the doorman. Pat and Joe fake an argument to distract the doorman while Tommy sneaks inside the theater. There Tommy meets Farnsworth and Schlenna. He asks for a spot in the show, and they send him to see the show's chairman, hoping that Tommy will beat up Cantor. When Tommy enters, however, Cantor has Olaf throw him out again.

Later, at a cafeteria, Joe, Pat, and Tommy are plotting their next move when a woman interrupts, insisting that Joe, whom she mistakes for Cantor, give her an autograph. This gives Pat the idea of kidnapping Cantor and having Joe take his place, so that Tommy can have a part in the show. Joe is hesitant, but agrees to try after they appeal to his acting ability. Joe calls some Indian friends of his and arranges for Cantor's abduction.

"Don't do anything to him," Joe warns, before adding, "that won't hurt." As Joe leaves to take another busload on a tour, Pat and Tommy roam around the lunchroom singing the lyrically inane "No You, No Me."

Back at the theater, Cantor is making a shambles of the show by order-ing elephants and camels for production numbers and offering surreal plans for chorus girls to dress as potatoes and dive into pools of sour cream, a vision probably inspired by his years with Busby Berkley.

Meanwhile, at a nearby barber shop, Joe is being remade into Cantor. With a huge portrait of the star as a guide, the barber cuts Joe's hair to match.

"I hate to do such a thing to a nice boy like you," the barber apologizes.

"He is repulsive," Joe agrees, "but do your best."

Tommy and the Indians enter to escort Joe to the theater. Joe leaves with them after only giving the barber a nickel tip. The barber takes out his frustrations on the poster of Cantor.

After Dinah Shore sings "The Dreamer," we see Cantor in his office getting a rubdown and regaling his staff with a selection of terrible jokes which, of course, they pretend to laugh at. (When they fail to pick up on a punch-line, the comedian growls, "What's the matter? Tired of your jobs?") The Indians enter in full warpaint to tell Cantor that he is being made an honorary chief. Cantor balks at the honor until they mention that a "squaw from *Life* magazine" is waiting in the alley to take his picture. Cantor changes into Indian regalia, and the Indians take his suit to give to Joe. While Joe is changing into Cantor's clothes, Pat pretends to take Cantor's picture. The Indians knock Cantor out and kidnap him, while Schlenna and Farnsworth witness the abduction from a window.

"We should maybe call the police—no?" Schlenna asks. After thinking it over for a second, the two producers look at each other, smile, and decide, "No!" Tommy advises Joe, now dressed as Cantor, to look for Farnsworth and Schlenna, whom he describes as a "beer barrel and a moose." Inside, Joe bumps into the pair, who are surprised to see the man whom they just watched being kidnaped. Joe recognizes them, explaining: "You are the beer barrel, and you are the moose."

"A moose!" Farnsworth declares. "I'm a Rotarian."

They attribute Joe/Cantor's strange behavior to the blow on the head he received. Joe promises not to interfere with the show anymore if they agree to put Tommy on. The producers jump at the offer.

The film shifts into high speed at this point—beginning with the buoyant "Ice Cold Katie," one of the film's best numbers, which features Hattie McDaniel and Willie Best. Most of the funniest comedy sequences and strongest musical pieces were saved for the second half of the film. By this time the Indians have taken Cantor to a Hollywood hideout, where they have tied the now conscious comedian to a large plank.

"Don't you boys realize who I am?" Cantor cries.

"Yeah," a brave responds, "that's what makes it such a pleasure."

The Indians go out for dinner, but not before leaving Junior, a huge Great Dane with a taste for blood, to watch Cantor.

"Fine thing," Cantor muses as the ferocious dog enters the room, "they're going out for a bite, and you came in for one." In an attempt to free himself, Cantor convinces Junior to bite the "delicious, imported" ropes which bind him to the board. Unfortunately, the Dane decides to take a bite out of the comedian's rear instead. Junior then knocks Cantor and the board over onto a saw horse, turning Eddie into a living teeter-totter. On one of his upswings, Cantor knocks over a jug of maple syrup on a nearby shelf. The syrup drips onto the comedian's feet, which Junior now begins to eagerly lick, tickling Cantor's toes in the process.

"Now I'm a wheatcake," Cantor moans.

The captive comedian is laughing uncontrollably when a pack of stray mutts appear at the window. Junior swings the board over and the dogs rush down the plank—over Cantor's bound body—and join in the syrup feast taking place at Eddie's feet.

After a brief scene back at the theater, where the show has started, Cantor escapes. While he is making his getaway, still dressed in the Indian suit and warbonnet, the Indians emerge from a nearby diner and give chase. Cantor runs up and down the streets of Hollywood crying "Help, Indians," while dressed as one himself. He eludes the redskins by ducking into an alley and climbing a handy fire escape. Unfortunately, the building Eddie is seeking refuge in happens to be a mental hospital, where at that moment the attendants are awaiting the arrival of a famous star requiring an emergency lobotomy.

The nurse (Ruth Donnelly) informs her three male assistants that the star, whose identity has been kept a secret for publicity reasons, suffers from delusions. Just at that moment Cantor enters through French doors, dressed as a chief and babbling about being chased by Indians.

"There, there, my poor man," the nurse comforts him. "Have you been running?"

"Yes," Cantor pants. "They've been chasing me, and chasing me, and chasing me."

"Who's been chasing you, Mr. Cantor?"

"The Indians," Cantor replies. "Three of them. They're right outside."

"You see, boys," one of the men explains in a patronizing tone, "the Indians have been chasing him."

"Not just the Indians," Eddie continues, "but dogs. Fifty of them. All licking my feet."

"Fifty dogs, all licking your feet."

"Yeah, but I fooled them, you know how?"

"No. How?"

"I got off the see-saw, and I left them there with the maple syrup," Cantor boasts, dispelling any doubts left in their minds that he's crazy. Before he can explain further, the attendants take Eddie's clothes and soak him in a cold shower in an attempt to calm him down.

At the theater, Dinah Shore performs "How Sweet You Are," a period production number done in Civil War costumes.

By now Cantor is thoroughly sopped and is removed from the shower. "What's my name?" he mutters. "Who launched me?" Cantor's calm state soon becomes an agitated one however, when the nurse informs him that he will soon be ready for his operation. In a second attempt to sedate the patient, the attendants give Cantor a vacuum massage which is so powerful it literally sucks him off the table.

In a little while—following Errol Flynn's "That's What You Jolly Well Get" number—Cantor is again somewhat composed.

"What kind of place is this?" Eddie asks the nurse.

"Just a place people come for nervous ailments," she explains.

"I don't know of a better place to get one," Eddie agrees, before making a desperate break for the door. The attendants grab him and bring him back.

"You don't understand," Cantor pleads. "I've got an opening tonight."

"You'll have an opening," they assure him, "as soon as Dr. Kirby gets here."

Cantor is then strapped down to a mechanical massaging table, and the contraption is turned on. "Say, this isn't bad," the comedian decides as the machine rocks him around. "It's like waltzing with an octopus." When his keepers briefly leave the room, Cantor again attempts to escape but only manages to put the machine into high gear. In yet another variation of the osteopath routine, Cantor is jolted and manipulated into a jellylike state before the nurse returns to rescue him. To calm him down, the attendants place Cantor on a motorized bouncing chair.

"Put me back on the table," Eddie cries, as the scene shifts back to the theater. There Bette Davis, in what many today consider the camp classic of the film, sings, or rather croaks, "They're Either Too Young or Too Old," a lament to the man shortage precipitated by the war. Backstage, an already nervous Joe receives a call from the Indians informing him that the real Cantor has escaped.

"What's the sense of getting panicky?" Tommy advises, trying to calm his friend's fears.

"To get panicky, you've got to have sense?" Joe asks.

While Joe paces, out on stage Ida Lupino, Olivia de Havilland, and George Tobias reprise "The Dreamer," with a zoot-suited parody that is at first amusing in its novelty, but quickly becomes tiresome.

At the hospital, Cantor, despite his protests, is being readied for his lobotomy. Dr. Kirby (Paul Harvey, the sheik from *Kid Millions*) enters smoking a cigarette and laughing about the operation. Cantor quickly explains that the pending procedure is a mistake and the doctor listens attentively until the comedian recounts how he escaped. Cantor is given gas and starts to drift off. Just then a pair of attendants wheel in the real patient. Finally realizing their error, the staff tries to revive the nearly unconcious Cantor.

"Have a cigar, fellows," Cantor responds groggily. "My wife just had another boy."

"Wake up, Mr. Cantor," Dr. Kirby informs him, "we're not going to operate."

"Go ahead, Doc," Eddie urges, "cut yourself a slice of ham."

Finally, Cantor is revived. He rushes off to the theater, still in his hospital gown, in an attempt to make the show. Before he exits, however, he stops to wish the real lobotomy patient well, but flees when it turns out to be the "Mad Russian" (Bert Gordon), his radio stooge.

Tommy goes on and performs the excruciatingly banal "Good Night, Good Neighbor," a number whose only redeeming quality is some fine dancing by Alexis Smith. His performance is good enough to elicit a quick offer from Jack Warner, who is sitting out in the audience.

The celebration is interrupted, however, when the real Cantor, still in his gown, enters with a policeman. Having been informed of the plot by the Indians, Cantor orders the cop to arrest Joe.

"Who's who?" the confused officer asks, while studying the doubles.

"I'm who! That's who!" the real Cantor insists.

Dinah Shore is called over to determine the real Eddie. Cantor offers to double her radio salary if he picks her.

"I don't know who you are," Dinah begins, "but if you're going to double my salary you're definitely not Cantor."

Olaf is then called over. The flunky suggests they both tell a joke. Cantor is too upset to joke, but Joe manages to tell such a stinker that Olaf decides that he must be the real Cantor. The policeman carries off the real Eddie Cantor to an uncertain fate.

Joe then goes out onstage to take part in the finale, along with Tommy and — for some unexplained reason — Pat. In a neat closing visual gag, Dr. Schlenna, who is conducting the orchestra, suffers a nervous breakdown when he looks over the pit musicians and discovers that all eighteen of them have turned into Cantors.

Filmed in the fall and winter of 1942-43, *Thank Your Lucky Stars* did not go into release until almost a year later in September 1943. The film garnered good notices, though the *New York Times* had few kind words for Cantor's tongue-in-cheek portrayal of himself and claimed that it almost ruined the film. Apparently audiences around the country either saw Eddie self-deprecating caricature in a different light, or they just didn't care. Either way they bought enough tickets to make *Thank Your Lucky Stars* one of the more popular films of the season.

Aside from appearing in patriotic, morale-building films like *Thank Your Lucky Stars*, Eddie Cantor worked tirelessly for the American war effort. The comedian crisscrossed the country, usually at his own expense, visiting army camps, hospitals, defense plants, bond rallies, and shipyards to entertain and encourage. In addition to these appearances, Eddie also urged others in show business to get involved in the work, and he went so far as to urge President Roosevelt to give draft exemptions to stars who were more valuable to the war effort on stage than behind a gun.

In addition to his regular charitable activities for the March of Dimes, the Aliyah, and of course the Surprise Lake Camp, Cantor added a number of war-related causes to his slate of fund-raisers. Along with stumping for the Red Cross and selling war bonds, Eddie also launched a drive to see that every serviceman in the hospital at Christmas received a present. Titled by Cantor "Give a Gift to the Yank Who Gave," the program distributed thousands of parcels to servicemen, both during the war and for years afterwards.

Perhaps one of the greatest gifts was delivered by Eddie in person at a San Francisco military hospital. During a routine hospital appearance, Cantor was going through his usual act when he noticed one shell-shocked soldier standing with his face to the wall, oblivious not only to the comedian, but to the world in general. Cantor tried almost everything in his repertoire in an attempt to reach the soldier, but nothing seemed to work until he launched into "Now's the Time to Fall in Love." The strains of the familiar radio theme somehow cut through the mental fog which had enshrouded the soldier since his initial injury in combat. Tears began streaming down the young man's face. After the show, one of the doctors thanked Eddie, telling him, "You've done just the thing we lacked here, Mr. Cantor: just the spark to bring him back. Once we achieve that link we come out winning, and the case is cured."

The wounded soldier wasn't the only one affected by the afternoon's events. After the show, the normally teetotaling Eddie went back to his hotel room and took a few stiff belts of scotch.

## REVIEWS

The fans of Eddie Cantor had better like him an awful lot if they want to continue liking him after seeing "Thank Your Lucky Stars." For the portrait which Mr. Cantor unblushingly draws of himself in this otherwise gay and good-natured Warner Brothers all-star show is of such an unpleasant nature that, if someone else did it, he could sue. As a crashing bore and egoist who insists upon injecting himself into a benefit show which S. Z. Sakall and Edward Everett Horton are trying to get up, Mr. Cantor plays Eddie Cantor with masochistic spite. His character is so disagreeable that it almost ruins the Strand's new film. — Bosley Crowther, *New York Times*, October 2, 1943

With virtually all the stars and featured performers on the Warner lot written into the script for bit sequences, the new Eddie Cantor–Dinah Shore WB musical, "Thank Your Lucky Stars," is a b.o. [box office] natural that'll garner top grosses everywhere. On the basis of its marquee strength alone it'll sell. But it's far from the smash filmusical it might have been, considering the super-duper aspect of the production as a whole.

As a Cantor vehicle it's been topped by some of his previous efforts but it's chiefly due to the banjo-eyed comedian that the thing is pulled together during its sagging moments. As such it's a triumph for Cantor. — Rose, *Variety*, August 18, 1943

# CHAPTER 35

# *Show Business*

Eddie Cantor found his extra charitable work during World War II gratifying. So much so in fact, that at one point the comedian went as far as to announce that he would quit show business after the war and devote himself entirely to social work.

"What we will need most after the war," Cantor told reporters, "are people who can sell victory bonds, people to help rehabilitate the world, and people to work with our war-scarred boys, and that's what I want to do."

Like his previously announced retirement in the late twenties, Cantor's current plans to leave the entertainment field never came to pass, much to the relief, no doubt, of his legions of fans. By 1944, however, it was evident that the one-time apostle of pep, though an energetic fifty-two year old, was on the downside of his career. Although he would remain active in show biz for at least another decade, the remainder of Eddie Cantor's career would show a decided shift away from vehicles designed for pure entertainment value and towards even more benefits, charities, and pet causes.

It is appropriate, given that the main body of Cantor's shows and films were behind him, that in 1944 the comedian finally realized what had long been a pet project of his — a filmed autobiography. Appropriately enough, it was entitled *Show Business*.

Originally conceived as an RKO vehicle back in late 1938 during Cantor's first fruitless sojourn at the small studio, plans for *Show Business* were revived in the spring of 1943, after Eddie completed retakes on *Thank Your Lucky Stars* at Warners. At that time, Cantor approached RKO production chief Charles Koerner with the idea for the film, and Koerner gave Cantor the go-ahead.

Initially the production found Cantor wearing three hats, those of the producer, writer, and star of the picture. After outlining the preliminary story, however, Cantor turned the more mundane writing chores over to Bert Granet (who received story credit), Joseph Quillan and Dorothy Bennett (both of whom shared credit for the screenplay), and Irving "Izzy" Ellison (who supplied additional dialogue). Although *Show Business* was not a Cantor biopix in the strict sense of the term — being based rather on several inci-

314

dents in the comedian's long career—Quillan and Ellison were well acquainted with Eddie's story because they had been longtime writers for his radio program. Despite the team of writers, Cantor kept close watch over the script to keep the story genuine, a quality he found lacking in many similar show business yarns.

"The trouble with most backstage stories," Cantor told a reporter, "is that the people who write them don't know anything about backstage life. Show business has been my whole life, and I'm sure the idea for the story is a true one."

Supporting Eddie in *Show Business* were George Murphy (Eddie's co-star from *Kid Millions* almost a decade previous) and Constance Moore in the romantic leads. Although a good selection, Murphy was not Cantor's first choice for the part. Initially, Cantor and RKO had planned to use film newcomer Frank Sinatra. After his successful screen debut in *Higher and Higher*, however, the studio thought Sinatra too "hot" for the part.

Playing opposite Cantor was comedienne Joan Davis. Davis was selected for her attractive homeliness, unlike Cantor's previous screen girlfriends, who had all been cast, at least in part, for their beauty. "I think," Cantor later remarked, "that the audience enjoyed the idea of two homely people getting together. It gave the rest of the people in the audience hope."

Aside from her looks, or lack of them, Eddie also admired Joan Davis' ability to ad-lib on the set. He recalled: "Joan, one of the greatest ad-lib comediennes in the business, put in many of her own lines and pieces of business and was an outstanding hit."

In one scene, where the four leads were sitting in a restaurant discussing their plans, Davis ad-libbed a bit where she absentmindedly loaded her coffee with spoonful after spoonful of sugar as she delivered her lines. When her speech was done, she lifted the cup to her lips, took a sip, and instead of grimacing, deadpanned, "needs sugar," and continued the scene.

In a project where Cantor was also the producer and Joan Davis was adding bits of business to the script, it's not surprising that George Murphy was called upon for extra chores behind the camera. Murphy, one of the more accomplished hoofers in Hollywood, was given the added assignment of teaching Eddie Cantor to dance. Surprisingly, Cantor, a star in musical comedies for more than a quarter of a century, had gotten through all those shows and films by "faking it." Eddie's hyperanimated style, complete with his bounding, jumping, and hopping around the stage, had disguised his lack of terpsichorean training. In the film *Whoopee!* Cantor's "dance" to "My Baby Just Cares for Me," though spirited and highly entertaining, primarily consists of the comedian just shufflingly his feet rapidly, with no set pattern.

In *Show Business*, which followed the career of four vaudevillians, Cantor was called upon to perform several dance numbers with Murphy, Moore, and Davis. Faced with a situation in which faking it would not do, Cantor the producer ordered Cantor the star to dance classes. "You should have seen me in Hollywood," Cantor recounted to Otis L. Guernsey, Jr., "in a sweater and tap-dancing shoes, going to dancing classes everyday." Although he is nowhere nearly as accomplished as his teacher, Eddie's dance lessons came in handy in *Show Business*, which is crammed with more than a dozen songs, most of them old standards.

At best one can say Cantor performs his dances in a serviceable manner, though after years of racing around the stage freestyle, Eddie seems uncomfortable when boxed in by set routines. His best footwork comes when he lets go with his trademark skipping. Ironically, this comes in Eddie's first scene where he wins a contest with the ploy. After this scene, he never repeats in the film the style which won him his first — and in real life his continued — success.

Filming on *Show Business*, under the supervision of veteran director Edwin L. Marin, began in December 1943 and proceeded into the early months of 1944. During shooting, Eddie Cantor took a few days off to attend a war bond benefit in San Francisco, in the course of which the comedian again made broadcasting history. Using radio station KPO as his flagship, Eddie invented the media marathon fund-raiser (what has come to be known as the "telethon") by staying on the air for twenty-four consecutive hours, a feat which had never been previously attempted. Beginning at 6:00 A.M. on Saturday, January 29, the comedian sang over one hundred songs, told countless jokes, read the news, and even did station breaks while raising more than $40 million for the Fourth War Loan Drive. Contributions poured in from listeners in forty-six states, and money was also raised from the overflow audience which kept NBC's San Francisco studio packed throughout the marathon.

Although he was accompanied for eighteen hours by his regular radio band leader, Cookie Fairchild, and singer Nora Martin, Cantor effectively carried the show, the final half hour of which was relayed via shortwave to all the Allied fighting fronts around the globe. After going off the air, instead of collapsing, Eddie spent most of Sunday thanking those who had helped make the broadcast a success, after which he returned, along with Ida, to Los Angeles, where he celebrated his fifty-second birthday.

Perhaps it was his increased charity work during the war which put Cantor in an even more giving mood, but for a film which is supposedly based on *his* life, Eddie practically gives *Show Business* away to his costars. With George Murphy and Constance Moore carrying the bulk of the plot and Joan Davis receiving most of the film's gags, Cantor is relegated to acting as support for the romantic leads and serving as a foil to Davis' continual mugging. This is not to say that *Show Business* doesn't work; it does, most of the time, but not purely as an Eddie Cantor starring vehicle. While producer Cantor may have seen fit to give his role a backseat, he managed to give the overall film an interesting story, along with very good production values, and thus made *Show Business* top notch entertainment.

The film opens at Miner's Bowery Theater, circa 1913. On stage George Doane (George Murphy — the five principals all retained their own first names) is entertaining the burlesque audience with "They're Wearing Them Higher in Hawaii." While George, a legendary ladies' man, makes time with the chorus girls on stage, his regular girlfriend, singer Nancy Gaye (Nancy Kelly), keeps an eye on him from the wings.

Also in the wings is Eddie Martin (Cantor), an amateur who is waiting to perform in Miner's weekly talent contest. George exits and strikes up a conversation with Eddie, who nervously rubs the song and danceman's shoulder for luck.

"You must be one of the amateurs," George surmises. "You look a little frightened."

"I always look frightened," Eddie admits. "Even when I was born I looked this way, only I was lying down at the time."

Eddie, a regular contestant at amateur nights, gives George a tour of the bumps on his head, received from hostile audiences of past performances.

"You must have the theater in your blood," George says, admiring Eddie's persistence.

"Yes," he replies, "and my blood is in a lot of these theaters."

Despite the fact that the first contestant has been pelted with rotten fruit, Eddie, at George's urging, goes on. Singing "The Curse of an Aching Heart," Eddie begins slowly, but picks up the pace in an attempt to avoid various snares the stagehands are throwing out towards him. With George cheering him on from the wings, Eddie's performance — complete with the standard Cantor hand-clapping and hopping about — soon electrifies the audience, and he wins first prize. George, forgetting his date with Nancy, takes Eddie out to celebrate at Kelly's, a local restaurant for actors.

At Kelly's they meet two vaudevillians, Constance Ford (Constance Moore) and Joan Mason (Joan Davis), and their manager, Charlie Lucas (Don Douglas). George is immediately taken with Connie, but she is put off by his flamboyant manner and the fact that he is only a burlesque performer. While Joan and Eddie trade quips, George softens up Connie with a pleasant song and dance of "It Had to Be You" (the film's romantic theme). The party is broken up when the irate Nancy enters and drags George out.

George decides to take Eddie into his act. The pair spend the next year touring the country in burlesque. At the end of their season, George confesses that he is still thinking about Connie. He tells Eddie that they are taking their act into vaudeville, with hopes of running into Connie. In order to get her out of the way, George sends Nancy on a vacation to Maine, while he and Eddie plan their new act in New York.

Back in New York, the pair returns to Kelly's, where they run into Connie, Joan, and Charlie. Charlie tells George that there is no room for two low comics in vaudeville, but Connie suggests that George and Eddie team up with her and Joan in an attempt to find better bookings. As the foursome rehearse their new act, George continues to make a play for Connie, with little encouragement, while Joan goes after Eddie, who reminds her of her old cocker spaniel, with similarly disappointing results.

Soon the new act of Doane, Martin, Ford, and Mason premieres on the vaudeville circuit. The act, which begins with Connie and Joan pedaling on stage on a tandem bicycle, followed by George and Eddie in a dilapidated Model T, is built around "I Want a Girl (Just Like the Girl That Married Dear Old Dad)." The number, like most in *Show Business*, is nothing spectacular, yet remains very entertaining and captures the flavor of the period.

The foursome continues touring around the country, with George now proposing to a still reluctant Connie. Joan follows a similar tack with Eddie, who is becoming increasingly bothered by her advances.

"I wish you'd stop annoying me," Eddie tells Joan. "Why don't you find some other man?"

"I don't want a man," Joan confesses, "I want you."

Even Joan's passion is cooled when Nancy arrives backstage fresh from her extended stay in Maine. Eddie intercepts Nancy before she can find George and manages to send her away, but not before his pleas are overheard by Joan, who believes Eddie is cheating on her. Joan responds by slapping a befuddled Eddie around while pretending to adjust his stage makeup.

Later, Charlie arrives at the theater. In her dressing room, he warns Connie about falling for George. When George and the others enter, Charlie urges them to build a bigger act complete with better scenery and chorus girls. He tells them such an act would put them in the big time although it would cost at least $10,000 to stage. While the others bemoan the cost, Eddie declares he has 6,000 in his wallet, but it turns out his fortune is all in cigar coupons. George sees a shortcut to the needed capital. He explains that they could dramatically increase their income if they booked themselves as five acts.

A quick montage shows the various skits and routines of the five acts. Soon the team has accumulated over $5,000, which is quickly exhausted when George sends the money to Nancy for an emergency operation. The girls are critical of his charitable display, but Eddie defends George, citing that one trouper helping another is what show business is all about. Resigned to their fate, the four performers think up five more new routines to perform.

In rapid succession, we are treated to a selection of their new acts, including a knife-throwing bit where George hurls daggers at a jittery Eddie, a rather tired Anthony and Cleopatra spoof starring Eddie and Joan, and an opera takeoff billed as the "Metropolitan Four." This last bit, featuring a burlesque done to a recording of the sextette from *Lucia*, was the comic highlight of *Show Business*.

All their months or years together — there are few time references in the film — have warmed Connie to George, and the pair get married secretly. On their wedding night, Eddie stops by to try out a new number ("Alabamy Bound") on George. After repeated attempts, George finally manages to get rid of his pesky partner, only to have Eddie return with a tray of sandwiches, presumably for an all-night work session. The newlyweds merely exchange frustrated looks, while their uninvited guest makes himself comfortable.

George and Connie's working honeymoon (at some point the couple inform Eddie and Joan of their marriage) is interrupted by a visit from Nancy. Nancy, though she congratulates the couple, is seething with jealousy. Nancy's intrusion makes little difference to the team, however, when Connie announces that she is pregnant and George chimes in that they have earned the necessary $10,000 to play the big time.

The team premieres their new act at the Palace in New York. In the film's flashiest production number, the team, complete with a female chorus, performs "Dinah," with all of the principals in blackface.

Soon Connie leaves the act to have her baby, while George, Eddie, and Joan continue the act. One night, while playing in New England, the call comes through that Connie has gone into labor. Eddie and Joan rush back to New York, while George, who is still on stage, promises to leave as quickly as possible. Nancy, who is also on the bill, offers to drive George back to the city. After several miles, George realizes that Nancy is going the wrong way on purpose. He orders her to turn around, but she spitefully refuses. George grabs the wheel, causing the car to careen off the road and into a tree. George gets out and starts to hitchhike back to New York.

At the hospital, Eddie and Joan nervously pace the waiting room. "Can I get you anything, Mr. Martin?" a nurse asks Eddie, noticing his lack of composure.

"Yes," Eddie replies, "get me a doctor. I'm very sick."

"Mrs. Doane's doctor will be right out," the nurse tells him.

"Oh," Eddie double-takes, "I'm not *that* sick!"

A nurse enters to announce that a baby girl has been delivered, but adds that the delivery was very difficult. The next morning George finally arrives to greet the emotionally spent Eddie and Joan. He rushes in to see Connie, tring to explain his lateness, but is quickly ordered out of the room by his irate wife. Out in the hall, the nurse informs George that the baby died soon after being born. Stunned, George wanders out alone.

A banner headline announces America's entry into World War I. At a dock, Joan bids farewell to Eddie, who, rejected for military service due to his bulging eyes, is going to France to entertain the troops. Joan hands him a salami and tearfully waves to him as he boards the troop ship. She frantically calls him back, however, after discovering that she has forgotten to give him a jar of mustard.

In France, Eddie entertains a group of wounded soldiers with a rousing rendition of "I Don't Want to Get Well." Halfway through his second chorus, Eddie hears one of the soldiers accompanying him; it turns out to be George, who has been wounded in action. Eddie urges him to get better and consoles him over the divorce which Connie has obtained.

After the war, Eddie invites Connie to a welcome-home celebration being thrown that night in George's honor. Connie, afraid of being hurt, tells him that she doesn't want to see George. Eddie urges her to attend. That night Joan and Eddie escort George into the nightclub where Charlie and

Connie are waiting. After a few minutes of getting reacquainted, the floor show begins, starring Nancy singing "You May Not Remember" (one of the film's few new songs, written by George Jessel and Ben Oakland). The party sits uncomfortably while Nancy sings by their tableside. Later, George escorts Connie home in a taxi. While George tries to start over, Connie announces that they are through and adds that she is going to marry Charlie. Stunned, George gets out and walks away.

Try as she might, Connie cannot forget George and soon breaks off her engagement with Charlie. She goes back to work, singing in nightclubs. George too has gone back to work, but as a saloon singer. Their career progress is illustrated in a series of vignettes in which they both sing "It Had to Be You." In each progressive scene, Connie's fortunes rise, while George's fall correspondingly. Finally, George winds up singing for drinks in a San Francisco dive.

While all this has been going on, apparently Eddie and Joan have continued as a prosperous team. During a visit to Connie, Eddie gets her to reveal her true feelings for George by using reverse psychology. Later that evening, Eddie meets with Charlie, who tells him that Ziegfeld wants him for a new show. Eddie also discovers from Charlie news of George's whereabouts and the depths to which he has sunk. Telling Charlie that Ziegfeld has to wait, Eddie rushes to San Francisco to help George.

Again using reverse psychology, Eddie pretends to be a bigger drunk than George. True to form, George forces Eddie to give up booze, promising that he will personally see to his recovery. Eddie and George return to New York, where, along with Joan, they all become the stars of Ziegfeld's new show—*Whoopee*.

Eddie performs the show's title number, with less impact than in the original film version of the same scene, and the show becomes a great hit. During the curtain call, Eddie asks George to sing a solo. George obliges with, of course, "It Had to Be You." Connie, sitting in the audience with Charlie, melts as George sings to her. By the end of the song, it is clear that the two will be reconciled, especially since Charlie gets up and walks out.

George and Connie are remarried, sharing a double ceremony with Eddie and Joan. George pays the justice of the peace his $2, while Eddie and Joan each give him $1. The justice kisses Connie, but hesitates to kiss Joan and decides to kiss Eddie instead. The two couples rush to make the next train for Niagara Falls, but Eddie and Joan double back to the hotel suite, where Joan, unable to wait any longer, carries Eddie over the threshold.

As with most of Eddie Cantor's recent films, *Show Business* was cross-promoted with his latest anniversary in the entertainment field—the latest being, for the purposes of the promotion at least, his thirty-fifth. For *Show Business*, the anniversary celebration was infinitely more topical because the film was based on incidents in Cantor's career.

The celebration was capped by a charity banquet at New York's Hotel Astor on May 7, 1944. Hosted by Jessel, the fete was carried live over NBC. The proceeds of the "Cantor Cavalcade" went to the Surprise Lake Camp which Eddie had attended as a youth.

*Show Business* premiered a few days after the banquet on May 10; appropriately enough, the film, most of which has a vaudeville setting, opened at the Palace (now the RKO Palace). Reviews were mixed, but *Show Business* performed well enough to become one of the studio's top three moneymakers of 1944. The flow of cash into the box office also assured that Cantor's option for another film at RKO would be picked up.

## REVIEWS

Picture is a speedy and well-assembled piece of diverting entertainment geared for profitable biz in all runs.

Title immediately tabs backstage setting. But that's not a drawback in view of present trend to spot every filmusical that way. In addition to Cantor, Murphy and Joan Davis there are plenty of laugh lines and situations, with the horseplay ideally set up between Cantor and Miss Davis. — Walt, *Variety*, May 19, 1944

An intensive publicity campaign celebrating Eddie Cantor's thirty-fifth anniversary in the entertainment world broke almost simultaneously with the release of his new picture, "Show Business," which came to the Palace yesterday. As Mr. Cantor's pictorial biography, the RKO production is a distinct letdown. A dignified and more or less factual story of the comedian's life from the penny-picking days in the Lower East Side to his present status would have been an undertaking worthy of the theme.

All in all, "Show Business" is not a monument in the history of Cantor and/or show business. Fact is, it would be stretching things a bit to call it a milestone. — P.P.K., *New York Times*, May 11, 1944

# CHAPTER 36

# *Hollywood Canteen*

The Hollywood Canteen, the servicemen's club, not the film, was begun in 1942 by Bette Davis and John Garfield. Patterned after New York's Stage Door Canteen, which was staffed by actors and actresses from the legitimate theater, the Hollywood Canteen was a place visiting servicemen could go to for free food and entertainment provided by the film community's greatest stars. Located on Cahuenga Boulevard just south of Sunset in the heart of Hollywood, the Canteen was a former stable converted by volunteer studio carpenters, technicians, and artists into a workable G.I. nightclub. The surroundings, though functional, weren't glamorous; the glamour was supplied by the 6,000 stars, writers, directors, and other studio personnel who staffed the Canteen.

Just as the Hollywood Canteen had followed in the footsteps of its East Coast predecessor, so Warner Brothers in 1943 decided to build a film around the soldiers' and sailors' West Coast night spot, following the lead of United Artists' *Stage Door Canteen* (1943). Encouraged by the success of their own review, *Thank Your Lucky Stars* (1942), Warners planned another all-star extravaganza. To further ensure the picture's success, the studio hired Delmer Daves, who had scripted *Stage Door Canteen*, to write and direct the film.

For rights to the use of the Hollywood Canteen's name, Warner Brothers paid the club an advance of $250,000, along with a promise for 40 percent of the film's gross. With such a financial arrangement, it would seem that everyone connected with the film would be happy—Warner Brothers was getting an almost certain box office hit, and the Canteen was receiving a much needed boost to its operating funds. Unfortunately, after roughly a month of production, the Screen Actors' Guild cried foul and brought the entire project to a halt.

Invoking Rule 33 of the agreement between SAG and the Producers' Association, SAG argued that Warners was not paying the raft of guest performers in the film commensurate with their star status. This had not been a problem for the studio on *Thank Your Lucky Stars* because all of the guest stars were under contract to Warners. Similarly, there was no difficulty on

*Stage Door Canteen*, but only because SAG had decided not to press the point.

In the case of *Hollywood Canteen*, however, SAG decided that any further concessions to Rule 33 would open a flood gate of problems in the future. Warners planned to use in cameo bits many more stars than it had under contract, paying them a fraction of what they usually received for starring roles. Thus many stars who normally earned up to $25,000 per picture would receive an average of $2,500 for their work in *Hollywood Canteen*.

While work on the film ground to a halt, Warners filed a $500,000 suit against the Screen Actors Guild. In their brief, they reasoned that if SAG forced compliance to the usual union scale, the studio could not afford to finish the picture. SAG argued that the studio was merely trying to get top-flight stars at cut-rate prices. After almost six months of wrangling, a compromise solution was hammered out that allowed the production to resume.

The battles between Warner Brothers and SAG had little effect on Eddie Cantor's participation in *Hollywood Canteen*. Eddie was a natural choice to appear in the film because he had served as master of ceremonies on the club's opening night and had performed there numerous times since (sometimes even broadcasting his radio show from that location). Eddie signed on the picture in May 1944, just as production was resuming.

Not surprisingly, since Delmar Daves wrote both scripts, the plot of *Hollywood Canteen* is similar to that of *Stage Door Canteen*. Both focus on the stories of servicemen—three in *Stage Door*, two in *Hollywood*—who enjoy brief wartime romances in the friendly confines of the respective canteens. In *Hollywood Canteen*, the two soldiers (Robert Hutton as the boy-next-door type and Dane Clark as the obligatory comic relief from Brooklyn) are in the film capital after being released from a nearby army hospital. They are free in Hollywood for three days before they have to report again for duty. Hutton's character has only one goal in mind: meeting his dream girl, film star Joan Leslie. Through a series of progressively implausible coincidences, he not only meets Leslie, but eventually winds up kissing her, dating her, and falling in love with her (and she with him), all in the space of three days.

While we are repeatedly told that such familiar favoritism is strictly against the Hollywood Canteen rules, it seems that all the stars in the picture go out of their way to make this one soldier their guest of honor. Still, such plots, no matter how hokey they seem today, were evidently effective to wartime audiences, and besides, the convoluted story is just an excuse to parade as many of Hollywood's stars as could be rounded up for the film. In this aspect, *Hollywood Canteen* remains an enjoyable picture, with guest spots by Jack Benny, Joe E. Brown, the Andrews Sisters, Roy Rogers and Trigger, Bette Davis, John Garfield, and Joan Crawford, to name but a few.

Eddie Cantor's scene in *Hollywood Canteen* occurs roughly one-quarter of the way into the film, just after Hutton's first kiss from Joan Leslie. The bit opens with an unidentified waiter, loaded down with a tray of sandwiches, wading through a crowd of servicemen. By the time he runs the gauntlet, the soldiers have picked the tray clean. The empty tray is lowered to reveal Cantor, who is greeted by his radio singer, Nora Martin.

"What happened to the sandwiches?" Nora asks.

"What happened? Look!" Eddie exclaims, adding, "I wish I could get rid of my daughters that fast."

"Pardon me, Mr. Cantor," a nearby soldier drawls, "but are you married?"

"He's new around here, isn't he?" Cantor observes.

Several of the soldiers call out for a song, and soon the entire room is chanting the familiar "We Want Cantor" chorus made popular on his weekly radio show. Removing his waiter's apron, Eddie climbs on stage and begins to tell a story. Before he can reach the punchline, however, Hutton, still dazed from his kiss with Miss Leslie, stumbles on stage behind Cantor. The crowd begins to chuckle and then roar as Hutton fumbles around the stage unbeknownst to Cantor. Finally, Eddie spots the confused soldier and calls him forward. He asks what's wrong, and Hutton explains he's just been kissed by Joan Leslie.

"No wonder," Eddie nods. "Make way for a soldier who's just seen action."

Hutton exits, and Cantor calls for Nora, explaining that they're going to sing "the baby song" ("We're Having a Baby" from *Banjo Eyes*). A prop front porch set is wheeled on stage, and Cantor ducks behind it, emerging a moment later as "Erwin." Nora, whom he calls "Sally," greets him and tries to subtly break the news that she is pregnant. She first tries to explain that they will soon be having a visitor, to which Erwin glumly replies, "Your mother is coming to stay with us?"

Sally then tries to explain they're getting an addition to the family that looks just like him. "Oh," Erwin nods, "you're buying a cocker spaniel." Finally, Sally tells him that they're going to have a baby. Erwin almost faints at the news and has to be escorted to the front porch bench. There, once recovered, he joins Sally in a duet of "We're Having a Baby."

The song, which does not contain all of the original lyrics which NBC censors had found objectionable in a television broadcast that May (see Chapter 42 on television), was a good choice for two reasons. First, it was already the property of Warner Brothers because they owned a half interest in the show it came from, and second, it committed to film at least a glimpse of that show, *Banjo Eyes* (plans for a full version of the stage musical had been permanently shelved).

After the song, Eddie kisses Nora, then apologizes for doing so in front of all those love-starved servicemen. By way of consolation, he invites a soldier on stage to receive a kiss from Nora. Cantor next picks out a sailor to come up on stage, but when the tar eagerly jumps up for his kiss, it is Eddie, not Nora, who delivers the smooch. The scene fades out, as the crowd laughs.

"We're Having a Baby," is one of the musical highlights of *Hollywood*

*Canteen,* which, like many musical reviews, offered a mixed bag of tunes of various quality. Many of the numbers, Cole Porter's "Don't Fence Me In" (performed twice in the film) and "Sweet Dreams, Sweetheart" in particular, are quite entertaining. Others, most notably "I'm Getting Corns for My Country" and "You Can Always Tell a Yank," haven't worn well at all.

*Hollywood Canteen* opened in late December 1944, with the ad slogan: "All of Hollywood's Heart Is in It . . . and 62 of Hollywood's Stars." The film played extremely well all around the country, earning over $4.2 million (just slightly disappointing in light of the fact that *Stage Door Canteen* had grossed $4.5 million).

## REVIEW

Author-director Delmer Daves has done it again. He scripted "Stage Door Canteen" for Sol Lesser in early '43, and he's parlayed himself into another smasheroo for Warners with "Hollywood Canteen." There isn't a marquee big enough to hold all the names in this one, so how can it miss? Besides, it's basically solid. It has story, cohesion and heart. That's not a bad parlay either. . . .

Eddie Cantor and Nora Martin do their "We're Having a Baby (My Baby and Me)" and click, although Cantor, somehow, permitted himself a bad makeup.[1]
—Abel, *Variety,* December 6, 1944

## *Notes*

1. Perhaps what *Variety* judged "a bad makeup" was actually just Cantor's natural appearance. His face is fuller, and his chin less defined than in his youth, but overall Cantor looks good for a man of fifty-two years of age.

# CHAPTER 37

# *If You Knew Susie*

Question: What do *A King in New York*, *Utopia*, *Love Happy*, and *The Sin of Harold Diddlebock* have in common?

Answer: They all were disappointing, if not dismal, final starring features in the careers of otherwise great film comedians.

While Eddie Cantor may not be ranked among such classic screen clowns as Charlie Chaplin, Laurel and Hardy, the Marx Brothers, or Harold Lloyd, he shares the common mistake that he also made at least one too many starring films. This is not to say that *If You Knew Susie* (Cantor's swan song) or any of the above mentioned films are without worthwhile moments, but rather that the overall quality of each film makes it palatable only to die-hard fans of its star. Unfortunately, in film careers, as in life, you never know that your welcome has been overstayed until you actually overstay it.

*If You Knew Susie*, as all the other films listed above, no doubt started optimistically, but upon its release, it was discovered that one too many trips to the well had been made. In 1944, with the strong box office results of *Show Business* happily jingling in RKO's coffers, the studio decided to exercise the option for another Eddie Cantor production. Less than four months after the release of Cantor's first production, and while the comedian was working over at Warners on *Hollywood Canteen*, plans were announced for his next RKO feature — *It Happened in Mexico*. Aside from the title, few details about the new project were divulged.

*It Happened in Mexico* sat on the shelf for six months while Cantor toured army hospitals and briefly toyed with the idea of producing another stage musical. When work on the picture resumed in February 1945, it was announced that the film, now untitled, would be a musical Western, with songs by Jimmy McHugh and Harold Adamson. In addition, Joan Davis would be back to reprise her costarring role from *Show Business*. A few more months went by until it was announced that the Western would be called *The Calico Kid* (a return to Cantor's old habit of appearing in vehicles with "Kid" in the title) and would be directed by Felix Feist.

Months went by, the war ended, but there was still no progress on Eddie's next film until September, when RKO announced that it was waiting on the availability of Technicolor stock (the color film was very scarce during the war) for *The Calico Kid*. According to studio sources, the film stock would be available in mid–November, at which time filming would begin. Not surprisingly, mid–November found Cantor three thousand miles away, selling bonds and having dinner with President Truman, while *Come on Along* (the film's latest title) remained in cinematic limbo.

Finally, after over eighteen months of waiting, Cantor's next film premiered; unfortunately it was only three minutes long and he wasn't even the star. In early 1946, Eddie, along with such Hollywood luminaries as Ingrid Bergman, Edward G. Robinson, Katherine Hepburn, and Walter Pidgeon, appeared in *For All the People*, a brief short produced by David O. Selznick for the National Conference of Christians and Jews to commemorate American Brotherhood Week.

RKO celebrated Brotherhood Week by dropping Cantor's film, now blatantly titled *Show Business Out West*, from the production schedule altogether. Studio executives cited the expected flood of big budget Technicolor Westerns as the official reason for killing the project. Probably other considerations, such as a poor script, were the true cause for their actions since it is highly unlikely that audiences would be confused by too strong a resemblance between, say, Gregory Peck in *Duel in the Sun* and Eddie Cantor in *Show Business Out West*. Either way, for whatever reasons, Eddie Cantor was told to go looking for another project for his second RKO release.

Perhaps if RKO executives had been able to see what would eventually be released, they would have changed their decision on Cantor's musical Western. By mid–May 1946, a new script by Warren Wilson and Oscar Brodney (with additional dialogue by Bud Peterson and Lester A. White) had been presented to RKO and approved for production. Originally titled *Rich Man, Poor Man*, the story centered around two retired vaudevillians (Cantor and Davis), who suddenly discover that the Federal government owes them a fortune.

The film's songs were provided by Harold Adamson and Jimmy McHugh. Unlike the score of *Show Business*, which contained nothing but proven material, none of the musical numbers for *Rich Man, Poor Man* were considered potential hits, which prompted producer Cantor to reach back into his vast collection of old standards for a bona fide smash. He chose "If You Knew Susie" (by Buddy DeSilva and Joseph Meyer), a song he first performed back in *Kid Boots*, which had been covered by many singers (Jolson had first introduced it, then suggested it to Cantor), but was almost exclusively identified with Eddie.

With such a strong identification between the song and the star, it was soon decided to rename the entire project *If You Knew Susie*. Although the song had nothing at all to do with the plot, except that Joan Davis' character was renamed "Susie" to match the film's title, the new name could at least hope to attract the strong, but aging, base of Cantor fans who would be brought out in search of a trip down memory lane with their favorite star.

RKO paid the unusually high, but not record, sum of $20,000 to Shapiro-Bernstein music publishers for unlimited use of "If You Knew Susie."

While a strong title and song may have ensured a high degree of recognition, unfortunately they did not ensure a strong film. The money RKO lavished on musical rights would have been better spent on providing a cohesive script. Although the film's plot was basically sound, the various gags hung on it were not. In a return to the style of such films as *Palmy Days* and *Strike Me Pink*, jokes were scattered into the script as if they had been placed there with a shotgun. Very little of the comedy in *If You Knew Susie* has anything to do with the picture's story, and this results in a jerky production which seldom slips smoothly into gear. Proof of the dearth of comedy in the film can be found in the fact that the funniest moments in *If You Knew Susie* come in a flashback to the opera parody in *Show Business*, which is inserted intact into the film, with little motivation other than a desperate need for laughs.

Again, as in *Show Business*, most of the film's laughs went to Joan Davis. Unfortunately, without George Murphy and Connie Moore to carry the plot (and act as something of a buffer between the comedienne and the audience), Davis' usual "anything-for-a-laugh" style of mugging begins to wear thin quickly in *If You Knew Susie*. Eddie Cantor, both as costar and producer, was evidently sufficiently enamored of Davis and her talents to try to tone down, or even balance out, her character in the film.

While most of the fault for the weakness of *If You Knew Susie* must be assigned to the quartet of writers, the film's director did little to avert the problem. Gordon Douglas, who had begun his career as a gagwriter and then a director at the Hal Roach Studios, was brought on board to helm the production. A "B" director, Douglas has the distinction of directing some of Hollywood's top comics (Laurel and Hardy, Bob Hope, Jerry Lewis) in some of their most disappointing vehicles.

*If You Knew Susie* was slated to go before the cameras in September, but production was pushed back several times, finally getting under way in early 1947 on location in Washington, D.C. (although no capital locations are evident in the final product). Aside from Cantor and Davis, the film's cast included character actor Allyn Joslyn, Sheldon Leonard (as the villain), Charles Dingle, and child actor Bobby Driscoll, borrowed from Walt Disney, where he was that studio's first "live" contract player.

The film, which was considered by some to be a sequel to *Show Business*, opens outside a vaudeville theater, whose marquee announces the final performance of veteran vaudevillians Sam and Susie Parker (Cantor and Davis). Inside, as six chorus girls dance before the curtain, the curtain itself is alive with a huge animated caricature of Sam in blackface. As the caricature sings the beginning of the song "My How the Time Goes By," its huge hands lift up and part the curtain, behind which the real Sam goes into his number. Unfortunately, as cleverly as the number and indeed the picture begins, it's all downhill from here. The song — which is neither good, nor bad, just there—is performed by Cantor in blackface while he dances along a treadmill using steps left over from his lessons with George Murphy. He is joined on the second chorus by the girls and on the final stanza by Davis, also in blackface.

Later in the dressing room, Sam and Susie remove their makeup for the last time and reflect on their many happy years together in show business. Susie thanks Sam for keeping his promise that someday they would retire from two-a-days.

"Sam Parker, you're the most wonderful husband in the whole world," she remarks.

"Small world, ain't it?" Sam notes.

The Parkers plan to move back to Sam's ancestral home, a revolutionary war farmhouse in Brookford. There, with their two children, teenage Marjorie (Margaret Kerry) and preteen Junior (Bobby Driscoll), and Susie's mother (Mabel Paige), they hope to become valued members of the community. The other actors on the bill enter to wish Sam and Susie well, and the theater manager asks if they won't reconsider and play a few more weeks. Sam insists they must leave for Brookford immediately to arrive in time for the annual reenactment of Paul Revere's ride, especially since this year he will play the famed rider.

A few days later at the Patriot's Day celebration the crowd awaits the arrival of Paul Revere/Sam, who is hours late. The town's leading citizen, Mr. Clinton (Howard Freeman), grumbles, while his son Handy (Dick Humphreys) tries to court Marjorie as Junior kibitzes. Finally Sam rides up on a horse, and the ceremony can begin.

"Hey, Pop," Junior calls out, "what took you so long?"

"Oh, that horse!" Sam exclaims, while limping bowlegged towards the podium. "No wonder that poor Cassidy has to hop along."

Sam begins his speech by thanking the townsfolk for their hospitality and expresses his happiness at returning to his family's homestead. Any goodwill created by this heartfelt address is quickly dispelled when Sam uses the occasion to announce that they have turned the farmhouse into the "Colonial Inn," a restaurant complete with floor show, chicken and steak dinners, and a $1 cover charge. The locals sit stunned as Sam fires off a colonial musket releasing an advertisement for the inn.

The next day, while Susie tries to thread a straight pin ("Anyone can thread a needle," she explains), Sam goes through a quick rehearsal of "If You Knew Susie" with the inn's orchestra and chorus girls/waitresses. The practice is unnecessary, however, for that night not one customer attends the inn's opening. Sam and Susie learn that Clinton has effectively instituted a townwide ban on the club (although given Sam's tasteless announcement, along with the intrusive neon signs on the inn, one couldn't really blame the townspeople if they stayed away on their own).

While putting Junior to bed later that night, Sam and Susie learn that both of their children have been shunned by the other children in town because their ancestors were "nobodies." Sam makes up a story about his ancestor Jonathan Parker being a spy during the Revolution.

Soon the contents of the inn are being auctioned off under Clinton's supervision. Sam and Susie glumly resign themselves to the action. Upstairs, however, Junior and Marjorie discover a strongbox in a secret hiding place, uncovered when two workmen remove a cabinet.

"It might be a bomb," Junior exclaims, before adding, "Mom better open it."

When Sam and Susie inspect the box, they discover a letter from George Washington, Thomas Jefferson, and Benjamin Franklin to Jonathan Parker thanking him for delivering a ship full of supplies to the Continental Army. They show the document to Clinton, who dismisses it as a forgery. Undaunted, Sam and Susie decide to go to Washington, D.C., to find proof that the letter is genuine and Jonathan Parker is a true hero. For reasons unexplained, the auction is never finalized and the Parkers and their furniture remain in the farmhouse.

Sam and Susie leave the children with their grandmother and head to Washington, where they march from agency to agency trying with no success to get their letter authenticated. Unable to find a hotel room, they sleep on park benches until they meet Mike Garrett (Allyn Joslyn) a friendly, yet somewhat unscrupulous, reporter for a national news service. Mike offers to share his luxury apartment, which actually belongs to the news service, with the Parkers for only $100 a week, a sum which he then promptly turns over to a local gangster to whom he is in debt.

Susie pours over history books late into the night while Sam tries in vain to get some sleep. Sam's slumber is disturbed further when Mike arrives for the next week's rent, which he needs for the next installment on his gambling losses. Mike's enterprise is interrupted the next morning when his boss, Mr. Whitley (Charles Dingle), arrives unexpectedly with a count and countess. Whitley has promised the nobility the use of the company suite. Mike explains that the apartment is uninhabitable because of a sudden infestation of various pests. His charade falls through when Susie enters in her dressing gown and offers to cook breakfast for the new arrivals. Whitley is enraged, but not as much as when Sam enters in his pajamas, shaking spastically due to an early morning run on an exercise machine. After Sam and Susie exit, Mike tries to explain that the Parkers are international spies involved in a story he is writing. Whitley orders Mike to throw them out and then fires him.

Unable to evict paying tenants, Mike tries to get the Parkers to leave by making them homesick. Sam and Susie explain that they can't leave until they authenticate Jonathan Parker's letter. Mike promises to expedite the search and takes them to the archives.

At the archives, clerks scour the files before finally finding a copy of the letter. A codicil explains that not only had Jonathan Parker delivered supplies to the Continental Army, but he was never paid for the goods. As a result his heirs are owed the original sum of $50,000, plus interest compounded semiannually. As clerks rush around to verify the claim, Sam and Susie wait in the hall, discussing how they will spend their $50,000 windfall. Meanwhile, inside the accounting office, a battalion of clerks start to compute the interest due on the claim, which quickly runs into the millions. When a passing clerk chides Sam for causing all the confusion, Sam takes it to mean that he and Susie won't receive any money. He consoles Susie (who has begun to bark like a dog at the bad news) with the pleasant "What Do I Want with Money," in which Sam tells his wife that he doesn't need wealth to be happy, just her. Sam and Susie decide to return home, and they enter the accounting office to bid farewell to Mike. Mike informs them that their claim with interest amounts to over $7 billion, instantly making them the richest people in the world. When asked what he will do with the fortune, Sam reprises "What Do I Want with Money," but instead of extolling the simple life, Sam now tells of the spending spree he and Susie will enjoy.

The news quickly spreads back to Brookford, where now, instead of deriding the Parkers, Clinton drops by to do the dishes for Grandma and the kids. In Washington, Sam and Susie are resettled in the news service's flat and given a blank check from Whitley to indulge their every whim. The next morning at breakfast Susie remarks that their interest is still compounding.

"Do you realize we made forty-five thousand dollars while we were in bed last night?" Susie asks Sam.

Sam grabs his wife's hand and starts to lead her out of the kitchen.

"Where are we going?" she asks.

"Back to bed!" Sam announces.

The Parkers become instant celebrities. Later that day they attend a charity fashion show along with Mike and Whitley, where they are encouraged to bid freely with Whitley's money. Also at the show is Steve Garland (Sheldon Leonard), a local gangster who eyes the Parkers while trying to figure out how to get hold of some of their fortune. While Susie does some comedic modeling, Mike receives a phone call from a rival reporter. The reporter tells Mike that the Parker's claim will be thrown out because of a little known law which states that the Federal government can't be sued unless it agrees to be sued. When Mike informs Whitley of the call, he threatens to fire him again. Mike tells him that no one else knows about the call, and they decide against telling Sam and Susie. When his bookie arrives for another payment, Mike decides to kill two birds with one stone. He arranges for the bookie and his gang to kidnap the Parkers, thus generating additional publicity and sympathy for the couple. Garland overhears the plan and decides to kidnap the Parkers himself.

Sam and Susie agree to the kidnapping and go back to the apartment to pack for it. When Garland and his stooge arrive, Sam and Susie not only go along with the abduction, they give their kidnappers lessons in how to be proper thugs. Soon Sam and Susie take charge of the whole affair, planning the escape route, eluding the police, and generally directing the gangsters. Mystified, Garland explains to his henchman that all their money must have driven the Parkers crazy.

Garland takes the Parkers to his warehouse hideout, where he instructs his henchmen to treat Sam and Susie with kidgloves. After Garland leaves to call in the ransom demands, Sam decides he is tired of the stunt and calls off the kidnapping. Ignoring the boss's orders, one of the thugs picks up Sam and throws him through a glass partition.

At Mike's office the first kidnapper arrives to inform him that Garland has snatched the Parkers first. When Garland calls, Mike tells him that the Parkers aren't worth a penny, and the entire affair was a publicity stunt. Back at the warehouse, a thug pleads with Sam not to tell the boss about the partition incident, while Susie picks glass from her husband's backside. Just as Sam decides to forgive the thug, Garland phones with new instructions to rough up and then "unload" the Parkers. In the middle of Sam's speech on forgiveness, the thug throws him through another glass partition and then starts shooting at the couple. A contrived chase through the warehouse's packing crates ensues, reminiscent of similar "cheapy" scenes used in various Three Stooges shorts.

Garland makes a deal with a rival news service for the Parkers and then calls his henchmen to change the orders again. Sam overhears Garland's "no rough stuff" orders and uses the opportunity to show off in front of Susie. He boldly comes out of hiding, telling the thugs in whispers to take a dive. With Susie watching, Sam decks one thug, but is picked up by the other and carried off. Another crash of glass follows, but when Susie investigates it is the thug, not Sam who has been thrown.

Sam and Susie leave on foot. As they walk the streets of Washington, they run across a theater where they once played. They reminisce about the time when they had an act with George Murphy and Connie Moore and then decide to go inside. Sitting down in the audience, they imagine the theater packed again and then watch themselves, along with the aforementioned stars, perform the opera parody from *Show Business*. After the flashback ends, they realize that they were happier then without the money and decide to return home.

Soon the news breaks that the Parkers have no claim. Public opinion turns against Sam and Susie with a vengeance, and they are forced to hide out in their Brookford home. Clinton's son Handy, who likes Marjorie, makes secret deliveries of groceries to keep the family fed, while Sam and Susie take turns tasting the food for poison. When Susie accidentally substitutes dry mustard for sugar in her coffee, she immediately believes she has been the victim of a poisoning. Susie goes through a melodramatic death scene while Sam tearfully watches.

"Don't leave me behind," he implores, "I want to go with you!"

"Okay," Susie agrees, "take a slug of that coffee."

"Susie," Sam revises, "I'm going to miss you."

Eddie rides in Hollywood's 1949 Christmas parade along with grandchildren Judy McHugh and Michael Metzger (collection of Brian Gari).

In an uncustomary act of generosity, especially given the mood of public opinion, Congress votes to pay the Parker claim. Sam and Susie, however, decline the money, thus becoming national heros. They reopen the inn, which, thanks to their popularity, is a resounding success. Sam and Susie reprise the title tune.

*If You Knew Susie* was released in February 1948, more than a year after it had gone into production. Notices were kind to the film, not praising it, but obviously pulling their punches. The box office on *If You Knew Susie* was spotty, yet the picture still managed to do modest business around the country, keeping in the top ten films for over a month, albeit against a relatively weak field.

After viewing his latest finished product, Eddie Cantor decided to retire from the screen. On February 24, 1948, while *If You Knew Susie* was the sixth most popular film in America, Cantor announced that the picture would be his last starring vehicle. Eddie told reporters that at fifty-six he found that he "just can't think right before noon, and this idea of getting up at 6:00 A.M. is just too tough, especially with my other interests."

Ironically, more than two decades before, following his feature film debut in *Kid Boots*, Cantor had explained that he was leaving the stage in favor of films because of the easier schedule they offered. One suspects, however, that the true reason for Cantor's hasty retreat on the heels of *If You Knew Susie* rested more with that film's poor quality than the effort required to make it. *If You Knew Susie* was one of his few films which Eddie Cantor would later disown, calling it "a picture . . . that was nothing."[1]

## REVIEWS

"If You Knew Susie" is just the proof needed, if, at this late date, there are a couple of doubting Thomases who imagine Eddie Cantor is not indestructible. For the comedy with music, which came to the Palace on Saturday, is proof that Mr. Cantor is as solid as the Rock of Gibraltar and just as changeless.

To put it briefly, Mr. Cantor is regaling the customers as of yore with wide eyes popping, a few capers, a few songs and some—not many—funny sayings. "If You Knew Susie" leaves one wondering what the cheering has been about all these years. Merely put it down as a frivolous entertainment, which tries earnestly to be amiable and occasionally succeeds.—A.W., *New York Times*, February 23, 1948

There's little here that Cantor hasn't done in one form or another for many years, whether it's been in radio, musicomedy or pictures. However, there's a certain relish and zest with which he and Miss Davis go about their chores that help minimize its familiarity.—Kahn, *Variety*, February 4, 1948

## *Notes*

1. The other film not on Eddie Cantor's list of personal favorites was *Forty Little Mothers*, which Cantor repudiated for its poor performance at the box office, not its quality.

CHAPTER 38

# *My Forty Years in Show Business*

In the spring of 1950, after completing his first and last season on radio's *Take It or Leave It* and despite garnering some of that program's highest ratings in years, Cantor declined an offer to continue in the series. Before undertaking plans for his fall television debut, he paused for a recap of his already legendary entertainment career. Appropriately enough, the show which marked the comedian's return to the stage for the first time in almost a decade was titled *My Forty Years in Show Business.*[1]

Eddie conceived the project in January 1950 as a one-man show, half-monologue, half–solo vaudeville act. Originally designed as a lecture to be presented at various colleges and universities, the one-man review proved so successful that it soon outgrew the collegiate setting. *My Forty Years in Show Business* opened at the University of Maine, drawing such crowds that a second show had to be added, both of which were standing-room-only, despite a snowstorm which had blanketed the area with more than a foot of snow.

*My Forty Years* graduated from college campuses when Cantor was informed that he would be given the "One World Award" in recognition of his many years of humanitarian activities. The award, presented by Professor James S. Sheldon of Boston University and radio personality Mary Margaret McBride, was to be given at New York's Carnegie Hall. Actually, the presentation of the award was arranged by a pair of promoters who used the occasion as an excuse to bring the one-man show to New York. The show was financed by eighteen-year-old Joe Franklin, who put up $6,000 of his own to rent out Carnegie Hall. Although Franklin received back his initial stake money, he saw little of the profits, which went to the "promoters." Still, in his Manhattan office, Joe Franklin proudly displays the poster from the Carnegie Hall concert, the top of which proclaims "Joe Franklin Presents!"

Franklin, now the host of his own long-running talk show, recalls the event vividly. "I was just a kid, but I was an Eddie Cantor fanatic. I got back my money, but I should have made a fortune. I think we charged a hundred dollars a seat for the first few rows."

335

The one night only Carnegie Hall concert sold out quickly, with such a great demand for additional seats that over three hundred chairs were placed on stage to handle the overflow. Cantor cleverly worked his stage audience into the show by turning to them at one point and handing each one of them a dollar bill. "I think you've been cheated," Eddie announced, "and I'd like to give you back some of the money. Here's a dollar for . . . you and you . . . and you. . . ."

On the night of the show, March 21, 1950, Joe Franklin remembers he was escorting Cantor to the stage door, when they were stopped by an elderly gentleman. "Mr. Cantor, I gotta see this show," the man began. "I can't buy tickets, but maybe you could sneak me in. I've been a fan of yours ever since I was a kid."

"How old are you?" asked the fifty-eight-year-old Cantor.

"I'm ninety," the man deadpanned, breaking up the comedian.

"That put Eddie in a really good mood," Franklin recalled, "he didn't laugh often."

Eddie started out the evening by recalling his youth back on Henry Street when Grandma Esther's employment agency left him no room in their tiny apartment in which to play. "Grandma, where can I play?" Eddie remembered asking. "She'd say 'go play in the hall.' If she knew it was Carnegie Hall where I was playing!"

From there Eddie ran through a lively résumé from Surprise Lake Camp to vaudeville to the *Follies* to Hollywood. Interspersed with the anecdotes throughout the two-hour performance was a full complement of the standards Cantor had helped make famous, including: "Dinah," "Ma," "Ida," "Margie," "If You Knew Susie," and "Makin' Whoopee."

*My Forty Years in Show Business* won unanimous raves from the New York critics, many of whom agreed that it was one of the best shows of the 1949-50 theatrical season. Even though the one-man show could have easily moved into a Broadway house for what would undoubtedly have been a successful run, Cantor declined, deciding instead to take *My Forty Years in Show Business* around the country. Playing for one night only in a majority of the stops, the exceptions being White Plains, Pittsburgh, and Miami Beach, Cantor played a total of thirty-three cities, spread out over roughly the next year in between his tour to Israel and his work on NBC-TV's *Colgate Comedy Hour.* In most towns, as at Carnegie Hall, Cantor played to turnaway crowds, prompting Bob Considine of INS to dub the tour a "one-man *South Pacific.*"

Eddie Cantor repeated the format of a one-man show two years later when he made a whirlwind tour of one-nighters through the Northeast and Midwest. This tour was unique, however, in that it was arranged to benefit the Red Cross Blood Drive. Instead of buying tickets, admission was given out free in exchange for the donation of a pint of blood. Playing theaters and small auditoriums, Cantor still managed to raise over 50,000 pints of blood in two weeks.

## REVIEWS

Broadway's week gave us Eddie Cantor in his own one-man show, and a rather wonderful show it is. I might even be inclined to vote for it as the best play of the season.

I wish he would bring it into a Broadway playhouse for a limited engagement. He would sell out. — W. Morehouse, *New York World-Telegram and Sun*, March 22, 1950

"My Forty Years in Show Business," all by, all with and all about Eddie Cantor, turned out to be one of the very best shows of the 1949-1950 season. — Robert Garland, *New York Journal-American*, March 22, 1950

It was a terrific example of the comedian's art, in which pathos and fun ran hand-in-hand, and an audience of 5,000 sat spellbound. — *Detroit Free Press*, November 15, 1950

## *Note*

1. Because Cantor actually started in 1909, the project could have more correctly been called *My Forty-One Years in Show Business*, but that was certainly less "catchy."

# CHAPTER 39

# *The Story of Will Rogers*

For the most part, Eddie Cantor stuck to his retirement from the screen following the release of *If You Knew Susie*. Although the comedian never starred again in another feature film, he did make two appearances in two separate film biographies—in both instances playing himself. The first of these honored his dear friend from vaudeville and *Follies* days: Will Rogers.

Plans to make a film biography of Rogers had been kicking around Hollywood ever since the humorist's untimely death in 1935, with various studios and stars involved in the project at one time or another. The vehicle ultimately landed at Warner Brothers in the early forties, where producer Mark Hellinger planned to make the film under the title of *The Life of Will Rogers*. That incarnation of the film in 1943 got as far as a completed screenplay (by Sam Hellman) before it was shelved. The Rogers story was renewed after the war, this time with Jerry Wald producing. The main problem, that of casting the lead role, was solved when Will Rogers, Jr., was signed to recreate his father on the screen. Will Jr., bearing a strong resemblance to his dad, became available in November 1946 after an unsuccessful bid to the United States Senate. Despite a renewed popularity for biopics—due largely to the success of *The Jolson Story* earlier that year—Will Rogers' life story was again shelved for almost another six years.

Finally, in 1952, producer Robert Arthur guided *The Story of Will Rogers* to the screen. Michael Curtiz, one of Warners' top directors, helmed the picture, which was based on the *Saturday Evening Post* story "Uncle Clem's Boy" by Rogers' wife. Frank Davis and Stanley Roberts completed the screenplay from John C. Moffitt's adaptation of the *Post* article. The high budget, Technicolor production starred Will Rogers, Jr., in the title role, with Jane Wyman as his wife.

Eddie Cantor was signed to play himself, the only contemporary of Rogers' to appear in the film because most of them were deceased (W. C. Fields had died on Christmas Day, 1946, while Fanny Brice passed away in 1951). Although most of the headliners with whom he had shared the stage of *Ziegfeld Follies* were gone, Cantor did a remarkably good job recreating the youthful Eddie of a quarter of a century earlier. The one concession to

Cantor's age was his makeup. He had filled out somewhat, with the inevitable loss of youthful muscle tone, and his face, though still fairly thin, was clearly twenty-five years older than that of the apostle of pep who had pranced across the stage of the New Amsterdam Theatre. To cover Cantor's wrinkles, it was wisely decided that the guest star would do his two scenes in blackface to cover the march of time across his features. The use of blackface on Cantor makes sense, not only logistically, but historically, since in his *Follies* days Eddie mainly appeared under burnt cork. Both Cantor scenes take place in theaters and thus do not draw undue attention to the use of the makeup.

*The Story of Will Rogers—As Told by His Wife* (the film's full opening title) tells the humorist/humanitarian's story with warmth and gentle humor. Being told from Betty Rogers' point of view, the film begins circa 1903 in Oologah, Oklahoma, where the couple first met when Will was a traveling cowboy. The film covers the major events in Rogers' life from his travels as a cowboy and then in a Wild West show to his entry into vaudeville, the *Follies*, and finally motion pictures.

Most of the dramatic conflict in the picture is provided by Will's father (Carl Benton Reid) and then his wife, both of whom urge the easygoing cowboy to "take his place in the world." When Will accidentally stumbles upon the use of topical monologues, he rides the device all the way to the *Follies*, but self-consciously retreats from his "funny talks that make people think" when President Wilson (Earl Lee) urges him to continue them. Moving into silent pictures, Rogers only becomes convinced that his gift is needed when pressing issues force him to go on lecture tours. Once the film reaches its serious side, other aspects of Rogers' career are barely touched upon—it hardly mentions his extremely popular career in sound films—stressing instead his career as a humanitarian.

Eddie Cantor (billed last in the credits) appears twice in the film, to good effect, though with some historical inaccuracies. Cantor's first appearance occurs when Will Rogers makes it to the *Ziegfeld Follies of 1916*, where Eddie advises Will not to be nervous. In actuality, Rogers first appeared in the *Follies* in 1915, two years before Cantor, and it was Rogers who took the younger Cantor under his wing, not the other way around.

Cantor next appears years later during the depression when Will is arranging benefits for its victims. After film clips of Al Jolson and Fanny Brice performing, Eddie is seen on stage performing the second half of "Ma (He's Making Eyes at Me)." Eddie then introduces Will, who makes a short speech before turning the event back over to Cantor.

While *The Story of Will Rogers* rearranges events in its subject's life quite freely, as Hollywood biopics go it is on the whole far more accurate than most. Director Curtiz manages to pay tribute to the man the film calls one of "America's great folk heroes" without becoming overly sentimental. The performances are fine. Will Rogers, Jr., though clearly not the man his father was, still provides a creditable substitute. One only wishes that Warner Brothers could have done so well a year later with *The Eddie Cantor Story*.

## REVIEW

Warners pays tribute on film to the late Will Rogers, via a kaleidoscopic impression of the humorist who made the world chuckle and think with his homilies. Enough of the character is caught to please his still-loyal fans, and filmgoers of a new generation should find sufficient entertainment along conventional biopic line for it to be acceptable. — Brog, *Variety*, July 16, 1952

# CHAPTER 40

# *The Eddie Cantor Story*

Not long after the release of the quasi-biographical *Show Business*, plans for an full screen biography of Eddie Cantor started to take form. Fueled by a rash of show biz biopics in the early and mid–1940s, such as *Yankee Doodle Dandy*, *Rhapsody in Blue*, *Till the Clouds Roll By*, it was only a matter of time until the highly profitable genre would get around to a treatment of Cantor's life.

Following the record box office success of Columbia's *The Jolson Story*—which not only made a star, albeit briefly, out of Larry Parks, but precipitated one of show business's greatest comebacks for its subject—Warner Brothers signed Cantor for a similar project. The first deal, which was signed in June 1947, called for Cantor to receive a $50,000 down payment, in addition to a whopping one-third of all the profits the film would earn. Tentatively titled *All My Life*, the film, like *The Jolson Story*, would feature a yet-to-be-named newcomer in the role of Cantor, although Eddie would provide his own offscreen voice for musical numbers. Cantor would also work with the film's screenwriters.

A little more than six months later, in early 1948, it was announced that Warners and Cantor had revised their agreement. Instead of surrendering 33 percent of the film's profits, the studio decided to pay Eddie a flat fee of $1 million payable in ten yearly payments of $100,000 over the next decade (a deal which would save Warner Brothers considerable cash if Cantor's story proved to be as popular as Jolson's, which raked in $8 million). At the same time, it was announced that Warners' new contract player Gordon MacRae would play Cantor in what was now titled *Banjo Eyes (Life of Eddie Cantor)*. The studio decided upon the new title since it was not only closely identified with Cantor, but it was also already property of the studio by virtue of their half-interest in Cantor's 1941 stage production of the same name.

Two weeks later *Variety* reported that progress on Cantor's life story had come to a halt because the writers were having trouble with the story line. Try as they might, producer Harry Kurnitz, Cantor, and the writing staff couldn't come up with an interesting angle from which to present the star's life story. The project was put on hold temporarily, then resumed in the fall

341

**Eddie talks business with songwriter/cousin Charlie Tobias (collection of Brian Gari).**

with still no success. As Cantor himself described it, the difficulty centered around "taking the halo off my noggin" to provide some dramatic interest in the picture. The film was reassigned to producer Lou Edelman, who was as unsuccessful as his predecessor in solving the story problem. Warner Brothers canceled the project altogether, not only because of the lack of a firm plot, but because of a recent downward trend in $2 million musical productions at the box office.

With prospects for a Cantor film biography growing dim, in stepped Sidney Skolsky. Skolsky, a Hollywood columnist, had successfully packaged and produced *The Jolson Story* for Columbia and was now, at Eddie's invitation, attempting the same coup for Cantor. Despite the failure of two previous producers, Skolsky promised to lick the story problem. "Give me a week," he told Cantor, "to see if I can get an angle."

What Skolsky devised was a plot not dissimilar from *The Jolson Story*, in which all of Jolie's relationships are forced to take a backseat to his need to perform. "I finally saw it as the portrait of a ham in a nice way," Skolsky explained to Earl Wilson. "He was an orphan boy. He never got any love. He went on stage to get some. But you can't bottle applause. He kept driving. What makes Eddie run? That was my story."

Originally, Skolsky and Cantor had planned to cast and produce the picture themselves and then make a deal with one of the major Hollywood studios for a releasing agreement. Thanks to Cantor's appearances on television, however, the comedian was again considered a "hot" property, and several studios, along with Louis B. Mayer (working independently after leaving MGM), expressed an interest in Eddie's biopic. Eventually, Skolsky wound up pitching the idea to Jack Warner, who had rejected it two years earlier. In late 1951, the columnist-cum-producer asked Warner to reconsider the Cantor project. Warner remained disinterested until Skolsky reminded him of a similar meeting they had more than five years ago. "Don't forget, Jack," Skolsky told him, "you also turned down my Jolson story."

Not wanting to lose out on a potential $13.5 million gold mine (the combined grosses of *The Jolson Story* and its sequel *Jolson Sings Again*), Warner agreed to the film and took out a full-page ad to announce the project. For his efforts, Skolsky was rewarded with a share of Cantor's profits from the picture.

Although *The Eddie Cantor Story* now had a studio, it still was without a star. Cantor joked to the *Long Island Press* that he would like to have one of Hollywood's hottest young comics, Jerry Lewis, play him. When asked why he couldn't play himself, Cantor responded: "The story starts when I'm twenty-four, and I already look twenty-five." While the search went on, Cantor did play himself in *The Story of Will Rogers*. Will Rogers, Jr., would return the favor by reprising the role of his father in Cantor's story.

While Warner Brothers and Sidney Skolsky were madly searching for a star to play Cantor, a young Hollywood actor was trying desperately to land the part. Keefe Brasselle, the twenty-nine-year-old son of a Hollywood hair stylist, was under contract at MGM when he cornered Skolsky in a drugstore and shouted, "I just gotta play Cantor!" Impressed by the Cantoresque energy Brasselle displayed in his pitch for the part, Skolsky asked the young actor to do "If You Knew Susie." Brasselle quickly complied. "He stank," Skolsky later remarked. The producer told Brasselle he "didn't know Cantor," yet hoping that perhaps he was dealing with the next Larry Parks, Skolsky agreed to start coaching Brasselle.

Skolsky rented a dance studio and began giving Brasselle lessons on how to imitate Cantor. After almost two months of daily workouts, the producer invited Cantor over for a demonstration. Eddie complimented Brasselle's mimicry, but insisted the youngster was missing a few of the finer points of his act. Cantor gave a few examples, but Skolsky was unconvinced that there were any flaws in Brasselle's performance.

"He was doing it the same way Keefe was," Skolsky recalled, "but didn't know it. Jolson was the same way."

Convinced that Keefe Brasselle was now ready for a screen test, Skolsky had to proceed carefully, given the fact that his would-be star was still under contract at MGM. Skolsky smuggled Brasselle on to the Warners' lot one night after hours and had him tested under the pseudonym "George Wonders." After viewing the test, Jack Warner announced, "This is it," and Brasselle went about obtaining his release from MGM. A month later, in April 1952, Skolsky announced that he had just "discovered, tested, and hired" Keefe Brasselle for the lead in *The Eddie Cantor Story*.

Eddie Cantor went out of his way to laud the choice publicly. "I am completely amazed by the way this Brasselle boy has my mannerism down to a 'T,'" Cantor told Louella Parsons. "He is so perfect making like Cantor that when I saw his test, I thought surely he must be married to Ida!"

After landing the role, Brasselle continued to study Cantor's films and took individual lessons from Eddie himself. In addition to learning Cantor's mannerisms backwards and forwards, Keefe Brasselle's appearance was altered to match that of his subject. The Warners' makeup department spent eight months perfecting Brasselle's makeup for the part.

Brasselle's hairline was shaved back to approximate Cantor's, and the scar which had creased Eddie's forehead since childhood was carefully duplicated, although it often appeared much more prominently than audiences would have remembered it since the scar was usually covered with a bang of hair or stage makeup. In addition, Brasselle was fitted with plastic ears designed to stick out further.

Cantor's most prominent feature, those "banjo eyes," were recreated with the use of eye drops, a set of false lower eyelashes and a pair of contact lenses. Unlike the thin plastic lenses which have been developed since, the lenses Brasselle wore were more akin to semispherical glass eyeballs which fit, rather uncomfortably, over the actor's own eyes. A nurse was continually on the set to care for the faux eyes along with those of Keefe Brasselle. After the filming of *The Eddie Cantor Story* was completed, Brasselle had the contact lenses made into a pair of cufflinks.

The choice of Brasselle in the title role also affected the selection of his supporting cast. Since Keefe Brasselle was noticeably taller than Eddie Cantor, a relatively tall cast had to be chosen to make Brasselle appear smaller than he actually was.

The plot of *The Eddie Cantor Story* takes great liberties with Cantor's true life. Although in most Hollywood screen biographies events and characters are usually stretched, squeezed, and condensed for the sake of a more dramatic storyline, in Cantor's biopic much more of this goes on than normal. As previously stated, *The Eddie Cantor Story* exaggerates its subject into a love-starved workaholic whose only satisfaction comes before an audience. In order to "redeem" Cantor before the end of the story, Sidney Skolsky wrote a heart attack into the picture, having it occur somewhere around 1930. In the film, Cantor's coronary slows him down, makes him listen to the advice his friends and family have been preaching to him, and helps him achieve a happy, balanced life.

In a case of life imitating art, on September 28, 1952, before filming began, but after the story had been completed, Eddie Cantor obliged Skolsky and Warner Brothers by actually having a heart attack (see Chapter 42 for more details on Cantor's heart attack). Among the many get well cards and telegrams Eddie received in the hospital was a wire from Jack Warner which read: "That's what I call cooperation!" One of the first activities attempted by Cantor after his recuperation was the recording of the soundtrack for *The Eddie Cantor Story*. Beginning in December 1952, Cantor recorded seventeen songs which were used, in whole or in part, in the final film. In addition to the songs recorded by Cantor himself, another five songs were performed by Richard Monda, who played Cantor as a boy.

It is indeed fortunate that *The Eddie Cantor Story* contains so much music, for therein is the film's strong suit. Even with its weighty score, the film suffers from a number of major flaws, the greatest of which is Keefe Brasselle. Although Brasselle obviously spent countless hours studying Cantor's performances, he evidently invested precious few moments observing Eddie's day-to-day mannerisms. Brasselle plays Cantor the public entertainer and private citizen exactly the same. Thus, while it is a piece of fine mimicry for Brasselle to clap his hands and rolls his eyes on stage, the same behavior in a sedate conversation at home reduces his performance to that of an exaggerated imitation.

To Brasselle's credit, when he is performing to Cantor's soundtrack, the effect is almost flawless. His lip-syncing is very good, and at times, especially when he appears in blackface, one almost believes one is watching the real Eddie Cantor in his prime. Offstage, however, when he continues to mug and use stage gestures, the effect is grossly overstated and often borders on the bizarre. To make matters worse, Brasselle is frequently caught playing to the camera, often looking directly into the lens.

Brasselle's first scene in the film is perhaps the most jarring and turns a clever transition into an almost horrific experience. The jump from Richard Monda's younger Cantor to Keefe Brasselle's is made in a dressing room. Monda has been out on stage performing in Gus Edwards' *Kid Kabaret*, while Edwards (Hal March) remarks that Eddie Cantor is outgrowing his part and will have to leave the show soon (historically untrue, since Cantor was already an adult in *Kid Kabaret*). The next scene shows Cantor (now Brasselle) in a dressing room stooped over a sink, washing off his blackface. An offscreen voice calls for Eddie to hurry up. Brasselle grabs a towel, and with the towel covering his face, straightens up and turns to face the camera. He then slowly lowers the towel to reveal his face, while glaring into the camera with bulging eyes and a grin so mawkish that it is almost frightening.

Another effect that hampers Brasselle's performance is his attempt at imitating Eddie Cantor's speaking voice. Not that it is that bad; it is actually fairly close to Cantor's own. Paradoxically, however, the closer he gets to a perfect impression without actually achieving it, the worse the effect. At times Brasselle's accent slips and instead of a close approximation of Cantor, he winds up with a whiny, softened version of Keefe's own speaking voice. Rather than trying to capture Cantor perfectly, Brasselle would have done better following Larry Parks' example. In *The Jolson Story*, Parks (or the director) wisely chose not to mimic Al Jolson, affecting instead an altogether different voice pattern which, since it was not trying to directly imitate Jolson, was more readily accepted and not at all distracting.

Brasselle's frequent lapses into caricature are unfortunate because for the most part the rest of *The Eddie Cantor Story* is a handsomely mounted production. Beautifully photographed in Technicolor, the film is especially good at recapturing the period between Cantor's childhood and his early career. Alfred Green, who had been so successful at the helm of *The Jolson Story*, was called upon to direct Cantor's tale. Given his direction of the Jolson biopic, one would suspect that it was producer Skolsky, not Green, who had Keefe Brasselle perform his role so maniacally. After all, it was Skolsky who had invested months of private rehearsals getting Brasselle ready for the part. Other than the lead performance, Green's direction is professional.

Filling out the cast were Marilyn Erskine, who does quite well in the crucial role of Ida; Aline MacMahon, as the longsuffering Grandma Esther; and Richard Monda, who turns in a very good performance as Eddie at age thirteen. The rest of the cast were unremarkable with two exceptions: Alex Gerry stands out as Ida's father, supplying much of the film's supporting comedy, while, on the other hand, Jackie Barnett as Jimmy Durante apes the "Schnozzola" so pathetically he actually makes Keefe Brasselle's Cantor shine by comparison.

Like most of Hollywood's attempts to chronicle the history of one of its own, *The Eddie Cantor Story* is designed purely for box office, with little regard to accuracy. It is remarkable, especially when the subject has aided the producers, as in the case of Cantor, Jolson, and Buster Keaton, that a star's life cannot be brought faithfully to the screen without wholesale fabrication and manipulation of facts. Of course, when the star is being paid handsomely, as was Cantor, for the rights to his life story, there is little incentive to bite the hand which is feeding you just to get the facts straight.

To give a full synopsis of *The Eddie Cantor Story* in a book that has already presented his life in detail would be counterproductive and confusing in light of the many variances from his true life story. Here then are the major differences between the plot of the film and Cantor's real life:

• In the film, Eddie begins his show business career at Miner's Theatre around 1904 to avoid being taken to an orphanage. In real life he made his premiere at Miner's in 1908 when he was living on the streets.

• After winning amateur night, the film's preteen Eddie receives an offer to join Gus Edwards' *Kid Kabaret*. In real life, Cantor did not join Gus Edwards until he was an adult veteran of various amateur performances, Carey Walsh's Saloon, the People's Vaudeville Company, and Bedini and Arthur.

• After he outgrows *Kid Kabaret*, screen Eddie gets a job at a Coney Island beer garden (circa 1914) run by a friend of his, and he is discovered there by a London producer. In real life, Carey Walsh's Coney Island Saloon represented one of his first jobs (circa 1909), after which he went on to become a single act in small-time burlesque and vaudeville.

• In the film Eddie and Ida get married after Eddie receives an offer from the "Ziegfeld of London." The show in London falls through, however, and the couple never leave America. In real life, Eddie and Ida went to England on their honeymoon after Eddie was booked by Max Hart, along with straightman Sammy Kessler.

• After getting married, the film's Eddie and Ida live in New York in a flat of their own. Eddie is unable to find work in the theater until Jimmy Durante recommends him for a part in *Canary Cottage*, which he himself has turned down. In real life, Ida lived with relatives while Eddie toured the country for almost two years with Al Lee. Durante had nothing to do with Eddie getting a part in *Canary Cottage*.

• In the movie Eddie leaves *Canary Cottage* after he is tricked by its star into thinking he has an audition with Ziegfeld. When he arrives in New York, however, Ziegfeld has never heard of him. In real life, Ziegfeld saw Eddie in the show and offered him a tryout for the *Frolics*.

• The film has Eddie making such a hit in the *Frolics* that Ziegfeld puts him into the *Follies of 1916*, and the following year he is made star of the *Follies*. In real life, Eddie's first appearance in the *Follies* occurred in 1917 as a featured player. He was not made the star of the *Follies* until the 1927 edition.

• Grandma Esther, who is living with Eddie and Ida in the film, dies on the opening night of the *Follies* with her ticket in her hand. In real life, Grandma Esther died prior to opening night and was not living with Eddie and Ida.

• The film's Eddie sings "How Ya Gonna Keep 'Em Down on the Farm" as his tryout song in the *Midnight Frolics*, before America's entry into World War I. In real life the song was not introduced until the *Follies of 1919*, as it was about the soldiers returning from France. In addition, in the film, Eddie sings "If You Knew Susie" in the *Follies of 1917*, when the song wasn't written until the mid–1920s. Many of the film's songs are similarly out of place.

• Eddie is portrayed as going directly from the *Follies* to *Kid Boots*. In real life Cantor left Ziegfeld after the Actors' Equity strike and played in two shows for the Shuberts.

• In the film Eddie is wiped out in the stock market crash, then opens in the stage version of *Whoopee* in an attempt to recoup his losses. In real life, the crash occurred in the middle of *Whoopee*'s run.

• The screen Eddie begins his radio career while still performing on Broadway. In real life, Cantor did not start his weekly radio show until after he had already made two films for Sam Goldwyn.

• The Eddie character has a heart attack, presumably around 1930. In real life, Cantor did not have his heart attack until 1952.

• After his movie heart attack, Eddie withdraws from performing and spends his days in his Great Neck home brooding. In real life, Cantor never quit show business until the late fifties, when he went into semiretirement. Even after his 1952 heart attack he was back at work as soon as he was able, with part of his schedule including work on *The Eddie Cantor Story*.

• The film has Eddie come out of a postcoronary depression when he reluctantly agrees to play a benefit. After the benefit, he is amazed at the restorative powers of unselfishness and devotes most of his career to charity performances. In real life, Cantor played benefits from an early point of his career on through all its other phases.

Despite the unfortunate errors in casting and the general disregard for historical facts, *The Eddie Cantor Story* is not a total failure. Rather, in meeting what was presumably its main goal, entertainment, the film often succeeds, thanks to a full score of Cantor's song standards. Whereas Keefe Brasselle's pop-eyed prancing is a decided liability in dramatic scenes, the same technique is a blessing in the musical sequences which are the highlights of the picture, as well they should be. The film's other strong point rests in the early sequences where Richard Monda plays Cantor.

Unlike Jolson, who strove unsuccessfully to be included in both of his biopics, Eddie Cantor is given two cameo scenes in *The Eddie Cantor Story*. The first occurs prior to the opening credits, when a guard waves Cantor's black sedan through the Warner Brothers studio gates. Cantor, along with Ida, then enters a private projection room and sits down to watch the film. "Ida," Eddie remarks as the lights go down, "I've never been so nervous in all my life." The picture then begins.

Eddie and Ida reappear at the end of the film when the camera pulls back during the final sequence to reveal that the couple have been watching the picture along with the audience. Their reaction is rather strange, however, when the lights come up. They simply stand up and put on their coats. They are as expressionless as if they had been watching a blank screen for the past two hours. Ida helps Eddie with his coat, telling him: "Button up, it's chilly outside."

"Oh, I'm fine, honest," he tells her. Then gazing at the audience, he dead-pans, "I've never looked better in my life."

Although Cantor's onscreen endorsement seems unenthusiastic, off-screen Eddie did his best to promote *The Eddie Cantor Story*. He plugged the film for three consecutive months on his *Colgate Comedy Hour* television shows, in addition to making guest spots on *The Dinah Shore Show*, *Strike It Rich*, *The Milton Berle Show*, and *The Eddie Fisher Show*. Keefe Brasselle also made the rounds, making multiple appearances on both *Twenty Questions* and *Strike It Rich*. Oddly enough, Cantor never had Brasselle on the *Colgate Comedy Hour* to give the film an extra boost.

In addition to the above television appearances, Eddie Cantor was also the subject of *This Is Your Life* the week the film opened, although a factual telling of the comedian's life story might only confuse those viewers who were planning to see the film. In keeping with the pioneer nature of his career, Cantor set another precedent in appearing on the program hosted by Ralph Edwards — he was the first subject of *This Is Your Life* who knew in advance that he was to be so honored. The official reason given for the change in the show's usual format was that Cantor, due to his heart attack the previous year, might not be able to stand the shock. It is obvious, how-ever, that the program was arranged as part of the overall publicity campaign for *The Eddie Cantor Story*.

Broadcast December 23, 1953, *This Is Your Life* included appearances by Catherine Luddy, one of Eddie's former teachers; boyhood friend and later financial adviser Daniel Lipsky; Jimmy Durante; George Jessel; Gus Van; and Dvora Ekheiser, from the Israel Youth Aliyah. Ida and daughters Natalie and Edna were also on the program from Hollywood. Daughters Janet, Marjorie, and Marilyn made their appearances from the lobby of New York's Paramount Theater, where the film's East Coast premiere was going on concurrent with the *This Is Your Life* broadcast. Also appearing from the Paramount were Bobby Breen, Georgie Price, Eddie Fisher, Sidney Skol-sky, and Keefe Brasselle.

The film's West Coast opening was televised live six days later from Warner's Beverly Hills Theater over ABC-TV with Virginia Mayo and her husband, Michael O'Shay, serving as M.C.'s. Eddie Cantor masks were given out to those attending the premiere. These, coupled with the "banjo eyes" painted on the headlights of the cars chauffeuring guests to the opening and the giant pair of revolving eyes placed on top of the theater, only confirmed what the city of Beverly Hills had already made official: December 29 was "Eddie Cantor Day."

Most reviewers gave the picture mixed notices, although Keefe Bras-selle's imitation of Cantor drew almost universal pans. Those who did have kind words for the film cited its production values, score, and nostalgic feel. Still the Cantor name, along with the heavy promotional campaign, was enough to win the film $90,000 for its first week at the Paramount. The sum was a record for a film unaccompanied by a live performer on stage. After playing well in major cities, *The Eddie Cantor Story* went into national release in late January 1954. The film stayed in the nation's top ten for two weeks and then dropped from sight.

The lower than anticipated returns on the film killed any talk of a sequel (à la *Jolson Sings Again*), although Cantor himself initially thought that a follow-up film was a viable possibility. In October 1953, two months before the film's premiere, Cantor told a reporter: "There's so much material that hasn't been touched four more pictures could be done." Whether some material was saved with a sequel in mind or was omitted due to time constraints, *The Eddie Cantor Story* did leave much of the comedian's career untouched. The film ends in the early thirties with no mention at all given to his film career (in silents or talkies) and his television work; his highly successful radio career is only briefly touched upon.

Perhaps hoping against hope that Keefe Brasselle would be honored with an Academy Award nomination for best actor, as Larry Parks had been for his portrayal of Al Jolson, Eddie sent Brasselle, via Western Union, a pair of gold cufflinks in the shape of tiny Oscar statues. The accompanying telegram read: "May this lead to Oscarville. Remember your friend with the big eyes is saying a little prayer to make all your dreams come true." Despite Cantor's prayers and the fact that Keefe Brasselle wore a gold mezuzah around his neck for luck throughout the filming, neither he or the film received any nominations.

## REVIEWS

Undoubtedly Sidney Skolsky, who not only produced this biography for Warner Brothers but also wrote the story and collaborated on the script, was motivated by admiration and affection for a star of the first magnitude. Unfortunately, however, little of the magic that endowed this luminary with genuine brilliance over the years is projected to an audience.

Although it has been filmed in the pleasing hues of Technicolor and is weighted with the songs and shows he helped make famous "The Eddie Cantor Story" is slightly less than a colorful illustration of the reasons for its hero's greatness. — A. H. Weiler, *New York Times*, December 26, 1953

The life of Eddie Cantor as a man and as an entertainer draws conventional treatment in this biopic. In its favor, naturally, is the Cantor name and reputation, the nostalgic portrayal of a colorful era in show business, and the songs Cantor made known during his long, and still continuing, career. The picture will get strong exploitation, so key dates look healthy. — Brog, *Variety*, December 23, 1953

# CHAPTER 41

# *Radio*

Throughout Eddie Cantor's career, he mastered almost every entertainment medium that existed, including vaudeville, reviews, musical comedy, films, and television. Although Cantor was a major star in each of those branches of show business, perhaps his greatest and clearly his longest success was in radio.

It is fitting, perhaps, that the history of radio broadcasting so closely parallels the life of one of its biggest stars. Radio telegraphy became practical thanks to the invention of Guglielmo Marconi, just three years after Cantor's birth. At first it was just a series of dots and dashes through the air, but radio began transmitting human voices at roughly the same time Eddie was finding his voice in amateur night performances. After the restrictions of World War I, commercial radio broadcasting burst on the scene in 1920, just as Cantor was himself bursting free of featured status in the *Follies* and becoming the star of his own vehicles.

As with just about every new entertainment medium, radio had difficulty attracting established stars from the stage to fill its programs and depended instead on talent it nurtured itself. Any reluctance on the part of Broadway's top performers to test the new waves of radio is understandable, especially since each station stood alone prior to the emergence of networks later in the decade. Rarely shy before any audience or medium, Eddie Cantor was one of the first Broadway stars to give radio a try. It is generally believed that Cantor's first broadcast occurred sometime either in late 1921 or early 1922 over WDY, an experimental station owned by the then fledgling Radio Corporation of America. Not surprisingly, Cantor's debut was an appeal for a charity, the Salvation Army. Although WDY served the New York area, its studios were across the river in Roselle Park, New Jersey. One of the station's most popular programs was the *Radio Party*, a Friday night broadcast which attracted a number of Broadway celebrities. Despite the lack of pay in those first few years of radio (guests on *Radio Party* were treated to a champagne dinner for attending), appearances were regularly used to plug a performer's latest show or record, a practice still common in broadcasting all these years later.

351

Although network broadcasting began in 1926 with the formation of the National Broadcasting Company, initially it attracted very few stars from the established entertainment fields. Aside from Ed Wynn in *The Perfect Fool*, there were very few Broadway comedians with a regularly scheduled radio program. Cantor, like most of his contemporaries, made regular guest appearances on NBC and CBS, which was founded three years later, but again most of these appearances were to plug a new play or film. Eddie set a salary record in 1926 on NBC, when he was paid $1,500 for a fifteen-minute spot on the *Eveready Battery Hour* to promote the film version of *Kid Boots*.

Eddie Cantor finally settled down to a permanent show of his own as the result of a working vacation he took to Florida in the winter of 1930-31. In Miami to play some club dates, Eddie ran into Rudy Vallee, who was then at the peak of his popularity as a crooning heartthrob. Rudy suggested that Eddie make a guest appearance on his NBC program *The Fleischmann Hour*. Cantor agreed, appearing on Vallee's show in February 1931. On the program, Eddie sang a selection of his standards and joked with his host between numbers. Mort Millman, an agent, caught the broadcast and was so impressed by Cantor's radio manner that he recommended Eddie to one of his clients, Chase and Sanborn Coffee. During this period, network programing slots were purchased by sponsors, who were then responsible for providing their own talent to fill the programs. At the time Maurice Chevalier was appearing for the coffee manufacturer, but was planning a return to his native France.

Chase and Sanborn, through their advertising agency, J. Walter Thompson, signed Eddie Cantor to a seven-week trial schedule beginning on Sunday evening, September 13, 1931. Cantor had arrived in New York a few weeks earlier after completing retakes on *Palmy Days*. The sponsor provided a team of writers who worked with Eddie and his favorite gagman and collaborator, David Freedman. Born in Romania, Freedman immigrated to New York with his family when he was one year old. Like Cantor, Freedman grew up on Manhattan's lower East Side, where his father wrote for a local Yiddish newspaper. Unlike Cantor, Freedman stayed in school, eventually graduating from the College of the City of New York in 1918. Freedman's writing career took off with the creation of his popular character "Mendel Marantz," who was featured in a series of magazine stories, stage skits, and eventually motion pictures. Known as a human joke machine, Freedman met Cantor in the late twenties and began a close friendship fostered by their mutual interest not only in comedy but also in hypochondria, a favorite hobby of each man.

"Cantor complained of stomach trouble," Freedman said years later, recalling their initial introduction, "and I recommended a tablet, and that sort of cemented our friendship. After that we compared a lot of ailments we had in common."

From then on, the two men shared what Freedman later characterized as a "Damon and Pythias" relationship. In the years that followed, Freedman would collaborate with Cantor on numerous humorous articles, the script to *Palmy Days*, and Eddie's 1928 autobiography "My Life Is in Your Hands, by Eddie Cantor as told to David Freedman." Despite these many collaborations, David Freedman's greatest contribution to the career of Eddie Cantor was on *The Chase and Sanborn Hour*, where his ability to churn out a steady stream of gags was vital to the program's early success.

A sample of David Freedman's work from the *Chase and Sanborn Hour* includes this dialogue on the science of crossbreeding:

INVENTOR: Mr. Cantor, I have already managed to cross oranges with watermelons.
CANTOR: That's nothing. I once crossed a bridge with an automobile.
INVENTOR: Amazing! What was the result?
CANTOR: The other side. But I've also crossed a dachshund with a zebra.
INVENTOR: What for?
CANTOR: To make striped frankfurters. But that's nothing. I've got an uncle in Scotland who crossed an overcoat with a parrot. So when he hangs his coat in a restaurant and somebody tries to take it, the pocket opens up and says: "Hot mon, MacPherson, somebody's trying to make awa' wie yer coat!"

Another sample of Cantor's early radio humor by Freedman involves this domestic exchange:

WIFE: The maid quit—she said you spoke to her insultingly over the phone.
CANTOR: I thought I was talking to you.
WIFE: You're going to drive me out of my mind.
CANTOR: That's no drive—that's a putt.
WIFE: You're so bright they named a town after you—Marblehead.
CANTOR: You're such a good card player they named a game after you—Rummy.

*The Chase and Sanborn Hour*, starring Eddie Cantor, was a hit from the beginning, with the coffee company giving their host a seven-week extension on his contract after only the first show. Eventually Cantor's contract was extended through the spring until he had to leave for California to begin work on his next picture for Sam Goldwyn, *The Kid from Spain*. No doubt Chase and Sanborn, along with millions of radio fans, were sorry to see Cantor go for the summer, a fact borne out by Eddie's ratings. For his first season (1931-32), Cantor garnered a 28.9 rating, second only to the established team of Amos and Andy. This meant that almost three out of every ten radios in America were tuned into Cantor each Sunday. Aside from earning him the love of his listeners, Eddie received $4,000 a week from Chase and Sanborn for each of the sixty-minute broadcasts, which were heard every Sunday night at 8 o'clock over NBC.

The first season for Chase and Sanborn was unusual in that Cantor played most of the parts on the program, in addition to his own. Aside from announcer Jimmy Wallington and orchestra leader Dave Rubinoff, Eddie was the whole show and often played half a dozen parts of differing accents, pitches, and dialects each week. In fact, Eddie even provided the on-air voice for Rubinoff, complete with Russian accent. Cantor's share of the weekly script was made even larger because for the first couple of years there were very few guest stars. For variety, Cantor would often bring Wallington into routines; this was the first time an announcer was made a straight man in a program, a practice which quickly became commonplace.

Another innovation that Cantor pioneered on radio was the use of the studio audience. In its first season-and-a-half, Cantor's show, like many other programs, was performed before a studio audience, but for no practical purpose because the audience was not allowed to react to the show. Before each broadcast, members of the audience were informed that they were guests of Chase and Sanborn and were requested not to laugh or applaud. Violators who even slipped out a giggle were quickly "sshhed" by the studio usher.

The silent audience policy came crashing down one Sunday evening during the second season when Cantor and Wallington were doing a skit about two lady truck drivers. As "Edwina" Cantor and "Jenny" Wallington, they were going through their scripted routine when "Edwina" decided to embellish the bit for the studio audience by adding some costumes. Jumping down into the first row where Ida and Mrs. Wallington were seated, Eddie grabbed the ladies' hats and wraps, jumped back on stage, and slapped the female garb on himself and Jimmy. While he and Jimmy continued the skit, the studio audience, unable to control themselves, began to howl with laughter. The audience screams only served to egg Eddie on to an even more flamboyant performance, which in turn was greeted with even bigger laughs.

After the show, Cantor received a call from John Reber of the J. Walter Thompson Agency, the sponsor's representatives, demanding to know what happened. As Eddie began to apologize for the laughter, Reber explained that he had called to congratulate Cantor, not reprimand him. The audience's laughter, by Reber's account, gave the program an added vitality. Listener mail confirmed this; those at home felt a part of the program when they could hear the reaction of the studio audience. The studio audience became an integral part of broadcasting after that, so much so that eventually "canned" laughter and applause were added when no live audience was present. Ironically, one of Eddie Cantor's final broadcasting ventures, television's *The Eddie Cantor Comedy Theatre*, used canned laughter to simulate a studio audience — 180 degrees from the early days of *The Chase and Sanborn Hour*, when his live audiences were kept quiet.

Unfortunately, one of the drawbacks of letting Eddie Cantor loose on a responsive audience was that often, as when he and Jimmy Wallington wore their wives' hats, Cantor wound up playing to the studio audience with bits of business that had to be seen to be appreciated. Eddie would use sight gags, bizarre costumes, and funny faces to elicit huge laughs from the studio patrons, while audiences at home often sat in mystified silence, wondering what was going on.

Still, while he often catered to his studio guests, Cantor was also adept at making his listeners across the country feel that he was speaking directly to each of them. Since he was bringing new innovations to the airwaves with almost every broadcast, this talent of Eddie's was also discovered by accident. One Sunday, as he came to the final page of his prepared script, Cantor looked up to see an engineer in the control booth with a look of panic on his face, motioning the comedian to stretch out his material. A quick look at the clock confirmed the reason for the engineer's anxiety—it was only 8:55.

With five minutes of air time to fill and no script left with which to fill it, the unperturbed Eddie started to give a leisurely, conversational pitch for Chase and Sanborn coffee. The impromptu talk, even though it was in effect a commercial, struck listeners as being genuine. Thereafter, almost every week the show was planned to come up five minutes short so that Cantor could have an intimate chat with his millions of listeners. Sometimes Eddie would promote the sponsor, but more often than not he used the time to wax philosophical or make a heartfelt appeal for one of his pet charities or causes.

One topic which Cantor addressed frequently hit especially close to home for his listeners—the deepening Great Depression. With a mix of understanding and patriotic optimism, Eddie encouraged Americans to look at what they had, rather than what they didn't have. On one broadcast Eddie played a doctor advising the depression-sick Uncle Sam:

> You've got the people, the natural resources, the power and the wealth to be the biggest nation on earth. You've become a little too high hat—you're not working as hard as you used to. Do the chores around the house. Plain, honest work can't hurt you. And keep cheerful. Get out of the shadows and into the sunshine. Face the sun and the shadows will fall behind you. Don't look back, look ahead, the view that way is a whole lot pleasanter. Why, Uncle, you're the richest, strongest man on earth and you don't know it!

Eddie's sanguine pep talks soon blossomed into a tongue-in-cheek run for the presidency. A series of humorous, yet earnest, platform articles and radio bits appeared, along with a book, *Your Next President.* Cantor's campaign was punctuated with a four-note chant of "We Want Can-tor," which outlived the 1932 political season and became a theme of sorts that stayed with Eddie the rest of his career.

Eddie Cantor's successful blend of the comic and the heartfelt was further underscored by two songs that served as his radio themes. The first, "Now's the Time to Fall in Love," by Al Sherman and Al Lewis, was a bouncy, humorous number that was pure Cantor. The song's lyrics—which advised that since "Potatoes Are Cheaper" and "Tomatoes Are Cheaper," couples should take advantage of the bargain prices and get married—were not only sung each Sunday by Cantor, but also amended weekly with even sillier stanzas. Eventually the demand for fresh choruses stretched the list of bargain-priced household goods to include such divergent items as Weiners and vacuum cleaners.

Eddie's other theme, which he usually reserved for his sign-off, was the sentimental "One Hour with You," by Oscar Straus, Richard A. Whiting, and Leo Robin. Although the song was first popularized by Maurice Chevalier, through weekly use it quickly became associated primarily with Cantor.

America made Eddie Cantor a frequent and welcome guest in their homes. The next two seasons (1932–34) the *Chase and Sanborn Hour* was the most popular radio show in the country, pulling in astounding ratings of 58.6 and 50.2 percent respectively. These figures, coupled with the strong box office receipts for his films during those years (*The Kid from Spain* and *Roman Scandals*) and his personal appearances, made Eddie Cantor arguably the most popular entertainer in America.

As a testament to his popularity, one week, during his closing speech, Cantor mentioned that his birthday was coming up.

"I'm not hinting about any presents," Eddie said jokingly. "That would be cheap, not to say audacious. However, my shirt size is 15½, my socks, size 11; and if you're sending any kind of cake, make it chocolate because I could eat that the rest of my life!"

Within days packages began to pour into NBC addressed to Cantor. By the end of the week, a special committee had to be formed to help distribute the over fifteen thousand parcels containing an assortment of shirts, socks, and cakes to the needy.

Similarly, when Chase and Sanborn offered listeners a promotional booklet entitled *Eddie Cantor at Home*, the flood of requests for the giveaway item reached over 250,000. A follow-up brochure, *Cantor Makes Coffee*, had an equally large circulation. Ironically, though Cantor may have made coffee, the star didn't drink his sponsor's brew — a fact which broke new ground for truth in advertising.

Cantor suggested to the J. Walter Thompson Agency that he go on the air and publicly proclaim he didn't use his sponsor's product. At first the agency was reluctant, claiming the pitch was in effect "negative advertising," but agreed to let Eddie go ahead with it after okaying the new ad with Standard Brands, makers of Chase and Sanborn. Although simple and straightforward, Eddie's coffee confession was received as somewhat of a revelation.

"Ladies and gentlemen," Cantor began, "I do not drink Chase and Sanborn coffee. The people who sponsor this program haven't enough money to make me say I do, because I don't." Eddie went on to tell his audience that although he didn't drink coffee, Chase and Sanborn was the brand of choice in his home. "Ida likes it," he concluded. "My girls like it. So it must be good. And I believe that if I drank coffee, I'd drink Chase and Sanborn's."

The new slant — truthfulness — was so popular that other advertisers picked up on the trend of telling the plain truth about their products. Cantor's coffee pitch worked so well that a group of South American coffee growers approached Eddie with an offer to manufacture his own brand, "Eddie Cantor Coffee." Although flattered, Cantor turned the men down, citing a conflict of interest with his current sponsors.

As Cantor's radio popularity soared, he wisely diversified his show,

**Eddie Cantor in 1933 at the peak of his popularity in this still which plugs his career not only as one of the world's top film stars but as America's top radio draw.**

bringing on other cast members and vocalists. Character actor Lionel Stander was brought aboard briefly to provide the voice for violinist/orchestra leader Rubinoff, who himself was starting to win great popularity from his exposure on the *Chase and Sanborn Hour*. (Cantor liked to tell the story of the night in 1933 when virtuoso Yehudi Menuhin stepped into an elevator at NBC and told the operator of the car to hurry up. "I'm Yehudi Menuhin," he explained, holding up his violin case. "I don't care if you're Rubinoff" was the operator's response.) Other talented radio actors who contributed their talents to Cantor's various shows over the years were Alan Reed, Charlie Cantor, Sid Fields, and Betty Garde.

Rather than feeling threatened by sharing his time slot with supporting comics, Cantor welcomed them to his show and went so far as to play straightman for them. One of Eddie's first guests was Gracie Allen, of Burns and Allen, who had been appearing with Cantor in his and George Jessel's vaudeville tour. One guest who was invited on Cantor's show for one Sunday and wound up staying for over three years was Greek dialect comedian, Parkyakarkus. Cantor discovered "Parky" one day in Boston at a luncheon where Eddie was the guest speaker. Also on the dais was a man introduced as a representative of the Greek Embassy. His talk, although essentially serious in its text, was delivered in a comic Greek dialect which fractured the English language.

"This guy ought to be in show business," Eddie remarked to his neighbor on the dais. "Who is he?"

"He's Harry Einstein," Cantor was told. "He writes advertising copy for the Kane Furniture Company."

After the luncheon, Cantor asked Harry Einstein if he would like to be a guest on next Sunday's *Chase and Sanborn Hour*. Einstein agreed, asking only for his traveling expenses, $50, for the appearance.

That Sunday, Einstein, performing under the name Parkyakarkus, was the hit of the show and an instant celebrity back at the furniture company in Boston. His bosses urged him to go on again next week, a request which brought no argument from Cantor. Again, explaining that he made a good salary with his weekday job, Einstein refused any salary save his expenses. After a few more appearances, Cantor insisted that Einstein be paid $250 a week. Einstein quickly gave up advertising copywriting and settled down to a career in show business as Parkyakarkus.

More often than not Eddie played the straight part to Parkyakarkus' unique brand of broken English and fractured logic. Although Cantor never entirely handed over the show to Parkyakarkus or any of his radio protégés, he wasn't threatened by his stooges getting laughs. If anything, Eddie was every bit as good playing straightman as he was getting the laughs. "The comic who becomes a straightman," he explained to *Variety*, "can be a great straightman — he knows how he'd want to be fed."

Here's a typical Cantor/Parkyakarkus exchange in which they discuss Parky's 1936 campaign for president:

PARKYAKARKUS: I am so mad right now . . . I could not kill myself! Where could I find a lawyer.

CANTOR: Lawyer? You wanna sue somebody?

PARKY: You got the sitzmuation! Look what it's printed in the paper about me: . . . "If Parkyakarkus is elected president, he will ruin the country."

| | |
|---|---|
| CANTOR: | Which newspaper was that in? |
| PARKY: | Mine. |
| CANTOR: | You printed it? |
| PARKY: | I did. |
| CANTOR: | So you're gonna sue yourself for printing those things? |
| PARKY: | Yeah, but I don't worry. |
| CANTOR: | You're not worried? |
| PARKY: | No, I cannot collect. I'm broke! |
| CANTOR: | Parkyakarkus, the next time you order a glass of beer have the bartender put the head on you. |
| PARKY: | Say, yesterday my dog went into a saloon and ordered a glass of beer. |
| CANTOR: | Your dog ordered a glass of beer? |
| PARKY: | Smertainly! He walked up to the bartender and said, "woof, woof." |
| CANTOR: | "Woof, woof?" That's a beer? |
| PARKY: | Well, don't you never hear of "bark beer?" You know when I go out to speak on my campaign I gonna take that dog with me because he is got a very short tail. |
| CANTOR: | What good is a dog with a short tail on a campaign? |
| PARKY: | He could make stump speeches. |

About the same time he was adding new voices, Cantor also made a decided change in the style of comedy featured. Originally, like most of his contemporaries on the ether, Cantor did a program packed with jokes, mostly unrelated to one another or to any identifiable character. As early as October 1932, Eddie told newspaper reporters that radio comedy as such was doomed. "Radio audiences were becoming smarter with each program," Cantor asserted, "and rather than be gagged to death they would just stop dialing in on the people who recited a series of jokes." Instead of a stream of wisecracks and gags, Cantor's show began to build its comedy on recognizable personalities and situations. The character Eddie played was more or less based on his real-life personality.

Despite Eddie Cantor's popularity on the radio, one person who failed to appreciate it was Sam Goldwyn. The film producer was loath to let his star perform weekly over a medium other than film—especially with no remuneration to the producer himself. Cantor, on the other hand, used the radio to promote his films and open up markets in segments of the country which had never seen him perform in person. Eddie's radio career was a prime, if not the main, reason for the eventual split between Goldwyn and Cantor.

Even before Eddie Cantor left Sam Goldwyn, he had already jumped ship on his radio career, leaving Chase and Sanborn and NBC for the more financially lucrative waters of the growing Columbia Broadcasting System. The switch, made in early 1935, landed Cantor in CBS's Sunday 8:00 P.M. time slot under the banner of Pebeco, a toothpaste made by the Lehn and Fink Company. In addition, the program's length was cut from one hour to thirty minutes, which necessitated a change in Eddie's theme lyrics from "I'd love to spend this hour with you" to "I'd love to spend each Sunday with you."[1] The only other difference between his NBC program and the one on

CBS was the substitution of announcer Ted Husing for Jimmy Wallington, who had been working for Chase and Sanborn, not Cantor. Aside from Wallington, who later rejoined Eddie when he became available, the rest of Cantor's growing family of radio regulars, including Dave Rubinoff and Harry Einstein, made the move intact.

Although the shorter format worked well for Cantor and resulted in a better overall quality of material, unfortunately schedule changes, coupled with his curtailed schedule (courtesy of Sam Goldwyn), hurt Eddie's ratings. The schedule, which originally had Cantor in his familiar Sunday 8:00 P.M. slot, was changed early in 1936 to the 7:00 P.M. position. Although the move placed him in direct competition with fellow comedian Jack Benny, Cantor explained that he preferred going up against Benny, rather than Major Bowes and his *Amateur Hour*, which had developed into a ratings sensation in Eddie's departed time slot on NBC.

Still the time change did little to help Cantor's ratings. After winning a 50.2 rating in his last full season for Chase and Sanborn, Cantor's broadcasts for his first (and last) full season for Pebeco managed only a withered 16.1. Although Lehn and Fink also hired Eddie to advise them on their overall radio strategy—one of his first suggestions was that they hire Husing and Rubinoff for his off-season replacement—the company and Cantor were not destined for a long relationship. A year and a half after his initial broadcast for Pebeco, Eddie and his troupe pulled up stakes to move under the Texaco banner for the 1936-37 season, appearing in CBS's 8:30 time slot each Sunday evening.

The new show, *Texaco Town*, featuring Cantor as the imaginary locale's honorary mayor, brought with it a few personnel changes. First, Dave Rubinoff had left the show when it started broadcasting from Hollywood. Preferring to stay in New York, the violinist was replaced first by Louis Gress, then by Jacques Renard and the Texaco Orchestra. The other changes were not subtractions, but additions—two talented youngsters discovered by Eddie, Bobby Breen and Deanna Durbin. Cantor later explained his taking on of the pair of protégés as a sort of repayment to a former mentor of his own.

"In the back of my mind," Cantor wrote in *Take My Life*, "there was always the memory of Gus Edwards and what he had done for so many kids, including me. He'd found talent and given it a chance, and I thought I'd like to do that, too."

Bobby Breen was the first aboard. In late 1935, while still on the air for Pebeco, Cantor decided to audition children in search of one to spotlight on his upcoming Christmas broadcast. One of the children was eight-year-old Breen, who reduced Cantor to tears with his rendition of the song "Santa, Bring My Mommy Back to Me." A few weeks later, with Cantor playing the part of Santa Claus, Bobby repeated his performance on the air, with a similar reaction from the studio audience and listeners across the country. He was immediately signed to a contract. In addition to his singing duties, Breen often played the son Cantor never had.

In this dialogue from *Texaco Town*, Cantor and Breen discuss the Bible:

BREEN:    I did start to read about that [the Bible], Daddy, but those words are so old-fashioned. You know, like the prayers.

CANTOR:    Prayers aren't old-fashioned. After all, prayers are only little messages that we send to heaven.

BREEN:    Oh, now I know why we send them at night.

CANTOR:    Why?

BREEN:    To get cheaper rates.

Soon after his debut as a regular on Cantor's radio show, Bobby Breen signed a contract at RKO pictures, where he became a leading child film star. Breen remained with Eddie Cantor for three years and according to Cantor could have stayed longer except for Breen's brother, Mickey. Bobby had been getting $500 per broadcast, but when Mickey, acting as his brother's negotiator, tried to win an unacceptable list of concessions from "Uncle Eddie" (including Mickey's right of refusal on the songs his brother sang), Cantor simply dropped Bobby Breen.

Deanna Durbin was first brought to Eddie Cantor's attention by Rufus LeMaire, the casting director of Universal Pictures. Universal had already signed Deanna for her first picture, but thought that extra exposure on Cantor's popular radio program would help ensure the success of its new talent.[2] Cantor was still working for Sam Goldwyn at the time, and LeMaire brought the thirteen-year-old Deanna to the United Artists studio for an audition. Even before she had sung a note, Cantor was impressed with Durbin's natural poise and charm. As they were walking across the lot to musical director Alfred Newman's bungalow where the audition was to take place, Deanna slipped her hand into Eddie's and said: "I hope you aren't nervous, Mr. Cantor, because everything's going to be all right. I'm going to be with you."

Deanna's singing impressed Cantor as much as her manner did, and the young operatic-style singer was hired. Deanna's debut coincided with Cantor's premiere broadcast for Texaco. Both were immediate hits. A few months later, when her first feature film, *Three Smart Girls*, was released, Deanna became an overnight sensation in the movies as well. Her films were so popular that they saved Universal from bankruptcy. The combination of her voice and charming personality made Deanna Durbin one of the most popular stars of the late thirties and early forties and won her a special Academy Award presented jointly to her and Mickey Rooney in 1938 for "bringing to the screen the spirit and personification of youth." When she retired from the screen in 1948 to pursue private life, Deanna was the highest-paid female performer in Hollywood.

Despite her sudden stardom, Deanna Durbin never lost her sense of priorities. Eddie liked to recall the time when he was on a personal appearance tour with Deanna during their first season with Texaco. One day the suitcase containing Deanna's only stage dress was stolen from the limousine.

"Deanna, don't cry," Cantor said, trying to console his protégée. "We'll get you another dress."

"But, Uncle Eddie," she sobbed, "it had such lovely ribbons."

The next day Ida took Deanna out and bought her a new stage dress and matching coat. For the rest of the tour, Cantor recounted the dress incident to audiences, adding, "Now, if Deanna keeps working for two more years she can pay off the dress and start working on the coat."

Four years later, when Deanna was one of Hollywood's top stars, she was showing her "Uncle Eddie" around her new Beverly Hills mansion. The tour included closets filled with sumptuous clothes. Finally, she opened one closet door to reveal a solitary outfit—the dress and coat bought for her by Cantor.

"Any time I feel I'm getting too cocky," she explained, "I open this door, Uncle Eddie, and remember the time I had just one stage dress."

Deanna Durbin remained on *Texaco Town* until the spring of 1938, when the demands of her burgeoning film career made it difficult to fulfill her radio obligations. Eddie Cantor threw a small party at which he tore up his contract with Deanna, releasing her exclusively to Universal.

The mix of Eddie Cantor, Parkyakarkus, Deanna Durbin, and Bobby Breen combined to make *Texaco Town* the number one rated show for the 1936-37 radio season and won Cantor a six-year pact with the oil company. Although he was back on top as the most popular radio comedian in America, the 1936 season was not all sunny for Cantor. Towards the end of the year, David Freedman, Cantor's longtime collaborator and gagman, sued his friend and former boss for $250,000 in back salary.

Freedman and Cantor had parted company in 1934 over a salary dispute, which wound up in the New York State Supreme Court. Freedman contended that he and Cantor had made an oral agreement in 1931 under which the comedian would pay the gagman 10 percent of his radio earnings. According to the writer, Cantor had held up his end of the agreement when he was making $2,000 a week, but started balking at the deal when his success had put him in the $10,000 a week salary range. Cantor denied that any contract, written or oral, existed between himself and Freedman and added that at times he had wound up paying the writer up to 18 percent of his own radio salary.

The opening day of the trial, December 7, 1936, featured Freedman on the stand telling how he met his former friend and how Cantor's radio earnings had risen dramatically during the period he was supplying him with jokes. While Cantor was present in court, he made no statement the first day, and as it turned out, he did not have the opportunity to testify at all. The second day of the trial, Freedman's lawyer stood up and announced to the court that his thirty-nine-year-old client had died during the night of a heart attack. After regrets were voiced from Cantor's attorney, the judge declared the case a mistrial. The news of David Freedman's sudden death shocked Eddie Cantor. "It is the most distressing thing I have ever heard of," Cantor told reporters outside the courtroom. "Despite this case, he must have known in his heart that I was his friend."

It was a few months later that Eddie Cantor bid farewell to another integral part of his radio team, though not because of such tragic circumstances. After more than three hit seasons with Cantor, including a supporting role in his last Goldwyn picture, *Strike Me Pink*, Harry Einstein decided that he wasn't making enough money. He broached the subject while on tour with Cantor, who agreed to tear up his stooge's contract at the conclusion of the tour. Cantor then arranged for Einstein's representation through the William Morris Agency. By March 1937, Morris had placed Parkyakarkus on Al Jolson's radio show at twice the money he was making for Cantor. Despite Einstein's jump to Jolson's program, he and Cantor remained friends.

The departure of Parkyakarkus left Eddie Cantor with only announcer James Wallington to participate in comedy skits. To fill in the gap, Cantor turned more and more to guest stars. Whereas in the early days of the *Chase and Sanborn Hour*, guests were all but avoided, a visiting film or radio star had since become the rule, especially since Cantor, now broadcasting from Hollywood, had a readily available talent pool from which to draw. Still, Cantor tried out various other supporting comedians, among them Pinky Tomlin and Helen Troy, before discovering the second coming of Parkyakarkus in Bert Gordon, a.k.a. the "Mad Russian."

The "Mad Russian," like Parkyakarkus before him, specialized in dialect comedy filled with malapropisms and inane logic. Round of face with frightwig hair that predated Marty Allen's coiffure by twenty-five years, Bert Gordon was described by Cantor as a performer with a natural comic delivery, so much so, that he could often deliver a line flawlessly without understanding why it was funny. The "Russian's" favorite introductory line, the thickly accented "How do you do?" quickly became his trademark and a popular catch-phrase across America. Gordon's schtick was described perfectly by his nickname. He was crazy and often drove Cantor slightly nuts in the course of their conversations, and he was Russian, so he usually worked in jokes about the repressive conditions then existing in Soviet Russia.

One week, when the guest star was opera singer Lawrence Tibbett, he and the "Mad Russian" had this exchange:

RUSSIAN: Lawrence Kibbuts, I was an opera singer in Russia. It was there I developed my nose. In Russia you sing only through your nose.
TIBBETT: Through your nose? Why?
RUSSIAN: In Russia, you can open your mouth?

Bert Gordon remained with Cantor through more than ten seasons, appearing almost every week. During World War II when the Soviet Union suddenly became an ally of the United States, the anticommunist jokes were toned down, but the Russian remained as mad as ever. In one broadcast from March Field airbase during the war, the Russian turned up as the valet of the base commander and put a plug in for the government's scrap rubber drive:

RUSSIAN:    I sent my wife's rubber bathing suit to the government and I hope they don't send it back.
CANTOR:    Why, Russian?
RUSSIAN:    My wife's in it.

Another time during the war, Cantor and announcer Harry Von Zell ran into the Russian down at Union Station:

RUSSIAN:    How do you do!
CANTOR:    Russian, what are you doing here?
RUSSIAN:    I am a travel agent. In fact, traveling is mine hobo.
CANTOR:    You don't mean "hobo," you mean "hobby."
RUSSIAN:    You travel on your salary, I'll travel on mine.
CANTOR:    Have you ever arranged a trip for anyone else?
RUSSIAN:    Yes. I was on a train for eight days with Hedy Lamarr going to San Francisco.
VON ZELL:    On a train with Hedy Lamarr eight days? You should have got there in one day.
RUSSIAN:    Ah-hah. I was so disappointed!

Despite their high ratings, in late 1937 *Texaco Town* and its residents moved from Sunday evenings to Wednesdays at 8:30 P.M. in an attempt to get away from NBC's new Chase and Sanborn lineup of W. C. Fields and Edgar Bergen and Charlie McCarthy. The move, the first for Cantor away from Sunday night, resulted in lower ratings. Six months later Cantor decided to make a move of his own and relocated himself and his cast out of *Texaco Town* altogether. Walking away from his long-term contract with the oil company, Eddie signed on with R. J. Reynolds' Camel cigarettes for $15,000 a week. The total sum was paid to Cantor, who in turn was responsible for the salaries of his cast members and staff. The one-year contract called for thirty-nine weekly programs, with a thirteen-week layoff between the end of June and the beginning of October.

Joining Eddie on the Camel program were Bert Gordon and Deanna Durbin, with newcomers Edgar "Cookie" Fairchild and his orchestra and Walter Woolf King as the announcer. Although King was primarily an actor— appearing as the villain in a number of comedies starring Laurel and Hardy and the Marx Brothers—his excellent diction and fine singing voice made him a versatile addition to replace Jimmy Wallington. Broadcast on Monday nights at 7:30, Cantor's Camel shows earned the lowest ratings of his career, though they were still good enough to keep him among radio's most popular stars.

While Camel was paying Cantor handsomely for his weekly program, there was trouble brewing between the star and his sponsor. As explained earlier, time slots for radio programs were bought in blocks by sponsors who were then responsible for providing the show. Under this system, stars became strongly identified with the products they appeared for and often participated in the radio commercials and related print ads. With such a close bond between talent and products, sponsors were hypersensitive to any material which might be construed as off-color or controversial. Fearing an audience/consumer backlash from any froward program content, sponsors carefully scrutinized scripts in search of any material which might be offensive.

Cantor's first dispute with Camel cigarettes arose over a remark that Eddie had planned to use in the 1938 Thanksgiving show. Known since the early days of the *Chase and Sanborn Hour* for making short speeches of a more serious nature, Cantor decided to use Thanksgiving to comment on the volatile situation in Europe. With Hitler and Mussolini slicing off smaller neighbors seemingly at will, Eddie wanted to say that it was "wonderful to live in a country where on a day like this the leader of the nation sits down to carve up a turkey, instead of a map." The remark, though clever and obviously true, set off alarms at R. J. Reynolds' advertising agency (William Esty). Afraid of offending isolationists and pro–Nazi elements, the agency banned the comments with the explanation that "some people mightn't like that."

Ironically, Eddie's comments became even more widely publicized as a result of their being banned. With his feelings censored from the air, Cantor set them down in a personal Thanksgiving telegram to President Roosevelt. Roosevelt was so delighted by the observation that he repeated Cantor's remarks, quickly turning them into front-page news.

Although Cantor's remarks to Roosevelt were quickly vindicated, the comedian was soon involved in other controversies which proved to be the straws which broke Camel's back. Eddie's troubles started anew on March 27, 1939, after his weekly show. As was often his custom, Cantor was entertaining his studio audience with some informal post-air jokes aimed at one of his favorite targets of ridicule: Adoph Hitler. In the middle of Cantor's fictitious dialogue between Hitler and a rabbi, Charles Gollob, a naturalized American citizen originally from Austria, rose from the back of the audience and started heckling Eddie.

"He yelled at the top of his lung," Cantor told reporters, "giving me the raspberry. He shouted: 'I'll fix that Jewish so-and-so!'" When other members of the audience told Gollob to be quiet, the heckler left with his wife. "I didn't want to hear any more propaganda," Gollob later explained.

A few minutes later, outside CBS's Hollywood studios, Gollob and his wife were beaten by three (or four according to differing reports) men, who were described as "Cantor admirers." Gollob, who suffered a split lip to go with his wife's bruised jaw, contended that one of his assailants was Bert "The Mad Russian" Gordon.

"My jokes about Hitler and Nazism aren't any different than jokes I've made about other people prominent in the public eye—like Roosevelt and Hoover, for instance," Cantor said, defending the remarks which set off the incident. "But the man's rudeness does not call for a beating. A man is entitled to say whatever he pleases. But when a man and his wife come into a theater as my guests and start a disturbance, that isn't quite cricket."

Cantor also denied that Bert Gordon was involved in the beatings, alibiing that the "Russian" was sitting backstage in his dressing room throughout the entire incident. Nothing came of the charges about Gordon, and no further direct involvement of Cantor or any of his staff was proven.

While Eddie Cantor may have insisted that his anti–Nazi humor was as innocent as similar pokes at American politicians, this was clearly not the case. Cantor was well known for his efforts to rescue children from Germany and Eastern Europe, efforts which earned him death threats from Nazi sympathizers. Still, while controversial, none of his words or actions had as yet proven too hot for his sponsors too handle — that is until June 13, 1939. That day, at the Temple of Religion pavilion at the New York World's Fair, Eddie and Ida were the honored guests of the New York chapter of the Hadassah. The Cantors, who had celebrated their twenty-fifth wedding anniversary four days earlier, were presented with a cake, after which Eddie was to speak.

When he stepped up to the microphone, Cantor unleashed a hard-hitting attack on those he considered "the enemy within." Singled out in the speech was renegade radio priest/demagogue Father Charles E. Coughlin, whom Cantor accused of "playing footsie with the Nazis." Throughout the thirties Coughlin had maintained a huge listening audience. He appeared initially on CBS, but then on an even larger network of independent stations after CBS refused to renew his contract in 1933. Increasingly controversial as the decade wore on, in 1934 Coughlin founded the National Union for Social Justice, which espoused a mixture of vague social programs and a heavy dose of anti–Semitism. In 1936, after denouncing FDR as a "scab president," Father Coughlin ran his own candidate for the chief executive under the banner of the "Union Party." Eventually Coughlin's rancorous broadcasts started to lose him his base of support, while earning him rebukes from the hierarchy of the Catholic church.

Despite Coughlin's then dwindling influence, Cantor's attack from the Temple of Religion on the priest and other negative influences (such as the German-American Bund, a homegrown Nazi organization) were still viewed as extremely controversial by R. J. Reynolds and its advertising agency. In *Take My Life*, Cantor defended his speech as one that had to be made. "The American public knows the enemies without," Cantor wrote. "Why shouldn't they know the enemies within?" Unfortunately for Eddie, R. J. Reynolds didn't view pro–Nazi and anti–Semitic elements as potential enemies, only potential smokers. Cantor's contract, which was up for renewal at the end of June, was dropped, leaving the comedian without a sponsor. Prospective sponsors failed to sign Cantor because he was branded "too controversial."[3]

Although Cantor in his autobiography states that he did not work in radio for the next year, this is not entirely true. While Eddie was branded as a pariah by permanent sponsors, he did make several guest appearances on other shows. The most notable was a New Year's Eve spot on the *Gulf Screen Guild Theatre* program, in which Cantor's entire routine revolved around his currently being sponsorless. The skit supposedly originated from the Cantor home, with Bea Benadaret playing Ida, along with a bevy of actresses impersonating the five girls.

1ST GIRL:     Mama, how about some butter?
IDA:           How many times have I told you girls we can't have butter until your father gets a sponsor?
2D GIRL:     You mean we're gonna grow up without butter?
CANTOR:     You should have thought of that when you kids voted for Jack Benny in the popularity poll. Do you know where *I* should have been on that poll?
3D GIRL:     Hey, Pop, you're leaving yourself wide open.
1ST GIRL:     As official representative of Local 802 of the Cantor girls . . . when are you going to get a job?
CANTOR:     Ida, I refuse to have the children talk to me like that.
IDA:           Your father's right, children . . . how many times have I told you—never kick a man when he's down!
CANTOR:     Who's down!! I've never done better in my life. . . . Why . . .
(Knock on door)
CANTOR:     I'll open it.
(Door opening)
MAN:         Eddie Cantor!
CANTOR:     Yes.
MAN:         I'm from the Salvation Army. You did a benefit for us last year, didn't you?
CANTOR:     Yes.
MAN:         Well—we've come to reciprocate. Here's a basket.

Although he missed the entire 1939-40 radio season, the following autumn Eddie was back on the air with his own show, a feat which he attributes to his friend and neighbor, Jack Benny. "More than anyone," Cantor remembered, "Jack understood how depressed I was, an entertainer without an audience, a citizen who loved his country chastised for using the freedom of speech with which he'd meant to help her."

According to Cantor, one night the top-rated Benny placed a call to the president of the Young and Rubicam agency in New York and demanded that Eddie Cantor deserved another radio show. Jack contended that Eddie should not be punished for saying what most others were thinking, but hadn't the guts to say. With the door opened by Jack Benny, by the end of May 1940, Cantor had negotiated his return to the regular network schedule with Young and Rubicam. Beginning in the fall, Cantor would appear weekly under the sponsorship of Bristol Myers, or rather two of their products, Ipana (a toothpaste) and Sal Hepatica (a laxative). The program, which was slated for the Wednesday 9:00–9:30 P.M. slot on the NBC red network, was titled *Time to Smile*, a reference not only to Cantor's material, but more specifically to the products advertised ("Ipana, for the smile of beauty; Sal Hepatica, for the smile of health").

Cantor's new radio deal called for a guaranteed $10,000 per week over the course of thirty-nine weeks, plus a bonus if his ratings for the season surpassed 20 points. For each additional rating point over 20, Eddie would receive $2,000, with a lump sum award of $39,000 if he exceeded 25 points.

In the six years beginning with the 1940-41 radio season, Cantor never achieved a rating over 25, although he managed to top 20 three times, and was again a consistent favorite with radio audiences. Another stipulation in the comedian's contract called for the careful inspection of scripts by the sponsor. The provision was obviously designed to head off any remarks which might be construed as controversial. Paradoxically, once Eddie was back on the air, many of the stands which had made him controversial in the first place were no longer considered dubious. His anti–Nazi remarks were now in the mainstream of opinion since Hitler had invaded Poland, launching World War II, and Father Coughlin, after years of alienating larger and larger segments of his radio audience, had been forced to halt his broadcasts in 1940 due to dwindling financial support.

Joining Eddie Cantor on his return to the air were veteran announcer Harry Von Zell (best remembered for similar chores for the Burns and Allen television program) and Bert Gordon as the "Mad Russian." Initially, Bobby Sherwood provided musical direction, although he would eventually be replaced by Edgar "Cookie" Fairchild. *Time to Smile* was scheduled in the slot vacated by Fred Allen's popular program. Unfortunately, Allen had jumped to the same night and time on CBS, providing stiff competition for Cantor.

In an attempt to combat Fred Allen, Cantor decided to start auditioning for a new female singer, one who would perhaps give the program a ratings boost similar to that provided by Deanna Durbin back on the *Texaco Town* show. According to Cantor, he auditioned between eighteen and twenty vocalists with his back to them in order to choose the best voice, without regard to the auditioner's physical charm or beauty. "So, I'm listening this day," Cantor continued, "and all of a sudden there's a voice that I can say is the most natural feminine singing voice I've ever heard since Nora Bayes, a gal singing not because she's being paid for it — she'd pay you — but because she loves it." Cantor immediately knew he'd found his new female vocalist, but he let the girl, who was named Dinah Shore, keep singing. "Someday we'll pay a terrific cover charge to hear this girl," he told producer Vic Knight. "Let's enjoy it just this once for nothing."

Listening to Dinah Shore did not remain a "free" pleasure for long; the singer was signed to a two-year contract at $200 per week. Out of this salary, Dinah had to pay two commissions, one to her agent, General Amusement Corporation, and the second to the NBC's artist bureau. When the first option on her contract came due in March 1941, Dinah Shore, claiming that she had not been notified that her option had been picked up, bolted from Cantor's employ and signed a $750 a week deal to appear on the Chase and Sanborn program. Cantor quickly cried foul, contending that his secretary had notified Shore a full day before her option was up. The case went to the arbitration board of the American Federation of Radio Actors, which found in Cantor's favor, and Dinah Shore remained part of the *Time to Smile* family. In Dinah's favor, the board also ruled against the double commissions she had been paying; in addition Cantor also gave his latest protégée a substantial bonus and promised to include her in his next picture (*Thank Your Lucky Stars*). The relationship between Cantor and Shore was quickly healed, with both performers expressing their admiration for the other.

Dinah Shore's debut on the inaugural broadcast of *Time to Smile* was a great hit. In fact the whole program went over well. *Variety* made the following comments about the October 2, 1940, premiere broadcast:

> Eddie Cantor has come back to radio, after a season's layoff, with a combination that seemingly can't miss. Cantor's comedy is standard as ever, but his new brand of gags are more fresh and crisp. Resourceful showman that he usually is, Cantor stepped out for the first time under the Bristol-Meyers banner last Wednesday with a cornucopia of sock entertainment. Cantor not only glutted the air with laughs but he so projected Dinah Shore that listeners got an entirely new vista of this girl's singing talents. Judging from her performance on that broadcast, Miss Shore stacks up as radio's new vocal sensation.[4]

Some of the bits used on that first show included a typical, yet very funny, routine between Cantor and announcer Harry Von Zell regarding Eddie's age. To prove that he isn't as old as Von Zell would lead the audience to believe, Cantor calls up the birth certificate bureau in an attempt to verify his age. The clerk at the bureau chides Eddie for not having sent them any business in over twelve years.

"You wouldn't want to lose your merit badge, would you?" The clerk asks. After some searching the clerk finds a birth notice for Eddie.

"Here's your record," the clerk announces. "Weight: two pounds, two ounces. . . . I'm surprised the game warden let 'em keep you. Description: two big black eyes—that's all."

When Eddie asks for a copy of his birth certificate, the clerk informs him that it isn't there, but in the National Archives in Washington, D.C.

"What's it doing down there?" Cantor asks.

"Lincoln wrote his Gettysburg Address on the back of it," informs the clerk.

Although the ratings of the first season of *Time to Smile* represented the weakest in Cantor's radio career to date, in subsequent seasons the program rebounded to again make its star one of the air's top comedians. It was during the show's second season that the United States was plunged into World War II. Cantor, like most of the entertainment industry, responded by filling his programs with topical military jokes and patriotic appeals designed to boost morale. In addition, many of his *Time to Smile* broadcasts originated from southern California military bases, such as Riverside's March Field and the marine base at San Diego. While Cantor's anti–Nazi, anti–Japanese bits drew strong laughs from his G.I. audiences, it was usually the appearance of Dinah Shore that elicited the most appreciative response from the servicemen. In addition to the change in material and location, the war also brought a change in Cantor's usual charitable appeals and contests. The USO, Army Relief, and his own "Give a Gift to the Yank Who Gave" appeal were heavily promoted causes, while Eddie's radio contests, a regular feature for years, changed from essays on current affairs to searches for the "typical G.I. Joe."

*Time to Smile*, as were Cantor's previous radio shows, was scripted by a team of gagmen supervised by Eddie himself. Included on Cantor's writing staff in the early forties were John Rapp, Joe Quillan, Izzy Ellison, Carl Forman, Charles Marion, and Paul Conlon, among others. The production of a weekly radio show, coupled with Cantor's personal appearances, films, and numerous guest shots on other programs (which averaged two per month), made the comedian's schedule hectic to say the least.

Thanks to strong writing, a solid cast, and the ever present energy of Eddie Cantor, *Time to Smile* continued to land in the top fifteen radio shows. After attaining star status under Cantor's banner, Dinah Shore left when her contract expired to star in her own program. She was replaced by Nora Martin, who in addition to her radio duties, also appeared on tour with Cantor and in the film *Hollywood Canteen*. When Nora Martin left at the close of the 1944-45 season, she in turn was replaced by Thelma Carpenter. The signing of Thelma Carpenter marked the first use of a black woman singer as a regular on a network show. Before her debut, *Time* magazine called Cantor and asked what he was trying to prove in hiring Thelma. Cantor replied that he wasn't trying to prove anything, other than that Thelma was a talented vocalist. The magazine then asked if Eddie was going to introduce her as a "colored singer." "I don't remember having introduced Dinah Shore as a white singer," Cantor replied, and the issue was dropped.

At the end of the 1945-46 season, after six years on the air for Ipana and Sal Hepatica, Eddie Cantor announced that he was making a switch in sponsorship to Pabst Blue Ribbon Beer. As initially reported by *Variety*, the change was not to take place until the fall of 1947 and would necessitate a jump back to CBS. It turned out, however, that Cantor and his regulars would begin for Pabst in the fall of 1946, still on NBC but in their Thursday 10:30 P.M. to 11:00 P.M. time period, following Abbott and Costello. The agreement with the brewer also called for a near-record $20,000 per week for Cantor, along with total control over the program's content aside from the commercials (a concession which he had won a few years back in his Bristol Meyers contract). Aside from his thirty-nine yearly radio appearances for the beer, Cantor also served as the brew's goodwill ambassador, making personal appearances and posing for a series of colorful print ads.

The Pabst show, which saw Cantor's radio ratings dip—probably because of the late time slot, coupled with the increasing popularity of television—featured familiar regulars Harry Von Zell, Cookie Fairchild and his orchestra, and vocalist Margaret Whiting, as well as frequent appearances from Bert Gordon as the "Mad Russian." The *Pabst Blue Ribbon–Eddie Cantor Show* managed to maintain the high level of comedy and zest that had made Eddie a radio staple, as a sample from the 1947 season illustrates:

(Telephone rings)
CANTOR:  (on phone) Is-is this the B-Beverly Hills police station?

COP: Yes. Sgt. Mulvaney speaking.
CANTOR: Sergeant, this is Eddie C-c-cantor.
COP: Yes, Mr. Cantor.
CANTOR: I got a letter. Somebody threatened to kill me. What should I do?
COP: Move to Glendale! We don't allow any murders in Beverly Hills.
CANTOR: Look! I'm a citizen of Beverly Hills. I own property in Beverly Hills. Pay taxes in Beverly Hills. I got a right to be murdered in Beverly Hills. I demand protection! I'm a big radio star. You've got to find out who sent me a threatening letter.
COP: Mr. Cantor, how many people listen to your program?
CANTOR: About fifteen million.
COP: That's amazing!
CANTOR: That so many people listen to me?
COP: No, that you only got one threatening letter.

After two years in NBC's Thursday night lineup, Cantor and Pabst moved to Fridays at 9:00 P.M. for 1948-49, the show's third and final season. By 1949, television was clearly the wave of the future, although as of yet few major film and radio stars had moved to the small screen. With his ratings for the 1948-49 season the lowest ever (12.2), Eddie Cantor decided a change of format was in order. After seventeen years of following essentially the same pattern each week, Cantor decided to part company with Pabst and begin doing a quiz show.

*Take It or Leave It*, sponsored by Eversharp-Schick razors, was an established program when Eddie Cantor became its host. Heard over NBC on Sunday night at 10 o'clock, the popular program had been the first quiz show to break into radio's top ten. The game itself, which popularized the phrase "the 64-dollar question," was a simple quiz conducted within a variety of categories. Questioning began at the $1 level and doubled—providing contestants furnished the correct answers—until the grand prize level of $64 was reached. At the end of the show, contestants were given the opportunity to answer a "jackpot question" worth considerably more money.

The main appeal of *Take It or Leave It* was the host chatting with each contestant before quizzing them. In addition, with Cantor hosting, each program began with Eddie singing a song, backed up by Cookie Fairchild and his orchestra. Also included were Cantor's usual appeals for various charities and his familiar theme, "One Hour with You." Like Groucho Marx's *You Bet Your Life*, which had premiered a few years earlier, Cantor's prepared "ad-lib" remarks usually were prompted by contestants' unusual backgrounds or occupations. Witness this exchange from March 1950:

CANTOR: What do you do for a living?
GIRL: I'm a cigarette girl at the Mocambo.
CANTOR: Really? How does it feel to be standing up here without your satin panties?
GIRL: Mr. Cantor, did you ever work at the Mocambo?
CANTOR: To tell you the truth, one night when I got my check there I thought I'd have to!

**Cantor with actress Irene Ryan at the end of his radio career.**

  After one season of *Take It or Leave It*, Eddie Cantor left it, effectively firing his sponsor in order to concentrate on his premiere season on NBC-TV's *Colgate Comedy Hour*. With one year of television successfully under his belt, however, Eddie returned to radio in yet another format. With more and more of the traditional situation comedy and variety programs switching over to TV, radio was quickly becoming more musically oriented, with an increasing number of record shows presided over by disc jockeys. For three seasons beginning in 1951-52, Cantor joined the ranks of the record spinners with a half hour program devoted to music and nostalgic monologues. Heard over NBC—Sundays at 9:30 P.M. for the first year and Thursdays at the same time in the two succeeding seasons—the program underwent three title changes from *The Philip Morris–Eddie Cantor Program* to *The Eddie Cantor Record Show* to *Eddie Cantor: Records and Reminiscences.* As its title suggests, the first year's show was sponsored by Philip Morris; subsequent seasons were sponsored by an assortment of advertisers on a syndicated basis.

Eddie's disc jockey shows were written by Joe Franklin. Now himself a show business institution after more than forty years as host of his *Memory Lane* radio and television programs, the Cantor program represented Franklin's first show business job. The impetus for the program was a segment entitled "Ask Eddie Cantor" in which the comedian answered mail pertaining to various show business luminaries.

Although the letters were supposedly sent in by listeners, it was actually Joe Franklin who was doing all the asking. "I used to create questions allegedly sent in by listeners," Joe recalled. "I would create four, five, or six questions every week. I'd make them up myself. Each one would be accompanied by him answering a question, then playing a phonograph record by that person."

After having worked with large writing staffs, employing a one-man crew proved both economical and profitable for all concerned. Joe Franklin explains: "Philip Morris was paying Eddie five thousand a week. He used to give me five hundred a week, which in those days when I was a kid was unbelievable money. I used to give my girlfriend, who later on became my wife, fifty dollars a week to go to the library and do the research for me. So, I made four hundred fifty dollars a week for just doing nothing. I was a pretty good young entrepreneur in those days."

Eddie's long association with NBC radio ended concurrently with his departure from that network's television division. With the signing of his multimillion dollar TV deal with the Ziv company, Cantor's exclusive radio services were also obtained. Although they were not given as much attention as his half-hour TV plays, the comedian also made a series of short radio programs for Ziv. The shows were not widely circulated, however, and of course were stopped when Eddie bolted from his TV deal with the syndication company in 1955.

Eddie Cantor's last regular contribution to the airwaves came six years later in another package of programs syndicated to over one hundred radio stations nationwide. Reviving the "Ask Eddie Cantor" format, these shows were heard weekdays, running five minutes in length per episode. Like the longer format, the programs, which were heard in 1961, relied solely on brief reminiscences of contemporaries and luminaries from Eddie's long show business history. Many of the recollections from this last series were included, along with various Cantor magazine articles, in Eddie Cantor's last literary effort, *As I Remember Them* (Duell, Sloan and Pearce, 1963). The show, produced in the comedian's sixty-ninth year, thirty years after his first radio series premiere on the *Chase and Sanborn Hour*, represented Eddie Cantor's final foray into the medium which he had an integral part in pioneering.

## *Notes*

1. The song was altered throughout Cantor's broadcasting career, sometimes changing "one hour" to the day of the broadcast, "Sunday" or "Wednesday"; other times it just became "these moments."

2. Deanna Durbin had come to Universal via MGM, where she appeared in a short film with another young singer, Judy Garland. After viewing the short, MGM decided to keep Garland and drop Durbin.

3. According to Cantor's account of the incident, the reaction of the public and R. J. Reynolds was swift and widespread: "That night's headlines read: Comedian Blasts Priest. The next day, my thirty-nine week radio program is canceled." Although it makes Cantor's brave speech all the more dramatic, there is no corroborating account of the speech in the *New York Times* (which at the time was devoting almost two pages exclusively to news of the World's Fair) or in the *Washington Post*. *Variety* makes two mentions of Cantor's radio contract: one on June 21, which states that R. J. Reynolds was stalling on the renewal of Cantor's contract, and a second, one week later, when it was announced that Camel had declined to exercise its option on Cantor, though no reason for the decision was given. In any case, Eddie finished out his current contract, making his last broadcast for the tobacco company on June 28, 1939.

4. Although Eddie Cantor is generally credited with discovering Dinah Shore, she had previously sung with Ben Bernie's orchestra, though, as this review points out, not nearly as successfully.

# CHAPTER 42

# *Television*

Contrary to popular misconception, the first television did not appear all of a sudden after World War II with Milton Berle jumping out of it. The medium had been in development since the late twenties. Frequently throughout the thirties, *Variety* proclaimed in banner headlines that television was only a year or two off. Fortunately for the great number of performers who made their living off radio (along with the millions who enjoyed the unique qualities radio delivered in its "golden age"), the premiere of network television was postponed, first by the depression, then by World War II.

As early as 1936, Cantor told the *New York Times* he was preparing for the eventuality of television, confident that the new medium would have a place for him. "Television will not be such a revolutionary change for the actor with stage and screen experience," Eddie said, "but it will be a hard taskmaster for those radio artists whose personalities have remained hidden behind the unseeing 'mike.'" In preparation for the advent of television, Eddie announced that starting the following season he would begin memorizing his radio lines, rather than relying on a hand-held script, a resolution he did not keep. Cantor went on to predict, and quite accurately, that the widespread popularity of TV would cause comedians to use up their material at an alarming rate.

While Eddie Cantor was not the first star to test out the medium of television, he does hold the distinction of being one of the first pulled from the video box by network censors. The incident in question took place May 25, 1944, during the first practical intercity chain telecast between New York and Philadelphia. Cantor, along with Nora Martin, was scheduled to sing "We're Having a Baby," from *Banjo Eyes*. The night of the broadcast NBC censors called attention to the song's second chorus and notified Cantor that the lyrics were objectionable.

Cantor cited the fact that he had not only performed the song numerous times on Broadway and on the radio (over NBC), but he would film the number with Martin for the upcoming film, *Hollywood Canteen*. Eddie went on to point out that he was doing the broadcast for free and was rushing back to

New York from an army benefit on Long Island to perform the bit. The manager of NBC television, John T. Williams, asked Cantor simply to repeat the song's first verse, but Eddie refused, saying it was "silly and unshowmanly."

That night during the live telecast Cantor and Nora Martin performed the song as they had rehearsed it. At the beginning of the second verse, NBC censors turned off the sound and threw the picture out of focus. The lyrics, which NBC thought "dirty" and Cantor defended as "cute," refer to the pregnant condition of Nora Martin's character.

The incident was complicated by complaints from the Canadian Broadcasting Company, which was simulcasting the audio portion of the program. A few weeks later, when NBC censored one of Cantor's radio guest stars (Joe Besser doing his "sissy" character), Eddie threatened to quit the network all together. Eventually cooler heads prevailed, and Cantor remained with NBC.

Despite his initial experience with television, Eddie Cantor was convinced of the potential of the medium. When almost all programs were broadcast live, Cantor, unlike many of his radio contemporaries like George Burns and George Jessel, saw the future of TV would be in filmed shows carefully timed and edited. While filmed shows as the norm were still a few years off, the practice eventually became the rule rather than the exception.

Another more immediate need in television which Cantor perceived was showmanship. "On radio, we used to just sound stupid," Cantor wrote in *Variety* in 1948, "now we can look stupid, too!" Eddie went on to explain that too much of television was amateurish: "No actor has a right to be televised unless he is properly made up—rehearsed—and fully prepared for it." Television, in Cantor's opinion, was too important not to be approached professionally. "The novelty alone," he wrote, "no longer suffices. Television is such a big thing that just anything is not good enough."

While Eddie Cantor realized the importance of television and its need for quality programs, still, he was cautious not to jump to video before the time was right. Although Eddie Cantor might have been ready, he believed the audience was not there yet in sufficient numbers to warrant the effort. "Right now," Cantor said in 1949, "in this great big United States of ours I do not believe there are more than 1,200,000 sets. If there were five viewers for each set, you have an audience of 6,000,000. Is that good?"

# THE COLGATE COMEDY HOUR

By 1950, thanks to such programs as Milton Berle's *Texaco Star Theater*, the number of TV sets in the U.S. had risen to almost four million, giving Eddie Cantor a potential audience size more to his liking. Still, Cantor was reluctant to commit to a weekly television show, contending that such an undertaking, no matter how successful it might be initially, would be impossible to sustain. "Television is slow death to the comedian who goes on week after week." Cantor wrote in his second autobiography. "It exhausts his material, his body, his soul, and, alas, his audience."

To alleviate the problem of overexposure on the new medium and still appear on a regularly scheduled basis, Eddie Cantor approached NBC with the idea for a rotating format. Under Cantor's plan, he proposed to do a show once every four weeks, with the other three weeks being filled by other comics. This format would not only enable Cantor (and the other comics in the rotation) ample time to prepare each show, but would allow Eddie to continue doing his weekly radio broadcasts, various charity performances, and one-man shows.

NBC accepted Cantor's plan, and under the sponsorship of the Colgate-Palmolive-Peet Company, the *Colgate Comedy Hour* was born. Originally, the stars were Cantor, followed in successive weeks by Dean Martin and Jerry Lewis, Fred Allen, and Bobby Clark. For various reasons this schedule changed often, with Abbott and Costello, Bob Hope, Donald O'Conner, Jimmy Durante, Ben Blue, and Danny Thomas all signing on for at least some shows. The mainstays of the *Comedy Hour*, however, were Cantor, Martin and Lewis, and Abbott and Costello.

As great an opportunity as the *Colgate Comedy Hour* afforded Eddie Cantor, it unfortunately robbed him of a chance to preserve for posterity some of his greatest Broadway roles. After the contracts with Colgate-Palmolive-Peet had been inked, but prior to the first broadcast, Cantor was approached by Procter and Gamble to recreate *Whoopee* and *Banjo Eyes* on separate telecasts of their *Musical Comedy Theatre* program. Cantor agreed, but was forced to withdraw from the planned shows when Colgate balked at having one of its stars performing under the banner of a rival soap producer. Although Colgate's stance is clearly understandable, it did kill the last chance for a recorded version of *Banjo Eyes*.

While Cantor was denied the opportunity to do a full treatment of *Banjo Eyes* on television, he did manage to work two of the show's more successful bits, the army camp scene and the "We're Having a Baby" number, into his first episode on the *Colgate Comedy Hour*.

The *Comedy Hour* premiered live from New York on Sunday evening, September 10, 1950, in NBC's 8:00–9:00 P.M. time slot. Cantor opened the show addressing a mock banquet of Colgate executives, explaining the show's format before seguing into a production number featuring stars from a handful of Broadway's current top musicals. Aside from the medley of Broadway's recent successes, most of the show was given over to nostalgic reprises from Cantor's own career, with the highlights including the aforementioned bits from *Banjo Eyes*, and, of course, a minstrel show finale allowing Eddie to don blackface and skip through a pastiche of his old standards.

Probably the most effective number of the program was the "Joe's Blue Front" skit from *Midnight Rounders* and *Make It Snappy*. Joining Cantor in the classic bit was Lew Hearn, who had worked the routine with Eddie in both shows. Ironically, the previous year Cantor and Hearn had feuded publicly after Hearn had performed the skit on the *Texaco Star Theater* program. After that telecast, Cantor protested that he had written the bit and accused Hearn of stealing his material. Hearn insisted that he had written the routine and had been performing it for years. Cantor countered that Hearn's claim was the height of ingratitude and that he had only allowed Hearn to use the bit over the years as an act of friendship. Such disputes over the authorship and ownership of various vaudeville routines were, well, routine.

Cantor's premiere on the *Comedy Hour* was a sensation, handily beating his competition on CBS, Ed Sullivan's *Toast of the Town*. Reviews were enthusiastic, with *Variety* hailing Eddie as a "TV Natural." The rave notices were not all that surprising, although many show business mavens speculated that Cantor would be good for one top notch show, after which the demand for new material and less nostalgia would prove his undoing. The skeptics were silenced, however, after Eddie's second appearance on the *Comedy Hour* the following month, which was even better received than his first. While the first show had relied heavily on routines from Cantor's past successes, the second show, aside from the songs, included all fresh material. The hit of the second telecast was Eddie's "Maxie the Taxi" routine, a bit in which Cantor played a loquacious hack driver who exchanged quips and observations with his fares.

"Maxie the Taxi" proved so successful that almost every future Cantor appearance on the *Comedy Hour* would include a ride in Maxie's cab. The regular use of "Maxie the Taxi" not only assured the show of a character with proven audience appeal, but it allowed Eddie at least one opportunity each show to relax a little from his usual frantic pace. Usually scheduled in the middle of the show, the bit, in Cantor's words, "eased the hour strain."

While "Maxi the Taxi" was a fresh bit for television viewers, it actually was close to thirty years old. The character was first introduced in *Make It Snappy*, a fact which came in handy when a New York cab driver sued Cantor for $2,225,000. The cabbie claimed that "Maxie" had been his invention back in 1949 when he submitted the idea to a New York advertising agency. Although the idea, which was written in book form, had never been published, the cabbie accused Cantor of reading it through "some devious means." The suit was eventually thrown out of court, and Cantor and his codefendants NBC, Colgate-Palmolive-Peet, and the ad agency were all cleared. Eddie's only comment on the suit came in the form of a question. "When you give a taxi driver a million bucks," he wondered in the event that he might lose, "how big should the tip be?"

Other regular features of Eddie's stints on the *Comedy Hour* included Al Goodman and his orchestra (a vital part, given Cantor's heavy emphasis on musical numbers and guest vocalists; radio regular Charlie Cantor, who often appeared along with Eddie in drag in a series of housewife skits; longtime foil Sid Fields; and various female vocalists, the most frequent of whom was Connie Russell. Even though Cantor had worked for so many years in radio with orchestra leader "Cookie" Fairchild, Al Goodman was no stranger to Eddie; he had conducted the orchestra during his run in *Canary Cottage* back in 1916.

Another frequent guest on the *Comedy Hour* was Eddie Cantor's latest protégé — Eddie Fisher. Cantor had first realized the young singer's potential when he heard Fisher perform at Grossinger's in the Catskills in 1949. At first Cantor had been reluctant even to listen to Fisher, but after hearing the audience response one night to the other Eddie, he immediately took him under his wing. After a cross-country tour with Cantor and his road-show (at the end of which Fisher cracked up Cantor's car), Cantor helped get his latest find established in the big time. Eddie Fisher remained loyal to his "mentor." Even after becoming a major recording and television star, he made regular appearances on Cantor's programs.

Eddie Cantor finished up his first season on the *Comedy Hour* in June 1951, after a dozen shows. While not all the shows were as successful as the first two, they were all immensely popular, with the series earning an overall 42.0 rating for the year, making it the fifth most popular television show in America.

Following his final show of his premiere season, Cantor compared television to the other mediums he had worked in for a column in *Variety*. Whereas radio lines could be read from scripts, television required the weekly memorization of up to seventy-five pages of dialogue. In addition, Eddie noted that a sixty-minute show took up to sixty hours of preparation, almost the amount of time it took to mount the long-running *Whoopee*. "There's no doubt about it," Cantor surmised. "Television is the orneriest ogre, the meanest monster and the toughest taskmaster of them all . . . but I LIKE IT!"

Eddie Cantor's second season on the *Colgate Comedy Hour* followed basically the same format of skits and musical numbers, though there was a major difference in the show. Whereas the first season, like all other network shows at the time, had originated from New York, the second was broadcast from Hollywood's El Capitan Theatre. This made Cantor the first star to originate from the West Coast, a practice that quickly became the norm. The move was made possible by the completion of AT&T's west-east microwave link.

While Eddie Cantor often remarked on the long hours and hard work involved in television, still his performances were filled with an amazing amount of the old energy which had first won him the sobriquet of the "apostle of pep." Eddie turned sixty halfway through his second season on the *Comedy Hour*, and while many jokes were made about his age, there was little evidence in his stage antics which bore out the gibes — until September 28, 1952, the premiere show of the third season.[1]

All that summer Eddie had been preparing for the season kickoff, in addition to attending story conferences on *The Eddie Cantor Story* at Warner Brothers and touring the country raising donations for the Red Cross blood drive and the Bonds for Israel campaign. The pace, which would exhaust a man half his age, caught up with Cantor the night of the telecast. The show itself, which featured guest stars Eddie Fisher, Dorothy Lamour, and Sammy Davis, Jr., was a resounding success. In praising the hour, *Variety* lauded Cantor as "a great showman," adding that the program "sped through the Sabbath hour with sparks of wit." During the program, Eddie started experiencing sharp chest pains. Feeling weak, the usually teetotaling Cantor came offstage and asked for a drink of whiskey. Although he managed to finish the program, within hours of its completion Eddie was in an ambulance rushing to Cedars of Lebanon Hospital. The indestructible, untiring Eddie Cantor had suffered a heart attack.

First newspaper reports stated that Eddie had collapsed from exhaustion and would be in the hospital for a week of complete rest. Soon, however, it was revealed that the comedian had had what was termed "a slight heart attack" and would be at Cedars of Lebanon for at least two weeks. In actuality, Cantor was not sent home until mid–November, after six weeks in the hospital.

Even though doctors expressed optimism over his chances for recovery, initially Eddie sank into depression because he thought he was going to die. After all, in the last few years his contemporaries Al Jolson and Fanny Brice had gone in much the same way. When his condition improved and he realized that he was going to live, Cantor remained gloomy. As an entertainer whose performance was so integrally linked to his physical vitality, Eddie reasoned that his career was through. "How could I entertain again?" Cantor asked following his coronary. "How could I raise money or sell bonds if I couldn't get around to make people laugh?"

Eddie's spirits gradually began to lift when he started joking with his doctors and nurses and got laughs. Another major contribution to his recovery was the deluge of letters, cards, and telegrams that flooded the hospital. Some were from friends and celebrities, but most were from just plain folks, strangers who only knew Eddie from his years on the stage, screen, radio, and television.

"I'd heard laughter and applause, sure, for forty-five years," Eddie wrote a few years after his heart attack, "but I hadn't realized that there was love behind the laughter. Now that love came rolling in, and it was better than any medicine, it was something you had to repay."

Buoyed by this outpouring of love from his well-wishers, Eddie's spirits and physical condition improved. To ensure his continued recovery, Cantor's physician, Dr. Eliot Corday, encouraged his patient to moderate his life-style. Eddie's exhausting schedule, which was overloaded with work, appearances, and late nights, was strictly curtailed. His diet was changed to include less food, but a daily drink or two was added. Early to bed, early to rise, and a daily afternoon nap were also prescribed to ensure that Eddie received the proper amount of rest.

Another major change came in Cantor's attitude. A perfectionist, Cantor was well-known in show business circles for demanding nothing less than the best from those who worked for him and often blowing up in temper tantrums when his expectations were not met.

In *The Way I See It*, Cantor's 1959 book of personal philosophy, he recalled the effect his temper had on his family. "On broadcast days," Eddie wrote, "my family stayed as far away as space allowed. They walked like in a mine field. Daddy detonated easy! In fact, the kids would even kid about it. 'It's Daddy's holy day. Watch it, or you'll wind up with a hole in the head!'"

Eddie planned his return to the *Colgate Comedy Hour* for January 18, 1953, after missing two of the programs in his schedule. While the format was essentially the same, one change which Cantor pressed for was the filming of some program segments. Originally, Eddie had asked to film the entire show, but NBC balked at the arrangement. Some portions of the programs, most notably "Maxie the Taxi" were filmed, however, giving Cantor a more leisurely pace on broadcast day.

The first show after Cantor's return featured guests Dinah Shore and another Cantor protégé, twenty-year-old Joel Grey. While Eddie was able to participate in his comedy bits and a pleasant song medley with Dinah Shore, he still was in no condition for a return to his usual frenetic-paced routines of skipping and hand clapping. Not wanting to disappoint his audience, however, Cantor sang a spirited rendition of "Now's the Time to Fall in Love" off camera, while Joel Grey hopped around the stage in a faithful recreation of his host's familiar style. While *Variety* admitted the "new" Eddie Cantor was far less energetic than the precoronary version, they hailed his return as a success, thanks to his "production savvy" and use of filmed segments.

As his recovery progressed, Eddie was able to occasionally perform in his signature style, but like an aging pitcher who must "pitch with his head" when his fastball loses some of its zip, Eddie Cantor could no longer rely on the sheer physical force of his performance to put over his act, especially on a live telecast. Consequently, despite his sharp show business sense, Cantor was more than ever at the mercy of the material his writers concocted for him. Unfortunately, the comedy material on the third and fourth seasons of the *Comedy Hour* was inconsistent at best and often relied on reworkings of past bits.

The number of Cantor's appearances on his own show in the last two seasons of the *Comedy Hour* also varied. Some programs spotlighted Eddie as much as always, while others leaned heavily on guest stars, novelty acts, and newcomers. In addition, many of the later Colgate programs could have been accused of using the label *Comedy Hour* under false pretenses because they contained only two comedy bits versus more than twice that number of musical spots.

While Cantor's average may have dipped in the '52 and '53 seasons, he was still capable of recreating his unique magic on home screens. Not surprisingly, the best of these shows featured heavy doses of nostalgia, both in

**Eddie shows he has recovered from his 1952 heart attack in this publicity still herald-
ing his 1953 return to the *Colgate Comedy Hour*.**

material and guest stars. One of the better offerings of the third season was
a show celebrating Eddie and Ida's thirty-ninth wedding anniversary. The
show not only featured Ida and the girls, but George Jessel, Jimmy Wallington (who brought along the script from Cantor's premiere Chase and Sanborn radio show), Dave Rubinoff (and his violin), and Dinah Shore. The

show's finale began with a serious tribute by toastmaster Jessel, which soon turned decidedly comical when Ida was presented with a large gift box which contained a small boy.

The highlight of Eddie's fourth and final season on the *Comedy Hour* was probably another appearance by George Jessel. That program harkened back to their vaudeville tour of two decades earlier and was liberally sprinkled with the pair's customary exchange of good-natured barbs. Aside from recreating parts of their early thirties appearance at the Palace, Eddie and Georgie dressed up in drag for a hilarious segment in which they portrayed two women from the Palace audience.

Despite the inconsistency of material, especially in Cantor's final two seasons on the *Colgate Comedy Hour*, the show remained a highly rated program for NBC. Peaking its second season (with a 45.3 rating that put it in fifth place for the 1951-52 television season), the *Comedy Hour* managed 44.3 and 36.2 ratings (for a seventh and eleventh place finish, respectively) for its third and fourth seasons. Like Cantor's monthly segment of the *Comedy Hour*, the series in general was plagued by wildly inconsistent shows and an even more erratic schedule of "regular" stars.

# THE EDDIE CANTOR COMEDY THEATRE

Although Eddie had only starred in an average of seven episodes of the *Comedy Hour* in each of the past two seasons, the demands of live television made even that reduced schedule too great a strain. In May 1954, Cantor completed his last show for Colgate, and while he wanted a rest from the rigors of live TV, retirement was not in his plans. A month later Cantor announced that he had signed to do another television series that would differ from the *Comedy Hour* in a number of ways. First, the series would not be a network show, but would be produced by the Frederic W. Ziv, Co. Second, it would be syndicated without any regular sponsor, with advertisers buying into the program on a market-to-market basis. Finally, and probably the most attractive part of the deal to Cantor, the thirty-nine half-hour shows produced each year would be filmed. In addition, the contract called for a like number of Cantor-hosted radio shows in the style of his recent disc-jockey program on NBC radio.

In trumpeting the deal, John Sinn, president of Ziv programs, expressed his delight at landing Cantor. "We are proud that Eddie Cantor is joining our organization. We believe that his long and successful experience as a showman in every branch of theatrical entertainment will prove immeasurably valuable both in front of and behind the scenes."

Cantor was so adamant in rejecting any more live television that he turned down an offer from RCA (NBC's parent company) to appear in four specials during the 1954-55 season. In passing on the offer which would have paid him $25,000 per show, Cantor told reporters that the only live television appearances he would make henceforth would be for charities and exchange guest spots.

The new program, which would be titled the *Eddie Cantor Comedy Theatre*, would be produced by Cantor, with the comedian hosting weekly comedy plays with a variety of guest stars. In addition to hosting the shows, Eddie would also star in roughly thirteen of the programs each year. Initially, Eddie was also named as the director of all the shows, though ultimately that duty was filled by others.

Eddie's seven-year deal with Ziv would earn him $9 million over the length of the contract, with half of that guaranteed exclusive of residuals. Cantor's Ziv deal set a number of records and not just in the amount that a star was being paid. Each episode was budgeted at around $53,000, then the highest amount for a syndicated series. In addition, to pay for each pricey installment, a record rate card (the price list given to prospective sponsors) was set. To back up all of this, the Cantor series was given an extensive saturation advertising campaign.

Despite the financial gamble Ziv was taking, its risk quickly proved itself a good one. Armed with a strong pilot episode shot in the summer of 1954, the Ziv sales team succeeded in placing the *Eddie Cantor Comedy Theatre* in sixty of the country's top markets by fall, with a large amount of the sponsorships being picked up by local breweries. By the time the show premiered in the first months of 1955, the *Comedy Theatre* was being shown over more than 180 television stations.

It is not at all surprising that the *Eddie Cantor Comedy Theatre* was a syndication sell-out, especially after the series' premiere episode was televised. While the show was, for the most part, an anthology series, viewers were given the impression that the *Eddie Cantor Comedy Theatre* was not just the name of a program, but an actual, ultramodern showplace, filling an entire skyscraper. The pilot episode opens with a trio of reporters standing beneath the theater's marquee while the audience hears the show's theme, "One Hour with You" (each program was actually only half that length).

The reporters ponder, musically, whether the *Eddie Cantor Comedy Theatre* is all that it's been promoted to be, before they barge into the building's lobby. A receptionist explains that the theater is indeed everything they've heard and more, thanks to Mr. Cantor, who is responsible for every aspect of the production. The reporters begin to chant the familiar "We want Cantor" theme until Eddie appears to much applause (here, as throughout the series, canned laughter and applause are used).

Cantor, appearing remarkably trim and vigorous, much more so than during his recent live appearances on NBC, gives the reporters a brief musical outline of the series, the two main points of which are that he is doing it all (including waxing the floors and playing dogs' parts) and that no expense

According to the NBC publicity department, Cantor, as the 1954 New Year infant, had "many plans for his next year's programs" under his bonnet. Ironically, one of them was to bolt the network and sign a syndication deal with Ziv television.

is being spared to produce a quality show. While Cantor naturally did not do all that he claimed to in this humorous routine, he wasn't exaggerating about the show's production values, which were polished and much higher than for most of the live television programs on the networks.

Eddie then invites the reporters to watch as he brings out his first guest star, Brian Ahern. Ahern asks Cantor to pay his cab fare to the driver waiting out in the alley behind the theatre. The two men go outside for a brief, yet humorous, bit, with "Maxie the Taxi" played by Eddie in a convincing double exposure.

"Hey, you're Eddie Cantor," Maxie remarks, adding, "My friends say I look like you."

"Really," Eddie responds, playing straightman to himself.

"Yeah," Maxie replies, "now that I see you I know they're not my friends."

"Well," Eddie remarks, "you're not a bad-looking fellow."

"Aw, stop flattering yourself," Maxie sneers.

Next, guest Brian Ahern is wasted in a terminally cute bit in which he plays babysitter to an infant and a dog who carry on a telepathic conversation provided by off-camera voices. After this routine, Cantor sings a duet with his own reflection in the dressing room mirror. Although this repeats essentially the same gimmick as the "Maxie the Taxi" bit, it is done so well and so cleverly (Cantor tries to sing "If You Knew Susie" while his image sings alternate self-deprecating lyrics) that the overall effect is quite delightful.

Joe Besser then joins Eddie for a skit in the patent office, where the two comics play inventors who have accidentally invented the same thing — an electronic popcorn popper. Cantor closes the show with a rousing rendition of "Ma, He's Makin' Eyes at Me," which thanks to the use of film, displays Eddie at his animated, hand-clapping, eye-rolling, best. In fact the whole pilot, and most of the shows in the series, flatter Cantor, allowing him to return to his precoronary form. Unlike the *Colgate Comedy Hour* broadcasts, many of which for whatever reasons find Cantor's comic timing off, the *Eddie Cantor Comedy Theatre* provides a glimpse at the vintage Eddie, the fellow who could and often did rise above subpar material on the sheer strength of his stage presence and personal energy.

Although *Variety* gave the pilot episode passing marks, with special praise reserved for Cantor, *Newsweek* used the show's premiere to fire a personal salvo at Eddie himself. While dismissing the program as being full of "very bad jokes," the review closed with a nasty quote from *Tonight Show* host Steve Allen. Allen wrote: "Of all the top-ranking comedians Eddie Cantor has always seemed to me the unfunniest. . . . He is basically a song-and-dance man. . . . He finally attained a position where his vivacity and lightheartedness combined to create the *illusion* that he was a comedian. . . . Let no one underestimate the importance of being venerable. . . ." Cantor was quick to respond that if he indeed was not a comedian, then he owed millions in refunds to the multitudes of people who had paid him to make them laugh over the years. Ironically, it seems that Allen's parting shot — "Let no one underestimate the importance of being venerable" — is still applicable to some veteran performers.

Unfortunately, while many of the programs in the *Eddie Cantor Comedy Theatre* are quite good, again usually due to the strength of such performers as Cantor, Peter Lorre, and Buster Keaton, on the whole the series suffers from an overall writing drought. Cantor, as the show's producer, was well aware of the story problems and often worked overtime trying to rewrite weak scripts. Eddie received scant help from the Ziv Company, whose executives were only interested in getting finished shows in the can, with little regard to their quality. It seemed that Ziv was experienced in selling shows, but less interested in what actually made a good show. Despite John Sinn's initial delight at having a man of Eddie's experience on board, Ziv was apparently not interested in any show biz expertise which might interfere with its bottom line. After one season of what he considered a losing battle, Eddie Cantor bowed out of the remaining six years of his Ziv contract.

Two years later the bitter taste of his experience with Ziv was still fresh in Eddie Cantor's mouth. Writing in *Take My Life*, Cantor summed up the *Eddie Cantor Comedy Theatre* thus: "Supersalesmen, even within my own organization, assured me I'd have the last word but that they couldn't establish a precedent by putting that in my contract; and for once in my life I allowed my better judgment to be swayed by the money involved. I'd give all the money back if I could take back the shows, which are still running."

Ironically, the best shows from the *Comedy Theatre* are far superior to most of Eddie's *Colgate Comedy Hour* performances. Perhaps the fact that the *Comedy Theatre* was filmed, allowing Cantor to scrutinize each weakness, colored his opinion of the program. Despite its large budget, the *Comedy Theatre* managed to make money for Ziv and on average pulled good ratings around the United States and Canada. Because of its syndicated distribution, which resulted in the *Comedy Theatre* being shown at different times, against different competition in each market, exact ratings are not available.

With the ringing down of the curtain of the *Eddie Cantor Comedy Theatre*, its star was, for the first time in his forty-six-year career, without a regular vehicle or venue. At the age of sixty-three, Eddie Cantor went into semiretirement.

# Notes

1. Although Cantor in his 1957 autobiography lists the date of his heart attack as September 30, all television schedules and newspaper accounts give it as September 28.

# CHAPTER 43

# *Semiretirement*

Following his retreat from the ill-fated Ziv contract, Eddie Cantor settled down into semiretirement. Although his professional activities over the remaining eight to nine years of his life would become less and less frequent, a total retirement seemed a contradiction in terms to the man who had forged a show business career largely on his unfailing personal energy.

Still, while the one-time apostle of pep had turned in an astounding effort against the unrelenting march of time, eventually old age caught up with Cantor, and with a vengeance. His later television performances, most notably a 1959 appearance with Jack Benny and George Jessel on a George Burns special, dramatically demonstrated how suddenly time had overtaken Eddie. It is almost as if the only way time could have caught up with him was to pounce on him suddenly. On the aforementioned television show, Cantor appears much older than his three longtime friends (although he was only two, four, and six years older than Benny, Burns, and Jessel, respectively). The most shocking change in Eddie was in his once vibrant voice, which was now only a hollow-sounding echo of its former self.

Although Eddie Cantor could no longer match his former energetic performing style, this did not stop him from taking an active role in show business. Unfortunately, most of Cantor's involvement in the entertainment industry centered around plans for projects which never got off the ground. In 1955-56 alone, Eddie considered two possible television shows and one film role. The first TV show, entitled *Stardust*, was designed as a weekly half-hour showcase for new talent. Cantor saw himself not only as the host of the program, but also as the impresario who would discover the new talent, a role long familiar to him. The idea—which Eddie hoped would be sponsored by insurance companies under the banner of the National Safety Council, another of his pet causes—never got past the discussion stage.

A second proposed Eddie Cantor television show also was to involve the participation of insurance companies, but not as sponsors. Dubbed *Retire for Life*, this was to be a quiz program designed to capitalize on America's current fascination with such big money games as the *$64,000 Question* and *Twenty-One*. *Retire for Life*, which would again find Cantor in the role of the

The Cantor clan in the mid–1950s. Standing left to right: Edna, Marilyn, Natalie, Marjorie, Janet. Seated left to right: Judy McHugh (Edna's daughter), Brian Gari (Janet's son), Ida, Eddie, Michael Metzger (Natalie's son) (collection of Brian Gari).

comically congenial master of ceremonies, was slated to be similar to other quiz shows of the time in that contestants would answer a progressively difficult list of questions to attain higher and higher levels and more and more valuable prizes. Unlike the other shows, however, which rewarded the winner with a lump sum of cash, the grand prize on *Retire for Life* was to be an annuity which would leave the recipient comfortable for the rest of his days. *Retire for Life* was the subject of serious discussions between Eddie, NBC, sponsors, and various insurance companies (who would handle the annuity), but the project was ultimately shelved due to the orders of the would-be host's physician, who forbad Cantor to return to a weekly series because of health reasons.

Cantor's film project which was not to be was with independent film producer Gregory Ratoff. In 1956, Ratoff signed Cantor to appear in *The Fifth Season*, based on the Broadway play set in Manhattan's garment district. Although scheduled to be filmed in New York that summer for a 20th Century–Fox release, *The Fifth Season* was never produced.

While many of Eddie Cantor's later plans did not pan out, he did manage to keep busy in 1956 and 1957 through various literary endeavors.

The first of these was a second autobiography, ghostwritten by Jane Kesner Ardmore. Originally called *The Best of My Life*, the book was later retitled *Take My Life*. Like his earlier autobiography, *My Life Is in Your Hands* (gagwriter David Freedman, to whom it "was told," is responsible for that book's more amusing title), *Take My Life* was organized around a central event in Eddie's life. Whereas the earlier opus had concentrated on the still flourishing late twenties American rags to riches story, the fifties biography finds Cantor recalling his life in well-organized flashbacks as viewed on the night of his 1952 heart attack. While well written, *Take My Life* is not nearly as entertaining as *My Life Is in Your Hands*, because David Freedman presented cleverly even the most mundane passages. Coming as it did, before the Great Depression and Eddie's extensive charity work, *My Life Is in Your Hands* is much lighter in tone, reflecting a period when Cantor and America were both younger and more carefree. *Take My Life*, on the other hand, has the aging Eddie looking back on his life from the threshold of death and trying to tally his good works versus his sins with his eye on the balances. While the better anecdotes from Cantor's long career are included in both works, the later book can at times become somewhat maudlin. Still, *Take My Life*, published by Doubleday, managed to get good notices—including an unabashedly rave review from *Variety*—and to post very respectable sales.

Eddie Cantor's writings during his semiretirement were not just reserved to books. Always a prolific contributor to magazines, Cantor continued in the late fifties and into the early sixties with numerous regular columns for the Bell Newspaper Syndicate and the Diner's Club magazine. The columns ranged from the usual show biz reminiscences to advice on living, and even Cantor's own view of philosophy. Later, in 1959, excerpts from these columns were gathered into a book, *The Way I See It* (edited by Phyllis Rosenteur and published by Prentice-Hall), which is a wide-ranging "Eddie's eye view of life," with topics ranging from sex and marriage to religion and health.

While he never returned to a regularly scheduled program after the *Eddie Cantor Comedy Theatre* ceased production, Cantor still made numerous appearances on the small screen, most often on fund-raising telethons and protégé Eddie Fisher's program. Aside from guest shots, Cantor participated in four noteworthy television programs of which he was the star. The first was a starring role in NBC's afternoon anthology show, *Matinee Theater*, on June 11, 1956. The hour-long play, *George Has a Birthday*, featured Eddie in the title role as an mild-mannered elevator operator who will inherit a fortune on his fifty-fifth birthday. Unfortunately for George, his two sisters (played by Mae Clark and Madeleine Holmes) have squandered their own inheritances and plan to do away with their unsuspecting brother to obtain his. Although it is described in preshow publicity as Cantor's first dramatic role, *George Has a Birthday* was merely further evidence (first presented in *Forty Little Mothers*) that Eddie could handle straight roles. *Variety*, while appreciating Cantor's performance, commented that overall he was "wasted in the part," adding that the show would have been better if its length had been trimmed in half.

Cantor continued his dramatic television career, this time in prime time, on CBS's *Playhouse 90* program. The hour and a half episode *Sizeman and Son* broadcast in October 1956 again found Eddie in the title part of Morris Sizeman, a businessman in Manhattan's garment district. Farley Granger played Eddie's son, a Korean War veteran who returns home with radical ideas on how his father should conduct his business. Peter Lorre was also in the cast, playing Cantor's closest friend. Again Cantor drew strong notices for his efforts, although he confessed that he had a little difficulty mastering the role.

"It was difficult for me," he told a reporter, "to get a Jewish dialect, but I've been around George Jessel so long I finally mastered it."

After an appearance on Edward R. Murrow's *Person to Person* in which Eddie and Ida were interviewed by the newsman from their Beverly Hills home (telecast the same month as *Sizeman and Son*), Cantor appeared on a CBS extravaganza to celebrate his sixty-fifth birthday. Originally, the tribute to Cantor was designed as a segment of the *Ed Sullivan Show*, but Sullivan dropped plans for the broadcast after he discovered that too many of the scheduled guests — including Jimmy Durante, Eddie Fisher, Jack Benny, and Burns and Allen — were signed to exclusive contracts with competing networks or sponsors. A month after the Sullivan deal fell through, Jackie Gleason stepped in, offering Eddie his regular Saturday evening time slot for a similar birthday tribute.

Broadcast from Hollywood on January 12, 1957, the program, *At Sixty Five*, featured an all-star cast including Cantor, Burns and Allen, Eddie Fisher, George Jessel, Burt Lancaster, Edward R. Murrow, Connie Russell, and songwriters Milton Ager, Harry Akst, Jimmy McHugh, Harry Ruby, and Harry Warren. Also on the Bulova/Old Gold sponsored show was daughter Marilyn, who was pursuing a show business of her own at the time. As could be expected, the tribute was a nostalgic presentation filled with the routines and songs that had made Cantor one of the most popular stars of his generation.

While Eddie Cantor pulled out all the stops in *At Sixty Five* to recreate the highlights of his career, there was one notable event which he hadn't planned to reprise — his 1952 collapse from a heart attack. The strain of appearing again in an hour-long live telecast proved too much for Eddie, who at one point in the program, looking ashen, sat down and asked for a glass of water. After the show, Cantor was checked in Cedars of Lebanon Hospital for a two-day stay. Although he had not suffered another coronary, he had pushed his weakened constitution to the point of exhaustion.

In its favorable review of the program, *Variety* wondered if this was perhaps the comedian's swan song:

> Eddie Cantor, who has made good in all fields of show biz, went on for what may be his finale on the Jackie Gleason Show. On the occasion of his 65th birthday, Cantor was toasted by many with whom he's been associated in his many

years in the business. But whether it was the strain of working diligently in the preparation of his show, or whether the old heart ailment asserted itself mildly, Cantor caved in following the session.

Despite the collapse of its star, *At Sixty Five* managed to win the most viewers for its time slot that evening handily, beating NBC competitor Perry Como, a feat which Jackie Gleason had failed to accomplish for many months previous.

A few months later, in March 1957, Eddie Cantor suffered another brief stage collapse, this one while waiting to receive his honorary Oscar from the Academy of Motion Picture Arts and Sciences. While he was backstage during the ceremony, which was televised nationally, Cantor complained of feeling ill. A doctor was on hand and with the help of an aide, removed the comedian's dinner jacket, gave him a quick examination, and a shot of what was termed "restorative medication." After a few moments outside the stage door for a breath of fresh air, Cantor walked on stage to receive his Oscar "for distinguished service to the film industry." Although he was whisked away immediately after the presentation, Cantor denied he had suffered another attack, attributing the episode to being overcome with the excitement of the evening.

Eddie soon made more headlines connected with his sixty-fifth birthday when he, along with wife Ida, showed up at the local Social Security office to collect his first retirement benefits check. Although the move prompted many to wonder why the millionaire comedian and his wife needed the government's draft for $323.40 (covering their first two months of benefits), the event was actually staged to demonstrate who was eligible to collect the retirement insurance and how to go about it. Cantor asked the reporters present at the ceremony to keep his extra income a secret from at least one of his pals. "Don't tell George Jessel," Eddie quipped, "he'll borrow it for sure."

Cantor turned his Social Security check, along with subsequent payments, over to one of his favorite charities, the Surprise Lake Camp for boys back in New York. In addition to receiving his Social Security checks, the camp also received a new $75,000 theater from the comedian. Christened the "Eddie Cantor Playhouse," the arena stood on the site where Eddie had given his boyhood campfire concerts.

Over the next few years Eddie Cantor's professional appearances dwindled down to a mere handful. His weakened health, along with Ida's—she had also suffered a heart attack a few years after Eddie's—restricted their once active schedules. The Cantors now stayed closer to home and family (children and grandchildren), dividing their time between Beverly Hills, Palm Springs, and occasional visits to New York. With both he and Ida in failing health, it came as a tragic shock when they discovered in March 1959 that their eldest daughter, Majorie, was dying of cancer. Although she had been ill with the disease for two years, Marjorie had confided only in her four sisters, shielding her parents from the devastating diagnosis.

When Marjorie entered Cedars of Lebanon Hospital on March 26, her second visit that year, Eddie and Ida were told. Marjorie died less than two months later, at the age of forty-four. Her four sisters were at her bedside. When Eddie was told of his eldest's passing, he broke down in tears. Both he and Ida had to be sedated.

In the next few years, both Eddie and Ida suffered additional attacks. In February 1962, Ida had another heart attack, her fourth in seven years, which left her bedridden for the next six months before she died on August 9 at the age of seventy. Three of her surviving daughters were present when she passed away. After more than fifty-seven years with the "Belle of Henry Street," forty-eight of them in marriage, Eddie collapsed in a state of shock at the news of his wife's death. Again, he had to be sedated. Too ill to attend Ida's funeral, Eddie remained in bed under a doctor's care for several weeks.

Eddie Cantor's health at last improved to the point that, while he no longer had the physical strength to perform, he was soon again busy writing close to four hours a day at home. Most of his efforts were on his column for the Diner's Club magazine and his upcoming book, *As I Remember Them*, though he also wrote various treatments for television shows which were never produced. A few years earlier Cantor, along with Elick Moll, writer of *Sizeman and Son*, had written a drama based on the experiences of Eddie and Bert Williams. The networks, though receptive to the idea, eventually turned it down since Bert's race made the project "too touchy" at the time. Cantor attributed the fact that he couldn't sell any of his plots to the absence of real showmen in television, pointing out that most of the industry was run by bankers.

Eddie learned this firsthand a few years earlier when his friend Manie Sacks, a programing V.P. at NBC, had offered him a position as program adviser. Before the deal was finalized, Sacks had some high-level discussions with his supervisors about Cantor's future role with the network. A few weeks later Manie called the friend with some advice of his own. "Eddie," Manie began, "I'm going to do you a favor and tell you not to take the job. I don't want to submit you to the politics and headaches you would have to undergo." Despite his various difficulties with NBC and the other networks, in the last years of his life Eddie devoted roughly five hours a day to watching television.

As Eddie Cantor's life drew to a close, accolades poured in from various sources almost as dividends to a life filled with service. In 1962, Eddie was presented with the Medallion of Valor from Israel, in recognition not only of his extensive sale of bonds for that nation, but also of his strong support of Israel in its first years. In September 1963, Eddie was honored by the American Federation of TV and Radio Artists for his pioneering in both mediums, along with his help in founding the union which he served as its first president. Two months later, Cantor was honored by another entertainers union which he had helped found and whose first president he had been — the Screen Actors Guild. In its first annual Screen Actors Guild award,

SAG cited Eddie for "outstanding achievement in fostering the finest ideals of the acting profession and advancing the principles of good citizenship." Jack Benny accepted the award for Eddie, who was too ill to attend.

Having received the recognition of his peers, the last honors for Eddie Cantor came from his country. In January 1964, just before Eddie's seventy-second birthday, his longtime best friend, George Jessel, traveled to Washington to lobby for a congressional medal for his pal. Perhaps sensing that this birthday would be the last for his friend, Jessel met with President Johnson and various congressmen in an attempt to garner Eddie the honor. Jessel left the capital with a citation from the Congress that singled out Eddie for his humanitarian efforts, with special emphasis on his work in founding and naming the March of Dimes. The award was presented to Cantor at his home by Jessel and Governor Pat Brown of California. Later, the president followed suit with a honorary medal echoing the sentiments of the Congress.

On Saturday, October 10, 1964, at 7:20 in the evening, Eddie Cantor died at his Beverly Hills home, the victim of a heart attack. With him at his bedside were daughters Natalie and Edna, along with a doctor and nurse. Messages of sympathy and testimonials poured in for Cantor, who was praised by show business and the press. *Variety* called the man whose notices had filled their pages for over fifty years "a staple of the entertainment field . . . transcending his basic appeal as a headliner." In a special editorial, the *New York Times*, noted: "In his day, no actor of the stage, screen and radio was better known or better liked than Eddie Cantor—or funnier."

Eddie Cantor left his estate to his four surviving daughters: Natalie, Edna, Marilyn, and Janet. His estate was valued at $530,534 (this figure does not include much of his wealth, which had been in Ida's name and had been placed after her death in trust under Cantor for their daughters). Unfortunately, while he had earned many fortunes during his fifty-plus years career, Cantor's financial legacy became a textbook example of poor estate planning. Of the over half a million dollars in his gross estate, $161,854, or more than 30 percent of it, was eaten away by various fees and taxes.

Years after his death, Eddie Cantor is almost a forgotten man. While many of his contemporaries such as W. C. Fields and the Marx Brothers have lived on through the cults which have sprung up upon the rediscovery of their work by later generations, Eddie Cantor has yet to experience such a renaissance. He is recalled to life primarily by "old-timers" who remember him in his prime and nostalgia buffs, whose love for performers past provides them with the magic insight to see what made this banjo-eyed comedian not only a star of the highest magnitude, but one of the greatest performers and entertainment innovators of the twentieth century.

# APPENDIX

# Cantor Career Data

## STAGE

The following list includes Eddie Cantor's major stage appearances but is not intended to be exhaustive. After achieving stage and film stardom, Cantor made numerous forays back into vaudeville, benefits and other personal appearances. Sometimes these stints would be for only one or two performances; others lasted weeks.

Music and lyric credits for the shows below list the composers and lyricists credited for the overall show. As many of Eddie Cantor's songs, especially those in reviews, were in specialty numbers, he was free to perform songs by composers other than those credited.

### Burlesque

**c.1908**   Numerous amateur night performances beginning with an appearance at Miner's Bowery Theatre.

**November–December**   Toured with Frank Carr's traveling review *Indian Maidens*. Tour ended with cast stranded in Shenandoah, Pennsylvania.

**c.1909**   Singing waiter at Carey Walsh's Saloon, Coney Island, New York.

**c.1909**   Toured Northeast on various burlesque stints.

### Vaudeville

**c.1909–10**   16 weeks with Peoples Vaudeville Company split between their four New York area theaters.

**1910–12**   Toured Orpheum circuit with act of Bedini & Arthur, first as a gofer, eventually working up to featured status.

**1912–14**   Toured Orpheum circuit with Gus Edwards' *Kid Kabaret*, a "Musikal Review" in eight parts. Book & lyrics by Thomas J. Gray. Additional lyrics by Will D. Cobb. Music and staged by Gus Edwards with Eddie Cantor, Hattie Kneitel, and a Kompany of Twenty Klever Komics including Mona, Ruth Francis, Georgie Jessel and Evelyn McVay.

**June 1914**   Played one week with straightman Sammy Kessler at Oxford Theatre, London, England.

**July 1914** Played one month with Andre Charlot's review *Not Likely* in London, England.

**August 1915–February 1916** Toured Orpheum circuit with straightman Al Lee in act Cantor & Lee, *Master & Man*.

**October–December 1931** Headlined vaudeville program at New York's Palace Theatre with George Jessel, Burns & Allen, Janet Reade, the 3 Rhythm Dancers, and Ben Meroff's Orchestra.

**January–March 1932** Cantor took show on 35 city tour.

# Legitimate Stage

*Canary Cottage*. A musical comedy produced by Oliver Morosco. Book by Oliver Morosco and Elmer Harris. Score and lyrics by Earl Carroll. Staged by Frank Stammers. *Cast:* Trixie Friganza, Herbert Corthell, Eddie Cantor, Eunace Burnham, Charles Ruggles, Louise Orth, Laurence Wheat, Grace Ellsworth, the Morin Sisters, and the Edwards Brothers. Opened May 24, 1916, at the Morosco Theater, Los Angeles. Cantor remained with show in Los Angeles until October 1916.

*Midnight Frolics (4th Edition)*. A cabaret review with eight acts and nine song numbers. Produced by Florenz Ziegfeld. Score by Dave Stamper. Lyrics by Gene Buck. Staged by Ned Wayburn. *Cast:* Sybil Carmen, Lawrence Haynes, Olive Thomas, Frances White, Rock and White, Eddie Cantor, Milo, Peggy Brooks, Genevieve Santi, Lucy Gillette, Bird Millman, and the Arnaut Brothers. Opened October 17, 1916, at the New Amsterdam Roof, New York. Cantor remained with the show 27 weeks until the Follies 1917 edition opened. Like other Ziegfeld stars, Cantor would go upstairs to the Frolics occasionally as an added draw to the rooftop cabaret, and to try out new material.

*Ziegfeld Follies (11th Edition). (Ziegfeld Follies of 1917)*. A review in two acts produced by Florenz Ziegfeld. Score by Dave Stamper. Lyrics by Gene Buck. Staged by Ned Wayburn. *Principals included:* Fannie Brice, Will Rogers, W. C. Fields, Bert Williams, Eddie Cantor, Walter Catlett, Fred Heider, Don Barclay. Broadway opening, June 11, 1917, the New Amsterdam Theatre. Broadway run: 15 weeks. Road tour September 1917 through May 1918 in the following cities: Boston, Philadelphia, Baltimore, Washington, Pittsburgh, Detroit, Chicago, Washington (second engagement).

*Ziegfeld Follies (12th Edition) (Ziegfeld Follies of 1918)*. A review in two acts produced by Florenz Ziegfeld. Score by Dave Stamper and Louis Hirsch. Lyrics by Gene Buck. Staged by Ned Wayburn. *Principals included:* Will Rogers, Marilyn Miller, Lillian Lorraine, Fannie Brice, Ann Pennington, Eddie Cantor, W. C. Fields, Alyn King, Van & Schenck, Kay Laurel, Frank Carter, the Fairbanks Twins. Out of town opening June 14, 1918, Atlantic City. Broadway opening June 17, 1918, the New Amsterdam Theatre. Initial Broadway run: 14 weeks. Road tour September 1918 through May 1919 in the following cities: Boston, New York (second run due to closing of Boston theaters during Spanish flu epidemic), Philadelphia, Baltimore, Washington, Pittsburgh, Cleveland, Detroit, Chicago, St. Louis, Columbus, Montreal, Boston (second engagement).

*Ziegfeld Follies (13 Edition) (Ziegfeld Follies of 1919)*. A review in two acts produced by Florenz Ziegfeld. Music and lyrics by Dave Stamper and Gene Buck. Harry Tierney and Joseph McCarthy, Irving Berlin. *Principals included:* Will Rogers, W. C. Fields, Eddie Cantor, Fanny Brice, Bert Williams, Van and Schenck, Marilyn Miller, Ann Pennington, George LeMaire. Out of town opening June 11, 1919, Atlantic City. Broadway opening, June 16, 1919, the New Amsterdam Theatre. Show closed from August 13 to

September 10, 1919, due to Actors' Equity strike. Road tour, December 1919 through May 1920 in the following cities: Detroit, Chicago, Baltimore, Washington, Philadelphia, Boston.

**Ziegfeld Follies (14th Edition) (Ziegfeld Follies of 1920)**. A review in two acts produced by Florenz Ziegfeld. Out of town opening June 15, 1920, Atlantic City. Broadway opening, June 22, 1920, New Amsterdam Theatre. Though not with the show for its rehearsals or its Atlantic City try-out, Eddie Cantor was inserted into the cast opening night to add some much needed comedy. Cantor subsequently left the show before the end of its New York run as the result of a dispute with Ziegfeld.

**Broadway Brevities**. A musical comedy review produced by George LeMaire. Music by Archie Gottler and George Gershwin. Lyrics by Blair Treynor and Arthur Jackson. Additional songs by Bert Kalmar and Harry Ruby. *Cast included:* George LeMaire, Bert Williams, Eddie Cantor, Dorothy Jardon (replaced by Edith Hallor), Ula Sharon, Alexis Fosloff, William Sully, Eddie Buzzell, Peggy Parker, Genevieve Houghton, Maxwell Francis. Cantor joined the show during its Philadelphia try-out run in mid–September 1920. The Broadway opening was at the Winter Garden Theatre on September 20, 1920. Cantor remained with the show through mid–November. The show completed its Broadway run and its road tour without him.

**Midnight Rounders**. A musical comedy review produced by Lee and J. J. Shubert. *Cast included:* Eddie Cantor, Nan Halperin, Lew Hearn, Harry Kelly, Joe Opp, Jane Green, James Blyler, John Byam, Clarence Levy, Betty Pecan, Alice Ridnor, Muriel DeForrest. Strictly a road show made up of parts of two earlier reviews, *Midnight Rounders* did not play Broadway. Opened December 3, 1920, at the Shubert Theatre, Philadelphia. Subsequent tour stops included Atlantic City, Boston, Detroit, Baltimore, Chicago, Milwaukee, Indianapolis and Cincinnati before ending in January 1922.

**Make It Snappy**. A musical comedy review produced by Lee and J. J. Shubert. Book by Harold Atteridge and Eddie Cantor. Music by Jean Schwartz. Lyrics by Harold Atteridge. Performance staged by J. C. Huffman. *Cast included:* Eddie Cantor, Nan Halperin, Lew Hearn, Joe Opp, John Byam, Muriel DeForrest, Georgie Hale, J. Harold Murray, Margaret Wilson, Tot Qualters, Dolly Hackett. Pre-Broadway tour February–April 1922 in the following cities: Philadelphia, Buffalo, Cleveland, Pittsburgh. Broadway opening April 13, 1922, the Winter Garden Theatre. Broadway run: 12 weeks. Road tour September 1922 through May 1923 in the following cities: Brooklyn, Boston, Detroit, Chicago, Philadelphia.

**Ziegfeld Follies (16th Edition) Ziegfeld Follies of 1922**. A review in two acts produced by Florenz Ziegfeld. Cantor made a three week appearance in the show as a substitute for Will Rogers beginning June 4, 1923. Another brief appearance in the show was made in mid–August 1923.

**Kid Boots**. A musical comedy in two acts and seven scenes. Produced by Florenz Ziegfeld. Book by William Anthony McGuire and Otto Harbach. Score by Harry Tierney. Lyrics by Joseph McCarthy. Staged by Edward Royce. Starring Eddie Cantor. Featuring Mary Eaton. *Cast:* Harry Short (Peter Pillsbury), Paul Everton (Herbert Pendleton), John Rutherford (Harold Regan), Harland Dixon (Menlo Manville), Harry Fender (Tom Sterling), Mary Eaton (Polly Pendleton), Eddie Cantor (Kid Boots), Beth Berri (Beth), Ethelind Terry (Carmen Mendoza), Marie Hallahan (Jane Martin), Jobyna Howland (Dr. Josephine Fitch), Robert Barrat (Randolph Valentine). Pre-Broadway tour December 1923, in the following cities: Detroit, Cincinnati, Washington, Pittsburgh. Broadway opening December 31, 1923, the Earl Carroll Theatre. Moved to Selwyn Theatre September 1, 1924. Broadway run: 60 weeks. First road tour March 1925 through May 1925 in the following cities: Boston, Newark, Brooklyn, and Philadelphia. Second road tour September 1925 through January 1926 in Chicago for 18 weeks before closing due to Cantor's illness. Tour resumed February 1926 through April 1926 in the following cities: Indianapolis, St. Louis, Kansas City, Milwaukee, Baltimore, Washington.

*Ziegfeld Follies (21st Edition) (Ziegfeld Follies of 1927)*. A review in two acts and twenty-three scenes. Produced by Florenz Ziegfeld. Sketches by Harold Atteridge and Eddie Cantor. Music and lyrics by Irving Berlin. Featuring Eddie Cantor. *Principals included:* Andrew Tombes, the Brox Sisters, Dan Healy, Phil H. Ryley, William H. Powers, Claire Luce, Francis Upton, Irene Delroy, Helen Brown, Franklyn Baur, Harry McNaughton, Leo Bill, Cliff Edwards, Ruth Etting. Out of town opening Boston, August 5, 1927. Broadway opening August 16, 1927, the New Amsterdam Theatre. Broadway run 21 weeks. Road tour January 1928: Boston Tour canceled after one city due to Cantor illness.

*Whoopee*. A musical comedy in two acts and ten scenes. Produced by Florenz Ziegfeld. Book by William Anthony McGuire. Based on Owen Davis' farce "The Nervous Wreck." Music by Walter Donaldson. Lyrics by Gus Kahn. Starring Eddie Cantor. Featuring Ethel Shutta and George Olsen. *Cast:* Ruth Etting (Leslie Daw), Olive Brady (Pearl), Gladys Glad (Betty), Josephine Adaire (Mable), Jean Ackerman (Estelle), Adele Smith (Alice), Katherine Burke (Irene), Myrna Darby (Virginia), Muriel Finley (Lucille), Freda Mierse (Vivian), Louis Morrell (Jusdon Morgan), Frank Colleti (The Padre), Jack Shaw (Jim Canson), Frank Frey (Pete), Bob Rice (Joe), Jack Gifford (Jack), Ethel Shutta (Mary Custer), John Rutherford (Sheriff Bob Wells), Frances Upton (Sally Morgan), James P. Houston ("Brand Iron" Edwards), Eddie Cantor (Henry Williams), Paul Gregory (Wanenis), Chief Caupolican (Black Eagle), Spencer Charters (Jerome Underwood), Albert Hackett (Chester Underwood), Jack Shaw (Timothy Sleane), Mary Jane (Harriet Underwood), Will H. Philbrick (Andy Nab), Bob Rice (Morton), Sylvia Adam (Ma-Ta-Pe), James P. Houston (Comulo), Edouard Grobe (An Indian), Jack Shaw (Tejou), Tamara Geva (Yolandi), Olive Brady (Eleanor). Out of town opening Pittsburgh, November 2, 1928, with a subsequent run in Newark. Broadway opening December 4, 1928, the New Amsterdam Theatre. Broadway run: 48 weeks. Road tour November 1929 through March 1930 in the following cities: Boston, Philadelphia, Chicago, St. Louis, Cleveland.

*Banjo Eyes*. A musical comedy in two acts and twelve scenes. Produced by Albert Lewis. Book by Joe Quillan and Izzy Ellison from the play "Three Men on a Horse" by John Cecil Holm and George Abbott. Music by Vernon Duke. Lyrics by John Latouche. Additional lyrics by Harold Adamson. Staged and lighted by Hassard Short. Book directed by Albert Lewis. Starring Eddie Cantor. *Cast:* Jacqueline Susann (Miss Clark), E. J. Blunkall (Mr. Carver), Eddie Cantor (Erwin Trowbridge), June Clyde (Sally Trowbridge), Richard Rober (Harry, the Bartender), Bill Johnson (Charlie), Virginia Mayo (Ginger), Sally and Tony DeMarco (The DeMarcos), Lionel Stander (Patsy), Ray Mayer (Frankie), Audrey Christie (Mable), Tommy Wonder (Tommy), John Ervin (The General), James Farrell (The Captain), Ronnie Cunningham (The Filly), Mayo and Morton ("Banjo Eyes"). Out of town opening: New Haven, November 7, 1941. Subsequent cities on tour: Boston, Philadelphia. Broadway opening December 25, 1941, the Hollywood Theatre. Last performance April 12, 1942. Broadway run: 16 weeks.

*My Forty Years in Show Business*. A one man show produced by Ken Robey, Felix Gerstman and Joe Franklin. Starring Eddie Cantor. Piano accompaniment by George Tibboth and Arthur Siegel. Carnegie Hall, New York, March 21, 1950, one performance. Subsequently toured 33 cities and numerous college campuses.

# FILM

*Widow at the Races*. Edison, c.1913. One reel. Experimental Sound. *Cast:* Eddie Cantor, Georgie Jessel, Truly Shattuck.

*A Few Moments with Eddie Cantor*. Lee DeForest Phonofilms, c.1924. One reel. Sound. Black and white. Starring Eddie Cantor.

*Kid Boots*. Paramount/Famous Players–Lasky, 1926. Presented by Adolph Zukor and Jesse L. Lasky. Directed by Frank Tuttle. Adapted by Luther Reed. From the play by William Anthony McGuire and Otto Harbach. Script by Tom Gibson. Titles by George Marion, Jr. Associate producer: B. P. Schulberg. Length: 9 reels. Silent. Black and white. *Cast:* Eddie Cantor (Samuel "Kid" Boots), Clara Bow (Jane Martin), Billie Dove (Polly Pendleton), Lawrence Gray (Tom Sterling), Natalie Kingston (Carmen Mendoza), Malcom Waite (George Fitch), William J. Worthington (Polly's Father), Harry Von Meter (Carmen's Lawyer), Fred Esuelton (Tom's Lawyer).

*Special Delivery*. Paramount Pictures, 1927. Directed by William Goodrich (Fatty Arbuckle). Original story by Eddie Cantor. Titles by George Marion, Jr. Length: 6 reels. Silent. Black and white. *Cast:* Eddie Cantor (Eddie Beagle), Jobyna Ralston (Madge), William Powell (Harold Jones), Donald Keith (Harrigan), Jack Dougherty (Flannigan), with Victor Potel, Paul Kelly and Mary Carr.

*That Certain Party*. (a.k.a. That Party in Person). Paramount Pictures, 1928. Running time: 9 minutes. Sound. Black and white. *Cast:* Eddie Cantor, Bobby Arnst.

**Untitled Short**. 1929. Sound. Black and white. A short film produced as the opening number to the Broadway review *Earl Carroll's Sketch Book*. *Cast:* Eddie Cantor, Earl Carroll.

*Midnite Frolics*. Paramount, 1929. Running time: 19 minutes. Sound. Black and white. *Cast:* Eddie Cantor.

*Glorifying the American Girl*. Paramount, 1929. Directed by Millard Webb. Story by J. P. McEvoy and Millard Webb. Music and lyrics by Walter Donaldson, Irving Berlin, Dave Stampler and Larry Spier. Running time: 96 minutes. Sound. Black and white with 5 percent color sequences. *Cast:* Mary Eaton (Gloria Hughes), Edward Crandall (Buddy), Olive Shea (Barbara), Dan Healey (Miller), Kaye Renard (Mooney), Sarah Edwards (Mrs. Hughes), Eddie Cantor (Himself), Helen Morgan (Herself).

*Getting a Ticket*. Paramount, 1930. Running time: 11 minutes. Sound. Black and white. *Cast:* Eddie Cantor.

*Insurance*. Paramount, 1930. Running time: 9 minutes. Sound. Black and white. *Cast:* Eddie Cantor.

*Cockeyed News*. Paramount, 1930. Running time: 4 minutes. Sound. Black and white. *Cast:* Eddie Cantor.

*Whoopee!* United Artists, 1930. Produced by Samuel Goldwyn and Florenz Ziegfeld. Directed by Thornton Freeland. Music and lyrics by Walter Donaldson and Gus Kahn. Dances staged by Busby Berkley. Running time: 93 minutes. Technicolor (two strip). *Cast:* Eddie Cantor (Henry Williams), Eleanor Hunt (Sally Morgan), Paul Gregory

(Wanenis), John Rutherford (Sheriff Bob Wells), Ethel Shutta (Mary Custer), Spencer Charters (Jerome Underwood), Chief Caupolican (Black Eagle), Albert Hackett (Chester Underwood), Will H. Philbrick (Andy McNabb), Walter Law (Judd Morgan), Marilyn Morgan (Harriet Underwood).

*Palmy Days*. United Artists, 1931. Produced by Samuel Goldwyn. Directed by Edward Sutherland. Original story with dialogue by Eddie Cantor, Morris Ryskind and David Freedman. Running time: 80 minutes. Black and white. *Cast:* Eddie Cantor (Eddie Simpson), Charlotte Greenwood (Miss Martin), Spencer Charters (A. B. Clark), Barbara Weeks (Joan Clark), Charles B. Middleton (Yolando), George Raft (Joe-the-Frog), Paul Page (Stephen Clayton), Harry Woods (Plug Moynihan).

*The Kid from Spain*. United Artists, 1932. Produced by Samuel Goldwyn. Directed by Leo McCarey. Story by William Anthony McGuire, Bert Kalmar and Harry Ruby. Music and lyrics by Bert Kalmar and Harry Ruby. Running time: 118 minutes (road show); 96 minutes (subsequently). Black and white. *Cast:* Eddie Cantor (Eddie Williams), Lyda Roberti (Rosalie), Robert Young (Ricardo), Ruth Hall (Anita Gomez), John Miljan (Pancho), Noah Beery (Alonzo Gomez), J. Carrol Naish (Pedro), Robert Emmet O'Connor (Detective Crawford), Stanley Fields (Jose), Paul Porcasi (Gonzales), Julian Rivero (Dalmores), Theresa Maxwell Conover (Martha Oliver), Walter Walker (Dean), Ben Hendricks, Jr. (Red), Sidney Franklin (Himself).

*Roman Scandals*. United Artists, 1933. Produced by Samuel Goldwyn. Directed by Frank Tuttle. Story by George S. Kaufman and Robert Sherwood. Adapted by William Anthony McGuire. Additional dialogue by Arthur Sheekman, Nat Perrin and George Oppenheimer. Music and lyrics by Al Dubin, Harry Warren and L. Wolfe Gilbert. Running time: 92 minutes. Black and white. *Cast:* Eddie Cantor (Eddie), Ruth Etting (Olga), Gloria Stuart (The Princess Sylvia), David Manners (Josephus), Verree Teasdale (The Empress Agrippa), Edward Arnold (The Emperor Valerius), Alan Mowbray (Majordomo), Jack Rutherford (Manius), Grace Poggi (Slave Girl).

*Kid Millions*. United Artists, 1934. Produced by Samuel Goldwyn. Directed by Roy Del Ruth. Written and adapted by Arthur Sheekman, Nat Perrin and Nunnally Johnson. Songs by Walter Donaldson and Gus Kahn, Burton Lane and Harold Adamson, and Irving Berlin. Running time: 90 minutes. Black and white, with final sequence in Technicolor. *Cast:* Eddie Cantor (Eddie Wilson), Ann Sothern (Jane Larrabee), Ethel Merman (Dot), George Murphy (Jerry Lane), Jessie Block (Ben Ali), Eve Sully (Fanya), Burton Churchill (Colonel Larrabee), Warren Hymer (Louie the Lug), Paul Harvey (Sheik Mulhulla), Otto Hoffman (Khoot), Doris Davenport (Toots), Edgar Kennedy (Herman), Stanley Fields (Oscar), John Kelly (Adolph), Jack Kennedy (Pop), Stymie Beard (Stymie), Tommy Bond (Tommy), Leonard Kilbrick (Leonard), Guy Usher (Slade).

*Strike Me Pink*. United Artists, 1936. Produced by Samuel Goldwyn. Directed by Norman Taurog. Based on Clarence Buddington Kelland's story "Dreamland." Adaptation and screenplay by Frank Butler, Walter DeLeon and Francis Martin. Additional dialogue by Philip Rapp. Music and lyrics by Harold Arlen and Lew Brown. Running time 99 minutes. Black and white. *Cast:* Eddie Cantor (Eddie Pink), Ethel Merman (Joyce), Sally Eilers (Claribel), Harry Parke (Parkyakarkus), William Frawley (Copple), Helen Lowell (Ma Carson), Gordon Jones (Butch), Brian Donlevy (Vance), Jack LaRue (Thrust), Sunnie O'Dea (Sunnie), Rita Rio (Rita), Edward Brophy (Killer), Sidney H. Fields (Chorley), Don Brodie (Marsh), Charles McAvoy (Selby), Stanley Blystone (Miller), Duke York (Smiley), Charles Wilson (Hardin), Clyde Hagar (Pitchman), and the Goldwyn Girls.

*Ali Baba Goes to Town*. 20th Century–Fox, 1937. Produced by Lawrence Schwab.

Directed by David Butler. Story by Gene Towne, Graham Baker and Gene Fowler. Screenplay by Harry Tugend and Jack Yellen. Music and lyrics by Mack Gordon, Harry Revel and Raymond Scott. Running Time: 80 minutes. Black and white. *Cast:* Eddie Cantor (Aloysius Babson), Tony Martin (Yusuf), Roland Young (Sultan), June Lang (Princess Miriam), Louise Hovick (Sultana), John Carradine (Ishak), Virginia Field (Dinah), Alan Dinehart (Boland), Douglas Dumbrille (Prince Musah), Maurice Cass (Omar, the Rug Maker), Warren Hymer, Stanley Fields (Tramps), Ferdinand Gottschalk (Chief Councilor), Charles Lane (Doctor) with the Peters Sisters, Jeni LeGon, the Raymond Scott Quintet and the Pearl Twins.

*Forty Little Mothers.* Metro-Goldwyn-Mayer, 1940. Produced by Harry Rapf. Directed by Busby Berkley. Screenplay by Dorothy Yost and Ernest Pagano. Based on "Monsieur Petiot" by Jean Guitton. Running time: 90 minutes. Black and white. *Cast:* Eddie Cantor (Gilbert Thompson), Judith Anderson (Mme. Granville), Rita Johnson (Marian Edwards), Bonita Granville (Doris), Ralph Morgan (Judge Joseph M. Williams), Diana Lewis (Marcia), Nydia Westman (Mlle. Cliche), Margaret Early (Eleanor), Martha O'Driscoll (Janette), Charlotte Munier (Lois), Louise Seidel (Betty), Baby Quintanilla ("Chum").

*Thank Your Lucky Stars.* Warner Brothers, 1943. Produced by Mark Hellinger. Directed by David Butler. Screenplay by Norman Panama, Melvin Frank and James V. Kern. Original story by Everett Freeman and Arthur Schwartz. Music and lyrics by Arthur Schwartz and Frank Loesser. Running time: 127 minutes. Black and white. *Cast:* Eddie Cantor (Eddie Cantor/Joe Simpson), Joan Leslie (Pat Dixon), Dennis Morgan (Tommy Randolph), Edward Everett Horton (Farnsworth), S. Z. Sakall (Dr. Schlenna), Ruth Donnelly (Nurse Hamilton), Don Wilson (Announcer), Henry Armetta (Barber), Bette Davis (Herself), Errol Flynn (Himself), John Garfield (Himself), Ann Sheridan (Herself), Olivia deHavilland (Herself), Ida Lupino (Herself), Dinah Shore (Herself), Humphrey Bogart (Himself), Alexis Smith (Herself), Jack Carson (Himself), Alan Hale (Himself), George Tobias (Himself), Hattie McDaniel (Herself), Willie Best (Himself) and Spike Jones and his City Slickers.

*Show Business.* RKO, 1944. Produced by Eddie Cantor. Directed by Edwin L. Marin. Screenplay by Joseph Quillan and Dorothy Bennett. Story by Bert Granet. Running time: 90 minutes. Black and white. *Cast:* Eddie Cantor (Eddie Martin), George Murphy (George Doane), Joan Davis (Joan Mason), Nancy Kelly (Nancy Gaye), Constance Moore (Constance Ford), Don Douglas (Charles Lucas).

*Hollywood Canteen.* Warner Brothers, 1944. Produced by Alex Gottlieb. Directed by Delmer Daves. Original Screenplay by Delmer Daves. Running time: 124 minutes. Black and white. All-star cast including: The Andrews Sisters, Jack Benny, Joe E. Brown, Eddie Cantor, Jack Carson, Dane Clark, Joan Crawford, Bette Davis, John Garfield, Sidney Greenstreet, Alan Hale, Robert Hutton, Joan Leslie, Peter Lorre, Ida Lupino, Nora Martin, Dennis Morgan, Roy Rogers, S. Z. Sakall, Barbara Stanwyck.

*If You Knew Susie.* RKO, 1948. Produced by Eddie Cantor. Directed by Gordon Douglas. Original screenplay by Warren Wilson and Oscar Brodney. Additional dialogue by Bud Pearson and Lester A. White. Music and lyrics by B. G. DeSylva, Joseph Meyer, Jimmy McHugh, Harold Adamson, George Tibbles and Ramez Idriss. Running time: 90 minutes. Black and white. *Cast:* Eddie Cantor (Sam Parker), Joan Davis (Susie Parker), Bobby Driscoll (Junior), Margaret Kerry (Marjorie Parker), Allyn Joslyn (Mike Garrett), Charles Dingle (Mr. Whitley), Sheldon Leonard (Steve Garland), Joe Sawyer (Zero Zantini), Mabel Paige (Grandma), Douglas Fowley (Marty), Dick Humphreys (Handy Clinton), Howard Freedman (Mr. Clinton), Phil Brown (Joe Collins), Isabel Randolph (Mrs. Clinton), Sig Ruman (Count Alexis), Fritz Feld (Chez Henri).

***The Story of Will Rogers.*** Warner Brothers, 1952. Produced by Robert Arthur. Directed by Michael Curtiz. Screenplay by Frank Davis and Stanley Roberts. Adaptation by John C. Moffitt. Based on the *Saturday Evening Post* story "Uncle Clem's Boy" by Mrs. Will Rogers. Running time: 109 minutes. Technicolor. *Cast:* Will Rogers, Jr. (His Father), Jane Wyman (Mrs. Will Rogers), Carl Benton Reid (Clem Rogers), Eve Miller (Cora Marshall), James Gleason (Bert Lynn), Slim Pickens (Dusty Donovan), Noah Beery, Jr. (Wiley Post), Mary Wickes (Mrs. Foster), Steve Brodie (Dave Marshall), Pinky Tomlin (Orville James), Margaret Field (Sally Rogers), Virgil S. Taylor (Art Frazer), Richard Kean (Mr. Cavendish), Jay Silverheels (Joe Arrow), William Forrest (Flo Ziegfeld), Earl Lee (President Wilson), Brian Daly (Tom McSpadden), Eddie Cantor (Himself).

***The Eddie Cantor Story.*** Warner Brothers, 1953. Produced by Sidney Skolsky. Directed by Alfred E. Green. Screenplay by Jerome Weidman, Ted Sherdeman, and Sidney Skolsky; from a story by Sidney Skolsky. Running time: 115 minutes. Technicolor. *Cast:* Keefe Brasselle (Eddie Cantor), Marilyn Erskine (Ida), Aline MacMahon (Grandma Esther), Arthur Franz (Harry Harris), Alex Gerry (David Tobias), Greta Granstedt (Rachael Tobias), Gerald Mohr (Rocky), William Forrest (Ziegfeld), Jackie Barnett (Durante), Richard Monda (Eddie, age 13), Marie Windsor (Cleo Abbott), Douglas Evans (Leo Raymond), Ann Doran (Lillian Edwards), Hal March (Gus Edwards), Susan Odin (Ida, age 11), Owen Pritchard (Boy Harris), Will Rogers, Jr. (Will Rogers), Eddie Cantor (Himself), Ida Cantor (Herself).

# RECORDINGS

| | | | |
|---|---|---|---|
| New York—July 1917 | | | |
| Victor | 18342 | The Modern Maiden's Prayer | B-20216 |
| | 18342 | That's the Kind of a Baby for Me | B-20217 |
| New York—November 1917 | | | |
| Aeolian Vocalion | 1220 | The Modern Maiden's Prayer | |
| | 1220 | That's the Kind of a Baby for Me | |
| | 1228 | Down in Borneo Isle | |
| | 1228 | Hello, Wisconsin | |
| | 1233 | The Dixie Volunteers | |
| | 1233 | I Don't Want to Get Well | |
| New York—August 1919 | | | |
| Pathé | 22163 | The Last Rose of Summer | |
| | 22163 | We Don't Need the Wine to Have a Wonderful Time | |
| New York—September 1919 | | | |
| Emerson | 1071 | You Don't Need the Wine to Have a Wonderful Time | 4467-3 |
| New York—October 1919 | | | |
| Emerson | 1071 | Don't Put a Tax on the Beautiful Girls | 4508-3 |
| | 1094 | When They're Old Enough to Know Better | 4509-1 |
| New York—November 1919 | | | |
| Emerson | 10102 | I Used to Call Her Baby | 4629-4 |
| | 10105 | Give Me the Sultan's Harem | 4630-2 |
| Pathé | 22201 | When They're Old Enough to Know Better | 67953 |

|  |  |  |  |
|---|---|---|---|
|  | 22201 | I've Got My Captain Working for Me Now | 67977 |
|  | 22260 | Don't Put a Tax on the Beautiful Girls | 67979 |
| New York — December 1919 |  |  |  |
| Emerson | 10102 | You'd Be Surprised | 4670-3 |
| New York — January 1920 |  |  |  |
| Emerson | 10134 | The Last Rose of Summer | 4734 |
| Pathé | 22260 | At the High Brown Babies Ball | 68091 |
| New York — February 1920 |  |  |  |
| Emerson | 10105 | When It Comes to Lovin' the Girls I'm Way Ahead of the Times | 4759-2 |
|  | 10119 | Come on and Play Wiz Me My Sweet Baby | 4760-3 |
| Pathé | 22318 | When It Comes to Lovin' the Girls I'm Way Ahead of the Times | 68188 |
|  | 22318 | I Never Knew I Had a Wonderful Wife (Until the Town Went Dry) | 68689 |
| New York — March 1920 |  |  |  |
| Emerson | 10119 | All the Boys Love Mary | 4779-2 |
|  | 10134 | You Ain't Heard Nothin' Yet | 4780-2 |
| New York — May 1920 |  |  |  |
| Emerson | 10200 | The Argentines, the Portuguese and the Greeks | 41171 |
|  | 10200 | Noah's Wife Lived a Wonderful Life | 41172 |
| New York — June 1920 |  |  |  |
| Emerson | 10212 | The Older They Get, the Younger They Want 'Em | 41207 |
|  | 10212 | Snoops the Lawyer | 41208 |
| New York — July 1920 |  |  |  |
| Emerson | 10292 | She Gives Them All the Ha! Ha! Ha! | 41239 |
| New York — August 1920 |  |  |  |
| Emerson | 10263 | Dixie Made Us Jazz Band Mad | 41375 |
|  | 10263 | When I See All the Lovin' They Waste on Babies I Long for the Cradle Again | 41376 |
| New York — October 1920 |  |  |  |
| Emerson | 10301 | I Wish That I'd Been Born in Borneo | 41453 |
| New York — November 1920 |  |  |  |
| Emerson | 10292 | Palesteena | 41494 |
| New York — December 1920 |  |  |  |
| Emerson | 10301 | Margie | 41534 |
|  | 41551 | You Ought to See My Baby | 41551 |
| New York — January 1921 |  |  |  |
| Emerson | 10349 | I Never Knew |  |
|  | 10352 | Timbuctoo |  |
|  | 10352 | My Old New Jersey Home |  |
| New York — June 1921 |  |  |  |
| Emerson | 10397 | Anna in Indiana | 41852 |
|  | 10397 | Oh, They're Such Nice People |  |

New York—April 1922
Columbia            A-3624      I Love Her, She Loves Me (I'm Her
                                    He She's My She)                    80328
New York—May 1922
Columbia            A-3624      I'm Hungry for Beautiful Girls          80342
New York—July 1922
Columbia Rejected               Oh, Is She Dumb!                        80349
                    A-3682      Susie                                   80440
                    A-3682      Oh, Is She Dumb!                        80439
New York—October 1922
Columbia            A-3754      Sophie                                  80636
                    A-3754      He Loves It                             80637
New York—December 1922
Columbia            A-3784      Joe Is Here                             80715
                    A-3784      How Ya Gonna Keep Your Mind on
                                    Dancing (When You're Dancing
                                    with Someone You Love?)             80716
New York—May 1923
Columbia            A-3906      I Love Me (I'm Wild About Myself)       81004
                    A-3906      Ritzi-Mitzi                             81005
New York—June 1923
Columbia            A-3934      Oh! Gee, Oh! Gosh, Oh! Golly, I'm in
                                    Love                                81073
                    A-3934      Eddie (Steady)                          81076
New York—July 1923
Columbia            A-3964      No, No, Nora                            81148
                    A-3964      (I've Got the) Yes We Have No
                                    Banana Blues                        81149
New York—January 1924
Columbia            56-D        O, Gee, Georgie!                        81459-3
                    56-D        If You Do What You Do                   81460-2
New York—April 1924
Columbia            120-D       I'll Have Vanilla                       81666
                    120-D       On a Windy Day Down in Waikiki          81667
New York—May 1924
Columbia            140-D       Oh Papa                                 81779
                    140-D       Monkey Doodle                           81780
New York—July 1924
Columbia            182-D       Charley, My Boy                         81878
New York—August 1924
Columbia            196-D       No-One Knows What It's All About        81904
New York—September 1924
Columbia            213-D       Doodle-Doo-Doo                          140037
New York—October 1924
Columbia            234-D       How I Love That Girl                    140106
New York—November 1924
Columbia            256-D       Those Panama Mamas
                                    (Are Ruinin' Me)                    140145
New York—December 1924
Columbia            277-D       Goo-Goo-Goodnight Dear!                 140213

| | | | |
|---|---|---|---|
| New York—January 1925 | | | |
| Columbia | 283-D | Laff It Off | 140223 |
| New York—April 1925 | | | |
| Columbia | 364-D | If You Knew Susie | 140499 |
| | Rejected | We're Back Together Again | 140558 |
| New York—June 1925 | | | |
| Columbia | 397-D | We're Back Together Again | 140558 |
| | 415-D | Row, Row, Rosie | 140641 |
| New York—September 1925 | | | |
| Columbia | 457-D | Oh Boy! What a Girl | 140925 |
| | Rejected | Jake the Plumber | 140926 |
| | Rejected | Eddie's Trip Abroad | 140928 |
| New York—September 1928 | | | |
| Victor | Rejected | Sonny Boy | BVE-46989 |
| | Rejected | It Goes Like This (That Funny Melody) | BVE-46990 |
| Unnumbered Test | | Sonny Boy | |
| New York—December 1928 | | | |
| Victor | 21831 | Makin' Whoopee | BVE-49001 |
| | 21831 | Hungry Women | BVE-49002 |
| New York—January 1929 | | | |
| Victor | 21862 | Eddie Cantor's Automobile Horn Song | BVE-49688 |
| | 21862 | I Faw Down and Go 'Boom!' | BVE-49689 |
| New York—April 1929 | | | |
| Victor | 21982 | Hello, Sunshine, Hello | BVE-51610 |
| | 21982 | If I Give Up the Saxophone (Will You Come Back to Me?) | BVE-51611 |
| New York—October 1929 | | | |
| Victor | Rejected | Does an Elephant Love Peanuts? | BVE-57128 |
| | 22189 | My Wife Is on a Diet | BVE-57129 |
| | 22189 | Eddie Cantor's Tips on the Stock Market | BVE-57130 |
| Hollywood—August 1931 | | | |
| Victor | 22851 | There's Nothing Too Good for My Baby | PBVE-68306 |
| New York—September 1931 | | | |
| Hit of the Week | K-6 | Cheer Up (Ballyhoo) | |
| New York—November 1932 | | | |
| Columbia | 2723-D | What a Perfect Combination | 152316-3 |
| | 2723-D | Look What You've Done | 152317-3 |
| New York—April 1934 | | | |
| Monument | M-13001 | Over Somebody Else's Shoulder (I Fell in Love with You) | 15075 |
| | M-13001 | The Man on the Flying Trapeze | 15076 |
| Los Angeles—September 1934 | | | |
| Monument | M-13183 | Mandy | LA-204-A |
| | M-13183 | An Ear Full of Music | LA-205-A |
| | Rejected | When My Ship Comes In | LA-206-A |
| | M-13184 | Okay, Toots | LA-207-A |

| | | | |
|---|---|---|---|
| Los Angeles — October 1934 | | | |
| Monument | M-13184 | When My Ship Comes In | LA-206-C |
| London — December 1934 | | | |
| Rex | 8389 | That's the Kind of a Baby for Me | F-117-3 |
| | 8389 | Making the Best of Each Day | F-118-1 |
| Los Angeles — January 1938 | | | |
| Decca | 1887 | Alexander's Ragtime Band (with Connie Boswell & Bing Crosby) | DLA-1152 |
| London — July 1938 | | | |
| Decca | F-6741 | Says My Heart/Little Lady Make-Believe | DR-2822-1 |
| | F-6741 | Lambeth Walk | DR-2823-2 |
| Los Angeles — November 1939 | | | |
| Columbia | 35325 | The Only Thing I Want for Christmas (Is Just to Keep the Things That I've Got) | LA-2049 |
| | 35325 | If You Knew Susie | LA-2050 |
| Los Angeles — February 1940 | | | |
| Columbia | 35428 | Little Curly Hair in a High Chair | LA-2171 |
| | 35428 | Margie | GA-2172 |
| New York — May 1941 | | | |
| Decca | 3798 | Makin' Whoopee | 69143 |
| | 3798 | Yes, Sir! That's My Baby | 69144 |
| | 3873 | Oh! Gee, Oh! Gosh, Oh! Golly, I'm in Love | 69145 |
| | 3873 | They Go Wild, Simply Wild, Over Me | 69146 |
| New York — March 1942 | | | |
| Decca | 4314 | We're Having a Baby (My Baby and Me) (with June Clyde) | 70539 |
| | 4314 | Now's the Time to Fall in Love | 70540 |
| Los Angeles — October 1944 | | | |
| Decca | 23529 | Around and Around and Around (with Nora Martin) | L-3648 |
| | 23529 | You Kissed Me Once (with Nora Martin) | L-3649 |
| | 23986 | If You Knew Susie | L-3668 |
| | 23987 | You'd Be Surprised | L-3669 |
| | 23988 | Dinah | L-3670 |
| | 23723 | Ma! (He's Makin' Eyes at Me) | L-3671 |
| Los Angeles — November 1944 | | | |
| Decca | 24597 | Alabamy Bound | L-3673 |
| | 23723 | Margie | L-3674 |
| | 23987 | Ida (Sweet as Apple Cider) | L-3675 |
| c.1946 | | | |
| Musicraft | | Tweedledum and Tweedledee (children's record) | |
| c.1947–48 | | | |
| Pan American | PAN036 | One-Zy, Two-Zy | St-71 |
| | PAN044 | Josephine, Please No Lean on the Bell | St-83 |
| | PAN044 | Makin' Whoopee | St-84 |

September 1949

| | | | | |
|---|---|---|---|---|
| Victor | 54-0005 | I Never See Maggie Alone | | VB-1935 |
| | 30-0010 | Oh! Gee, Oh! Gosh, Oh! Golly, | | |
| | | I'm in Love | | VB-1946 |
| | 30-0010 | The Old Piano Roll Blues | | VB-1947 |

January 1950

| | | | |
|---|---|---|---|
| Victor | 20-3705 | Enjoy Yourself | VB-3171 |
| | 20-3705 | I Love Her | VB-3172 |
| | Rejected | Now I Always Have Maggie Alone | VB-3173 |

March 1950

| | | | |
|---|---|---|---|
| Victor | 20-3751 | The Old Piano Roll Blues | |
| | | (with Lisa Kirk) | VB-3922 |
| | 20-3751 | Juke Box Annie (with Lisa Kirk) | VB-3923 |

April 1954

| | | | |
|---|---|---|---|
| Capitol | 32159 | Maxie the Taxi (parts 1 & 2) | 12416-7 |

## Albums of Original Material

1953

| | | |
|---|---|---|
| Capitol | L-467 | The Eddie Cantor Story |
| | | (film soundtrack) |

1957

| | | |
|---|---|---|
| RCA Victor | LX-119 | The Best of Eddie Cantor |

1960

| | | |
|---|---|---|
| Audio Fidelity | AFLP-702 | A Date with Eddie Cantor |
| | | (recorded 1960 released 1962) |

(This album is a studio recreation of the 1950 Carnegie Hall concert with sound effects added to simulate an audience. While it clearly attempts to pass itself off as the original concert soundtrack, a careful reading of the liner note gives clues to the fact that it is not what it pretends to be.)

1992
Original Cast
Records                    Eddie Cantor — The Complete
OC-9217-1 & 2              Original Carnegie Hall Concert

Thankfully, the complete March 21, 1950, Carnegie Hall soundtrack has been discovered by Brian Gari, Eddie Cantor's grandson, and released in a two CD set.

## RADIO STARRING ROLES

| Season | Sponsor | Day/Time | Network | Format |
|---|---|---|---|---|
| 1931-32 | Chase & Sanborn | Sunday 8:00-9:00 | NBC | Comedy |
| 1932-33 | Chase & Sanborn | Sunday 8:00-9:00 | NBC | Comedy |
| 1933-34 | Chase & Sanborn | Sunday 8:00-9:00 | NBC | Comedy |
| 1935-36 | Pebeco Toothpaste | Sunday 7:00-7:30 | CBS | Comedy |
| 1936-37 | Texaco | Sunday 8:00-8:30 | CBS | Comedy |

| | | | | |
|---|---|---|---|---|
| 1937-38 | Texaco | Wednesday 8:30-9:00 | CBS | Comedy |
| 1938-39 | Camel Cigarettes | Monday 7:30-8:00 | CBS | Comedy |
| 1940-41 | Sal Hepatica/Ipana | Wednesday 9:00-9:30 | NBC | Comedy |
| 1941-42 | Sal Hepatica/Ipana | Wednesday 9:00-9:30 | NBC | Comedy |
| 1942-43 | Sal Hepatica/Ipana | Wednesday 9:00-9:30 | NBC | Comedy |
| 1943-44 | Sal Hepatica Ipana | Wednesday 9:00-9:30 | NBC | Comedy |
| 1944-45 | Sal Hepatica/Ipana | Wednesday 9:00-9:30 | NBC | Comedy |
| 1945-46 | Sal Hepatica/Ipana | Wednesday 9:00-9:30 | NBC | Comedy |
| 1946-47 | Pabst Blue Ribbon | Thursday 10:30-11:00 | NBC | Comedy |
| 1947-48 | Pabst Blue Ribbon | Thursday 10:30-11:00 | NBC | Comedy |
| 1948-49 | Pabst Blue Ribbon | Friday 9:00-9:30 | NBC | Comedy |
| 1949-50 | Eversharp-Schick | Sunday 10:00-10:30 | NBC | Quiz |
| 1951-52 | Philip Morris | Sunday 9:30-9:00 | NBC | Records/Talk |
| 1952-53 | Syndicated | Thursday 9:30-10:00 | NBC | Records/Talk |
| 1953-54 | Syndicated | Thursday 9:30-10:00 | NBC | Records/Talk |
| 1954-55 | Syndicated | Various/Half-hour | ZIV | Records/Talk |
| 1961 | Syndicated | 5 days a week/5 min. | | Talk |

# TELEVISION STARRING ROLES

| Date | Program | Network |
|---|---|---|
| 5/25/44 | *Philco Relay Program* (Eddie Cantor, Nora Martin) | NBC |
| 9/10/50 | *Colgate Comedy Hour* (Eddie Cantor, LewHearn, Bob Gari, Yma Sumac, Joseph Buloff) | NBC |
| 10/8/50 | *Colgate Comedy Hour* (Eddie Cantor) | NBC |
| 11/5/50 | *Colgate Comedy Hour* (Eddie Cantor, Bob Gari, Ida Cantor, Charlie Cantor, Bil & Cora Baird, Leslie Scott, Fred & Sledge, Dick Barstow) | NBC |
| 12/3/50 | *Colgate Comedy Hour* (Eddie Cantor, Dick Van Patten, Jack Albertson, Connie Sawyer, Les Zoris, The Amadis, June Keegan, Joe Bushkin) | NBC |
| 1/28/51 | *Colgate Comedy Hour* (Eddie Cantor, Joe Marks, Lee Fairfax, Estelle Sloan, Dave Powell, Jack O'Brian) | NBC |
| 2/25/51 | *Colgate Comedy Hour* (Eddie Cantor, Lena Horne, Charlie Cantor, Bil and Cora Baird, Landre and Verna, Jack Albertson, Phil Kramer, Marcia Walter) | NBC |
| 3/25/51 | *Colgate Comedy Hour* (Eddie Cantor, Jimmy Durante, George C. Marshall) | NBC |
| 4/1/51 | *Colgate Comedy Hour* (Eddie Cantor, Joel Gray, Evelyn Gould, Tony & Eddy, Michelle Auclair, William Warfield) | NBC |
| 5/27/51 | *Colgate Comedy Hour* (Eddie Cantor, Eddie Fisher, Connie Haines, Charlie Cantor, Joel Grey) | NBC |
| 6/17/51 | *Colgate Comedy Hour* (Eddie Cantor, Milton Berle, Jack E. Leonard, Dagmar, Phil Foster, Ida Cantor, Marilyn Cantor, Junie Keegan) | NBC |

| | | |
|---|---|---|
| 9/9/51 | *Colgate Comedy Hour* (2nd season premiere) (Eddie Cantor, Cesar Romero) | NBC |
| 9/29/51 | *Colgate Comedy Hour* (Eddie Cantor) | NBC |
| 10/28/51 | *Colgate Comedy Hour* (Eddie Cantor, Cesar Romero, Verna Felton, Sheila Graham, the Caprino Sisters) | NBC |
| 11/25/51 | *Colgate Comedy Hour* (Eddie Cantor, Eddie Fisher, Cesar Romero, Betty Graham) | NBC |
| 12/9/51 | *Colgate Comedy Hour* (Eddie Cantor) | NBC |
| 12/23/51 | *Colgate Comedy Hour* (Eddie Cantor, Farley Granger, Bobby Breen, Sharon Baird) | NBC |
| 1/20/52 | *Colgate Comedy Hour* (Eddie Cantor, Kirk Douglas, Robert Clary, Esther Dale, Sharon Baird) | NBC |
| 2/17/52 | *Colgate Comedy Hour* (Eddie Cantor, Sammy Davis Jr., the Will Masten Trio, Reggie Rymal) | NBC |
| 3/16/52 | *Colgate Comedy Hour* (Eddie Cantor, Sammy Davis Jr., the Will Masten Trio, Dorothy Kirsten, Harry VonZell, Mabel Butterworth, Sharon Baird) | NBC |
| 4/13/52 | *Colgate Comedy Hour* (Eddie Cantor, Joe E. Brown, Constance Moore, Dave Barry) | NBC |
| 5/18/52 | *Colgate Comedy Hour* (Eddie Cantor, Cesar Romero, Gisell and Francois Szony) | NBC |
| 6/8/52 | *Colgate Comedy Hour* (Eddie Cantor, Ida Cantor, Harry VonZell, Danny Thomas, Kay Starr, Pat O'Brien, Tom D'Andrea, Hal March, Harry Askt, Jimmy McHugh, Harry Ruby, Nacio Herb Brown, Jay Livingston, Johnny Dugan, Sharon Baird) | NBC |
| 9/28/52 | *Colgate Comedy Hour* (3rd season premiere) (Eddie Cantor, Eddie Fisher, Dorothy Lamour, Sammy Davis Jr., Tom D'Andrea, Henry Slate, Sidney Fields) | NBC |

(misses two shows due to heart attack)

| | | |
|---|---|---|
| 1/18/53 | *Colgate Comedy Hour* (Eddie Cantor, Dinah Shore, Joel Grey, Arnold Stang, the Six Tokayers | NBC |
| 2/15/53 | *Colgate Comedy Hour* (Eddie Cantor, Connie Russell, Billy Daniel, Tom D'Andrea, Hall March, Sara Berner, Danny Richards) | NBC |
| 3/15/53 | *Colgate Comedy Hour* (Eddie Cantor) | NBC |
| 4/12/53 | *Colgate Comedy Hour* (Eddie Cantor, Sammy Davis Jr., Gloria Grahame, Will Mastin Trio, Connie Russell, Ned Washington, Dimitri Tiomkin) | NBC |
| 5/10/53 | *Colgate Comedy Hour* (Eddie Cantor, Connie Russell, Jan Peerce, Si Milano, John Robertson, Billy Daniel, Nanci Crompton, Bonzo the Chimp) | NBC |
| 6/7/53 | *Colgate Comedy Hour* (Cantors' 39th Wedding Anniversary Show) (Eddie Cantor, Ida Cantor, George Jessel, Dinah Shore, the Notables, | NBC |

|          | Ticker Freeman, Rubinoff, Jimmy Wallington, Ralph Edwards) | |
|----------|---|---|
| 10/18/53 | *Colgate Comedy Hour* (Eddie Cantor, Jack Benny, Connie Russell, Billy Daniel, Sheldon Leonard, Rex Ramer) | NBC |
| 11/29/53 | *Colgate Comedy Hour* (Eddie Cantor, Frank Sinatra, Eddie Fisher, Harold Arlen, Connie Russell, Brian Donlevy, the Debonairs) | NBC |
| 12/17/53 | *Colgate Comedy Hour* (Eddie Cantor) | NBC |
| 12/23/53 | *This Is Your Life* (Ralph Edwards, Eddie Cantor, Ida Cantor, Jimmy Durante, George Jessel, Dan Lipsky, Bobby Breen, Eddie Fisher, Keefe Brasselle) | NBC |
| 1/31/54 | *Colgate Comedy Hour* (Eddie Cantor, Groucho Marx, Wally Cox, Connie Russell, Billy Daniel, Ida Cantor, Marilyn Cantor, Johnny & Bill, Jesse, James & Cornell) | NBC |
| 3/7/54 | *Colgate Comedy Hour* (Eddie Cantor, William Holden, Jack Palance, Audrey Hepburn, Brandon de Wilde, Eddie Fisher, Billy Daniel, Ricky Vera, the Three Houcks) | NBC |
| 4/4/54 | *Colgate Comedy Hour* (Eddie Cantor, Connie Russell, Billy Daniel, Chiquita & Johnson, Manolo Mera, Ricky Vera) | NBC |
| 5/16/54 | *Colgate Comedy Hour* (Eddie Cantor, Milton Berle, Eddie Fisher, Connie Russell, Andre, Andree & Bonnie) | NBC |
| 1954-55 | *The Eddie Cantor Comedy Theatre* 38 Half-hour syndicated programs, Eddie Cantor, host & performer. Various guest stars | ZIV |
| 6/11/56 | *Matinee Theater*/"George Has a Birthday" (Eddie Cantor, Mae Clark, Madeleine Holmes) | NBC |
| 10/5/56 | *Person to Person* (Edward R. Murrow, Eddie Cantor, Ida Cantor) | CBS |
| 10/18/56 | *Playhouse 90*/"Sizeman and Son" (Eddie Cantor, Farley Granger, Peter Lorre) | CBS |
| 1/12/57 | At 65 (Commemorating Cantor's 65th Birthday) (Eddie Cantor, Burns & Allen, George Jessel, Burt Lancaster, Edward R. Murrow, Connie Russell, Marilyn Cantor) | CBS |

# Colgate Comedy Hour: Ratings

While Eddie Cantor was only one-fourth of the Colgate Comedy Hour line-up, he was the show's creator and one of its most reliable hosts, so the show's ratings success is undoubtedly reflective of his popularity. It is noteworthy that the program was a consistent ratings success while Cantor was on the show. After he left the program prior to its fifth season, however, the show fell sharply in the ratings, never again finishing in the top 15 for the season.

Colgate Comedy Hour               NBC                  Sundays 8:00–9:00

| Season | Average rating | Ranking for Season |
|--------|----------------|--------------------|
| 1950-51 | 42.0 | fifth |
| 1951-52 | 45.3 | fifth |
| 1952-53 | 44.3 | seventh |
| 1953-54 | 36.2 | eleventh |

# Selected Bibliography

Arnold Edward (in collaboration with Frances Fisher Dubuc). *Lorenzo Goes to Hollywood*. New York: Liveright Publishing Corp., 1940.

Berg, A. Scott. *Goldwyn*. New York: Knopf, 1989.

Burns, George (with David Fisher). *All My Best Friends*. New York: Putnam, 1989.

Cantor, Eddie. *As I Remember Them*. New York: Duell, Sloan and Pearce, 1963.

Cantor, Eddie. *Caught Short*. New York: Simon & Schuster, 1929.

Cantor, Eddie (as told to David Freedman). *My Life Is in Your Hands*. New York: Harper & Brothers, 1928.

Cantor, Eddie. Personal papers. UCLA Library, Special Collection.

Cantor, Eddie (with Jane Kesner Ardmore). *Take My Life*. Garden City: Doubleday, 1957.

Cantor, Eddie (edited by Phyllis Rosenteur). *The Way I See It*. Englewood Cliffs: Prentice-Hall, 1959.

Easton, Carol. *The Search for Sam Goldwyn*. New York: William Morrow, 1976.

Fisher, Eddie. *Eddie*. New York: Harper & Row. 1981.

Fowler, Gene. *Schnozzola, The Story of Jimmy Durante*. New York: Viking Press, 1951.

Goldman, Herbert G. *Jolson: The Legend Comes to Life*. New York: Oxford University Press, 1988.

Green, Able & Joe Laurie, Jr. *Show Biz*. New York: Henry Holt, 1951.

Higham, Charles. *Ziegfeld*. Chicago: Henry Regnery, 1972.

Jessel, George. *So Help Me*. Los Angeles: Friars Publication Corp., (no publication date given).

LeRoy, Mervyn (as told to Dick Kleiner). *Mervyn LeRoy: Take One*. New York: Hawthorn Books, 1974.

Meredith, Scott. *George S. Kaufman and His Friends*. Garden City, NY: Doubleday, 1974.

*New York Times*, 1919–1964.

Torrence, Bruce T. *Hollywood: The First Hundred Years*. NewYork: New York Zoetrope, 1982.

*Variety*, 1915–1964.

# Index

DATE DUE